PSYCHOANALYTIC EXPLORATIONS IN MUSIC

Applied Psychoanalysis Series
Monograph 3

Edited by
Chicago Institute for Psychoanalysis
George H. Pollock, President

Psychoanalytic Explorations in Music

Edited by
STUART FEDER, M.D.
RICHARD L. KARMEL, PH.D.
GEORGE H. POLLOCK, M.D., PH.D.

INTERNATIONAL UNIVERSITIES PRESS, INC.
Madison, Connecticut

Copyright © 1990, Stuart Feder, Richard L. Karmel, George H. Pollock

All rights reserved. No part of this book may be reproduced by any means, nor translated into a machine language, without the written permission of the publisher.

Library of Congress Cataloging in Publication Data

Psychoanalytic explorations in music / edited by Stuart Feder, Richard L. Karmel, George H. Pollock.
   p. cm.—(Applied psychoanalysis monograph series; monograph 3)
   Includes bibliographical references.
   ISBN 0-8236-4407-3
   1. Music—Psychology. 2. Psychoanalysis. I. Feder, Stuart, 1930–
II. Karmel, Richard L. III. Pollock, George H.
   [DNLM: 1. Music. 2. Psychoanalytic Interpretation. WM 460
P9751]
ML3830.P89   1990
780'.1—dc20
DNLM/DLC
for Library of Congress   89-24574
                                                                   CIP
                                                                   MN

Manufactured in the United States of America

Contents

Contributors	vii
Introduction	ix

I. PSYCHOANALYTIC CONTRIBUTIONS ON THE PSYCHOLOGY OF MUSIC

1. On the Enjoyment of Listening to Music (1950)—
   Heinz Kohut and Siegmund Levarie — 1
2. Observations on the Psychological Functions of Music
   (1957)—Heinz Kohut — 21
3. Some Considerations of a Psychoanalytic Interpretation
   of Music (1971)—Martin L. Nass — 39
4. Freud's Theory of Jokes and the Linear-Analytic
   Approach to Music: A Few Points in Common
   (1979)—Daniel Sabbeth — 49

II. PSYCHOANALYTIC DEVELOPMENTAL PSYCHOLOGY AND ITS APPLICATION

5. The Development of Musical Ability (1968)—
   Pinchas Noy — 63
6. Transitional Tunes and Musical Development
   (1970)—Marjorie McDonald — 79
7. A Psychoanalyst's View of Clara Schumann (1968)—
   Anna M. Burton — 97
8. Charles and George Ives: The Veneration of Boyhood
   (1981)—Stuart Feder — 115

III. PSYCHOANALYTIC THEORY APPLIED TO MUSICAL COMPOSITION

9. On Hearing and Inspiration in the Composition of
   Music (1975)—Martin L. Nass — 179
10. Mourning and Memorialization through Music
    (1975)—George Pollock — 195

11. Form Creation in Art: An Ego Psychological Approach
    to Creativity (1979)—*Pinchas Noy*   209
12. The Nostalgia of Charles Ives: An Essay in Affects and
    Music (1981)—*Stuart Feder*   233
13. The Development of Creative Imagination in
    Composers (1984)—*Martin L. Nass*   267

IV. PSYCHOANALYTIC STUDIES OF COMPOSERS

Ludwig van Beethoven (1770–1827)

14. On Beethoven's Deafness (1978)—*Maynard Solomon*   287

Johannes Brahms (1833–1897)

15. Johannes Brahms—Music, Loneliness, and Altruism
    (1985)—*Peter Ostwald*   291

Gustav Mahler (1860–1911)

16. Mourning through Music: Gustav Mahler (1974)—
    George Pollock   321
17. Gustav Mahler: The Music of Fratricide (1981)—
    Stuart Feder   341

Wolfgang Amadeus Mozart (1756–1791)

18. Mozart: A Study in Genius (1951)—*Aaron H. Esman*   391
19. Mozart's Zoroastran Riddles (1985)—*Maynard Solomon*   401

Gioacchino Rossini (1792–1868)

20. Rossini: A Psychoanalytic Approach to "The Great
    Renunciation" (1965)—*Daniel W. Schwartz*   423

Robert Schumann (1810–1856)

21. Robert Schumann and Clara Wieck—A Creative
    Partnership (1985)—*Anna M. Burton*   441

Richard Wagner (1813–1883)

22. On Falling in Love: The Mystery of Tristan and Isolde
    (1986)—*Richard D. Chessick*   465

AFTERWORD: THE FIELD OF INQUIRY:
SHARPENING THE FOCUS—WIDENING THE SCOPE   485

References   489
Name Index   509
Subject Index   515

Contributors

ANNA M. BURTON, M.D.
President, New Jersey Psychoanalytic Society
Faculty, The Psychoanalytic Institute of New York University Medical Center

RICHARD CHESSICK, M.D., PH.D.
Professor of Psychiatry, Northwestern University
Fellow, American Academy of Psychoanalysis

AARON H. ESMAN, M.D.
Professor of Clinical Psychiatry, Cornell University Medical College
Faculty, New York Psychoanalytic Institute

STUART FEDER, M.D.
Faculty, New York Psychoanalytic Institute

RICHARD L. KARMEL, PH.D.
Senior Staff Psychologist, Department of Psychiatry, Montreal General Hospital
Member, Canadian Psychoanalytic Society

HEINZ KOHUT, M.D.
(Deceased)

SIEGMUND LEVARIE, PH.D.
Professor Emeritus of Music, City University of New York

MARJORIE MCDONALD, M.D.
Associate Clinical Professor of Psychiatry, Tufts University School of Medicine

MARTIN L. NASS, PH.D.
Visiting Clinical Professor of Psychology, Training and Supervising Analyst, New York University Postdoctoral Program in Psychotherapy and Psychoanalysis
Faculty, New York Freudian Society

PINCHAS NOY, M.D.
Training and Supervising Analyst, Israel Institute for Psychoanalysis
Associate Professor, Hebrew University, Jerusalem

PETER OSTWALD, M.D.
Professor of Psychiatry and Medical Director, Health Program for Performing Artists, University of California, San Francisco

GEORGE H. POLLOCK, M.D., PH.D.
Professor of Psychiatry, Northwestern University Medical School
Faculty, Institute for Psychoanalysis, Chicago

DANIEL SABBETH, M.D., PH.D.
Private Practice of Child, Adolescent, and Adult Psychiatry, New Rochelle, New York

DANIEL W. SCHWARTZ, M.D.
Director, Forensic Psychiatry Service, Kings County Hospital Center
Associate Professor, Psychiatry, State University of New York Health Science Center at Brooklyn

MAYNARD SOLOMON
Visiting Professor, State University of New York at Stony Brook

Introduction

This book is about the relationship between the psychoanalyst, the composer, the musical performer, and the music listener. It is also about a felt need: to bring about an improved, better informed, and more sensitive intuneness to a study of the musical arts through the medium of psychoanalytic inquiry.

As indicated by our chosen title, we are following a path laid down by a predecessor, Ernst Kris, who personally took the step from art historian to psychoanalyst and who, over a twenty-year period (1932–1952), introduced "a new type of interdisciplinary contact" (Kris and Kurz, 1934).

As he stated in his Preface to *Psychoanalytic Explorations in Art* (1952), the psychoanalytic perspective offered "new potentialities . . . to the problems traditionally treated by the humanities . . ." (p. 9). Yet, as he readily pointed out, the task was not without its difficulty and complexity and, from the perspective of an art historian circa 1930 had as yet to be adequately undertaken.

Kris took note of developments in psychoanalytic theory and clinical technique (ego psychology) and wished to demonstrate that art and the creative process might be studied in order to explore and clarify clinical concepts. And, it was Kris's particular aptitude and talent for achieving this "shift in focus," both within psychoanalytic theory and in its application outside the clinical realm, which remains distinctly his legacy.

The contributions of Kris emerged after the "initial stage" or beginnings of efforts to apply the ideas of Freud in what might be termed *the initial Freudian ambience*—the formation of the Wednesday Society or Psychological Wednesday Society (1901–1906) (Jones, 1955). For, it was during this germinative period that Freud hosted weekly discussion groups which included a mixed company of medical specialists and other Viennese prominent in the arts, literature, education, journalism and publishing, and politics. Having a common interest in gaining a more in-depth, personalized appreciation of Freud's writings and teachings, and in discussing and debating with Freud, this first group of students of psychoanalysis demonstrated an active and lively interest around the subject of creativity and the products of artistic creation; namely, art, literature, and music. Some years later, as membership changed and evolved, a more formalized group emerged to be known as the Vienna Psycho-Analytical Society (1908).

Among the founding members of the Wednesday Society was musicologist Max Graf who assumed "the task of investigating the psychology of great musicians and the process of composing music, utilizing psychoanalysis for this task" (Graf, 1942, p. 470).

Graf reports that he presented material to the study group on "the psychological processes of Beethoven and Richard Wagner in writing music" (p. 471), which eventually resulted in the first published "applied" psychoanalytic study of a composer, "Richard Wagner im Fliegenden Hollander" (1911) (*The Flying Dutchman*). In reviewing Graf's paper, Wilheim Stekel (1911), another charter member of the Wednesday Society, stated that the author "has offered us for the first time a deeper insight into the problem 'Wagner' and has proceeded far beyond what is being offered by extant Wagner biographies" (p. 252).

Graf's approach involved an investigation of Wagner's autobiographical writings, including letters and reported dreams, a detailed study of the opera and its "poetic imagery," the women in Wagner's life, and the nature of each relationship as it could be determined. It utilized certain psychoanalytic views prevalent at that time about "the typical family history of neurotics" emphasizing the concepts of repetition compulsion, identification, early object loss, maternal fixation, and reality conflicts resolved through (adolescent) fantasy. Graf also considered concepts such as artistic creativity as a source for conflict expression and conflict resolution where solutions in reality cannot be found.

Graf brought considerable knowledge and sophistication to the Wednesday discussion groups and he can be thought of as the first musicologist to apply Freud's clinical findings and theoretical formulations to the study of an operatic work, delineating the many motifs employed by the composer and relating them to the vicissisitudes of the composer's complex life. He postulated that *The Flying Dutchman* was Wagner's artistic rendition of "salvation . . . by a mother figure" (the heroine, the composer's wife, rescuing the wandering mariner, Wagner) (Flugel, 1936, p. 288). (Kalfus [1984] offers additional insights regarding the representational significance of *The Flying Dutchman*.)

Graf's study permits the hypothesis to be formulated that a

Introduction

powerful impetus may exist for the artist–composer to continually create new artistically based representational worlds. This viewpoint is based upon the argument that at a particular period in the composer Wagner's life, he found it essential to utilize certain motifs based upon critical inner requirements. No doubt the more specialized medium of opera lent itself well as an artistic–creative outlet which enabled Wagner to accomplish at least two objectives: (1) to express in highly artistic–creative form, personalized needs, conflicts, and solutions in fantasy, and in doing so, (2) to transform the very medium of opera. That is, Wagner, bringing together the personal and artistic–creative, introduced a new operatic representational form (style) which provided a new artistic conceptualization of what opera could say and do and how it might do so; namely, its content and form. Thus, in this first psychoanalytic essay on musical creativity, Graf (1911) pointed out how great musical talent may produce innovative musical pieces involving new compositional forms in relation to life's vicissitudes, rather than on the basis of psychopathology.

Since this formative period in the history of applied psychoanalytic studies, an appreciation of the interplay between life events and creative activity has been established. Nevertheless, there has been a distinct uneasiness with regard to psychoanalytic exploration of the creative process and to the study of creative individuals. For example, as Feder (1983) points out, psychoanalytic inquiry is often viewed by nonanalysts as "intrinsically intrusive" if not "assaultive," and, thus, an essentially "demeaning endeavor." An accusatory morbid pathophilia might be directed toward investigatory motives. However, in reviewing the papers included in this volume, as well as many which could not be included, a different impression emerges: it is rare to read a psychoanalytic paper which fails to reveal the author's fondness if not deep appreciation for the composer's artistic–creative talents. In fact, it is often the richness of the musical experience which acts as a stimulus to the subsequent inquiry and investigation carried out by the psychoanalyst (Martin, 1966).

Since the position of the psychoanalyst outside the clinical realm is so often misunderstood, the reader may find it useful to consider the position put forward by Feder (1983) with regard to nonclinical (applied) psychoanalytic inquiries (which this anthology hopes to reflect). That is, (1) an interest in describing and understanding the unique qualities of the composer without preconception; (2) a recognition that applied psychoanalysis is *not* equivalent to nor should it be confused with clinical psychoanalysis; (3) an interest in both normal developmental and pathological processes without favoring one over the other; and (4) an ultimate interest in "the psychology of creativity itself." As expressed by Lichtenberg (1984), "It is the interplay between life experience, past and present, and creative change that interests a psychoanalyst . . . " (p. 298).

One should also be aware of those instances whereby a musical idea, for example, a simple melody, which resulted in aesthetic pleasure common to any listener, had an additional "lingering effect" on the psychoanalyst, ultimately leading to a deeper understanding of the clinical material (Reik, 1952, 1953). In such instances, musical composition or musical performance may become woven into the countertransferential experiences of the analyst at particular junctures in the analysis. Thus, within the clinical analytic format, the analyst may have an "inner musical experience" (Jaffe, 1983, p. 591) which can resonate or mirror aspects of the analysis not readily identifiable by other means. In this anthology, the reader will have the opportunity to view the "inner musical experience" of a number of great composers reconstructed on the basis of historical sources, musical texts, and the author's psychoanalytic perspective. It is, of course, the latter point which distinguishes this volume from a multitude of other scholarly writings on music, composers, and musicians.

To return to Vienna, circa 1911, working chronologically forward to the era of the 1950s, the reader might wish to consult both Sterba's (1965) review article on "Psychoanalysis and Music," which discusses most of the major articles published in German prior to 1940 (unavailable in English translation), as well as the extensive review and bibliography provided by Noy (1966, 1967a, b, c, d).

Sterba noted that despite the significance of musical activity for society and culture, relatively little had appeared in the psychoanalytic literature compared with studies of other forms of artistic expression. He pointed out some of the difficulties inherent in a psychoanalytic study of music, such as utilization of familiar manifest versus latent (unconscious) categories as applied to other works of art. This approach, according to the author, "cannot be applied in the realm of music, where the work of art is not a copy of reality" (p. 97).

Sterba's review illustrated the nature of psychoanalytic thinking, and the methods employed, during the years from World War I until 1957. It offered the following summary: (1) music provides gratification involving "deep regression" to the earliest developmental experiences; (2) music reaches back to a period of development prior to the establishment of ego boundaries and the separation of inside and outside world; (3) the regressive pleasures of music (i.e., narcissistic) combine with "the highest synthetic functions of the ego" (musical composition); (4) the composing of music (as an advanced ego function) acts as a "safeguard" against massive, threatening regression; and (5) "the combination of and interaction between deepest regression and highly developed organization makes music a unique experience"; and (6) music creates "the inner illusion of ego world identity, of an extension of the psychic organization which brings the cosmos under the domination of the self" (p. 111).

Clearly, prior to the 1950s, "music as a regressive experience" was overemployed as an explanatory model. However, by the 1950s, one began to see the emergence of newer, more sophisticated thinking which reflected an appreciation and an ability to incorporate Freud's evolving views on the organization and structure of the psyche. Thus, Kohut (1952) argued that musical *thought* should be placed among the "secondary processes" which serve as an "energy-binding function" for the musician. Within this framework, music could be viewed as having genetic significance while, at the same time, serving the needs and requirements of the more mature, adult, creative ego. Thus, primitive pleasures coexist with more sophisticated aesthetic gratifications. More recent formulations have argued that while it is reasonable to expect some influence or input from the neurotic or even psychotic side of the personality in relation to creative output, nonneurotic or conflict-free factors should be given greater consideration (Corbin, 1974).

From the standpoint of musical composing, Kohut (1952) also underscored a point which has yet to be fully explored: music as a representation of various superego functions. Here the composer is viewed as an artistic representative of a society's superego demands. This conceptualization was introduced by Michel (1951) who suggested that the music of Bach could be viewed as a "superego representation" of medieval Catholicism—the composer's music functioning as an "artistic compromise." There is the suggestion that the composer composes, at least in part, on the basis of an "unconscious artistic superego" which includes and, perhaps, requires various compromise formations, which are historically linked to religious authoritarian–submissive imperatives applied to the artistic sphere. Today's musicians and composers may not face such harsh artistic strictures; nonetheless, restrictive or at least prescriptive superego influences, indeed, seem to remain operative (Bradshaw, 1973; Babikian, 1983).

With the presentation of this historical overview, the reader may now wish to learn more about the planning and organization of this volume. Our purpose is to provide an up-to-date compendium of representative articles drawn from the major psychoanalytic sources as well as the inclusion of a number of previously unpublished papers that relate to psychoanalysis and music. Though the field of applied psychoanalysis is broad, diverse, and rather well established with regard to the study of writers and literary creativity, the musical arts have received only marginal consideration from the psychoanalytic theorist and clinician. Furthermore, as a resource for the study of creativity, the musical arts have been underemphasized and underutilized. Therefore, it is to stimulate future studies as well as to provide an "entry point" from the psychoanalytic point of view with regard to music that this collection of papers has been compiled. It is hoped that this volume will be a sourcebook, providing a foundation and basis for further critical inquiries into the world of musical creativity.

The volume is organized in the following manner. It begins with a section (chapters 1 to 4) on the psychoanalytic psychology of music—how the musical experience is conceptualized and what music represents from a psychoanalytic perspective.

The reader will note that by the 1950s a shift has taken place away from a more "regressive," id psychology model to one emphasizing the concepts and formulations of ego psychology; namely, adaptation, cognitive style, and ego mastery. Furthermore, there is a shift in emphasis toward more in-depth study and analyses of actual musical compositions and texts, the latter now regarded as extraclinical data invaluable as a supplement to and elaboration of the "inner musical experience" (Jaffe, 1983). Music, with its specific forms and styles, may be understood as reflecting the auditory representational world of a given musician and/or composer. Acoustic–musical experience and expression occupy "an exceptional position" in relation to other sensory modalities (Isakower,

1939). Consequently, musical creations may be a "primary source" for insights into certain aspects of psychic functioning; for example, various mood states generated within the individual over time (Feder, 1981), the outcome or consequence of early superego structures (Isakower, 1939), the artistic–creative expression of "the sound image of the self" (Anzieu, 1979), and the formation of archaic precognitive structures (Rechardt, 1985).

In section II, the roots of musicality and the influences on musical development are examined both theoretically and through a psychoanalytic "reconstructive" methodology. Chapters 5 and 6 examine the question of musical endowment and infant psychology and how music development may find direction. Historically, the early psychoanalytic perspective (Bernfeld, 1915; Jacoby, 1926) reacted against an "inborn talent model," arguing that early environmental experiences, be they familial and/or pedagogic, could influence (actually stifle) the developing child thereby rendering the individual "unmusical," apparently talentless, ultimately lacking even the capacity to appreciate music. Musical talent and musical accomplishment were viewed as susceptible to blockage by unconscious factors as well. Isakower (1939) made no specific reference to the roots of musicality; nonetheless, the special role of the "auditory sphere" in the developmental process with regard to the other sensory modalities was emphasized: "one of the most important apparatuses for the regulation of relations with the environment and with the introjected representations of interests in that environment . . ." (p. 4). The question may be asked: If the auditory–sensory mode occupies a "special role" in a general sense, that is, developmentally, does musicality, the development of musical talent, require a "subspecialized" auditory sphere? The reader may wish to consider such issues while examining the first article, which discusses both constitutional and environmental issues. The second article focuses on Winnicott's concept of "transitional phenomena" as applied to the auditory sensory sphere and the role of transitional tunes such as lullabies and cradle songs, as a component of an important stage in the child's (self-creating) musical development. Additionally, it may have implications for the early mother–child relationship (Kleiner, 1961; Anzieu, 1979), facilitating the development of an "inner aesthetic sensitivity" which influences the capacity for appreciating music: to be able to listen and enjoy various forms and types of music. In chapter 7, musical development is no longer a theoretical issue. Now, we are in the realm of the child prodigy whose musical giftedness is manifest and responded to in a way that is specific to the nature of musical talent—a child with an audience and public, a child revered. In chapter 8, childhood is revered through the creative artistry of the composer where the composer re-creates his deep attachment to the "father–son in reverence."

In section III, chapters 9 to 13, the composer's world is the object of further theoretical and biographical exploration. What may inspire the composer to compose? How is the direction of musical creativity influenced in the face of certain life events such as personal loss? Is composing based upon (or does it require) an "early auditory style" or precocity with regard to auditory sensitivity which functions as a precursor of musicality? What may be the nature of the composer's "working ego" in the context of a highly specific musical style or form?

The evolution from auditory sensitivity in early childhood to competence as composer certainly involves a series of progressive–sequential stages. Yet, it may be difficult to clearly delineate the path to mature musical creativity. When certain life events, such as death of a loved object, confront the creative individual, how is creativity affected? May it stimulate the production of new compositional forms or styles in the case of the composer? Is there always a "merging" of the personal and the artistic in the sphere of musical composition? One outcome of the experience of personal loss may be a "mourning creation." Perhaps, one might be able to differentiate or distinguish composers on the basis of their inclination to include the "personal realm" as their main or primary source of inspiration as opposed to those composers who respond only on occasion to significant life experiences, apparently tending to respond primarily to external rather than internal factors.

For example, the composer Henry Cowell (1926) emphasized that as a school-age child he embarked upon "a rigorous process of self-training . . . to make my mind into a musical instrument [and eventually] control which sounds I should hear, and turn on a flow of them at will. . ." The composer concluded, "I can only say that the musical ideas as they run through my mind seem to be an exact mirror of my emotions of the moment, or of moments which I recall through memory" (p. 236). Cowell seems to be informing us of a

Introduction

latency-age child's strictly self-imposed efforts at ego mastery (Berezin, 1958) based upon a "compensatory" motive: he was without a musical instrument and "could not attend enough concerts to satisfy the craving for music . . ." (p. 235). In this instance, we learn from the composer about the process of internalization and the efforts at actively creating "inner musical experiences."

In section IV, chapters 14 to 22, we conclude with biographical studies of a selected group of classical composers, many, of course, of considerable reputation. We have now returned to a tradition first introduced by Graf (1911), where the composer's life and the musical text are *both* examined and scrutinized with the objective of gaining increased access to and fuller appreciation of the manner and means by which these individuals worked. Papers presented in this section reflect for the most part studies of composers and their music rather than studies exclusively devoted to an analysis and appraisal of the composer's personal relationships (Sterba and Sterba, 1952) or the composer's significance within a largely sociocultural and historical context (Stein, 1976; Kalfus, 1984). In the past, the trend has been to focus more on the composer than on the composer's musical output; musical analysis tending to assume a secondary role or peripheral position when compared to the amount of attention devoted to examining and reconstructing the composer's psychological world.

In conclusion, it is hoped that future studies stimulated by this book will continue to examine all facets of musical creativity: the role of personality factors, specific talents, life circumstances, cultural forces, and, ultimately, the musical creation itself. It is anticipated that clinical–theoretical developments in psychoanalysis will influence the direction of future studies on music as will the many outstanding, scholarly contributions from the fields of music history, theory, and compositional study.

Stuart Feder, M.D.
Richard L. Karmel, Ph.D.
George H. Pollock, M.D.

I
PSYCHOANALYTIC CONTRIBUTIONS ON THE PSYCHOLOGY OF MUSIC

Chapter 1

On the Enjoyment of Listening to Music

Heinz Kohut, M.D., and Siegmund Levarie, Ph.D.

Not everybody is musical, but probably nobody lacks entirely the ability to experience some pleasure through music. There is no nation, culture, or period in which some form of music has not existed. Such a universal phenomenon must fulfill a deeply rooted human need; it must be the response to important psychological constellations. Whether the psychological basis for music be a single factor supplying a prime motivation; or a multiplicity of variable factors of which none may be indispensable, but which together bring about the necessary motivation; or a combination of one essential psychological need with various auxiliary motivations—these are questions which theorists and philosophers have asked and attempted to answer in various ways.

Aristotle saw the basis for all art forms in the principle of imitation. He claims that music has a special position among the arts because it imitates not the external aspects of objects, but character—in his language, the passions and virtues. Quite similarly, although in different terms, Schopenhauer (1877), too, gives music a position of special distinction. Other art forms, he says, are only indirect objectifications of the will, while "music is the copy of the will itself." While it is difficult to translate such philosophical concepts as Aristotle's "character" or Schopenhauer's "will" into the vocabulary of modern psychology, one feels inclined to believe that they are related to the asocial, nonreasonable, emotional, or instinctual motivating forces—in short, to that part of the anatomy of the mental apparatus which Freud calls the id. Similar consid-

---

First published in *Psychoanalytic Quarterly*, 19:64–87, 1950. Reprinted by permission.

erations probably led Kant (1790) to rank music lowest among the arts. He, too, finds its point of gravity on the side of the emotions and thinks that it makes the least contribution to the dominance of reasoning power and intellectual progress. The intermediate position is taken by Plato who, recognizing the intrinsically emotional nature of the musical experience, is aware of the fact that the motivating power of the emotions may be made to subserve reasonable and moral goals. He therefore evaluates music according to the nonmusical and nonemotional parts of the total experience depending on whether the final result is in the service of moral or immoral tendencies.

In contrast to these views are those of such writers as Karl Philipp Emanuel Bach, Rousseau, Darwin, Spencer, Hanslick, and Whitehead. The common denominator which sets apart their point of view from that of the philosophers first mentioned is their attempt to evaluate music not by itself but as a biological or social phenomenon. Darwin (1872, p. 330 ff.), for example, finds in music the residue of a formerly more important means of interpersonal communication in the service of the survival of the race: a device with which the male of the species attracts the female. Spencer (1902) also believes that music has its origin in interpersonal communication, as appears from his statement that language plus emotion is responsible for its production. Whitehead (1927) considers music to be a semantic symbol, useful for communicating something about emotions. Similarly, both K. P. E. Bach (1753) and Rousseau (1781), and later Kierkegaard (1843), Riemann (1900), and Croce (1902), stress the point that music serves as a special means of communicating the emotions of the composer through the performer to the listener. Hanslick (1896) seems also to belong to this school of thought because of his emphasis upon the logic of the formal arrangement of sounds which characterizes music. In summary, this second group of theorists stresses the intelligible, purposeful, and reasonable aspects of the musical phenomenon, or, in Freudian terminology, the participation of the ego.

In this investigation of the psychology of musical enjoyment we are less interested in the work of such psychologists as Helmholtz (1865), Stumpf (1883–1890), and Wundt (1911). Valuable and important as their work may be, they take the enjoyable quality of music for granted and restrict themselves to the description of likes and dislikes in reaction to sounds. But, on the other hand, the conclusions of the philosophers fail equally to elucidate the problem. It makes little difference whether the emphasis is placed on the emotions or the intellect; whether id participation or ego participation is demonstrated. As a complex psychological phenomenon, the enjoyment of music should warrant the participation of the total personality. What remains obscure is something more specific: an explanation of the mechanism of the production of pleasure in the listener which will take into account the essential universality of this experience, as well as the circumstances which can prevent the experience from being pleasurable.

Psychoanalysis has taught us that phenomena in adult life which are seemingly unintelligible and indefinable take on new meaning when understood in terms of chronologically early experiences. Hence it seems that the investigation of a phenomenon so widespread and at the same time so hard to describe in the language of the adult as is musical enjoyment should lead us back to the primitive and archaic—in short, to infantile organization. The expectation, however, that psychoanalytic literature will contain many contributions to the topic leads to disappointment. Sterba (1939) summarized the situation: "In psychoanalytic literature one can find very little that has been written about music, and what has been said on the subject is not very enlightening. It is considered proven that music is based on anal and narcissistic instinctual foundations, but analytical investigation has not gone further than this" (p. 32).

All psychoanalytic writers on the subject consider music almost exclusively from the point of view of the creative artist and explain the pleasure which the listener experiences through his identification with the composer (Van Der Chijs, 1923). Eggar (1920) states: "There is . . . a primary physical impulse in the musician; that is, to make a noise. . . ." Mosonyi (1935) derives the origins of music from the tension-relieving cry of the infant. Sterba's very significant contribution (1939) is also derived from the standpoint of the performing artist and appears to assume identification of the listener with the artist.

Since our interest is confined to the pleasure produced by *listening* to music, and not with the pleasure of creating music either by composing or performing, we omit examining the origins of music as a social or biological phenomenon, or the psychological mechanisms in the creative artist. No doubt the primitive precursor of the impulse to create music was present in the history of the race long before the nonproducing listener became important. As music develops and becomes an integral part of a culture, the noncreative listener increases in importance. This development in turn influences musical composition, for the creative artist, while still following inner needs of expression, is aware that he is composing for an audience, however much he may deny it.

What is the precursor of music to the infant? We are told that

[A]uditory stimuli [are] rarely effective during the first twenty-four hours, for the newborn infant seems to be deaf, the middle ear being filled with embryonic mesenchyme tissue and becoming gradually pneumatized on the first day or two of life. [Soon] the Moro reflex is displayed in response to a loud noise, a sudden jarring of the crib . . . : the infant lying on his back extends his arms forward, stiffens the lower extremities and contorts his face into a grimace; after a second or two he brings the arms slowly together into a sort of embrace, emits a cry and then gradually relaxes. The reflex normally persists for about a month or six weeks, being gradually replaced by the startle response shown by adults following a loud noise like a pistol shot [Holt and Howland, 1940, p. 32].

That children and adults react to sudden noise directly, by reflex action—without immediate interference of logical thought between stimulus and reaction, as though it were an undoubted signal of approaching danger—lies within the everyday experience of all of us. A shrill and loud sound may be experienced as an unpleasant attack, almost like a sudden blow. Under certain circumstances of great emotional vulnerability, even a very soft noise, particularly when suddenly interrupting silence, is reacted to by a startle response as connoting danger even though a moment later one might be embarrassed and smile about the apparently foolish overresponse. The latter reaction occurs particularly when the noise interrupts an atmosphere of self-concentration and self-preoccupation. Here belong the frequent observations of the hypersensitivity to noise in periods of stress during psychoanalytic sessions, or in traumatic neurosis, when the mental energies are taken up with the task of mastering a recent threat to the individual's physiological and psychological integrity (Freud, 1920). Both states resemble the psychology of the infant in one significant aspect: the major cathexis is intrapsychic, while a weakened remainder of the ego faces a threatening reality.

The infant's reaction to sound differs significantly from its reaction to other stimuli. After having been expelled from the Eden of intrauterine existence with its protective perfect equilibrium and its minimum of disturbing stimuli, the infant has to make the first great adjustments to external reality in order to survive: it has to breathe and it has to take nourishment. For the rest, a loving human environment (the mother) attempts to create a state as similar as possible to the former intrauterine existence. The infant must be protected from unusual temperatures and from severe mechanical stimulation or it will not survive. Against lesser mechanical irritation it can protect itself (Holt and Howland, 1940): "Coördinated withdrawal of an extremity from a painful stimulus [occurs] at the latter part of the first week of life" (p. 32), and the intruding disturbances from visual stimulations are kept away with the aid of the covering eyelids. It remains exposed to auditory stimuli, however, to a much greater degree. This exposure must create an early close (or "symbolic") association between sound and the threatening external world, as opposed to quiet and security. Hence, in the regressive psychological states mentioned above in which hypersensitivity to noise is revived, the danger reacted to is, on the deepest level, the greatest and earliest of all: the danger of total psychobiological destruction. Such a concept is, of course, to be taken not as a final, exclusive explanation for every fear reaction in response to sounds but rather as the primitive precursor and central nucleus around which later reactions crystallize. As the child grows up, physically, emotionally, and intellectually, it is threatened by dangers which are specific for the various periods of psychosexual development (weaning, toilet training, castration anxiety). Specific noises may come to evoke specific fears, and sensitivity to them may give clues as to the point of regressive fixation. Some people are particularly sensitive to the noisy chewing of others; some overreact to sounds reminding them of intestinal flatus; still others hear in the specific inflections of a male voice the voice of an angry father and react to it with anxiety or aggressive defense. Sounds may also represent realistic dangers. A striking example of the special significance of sudden sound in creating a feeling of panic is corroborated by many Jews who, in Germany under Hitler, lived in continuous fear of being arrested and sent to a concentration camp.

They experienced less fear when encountering storm troopers in the street than when at home they suddenly heard the ringing of the doorbell. The unknown significance of the signal in an atmosphere of continuous danger produced without fail a paralyzing effect.

Not only sudden noises produce fear. Repetitive, monotonous sounds produce mounting tension and may, under special circumstances, lead to a feeling of panic. This effect is used artistically by Eugene O'Neill in *The Emperor Jones* (1920), in which the thumping of a drum, coming closer and closer, is the symbol both of the internal guilt and of the threatening external punishment, and the monotonous sound of increasing intensity leads to panic and death. That primitive warriors used noise to create terror in the enemy is well known. In the last war the Germans deliberately attempted to produce panic in the Allied troops by attaching sirens to their dive bombers. All these examples support the opinion that the archaic mental apparatus, whether in the infant, in primitive man, or under special circumstances in the adult, has the tendency to perceive sound as a direct threat and to react reflexly to it with anxiety.

Pleasure is experienced when psychological tension is relieved or when such relief is shortly anticipated. Energies bound to a certain task become freed and can now be employed in pleasurable discharge. When after carrying a heavy load on one's back one is suddenly relieved of it, the act of walking, which is usually a neutral experience on the pleasure–pain scale, becomes for a while definitely pleasurable. The amount of surplus energy freed by the removal of the load is discharged in exuberant motions, in extra elasticity of gait, and the accompanying emotion is one of pleasure. Could it be that the enjoyment of music is based on similar mechanisms; that the original fear evoked by sound plays the role of the burden that is removed, creating pleasure through the release of energy?

Before examining the artistic use of sounds we shall have to trace the development of the infant in his relations to the external world of which sound is one of the most threatening aspects. We must not forget that at first the whole external world represents an influx of disturbing stimuli to the infant, and that what is done by the environment to diminish this threat is an attempt to keep these stimuli— internal (hunger, thirst) and external (temperature deviations, mechanical stimuli)—at a minimum. Silence at this stage would,

On the Enjoyment of Listening to Music

therefore, seem to be the ideal medium; and it is true that in regressive states of later life (states of ego constriction) like severe physical disease, traumatic neurosis, and sleep, an absence of sudden or loud noises is experienced as beneficial and pleasant by the individual and is provided for by an understanding environment.

But the external world must be dealt with, and the developing ego begins to recognize it, not only as the unknown danger from which it tries to withdraw, but also as the source of satisfactions for which it reaches out. The chaotic, disturbing sounds are gradually replaced by meaningful ones. If the environment is a satisfactory one, most of the sounds take on the early "symbolic" association with pleasurable events. Such associations are manifold and vary not only with the stage of libido development (or regressive libido fixation) but also with the specific present-day situation of the adult. The mother's voice becomes associated with oral gratification for the infant; the mother's lullaby, with the drowsy satisfaction after feeding. Early kinesthetic eroticism (rocking the cradle [Coriat, 1945] for example) anticipates the enjoyment of dancing and may become associated with definite rhythmic patterns. The tiny anal exhibitionist may later by identification enjoy the sound of instruments which connotes his former pleasure in excretion (Ferenczi, 1911), a pleasure otherwise not consciously admissible. Identification with the soloist, but often also with the solitary or predominant sound of a musical production, may have phallic-exhibitionistic, pleasurable implications. Silence, at later stages of development, may in turn be experienced as threatening because, after once the need for a good human environment has been discovered by the ego, silence implies being alone. Music as a group experience connotes the relief of this later fear, and one of the factors of musical enjoyment is certainly that it is a group experience. While this factor does not seem to be a specifically musical one (most other art forms relieve loneliness in much the same way), the purpose of certain forms of music appears to be to relieve just such specific anxieties. Here belong the group singing of clubs and fraternities, the courage-inspiring singing of the national anthem, and probably to some extent the war chants of primitive tribes. "Whistling in the dark" is an attempt to dispel the anxiety of loneliness by creating the illusion of a supporting group.

Music gives various things to different individuals. One may sit with closed eyes and open mouth and drink in music, in regressive enjoyment, as he once sucked his mother's breast. Another enjoys mainly the rhythm: he cannot sit still; he has to move his fingers and hands, his feet, his head in enjoyable kinesthetic discharge of the tension created by the rhythmical sounds. For a third, music is mainly enjoyable as a group experience: he derives from it a feeling of strength, the support of many, the relief of loneliness. A fourth may find the sublimated gratification of a long-forgotten curiosity aroused by rhythmical sounds of the primal scene. A fifth identifies himself with the composer or performer and finds a vicarious fulfillment of ambitious and exhibitionistic wishes. These factors and perhaps others, or combinations of them, undoubtedly play a great role wherever music is enjoyed, but they do not explain what is the specifically *musical* element about pleasure in listening to music.

For this problem, let us return to the earliest fear of sounds, to a stage of the unformed ego to which sound is a chaotic, threatening experience that cannot be mastered. The relief of this primitive fear of destruction is brought about by the formal aspects of music which enable the developed, musical ego to master this preverbal sound experience. Through music a psychological situation is created in which the individual is confronted with a complex, nonverbal influx of auditory stimuli which, essentially, cannot be understood in other terms. Such a situation resembles the one in which the unorganized ego faces the world. If flight is not possible, or if the impulse to withdraw is resisted, a large amount of energy is mobilized to neutralize an anxiety which is anticipated as the listener prepares himself to confront the sounds. But music *is* intelligible, it has forms and laws which the ego can learn and which it can make a part of its organization. With the aid of this organization the sound stimuli are mastered, and the energy which was mobilized, in anticipation, to deal with the influx of unorganized sound, is liberated.

An important objection will have to be met at this point. If the source of the pleasure in music stems from the liberated energy, if this liberation of energy is made possible because the anxiety proves to be unnecessary, and if, finally, the anxiety becomes unnecessary because of the intelligibility of the formal aspects of music—why, it may be asked, do these considerations not apply equally to every intelligible sound, and why, therefore, is not every intelligible auditory impression as enjoyable as music? The answer is that there are quantitative as well as qualitative differences between the psychological effects of music and the psychological significance of other intelligible sounds.

It may be assumed that the understanding of spoken language, the recognition of the sounds produced by the waters of a brook, and the like, have some pleasurable quality; but this pleasure is, under ordinary circumstances, not great enough to be noticeable. It simply creates a vague feeling of general well-being. The pleasurable feeling is increased whenever the experience of recognition is not entirely taken for granted, for example, when one hears the familiar sound of one's mother tongue in a foreign setting. A similar pleasurable effect, though essentially a nonmusical one, is created in program music through imitation, as of the song of birds (Respighi's *The Pines of Rome*), or of a thunderstorm (Richard Strauss's *Eine Alpensinfonie*), or the simulation of human conversation (Ravel's orchestration of Mussorgsky's *Pictures at an Exhibition*).

There is, however, a more significant difference between such sounds and music. The meaning of all the intelligible sounds other than musical can be verbalized. When hearing the murmuring of a brook, one can say, "I hear a brook"; or "the wind," or "a person talking." The mere fact that the content of an experience can be put into words exempts it, psychologically, from being threatening on the deepest levels on which the musical effect originates. Pure music cannot be translated into words. The world of pure sounds cannot be mastered with the main instrument of logical thinking—the neutralizing, energy-binding functions of the mind—which Freud calls the secondary process of the psyche (1900). This fact accounts, perhaps, for the special position of music among the forms of art. It, surely, is the explanation for the specific quality of pleasure in music. Stimuli which cannot be mastered through translation into words (or comparable symbols used in logical thought) mobilize much greater forces, and perhaps also forces of a different distribution corresponding to a very early ego organization. This energy is required to withstand the influx of a chaotic stimulation; it becomes liberated when the form of music transforms the chaos into an orderly stimulation that can be dealt with comparatively easily. Logical study of a work of music and abstract, theoretical knowledge of a musical composition are aids to understanding which lie outside the intrinsically musical. They are not an essential part of the capacity for musical enjoyment; but, as they belong to the secondary process, they add the minor aesthetic pleasure of recognition to the major, primary pleasure, which one might call the "ecstatic" pleasure. They do, however, sometimes enable a listener to create for himself an atmosphere of security in knowing, in which the deeper transformations of energy can take place, and in which the ecstatic pleasure can be experienced.

One could, perhaps, on the basis of the foregoing considerations, attempt to differentiate theoretically, first, the nonmusical listener; second, the primitively musical listener or the musical ecstatic; and, third, the person who enjoys the aesthetic pleasure of consciously recognizing and following the formal structure of musical creations. Often, however, the second and third types coexist. The faculty for musical enjoyment can be better delimited. It is the capacity to confront the world of sounds without the aid of processes of verbalization and without a logiç in terms of visual imagery. It is the capacity to solve the musical task through musical mastery. It was stated, for example, by many musical people that they felt frustrated by Walt Disney's *Fantasia* because the visual impressions distracted them from the music. Other listeners were pleased with the aid given by the simultaneous visual "commentary" which the film provided and which made them tolerate complex musical stimulation that could otherwise not have been mastered by them and would perhaps have created an unpleasant tension.

Music for films, according to this point of view, poses a special problem. As long as the emphasis is placed on the action of the moving picture, the music cannot be mastered and enjoyed by the listener. It will either prove to be an unpleasant distraction for the nonmusical part of the audience, or it will create enough tension in the musical listener to induce him to close his eyes. This fact has been recognized by those who write and perform film music. The devices used to prevent unwarranted tension effects in the audience are: first, great simplicity of the musical task for the listener (most film music is merely descriptive underlining of the action of the moment); second, low intensity of the sounds to enable the listener to withdraw his attention from them. The relationship between music, on the one hand, and words and action, on the other, has to be carefully treated in other art forms such as opera. Composers who place the emphasis upon the music must keep the libretto simple: the feelings portrayed have to be strong and directly understandable (love, hate, jealousy, triumph, submission) or the musical listener will be distracted. Verdi successfully represents this approach. Another device is the alternation of action parts (recitatives) with musical parts (arias and ensembles), as in the operas of Mozart.

All these examples demonstrate that a certain concentration of the listener on his task is necessary. Distractions hinder the musical work of mastering the influx of sounds and lead to anxious tension. The tension-producing effect of music is also noticeable when music accompanies an entirely different task, for example, reading when "the radio in the next room" can drive the reader to distraction. A similar frustration is brought about when extraneous noises compete with the musical sounds. It is particularly instructive to analyze one's emotional reactions under such circumstances as when during an open-air concert the noise of a passing train intrudes on the listener, or when during a concert-hall performance the whispering of impolite neighbors, the rustling of the pages of the program, or the step of a latecomer creates a similar disturbance. Tension, anxiety, and reactive anger betray the listener's psychological dilemma: if he turns his attention to the nonmusical sounds he cannot master the musical stimulation; if he tries to continue his concentration on the musical task, the extraneous noise is not logically understood and takes on primitive threatening qualities. Minor extraneous noises of low sound intensity, which ordinarily would not interfere with the process of listening to music, are sometimes rationalized as the source of disturbance by a listener who, in reality, feels himself unable to master a particular musical composition.

Music intended to supply the background to other activities is usually of such light nature as to present no special problems. Dinner music falls in this category. Even an ardent music lover would object to having a Brahms symphony accompany his chewing, while he might not mind on that occasion simple compositions which would otherwise bore him. Experiments have been made testing the effect of music accompanying work, with results pointing toward the conclusion that the efficiency of the workers increased in the beginning but that excessive fatigue canceled this gain in the end (Antrim, 1943; Kerr, 1945). This fact corroborates our hypothesis. Energy freed through the listening process produced first a joyful mood and with it greater capacity for work. It is not the basic store of energy of the worker, however, that is increased, but only the rate of its discharge or availability. As the basic energy becomes exhausted, not only does the work become tiresome, but the task of mastering the music constitutes an additional burden. Music, in these circumstances, has an effect similar to such pharmacological stimulants as benzedrine: it is useful when a special effort is needed for a short period, but the depletion of energy takes place at a more rapid pace.

In special circumstances even the attentive listener will be frustrated in his attempt to achieve pleasure. Such is the case when he is confronted with music, the form of which is entirely unfamiliar. Unable to cope with the unfamiliar sounds of atonal music, for example, large numbers of listeners trapped in the concert hall experience a gradual rise of anxious tension at the strange sounds which they cannot master. Mass flight, rationalized as moral protest, and compulsive laughter, in an attempt to relieve the tension, were frequent results in the early days of Schönberg and his pupils. Another defense on such occasions was the production of counter-noises (hissing, booing), over which the listeners at least had control, to drown out the uncontrollable and unintelligible music. If flight is not possible and if no supporting group of equally helpless listeners makes it practicable to turn the threatening passivity into active attack, then the only recourse is to close one's ears, as it were, by actively turning one's attention away from the sounds. This withdrawal can be partially achieved by daydreaming, which becomes almost automatic when exposure to music has been too prolonged and fatigue prevents the psychic apparatus from dealing with the stimuli in an adequate fashion.

Up to this point we have discussed in some detail the auxiliary factors which contribute to musical enjoyment and have stated, in the most general terms, that the basic pleasure stems from the energy liberated through mastery of the musical task. This latter process requires more detailed attention. Questions which have to be answered are: (1) What are the formal aspects of music that allow the listener to master the auditory stimuli? (2) In what way does the basic psychological process (threat–relief–pleasure) become reinforced and reduplicated in the musical composition? (3) How does the freed energy find discharge through essentially musical means? These three questions cannot be entirely separated because the same musical device often serves more than one psychological purpose.

To answer the first question, we recognize that nearly the whole of musical theory could in some way or other be credited as contributing to the solution of the task of the listener. We will mention only the most important means and those in which the psychological aid received by the listener is most clearly intelligible.

Immediately we can say that for the listener the psychological task is a limited one and that the scope of any musical work can be surveyed by the listener at least in approximation. Each composition has a clear-cut *beginning* and a definite *end*, and the listener knows this to be a fact. The attitude of the musical listener and artist at the beginning of the performance is noteworthy: both insist that a state of complete silence precede the first musical sounds. This silence has two functions. It brings into sharper focus the basically threatening situation in which sound interrupts silence and, therefore, by increasing the threat, increases the possibilities of enjoyment through mastery. It also allows the listener to prepare himself psychologically for the task of mastering the musical sounds by withdrawing his attention from sounds that can be understood with the aid of processes of verbalization and directing it to the specifically musical task: mastery through recognition of musical organization.

The main aid given to the listener in mastering the musical sound experience lies in the use of *tones* rather than noises. Tones supply the basic elements for building a composition. A tone is an already organized acoustical phenomenon. Unlike other sounds, it is characterized by regular sine vibrations which are responsible for giving it definite pitch, loudness, and timbre. These qualities permit us to master it, while noise, lacking them, remains chaotic. Very few compositions rely on noises rather than tones unless an effect of shock is desired. It is significant that noisy instruments, such as cymbals, are used primarily at the point of climax, as in the prelude to *Die Meistersinger*. Noise at the very beginning of a composition, as the roll of the snaredrum in Rossini's overture to *La Gazza ladra*, creates an intentional state of alarm, which, in this case, is quickly resolved into exaggerated hilarity.

The artistic necessity for the mastery of auditory stimuli also sheds new light on the concept of *tonality*. Tonality is a definite organization of tones as opposed to the chaotic influx of random tones. Its validity is derived from the natural organization of the overtone series. The physical interval of the octave, which is expressible by the simple frequency relationship of two to one, sets the consonant frame within which all the other tones are organized. As the histories of various civilizations show, the number of tones within the octave appears to be acquired arbitrarily according to principles which are not necessarily musical. Curt Sachs (1929) has pointed out the correlation between the number of tones used within an octave and certain holy and symbolic numbers: thus the Chinese divide the octave into five tones; classical Western culture has seven; modern music twelve. It can be easily proved that we can condition ourselves to any kind of tonality. Chinese music, for instance, will sound weird to a Western ear at first hearing, but repeated hearing of a Chinese composition will soon make us receptive to its tonal organization. Tonality can thus be understood as a group of tones bound by an acoustical law and repeatedly experienced, and hence as an important means permitting the mastery of otherwise chaotic acoustical stimuli. Within each tonality one special tone is chosen as a signal, a frame of reference within which all other tones can be understood. It is commonly called the tonic. It is a fixed point from which one measures all other tones and which determines the consonant or dissonant character of all other tones. It is an accepted rule of composition that a musical work should begin on the tonic. Gregorian melodies, sung and codified fifteen hundred years ago, follow it, as do recent works of such representative contemporaries as Hindemith and Stravinsky. The musical reasons for such universal observance are strong. The content of music being fundamentally the movement from consonance to dissonance to consonance, a norm must be set at the beginning of the composition against which all later tones and harmonies may be interpreted as either consonant or dissonant. This norm is quite understandable in terms of the psychological need of the listener for a mastery of the musical material.

Further organization of the material is supplied by the regular *rhythm* which has characterized Western music of the last few centuries. Bar lines usually follow one another at equal distances. Wherever we encounter irregularly shifting rhythms, either the music is organized by the rhythm of an underlying familiar text (as in vocal music), or it becomes upsetting to the audience, even to the point of riotous demonstrations, as with Stravinsky's early rhythmical shocks in his "barbaric" *The Rite of Spring*. The most regular rhythms are used in compositions in which the avoidance of psychological shocks is desired, as in lullabies and hymns.

Another device which has long been recognized as musically essential is *repetition*. We can hardly conceive of a composition in which certain motives, phrases, melodies, or whole sections do not recur more or less frequently. Instrumental music without any repetition whatever, and some Gregorian melodies (without reference to text), put a strain on any audience. The element of repetition permeates the music of most of the cultures we know, and can be easily traced in the development of Western music. Many historians of music have used it as a standard by which to measure the progress of musical communication. Sequences in Gregorian chant employ it. Songs of troubadours acquire their form by it. Renaissance composers construct entire masses on the repeated use of a *cantus firmus* or its fragments. The construction of baroque and classic melody invariably contains repeated motives. Even modern music has never dispensed with the element of repetition. Music critics have accepted the need for repetition almost as an aesthetic dogma. The economics of dynamic psychology may supply an explanation: when hearing a phrase or a melody for the second time, the listener saves a part of the energy required for a first hearing. He recognizes it—that is, requires less effort to master it than when it was new. The surplus energy is one of the sources which enable the listener to experience joy.

This procedure is closely related to another that provides pleasure in anticipation by recourse to previous experiences of the listener. Having thus far touched the factors of melody, tonality, and rhythm, our speculation must now turn to the musical concept of *form*. Musical form can be explained only by reference to the repetition and recurrence of certain musical elements, be they melodic, harmonic, rhythmic, or other. A new question arises with regard to the history of musical form: established musical forms are discarded after extensive periods of dominance. Thus, for example, the fugue dominates the baroque period, and the sonata form the nineteenth century. Adherence to one definite formal scheme through several generations would appear rigid if it had not supplied audiences of many generations with the special joy of utilizing previous experiences. The acoustical threat is reduced if the listener knows what is in store for him. He spends some energy, to be sure, distinguishing between one specific fugue or sonata and another which he has heard before; but he saves more energy in the anticipation of a familiar pattern. The pleasure of the audience is particularly great when such anticipation seems foiled for a moment to be followed instantly by the appearance of the familiar pattern. Such an experience is illustrated in an excerpt from a letter from Wolfgang Amadeus Mozart (1778) to his father:

> The Andante also found favor, but particularly the last Allegro, because, having observed that all last as well as first Allegros begin here with all the instruments playing together and generally unisono, I began mine with two violins only, piano for the first eight bars—followed instantly by a forte; the audience, as I expected, said "hush" at the soft beginning, and when they heard the forte, began at once to clap their hands. I was so happy that as soon as the symphony was over, I went off to the Palais Royal, where I had a large ice... [Paris, July 3, 1778].

Mastery is also facilitated by the traditional use of familiar *instruments*. The composition of a symphony orchestra and smaller musical ensembles is fairly well standardized. Unfamiliar instruments emphasize the inherent threat and arouse anxiety. This anxious tension was exemplified by the excessive giggling among student listeners at a presentation of strange Chinese musical instruments.

The pleasure of energy release in listening to music is usually not immediately discharged as it is through laughter. The musical composition reduplicates the original task and its solution by creating a secondary tension in the listener. In music this is accomplished by leading the composition from consonance through dissonance back to consonance. This mechanism corresponds to the one which Freud described in the play of children. A child plays "being gone" to master the painful experience of its mother's absence (1920):

> [O]ne gains the impression that it is from another motive that the child has turned the experience into a game. He was in the first place passive, was overtaken by the experience, but now brings himself in as playing an active part, by repeating the experience as a game in spite of its unpleasing nature.... We see that children repeat in their play everything that has made a great impression on them in actual life, that they thereby abreact the strength of the impression and so to speak make themselves masters of the situation.... the unpleasing character of the experience does not always prevent its being utilized as a game. If a doctor examines a child's throat, or performs a small operation on him, the alarming experience will quite certainly be made the subject of the next game... [pp. 16, 17].

Similar mastery is achieved by the musical movement into dissonance and back to consonance. The composer first establishes the tonic against which subsequent tones are anticipated as consonant or dissonant. The need for resolution of the dissonances drives the composition forward to the desired resolution. This resolution, already known to the listeners, is simply a return to the tonal consonance of the beginning. Only the manner in which the solution is brought about—the artistic detour—varies from composition to composition.

The listener must be permitted to expect that he will be able to solve the task. If the originality of the composer presents him with an unusual task, the composition will at first meet with violent resistance. Beethoven's First Symphony, for example, adds a puzzling minor seventh to the opening tonic chord of C major, and Wagner avoids the clear establishment of a basic tonality at the beginning of *Tristan und Isolde* by a series of unexpected modulations. As we know, both composers were harshly censured by their contemporaries. The shock effect of such dissonant and unfamiliar beginnings was criticized as "chaotic," "revolutionary," "undisciplined," and "indecent." The audiences felt defenseless. In both instances, however, the composer had merely set for himself a new artistic problem, which he solved in his own manner. To Beethoven, the first chord justified the long, slow introduction preceding the statement of the first subject of the sonata movement; to Wagner, the indefinite opening served as a means of expressing, in Wagnerian terminology, the "unfulfilled yearning" and the "love woes" of the emotionally high-pitched lovers, and of justifying the sheer length of the dramatic musical development to its climax.

The various manners in which composers can playfully reproduce the development from initial threat to final resolution are called *style*. In both classic and romantic styles, for instance, the return to the established tonality is a foregone conclusion. A classical composer will lead the listener all the way to the solution. Little in music is more affirmative than the end of a Beethoven symphony. A romantic composer, on the other hand, will lead the listener close enough to the solution to permit him to guess it, but he will not necessarily present the solution with the same emphasis as the dissonance.

Either overcomplexity or oversimplification of the task becomes responsible for changes of style. In the first case, such changes usually take the form of a deliberate musical revolution against a threat which has grown too great to be mastered. The esoteric constructions of the *ars antiqua* were as self-consciously thrown overboard by the *ars nova* of the fourteenth century as were later the sophisticated accomplishments of the *musica reservata* of the sixteenth century by the Florentine reform. In both instances the musical revolution brought about a return to simpler musical constructions.

In the case of oversimplification, a change of style becomes necessary because the tensions created in the listener are too minute to allow him to experience noticeable pleasure with the solution of the task. Modern popular music affords a good example of such a change within a narrower frame. A new song does not become a hit until it has become familiar enough so that people can prove their mastery of it by whistling it. After repeated playing has made it so familiar that no energy need be mustered to meet it, the listeners lose interest, and it has to be replaced by another tune.

A closer scrutiny of the psychoeconomics reveals that if the curve of the tension is too steep and the release too sudden, the type of enjoyment changes. The suddenly liberated energy has to be discharged immediately by laughing (as in the example of the overture to *La Gazza ladra*), or other motor activity, such as the clapping of hands (see Mozart's letter). The stormy enthusiasm at the end of a concert performance may serve at least in part as a means of release of tension which the listener was not able to discharge more gradually. But while the opportunity for such socially acceptable relief of tension is welcomed by most listeners, it does not seem to be a necessary component of the mechanics of pleasure in music.

That the discharge of energy takes place in true enjoyment through essentially musical means can be demonstrated by the symphonies of Beethoven. It is well known that with the approaching end of the symphony the music rises in sheer intensity of sound and that the listener experiences it as triumphant and victorious. The triumphant intensity of the ending is the solution of the musical task, coinciding with the return of the composition to, and the final establishment of, consonance. This is the moment in which the greatest quantity of energy is liberated and the peak of enjoyment is reached. That the musical composition reaches its triumphant peak at this particular moment can mean only that now the listener and the music have become *one* emotionally—that the music is now expressing and discharging the liberated energies of the listener. In identification with the music, the listener has reached the final mastery of an external task. He has reached it by regression to a primitive ego state which permits the ecstatic enjoyment of music. To this ego state belongs the most primitive form of mastery by incorporation and identification. At this moment the ecstatic listener does not clearly differentiate between himself and the outside world; he experiences the sounds as being produced by himself, or even as being himself, because emotionally they are what he feels. With the breakdown of the ego boundaries, the "oceanic feeling" (Freud, 1930, p. 64) of being one with the world (*'Seid umschlungen, Millionen!'*) is reached, and with it a socially acceptable form of magical omnipotence and a repetition of early, primitive kinesthetic pleasures as the listener flies through space with the sounds (Sterba, 1939).

Introspection and observation indicate that the ecstatic enjoyment of music of all styles, not only the nineteenth century symphony, rests on the same principle. The example given demonstrates the case of the solved task and the resulting triumphant feeling which the listener finds both in himself and in the music he hears. Similarly, various tensions can be created on the way to the solution, creating different moods in the listener and, at the same time, reproducing the mood in the composition. The opening of Beethoven's First Symphony and the beginning of Wagner's *Tristan und Isolde* illustrated this point. The listener reaches the union with the musical sounds which enlarges his identity to embrace a whole primitive, nonverbal universe of sounds after the original threat is overcome, when during the playful repetition of the task of mastery he has recognized that the emotions expressed in the music are his own. The ability to regress to this early ego state, while at the same time preserving the complicated ego functions required to recognize and master the influx of organized sound, is the prerequisite for the enjoyment of music.

Summary

We have attempted to clarify only certain genetic, topographic, and psychoeconomic aspects of the problem of the enjoyment of music. From the genetic point of view it was demonstrated that unorganized sound symbolizes primitive dread of destruction. The fear is made unnecessary by the intelligible, though nonverbal, organization of sound in music. Elements in this organization are the clear-cut beginning and end; the use of tones rather than noises; a tonality to which the listener is conditioned; a statement of the tonic at the beginning of the composition; regular rhythm; repetition; traditional formal patterns (for example, fugues or sonatas); and familiar instruments. Topographically, the coexistence of the understanding ego functions (which recognize orderliness in the essentially alarming nonverbal stimulations) with the ability to experience primitive id mechanisms (which bring about magical omnipotence and loss of ego boundary) appears to be the condition for the ecstatic enjoyment of music. This pleasure is reached not directly but only after the musical composition has playfully repeated the original task and its solution by deviating into dissonance and returning to consonance. Joy and other moods created in the listener discharge themselves predominantly through the listener's identification with the musical sounds. Psychoeconomically, the steepness of the curve of liberated energies seems to contribute to the definition of the special quality that characterizes musical enjoyment.

There is perhaps no better way to summarize these theoretical considerations than by a quotation from a poet.

... Denn das Schöne ist nichts
Als des Schrecklichen Anfang, den wir noch grade ertragen,
Und wir bewundern es so, weil es gelassen verschmäht,
Uns zu zerstören. ...[1]

(*Duineser Elegien*, Rainer Maria Rilke.)

---

[1] ... For Beauty's nothing
But beginning of Terror we're still just able to bear,
And why we adore it so is because it serenely
Disdains to destroy us. ...

(Trans. by J. B. Leishman and S. Spender.)

Chapter 2
Observations on the Psychological Functions of Music

Heinz Kohut, M.D.

What can the psychoanalyst contribute to the broad and manifold aspects of musical activity and musical experience? On first sight it would seem that he has no claim to competence in any of the many aspects of the field. Yet here too, as in the investigation of many other complex human activities, the psychoanalytic approach promises insights not obtainable with the conceptual tools that are derived from the field to be examined; that is, in the case of music, the laws of acoustics and the rules of musical aesthetics. To be more specific, intermediate and mediating between the unfolding potentialities of innate musicality and the activities of the developed musical function there are areas of conflict. The area of "primary autonomy" of musical function (innate musical talent, sequence of musical maturation, etc.) is the field of the geneticist, of the neurologist, and of those who investigate child behavior; here belong also such biological theories as those of Darwin, who looked upon music as the residue of a formerly more important means of communication in the service of the survival of the race (1872). The area of "secondary autonomy" (the mature musical functions) is the domain of the experimental psychologist and, par excellence, of the musicologist. To be sure, one must avoid schematism, except for the purpose of initial exposition. While the chronologically and structurally intermediate area of conflict is the province of the analyst's genetic orientation, yet the findings and insights thus obtained are often fruitfully applied, particularly in the investigation of the developed function.

First published in *Journal of the American Psychoanalytic Association*, 1–4/5:389–407, 1957. Reprinted by permission.

The following study continues earlier inquiries concerning the psychology of musical activity (see chapter 1; Kohut, 1951) which, on the whole, were oriented according to the outline given above. In the first part some of the thoughts that were expressed in earlier communications are summarized; in the second part a wider frame of reference will be used in order to broaden the scope of the present essay beyond the area of the preceding work.

I

It is generally acknowledged that music is a highly developed art form and that it therefore involves the whole personality of the musician, be he composer, performer, or listener. Three effects of music are widely recognized and seem well understood. They are: (1) that music provides sensual pleasure for the listener and the performer; (2) that the execution or composition of music provides for the player or composer the enjoyment of his own skill; and (3) that musical activity may be a social experience (e.g., in ensemble playing, group singing, and the like). Few additions to these generally accepted facts need be made. The direct libidinal satisfaction in music is an aim-inhibited and displaced one. The enjoyable awareness of the composer's mental skill or of the performer's physical dexterity contributes to the general level of healthy narcissism and, therefore, to self-esteem. And, finally, the reassurance of "belonging" which musical group activity gives to the participants is genetically derived from the old reassurance of being the member of a family; the leader or conductor represents the parental authority and the ego ideal, the other members of choir or orchestra are the brothers and sisters. All these effects of musical activity are undoubtedly important. They are, however, not specific for musical activity but are also experienced in all other forms of art, in sports, hobbies, and professional pursuits. In order to advance our understanding of what is specifically musical about the effects of musical activity on the psyche we shall first approach the problem by an application of the structural point of view.

First, music as it relates to the id. In this context we must look upon music predominantly as a cathartic experience or, metapsychologically, either as a transference phenomenon, a compromise formation, or a sublimation. The tensions which are produced by repressed wishes are allowed vicarious release in the musical emotion when otherwise they would have remained pent up, threatening the ego with unmodified forms of discharge. Some primitive rhythmic experiences, for example, belong to that part of psychic life which Freud subsumed under the concept of infantile sexuality. The rocking of disturbed children and of schizophrenics, and the ecstatic rites of primitive tribes, may serve as examples. Rhythm, of course, plays also an important role in mature sexuality, the only experience of the adult ego that equals the quality and relative intensity of infantile psychic life. The emotional release of such tensions, however, may occur by very subtle musical means, as in the barely perceived rhythms in the accompaniment of a sweet tune, or in the rhythm contained in the aesthetic abstractions of a Bach fugue. In these instances we can experience a catharsis of primitive sexual tensions under cover, because our conscious attention is directed toward a tune or a thematic variation and diverted from the rhythmic phenomenon. The weaker the aesthetic disguise of such rhythmic experiences, the less artistic becomes the music, as, for example, in some forms of jazz. For a similar reason one must also question the artistic value of Ravel's popular *Bolero*, in which a thinly disguised, monotonous, and prolonged sexual rhythm ends with a clearly orgastic dissolution and transformation. On the other hand, when, as has happened in some forms of modern music, a reliable rhythm disappears for all practical purposes, that is, cannot be perceived by the listener because the rhythms have become overcomplex and changing in a hyperintellectual art form, then deprived and disappointed audiences have been known to leave the concert halls in understandable rebellion.

It must be stressed that the foregoing considerations are merely to be understood as illustrative examples for the cathartic role of musical experience as it relates to repressed contents. Another example, cited in an earlier contribution (see chapter 1), is the experience of aggressive impulses in martial music. Striking evidence for the occurrence of sexual–kinesthetic discharge through musical activity was given by Sterba (1939).

As a second application of the structural point of view we arrive at a discussion of music as it concerns the ego. Here the thesis is again proposed that musical activity offers itself to the ego as an enjoyable form of mastery, as the enjoyable overcoming of the threat of a traumatic state (i.e., the prevention of the experience of panic), analogous to the theory of play that Freud advanced in

1920. The thesis that was suggested before (see chapter 1) is in brief as follows: sounds were once a threat to the weak psychic organization of the infant. Later psychological organizations that constitute a regressive approximation of the infantile state are characterized by hypersensitivity to noise, and the startle reaction when sudden noise intrudes on the unprepared continues throughout life the Moro reflex of infancy. Similarly do we find hypersensitivity to noise during acute traumatic neurosis, in severe physical illness, and in states of extreme fatigue. On the basis of the preceding examples we may conclude "that the archaic mental apparatus, whether in the infant, in primitive man, or, under special circumstances, in the adult, has the tendency to perceive sound as a direct threat and to react reflexly to it with anxiety" (chapter 1, p. 6).

The adult ego is usually more at home in the world of words, concepts, and images; the adult musical ego is, however, in addition, distinguished from the infantile psyche by being capable of understanding the orderliness of form and content in musical sounds. The adult ego can cope with the musical sound stimulation by perceiving that the composition has a beginning and an end and that music is made up of an organized system of tones and has a recognizable rhythm. Repetition of passages that have already occurred, the familiarity of form and style of compositions, and the use of familiar instruments aid the ego in its task of mastery. With this background of security the musical ego can now playfully repeat the original traumatic threat and enjoy it. A minor increase of tension is created by the musical movement into dissonance and followed by enjoyable tension relief as the music returns to consonance. Thus the playful mastery of the threat of being overwhelmed by sounds becomes an enjoyable ego activity which contributes to the total enjoyment of music.

If, because of the overcomplexity of the musical task, the musical content cannot be mastered, then the exposure to music becomes unpleasant. Compulsive laughter, the production of counternoises (hissing, booing), or flight were by no means rare, for example, in the early days of Schönberg and his pupils. Analogous observations can be made if the ability to understand music is disturbed due to brain damage. Goldstein (1948) states that "musical sounds, according to Quensel and Pfeiffer, are perceived by patients with perceptual defect in musical performance as disordered noises, and hence experienced as very disagreeable" (p. 147).

The preceding outline of the ego's playful mastery of threatening sounds deserves elaboration in one direction. Among the external noises which the weak infantile organization confronts, is also the sound of the infant's own cry. We must assume that the experience of his own cry is, at first, not yet comprehended as belonging to the self; the cry is not "willed" but is automatic and occurs in a setting of hunger frustration. It may well be that the threatening quality of primitive sound is enhanced by this early psychological association. The pleasure quality of mastered sound as well as the peculiar position of music in a no-man's land between self and external world may, therefore, be seen genetically in the context of hunger and cry changing into satiation and subsiding noise (i.e., mastered cry).

In the third place, music relates to the superego when our participation in it is weighted toward the recognition of rules and obedience to them. The emotional place of the code of morals is taken in art by the aesthetic code, in music by the rules of form and harmony. Musical activity may thus become a kind of work, and the submission to a set of aesthetic rules gives to the musician a feeling of satisfaction and security which is akin to the moral satisfaction of having done right. What we call the aesthetic experience is intimately connected with the satisfaction that results from the compliance to the formal demands of a musical superego. The artist follows his inner standards of beauty, and the truly creative musician is capable of enlarging the domain of the beautiful beyond the limits that were recognized before him. Part of this process of change and development in musical form may, of course, also be motivated by a rebellion against the existing order of aesthetic rules; that is, the rebellion against a poorly integrated superego. The result is sometimes a quasi-neurotic compromise formation between rebellion and submission. Michel (1951) believes, for example, that the music of the Protestant Bach should be understood as a secret continuation of Catholic artistic tradition. He also quotes Coeuroy's opinion (1951) that Schumann forestalled the outbreak of his psychosis by the intensive study of the works of Bach which, according to Michel, was an attempt to make peace with the father superego. As an alternative to and variation of Michel's theory it might be suggested that the inner experience of the disintegration of ego functions may lead to desperate efforts at self-healing through musical contact (or identification) with omnipotent figures. The discussion of the potential meaning of music in psychosis will, however, be undertaken later.

Up to this point we have summarized the significance of musical experiences for the fully structuralized psyche—that is, for a psychological organization characterized by verbal, abstract, logical thinking; by object recognition; and by a relatively high degree of independence from objects made possible by an effective internal tension regulator, the superego. The conclusions derived from the application of the structural point of view are these: first, music allows catharsis for primitive impulses; music is an emotional experience. Second, musical activity constitutes an exercise in (substantive) mastery; music is a form of play. Third, music, as an expression of rules to which one submits, becomes a task to be fulfilled; music is an aesthetic experience. With the aid of the structural point of view we comprehend how the pressure of unacceptable strivings, the despair at being incapable of inner or outer mastery, and the demands of an outmoded or tyrannical sense of duty leads us in our musical activities to substitutive forms of discharge, mastery, and compliance in a nonverbal medium that lies, usually, outside the field of most structural conflicts.

II

We can advance our understanding of the psychology of music by availing ourselves of three other psychoanalytic tenets which are closely related to each other. They are (a) the principle of the gradual development of psychological function from primary processes to secondary processes; (b) the principle of the developmental hierarchy of psychological stages; and (c) the principle of regression.

Primary and Secondary Musical Processes

Psychoanalytic psychology postulates the gradual development of psychological functions. Primary processes are primitive forms of psychological tension mastery by direct, rapid discharge, residually exemplified by the child's relative incapacity to tolerate delay. Secondary processes are refined and complex means of tension mastery via the tension-tolerant functions of concept formation and logical thinking, of problem solving, planning, and deliberate action.

Musical activity, too, undergoes a development the end points of which may be considered as primary and secondary musical processes. In the mind of the adult, primary processes continue to exist in the id, experienced, for example, in the wish-fulfilling hallucinatory discharge phenomena in dreaming; they are, however, covered up by the secondary processes of the waking ego. Similarly we find musical primary processes covered by musical secondary processes. To repeat an earlier example: a simple rhythm is often concealed by a highly sophisticated and rarefied tune or by complex elaborations of a theme. This layering resembles the structuralization of poetry: the meaningful content of poetry is the secondary-process surface of the phenomenon; the form, however, with the *Klangassociation* rhymes and the rhythm of the words, belongs to the primary process, the primitive psychic forms of the unconscious. In poetry a verbal secondary-process layer (content) may cover a deeper musical primary-process layer (rhythm, rhyme), in music a musical secondary-process layer (tune) may cover a deeper musical primary-process layer (rhythm). Musical rhythm, however, need not always be a primary-process component of music. Sophisticated changes in rhythm may, for brief periods, enter into the realm of the secondary musical processes and the description of the layering becomes thus more complex: the primary-process experience of rhythm is covered by secondary-process changes and complexities in the rhythm itself. This, however, is not the rule; in most compositions, especially in the simpler ones, the rhythm experience is clearly due to the formally more primitive component of music (for example, the simple accompaniment) which underlies the melodic line to which most of the conscious attention is directed. Some musical inhibitions (inability to play in rhythm, for example) are related to the more primitive, sexual elements of music and must, therefore, be regarded as hysterical.

As another example of such double-layering that is related to our topic that may be mentioned are the two strata of parental command or censure. The words and their meaning are the superficial layer (secondary process); the tone of, for example, the father's voice is the more primitive layer and "c'est le ton qui fait la musique." As pointed out in a previous communication, this may lead to the result that some people "hear in the specific inflections of a male voice the voice of an angry father and react to it with anxiety" (see p. 5). An important sector of our superego develops from the parental commands, censures, and approvals, transmitted by the sounds of the parents' voices, which may be piercing or cutting, heatedly angry or coldly killing by mortifying distance. This sector of our superego contains, therefore, not only a *content* that can be expressed and experienced on the level of secondary-process function (i.e., the code of behavior that is demanded and the specific censure for transgressions) but also a *form* which could be called the sound or the tone of the voice of conscience. An example for the artistic application of the concept that the voice of conscience may have a frightening sound was given in an earlier contribution (see chapter 1). It was pointed out that in O'Neill's *The Emperor Jones* (1920) the thumping of a drum, coming closer and closer, does not only indicate the approaching external punishment but is also the symbol of the internal guilt. Similar considerations apply also to the approving parental introjects. We may conclude, therefore, that the deeper layers of the superego, or its formal quality, are related to a preverbal acoustic sphere. This relationship explains the deeply calming, soothing, or near-hypnotic effect of some forms of music, patterned on the whole after the early experience of the mother's lullaby. Music cannot alter the moral code but can temporarily replace the coldly rejecting inner voice (for example, the voices that the paranoiac hears) with a loving one.

Bertram Lewin (1953) has recently proposed views that may be fruitfully compared with the theories presented here. Basing his position predominantly on Isakower's essay (1939), he sees the genetic roots and the deepest layers of the superego in intimate connection with the acoustic sphere. The sequence of (1) sleep at the breast and (2) arousal by the father's voice corresponds, in his formulation, to the disturbance which the adult suffers when guilt feelings intrude. This view seems quite compatible with the theory that the pleasure in listening to music is partly based on the joyful adult mastery of the acoustic threat to the infantile psyche. More recently, however, Lewin (1954) postulates a preacoustic superego (corresponding to the infant's arousal by hunger or cold) which is overlaid by one that consists of words in an imperative mood. By contrast, the formulation suggested in the present essay does not attempt to reach into depths in which the superego may extend beyond the acoustic sphere, but stresses the difference between the deeply threatening sound of the primitive layers and the less threatening verbalizable contents of the surface layers.

In this context I should also like to mention Freud's advice that the analyst should listen to his patients with "ever-hovering attention" by which he implies that the analyst should try to be receptive to the primary-process components of the communications of his patients. To these belong, par excellence, the sound of the patient's voice, the music that lies behind the meaningful words. Here perhaps lies a road to the solution of part of the riddle of interpersonal communication which Freud repeatedly discussed in his papers on telepathy.

The fact that there are two types of speech, or two "languages," is also well known to the neurologist. In some aphasias unemotional speech is disturbed, whereas emotional speech (swearing, for example) remains largely unimpaired. Closely related are clinical observations concerning some cases of motor aphasia. Not only may the ability to sing a tune be preserved in motor aphasia, but occasionally one can even find a patient who, although unable to say words or sentences, is capable of singing them. Goldstein (1948) says that "the difference between singing and speaking is due to the different physiologic and psychologic structures of both performances. According to the close relationship of singing ... to emotional language, ... singing will be preserved longer than language" (p. 146).

Music and the Developmental Hierarchy of Psychological Stages

The principle of the developmental hierarchy of psychological stages comprehends the recognition that the human psyche develops, beginning with birth or even earlier, from comparatively simple to more and more complex organizations, especially in respect to an at first nonexisting, then slowly dawning, then ever-growing recognition of an outside world, with the increasing awareness of the separateness of the "I" or "Self" from the "You" or the "Outside World."

The meaning and function of music can be defined not only in terms of primary- and secondary-process functions but also by relating it to the depth of the whole psychological layer that is activated. In other words, what appears objectively to be the same piece of music will affect different people differently, or the same people differently at different times, or the same person at the same time differently at various layers of his personality. Conversely, we might learn in time to isolate in the complexity of a musical composition those factors that are responsible for reverberations of the more primitive psychological structures as well as those that are directed toward the higher forms of the psychological organization. And, finally, we may return again to the starting point, and aspire to apply our knowledge to the various forms of psychopathology with the ultimate goal of broadening our understanding of the wholesome effects of musical activity on a variety of personality types.

The earliest psychological organization (pre-ego, preobject, and, of course, preverbal) is characterized by increases and decreases of inner tensions. The psyche can neither register its needs (i.e., experience them as wishes) nor provide for their relief; the tensions remain, without psychological elaboration, on the physical level. The rage caused by the mounting "unpleasure" can be understood as a form of automatic tension relief which is also not psychologically elaborated by fantasies. A partial return to such functioning in selected and circumscribed areas of tension is found in the organ neuroses, which will be briefly discussed first; and in a group of diffuse personality disorders, an example of which will be described more extensively later.

The hypertensive patient, for example, is in one segment of his psychological functions unable to elaborate anger psychologically (for example, by vengeful fantasies), and part of his anger translates itself directly en masse into physiological phenomena. Such a patient must learn psychological forms of discharge, the psychological buffering of his rage. It would be naïve, however, to expect that newly acquired musical activity could constitute a psychological channel for discharge, for example, by such simple means as playing the trumpet, percussion instruments, and the like. Only under exceptional circumstances (as in the case described later) will a potential for psychoeconomically significant musical activity be liberated in the course of psychotherapy. Musical experience (especially by "oral" listening) may, however, relieve a person's deepest tension anxieties (and thus secondarily, diminish his frustrated raging) by permitting the regressive experience of a primitive narcissistic equilibrium. Such regressions, described by Freud (1930) as the "oceanic feeling" in some religious states, can therefore also be attained through music (chapter 1). Forms of therapy that seem to be concerned with the patient's structuralized personality can also help only indirectly, most often by creating the experience being soothed by closeness, or of being comforted by a powerful therapist. The content of the verbal contact (explanations, for example) is not by itself effective.

Psychoeconomically similar to the organ neuroses is another form of psychopathology in which there is also no psychological elaboration of the inner tensions in the sense of neurotic or psychotic symptom formation. In these cases we find that an insufficient ego system is unable to deal with any of a wide variety of tensions; thus these cases differ from the organ neuroses, in which the area of pathology is more narrowly circumscribed. The following case illustrates this type of disorder as well as the role which musical activity began to play in the patient's life concurrent with psychoanalytic therapy.

The patient, a married man in his middle forties, was employed by a large university in an administrative job. He had been in psychotherapy of one sort or another for most of his adult life. He gave as reason for his seeking therapy that he did not like his job, did not do well in it, and wanted to obtain a better working adjustment through analysis. It became gradually clear that this complaint was a rationalization which he had constructed not only because it was socially acceptable, but mainly because the real disturbance was too vague to be clearly perceived and described by him. The only way in which he learned to describe his discomfort was by talking about an unbearable tension, either in the pit of his stomach, in his throat, in his extremities, or in his head. It came close to what Freud called the actual-neurotic hypochondriacal core of schizophrenia, without, however, ever becoming involved in further psychological formations; for example, by developing into a delusion. It is true that occasionally he worried about having a physical illness such as cancer. But the theories that he formed had no great importance to him; he changed them often, and most of the time he had none. The original complaint of not liking his job was, however, related to the tensions, although in a way which at first could not be appreciated. His father had been a well-known scientist whose achievements the patient could not match. After the father's death part of his considerable fortune went to the patient, who could expect even greater future wealth because most of the inheritance had gone to the mother. The patient was thus financially independent and his job held no emotional or intellectual interest for him. His complaint meant that under these circumstances his work could not absorb his interest and energies, and that it was, therefore, useless to him for the relief of his inner tension.

There is no need to discuss at length the nature and genesis of his tensions. While they were predominantly oral and anal–sadistic, their main characteristic was their diffuseness and the lack of elaboration by fantasies, even during childhood or in his adult dream life. The genesis of his tensions seemed related to certain typical childhood situations in which the adults repeatedly stimulated his greed or created rage by sudden frustration while, at the same time, they prevented an expression of the need or of the frustrated anger by their contemptuous coldness and withdrawal from such ungentlemanly behavior in the child. Only the lifelong psychotherapy which was tantamount to an addiction appeared to be able to ease his tensions. In therapy he could continuously talk about himself: he could complain to a magically powerful and kind parent and receive interpretations which to him had the meaning of being consoled and pacified.

A résumé of the course of psychoanalytic therapy and the psychoeconomic changes resulting from it follows. Interpretations were first directed at his use of psychoanalysis for direct tension relief; that is, he had to learn to listen to the content of the interpretations rather than being soothed by the sound of the analyst's voice. This phase of therapy was characterized by a typical form of resistance. While he had originally commented frequently on the pleasing qualities of the analyst's voice, his use of language, the lovely slight trace of a foreign accent, and so on, he now became very critical. He pointed out the analyst's errors in pronunciation or his wrong use of idioms, and often asked the analyst to repeat what he had said with the pretext that the wording of an interpretation had been unintelligible to a native American. As he began to listen to the content of the interpretations, however, he became more specifically aware of his tensions, of his need for tension relief, his fear of overstimulation, and his lack of meaningful relations to objects or to activities that could absorb his energies. Some progress was also made toward an understanding of his childhood, in particular of the family atmosphere in which the early tensions arose and relief by any form of discharge was prevented. A critical appraisal of his values and his mode of life followed and with it a gradual decrease of his tensions. The improvement remained at first puzzling to the analyst. His mode of life continued seemingly unchanged: his occupation was pursued without gusto and his marital sex life continued in the same automatic, emotionally unsatisfactory manner as before. There was, however, as became gradually evident, a new aspect to his life, a passion for music, which gave it content, the experience of strong emotions, and, secondarily, even an evergrowing richness of meaningful social contact. In the course of several years he became reasonably proficient with the several musical instruments that he had formerly played only in the most superficial fashion; he began to compose music; and he became a regular participant and finally a leading exponent of the active musical organization at the university. It is true that he had always been fond of music. Even as a young child he would for long periods listen to recorded music and immerse himself in the pleasing sounds. It is interesting to note again that, so far as could be ascertained, no verbalizable daydreams had accompanied these pleasurable experiences. He had been, and still remained, occasionally, most fond of listening to music from various operas; it seems that the dissolution of human voices into the extraverbal medium of the surrounding orchestral music contributed greatly to the pleasure obtained by him. It was an early regression from the painful world of people and their words to an extraverbal world whose stimulations could be kept within bounds and could therefore be enjoyed. In the course of later childhood, adolescence, and during adult life, however, music played only a small role in his psychic economy because his deeply fearful and insecure personality had adapted itself increasingly to an environment that stressed athletic achievement and the role of capable administrator and polite representative.

The psychoeconomic efficacy of psychoanalysis in this instance may be said to have been attained by these therapeutic steps: (1) the patient became aware of the true nature of his distress; (2) he learned the inadequacy of his imitative social adaptations; (3) he developed the courage to enjoy musical activity which could absorb a good deal of his tension. The major resistances were encountered in the first two phases; he developed a great deal of reactive hostility against the analyst whom he correctly held responsible for the anxiety that was aroused in him when he undertook to reassess the inefficacy of his imitative masculinity, which until then he had considered as truly himself. The third phase, however, in which he turned to music, not only developed without recognizable resistance but may be said to have taken place outside of therapy. It is the third phase, however, which, in the framework of the present essay, is the most interesting one. The diminution of the diffuse tensions from which the patient suffered, cannot be accounted for as would be the disappearance of hysterical symptoms after correct interpretation. No unconscious meaning was attached to the tensions; they were a fixed actual-neurotic "symptom" for which psychoeconomic relief had to be found.

The case presented demonstrates the psychoeconomic efficacy of musical activity for the relief of pregenital libidinal and aggressive tensions; and it can be assumed that in the psychoeconomic household of the normal individual musical activity may have a similar significance. The question remains, however, why music plays this role only for some people. In the case described, musicality was not created by analysis but had been potentially available since childhood. Leaving aside the question of inborn talent, the early childhood surrounding was favorable to the development of potential musicality. Free expression of emotions was prohibited, yet both parents condoned the child's turning to music. The early interest in music, however, was passive (listening) and no significant musical skills were attained. Musicality was thus not integrated into the ego ideal and was given up during latency and adolescence under the social pressure of peer groups.

Patients suffering from organ neuroses and those of the type exemplified in the preceding case report are both characterized by absence or paucity of psychological elaboration of their tension states, that is, by the absence of neurotic or psychotic symptom formation. On the next higher level—the level of schizophrenic psychosis—our understanding of the significant psychopathological formations is on firmer ground. They correspond to a still preverbal developmental stage (or layer) of the personality which is characterized by a gradual separation of what is experienced as "I" from what is recognized as either the helping–loving or the neutral–hostile "Object." Anxiety, in this phase, concerns the loss of this tentative differentiation and is, therefore, psychologically more elaborated than the tension increases of the preceding developmental stage. A replica of the acute anxieties of this stage in adult psychopathology are the nameless fears which overwhelm the schizophrenic and paranoiac in the early phases of his illness (Sechehaye, 1956); they are experienced as a fear of uncontrollable loss of contact with reality or as a fear of permanent object loss.

The schizoid individual is a potential schizophrenic who employs a chronic defense; he distances himself from reality in order not to be hurt. Musical activity is relatively frequent among schizoids; and schizoids seem to be relatively frequent among musicians. Musical activity supports the maintenance of the often precarious balance of the schizoid by permitting pleasurable activity and enjoyable experiences in a sphere outside the vulnerable interpersonal segment of the ego. The pleasure that music provides to the balanced schizoid is predominantly abstract and intellectual; the emotions experienced are not violent or ecstatic but correspond to the withdrawn personality of the schizoid.

The schizoid balance may be disturbed by an experience of rejection—often negligible to the observer—which results in a sudden decrease of object cathexis. The schizophrenic's ego recognizes that the tide of withdrawal has become uncontrollable but cannot stem the current because the raging self-destructiveness caused by the feeling of having been rejected or slighted is greater than the will to hold on to reality. If these events take place in the course of psychotherapy, the flow of the narcissistic regression can most often be halted. This is, however, a specific situation because the regressive movement is usually started in the therapeutic situation itself by the severely taxed therapist's mistakes and ambivalence. While intimacy with an understanding psychotherapist cannot be provided to the great majority of schizophrenics, artistic substitution for human contact is often available and is used as a preventive measure, unrecognized as such, by many ambulatory schizophrenics. Music, in particular, allows in this stage a controlled and limited regression. It provides a nonverbal experience that does not tax the crumbling secondary processes, while at the same time remaining socially acceptable; and it establishes the symbolic contact with an archaic "you" that the schizophrenic's ego is in danger of losing permanently. Once this active stage of regression has been passed, however, and the schizophrenic has truly been torn from reality, music, in so far as it is part of social reality, cannot be understood any more by the patient.

In this stage of regression the schizophrenic experiences the world as cold, empty, and far away. If the schizophrenic listens to music during this phase, no meaningful emotional experience results. Unlike the brain-injured patient (Goldstein, 1948, p. 147), the schizophrenic recognizes and remembers music; yet there is no sensual quality to the experience and no emotional response to it. If the musical schizophrenic is forced to listen to music or to participate in musical activity during this phase, no wholesome result can be expected; on the contrary, the schizophrenic interprets such lack of tact and understanding by physician or music therapist as hostile indifference, and the new experience of rejection drives him more solidly from attempts at renewed contact. Later, however, a new psychological balance may be attained. Restitutive processes emerge which are, according to Freud, attempts at self-healing; an illusory reality takes the place of the lost one in defense against deep hypochondriacal tensions which appear when contact with the world is lost. In this comparatively stable phase music can again play a role for the schizophrenic patient, but the experience is deeply regressive. The schizophrenic spins his autistic dreams and converses with his hallucinations while listening to the sounds of the music.

It may be asked whether music in this phase fulfills a wholesome function or whether it does not rather intensify the regressive withdrawal. Two considerations support the assumption that musical activity may be beneficial even at this stage of schizophrenia. Chronic schizophrenics tend to strike a balance in toto with social reality and may adapt to some social demands. Listening to music may sustain such superficial social adaptations by providing the psychotic patient with periods during which he can relax in his psychosis without being forced to dissimulate. It is true, however, that these adjustments concern only the preconscious and that the nuclear objects of childhood remain lost to the unconscious. The second consideration, in contrast, concerns the fundamental dynamic constellation. Unlike the neurotic, whose internal motivation toward health is never completely lost, the schizophrenic does not react with true internal change to external pressure, even if it is applied with great tact; pressure forces him only to dissimulate. A comprehension of the changing needs of the schizophrenic during the various phases of his illness may, however, enable the environment to satisfy wishes that the schizophrenic cannot afford to express or even to recognize. If thus the comfort of soothing regression in the form of music is provided, a movement toward the recathexis of memories of friendly voices may be initiated and the musical sounds may, in some cases, become the first emotionally significant representatives of a regained reality.

Music and the Principle of Regression

The last principle to be applied in this examination of the psychology of music is the psychobiological principle of regression, which Freud introduced into the realm of psychoanalytic theory. The most highly developed functions and organizations are the most vulnerable ones; under stress they tend to be given up and older modes of psychological adjustment reappear in their stead. A voluntary, temporary, controlled return to earlier forms of adjustment, however, may rejuvenate the higher functions: controlled, temporary regressions tend to prevent or counteract uncontrolled, chronic ones. Freud's paradigm for this kind of fluctuation was sleep, in which most ego functions are reduced and older modes of psychic function make their reappearance.

Within the framework of this essay it need only be repeated that the extraverbal nature of music lends itself particularly well to the type of controlled regression which Kris (1936) called "regression in the service of the ego." Music, however, is not necessarily regressive in this sense; or, at any rate, it need not be more regressive than any other artistic activity. Art helps the individual in the substitutive solution of structural conflicts; substitution, however, is not regression. Yet in addition, art may offer the disturbed psyche a temporary, controlled regression to which the extraverbal nature of music lends itself particularly well by offering a subtle transition to preverbal modes of psychological functioning.

Summary

The investigation of the psychological functions of musical activity requires a broad approach; it is undertaken in this essay with the aid of two sets of psychoanalytic concepts.

1. The meaning of music for the developed, structuralized psyche can be derived by focusing successively on the three parts of the structure: id, ego, and superego. We are thus enabled to isolate three functions of music: emotional catharsis for repressed wishes, playful mastery of the threats of trauma, and enjoyable submission to rules. Catharsis, mastery, and submission are experienced in a nonverbal medium (i.e., outside the sphere of most structural conflicts).

2. The significance of musical activity for earlier psychological organizations is derived from its capacity to allow subtle regression via extraverbal modes of psychic function. It appears to contribute to the relief of primitive, preverbal tensions that have found little psychological representation and it may provide for the maintenance of archaic object cathexes by virtue of its relationship to an archaic, emotional form of communication.

No attempt is made to discuss the possibility of a scientific music therapy based upon a theory of psychological function and structure. This investigation may, however, illuminate the role of music in a variety of pathological adjustments by its capacity to enter into structural conflicts, by its capacity to serve as substitute for archaic object cathexis, and by its capacity to allow regressive catharsis of the archaic libidinal and aggressive tensions of preverbal organizations. The psychodynamic and psychoeconomic value of musical activity for the normal mind lies in the variety of enjoyable possibilities that may be found on all these levels.

Chapter 3
Some Considerations of a Psychoanalytic Interpretation of Music

Martin L. Nass, Ph.D.

Listening and hearing, particularly in their relationship with music, have interested and puzzled man for centuries. The attracting power of music and sound has appeared in literature and mythology from very early times. Orpheus charmed the wild beasts and trees with his music; Ulysses followed the advice of Circe and had his crew stop their ears with wax to avoid hearing the song of the Sirens and thus be led to destruction, as he himself was lashed to the mast of his ship while he listened to the sounds and pleaded to be released.

Sound is an enveloping experience and fills an entire presence. It is more difficult to avoid the onslaught of auditory stimuli than visual ones. Closing one's ears is a more complex task than closing one's eyes. Thus, the quality of the auditory cognitive experience is of a different order in terms of its intensity and its ability to "hold" its receiver. It narrows object distance and is more closely related developmentally to experiences of holding and experiences of touch (Isakower, 1939; Niederland, 1958). The more primitive, ambiguous nature of sound and its great capacity to encompass the totality of experience, as well as its formation into spoken words and language, have resulted in discussions in the literature of the role of sound in early development. Both Anna Freud (1963) and Spitz (1963) talk about sound as a line of communication between mother and child; Freud describes the superego as developing through the voice of the parent (1923), and the ear as an organ of reception both

---

First published in *Psychoanalytic Quarterly*, 40:303–316, 1971. Reprinted by permission.

of sound waves and erotogenic stimuli has had a place in psychoanalytic literature (Abraham, 1924; Jones, 1914).

The holding and immersing power of music often results in an ambiguous state of cognition in which the discrimination between inside and outside becomes less precise. The nature of the listening and hearing experiences facilitates and promotes this type of ambiguity and lends itself to greater imprecision than do visual sensory experiences. A distant object is brought in very closely since, unlike vision, the auditory perception is not precise in distance, although it can be precise in terms of direction.

The meaning of music in the life of man has been discussed by the philosophers as well as the romantic writers (Portnoy, 1963). Psychoanalytic theorists are newcomers to this scene. Susanne Langer's writings in this area have highlighted the role of music as a vehicle for the expression of feeling (1942, 1953, 1967). She holds that music articulates forms and can reveal the nature of feelings in a manner which language is unable to approach. Langer believes that the logical explanations of music do not do justice to its sensuous value or to its sense of personal import. "The real power of music lies in the fact that it can be 'true' to the life of feeling in a way that language cannot; for its significant forms have that *ambivalence* of content which words cannot have" (1942, p. 206).

Thus, music is experienced through a different quality of cognition than is the case with language. As Langer indicates, "Artistic conception . . . is a final symbolic form making revelation of truths about actual life" (1967, p. 81). She adds that we may talk about them but their reality exists only through the artistic percept.

Elsewhere she states:

> Non-discursive form has a different office, namely to articulate knowledge that cannot be rendered discursively because it concerns experiences that are not formally amenable to the discursive projection. Such experiences are the rhythms of life, organic, emotional and mental . . . which are not simply periodic, but endlessly complex, and sensitive to every sort of influence. All together they compose the dynamic pattern of feeling. It is this pattern that only nondiscursive symbolic forms can present, and that is the point and purpose of artistic construction [1953, pp. 240–241].

Unfortunately, Langer's fundamental observations have not been attended to; much of the literature dealing with critical interpretation as well as psychoanalytic explanation has been a move toward rendering nondiscursive phenomena into discursive terms.

The history of the psychoanalytic interpretation of music and hearing parallels the history of interpretation and understanding in psychoanalysis and reflects its shifts of emphasis and broader applications. Where early psychoanalytic thinking reflected primarily an id psychology, writers on the psychoanalysis of music focused mainly on the id derivatives of the meaning of music (Pfeiffer, 1922; Montani, 1945; Racker, 1951; Michel, 1960) and related musical experiences to transformed screams, to anal sounds, and to primitive rhythmic roots. Ego aspects of the musical experience were not considered until recently. However, the role of hearing in the development of an adaptive style has not received careful consideration as has been the case with other perceptual modes (Klein, 1949, 1958; Gardner, 1953, 1962; Gardner, Jackson, and Messick, 1960). It is one of the purposes of this paper to attempt such an extension. At the same time it must be emphasized that a study of the ego aspects of a given function of necessity assumes the existence of all which preceded it in the development of the idea, so that references to ego functions assume the operation of drive-related aspects of music and hearing. This fact has frequently been overlooked in criticisms of ego psychology (Lustman, 1968).

The relationship between music and ego functioning was initially discussed by Kohut (chapter 2), who presented a structural interpretation of music. (For an extremely comprehensive review of the literature in this field the reader is referred to Noy [1966, 1967a, b, c, d].) He related the ego function of music to the mastery of threatening sounds and then to the playful repetition of the original threat as a form of working through. The ego's function of mastery is seen as a means of gaining control over the originally threatening sound through the repetition so often seen in mastery through play. Kohut also considered the musical structure to be related to superego attention to rules and their need to be recognized and obeyed, and to the primitive release of id impulses. Kohut's paper is an important one in that it is a move toward applying a structural point of view to the musical process and the musical experience, whereas the literature up until that point did not concern itself with these issues. However, Kohut's attention to structure can be extended further into the sphere of ego functions and cognition so that the musical process can be understood in terms of contemporary ego psychology. Such an application has been made to other creative arts (Coltrera, 1965), resulting in a new dimension of understanding of the creative process.

At this point, the central thesis of this paper may be stated: the early hearing and listening experiences may serve to develop a cognitive style used by the ego as a means of adapting to and mastering the outside world. These experiences may or may not be related to music. However, the art form of music provides a built-in vehicle through which this type of cognition may be developed and expanded. Hearing and music may be seen as attempts to employ early sensitivities and early pathways in the struggles of the infant and young child to relate to and master aspects of the world. Its early use may be as a channel of contact between mother and child (A. Freud, 1963) with its consequent employment as a vehicle of communication and hence increased musical sensitivity. This approach may also represent early attempts at adaptation and restoration in sensitive children (Bergman and Escalona, 1949). It certainly seems to be related to a hypersensitivity to auditory stimulation as suggested by Niederland (1958) who reports that the serious interest in music of one of his patients began at the time of an extended bombardment during his childhood when he was exposed to the sound of repeated gunfire over a long period of time.

In his paper on early auditory experience Niederland discusses its genetic aspects and deals with the qualitative differences between early and later auditory experiences. He suggests that early experiences are concrete in nature and closely related to physical contact. Their influence is felt early in life and never stops. The infant, he feels, operating through contact perception may perceive the sound as a kind of contact. This postulation is quite consistent with Isakower's (1939) statement relating the primitive organs of orientation in crustaceans and auditory perception. In fact, the physiological proximity between the organs of equilibrium and audition exist in man. Early sensorimotor acts involving sound and hearing are very close to body movement and body rhythm. The adaptive quality of a cognitive approach involving movement in relation to sound bears on this issue. In fact, Paul Hindemith suggests that early encounters with music result in the novice's search for "sensations corresponding to those [known] as being caused by his own acts of motility" (1952, p. 22).[1]

Current ego psychology has provided room within its structure for variations in precision of cognitive states without recourse to psychopathological interpretation and within the normal developmental framework. Hartmann's (1939) formulation of the ego as man's organ of adaptation heralded the formalization of the adaptive point of view and began to bring psychoanalysis much closer to general psychology. Defenses began to be seen as adaptations employed by the ego as well as countercathectic forces dealing with impulses. The adaptive aspects of sensory functions were considered (Klein, 1949) and in recent years the issue of cognitive controls has been a central one in psychoanalytic theory. Cognitive controls have been described as "structures which are essential attributes of personality organization and control certain aspects of adaptive behavior. They are thought to guide the expression of drive in response to particular classes of adaptive requirement" (Gardner et al., 1960, p. 2). While the various types of cognitive controls that have been identified need not be described here, they have been related to states of consciousness. In a significant contribution to the psychoanalytic theory of consciousness, Klein relates characteristic patterns of drive, defense, and control to varying levels of consciousness. He states that psychoanalytic theory provides us with the means for conceiving "various parameters of awareness in terms of which it is possible to describe different *states of consciousness*, each definable as a distinctive *pattern* of experience, and each reflecting and vouchsafed by the existing balance among drive, defense, and controlling structures" (Klein, 1959, p. 17).

One of the characteristics of listening to music is that it facilitates the emergence of less structured states of consciousness and thus provides experiences which may be easily connected with more fluid states of consciousness. The cognitive quality of the hearing experience is of necessity a more ambiguous one since the symbols used can reflect varying nuances of meaning and are experienced through the auditory sphere, an area that in itself is more easily transformed into ambiguous experience than is the visual sphere. In fact, the auditory experience can facilitate the ambiguity by the

---

[1] This is undoubtedly connected to body movements while listening to music, and to dance forms.

very nature of its less precise definition. Thus, the ambiguity may induce a more fluid state of consciousness, allowing more drive-related material to emerge. As Klein indicates, "Since perception is a cognitive event, an elaboration by schema, it follows . . . that under certain conditions of release from reality contact, registrations may be recruited to conceptual realms quite different from those that ordinarily dominate waking attention; the forms given in perceptual awareness may owe much of their structure to more 'primitive' drive schema" (1959, p. 29). It is suggested that the musical experience allows less precise and more ambiguous states of consciousness to emerge together with their concomitant drive organization. It may be that the form of the music with respect to degree of structuralization has some effect on the level of ambiguity of the experience.[2]

The role of audition in personality development has not been extended into the psychoanalytic–cognitive area as has been visual perception. The early forms of cognition that may arise out of a combination of unusual sensitivities and particular lines of communication between mother and child serve as a cognitive style and become part of the individual's character, resulting in his own particular orientation to the world.

The "auditory style" serves a variety of functions. It enables the child to maintain the object at a distance. The infant or young child is able to keep some contact with his mother by hearing her footsteps approach or leave, by hearing her voice from another room, and by thus "holding" the mother even when she is not visually present. At the same time, the auditory orientation tends to be ambiguous in that the precision that is possible in visual perception is not present in auditory cognition. Audition is more precise in the time dimension while vision has more spatial precision (Fraisse, 1963). Thus, the flow of ambiguous imagery is fostered in this kind of cognition, which undoubtedly bears a relationship to early sensitivity (Bergman and Escalona, 1949). Hearing is one sensory modality wherein ambiguous experiences and unclear perceptions may be tolerated and embellished through fantasy

---

[2] This is true, of course, in more "open" types of listening experiences analogous to free association. The issue of focused listening or listening with a particular set is not being considered in this discussion as it raises an entirely different area related to attention and set.

activity. Hypersensitive individuals who react to loud sounds as painful or to minute variations in musical pitch as a physical assault would reflect these qualities. One sees them in musicians whose orientation to the world is to a great extent through the auditory sphere.[3] That hearing is closely tied to superego development has been discussed in the literature from Freud's observations in "The Ego and the Id" (1923), through Isakower's classic work (1939), and in the initial differences in moral judgments between hearing and deaf children noted by the writer (Nass, 1964).

One can observe the operation of the auditory style in the analytic situation in a variety of ways. The patient with auditory orientation will "tune in" on the rhythm of the analyst's breathing, on his shifting in his seat, and on noises inside and outside the room. He may be more involved with the sound of the voice than with the content of the communication. One patient, hearing the faint sound of a bottle break in the street, recaptured two early childhood memories of bleeding after being cut by broken and flying glass. Another reexperienced his mother's anger through the sound of a door slamming which recaptured her slamming of cabinet doors in the kitchen.

The behavior of the analyst with respect to listening to his patient reflects a similar operation of the auditory style and of the immersion in the flow of the patient's material. As in listening to music, one can follow the melody line, the obbligato, the counterpoint. The analyst is free to move from one line to the other, to hear them all simultaneously, and to intercede at the level of communication that is closest to the point of interaction between the patient and himself. One's attention may be drawn to a behavior that rings false with respect to the rest of the material and may thus be related to a defensive reaction.

The quality of the communication between analyst and patient is close to the quality of interaction among musicians in small ensemble playing. The attention to minimal cues, the anticipation of actions and reactions, and the subtleties of communication reflect the narrowing of object distance and the extreme degree of closeness so characteristic of the analytic experience. The parallel between the musical and analytic experiences can be drawn still

---

[3] Noy (1968) has made a similar observation.

further when one listens to the development of a new theme. Just as a theme in a musical composition may be introduced very tentatively and a bit at a time before its full impact is felt, so a new analytic theme may follow the same form. The attentive listener is able to pick this up early and follow its development closely. As it is allowed to develop on its own, it is seen as stemming from the patient's own creative flow. The analyst goes through the process in himself and experiences it with the patient as the sensitive listener goes through the processes of the performer and the composer in a work of music (Hindemith, 1952). The theme will be played over and over again in a variety of forms and variations until it becomes an integral part of the composition. This type of auditory orientation seems to be related to the "special gifts" of artistic individuals described by Greenacre (1957) and to Bergman and Escalona's discussion of unusual sensitivities in children (1949). It becomes a part of the ego's cognitive repertory and serves as a major orientation to the outer world.

Prior to the linking of cognitive psychology with psychoanalytic ego psychology, ambiguous experiences and less precise forms of cognition were interpreted as regressive phenomena or in terms of archaic forms of functioning. Most frequently investigators in cognitive psychology were not familiar with psychoanalytic formulations, or attempted to reduce them to "objective" terms. Most psychoanalytic investigators had not had direct experience with the findings of cognitive psychology in fields that affect psychoanalytic investigation. Thus, any indication of primary process thinking was regarded as regressive and most probably of a pathological nature. Ambiguous states and earlier perceptual modes were generally viewed as pathognomic signs. It now seems possible, however, to understand phenomena previously characterized as regressive or psychopathological as existing within the framework of "normal" ego functioning. In this conceptualization, a different level of cognitive organization is operating within the ego. The conceptualization predating a structural point of view would describe the musical experience as bringing about the "dissolution of barriers between self and outside world" (Sterba, 1939), or as "an attempt to relegate oneself with the cosmic spirit from which man has been separated, and to reunite with the god, i.e., with the lost parents" (Racker, 1951), without dealing with the ego states involved.

It is clear that these statements are references to regressive phenomena. A shift to a less precise cognitive organization does not of necessity demand ego disorganization by regression, nor the dissolution of boundaries. In fact, the ego state is closer to the analyst's "evenly suspended attention" described by Freud (1923) as requisite for the conduct of an analysis. A critique of the concept of regression in the creative arts has been made by Weissman (1967) who argues for a "dissociative function" in the ego which is subject to the ego's synthetic function and operates in the service of creativity. Thus, experiences related to early ego states normally exist together with more highly organized, later experiences and are brought back into play through the reexperiencing of situations that recapture some of the early cognitive organization. As Brenner states, "Later acquisitions in mental life do not supersede earlier ones. Often, they hardly seem to alter them. Instead, the two exist side by side" (1968, p. 428). The rhythm of a musical piece or the feeling of being surrounded by sound may recapture and call forth early cognitive states *without the dissolution of self-outer world boundaries*, and without the need to postulate regressive phenomena. Hindemith talks about music being related to sensations of early motility. He states, "The baby's own crying, whining, and playful crowing is probably the primordial material which assumes a very primitive musical meaning after comparison with the already experienced feeling of general motion" (1952, p. 38). Sensorimotor theory has clearly shown that the infant's earliest encounters with the object are related to and indistinguishable from his own actions (Piaget, 1952; Wolff, 1960). It is this quality of experience that seems to be recaptured and relived in the music.[4] Nor is it necessary to refer the experience back to an earlier known content in order to make it meaningful. Such attempts may very often result in artificial transpositions from one form to another, which is of questionable validity.[5]

The capacity for shifts in ego states is most common among the creative, and the structural position makes such cognitive shifts

---

[4] An analogous point is made by Schachtel (1959) in his critique of the concept of regression in the service of the ego.

[5] For example, Noy (1968) attempts to relate the attraction of the form of the fugue to the recapturing of the experience of a mother following her toddler from a distance. It is this type of approach in attempting to translate and equate creative activity with known, discursive-type experiences that results in both losing their intrinsic meaning.

part of normal functioning (Coltrera, 1965). This view also presents an outlook different from that of Piaget, where completion of the attainment of a developmental stage appears to be an all-or-none phenomenon allowing for no possibilities of simultaneous levels of functioning. Once a given stage is attained, the child has passed through the previous level and no longer employs that particular mode of thinking. Thus, although he does not state so explicitly, Piaget's position would regard the continuation or reappearance of earlier forms of cognition as regressive or pathological in clinical terms and not as a more open mode of functioning. The author disagrees with this position. The expanding view of normal functioning provided by ego psychology makes possible the establishment of a closer link between psychoanalysis and cognitive psychology.

Summary

This paper attempts to outline some of the salient issues relating to an extension of the psychoanalysis of music and musical–auditory experience to the sphere of ego psychology. In so doing it relates the meaning of the musical experience to early hearing experiences and to the adaptive use of the exposure to sound. The musical experience is presented as facilitating the emergence of less structured, ambiguous cognitive states and their concomitant drive organization. These phenomena are presented as early modes of ego organization whose presence does not necessitate the postulation of a regressive process and which bears a strong resemblance to the listening and hearing experiences in psychoanalysis.

Chapter 4

Freud's Theory of Jokes and the Linear-Analytic Approach to Music: A Few Points in Common

Daniel Sabbeth, M.D., Ph.D.

As a student of linear analysis,[1] on one hand, and Freud's (1905) theory of jokes, on the other, I have come to notice a number of similarities between certain verbal and musical pleasure-producing mechanisms. This is not to say that the significance of a musical masterwork and a common joke are equal; obviously, this cannot be so. Nor am I proposing that music be considered funny. Rather, as Freud has shown, it is that jokes have much in common with many noncomic productions of the psyche; and music shares in these similarities. To demonstrate this, I will compare a few jokes and a few measures, in the hope that this discussion of some of music's small-scale pleasure-producing mechanisms will also shed light on the older and larger question: What are the pleasures of music?

What creates a joke, and why do we enjoy it? Using an example from Heine's *Reisebilder*, Freud (1905) suggests some answers. Here, a poor lottery agent boasts to the poet of his relations with the powerful Baron Rothschild; he proclaims:

> And, as true as God shall grant me all good things, Doctor, I sat beside Salomon Rothschild and he treated me quite as his equal—quite famillionairely [p. 16][2].

Freud states that there are two possible explanations as to why this statement is a joke: "either the thought expressed in the sentence

---

First published in the *International Review of Psycho-Analysis*, 6:231–237, 1979. Reprinted by permission.

[1] Salzer (1962) provides a comprehensive explanation of the linear-analytic techniques developed by the Austrian composer and theorist, Heinrich Schenker (1868–1935).

[2] Henceforth, I shall refer to Freud (1905) by page number alone. All quotations which appear without page number are from pps. 16–19.

possesses in itself the character of being a joke or the joke resides in the expression which the thought has been given in the sentence." He points out that the same thought can be expressed in different words: "Rothschild treated me quite as his equal, quite familiarly— that is, so far as a millionaire can." Now, however, the joking quality is lost and we are left with the bitter cynicism of a poor man confronted by wealth. Since the thought in itself does not produce the joke, Freud reasons that it must be the form given to the expression which produces its character.

Three transformation techniques produce the joke's form: *condensation*, *displacement*, and *substitute formation*. Comparing Heine's joke with Freud's restatement of its content, we see that the joke format is considerably *condensed*. The postscript, "so far as a millionaire can," is unnecessary because its thought-content is displaced forward, to the location of the word *familiarly*. The transformation of the word *familiarly* into the *substitute formation famillionairely* makes the condensation feasible. Using a diagram, Freud illustrates the derivation:

FAMILI ÄR (familiarly)
MILIONÄR (millionaire)
───────────────────
FAMILIONÄR (famillionairely)

In other words, the thought starts in the mind in the following form:

R. treated me quite familiär,
 that is so far as a Millionär can.

Then, a compressing force takes advantage of the aural similarity between the two phrases and eliminates the latter grouping; only its most important constituent, the word *Millionär*, remains. Further, by the process of *substitute formation*, this force displaces *Millionär* forward to the opening phrase:

R. treated me quite famili on är.
                      / \
                   (mili) (är)

Freud writes, "Words are a plastic material with which one can do all kinds of things" (p. 34). Later, I will show how music is similar; there, too, the transforming processes of condensation, displacement, and substitute formation are constantly and subtly at work.

Although I have explained the joking technique, I have not yet

Jokes and Linear Analysis of Music 51

discussed why listening to the joke is pleasurable. Here, Heine has created a new nonsense word, "capable of multiple interpretation, which allows the hearer to find the transition from one thought to another" (p. 54). Why is this pleasurable? Because an "economy in psychical expenditure" results (p. 119).

Normally, in the world of reality-oriented thinking, familiar and millionaire are unrelated: the former means well acquainted; the latter, a person of wealth. As one thinks separately of each word, a certain amount of energy brings it from its preconscious storage location into focal awareness. "Famillionairely" and, thus, the joke saves energy by simultaneously bringing toward consciousness two preconscious thoughts. The mechanism is similar to a short circuit: an unexpectedly abbreviated path connects alien ideas, and a pleasurable discharge occurs.

To make the short circuit possible, *mili . . . är* is used in two, logically unrelated words. This multiple use of sound materials is a facet of the joke technique that is also important in music. Here in the joke, however, it allows us to recognize that there *is* a real connection between *familiär* and *Millionär*—by the pleasing, inner-oriented mechanism of sound association, rather than the reality-oriented logic of meaning. Freud points out—as did Aristotle—that recognition is pleasurable in itself. Therefore, it is quite understandable that in jokes, as in other activities, people exercise this capacity for its own sake (p. 121).

Freud defines the purpose of joke formation as "activity which aims at deriving pleasure from mental processes" (p. 96). Thus, the joke's transformation techniques have two aims: to produce pleasure, by allowing us to recognize and rediscover the familiar in unexpected places; and to divert our attention from verbal meanings toward sounds.

Music also wins pleasure from sound association and mental processes. This excerpt, from Martin Peerson's (1572–1650) "The Primrose" (quoted in Salzer, 1962, vol. 2, pp. 114-115), contains some analogies to the joke:

(Ex.) 4.1

There is an inner coherence in these two measures, and its cause is readily seen. Although the melody of bar 2 is different from that of bar 1, it is not new but merely a variation (sequence) of what has just been stated. The same motif, a falling fifth, generates both measures. Instead of having to comprehend and retain two melodic units, the listener need actively grasp only the first. The descending fifth is then used to assimilate what follows (bar 2). As in the joke, energy is saved: we rediscover the familiar in an expected location as a single motif connects the two segments of time.[3]

Repeated motifs (recognizable sound patterns) also exist in jokes. Here is the story of a physics professor who told a prince, standing in front of a telescope during a demonstration:

> Your Highness, I know quite well that you are *"durchläuchtig* (illustrious)," but you are not *"durchsichtig* (transparent)" (p. 207).

This also wins pleasure because "something familiar is rediscovered, where we might instead have expected something new" (p. 120). By the repetition of a *sound* at a later time, both the musical excerpt and this joke save energy:

(Ex.) 4.2

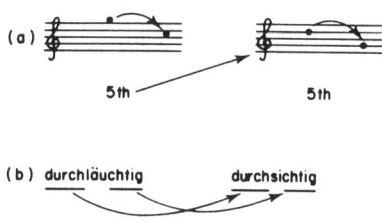

Another way of understanding Example 4.2 is to see that, in both (a) and (b), two nonsimultaneous events are generated by a single,

---

[3] In chapter 1, pp. 15, Kohut and Levarie state that the energy surplus saved by hearing a melody a second time yields pleasure. Weiss (1947) notes the similar function of repetition in visual art. Noy (1968) suggests that art is grasped by both inner-oriented primary and reality-oriented secondary perception, and that this creates a discrepancy "between the complexity appearing to secondary perception and the simplicity of the primary intuitive grasp" (p. 641). When the primary percepts are readily grasped through the unconscious perceptive functions, the surplus of energy mobilized to master the secondary percepts is discharged and sensed as aesthetic pleasure.

underlying sound motif. Consciously, such events must be perceived sequentially in time; unconsciously, however, they can exist simultaneously, as the representation of a single sound pattern.[4]

(Ex.) 4.3

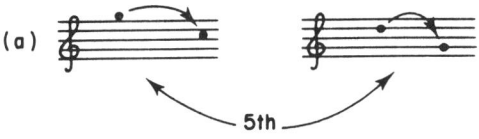

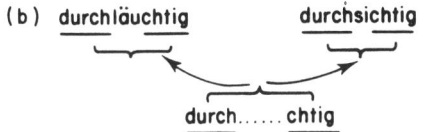

We have seen that form alone holds the key to the joking process, by "focusing our psychical attitude upon the *sound* of the word, instead of upon its *meaning*" (p. 119). In a joke, meaning exists to lure us toward the enjoyment of play with the repetition of similar sounds. Such activity is really play with *lack* of meaning, with nonsense.

"Pleasure in nonsense ... is concealed in serious life to a vanishing point," writes Freud (p. 125). Where, then, does it exist? Freud describes the behavior of the child who "puts words together without regard to the condition that they should make sense, in order to obtain from them the pleasurable effect of rhythm or rhyme" (p. 125). Preverbal children, as yet incapable of reality-oriented thinking, have few ways of exercising their power; one is by repeating sounds. For the child, listening to these sounds is in itself pleasurable; the joy of creating this sequence of related sounds adds the bonus of a feeling of mastery. Later, in the development of logical thinking, these nonsensical games are relinquished. Then they become particularly attractive, as an escape from the pressure

---

[4] Sequence in time dominates the secondary processes and conscious perception in their contact with reality. According to Noy (1969), the older, egocentric, and unconsciously perceived modes of primary organization have to be free from all time considerations: "the ability to transcend time limits and organize past experiences with present ones is a higher ability in terms of the self and its needs than being confined to the limitations of space and time" (p. 176).

of critical reason—"the rebellion against the compulsion of logic and reality is deep-going and long-lasting" (p. 126).

For most of us, it is easier to let our minds wander than to follow through on a logical train of thought. Children playfully avoid logic for this very reason: it is easier for them, too. Because they are much closer to their inner-oriented sound associations than to reality-oriented thought, youngsters frequently lapse into rhyme. The joke, however, must achieve a solution appropriate for an adult: to permit the yield of fantasylike pleasure from play, and simultaneously avoid the inhibition against nonsense "the absurd putting together of thoughts must nevertheless have a meaning" (p. 129). And of course jokes do have meanings, but they are "merely intended to protect the [liberation of nonsense] from being done away with by criticism" (p. 131).

Like the joke, music is a socially accepted procedure whereby adults derive pleasure from sound analogies that lack verbal meaning. It is easily seen that "The Primrose" demonstrates *displacement*: the descending fifth starts first on G and then on D. This is the first of the joking technique's three transformation processes, but what of *condensation* and *substitute formation*:[5] Let us look at the larger musical phrase and its corresponding graph:

(Ex.) 4.4

[5] These are, of course, transformations by the primary process. Noy (1966, 1967 a, b, c, d) has summarized earlier discussions of such transformations in music.

Note the last two measures. At first they too are pleasing, but it is not obvious why. Here the importance of linear (Schenkerian) analysis is demonstrated: the graph shows that the melody of bars 3–4 is not new; it is merely a rhythmic augmentation and a melodic elaboration of the original G–C descent. Thus bars 3 and 4 contain a transformation of the initial motif, which now, retrospectively, appears as a *condensation*.[6] A trained musician can explain obvious relationships between motifs (such as that between bars 1 and 2) and other surface-level events without recourse to Schenker. However, as variation procedures become more elaborate and attendant interrelationships appear more remote, the graphic techniques of linear analysis help bring the most deeply disguised aural similarities into focal awareness: Schenkerian study provides an organic view of musical conception.

Recognizing the opening in the *substitute formation* of the final bars creates satisfaction. The transforming process deepens the pleasure of rediscovery and brings it into a new context. A literal repetition in such a short time-space would have seemed a trite conclusion. Instead, restating the original fifth (G–C) in the context of a substitute formation, the composer expands the potential of this simple motif. The fifth becomes varied in its possibilities, and generates more satisfaction than would have been possible without the transforming process. Just as meaning allows a joke to exist, subtle development of the motif allows the musician to enjoy the pleasure gained from a restatement of his sound material without the use of literal, or obvious, repetition.

Another aspect of the piece is departure and return.[7] By the end of bar 2, we enjoy hearing the derivation of this measure from the first. However, this pleasure is only partial, because the second statement brings us into the domain of a new tonal area, the

---

[6] If the ascending bass line (C-G) of bar 3 is heard as a retrograde of the initial motif, then it plus the descending augmentation above (G-C, bars 3-4) also comprise a condensation, in line with Friedman's (1960, pp. 430–432) view. If the reader can follow this example of overdetermination, he will find additional transformations of the initial motif: in the bass, in bars 1 (the motion from C to G) and back which can be seen in the graph) and 2 (the similar motion from G to D and back). Also, the bass expands this scalar fifth to fill in the space of a seventh (bar 3, D up to C). Such overdetermination of the musical surface is brought into focus by linear analysis.

[7] Kohut and Levarie (see chapter 1) discuss departure and return in terms of movement from consonance to dissonance and back to consonance.

dominant.[8] As the pleasing transposition of a familiar motif lures us into an area of tonal instability and concomitant heightened tension, questions arise: Will the melody return with its *original* pitch-content? Will the harmonic structure return to the tonic chord, the signifier of stability? How can the conflict between tonic and dominant be resolved?

The anxiety generated by bar 2 is briefly resolved by a reassuring return to the tonic (bar 3). Immediately after this arrival, the melody begins a rhythmic augmentation of the descending-fifth motif, with its *initial* pitch-content (G–C). Yet, this elaboration of the original descent brings forth a new conflict between tonic and dominant: as the melody descends to D (bar 4), it is harmonized by the dominant chord, which acts as a prolonged, tension-producing sonority once again. Now, however, the resolution is immediate and conclusive. The expansion of the motif brings the melody to C, and this structurally decisive tone is accompanied by a final return to the harmonically stable tonic chord.

In "The Primrose," then, one motive not only relates the two opening measures to one another; it also resolves the tonal conflict concomitant in their creation. The resolution is achieved in two ways: the original statement (G–C) is reaffirmed, by the augmentation of the initial descent; simultaneously, the prolonged dominant—previously, a sign of departure—is resolved into the governing C-major framework.

Freud writes:

> [W]e derive unmistakable enjoyment in jokes from being transported by the use of the same or a similar word from one circle of ideas to another, remote one. . . . The pleasure . . . seems to be the greater the more alien the two circles of ideas that are brought together by the same word . . . [p. 120].

He describes the children's games which, like many jokes, intensify the joy of recognition by first putting obstacles in the way. This creates a psychical "damming-up" which evaporates with the release of pleasurable energy when recognition is at last achieved. As the anxiety caused by this "damming-up" is increased, so is the eventual pleasure of rediscovery.

---

[8] The dominant chord (V) is built on the fifth degree of the scale; the tonic (I), on the first. In C major, C is the tonic; G, the dominant.

How similar are these children's games of hide and seek, the jokes that reveal unexpected unities, and the recognition and tonal reconciliation that we experience at the end of Peerson's "Primrose." Through the technique of Schenkerian analysis, the musician focuses on the similarities between apparently dissimilar musical events. He sees how an infinitely varied set of foreground elaborations may express a single background. While the elaboration demonstrated in "The Primrose" is easily heard, many others are perceived only with difficulty. Yet, especially in such cases, linear analysis demonstrates one of its values: Because it makes us focally aware of the supple, not normally conscious recognition processes that are part of music listening, it also reminds us of the lively source of games with sound active deep within our psyche—"the unconscious thought processes . . . produced in early childhood":

> The thought which, with the intention of constructing a joke, plunges into the unconscious is merely seeking there for the ancient dwelling-place of its former play with words. Thought is put back for a moment to the stage of childhood so as once more to gain possession of the childish source of pleasure [p. 170].[9]

Listening to music, we resolve symbolic representations of the unconscious conflicts that exist deep within us with the easy delight of a child who can gain pleasure by simple sound manipulations.[10] The composer has done much of the work: he has put the music together. With the effort of active listening alone, we can take in what he has prepared.

In an extensive work there are many devices that yield pleasure. Among these are the disguised repetitions and remote interrelationships that can be clarified through Schenkerian techniques. And such restatement occurs on many levels, from the immediate variation in

---

[9] Work in the late sixties and early seventies suggests that the use of early modes of ego organization in jokes and creative activity is better seen as proof of an author's supple thought processes—explicitly, his highly developed facility for utilizing primary forms within a secondary structure—rather than as an instance of regression (Nass, 1971, 1975; Noy, 1968b, 1969).

[10] Noy (1967a, b, c, d) summarizes the common view that consciously perceived theme attaches itself to an affect which is different for each individual. Successive transformations of this theme may then represent the working out of an unconscious conflict that the listener attaches to this affect (Friedman, 1960). Kohut (1957) discusses the contribution of rhythm to the vicarious release of tensions generated by repressed wishes.

successive measures of "The Primrose" to the large-scale reworking of the materials of the exposition of a sonata-form movement in its recapitulation. Yet rhythmic, dynamic, and timbral devices also generate pleasure, and these are not (as far as we know) susceptible to linear-analytic study (Schachter, 1976). Even if repetition with variation could explain some instances of pleasure generated by nonpitch phenomena, it certainly could not explain all: the hypnotic effect of a Bartok *moto perpetuo*, the excitement of a Beethoven *sforzando*, and the richness of a late Mozart orchestral sound each require that we look further if we wish to propose an all-inclusive theory of musical pleasure. Moreover, music—unlike a joke—does not make us laugh; presumably the differences between the pleasures generated are not only quantitative but also qualitative.

Someday, perhaps, we may be able to asseverate—with both more perfect assurance and greater understanding—that in music listening also:

> [T]he euphoria which we endeavour to reach by these means is nothing other than the mood of a period of life in which we were accustomed to deal with our psychical work in general with a small expenditure of energy—the mood of our childhood, when we were ignorant of the comic, when we were incapable of jokes and when we had no need of humour to make us feel happy in our life [p. 236].

Yet for now I can only claim to have made a start: through the use of linear-analysis, I have identified a few pleasure-producing musical techniques and pointed to the similarities between these and the joking process. Further, I believe that in answering the larger question—what are the pleasures of music?—the structure that lies beneath the surface will remain the object of examination. For there we have already found many similarities—between music, the games of children, and the jokes of adults who are no longer allowed to play.

Summary

In his 1905 monograph, through a discussion of the primary process transforming techniques of condensation, displacement, and substitute formation, Freud demonstrated that jokes have much in common with many non-comic productions of the psyche.

As both jokes and music are socially accepted procedures whereby adults derive pleasure from sound relationships that lack verbal meaning, it is not surprising that music also shares in these similarities.

Schenkerian, or linear-analytic, study provides an organic view of musical conception. This paper shows how the graphic techniques of linear analysis are particularly well-suited to bringing deeply disguised aural similarities into focal awareness. Close musical analysis is used to demonstrate that the same transforming processes that allow pleasurable rediscovery of the familiar in a joke also are active in music. Thus, through linear analysis, we can discover many beneath the surface integrative techniques in a musical composition, and we can see the origin of some of these musical procedures in the thought processes developed in early childhood.

II
PSYCHOANALYTIC DEVELOPMENTAL PSYCHOLOGY AND ITS APPLICATION

Chapter 5

The Development of Musical Ability

Pinchas Noy, M.D.

Ernst Kris (1952) wrote: "the study of art is part of the study of communication. There is a sender, there are receivers, and there is a message" (p. 16). As a medium of communication, music, like any language, is spoken and listened to. He who is capable of creating structures, of finding original forms of expression in this language, is a creative artist; he who knows how to speak it, through making its signs audible and intelligible, is a performing artist; while the perceiver, who is sensitive enough to hear and understand it, is the "listener." Yet, all three, the creator, the performer, and the listener, although having command of this language and mastering its secrets, do so without awareness of what this language is, what it is saying, how it is saying what it says, and how the listener comprehends that of which he does not know what it is. And all three are incapable of translating the language of music into any other intelligible language.

To provide answers to these questions, to disclose the intrinsic essence of this language, requires investigations penetrating the secret of the artist's peculiar ability to create and perform, and of the listener's ability to comprehend, enjoy, and respond emotionally. Evidently, such problems cannot be resolved without thorough study of the multiple issues involved. No one branch of science can provide an all-embracing resolution; only a multidisciplinary approach evolving from musicology, psychology, sociology, anthropology, and other sciences has a chance of attaining conclusive information.

First published in *The Psychoanalytic Study of the Child*, 23:332–347, 1968. Reprinted by permission.
Thanks are due to Mrs. M. Frisch and Dr. M. Kaufman for their help in completing this paper.

The purpose of this paper is to examine one aspect out of the multiple facets, in an attempt to find an answer to part of the problems, through utilizing the theoretical, clinical, and experimental knowledge that has been accumulated in psychoanalysis. The paper will deal only with the origin of musical language and the developmental roots of musical ability and talent.

THE MUSICAL LANGUAGE

Most authors who concerned themselves with the origin of musical language traced it to preverbal communication. Racker (1951) writes: "We may also assume that music uses means prior to the spoken word and to object representation" (p. 150). Gutheil (1954) designates music as "a communication of which we know that it is non-verbal, or perhaps pre-verbal" (p. 98). In accord with this opinion, Masserman (1955) refers to music as "this nonverbal, nonanalogic form of communication" (p. 616). Margolis (1954), in an attempt to summarize the pertinent psychoanalytic ideas, states, "Most authors feel that music is related to the very earliest periods of psychological organization when the ego cannot as yet distinctly delineate the boundaries between self and reality" (p. 286).

This early source of musicality requires a discussion of what is known about the infantile ways of communication. Various authors have dealt with the specific modes of the central perceptual and organizational processes in infancy. In spite of differences in terminology to explain the peculiarities of the processes, the affinity of ideas is evident. Schachtel (1959) terms the primary mode of perception *autocentric perception*, and describes it as follows: "In the autocentric mode there is little or no objectification; the emphasis is on how and what the person feels; there is a close relation, amounting to a fusion, between sensory quality and pleasure or unpleasure feelings, and the perceiver reacts primarily to something impinging on him" (p. 83).

René Spitz (1965) refers to this primary organization as the "coenesthetic organization," of which he writes: "Here, sensing is extensive, primarily visceral, centered in the autonomic nervous system, and manifests itself in the form of emotions" (p. 44).

The reader can easily accede to the fact that these statements also contain a true description of the experience of music, although this was not intended by the authors. That such an association is possible may have to do with the probable origin of musical perception in those primary modes of perception.

Observation of a six-month-old shows that the infant apprehends and "understands" his mother and other members of the family. The infant "understands" and distinguishes whether the mother approaching him is happy and merry or tense, angry, and impatient, and he responds to her love with a smile and to her tension with crying. Every mother feels that her baby "understands" her talk and distinguishes between words of love and manifestation of anger. But the infant not only is sensitive to extreme variations, he is already aware of slight changes in mood as these are expressed in the mother's voice. Since the infant still lacks the capacity of relating to language as a semantic system, to its symbols and concepts, he is indeed responding merely to the various sound components—intensity, pitch, rhythm, and timbre. Hence the remark of Spitz (1965):

> Signs and signals that reach and are received by the infant in the first months of life belong to the following categories: equilibrium, tension (muscular or otherwise), posture, temperature, vibration, skin and body contact, *rhythm, tempo, duration, pitch, tone, resonance, clang*, and probably a number of others of which the adult is hardly aware and which he certainly cannot verbalize [p. 135; emphasis added].

But these coincide with what musicologists refer to as the elements of the musical language—tone, pitch, intensity, timbre, rhythm, and duration. All these are part components of the preverbal, auditory, communicative medium of the infant, gathered by Spitz under the umbrella term of *coenesthetic communication*. Dealing with these components of primary communication, Spitz states: "Adults, who have retained the capacity to make use of one or several of these usually atrophied categories of perception and communication, belong to the specially gifted. They are composers, musicians, dancers, acrobats, fliers, painters and poets" (p. 136).

It thus may be concluded that music is a language whose origin goes back to the auditory channel of communication at the preverbal infantile stage (i.e., at the oral and beginning anal phases). This early origin in a period preceding logical thinking may explain why it is so difficult to grasp this language by means of logical thinking and to translate its signs into the secondary terms of speech. It is highly improbable, in fact, that any language preceding the period governed by logic can be comprehended logically. Yet if we could turn back and identify with the infant, hearing the world around us through infantile ears, might not the secrets of music unveil themselves before us, enabling us to understand its paths of expression? Let us try and follow this fancy in an attempt at understanding the meaning of musical structures in analogy to infantile modes of perception.

Three examples will suffice to demonstrate briefly a new principle—to draw conclusions pertinent to the meaning of musical structures from the auditory experience of the infant. For if music as a language has its roots in the "language" of the infant, it seems right to assume that it may arouse and revive experiences originating in those early periods.

1. A frequently heard musical rhythm—the same tone repeated in short, evenly spaced beats followed by a longer accentuated tone—is regarded as portending "fate," as the opening of Beethoven's Fifth Symphony, for instance, or of Mahler's Fifth Symphony, or of the *Appassionata*, and of many others. Such structures bestow on the listener a dim feeling of anxiety, of apprehension, a sense of "fatefulness" and impending tragedy. If, ignoring the verbal content, we now try to imagine ourselves listening to a mother chiding her baby, we will hear the rhythmical repetition of the same, mostly high tone, followed by a long, intensive, and usually lower one. Does this analogy not suggest that our reaction to music of this kind with a dim feeling of anxiety may be due to a reenactment of the apprehension with which we responded as infants to mother's rebukes?

2. In many scores, particularly in those for cembalo and piano, we find movements of fast, bouncing configurations, accentuated by a fast, steadily repetitive rhythm, played by the right hand within the span of soprano. The accompanying left hand, in sonorous and slow basses, proceeds in large, confident, and rhythmical movements (e.g., Couperin's *Les Barricades Mystérieuses*), which bestow upon us an experience of calmness and repose. Returning once again to infancy, we can imagine the concord of voices—the baby's high, shrill, emotion-ridden shrieks and the mother's comforting, reassuring, and restraining cooing in low, quiet, and slow tones. May we not assume that it is the echo of an emotional experience of this kind that reverberates in the sounds of such music?

3. For centuries the fugue has been a favorite of musicians, transmitted from one period to the next, surviving and adapted to all styles and fashions. A form so attractive to composers and listeners alike over hundreds of years should express a deep psychological truth and gratify some basic need. Like the canon, the fugue, as its offspring, is founded on a single theme, carried by each voice and each instrument, yet taken up by each one after the other at evenly spaced intervals, so that at one and the same time it accompanies itself and is always behind itself at the same unchanging step. Turning once more to the infant and his development, we now recall the stage of first free mobility, crawling and toddling the first steps. As soon as the toddler achieves some mastery over his movements, he insists on being left on his own; he rejects support and the helping hand and is upset by any attempt to guide him. At the same time, however, he still wants his mother to stand by, ready to protect and pick him up the moment he stumbles. He wants to walk on his own, but be assured that the "big one" follows his steps at an equal and safe distance, lending him the feeling of security that makes him continue to walk "alone." Returning to the fugue, may we not assume that its specific structure of accompanying itself at a constant distance is reminiscent of some of this early experience of security, the reassurance that there is someone to follow, to look after, and protect us?

A similar, not far-off experience lies in the religious belief in the Divine Providence, in the guardian who watches man's steps (which is identical with the Ur-defense suggested by Masserman [1955], "the delusion of the omnipotent servant"). This experience, basic to all religions, may explain the fact that it was especially in the service of the church that the fugue developed and reached its height and prime.

That music is apt to induce regression to experiences dating back to earliest infancy has often been put forth in the psychoanalytic literature. Pfeiffer (1923) believes that music achieves its specific effect by inducing regression to narcissistic–erotic pleasure. In his opinion, music can do this by virtue of its property to symbolize the libido of the pregenital phases preceding the stage of object relation. Germain (1928) maintains that music inspires regression to the weaning period, while Sterba (1939) suggests that music is conducive to regression reaching back to the stage when the ego was not yet differentiated from the outside world. It is due to this particular regression that music bestows on the listener a deep experience of becoming united with the outside world, of being at one with the universe.

Kohut (1955) writes: "Music, however, as an extraverbal mode of mental functioning, permits a specific, subtle regression to preverbal, i.e., to truly primitive forms of mental experience while at the same time remaining socially and aesthetically acceptable" (p. 20).

The preverbal origin of the musical language explains its universality, its ability to cross frontiers, cultures, epochs, and language barriers, its being a language intelligible to everyone. Yet although it originates in a "language spoken" by every human being at one time, there are enormous individual differences in the specific capability to use it. Not everybody hearing it is sensitive enough to enjoy listening to it, to understand it, and to respond to it. Only a few people can reproduce musical sounds, and even fewer are gifted enough to be creative in it. The ability to use this language, be it as the creator, the performer, or the discriminating listener, is by no means a property common to all mankind. Rather, it requires a special talent, of which those endowed with it have each their own measured share. And those gifted with musical talent are not a priori aware of possessing an ability that not everyone has. Discriminative hearing, the capacity to distinguish sounds, to listen to numerous sounds at one and the same time, and to store and reconstruct them in the mind—these are for the gifted natural activities, as hearing and seeing are for ordinary people. But the person who lacks these faculties regards the gifted as exceptional, blessed, and favored with a "gift from the Gods."

The question about the source of such special artistic endowment was rather neglected in classical psychology. It was generally accepted that man was born with such properties, that he had inherited them. This was the belief of psychologists like Seashore (1938) and Schoen (1940), who both devoted their works to the study of music. In fact, this opinion was shared by a number of psychoanalysts, who regarded specific artistic talent as due to constitutional factors. Other authors, however, denied any constitutional basis and maintained that musical ability, like others, is acquired in the course of the learning process. Lundin (1953) collected a considerable amount of literature to prove this point.

From more recent psychoanalytic studies it appears that there is more to the problem and that matters are not so one-sidedly clear-cut. Artistic endowment is viewed as an end product that is determined by various factors, some constitutional, some environmental. These two factors, the constitutional background and the environmental influence, will here be presented separately in order to facilitate the discussion, yet they are always interrelated.

THE CONSTITUTIONAL BACKGROUND

Psychoanalytic research has endeavored to investigate those constitutional factors that are later affected by various environmental influences into promoting artistic talent. At present there is rather general agreement that the most important coefficient, probably the only one, is the presence of "a special sensory endowment which determines the perceptual organization of the individual" (Rosen, 1964, p. 4). This endowment grants the artist "greater sensitivity to sensory stimulation . . . [and] unusual capacity for awareness of relations between various stimuli" (Greenacre, 1957, p. 53).

Bergman and Escalona (1949) pointed out that children showed individual constitutional variations in their sensitivities in different sensory modalities. These variations in sensitivity may concern several senses or merely one specific sense, while the individual exaggeration of response is specific for the quantity of a given stimulus, its quality, or for both together. The oversensitivity is independent of a particular acuteness of the sensory perception (as differences in acuteness of vision, for instance); it depends, rather, on a specific reaction to stimuli and the ability to assimilate and withstand stimuli of a particular quality. The authors assume that the variations in response stem from a difference in the thickness of the "protective barrier against stimuli," or, in other words, they assume a barrier that checks the penetration of stimuli and permits no more to penetrate than can be best assimilated and integrated. A person having a lower than normal threshold will be overrun by stimuli that do not threaten to overtax another individual's tolerance. Such a sensitive person is liable to be hurt by an impact of stimuli that for a less sensitive person may still be within the normal range. The authors present a number of cases to demonstrate that extreme oversensitivity in various modalities is apt to impede the normal development of the ego and may result in psychotic development even in childhood. Yet when the deviation is less extreme, the ego succeeds in achieving normal development, although it will have to build up specific defenses to protect itself against its unusual sensitivity in order to reject, neutralize, or master the redundant stimuli.

In a mere footnote the authors put forth a tentative suggestion:

> It is attractive to follow the idea of a "thin" protective barrier against stimuli as a possible constitutional fundament of special gifts. To do so would lead to an assumption of this sort: Only the individual liable to suffer from "bad" stimuli in a certain modality would be likely to be able to develop sufficient interest in procuring or producing "good" stimuli. For example, only he who suffers from noise would be likely to become a good musician [p. 348].

It seems to me, however, that this hypothesis deserves further attention, since it can provide the basis for a theory of the constitutional background of artistic endowment; in my opinion, this assumption fits in with all we know about the development of perceptual modalities, with the observations gathered in other realms of psychology, particularly with those of Gestalt psychology.

Perception is an active process requiring internal regulatory mechanisms to absorb and screen percepts, rejecting them in part and, with the remainder, establishing the Gestalts that enter consciousness. Much effort has been invested in Gestalt psychological investigation of this process. Hartmann (1939), linking such conceptions with psychoanalysis, described perception as an active regulatory function on the part of the ego (p. 58).

The newborn is exposed to a multitude of stimuli, all working on his sense organs. In the developmental process the perceptual field becomes more and more recognizable and intelligible. This comprehension requires, in turn, much activity to organize the perceptual field. The infant must develop the capability for focusing his attention on numerous percepts, preventing the redundant ones from being absorbed and organizing those assimilated into simple Gestalts that he can recognize, remember, and compare.

In the auditory field, in which we are interested here, the infant absorbs tens or perhaps hundreds of stimuli at any given time. His capability for listening to certain stimuli depends, first of all, on the development of the ability *not* to hear, to shut out, all other stimuli. This is a natural faculty for every adult who, attending a lecture, for instance, listens to its presentation while being deaf to outside noises like the rattling of cars in the street, banging of doors, his neighbor's creaking chair, and so on. To put it schematically, one might suppose that a person who, at a given time, is simultaneously exposed to let us say fifty auditory stimuli will succeed in shutting out forty-eight or forty-nine, while his attention is absorbed by only one or two.

To the extent that the protective barrier against stimuli differs from one individual to another, it may be assumed that children differ in the ability *not* to hear the redundant stimuli. There are, thus, variations in the degree to which the child is capable of ignoring the surfeit stimuli; or such a selection, while easily carried out by one child, may prove to be too much of an effort for another. It may just as well be imagined that a child is simply incapable of shutting out the forty-eight or forty-nine stimuli, that he can do so with no more than thirty at a time. The child thus remains exposed to about twenty simultaneous stimuli. In that case he has only two alternatives—either to submit to "break down" or to develop specific abilities in the ego to overcome and master the threatening results of a constitutional deficiency. The only way out of this dilemma is an effort toward orientation in and mastery of the auditory perceptual field. The infant will have to develop an ability to concentrate his attention to directing and mastering twenty different, simultaneously occurring sound stimuli.

An extreme example of such an accomplishment is presented in the person of the prominent conductor of an orchestra, who has the extraordinary gift of simultaneously listening to the orchestra as one body and to each of the instruments separately, distinguishing each by its playing as if he concentrated on it alone—an achievement that the ordinary person can neither imagine nor grasp how it is being brought off.

The ego, exposed to the impact of auditory stimuli, is compelled to attain considerable abilities in order to protect itself and to build up a second line of defense to replace the primary, the deficient barrier against stimuli. In that case the ego develops a superior capability to organize auditory stimuli, to discern among their various shades, and, in particular, to transform "painful" stimuli so that the individual can derive gratification and pleasure from them. It may be assumed, therefore, that specific musical abilities are part of coping mechanisms which the ego is forced to develop as a defense for mastering oversensitivity.

This theory is borne out by the common observation that people with a flair for music are, in general, sensitive to sound stimuli and easily "irritated" by exceptional noise. Biographies of musicians brim with anecdotes about such oversensitivity. Macalpine and Hunter (1952) described one example of the composer Rossini, who suffered from phobic fear of the noise of trains, and a severe compulsion expressed in the auditory sphere.[1]

Some similarity may be found between the theory suggested here and the formulations put forth by Kohut and Levarie (chapter 1), Kohut (chapter 2), Niederland (1958), and Berezin (1958) with regard to enjoyment. These authors regard listening to music as an activity of the ego in the service of mastering auditory stimuli that, in their deeper meaning, are threatening and frightening. These writers, too, are convinced that, owing to constitutional and environmental factors alike, this threatening implication is attributed to various noise stimuli. Still there is an essential difference between their theories and the present one. Whereas they maintain that listening to music is an activity which, like playing, serves the ego's needs for mastery, it is here contended that the musical talent itself stems from the essential need of the ego to achieve mastery. Unlike playing, mastery of this sort is not primarily intended to attain pleasure; it is definitely enacted out of the defensive need, to help the ego cope with the onslaught of a surfeit of auditory stimuli.

The Environmental Background

The environmental factors influencing the development of musical ability have been rather neglected in the psychoanalytic literature. The few authors who have dealt with the subject stressed the influence of the primary mother–child relationship.

Racker (1951) discusses music as a communicative medium antedating the spoken word and object representation. He concludes that "the sharpening, or more exactly, the erotization of hearing may possibly have one of its roots in the attention a small child pays to the arrival of his mother" (p. 150).

Anna Freud (1965), dealing with the lines of development in

---

[1] It is dangerous to depend on biographies, which are frequently retrograde glorifications of childhood genius, as a scientific source for conveying facts about the predecessors of artistic achievement. But it would be possible and worthwhile to plan an anterograde research in which predictions could be made based on young children's specific sensitivities. These predictions would be related some years later to the possible emergence of musical abilities.

children, states that such lines of development "are included in their constitution as inherent possibilities" (p. 86). The proportionate strength, however, of the one or the other developmental line depends on environmental factors, most important among which is the mother and her primary relation to her baby: "In the beginning of life, at least, the infant seems to concentrate on the development along those lines which call forth most ostensibly the mother's love and approval. . . . This implies that activities which are acclaimed by the mother are repeated more frequently, become libidinized, and thereby stimulated into further growth" (p. 86).

Among the examples used by Anna Freud to demonstrate these influences, we find the following: "It is not unknown that early contact with the mother through her singing has consequences for the later attitudes to music and may promote special musical aptitudes" (p. 87).

In the light of the opinions quoted above it seems safe to assume that among the environmental factors it is the primary preverbal mode of communication between the infant and his mother that initiates the development of musical talent. Rather little was done in psychoanalysis to investigate these modes of communication until René Spitz (1965) observed that they differ essentially from later ones. The primary modes communicate no more than affects, expressed in patterns of coenesthetic organization through the various sensory channels—hearing, seeing, touching, and so on.

From observations of mother–child dyads it appears that there are individual differences in the modes of communication. Each dyad shows a preference for one particular channel of communication, which then becomes dominant in this specific relationship while others are used considerably less. Such individual differences are due to specific factors which vary from mother to mother and from infant to infant. Some mothers like to talk to their babies, to whisper and sing to them, whereas others do not open their lips while handling their babies. Often we hear a mother reply to our question about her contact with her child: "Naturally, I won't talk to him, he doesn't understand anything yet." Similar differences are found with regard to tactile contact. Some mothers enjoy keeping the baby in their arms, cuddling and fondling him, whereas others handle the baby as little as possible and only when it is really asked for. (Such mothers will not hesitate to find a rational excuse like the danger of infection, etc.) Because of the individual differences in the mother's contact with her baby, every infant "receives" the mother differently. As stated above, there usually is one dominant channel of communication through which the infant affectively "receives" the mother and, through her, the outside world; yet that channel is different for every baby.

Primary communication is mutual, as is communication in general, since the baby expresses his needs through the same channels—sounds, movements, contacts, and so on. Even such a primary ability as that of expression is subject to individual variations; Korner (1964) observed that infants vary in their abilities to demonstrate their inner states, some conveying "their needs more readily to their caretakers" than others (p. 65). It may be assumed, furthermore, that children differ in their capacities for utilizing the various modes of communication, yet every baby eventually succeeds in making himself understood through signs of one or the other sort. Some children convey their needs mainly by vocal means, while others resort more frequently to movement. These variations seem to stem from constitutional factors, on the one hand, and from the experiences the infant has had with regard to the mother's readiness to respond to his various "messages," on the other hand. Hence the specific pattern of communication characteristic of each mother-child dyad is modeled on a combination of two factors, those contributed by the mother and those inherent in the infant.

When the auditory channel is the supreme mode of primary communication, it may be assumed that the child is predisposed to building musical ability. In an infant who related affectively to his surroundings through the auditory channel of communication and who "received" the mother mainly through auditory stimuli, this channel may continue to play a prominent role in his emotional exchange with the outside world. And later, when the adult is stirred up by longings for the lost paradise of oral infancy, for that symbiotic mother love, such longings may take on the shape of craving for those "fondling tones." Music, with its sound patterns set according to primary design, can thus bring him back to that primary period when through the sensory modality of hearing he had felt reassured by his mother's love.

Psychoanalysts who have musical patients in treatment certainly observe a periodical increase in the pressing need of their patients to hear and enjoy music. With several patients I have had the experience that such periods were marked by concurrent diffuse and indistinct longings, such as "I feel like yearning for I don't know what; nothing can please me but music." Some time later all these patients vividly recalled early memories of their long-dead mothers.

Interestingly, it is not through musical ability alone that the preservation of infantile auditory modes of communication is manifested by those persons. They have other characteristics that retain traces of auditory coenesthetic perception. While talking with others, they are unusually sensitive to the various components of speech, such as sound, timbre, intensity, and rhythm. This perception, without necessarily being conscious, is actively engaged in, though it serves a communicative function. Whenever I am told by a patient about impressions such as "I can't complain, he is kind with me, but I feel that he is really mad at me; something in his voice tells me so . . . ," I usually ask the patient whether he is fond of music. And it has always proved to be true that those who are more sensitive and responsive to the sounds of speech rather than to its content have some affinity to music.

INTEGRATION OF THE FACTORS

The constitutional and environmental factors do not exist independently of each other, and it is obvious that they mutually influence each other. A specific sensory sensitivity that is considered to be determined by a constitutional factor is permanently subjected to environmental influences. Spitz (1965) maintains that the primary barrier against stimuli forms an integral part of the structure of the sensorium. Within a very brief span of time, though, the protective task is taken over by the "ego nuclei," so that the protective barrier is turned into a function of the ego. Since in the course of development the ego is exposed to numerous environmental factors, these will certainly exert an influence on the specific ability of the protective barrier to screen stimuli, to reject or to assimilate them. It may therefore be concluded that the unusual sensory sensitivity that is assumed to be at the root of musical ability is given at birth as an anlage and is molded into its final shape through the mutual influences of a variety of environmental factors.

On the other hand, it is rather improbable that the specific mode of communication of the mother–child dyad can be singled out as a mere environmental factor. This specific mode is not established solely by the mother's habitual approach to her child; it is no less determined by the infant's modes of expression, and these depend to a considerable degree on constitutional factors. In reality, however, as was indicated briefly, it is impossible to distinguish between constitutional and environmental factors because every single etiological factor bears distinct evidence of the mutual and interwoven influences of constitution and environment.

In spite of this mutuality of influences it seems worthwhile to distinguish between the primary sensory sensitivity and the mother–infant mode of communication, and to view them as two separate factors, each being instrumental in the development of musical ability. The proportionate degree to which each of them exercises its influence varies from one individual to another; accordingly, countless variations of individual patterns of musical ability are observed.

In some people musicality is many sided; they have a "natural" capacity for absolute pitch, for pitch discrimination, and so on, yet they show little interest in music and are not particularly keen on it, whereas others enjoy nothing better than music and even become "addicted" to it. Some persons get tense and irritable if for some reason they are prevented from listening to music for some time, but in musical aptitude tests they show no particular musicality, a factor that may be responsible for their falling short of performing or composing music, although they eagerly endeavor to do so.

Between these extremes multishaded variations are observed in the combination of primary ability and the need for attaining gratification through listening to music. Those combinations presumably mirror the varieties of integration of the two factors that determine the development of musical ability. Apparently, the specific musical capability owes its development to the unusual sensory sensitivity, whereas the specific interest in music and the ability to attain gratification from listening to it are based in the primary modes of communication. In reality we scarcely ever see a case in which one of the two factors can be isolated as the single determinant of development. It is not surprising, then, that a person will rarely display considerable musical talent while denying all interest in music, just as it is highly improbable that a person greatly interested in music will be denied all musical talent.

The opinions presented here are merely hypothetical, though they are rooted in the clinical and theoretical knowledge gathered in the field of psychoanalysis; yet they lack experimental confirmation. Certainly, every assumption will be scientifically better founded when it has withstood the test of controlled experiment. In fact, such an experimental investigation of the psychoanalytic conceptions about art and artists has not been undertaken. It seems, however, that the assumptions presented here might serve as the basis for designing a research project to examine and prove the constitutional roots of musical talent and to demonstrate the effects of primary modes of communication on the development of musical ability. I realize that considerable effort would need to be invested in an experimental study of this kind. Yet I think it worthwhile because the results, beyond yielding additional information about music and musical ability, may shed light on the problems of the developmental background of artistic talent per se and of gratification through art in all its forms.

Chapter 6
Transitional Tunes and Musical Development

Marjorie McDonald, M.D.

THE SUZUKI METHOD OF VIOLIN TEACHING

Following World War II Shinichi Suzuki, a Japanese violinist who managed to survive many tragedies inflicted on him by the war, determined that he would dedicate his life to teaching music to young children. Forsaking the possibility of a career as a college teacher or a performer, Suzuki instead took over an abandoned kindergarten in Matsumoto and turned it into a music studio. There he taught the violin to small children, some as young as three years of age. He gave a simple explanation for his unorthodox choice of pupils. "Children learn their native language in a natural fashion—properly taught, they can learn music the same way!" (Nickels, 1968, p. 5).

Suzuki proceeded to develop a system of teaching stringed instruments to young children which has become widely known under the name, "talent education." This system has had both strong supporters and strong critics, as evidenced by the mixed reactions to the first Annual Conference, in Japan in 1954, when several hundred young violinists played works ranging from "Twinkle, Twinkle Little Star" to the Bach Double Concerto. Some hailed it as a musical achievement and others regarded it as sheer exhibitionism. The Suzuki method first gained attention in the United States in 1958 when a film about it was shown to a meeting of string teachers at Oberlin, Ohio. Since then the system has become increasingly popular in this country. There have been innumerable Suzuki workshops for string teachers, and Suzuki has appeared in person, sometimes with his own pupils, at many of them. He has been accorded many honors, and respected musicians

First published in *The Psychoanalytic Study of the Child*, 25:503–520, 1970. New York: International Universities Press.

such as Joseph Szigeti and Pablo Casals have lauded his revolutionary contribution to the art of string teaching. Eminent musicians, trained by Suzuki methods, are beginning to appear on the international music scene (Nickels, 1968; Suzuki, 1969).

An English translation of Suzuki's book, *Nurtured by Love*, has been published (1969). In his Introduction Suzuki describes the great revelation that he experienced, in his early thirties, at his "discovery" about the learning of language.

> Oh—why, Japanese children can all speak Japanese! The thought suddenly struck me with amazement. In fact, all children throughout the world speak their native tongues with the utmost fluency. Any and every Japanese child—all speak Japanese without difficulty. Does that not show a startling talent? How, by what means, does this come about? I had to control an impulse to shout my joy over this discovery.
>
> But no one else seemed the slightest bit impressed. It was just taken for granted; people in general think that the ability children display is natural. At my excitement, half of my listeners were startled, and others just thought me absurd. Nevertheless, my discovery actually had a great meaning; it made me realize that any child is able to display highly superior abilities if only the correct methods are used in training [p. 9].
>
> Why do all children possess the marvelous ability to speak their mother tongue quite effortlessly? Therein lies the secret of how to educate all human ability [p. 97].

It is Suzuki's goal to teach children as young as three years of age to play the violin and to do so in a manner which resembles as closely as possible the way children have learned language. Recognizing the importance of the parent in this process, Suzuki begins by teaching the parent, who plays a small-size violin such as the child will later use. As the parent plays and enjoys the instrument, the child spontaneously wants to join the activity. He then attends both private and group lessons with his parent and soon is participating himself, enjoying the violin as a new toy. As he has learned language from his parents, so he learns the violin, at first from them, and later from his teacher and from group play sessions where he is exposed to older and more advanced pupils. The emphasis is always upon having fun through playing music.

There is much that is sound, on both a psychological and a

musical basis, in Suzuki's methods. To a psychoanalyst his method has more merit than his psychological explanation of it. He idealizes childhood as a time of supreme happiness, denies drives and conflicts, and minimizes the significance of hereditary and constitutional factors. It is his belief that, with loving teaching, talent can be "inculcated" (p. 110). The term for this method, *talent education*, must be understood to mean "talent inculcation."

Suzuki's own musical development is of special interest. He came from a family of samisen makers (the samisen is a Japanese three-stringed instrument, resembling a banjo). His father's researches into the history of this instrument led to an interest in the Western violin, and eventually his father converted the family business into a violin factory. Not only did his father thus bring the violin to the people of Japan, but his factory became the largest producer of violins in the world (at one time reaching 400 violins and 4,000 bows a day). Suzuki himself always thought of his father's violin factory as a toy factory until, at the age of seventeen, he heard a recording of Mischa Elman playing Schubert's "Ave Maria." He writes of this experience:

> To think that the violin, which I had considered a toy, could produce such beauty of tone! . . . Elman's "Ave Maria" opened my eyes to music. I had no idea why my soul was so moved [p. 79].

This profoundly moving experience led Suzuki to take up the serious study of the violin at the late age of seventeen years. (He constantly denies, however, even when in his early twenties he went to Germany to study, that he was a serious and ambitious musician.)

In Germany he had another profoundly moving experience in which he received an exalted appointment from Mozart. After listening to a performance of the Mozart Clarinet Quintet he experienced a temporary paralysis of both arms and was unable to applaud the performance. He had a typical "belle indifférence" reaction to his short-lived conversion reaction. He writes of the experience:

> It was Mozart who taught me to know perfect love, truth, goodness and beauty. And I now deeply feel as if I were under direct orders from Mozart, and he left me a legacy, and in his place I am to further the happiness of all children [p. 91].

It is my impression that this special summons by Mozart came at the height of a loneliness he could hardly permit himself to acknowledge. (Indeed he refers especially to the "piercing sadness" of the Quintet's second movement, and sees Mozart as answering life's sadness with a "loving affirmative" [p. 92].) He was an Oriental in Germany, having difficulty in finding a suitable teacher, and perhaps increasingly faced with his own limitations as a latecomer both to the violin and to Western music. So the man who started too late was ordained by the most noted musical child prodigy of all time to become the teacher of little children. And the man whose father once produced the world's largest supply of violins may well have become the man who has produced the world's largest supply of violinists.

That a preschool child can learn to play anything on the violin, let alone a Baroque concerto, holds as much fascination for a psychoanalyst as it does for a musician. Both must ask the question: how is such an achievement possible? The psychoanalyst must also ask: how can it possibly harmonize with ordinary prelatency tasks of personality development? Do the music lessons act as a developmental interference, or is it possible that, as with learning language, the learning of music might even *promote* personality development?

In an article for string teachers I attempted to answer these questions through a consideration of both the failures and the successes with the Suzuki system (McDonald, 1970). I discussed the inevitable failures that result when preschool music lessons are experienced by the child as a developmental interference—for example, when they repeat a toilet-training struggle between child and parent; when they foster a neurotic exhibitionism.

Much more intriguing are the reasons for the success of the Suzuki method. Musicians tend to point first to the remarkable personality of the method's founder. Childless himself, Suzuki has demonstrated a lifelong, selfless devotion to children and he works tirelessly in behalf of their development. "Today Dr. Suzuki seems to thrive on a schedule that might well kill a younger man. One of his biggest sorrows is that he no longer has much time to spend with the small children he loves. He coaches the teacher-trainees, travels around the country as needed to hold conferences, to help a discouraged teacher, to inaugurate a new class, to discuss revision of his method books" (Nickels, 1968, p. 5).

Yet the Suzuki charisma does not cover the story. The Suzuki system appears to incorporate certain essential ingredients that we would expect to find in any well-run psychoanalytically oriented nursery school. One or both parents must participate actively with the child in a pleasurable musical experience. The parent plays the violin with the child and attends and participates in the music lessons as well. Thus the child's first experience with a teacher is not complicated by a needless separation anxiety brought on by the parent's sudden desertion. Further, the strong parental cathexis of child, teacher, and music acts as an essential catalyst. It makes possible a gradual transfer of parental authority to the person of the teacher, and it promotes a pleasure not just in music but in the activity of learning, producing, and sharing it. These methods all promote learning as a progressive development of an ego skill, and minimize the possibilities that it will be detoured into developmental drive conflicts.

The question of inherent musical talent in the child as a determining factor in the method's success must also be considered. However, Suzuki has demonstrated time and again either that no unusual musical talent is needed for very young children to learn and enjoy music, or else that the population at large has a higher level of musical talent and a greater capacity to enjoy music than is generally recognized.

There is nothing I have presented so far about either the failures or the successes of the Suzuki system that will come as news to a psychoanalyst. But neither have I offered any explanation about why learning the violin might have a special place in the life of a musical preschooler. Suzuki points the way to an explanation with the simple statement of his philosophy, "Children learn their native language in a natural fashion—properly taught, they can learn music the same way." This statement, placing music on a par with language, has a natural appeal, but nevertheless it bears some scrutiny.

Ordinarily children learn to verbalize long before they can possibly learn to play the violin. They do so in part as a way of preserving and enjoying the vital emotional tie to the parents. In the first two years of life the child maintains this tie largely through primitive imitations and identifications with the parents. To be with the parents means to be at one with them, a part of them, and like them. The learning of language becomes for the child a part of this pleasurable imitation and identification. But as a child learns language he acquires a new way of communicating with his parents. The *verbal* communication promotes his reasoning powers. He develops a sense of separateness and independence in his mental functioning, and he gradually relies less and less upon primitive imitations and identifications to preserve the all-important tie to his parents.

When he arrives for his violin lessons, at three or four years, his ways of learning still draw quite heavily upon these early processes, but in addition they have advanced to include more independent intellectual reasoning powers. The mind of a three- or four-year-old is less amorphous, less a porous sponge, than that of a one- or two-year-old. Hence Suzuki's statement that children can learn the violin as they learn language seems to me to tell only part of the story. It does not allow for a developmental increment between a one- or two-year-old and a three- or four-year-old. (I am unprepared to take up the cultural differences in Oriental and Western societies as they affect timing and balance between early identification processes and later mechanisms involving more secondary process thought.)

Yet, in likening the learning of language and music, Suzuki seems to be saying more than is immediately apparent. He rightly suggests, in this comparison, that musical development can begin at the same age and in the same way as language development—long before violin lessons are possible. If given the opportunity, the infant and toddler will "absorb" music at the same age and in the same way that he absorbs, shares, and responds to language, as an auditory expression of the emotional tie with his parents. This very early musical development then provides a favorable foundation for introducing the violin as the *next* forward step at three or four years. Learning to play the violin becomes comparable to learning more words and sentences as the *next* forward step in lingual development.

In his book Suzuki gives a captivating account of an experience with a five-month-old baby's response to music. The baby, Hiromi, was attending her six-year-old sister's group violin lessons, cradled in her mother's arms.

> Hiromi's sister, Atsumi, six years old, was daily practicing at that time the Vivaldi A-minor concerto, as well as listening to the record every day. So Hiromi grew up hearing this music daily from the very beginning. I wanted to know what effect this had on a five-month-old baby. I announced that I would like to play something, and stood up with my violin. When everybody was

quiet, I started playing a minuet by Bach. While I played, my eyes did not leave Hiromi's face. The five-month-old already knew the sound of the violin well, and her eyes shone while she listened to this piece that she was hearing for the first time. A little while later I switched from the minuet to the Vivaldi A-minor concerto—music that was played and heard continuously in her home. I had no sooner started the piece when an amazing thing happened.

Hiromi's expression suddenly changed. She smiled and laughed, and turned her happy face to her mother, who held her in her arms. "See—that's *my* music," she unmistakeably wanted to tell her mother. Soon again, her face turned in my direction, and she moved her body up and down in rhythm. This baby, just five months old, had shown that she knew the melody of the Vivaldi A-minor concerto [p. 17].

(At four years Hiromi was herself playing the same concerto, and at ten years she was writing to the professor to send him her poetry and musical composition which had won first place in a national contest.)

My curiosity about the *earliest* stages of a child's musical development, aroused by my interest in the Suzuki system, led me to formulate a hypothesis. It seemed to me that some children, who have experienced music from birth onward as an integral part of the loving motherly and fatherly caretaking environment, might make use of music in a very particular way. My hypothesis is that these children find in music their own special "transitional phenomenon." Some may even select from a musical repertory a special "transitional tune," just as another child selects from among his toys a special transitional toy. (It seems very likely to me that Hiromi, for example, could have selected a transitional tune as a very young infant, and perhaps it was even the tune supplied by her sister, Atsumi, in her daily playing of the Vivaldi Concerto.)

Winnicott's Transitional Phenomena and the Auditory Sense

Psychoanalytic interest in "transitional phenomena" has focused almost exclusively upon tangible objects which infants use as their first "not me" possession—objects which make their appeal through sight, smell, feel, and taste. A musician would have to ask why the sense of hearing is not included in this list of significant sensations.

In his original article on the subject (1953), Winnicott has not ignored the auditory sense. The following quotations from this article will serve the dual purpose of reviewing his concept of transitional phenomena and crediting his recognition of auditory sensations as included in these phenomena.

> I have introduced the terms "transitional object" and "transitional phenomena" for designation of the intermediate area of experience, between the thumb and the teddy bear, between the oral erotism and true object-relationship, between primary creative activity and projection of what has already been introjected, between primary unawareness of indebtedness and the acknowledgement of indebtedness (Say: "ta!").
>
> *By this definition an infant's babbling or the way an older child goes over a repertory of songs and tunes while preparing for sleep* come within the intermediate area as transitional phenomena, along with the use made of objects that are not part of the infant's body yet are not fully recognized as belonging to external reality [p. 89, emphasis added]. . . .
>
> [T]here may emerge some thing or some phenomenon—perhaps a bundle of wool or the corner of a blanket or eiderdown, *or a word or tune* [emphasis added] or a mannerism, which becomes vitally important to the infant for use at the time of going to sleep, and is a defence against anxiety, especially anxiety of depressive type. Perhaps some soft object or type of object has been found and used by the infant, and this then becomes what I am calling a *transitional object*. This object goes on being important. The parents get to know its value and carry it round when travelling. The mother lets it get dirty and even smelly, knowing that by washing it she introduces a break in continuity in the infant's experience, a break that may destroy the meaning and value of the object to the infant.
>
> I suggest that the pattern of transitional phenomena begins to show at about 4-6-8-12 months. Purposely I leave room for wide variations . . .
>
> As the infant starts to use organized sounds (mum, ta, da) there may appear a "word" for the transitional object. The name given by the infant to these earliest objects is often significant, and it usually has a word used by the adults partly incorporated in it. For instance, "baa" may be the name, and the "b" may have come from the adult's use of the word, "baby" or "bear" [p. 91].

Winnicott stresses the normality and ubiquity of transitional phenomena and postulates that they may exist more often than is generally recognized by the caretaking adults. He considers their obvious use as a defense against infantile anxieties and as a focal point for expression of later (anal and phallic) drive conflicts arising in the course of ordinary development. In addition, he views the transitional experience as important in the development and maintenance of reality testing and as an early determinant in the evolution of creativity. In his preface to an article by Stevenson (1954) he writes:

> The transitional object is also not the same as the next soft toy. It can be said that the next one must be acknowledged as coming from the world. The infant is expected to say "ta" and in this way to make an acknowledgment of the gift. The transitional object comes from the environment, as we know, but it is essential to understand that from the infant's point of view it was created by the infant. There is no question of saying "ta," because the object was in use before the word "ta" could be formulated and before the acknowledgment to the world had become meaningful. In respect of these transitional objects the parents, as it were, conspire not to challenge the origin. They easily see that the thumb is part of the child and that the next toy or teddy bear or doll is a gift, but with regard to the object in question they undertake to refrain from challenging the infant as to its origin. There is a madness here which is permissible because it belongs to this stage of the infant's emotional development. The madness is that this object is created by the infant and *also* it was there in the environment for the infant's use [p. 200f.].

As I have recounted, it was a curiosity about the success of the Suzuki system which led me to hypothesize that some children select a special "transitional tune" as an early step in their musical development. Winnicott's inclusion of musical sounds and tunes in his original description of transitional phenomena offers a verification of the concept of a transitional tune.

Another verification can be found in the psychoanalytic literature in a brief clinical paper, "About the Sound 'Mm . . . ,'" by Greenson (1954).[1] He describes an unusual sensation which ap-

---

[1] In this work Greenson does not use the word *transitional* and it appears likely that he was unfamiliar with Winnicott's work, published in 1953. Greenson's paper was presented in 1953 and published in 1954.

peared during the analysis of an adult patient and lasted for several days, during which time it proved to be analyzable.

> [The patient] felt a constant pleasant humming sensation in his lips. Although no audible sound came from him, he felt as though he were making the sound "Mm . . .". . . .
> The humming sensation was a manifestation of a sense of contentment and well-being. . . . The sense of well-being was recognized to be a repetition of those few occasions in his life when he believed himself to be his mother's favorite. . . . [It] also represented a successful denial of quite the opposite feeling, of being abandoned and deserted [p. 234].

Further analysis of the "Mm . . ." sound, through a dream fragment concerning a piece of velvet cloth, led to the soft woolen blanket which the patient had fondled as a part of his pleasurable experience of sucking on his mother's breast. Throughout his life he had required this blanket or substitutes for it in order to be able to go to sleep. Thus the "Mm . . ." sound and the soft woolen blanket both appeared to be components of the patient's transitional phenomena. Greenson's postulations about the sound "Mm . . ." as both a shared experience with the mother and a means of pleasurably remembering her in her absence recall Winnicott's criteria for transitional phenomena.

> The musical quality of this "Mm . . . " sound is probably related to the fact that the contended mother hums cheerfully herself as she feeds her baby or rocks it to sleep. She hums by way of her identification with the baby's pleasurable satiation and thus echoes a sound she felt as a child. The "Mm . . . " indicates a sense of contentment and satisfaction [p. 235]. Apparently it is the sound produced with the nipple in the mouth or with the pleasant memory or expectation of its being in the mouth [p. 238].

Greenson does not mention whether music came to have any special significance in the course of this patient's development.

Transitional Tunes: Lullabies and Cradle Songs

A transitional tune has to be a familiar tune, frequently filling the atmosphere between parent and child. It has to provide a shared and comforting experience. In that the infant hears it himself, he probably initially experiences the sensation as though it were a part of himself, just as mother herself does not at first exist as a person distinct and separate from himself. At first he does not, and indeed is not capable of, asking about the tune's origins or who "possesses" it. When he finds a way to reproduce the tune—by command performance, or later on by singing it himself or playing a recording of it—he can feel himself to be in charge and the originator of the experience. Where once he was dependent upon his parents to produce the musical comfort, he gradually becomes able to control its production himself. The particular tune is *his own choice*, just as the transitional toy is the child's own special choice made from a whole collection of toys. The value of this transitional phenomenon is that it is a creative way for a small child to master separation and aloneness and at the same time begin to acquaint himself in a pleasurable way with the external world. When the transitional phenomenon is an auditory, musical, one, it would seem that music has claimed an early and very likely a lasting importance in the child's life. It may even be that a transitional tune is an essential early step in musical development. Early music instruction, for a child who has taken this first step, would seem natural, even necessary, and almost irresistible.[2]

I hope to collect further evidence in support of my hypothesis about transitional tunes and their place in musical development by exploring three sources of information. First, I am interested in collecting examples of transitional tunes observed by music teachers and parents of young children. Here is an illustrative example:

> A precocious little girl (she had a large vocabulary before the age of one year) was accustomed to hearing music all the time. Her father, a professional musician, taught and practiced in his home

---

[2] The musician, Wilhelm Friedemann Bach, grew up in the musical atmosphere of the large Bach family and received his musical instruction from his father, Johann Sebastian Bach. In her recorded comments on the "Two Part Inventions," composed by Bach for his nine-year-old son, Wilhelm Friedemann, Wanda Landowska remarked, "What today is for us erudition was for Wilhelm Friedemann daily bread and life experience" (RCA Victor LM-2389). Daily bread is not only a commonplace, but a necessity of life.

A musician friend who grew up in a large family of musicians once told me of the surprise she felt, as a very small child, when she discovered that every family in the neighborhood did not routinely spend their evenings together playing chamber music.

and the child could not help but sense that both parents loved music, as they loved her. She was little more than a year old when she developed the habit, upon awakening and discovering herself alone in her crib, of calling out, "Play Bach, Daddy!" Her loving father would respond by playing the child's favorite tune—the second Bouree from Bach's Suite IV in E Flat Major, for unaccompanied cello. Bach's Bouree was this baby's special lullaby. I believe it was a "not me" sound, shared between her and her parents, yet often available on command when she felt separated from them. That is, she could "create" its performance. This child has since grown into a successful and likable college student, and her ambition is to become a member of the Bach Aria Group.

Second, I hope that biographies and autobiographies of musicians may yield examples of transitional musical phenomena in the early development of these talented and creative people. A beautiful example is quoted in an interview with the violist, Ernst Wallfisch, in which he describes the role of music in the first six years of his life (Arazi, 1969, p. 7):

> Music played such a big part in my life from the beginning it seems, and I can recall much . . . my father was a business man and an amateur violinist . . . music was his big hobby . . . chamber music especially . . . his circle of friends included many like him and chamber music seemed to be part of living. . . . I can remember as a very small boy all of these people in our home talking, laughing, smoking cigars, and making music . . . at first all I recognized were the different sounds and the many moods of what they played . . . as I grew older, I began to separate the composers, the rhythms, the harmonies . . . *I can remember being lulled to sleep by all these sounds*, and being put to bed with all of these sounds swirling through my thoughts . . . *sometimes I would awaken a few hours later, and I could still hear the music sounding through the house* . . . to this day, whenever I hear certain works played by a quartet, it brings back a flood of memories of many things and people . . . *yes, I was thoroughly imbued with the spirit of music from the cradle* so it seems [emphasis added].

Third, I hope to make a collection of lullabies and cradle songs. The very word, *lullaby* confirms that it is a song intended to serve as a transitional tune. It is of echoic, onomatopoeic origin, being composed of "lull" and "bye." (A similar imitative word, based on "lull," exists in several other languages.) It is a song which soothes the baby while expressing a separation, a good-bye (or a goodnight, as the child narcissistically withdraws into sleep).

The words of many lullabies tell of the absence of an important person (parent, older sibling) and assure the infant of that person's return. But for the preverbal child, it is the comforting, *tune*, originally supplied by the parents, which must convey the feeling message. The *words* are as much to express and soothe the empathic distress of the adult for the lonely baby as to convey a verbal message to the infant. The words of the lullaby, "Bye, Baby Bunting," are illustrative:

Bye, baby bunting,
Father's gone a-hunting,
To fetch a little rabbit-skin
To wrap the baby bunting in.

Bye, baby bunting,
Father's gone a-hunting,
Mother's gone a-milking,
Sister's gone a silking,
Brother's gone to buy a skin
To wrap the baby bunting in.

In this traditional tune the rabbit skin seems to be offered as a potential transitional object.

In some lullabies it appears that the melodic line of the music may be intended to convey to the infant a sense of separation and safe reunion. Just as his rocking cradle will return to a low point of rest, so will the missing person return and his tension be relieved. Contained in the soothing melody may be a wide interval, expressive of a momentary high point of tension in the music, which is then followed by a rhythmic rocking return to a lower resting pitch. Two of the best-known lullabies, "Rockabye Baby" and Brahms's "lullaby," both contain such suspenseful intervals.

Musical Development

Finally, I would like to return to the question of whether the Suzuki system of teaching the violin to preschoolers could be consistent with and even promote personality development. I believe that this question can be answered affirmatively, with certain qualifications. The child must, of course, have the motor coordination necessary for playing whatever instrument is introduced and the instrument must be of a suitable size. (Suzuki violins come as small as "one sixteenth" size.) The music lessons must not conflict with other developmental lines or with the resolution of drive conflicts, which is so important a task in prelatency development.

Most important, the music lessons must harmonize with a natural developmental line for music within the child's total personality development. Ideally, and perhaps even necessarily, a line of musical development is opened up by favorable musical experiences in the first few years of life, before music lessons are a possibility. (I include among such favorable experiences a "transitional tune" stage.) Then preschool music lessons do not pose a new assignment, nor do they induce a new developmental line. Instead they contribute to a line of musical development which is already in progress, and through their contribution they foster a healthy expansion of the child's developing personality.

A developmental line for music can be constructed as follows. (The successive steps along this line bear many similarities to the steps in the developmental line, "From the Body to the Toy and From Play to Work," as described by Anna Freud [1965, pp. 79–84]).

1. At first the infant's babbling is an autoerotic activity which is only rhythmic or musical by accident. The mother's talking and singing and her performance of instrumental music in the child's presence is not discriminated from the autoerotic "music" activity of the child.

2. The child "creates" his own special music, a transitional tune, by transferring onto this "creation" the musical properties both of himself and of his mother (or parents). The tune, as a musical transitional phenomenon, becomes cathected both with narcissistic and with object libido. It is the child's special lullaby. (The child may also choose a musical toy for a transitional object—a cuddly toy containing a music box which plays his lullaby for him.)

3. Interest in a limited range of musical transitional phenomena broadens into a wider interest in the world of music. The transitional functions of the first musical interests fade out gradually, although the child's own "lullaby" may retain its special function at bedtime and at times of special stress.

4. Somewhere after the third birthday the first musical instrument can be given to the child. For him this instrument has the appearance of a new toy. He may regard it as a successor to an actual

toy instrument, or perhaps to a cuddly toy containing a music box inside it. His first pleasure, if the instrument is a violin, may be in scraping and scratching sounds and in the motor activity of producing them. The sophisticated musical ears of the parents must relax sufficiently to permit sharing the child's pleasure in this unmusical production. At the same time it may be necessary for the parents to protect the child from destroying the instrument altogether, as a result of lingering ambivalent, clinging, destructive impulses from the anal stage of development.[3]

5. Pleasure in disorganized play with the musical instrument evolves into a pleasure in more organized ego activity. Child and parents enjoy together the child's production of harmonious, rhythmic tunes upon the musical instrument. (If all goes well the child may progress from "Twinkle, Twinkle Little Star" to the Bach Double Concerto!) In time the child's main pleasure derives from his musical achievement, rather than from the indiscriminate playful production of sounds. Along with this pleasure in achievement he becomes less dependent upon the tie to his parents for experiencing his own musical pleasure.

6. The achievement of pleasure in "play" at music evolves into an ability to achieve pleasure through "work" at music. Greater impulse control, neutralization, sublimation, and the transition from the pleasure principle to the reality principle effect this change from play to work. In the adult personality music finds its place as an important sublimation. It may become a vital hobby or a full-time professional activity.

The sequence of steps in Suzuki's "talent education" methods conforms closely to the natural developmental line for music which I have just outlined. First the parents are encouraged to provide and share with the child a pleasurable exposure to music in some form, from birth onward. According to Suzuki, the parents introduce music as they introduce language to their child. Later the child's interest in the violin is naturally aroused through witnessing

---

[3] Suzuki regarded the violin as a toy until the late age of seventeen. Some artists have a conscious recall of the early experiencing of their instrument as a toy. In an interview with a local music critic, a young violin soloist with the Cleveland Orchestra, a member of a noted family of musicians, described such a recall. At the age of four years he broke his violin across his knee, and his parents then replaced it with a metal violin.

his parent's pleasure in playing the instrument. To this end the parent, whether a beginner or not, must take violin lessons himself, as a preliminary to the child's lessons. Suzuki calls this step "training the parent rather than the child." He says: "Until the parent can play one piece, the child does not play at all" (p. 106). As the child's interest is awakened he begins to attend the parent's lessons as an auditor. (These may be both individual lessons and group lessons, where other parents and children listen and play together). When the child wants to try the violin he is given his first tiny, but real, instrument, just as he would be given a new toy. Suzuki says, "We encourage them to 'play' with the violin. . . . We encourage them to think of it as fun" (p. 106f.). The parent's lessons are expanded to include the child, who shares with his parent both the relationship with and the instruction offered by the teacher. As the child progresses on the violin he joins group lessons with other young musicians, much as a nursery school child gradually acquires the ability to play with and enjoy other children. Suzuki emphasizes this timely group play as an important part of the fun for children. His observation is that parents who bring a child only for private instruction and regard the group sessions as unnecessary are parents who do not understand his methods and cannot succeed in applying them with their children. As the child grows the spirit of fun leads him on, almost imperceptibly, into the spirit of work and in turn to the development of his full musical ability.

Suzuki's own informal headings, in the brief account of his violin training methods which he includes in his book, could well serve to express his own conception of a developmental line for music: "We encourage them to think of it as fun." "We encourage them to 'play' with the violin." "A game to begin with, the spirit of fun leads them on." "Five minutes every day [leads to] three hours every day." "The development of ability is absolutely reliable." "We amaze the world."

Summary

The Suzuki method of teaching young children to play the violin roused my interest in musical development and led me to the concept of a "transitional tune" as an important early experience in the development of some musicians. In his original article on transitional phenomena Winnicott included sounds and tunes among the wide range of normal transitional experiences.

Confirmation for the concept of a transitional tune comes from direct observation of young children, from biographical and autobiographical accounts of the early lives of musicians, and from music itself, in the form of lullabies and cradle songs. The word *lullaby* is an onomatopoeic word, composed of "lull" and "bye," and thus a lullaby is a song offered to an infant as a lulling comfort at the time of a separation. By definition, the lullaby is a song intended for use as a transitional tune, and the words of many lullabies express this function of the music.

Finally, I have proposed a developmental line for music, in which the "transitional tune" stage occupies an early and probably an important position. The success of Suzuki's method of teaching the violin to young children seems to be based on its close adherence to and support of this natural developmental line for music.

Chapter 7

A Psychoanalyst's View of Clara Schumann

Anna M. Burton, M.D.

Dear Mother,
  You have as yet read nothing from me, but now I can write a little I will send you a little letter, which will please you. I had presents on my eighth birthday . . . from dear Father I got a beautiful dress, and from Bertha I had an ashcake and a plum-cake and a lovely knitting-bag. And I played Mozart's E-flat major concerto which you used to play, with orchestral accompaniment, and Herr Mathai, Lange, Belka and a lot of others played with me. It went very well and I never stuck at all, only my cadenza would not go easily, where I had to play a chromatic scale three times, I was not a bit frightened, but the clapping troubled me. . . . Please give my love to Grandmamma, and my brothers send their love to you. Now you will write to me, won't you?
  Your obedient daughter,
  Clara Wieck
  (Leipzig, September 14th, 1827)

From the very beginning, Clara Wieck Schumann was more than a child prodigy. The authentic musicality which she showed as a girl continued to characterize her music throughout a long and influential career, as one of the great pianists and teachers of nineteenth-century Europe. In turn, three different men laid claim to her work and her emotional life, in order to fulfill their musical destinies. These were Friedrich Wieck, her father and teacher, Robert Schumann, her husband and father of her children, and Johannes Brahms, her friend and younger colleague.

From the uniquely structured childhood to the last years as bearer of a musical tradition, what was most impressive about Clara Schumann was that amidst shifting pressures and stimuli, an integrated personality appeared, with definite and persisting features. At any age, she possessed purpose, resilience, a concern for rectitude and a profound reliance on music for emotional balance and sense of identity.

Since Madame Schumann's piano style is most relevant to what follows, we may learn of it through Harold Schonberg's summary of various first-hand reports:

She never was one of the heroic pianists, and she never modified the technic that her father had given her. It was playing that avoided any kind of violence . . . or . . . excessive physical movement. Fingers were kept close to the keys, and the keys were squeezed rather than struck. . . . Only the musical sound should be heard. Apparently, even with this hands-close-to-the-keys technic, she was able to draw a full, colorful tone. . . . George Bernard Shaw, when he first heard her, immediately realized what a "nobly beautiful and poetic player" she was. "An artist of that sort is the Grail of the critic's quest" [he said]. Clara always did her best to subordinate herself to the intentions of the composer as she saw them. The great Austrian critic, Eduard Hanslick, like everyone else, remarked on this, and on her penetrating understanding of every kind of music [1963, p. 228].

With steady vitality, Clara Wieck Schumann grew past each limit set by circumstance or attachment. A Galatea to her Pygmalion father, and a partner in creation to Robert Schumann, she was instructed and nurtured by both men in turn, and finally achieved a rare degree of artistic and personal integrity. Moreover, she seemed to be unstoppable: a wife who gradually took over, through necessity, those functions which Robert Schumann had to relinquish; later, a widow whose career flourished despite the exhausting claims of parenthood, and in sum, a nineteenth-century woman who earned the respect of her male colleagues and the deepest friendship of Johannes Brahms.

These qualities, in a remarkable musician, stimulate a closer scrutiny of the records, fortunately made available to the author through sharing readings and discussions with a musicologist and biographer of Clara Schumann, Nancy Reich (Reich, 1985). Thereby, a unique view is gained of the unfolding of her personality during a full and energetic life. The story centers on a complex father-daughter relationship, which poses the central clinical question: to what extent did Clara Schumann achieve psychological autonomy, specifically, independence from the attachment to her father? And a second, more profound question must be posed: how much did her accomplishments represent a process of psychic repair, in the face of severe losses, beginning with the loss of her mother? Over several years the psychoanalytic reading of biographical material has led to syntheses which address these questions by following three themes (taken up in this and chapter 21). This, the first, connects the early history with the later characterological solutions. A second illuminates the overdetermined object relationship which made Clara into Robert Schumann's "creative partner." A third traces their relationship after marriage, in which Clara was indispensable, but no longer a partner in creativity. Beyond these explorations, further ideas have formed concernng Clara Schumann's relationship with Brahms, and the ways in which her identification as a woman and mother affected her role in the lives of these men.

Any late twentieth-century "life" properly addresses etiological questions, which can be informed by applied psychoanalysis, especially since the latter has widened its scope from pathographies of artists to include the conflict-free domain of ego functioning and normal self and object relationships. In the "case" of Clara Schumann, the most impressive aspects of her personality and the most worth understanding are her splendid adaptation and her integrity, both personal and artistic.

However, the available data from letters and diaries are limited in usefulness. Biographical facts cannot be compared to the rich and released interchange created between living analysands and practicing psychoanalysts. The directional webbing of free association is lacking, as is the analyst's most reliable source of information—the transference–countertransference relationship. Clara Schumann's thoughts, as expressed in her writings, adhere to their special contexts. These have their own aims and constructions, at times quite explicit, since diaries within this cultural group were "official," and intended to be read by descendants as well as the general public.

As psychoanalytic data, then, diaries are complex resultants of many mental operations. To further complicate the matter, Friedrich Wieck, as he took Clara's destiny in his hands, also took over her diaries, so that for many years, it was his handwriting and his words, dictated to Clara, which kept the record for posterity. He also used the diary as an avenue of communication, with rules and principles, criticisms and praise, threats and promises, as vehicles between father and daughter.

When Clara finally took over her diary, her entries served many functions. First of all, they were a means of emotional catharsis. Moreover, the act of diary keeping in itself must have influenced her affective life since writing obliged the diarist to attend to her feelings and choose words to express them. One might regard these steps as working toward "taming" of affects, favoring mastery and integrated functioning. Keeping the diary also served to integrate differing self-images—as performer, wife, mother, and sometime composer. Not only did the diary provide an abreactive and integrative self-therapy to the diarist, it evidently took on another meaning and was related to as though it were itself an object; thus Clara Schumann addressed her diary as "my dearest companion." Writing was a constant exercise in self-observation and appraisal. Clara examined her performance, in each of her roles, measuring it against that of others and against her own ideal, so that from self-assessment came some degree of pride or chagrin. Finally, she would exhort herself to achieve more, or else forgive her own shortcomings. This led her to set down new resolves and dedications, just as her father had judged and set tasks for her in the earliest diary.

The available material also includes newly translated and published documents which provide irreproachable data and allow a correct historical context. The broad flow of diaries and of the correspondence between Clara Schumann, her loved ones, and her colleagues contained all the currents of her feelings and relationships. It also permitted exact chronologies which suggested developmental obstacles. Nowhere is this close chronology more important than in reconstructing features of Clara Wieck's childhood.

The Early Years

Even before Clara was born, her father decided that her destiny was to become the ideal child virtuoso. Friedrich Wieck was an unusually determined and pragmatic man—a teacher, lender and seller of pianos and scores, and a prime mover in the bourgeois artistic world of Leipzig. Little is known of the emotional atmosphere of the Wieck home except for the cardinal fact that it led to divorce before Clara Wieck was five. Her earliest care was largely delegated to a maid, Johanna Strobel, who was notably taciturn. In fact Wieck blamed Johanna's silent nature for the startling fact that Clara did not speak even single words until the age of four-and-a-half, and before that gave no evidence of language comprehension. This data comes from the father himself, writing the very first entry in Clara's *Diary*. He wrote in the first person, as though personifying his daughter:

> My inaptitude for speech, and my want of concern in all that was passing round me, often caused my parents to complain that I

was dull of hearing. Even up to my eighth year this defect was not entirely cured, although it improved as I came to speak better and to take more notice of what was going on. At Easter 1821 my parents moved to a house in the Salzgasschen, and it was here that I was fated to lose my mother. She left my father on May 12, 1824, and went to Plauen to arrange for a legal separation [Litzmann, 1913, Vol. 1, pp. 1-2. Quoted in Reich, 1985].

The entry gives important clues to the character of Wieck, unempathic and blunt in his appropriation of Clara's personality.

Clara was allowed one last summer with her mother and her maternal grandparents; then, at age five, she was permanently given over to her father. She had only minimal contact with her mother from then on, and remained the small mistress of the house until Wieck remarried four years later. It is not surprising, in view of her history, that observers of Clara as a child noted a prematurely adult quality, a solemnity or sadness in her demeanor (E. Schumann, 1833, p. 225).

Though few "hard" facts are available, they nevertheless spell out some important aspects of Clara's childhood. She was conceived three months following the death of the Wiecks' first-born daughter, and before she had reached the age of seventeen months, her mother's double series of piano performances and pregnancies had begun. A chronology may best convey the tempo and atmosphere of Clara's early family experience:

17 months	(Mar. 1821)	Mother's third pregnancy
23 months	(Aug. 1821)	Brother Alwin is born
25 months	(Oct. 1821)	Mother performs two concertos
35 months	(Summer, 1822)	Mother's fourth pregnancy
3 yrs. 4 mos.	(Jan. 1823)	Brother Gustav is born
3 yrs. 11 mos.	(Aug. 1823)	Mother's fifth pregnancy
4 yrs. 2 mos.	(Nov. 1823)	Mother gives two performances
4 yrs. 5 mos.	(Feb. 1824)	Brother Viktor is born

The above suggests that Marianne Wieck was heavily burdened during one period, when she produced a baby in August and a piano concert in October. Clara was then twenty-two to twenty-five months old—three important months within the larger span of the period of separation and individuation, which specifically feature the rapid, simultaneous development of locomotion, motor control, sphincter control, and speech. Apparently, locomotion was not a problem for Clara, who could keep up with the adults on miles-long daily "constitutionals" by the time she was three. However, the verbal communication did not develop. The author presumes this localized failure in the development of a crucial ego function to be a consequence of separation–individuation difficulties.[1] Clara's situation might have been even less favorable if her relationship with her father had suffered. One might speculate that a "dumb" and uncomprehending child would be a disappointment to such a father.

There were in fact two nonverbal channels of communication open to this toddler: her mother's music, and Johanna's silent mode of child rearing. An innately gifted child whose not-too-available mother sings and practices the piano amidst the other sounds of a musical household is extremely likely to identify piano sounds with "mother," and learn to hear and respond to elements of feeling in her mother's music (Greenacre, 1957). Normally, young toddlers who find themselves at some distance from their mothers use speech sounds to maintain contact, and clinical work with wordless autistic children shows that music may provide an alternate, and therapeutically useful, mode of communication.

It is therefore quite probable that Clara Wieck had early entry to a musical realm which signified "mother," and a world of associations to "mother," and that she derived psychological nurturance from her languagelike comprehension of musical ideas and feelings. This leads to the concept that her musical intuition and her lifelong need for music represented the continuance of a "transitional process" begun in her first two years (Winnicott, 1953). Clara's requirement for music was commented upon by Robert Schumann, in a letter dated January 24, 1839, when she was a young woman of almost twenty: "You would rather have continual thunder and lightning, and always something fresh which has never been done before."

Viewed in the context of inner conflict during childhood, hear-

---

[1] This is in line with the observations and clinical theories of Mahler, Pine, and Bergman (1975), who state:

> The less emotionally available the mother is at the time of rapprochement, the more insistently . . . does the toddler attempt to woo her. In some cases, this process drains so much of the child's available developmental energy that, as a result, not enough energy, not enough libido, and not enough constructive (neutralized) aggression are left for the evolution of the many ascending functions of the ego [p. 80].

ing and "thinking" music established a relatively safe surrounding; that is, one free of psychic conflict, and offering helpful possibilities of control and gratification. Musical thinking would thus acquire a valuable defensive function. A parallel situation in clinical work is the child who remains speechless when words have been weapons at home, or when words bring retaliation or guilt over choosing sides. Thus, some children speak only to their "safe" objects. In this connection, it is of some interest that Clara's language finally emerged normally when she was given a piano lesson together with other children.

Clara Schumann's speech difficulty transcended her childhood years; not only was it delayed, but words alone never quite said enough for her. She would often appeal to the language of music as a supplement, based on her long experience with musical expression and imagery. Lili Peller (1965) described how a "reciprocal relationship between speech development and the growth of the ego takes place in a setting of playful activity between mother and child." This essential "regaling function" of the mother was taken over in time by Clara's fellow student, Robert Schumann. Building on her early keyboard sensibilities, he engaged her at a tender age in this learning–playing activity. And many years later, in her middle and old age, echoes of these girlhood fancies may still be heard, in Clara's letters to Brahms; for instance when she imagines her spirit accompanying him, invisible in the shadows, partaking of his performance.

As long as Clara protected herself through exile from the verbal world, she remained at a disadvantage in the binding of affect and in precise, efficient communication; hence, also in anticipating events and mastering perceptions. (The absence of speech further compromises the child's individuation by delaying the ability to name objects and wishes, and the sense of mastery of the environment [Katan, 1961; Mahler et al., 1975]). As a result, she was vulnerable to minor shocks of rejection which might have been softened by explication in words. This is both a plausible construct, and one corroborated by the author's particular examination of Clara Schumann's writings, focusing on her use of metaphoric expressions.

The rationale for this special study was that metaphors provide data of a different order than that of conscious communication; they offer a particular "reading" of a subject's personality development. The psychological significance of an individual's choice of metaphor was demonstrated by Ella Freeman Sharpe (1940), who concluded from clinical observations that metaphor evolves from the displacement of emotions onto perceptions of the body, especially those associated with sphincter control. In adult life, the spontaneous use of a metaphor evokes "the epitome of a forgotten (important) experience," and the study of an individual's metaphors reveals something of her early perceptions of environment and her instinctual tensions. Thus, characteristic choices of metaphor derive from, and indicate the periods of development most fraught with anxiety. Using this approach, an intensive study of Clara Schumann's metaphoric expressions made it immediately apparent that a large proportion of her metaphors had to do with conflict over speaking. Specifically, of 214 consecutive metaphoric usages, 50 fall into this category of inhibition in speaking, including the very frequent use of the words *unspeakable* or *unspeakably*. Two illustrations are cited below; it will be noted, moreover, that these excerpts clearly connect the inhibition of speaking with strong emotions.

> February 5, 1870: We spent a ghastly night with frozen windows and we were so sad that the words almost withered on our lips [Quoted in Litzmann, 1913, Vol. 1, p. 238].
>
> October 23, 1875: But even thinking about it enrages me, so let us say no more about it... [Quoted in Litzmann, 1913, Vol. 2, p. 60].

In order to distinguish significant choice of phrase and personal style from cultural influences and letter-writing conventions, a parallel study was also made of the metaphors used in the letters of a peculiarly apt control subject, Elisabet von Herzogenberg (Kalbeck, 1909). This woman, a younger contemporary of Clara Schumann's, was an amateur pianist and, also, a prolific letter writer. She shared with Clara the same cultural milieu, language, and devotion to romantic music, especially that written for the piano. Moreover, many of her letters, like Clara's, were addressed to Johannes Brahms. (By further coincidence, both women married men who gave up the profession of law in order to compose music!) It was interesting to note that the letters of Frau von Herzogenberg presented a quite different array of metaphoric expressions. In her case, speechlessness, or the difficulty of verbal expression was represented only once in 169 consecutive examples of metaphor. (Preponderant groups of her metaphors had to do with procreative and nurturing functions, and with sensations in the chest and head. These findings are noteworthy, in view of the fact that Elisabet von Herzogenberg tried unsuccessfully to have children, and in later life developed congestive heart failure.)

The "speech-inhibited" metaphoric expressions of Clara Schumann are a regular finding in her writings, from the earliest to the final years. Approximately half of them are associated with fears of separation, or of rejection, in the form of a cold or angry response:

> February 1, 1861: Parting was so sad to me that every word that I've had to speak to other people has been hard for days now [Quoted in Litzmann, 1913, Vol. 1, p. 360].

> July 1, 1858: [W]hy should you want, by your coldness, to destroy the lovely confidence which permits me to express everything to you? . . . I have not the courage to express to you my delight about most of these (Volkslieder). Perhaps next time it will be easier to speak my mind freely. . . . If only I could view longing as sweetly as you do. It gives only pain to me and often convulses my heart with unspeakable sorrow [Quoted in Litzmann, 1913, Vol. 1, p. 225].

> What I endured this evening, is indescribable. Father in his excitement and anxiety made me so miserable—for him it was no small thing, and I certainly believe that he had never before been so wrought up [Quoted in Litzmann, 1913, Vol. 2, p. 98].

Some of these metaphoric evocations of speechlessness appear together with the related idea of being understood empathically, without the necessity of words; also, in several letters, both of these elements combine with bittersweet references to childhood, or the past:

> November 8, 1858: [having not written for fear of an unkind reply] . . . that it was hard for me, you know without my telling you; indeed it would have been a great joy for me to write it to you.

> [I]ndescribably beautiful. . . . is it true that the poet who speaks in this will be mine . . . so fully do I understand your every thought, that I could lose myself in you and your music. . . . one can see the child as it begs with its little hands pressed together. . . . In this piece there is something so original, so adventurous—I cannot find the words [Quoted in Litzmann, 1913, Vol. 1, p. 213].

The psychoanalytic understanding of such nostalgia is that it represents a defense against the reemergence of anxious or painful memories. The old traumata are camouflaged by a rosy glow, while the pain reappears, disguised as a longing for the past. These interpretations begin to reconstruct Clara Wieck's early experiences in a discordant home. In addition, some of her later writings strike the "analytic ear" as residuals from the psychic trauma of her family's breakup. Clara Schumann, at forty-five years of age, wrote to Brahms about the imminent divorce of *his* parents, and protested that she had suspected nothing "wrong," and "in any case [I] was quite innocent..." [Quoted in Litzmann, 1913, Vol. 1, pp. 171–172). Five months later, having had to witness the crisis, she wrote him, "I assure you it has made me feel quite ill, for one's heart gets torn in two" (Quoted in Litzmann, 1913, Vol. 1, p. 176). Again, regarding the divorce of the violinist, Joseph Joachim, Clara at first scornfully dismissed the rumors (Vol. 1, p. 243), only to be overwhelmed later by helpless feelings and anxieties. Her trouble in resolving loyalty conflicts showed quite plainly as endless vacillations, during the Friedrich Wieck–Robert Schumann contest over her. Going further, one might also attribute Clara's occasional obsessiveness over propriety, to the impact of her parents' divorce.

There is no hint that the Wieck children were prepared in any way to meet the cataclysm of divorce. Indeed, the nature of Friedrich Wieck's blunt entries in the *Diary* indicate that he openly blamed Marianne and scorned her character. And yet it is a key to the understanding of Clara's personality that, despite the compromised early relationship and the separation after the age of five, she formed an enduring, positive identification with her mother. Perhaps the availability of the "transitional" world of music enabled her to preserve optimal inner mental representations of her mother. Significantly, Clara's first letter to Marianne, which was probably dictated by her father, does at least allow for some preserving of contact via the keyboard. In this note, Clara anticipated playing piano duets with her mother, and noted that she had just performed the same concerto as her mother (Litzmann, 1913, Vol. 1, pp. 11–12).

A child's mental representations of an absent mother become polarized between idealized and angrily devalued extremes, burdening the child with the need to resolve these disparate "good" and "bad" images. Wieck's attacks on his ex-wife may have served to articulate for Clara all of her own angry feelings, thus permitting a very private, partly repressed idealization of mother. Such an ideal image of an absentee parent "inflates," so to speak, until it matches the parent's own ego ideal, that is, the child holds the image of the mother perfected. In the case of Clara Wieck, that "good" image—which substantially determined her own ego ideal—was of a woman who bore children, performed, and had the strength to break with a powerful father figure. (In understanding Clara Schumann as a mother, herself, it is noteworthy that both Marianne and Clara were able to tolerate guilt feelings associated with leaving their children.) The silent identification with her mother manifested itself clearly when Clara's rupture from her father took place, shortly before her marriage, and again much later in life when she (like Marianne in her second marriage) supported the family while caring for an ailing husband.

The Young Virtuoso

After the summer of 1824, five-year-old Clara was returned home to her two younger brothers, already motherless for two months, and to the father impatient to set about structuring her career. Clara's "ear" was the means of instruction, since Wieck understood that the pleasure of the melodies would be her best reward. Hence he wrote music to please as well as instruct her, and so became the first "composer" whose works she played. In time, voice lessons, counterpoint, and languages were added to a schedule which was carefully arranged never to become hectic or overburdened. Friedrich Wieck believed in a healthful, natural pace. The long daily walks and regular regime remained Clara's habit all her life. (This later became Robert Schumann's regimen as well.) Wieck's characteristic hypomanic and dictatorial style was softened for Clara in this one area—the study of music. At the keyboard, her need for a mother could find expression, while at the same time she accommodated the needs of her remaining parent. The making of music thus became fully available to Clara during the mourning of her first loss (because Johanna was soon dismissed, this was a double loss). And in facing all later losses, Clara's resilience was closely tied to the act of playing piano.

In the spring of 1830, when Clara was ten-and-a-half years old, her father became her impresario, taking her on tours for weeks and months, and adroitly capitalizing in every way on her budding career. The letters Wieck sent home from these tours to his second wife furnish vivid confirmation of his aggression and energy. Written hastily, under pressure of a self-imposed schedule, they depict an impervious juggernaut of a man, who persevered despite illnesses, local jealousies, wardrobe expenses, and other trials. He used every angle to further their joint careers, such as collecting autographs, selling engravings, and making political use of Clara's compositions. Wieck also sold instruments along the way, and at times, the concerts served to display the pianos as well as the pianist. Once he had to repair a keyboard in full view of the audience, during an intermission. Following this embarrassment, in "fear, sweat and anger," as he wrote, a damper became stuck, and he had to manually depress it "a few hundred times during the concert." Thus, while Clara played, her father functioned, in effect, as part of her instrument (Wieck, 1830, p. 48).

These concert tours cemented the bond between Clara and her single, dominating parent. In determining every facet of her life, her father must have profoundly affected Clara's tastes, her affective style, and her priorities. Clara's "diary" contained her father's entries, while his correspondence was in part written by Clara. Thus they mingled experiences, thoughts, and activities in pursuit of one great shared purpose.

Wieck's emotional investment in his daughter's life arouses clinical interest, if for no reason other than his need to defend that mission against criticism, as in his letter of October 13, 1831, to his second wife: "[the wife of Geheimrat . . . Schmidt] . . . reproached me that I have Clara play too much. . . . I said to her: 'for twenty-five years I have studied education and put it in practice—for seven years I have lived only for the training of my daughter—I do not need, now, any advice.' " (Wieck, 1830, p. 34).

The postscript to this letter adds:

> With meekness I take from God all these joys! . . . You see: we gain power in the wide world—as God wills. . . . My dear soul, you cry with joy—I see it—and permit me to say, from the heart. You certainly don't believe I am becoming boastful—I often cry, however, for joy. Clara does not yet understand all this . . .

One marvels that Friedrich Wieck, that pragmatic "survivor," could be so incoherent and passionate in glorifying his daughter. To whatever extent Clara partook of her father's heady excitement, their shared grandiose vision could only have further organized and sealed her identification with him.

At a peak of exhibitionism and inflated narcissism, Wieck (1830) revealed what his daughter signified to him, in these lines: "It cannot be described what a sensation both of the monkeys from the Leipzig menagerie are making here! . . . [people] are too dense . . . ever to conceive what an extraordinary child Clara is, and even less, that your Fritz from Pretzsch possesses and moulds her . . ." (p. 27).

The statement was unequivocal: he had created and now possessed, and virtually annexed, the ideal child–musician. His grand plan, as might be expected, caused Clara some stress. It was not the display of her talent which caused inner conflict, since that which she exhibited was of and for her father; the honors went first to him. Clara functioned as an extension of her father—symbolically, as a phallic supplement. He wrote her diary, ordered her life, traveled with her, and through her gifts, rubbed shoulders with all the "greats" of his time. She had adapted to this close working union, almost a body union at times (as when Wieck worked the broken damper-pedal while she performed in concert). Anxiety arose only when she felt she had not fully succeeded. This was evident in 1830, when because of a stiff keyboard, she burst into tears, saying that she knew despite the applause that it had been a poor performance (Litzmann, 1913, Vol. 1, p. 17).

In concert, the young artist fulfilled the audience's expectations that she would improvise and play her own compositions. However, composing often brought expressions of uncertainty, and even a consuming self-dissatisfaction. The first efforts to compose were reported at eight-and-one-half years of age, and with them, appeared a neurotic dissatisfaction. Her father wrote in the *Diary* in 1830: "My father specially blames me now for a certain jealousy of disposition—love of pleasure—childish sensitiveness—and a curious inclination never to enjoy the present time or present possessions. This last troubled my father the most, because it made me appear seldom contented, since a perpetual 'But' or 'If' got in the way" (Quoted in Litzmann, 1913, Vol. 2, p. 140). Later attempts elicited the same dissatisfied, irritable affect, along with spasms of self-derogation and mortification. At nineteen, she wrote to Schumann:

> It is with me as with you, there are just such alleys in my heart, but they are smaller and there are more of them. My mind has hardly

had time to look round in one of them before it stumbles on another, and so it goes on, perpetually.... I do not know what will come of it. I always comfort myself with the thought that I am a woman after all, and they are not born to compose [Quoted in Litzmann, 1973, Vol. 1, p. 140].

And a year later, at twenty, she wrote: "I once thought that I possessed creative talent, but I have given up this idea; a woman must not desire to compose. Not one has been able to do it, and why should I expect to? It would be arrogance, though indeed, my father led me into it in earlier days" (pp. 355–356).

The last year of the courtship, Clara had difficulties with their project to mutually compose a song collection. Although deferential to Robert's genius, she stubbornly resisted his suggestions for her "Idyll," both as to title and musical features. Schumann asked her to "write and tell me if you like your *Idylle* as I have altered it." Clara replied in June 1839:

I have received the *Idylle*, and thank you for it my dear; but I am sure you will forgive me if I tell you that there are some things in it which I do not like. The end, which I liked best, you have completely altered.... I wanted to ask you if you think it would be a good thing if I were to let it be printed here, together with several other little things, *as I had it first*.... You are not angry with me, are you? (emphasis added) [Quoted in Litzmann, 1973, Vol. 1, pp. 353–354].

When Clara's own efforts to compose wavered, she partook reverently of Robert's creative genius. Many of her compositions during the fourteen years of marriage to Schumann consisted of music which followed one of their periods of intense mutual study, or else they were small birthday pieces, written to please him.

It came more naturally for Clara to be the presenter of Schumann's works to the cognoscenti to whom she had formerly demonstrated her father's teaching method. On the psychological level, Clara had already begun to personify her father's ego ideal (a factor of great importance in her later relationship with Robert Schumann). Intrapsychically, her superego was organizing around the internalization of her father's precepts; thus, she carried the responsibility for upholding her father's standards as a teacher. She also fully internalized Wieck's work attitudes, such as moderation, naturalness, and regularity of exercise, as well as those artistic ideals which he proclaimed; namely, truthfulness to the spirit of the music, wholeness, good proportion, and the placing of art above material gain. Clara Schumann's identification with these values in both work and deed is quite clear in her writings. She became, like her father, a resilient and resourceful person. When it came to handling money, however, her scruples reflected only the better side of her father's character. Clara was never violent, as her father sometimes was, but she too could be harsh and unfeeling, even toward her own children.

During those early tours (1830–1832), Wieck assumed himself to be indispensable as manager of a daughter whom he still regarded as a naive, original, and pure being. However, with time, subtle changes transpired. The impresario Wieck was apparently daunted by the musical world of Paris. There, it was thirteen-year-old Clara who had the spark of enterprise. The letters of the exasperated father make it plain that his solemn little woman was becoming a headstrong adolescent: "Clara now is often so inconsiderate, domineering, full of unreasonable opposition, careless, totally disobedient, rude, prickly blunt, monstrously lazy . . . she is thinking only of the theater and—the gentlemen. . . . I will be irritated with her for the rest of my life . . ." (Wieck, 1830, p. 51).

A competitive note was sounded when they both prepared their French, Wieck remarking with some chagrin on how well Clara was mastering the language. (In view of Clara's delayed speech development, this matching of language skills with her father might have done much to bolster a sense of competence.) Wieck lost momentum and felt disoriented and homesick in Paris, while Clara adapted easily. "What I do for Clara, she can never make up to me," he mourned, in unconscious realization that their relationship was tilting in a new direction. Whereas earlier, Clara had functioned as the extension of her father's ambitions, he was now the adjunct to her career. Schumann noted this new development in his diary, on their return. Her father expressed her newfound arrogance in a humorous list of questions he had most often been asked:

> [O]nce it was snowing—a willfull snow-flake fell into my arms, and behold—that was this Clara, exactly as she stands before you.
> Q: Have you more children, equally musical?
> A: They have as much talent, but have not been taught.
> Q: How is that?
> A: Because I have only one life to give [Quoted in Litzmann, 1913, Vol. 1, pp. 66–68].

Budding adolescence and sexuality receive no other documentation in the written record, as handed down. If Clara knew desire, there were few young women in whom she could confide. The tone of many of her letters to Robert was playful, arch, and provocative, as well as mock maternal. His replies adopted her euphemism for his freely sexual way of life—namely his drinking: "If Florestan did not do just the opposite of everybody else, if Eusebius drank less Bavarian beer, if a certain Davidite did not stick to his business, when all the rest had departed, etc., why then I should be very different from what I am" (C. Schumann, 10 July, 1834, in May, 1888, p. 234).

Clara's period of sadness at sixteen has been attributed to jealousy over Robert's interest in Ernestine von Fricken; it did not take very long for her early flirtatiousness to give way to sober dignity. In fact, she was never to enjoy the freedom of passion that she envied, for instance, in her friend, Pauline Viardot-Garcia, and which she thoroughly decried in the unbridled Liszt.

The faultless propriety of Mme. Schumann's demeanor in later years may have had one root in the forced intimacy with her father during the long tours, when they lived and traveled together. There are absolutely no hints in the record of incestuous anxiety. One slender intimation that this remained a sensitive area for the mature Clara Schumann is found when, years later, she criticized Wagner's opera *Tannhauser*, voicing repulsion at the incestuous lives of the "tattered, villainous gods" (Quoted in Litzmann, 1913, Vol. 1, pp. 425–426). Her professed "boredom" with Wagnerian music may have even sprung in part from this old source of anxiety.

To summarize, Clara Wieck's development was determined by her innate abilities and the music-rich environment, in which her dyadic relationship with her mother was musically defined and expressed. The silence of her nurse rendered words less significant, thereby fostering nonverbal communication, especially musical sounds and phrases. Clara's late speech development, and the history of early periods of maternal deprivation strongly suggest some failure in the separation–individuation process.

Wieck's regimen fostered a new one-to-one bond, both complex and intense, through which Clara's development was inescapably funneled into, and organized around her piano career; her mother's example, and the earlier faulted individuation prepared the way for her father's enthusiastic takeover. This dyadic bond contributed to Clara's ironclad identification with her father, and was henceforth to color the oedipal issues of her life.

Clara Wieck's struggle for independence from her father progressed from these adolescent scuffles into the raging battles of the courtship period. The greatest single victory was her Parisian tour, without father, at the age of nineteen, but the war was not won until several years after her marriage. She often needed support from Schumann, to whom she confided, in distress:

> "Do you know what I long for? A lesson from Father!" (Quoted in Litzmann, 1913, Vol. 1, p. 238).

As late as February of 1840, when Wieck's outpouring of vitriol had succeeded in burning them both, Clara's letters reported severe stage fright, as well as headaches and "neurasthenia." With Robert demoralized and depressed, Clara met her last great crisis of divided loyalty. This was relieved when Schumann himself emerged from his depression into active legal combat with Clara's father, and reassured her that she would always remain a virtuoso, even without the help of Father Wieck. At the same time, he embarked on his "year of song."

The nature of Clara Wieck's innate gifts, the pattern and deficiencies of her mothering, and the intrusive management of her father, produced a personality relatively proof against change. One sees this in Clara Schumann's well-rooted musical life. While she was always eager for new music, whether from Chopin, Schumann, Mendelssohn, or Brahms, she unfailingly approached it from those interpretive referents learned in childhood. Her tastes changed slowly, and her technic and ideals, virtually not at all. What evolved then, in the young woman who attracted Robert Schumann, was a highly integrated and stable personality, although not truly autonomous, oriented toward performance, and a performer's version of love, marriage, and motherhood.

Chapter 8
Charles and George Ives: The Veneration of Boyhood

Stuart Feder, M.D.

A song entitled "The Things Our Fathers Loved," one of the *114 Songs* which Charles Ives (1922) published at the age of forty-eight, is set to the following text:

> I think there must be a place in the soul all made of tunes, of tunes of long ago; I hear the organ on the Main Street corner, Aunt Sarah humming Gospels; Summer evenings, the village cornet band, playing in the square. The town's Red, White and Blue, all Red, White and Blue. Now! Hear the Songs! I know not what are the words. But they sing in my soul of the things our Fathers loved [pp. 91–92].

No source for the text is given in Ives's carefully edited table of contents, but among a few notes and comments at the end of the volume he writes, "Where no author is indicated the words are by Harmony Twitchell Ives or her husband" (p. 260). It was Ives himself who wrote the words for this song, just as he had for many others of the *114*.

This collection has a special place in the body of Ives's work and a curious history as well. It captures our interest because of its intricate connections to every aspect of the composer's life and his long career in music. It stimulates us to explore certain relationships between music and biography and, in fact, despite its pretension to genteel privacy, fairly invites us into the composer's life. Indeed, it causes us to wonder, as Ives did himself, why this particular collection was written at all, much less printed and

---

Appreciation is expressed to Mrs. Sidney Cowell for her help and encouragement in Ives studies.
First published in *The Annual of Psychoanalysis*, 9:265–316, 1981.

published at his own expense, distributed free to anyone who wanted a copy. Perhaps of greatest interest of all to the psychoanalyst are the pervasive elements of childhood appearing and reappearing in so many guises throughout its pages. Even a superficial look at the score, in which the date of each of the songs is given, reveals it to be in some sense a work of autobiography; the dates start at 1921 and go back chronologically to 1888, to the very first song Ives is known to have written, at the age of fourteen. One finds in this collection a sense of the past, an awareness of both unity and development in life and work, and, above all, a reverence for the experiences and objects of childhood—features, in fact, that were characteristic of the entire body of Ives's music.

My purpose in this study is to explore, from a psychoanalytic viewpoint, certain aspects of the life and work of Ives. A central focus is the childhood of the composer insofar as it may be studied through the methods of applied psychoanalysis. Particular attention will be paid to Ives's unique relationship with his father and its role not only in Ives's career choice, character, and style but in the nature of his music as well. The development of Ives's music will also be discussed. Against this background we can explore the vicissitudes of Ives's later mourning for his father and its reflection in the music, here with particular reference to the creative pace of the composer.

In addition to the usual biographical materials, the music itself will comprise a part of the data. To neglect it would be inconceivable, if for no other reason than the fact that notes, diary entries, reminiscences, and the like, which would ordinarily comprise the standard biographical material, are here often written directly on the manuscript page! Beyond this, however, are the constant autobiographical references to be found in the music, rendered that is, in purely auditory terms. These range from relatively obvious examples that stem from Ives's habit of musical quotation, to others which, being quite subtle, may challenge interpretation. Frequently too the composer provides programs to the music and often personal comments about the background of its composition. Many of the texts of Ives's songs were his own and in the case of the volume of *114 Songs* he provided a lengthy postface in the nature of an apologia. Such an amalgam of music, word, and personal reference naturally stimulates curiosity about the nature of music itself. It is hoped that a study such as this may be one possible point of entry into the enigma of musical "meaning." At least it may throw some light on what music "means" in the context of the life of one man and how this meaning is conveyed.

Ives's creative output was vast, and the forms and instrumental combinations in which he cast his work are far ranging. For purposes of this study we will confine our illustrative material to the songs and to several transcribed or excerpted works which appear as songs. Other works, while cited, are not discussed in detail. I have chosen to focus on the songs because of their availability both physically (Ives, 1922) and musically and also because of the enriching associations in many of the texts.[1] This selection is far from arbitrary, however, since a representative sampling of Ives's works appears in some form in the *114 Songs*, and since in so many respects the entire body of his work may be said to form a unity. Certainly, for our purposes in this essay these songs, as characteristic of Ives as anything he wrote, are fertile for illustration.

IVES AT MIDLIFE:
UNIQUENESS IN THE EXTREME AND THE WANING OF CREATIVITY

Following a path familiar in clinical psychoanalysis, we will start with a point in midlife and then go on to develop its antecedents. By the time Ives had reached his early forties and was beginning to conceive his collection of *114 Songs*, he had carved a unique life for himself. He was a principal in the rising firm of Ives and Myrick, an insurance agency flourishing in the heyday of a growing new field. At that time, a period of unrestrained economic expansion, it was possible to accommodate a sense of idealism and an ingenuous interest in helping others, as well as the desire to make money. Ives himself was largely responsible for developing the concept of estate planning which is now so widespread. The firm was destined to become one of the largest and most successful in the business; by this point in his life Ives was a wealthy man.

---

[1] The interested reader is referred to other Ives studies by the author, the first of which includes a portion intended originally to be a part of the present paper. It contains an analysis, musically and from the point of view of psychological interpretation, of the song whose text began this study: "The Things Our Fathers Loved." See also "The Nostalgia of Charles E. Ives" (Feder, 1981b); "Decoration Day: A Boyhood Memory of Charles Ives" (Feder, 1980b); and "Charles Ives and the Unanswered Question" (Feder, 1984).

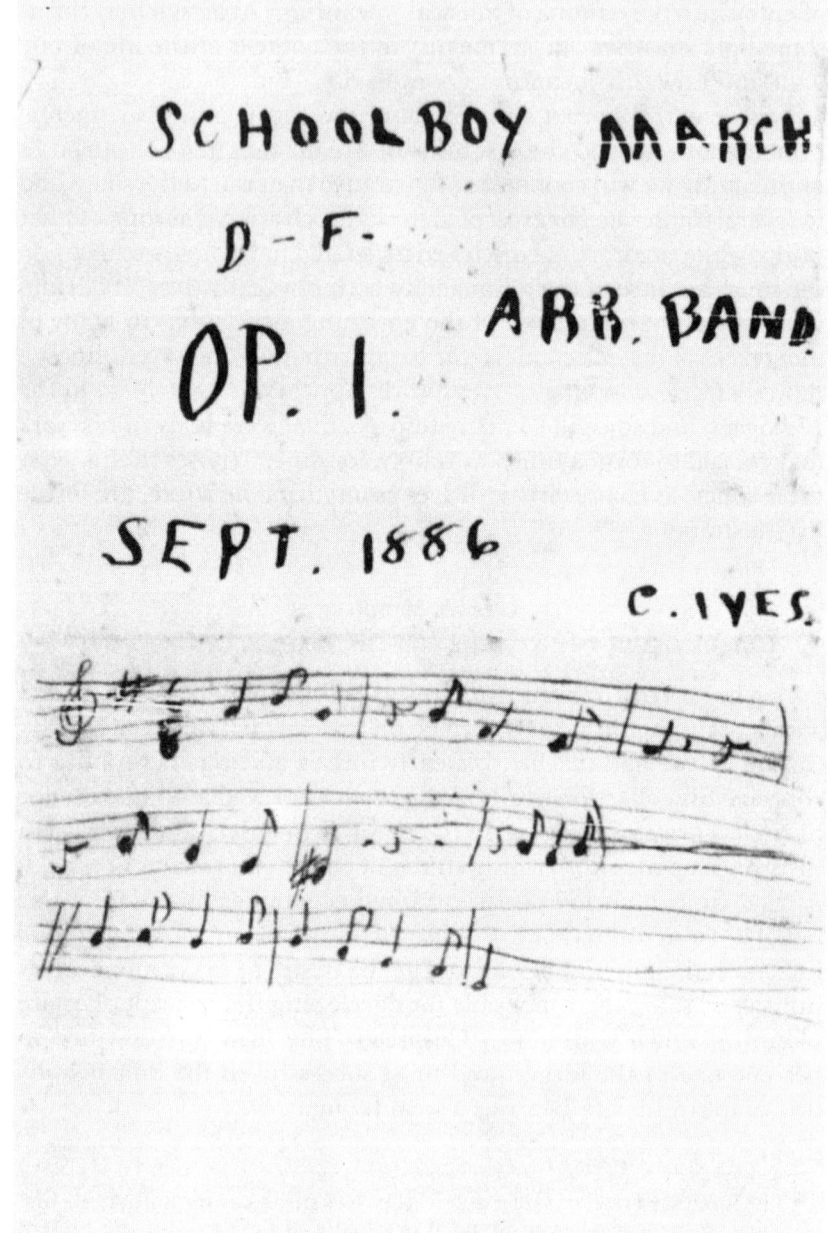

Figure 8.1 Title page (on a slip of paper from a pad) of one of Ives's first compositions, written when he was around 12. Courtesy of the Yale University Music Library.

Unlike the historical stereotype of musician and composer, Ives was then economically stable and secure. He lived in comfortable but unostentatious circumstances in New York City and in Redding, Connecticut, where he had recently purchased a country property with house and barn only a few miles from his boyhood home in Danbury. Consistent with the foregoing, he had been married at the age of thirty-four to a woman who appeared to be his complement in many important ways and with whom he had a closely shared and mutually respectful relationship. The marriage had not produced the children who would have been the natural maturational consequences of Ives's ongoing involvement with his own childhood. Yet extended family ties were rich and frequently entailed the assumption of responsibility for others. Moreover, he had not been completely denied the gratification of fatherhood; the Iveses adopted a two-and-a-half-year-old daughter, Edith, when Charles was forty-two.

Finally, Ives had by that point pursued independently and largely in artistic isolation his own musical craft, composing consistently and with day-to-day regularity from his college years on. By 1916, when he was forty-two, he had completed his most productive twenty-year period. He had produced, among a vast output, four symphonies and two "Sets," as well as comparable works for orchestra, two string quarters, four violin and two piano sonatas, numerous works for chamber orchestra, band, organ, chorus, and various other combinations, and perhaps two hundred songs! The most recently completed major work prior to the *114 Songs*, and, like it, representing some sort of culmination, appears to have been the Second Pianoforte Sonata. Its subtitle is "Concord Mass. 1840–1860," and it is evocative of the New England Transcendentalists who had been a consistent influence in Ives's personal philosophy throughout his life. The exact dating of the composition is uncertain since it was Ives's habit to work on various pieces in different states of completion, as well as often to use the same musical material in different forms or instrumentation.

As a result Ives's music seems to be one vast opus, the result of a consistent lifetime of effort eventuating in a single creative product. By the same token, his work is replete with quotations of other musical ideas—tunes, motifs, forms, snatches of melody—largely drawn from his past mental life. These hymn tunes, patriotic, and military music, popular and college songs, and so on, are nearly

nearly exclusively derived from college and boyhood days, or, in some cases, from an even earlier time. John Kirkpatrick (1960, pp. 264–266) has catalogued them in one small section of his extensive scholarly work on Ives. Far from a disjointed pastiche, they had been forged within a unique and strongly personal style. Rarely has there been a better example of the adage, the "style is the man": style and man are consistent with a pervasive point of view that is a reaffirmation of an Emersonian philosophy, "the fabric of existence weaves itself whole" (Cowell and Cowell, 1969, p. 97).

In connection with the "Concord" Sonata Ives wrote a long essay (1920a), one of his several prose works, which he called *Essays Before a Sonata*, an elaborate and complex personal statement regarding music and just about everything else that interested Ives—politics, personal philosophy, oblique personal reference. The *Essays* are essentially a set of enriched program notes. Ostensibly about the relationship of the music to the New England Transcendentalists, four sections bear the same titles as the movements of the Sonata, the names of Ives's heroes: Emerson, Hawthorne, "The Alcotts," and Thoreau. The range of subject was comparable to but not as extensive as that of the *114 Songs*. These three final creative efforts—the "Concord" Sonata, the *Essays*, and the *114 Songs*—were completed and privately printed and distributed between 1919 and 1922. He was forty-eight by the time this task was accomplished.

The end of Ives's fourth decade marked the waning of this very considerable creative impulse. The nature of this creativity is not conveyed by the mere quantity of output. Several elements are noteworthy. First is the consistent, unwavering nature of this impulse itself. Once sparked during Ives's college years, it appeared to lead a life of its own. It seemed independent of time, place, circumstance, and, above all, cultural musical influence. A part of his inner life unfolded and progressed quite naturally, both style and content the result of a highly personal integration.

The very summer after Ives's graduation from Yale, he started to work for the Mutual Life Insurance Company and took up residence with a group of contemporaries, none of whom was a professional musician, in what they called "Poverty Flat," a domicile that occupied three different locations between 1898 and 1908 (Ives, 1972, p. 202). Here, among young friends who were from time to time medical students or beginning business and professional men, with minimal privacy, and while working full time during the week (as well as holding a post as organist at the Central Presbyterian Church from 1890), Ives composed in a regular fashion. It was during these years that he composed the Second and Third Symphonies, the earlier sonatas, numerous experimental works, and many of the songs. He composed routinely evenings and weekends, a habit he was to continue even after his marriage. No doubt this was but a manifest aspect of an ongoing creative process in which he was mentally engaged more or less continuously. Later, when he was more established and thus freer to do so, he is said to have jotted down musical ideas during the business day. As one informant in Vivian Perlis's oral history of Ives (1974), his personal secretary, put it: "And at work sometimes Mr. Ives would be dictating a letter, and all of a sudden something in the music line would come into his head, and he'd cut off the letter and go into the music. I think that music was on his mind all the time" (p. 50).

The nature of Ives's musical isolation is complex and, I believe, highly overdetermined in motivation. It also bears an important relation to another feature of Ives's creativity, namely, innovation. Although he was rigorously trained in traditional music both by his father and later at Yale, where he studied with Horatio Parker, Ives never engaged in the practice of music in any traditional sense. That is, he never had to concern himself with the broader social, cultural, and economic implications of earning a living from music as a "professional." What is more, in his composition he did not appear to be interested in pursuing lines of innovation which were the natural extensions of tradition. These, for example, might have taken him along the path of Stravinsky on the one hand or, eschewing tonality, Schoenberg on the other. Even his characteristic use of quotation and folk material took him in a very different direction from that of composers such as Bartok. It is true that early examples of many innovative features of modern music are to be found in Ives, usages paralleling or antedating Stravinsky, Schoenberg, Prokofiev, Bartok, and others, but they were part of a very different trend in Ives's work.

This trend, one which was intensely personal rather than traditional, could perhaps be best cultivated in isolation from ongoing musical tradition. In any event, it was on this individual path that Ives was propelled. What prevails under such circumstances, given initial traditional foundation but in the absence of ongoing external traditional influence, are those influences of inner, mental life which, while always present in the artist, are here to be found intensified. It is as if autobiography itself exerts its own most powerful influence. In this sense, one may metaphorically view the "locus" of Ives's music as lying squarely within his mental life to a greater degree than might be the case with most creators. There it may be seen to interact and articulate with the individual life history of its composer. It is this factor that lends the identical uniqueness to Ives's music that is characteristic of his life—both mental life and life lived. Accordingly, it may be from this point of entry that we might best gain insight into certain aspects of the life and work of Charles Ives.

Another aspect of Ives's creative impulse and the final one to be considered at this point is its waning in the composer's late forties. While not every scholar agrees on this phenomenon, the historical record seems clear: Following the efforts of the *114 Songs* and the "Concord" Sonata with its accompanying *Essays*, no further major work was completed. He did not quite give up composing, however, nor was the decline precipitous. Eleven songs were written between 1922 and 1927, and some continued innovative trend is revealed in the brief quarter-tone pieces of 1923–1924 (Ives, 1972, pp. 165–166). But a Third Orchestral Set and Third Piano Sonata remained uncompleted as creative capacity wound down. What is striking, in any event, is that by 1927 Ives was only 53, and he was to live twenty-five years longer.

Ives (1972) himself wrote of this dwindling creative faculty in 1932, dating it back to a heart attack in 1918 which occurred within weeks of his forty-fourth birthday.

> In October 1918, I had a serious illness that kept me away from the office for six months, and I have not been since in my former good (very good) state of health, nor have I seemed to get going "good" in my music since then. (I'd start things, but they didn't seem to work out—[I] couldn't seem to keep them up and sailing. So [I] stopped and stopped, etc.) I don't know how to account for it except that what strength I had was used up during the day in what I had to do at the office, and it seemed impossible to do any work in the evenings as I used to do.
>
> During the last ten years or so [1922–1932] I've completed nothing. A set of chamber music was started and is fairly and mostly set down in a sketch (some five or six years ago), and I've started a *Third Piano Sonata* which doesn't seem to get along very

well. In 1919 and 1920, and especially in 1921, I did write quite a few songs and arranged songs for voice and piano and several for chorus—and also at that time made arrangements of songs from old scores, sketches, overtures, etc. Sometimes whole parts of these were put into a song, and sometimes they were revised, changed, or cut down to make a song . . . [pp. 111–113].[2]

Thus Ives himself pays scant attention to these later works, emphasizing his failing capacity and the final flurry of creative activity of the *114 Songs*. Earlier in the same section of his *Scrapbook* (1972), a portion of the *Memos* edited by Kirkpatrick, he notes that the body of his work was completed "in the twenty years or so between 1896 and 1916. . . . In 1917 the War came on, and I did but little in music. I didn't seem to feel like it. We were very busy at the office at this time with the extra Red Cross and Liberty Loan drives and all the problems that the War brought on. As I look back, I find that I did almost no composing after the beginning of 1918" (p. 112). The Cowells (1969) quote the same passage with the year 1917 (p. 76). This would tend to suggest some winding down of activity antedating the heart attack and starting when he was about forty-two.

Certainly by 1926 to 1927 he experienced his musical faculty as extinguished, and the matter-of-fact tone above may be supplemented with his wife Harmony's poignant observation of 1926: " . . . he came downstairs one day with tears in his eyes and said he couldn't seem to compose anymore—nothing went well, nothing sounded right" (Ives, 1972, p. 279). His interest in music was subsequently to be directed toward the dissemination and performance of his own music and that of others, what the Cowells (1969) in their biography call "the career of the music." (Fortuitously, Henry Cowell, who was instrumental in fostering interest in Ives's music, made his first approach to Ives in a letter during the summer of 1927. Ives's involvement in the publication of the *New Music Quarterly* and his first biography were the results.)

The portrait of Charles Ives as a person and artist at midlife is a complex one, and several things should be noted in advance of exploring his earlier life and in particular its own enduring meaning in his later mental life. Creativity in every sense should be

---

[2] Quotations from *Charles E. Ives—Memos*, ed. J. Kirkpatrick (New York: W. W. Norton, 1972), ©1972, The American Academy and Institute of Arts and Letters. Reprinted by permission.

emphasized above all, including those creative solutions Ives found for himself at several junctures of his life cycle. Health, in Hartmann's (1939) sense of "adaptation, and especially synthesis" (p. 17), is often less easily discerned by the psychoanalyst than pathology. This is perhaps a vestige of the early development of psychoanalysis itself which is manifested most clearly in psychoanalytic-biographical writings—pathographies. With few exceptions, it is rare to find psychoanalytic treatments of conflict-free areas of a person's life or, even in the presence of conflict, of a relatively successful, adaptive solution; rarer still to find a study whose focus is the healthy personality or aspects thereof.

In the case of Ives one may readily be seduced along the primrose path of pathography from several sources. Vignettes of Ives as an eccentric old man, reclusive, suspicious, hyperirritable (and, in a well-known anecdote on the circumstances of the photographing of his most famous portrait by Eugene Smith, terrified by the camera itself) may lead one in this direction (Perlis, 1974, pp. 42–43). Of course, by this time Ives was probably in fact senile, and even interest in his "third career," that of the dissemination of music (a career not of primary creativity but of generativity) had long since diminished in intensity. Thus even with this final adaptive solution, he may have failed his biographical posterity by an error of longevity.

A further appeal to pathography lies in his unusualness. Here is fertile ground for speculation. However, it invites the logical error of mistaking normative for normal and, consequently, deviant for unhealthy. Such a course fails to summon the best a psychoanalytic study offers as it fails to discriminate the unique from the sick and to attempt to understand that uniqueness.

While, as we shall see presently, Ives's life was certainly not free of conflict (an impossible condition in any event) and while certain resolutions were never quite achieved, it may be said to have been, on balance, a "successful" one, uniquely if curiously adapted to its circumstances. Its very conscious philosophical aim was that "wholeness" which the mental function of synthesis is organized to achieve. The earlier picture of Ives in his forties—married, monied, and musically gratified—reflects this. On the other hand, there is no question about the presence of conflict, and certain problem areas will emerge clearly enough in the ensuing account. Especially noteworthy are those of sexual identity and the threat of homosexuality, the aggressive component in character, and limitations in mourning. However, these are not intended as the focus of this particular study except insofar as they participate in characterological uniqueness, innovation, and creativity. For pathology is never the whole story. If unusualness and uniqueness in a life reflect attempts at resolution or courses of mastery which are not undertaken by most individuals, much is lost in reducing these to "pathology." Such distinctive individuality, however, does merit an attempt at understanding and explanation. To study a life such as Ives's is to study uniqueness in the extreme.

IVES, FATHER AND SON[3]

Charles Edward Ives was born in a house on Main Street in Danbury, Connecticut, on October 20, 1874. Danbury was a small town noted for its hat industry in an otherwise rural area of post-Civil War America. He could trace his American origins quite firmly back to the arrival of a ship-captain ancestor, William Ives, in 1653 and to the first settlement of New Haven. His paternal grandfather George White Ives (1798–1862) was a prominent Danbury businessman and the founder of its first bank. In fact, it was in the house which also served as bank building that George Edward Ives, Charles's father, was born in 1845. Against this background of tradition, George Junior, the youngest of five children, was somewhat of a maverick in his serious interest in music which asserted itself before the age of fifteen when he undertook rigorous training. The best available teacher in the area was sought out, a German who lived in Morrisania, Bronx, where George went to study. Two years later in 1862, the second year of the Civil War, his accomplishment was such that he was invited through family connections to organize a band for the First Connecticut Heavy Artillery Regiment. He served as Bandmaster for three years, the youngest in the Union Army. According to a favorite story of

---

[3] The interested reader is referred to the chief biographical sources for more detail: Cowell and Cowell (1969), Ives (1972), Perlis (1974), Perry (1974), Rossiter (1975). The following sketch is excerpted and condensed by Feder (1980b). Comprehensive catalogued data on the music can be found in Kirkpatrick (1960). The annotations of the same author in the presentation and editing of Ives's own *Memos* (1972) are enriching, as are his brief essays on various pertinent people, places, and miscellanea in the appendices of the same volume. The need for a concise introduction to the music of Ives is satisfied by Hitchcock (1977).

Charles, Lincoln himself praised the band to General Grant, who commented that it was the best band in the army.

Figure 8.2 George Edward Ives at age forty-five in his bandmaster's uniform. Courtesy of the Yale University Music Library.

Returning to Danbury after the war, George, a veteran at twenty, had already participated in at least three traditions other than those of family and community which characterized his Danbury boyhood. One was that of military life in general in which he was, if not a fighting man, at least a leader with considerable visibility and esteem; a bandleader is a leader nonetheless. The second was that of what has been called the "American band tradition," a subculture of musicians admirably described in certain musical and social aspects by Elkus (1974).

The third "tradition" to which young George belonged, as did his son Charles after him, is one that exists in a metaphorical sense only, independent of time and culture, and conferred by biology and heredity. It is the "tradition" of the musician. When a musical gift is present it usually asserts itself early. It is characterized by auditory sensitivity, a specialized cognitive capacity for musical thought, and various attributes resulting from these, such as interest and mastery. It serves as an internal stimulus with its own developmental requirements which may or may not be met in the environment. It is a potential which every person of extraordinary musical gift must come to terms with, integrate in some manner, and possibly realize. While each phase of life may present its particular problem for individuals so endowed, the periods of late childhood and early adolescence are critical from the point of view of exercise and mastery of this inclination in terms of learning, practice, and achievement. (It seems likely that this is more true in the case of instrumentalists.) The contribution of earliest childhood is little understood; the possibility that this period exerts an even greater influence on the composer is intriguing.

I believe it is likely that such individuals are more like each other than they are like other members of their own time and culture in certain important ways. It is this similarity, for example, that may foster the musical rapport among diverse performers that is but one manifestation of the cliché, "the universal language." (Its ambivalent underbelly may by the same token lead to bitter social rivalry.) In the case of Ives, this unusual capacity was later to subserve a bridge of mutual identification across a generation between father and son. Quite simply, they were more like one another than like anyone else either of them encountered in their lives. In later years this kind of rapport would facilitate the development of Charles's other relationships, such as that with Henry Cowell, at a time when Charles was otherwise withdrawing from new human contact.

When George returned to Danbury after the war it would seem as if the best of his life was in some sense already over. For one thing, he had been physically ill for the last year of his service with some unspecified medical problem. For another, his reentry into Danbury life rendered him somewhat of a misfit, albeit an admired one. As Kirkpatrick indicates, George rapidly became the center of musical life in town, a role for which he was well prepared (Ives, 1972, p. 247). But it was a social role about which people in a small New England town had mixed feelings. It carried with it the taint of deviance, frivolity, questionable respectability, and, above all, effeminacy. Rossiter (1975) has traced out some of the social implications of this role, indicating that George was considered déclassé even among members of the family. He had broken with a longstanding commercial tradition, and its inevitable financial consequence was to place him and his own family somewhere in the range of poor relations (p. 21). He points out that, although the town musician was accorded the title "Professor," the role he served was "somewhat similar to that of a jester." (Rossiter, a historian, draws his conclusions on a sociological level. He does not pursue psychosexual implications in individual mental life to any degree.)

Less manifest, but strongly influential, was the sense that music was not a man's work. More specifically, music had in fact become a woman's work by default. Characteristic of towns of its kind, Danbury's formal musical life was dominated by women. An alliance had been struck between woman and musician comparable to that made with the clergyman described by Douglas (1977) in *The Feminization of American Culture*. Its product was the music of "the cultivated tradition," the American music of church and parlor, although it might be heard in public concert as well. Its mainstay was the song, the content of which was largely genteel, sentimental, and nostalgic. Hitchcock (1974) contrasts this tradition with that of the "vernacular tradition" (pp. 96 ff.), which included the religious music of camp meetings and revivals, dance music, band music, and the music of the minstrel show and lyric theater. The latter may be said to be a more "masculine" music, meaning in the common sense that it was an "out-of-doors" and "outside of the home" music.

George, of course, was competent within either of these stylistic traditions, but, with the possible exception of the band, the institutional, hence income-producing aspects of music were dominated by women. He often worked behind the scenes and to the dismay of Charles was at times not even credited for his efforts in a performance. But another portion of George's musical life was intensely personal, privately developed, and independently pursued. He was fascinated by sound in every aspect and carried on private explorations ("experimental" would be both too scientific and anachronistic to convey their flavor) in the forms of sound and their combination, transformation, and varieties of presentation. In short, his interest extended to the vast possibilities of the auditory sphere. For example, he invented a device to play quarter-tone scales. Aspects of sound such as the effect of spatial distribution fascinated him, and he enjoyed hearing, for example, the effect of sound coming over a body of water or the way in which two bands approaching one another playing different pieces would blend and clash. However, in some sense, these were public experiments too—the water was the Danbury Pond, and the bands were his own, clashing on Main Street. It is not surprising that he earned the reputation of being an eccentric in post-Civil War industrial Danbury and the black sheep of the banking family.

George's marriage at the age of twenty-nine, the birth of Charles ten months later, and Moss sixteen months after that must surely have gone a long way toward establishing respectability. But it was not until 1889 when he was forty-four that he entered the more conventional commercial life of Danbury. The town had undergone very substantial economic growth during these first fifteen years of Charles's life, and the changes which were engendered in the name of progress were already rendering the town and its life unfamiliar. Music, unlike manufacturing, was not a growth industry, and George found it necessary to take a "regular" job at this time. The job was only superficially in the mainstream of the man's world. It was indoors, confining, and subordinating. George worked as a part-time clerk, an assistant to his own nephew, Howard Merritt Ives (known as "Cousin Howdie"), fifteen years his junior, in the business owned by his own older brother Joe (Joseph Moss Ives). Anecdotes of the period suggest a resigned but helpless bitterness, humorously conveyed.

This shift was no doubt motivated by the anticipation of educating his two sons, for barely two years later Charles was enrolled in preparatory school—first in Danbury, later in New Haven. In the fall of 1894, at the age of twenty, Charles entered Yale. By that time George had for the most part given up his efforts to function as a professional musician and taken a full-time job with the Danbury Bank. This event in George's life was not without its irony: It was the bank founded by his own father and namesake. It had by now moved from the original wooden chest in the dining room, out of the house itself, to which it had expanded as the bank's quarters, and into its own building, part of the ever-changing face of Main Street, Danbury. And, with the current of these changes, which in George's personal life now included family responsibility and aspirations for the careers of his two sons, was swept away George's career as a practicing musician, "professional" as far as it was possible in a small town. On November 4, 1894, a few months after Charles matriculated at Yale, George died in Danbury of a stroke. He was forty-nine years old.

While Charles appeared rather reticent about sensual or romantic love in both his life and work (Rossiter, 1975, p. 169), he was always frank and completely unabashed about his love for his father. The evidence for this is in reported conversations, his letters, and in the music itself. The love runs broadly and deeply, the forms in which it is represented complex. His frankness reveals the conscious surface deeply felt; its unconscious ramifications, as we will see, are far-reaching and intricate. Like every love relationship, it was not without ambivalence, and, where a life is so strongly influenced by positive ties, we are justified in seeking the effects of their opposite. While in general the healthy, adaptive aspect of Ives's life is stressed, conflictual elements in the father–son relationship took their toll, a point which we will consider in more detail later. In any event, Ives's father was without doubt the most important object in his life. While his wife Harmony was later to run a close second, she did not enter his life until he was thirty-four. But even that relationship reveals strong elements of paternal influence in object choice, and it is of interest that their relationship stems from Ives's involvement with her brother and father which started early in his career at Yale.

That Ives's mother is strangely missing from the above account is a precise reflection of her position in the Ives's biographical literature. Mary Elizabeth Parmelee, "Aunt Mollie" to the extended family, was the daughter of a farmer in nearby Bethel. Kirkpatrick, whose scholarship is thorough and who also knew Ives in his later years, comments that Ives (1972) "wrote and talked so devotedly about his father that one tends hardly to notice his mother. Though unimaginative beyond household duties, she was a small but intense focus of energy and determination" (p. 247). Kirkpatrick can only eke out a single family anecdote about how Aunt Mollie once flagged down the train at Brewster, where it wasn't supposed to stop, when she wanted to come to New York. Perlis's (1974) recordings of personal reminiscenes provide little more—some suggestion of the openness and generosity of the household (p. 6) and the later pride his mother was to take in her oldest son's musical accomplishments, although Ives did not believe she really understood what he was doing (p. 72). Charles was always to remain respectful and dutiful toward his mother who died in 1929 at the age of seventy-nine. (Charles was fifty-five by then and within a year of retiring from his business career.) As time went on respect gave rise to the assumption of responsibility for her. But nowhere in his extensive prose writings, memos, or reported conversations do we find any other attitude expressed toward his mother, certainly nothing of the reverence and deep affection constantly revealed toward his father.

There is scant reference to the maternal in any of Ives's music even in that which we can readily identify as representational or programmatic. Two songs of the Yale years might be mentioned briefly in this context, "The Old Mother" (Ives, 1922, No. 81, pp. 183–185) and "Songs My Mother Taught Me" (Ives, 1922, No. 108, pp. 250–257). The latter contains many of the melodic and harmonic conventions of the sentimental song (such as the augmented passing tones of measure 3 and elsewhere and the tonic-seventh chord in measure 7). Perhaps it was this effusion of sentimentality which Ives needed to contain or derisively disavow when only eight years later, in 1903, he cast the latter for clarinet, harp, and string quartet, calling it *An Old Song Deranged* (Kirkpatrick, 1960, p. 64). Attention is called to a further aspect of his mental image of women as revealed in a musical representation of the "Goddess of Liberty" in the "Putman's Camp" movement of *Three Places in New England*, the details of which will have to await another study. In any event, such references as can be isolated for study are rare compared to those which, as I will demonstrate, relate to Ives's father.

Therefore, in the remainder of the present study, we will adhere gratefully to the rich material we do have, although one cannot help but wonder what, if any, defensive function the relative absence of material about mother might serve. While knowledge of such a "layer" in the study of a life is unquestionably important and perhaps even critical, what we might speculate about from absent data is not nearly so enriching as what we can further learn from the base of what we already know. Here, there is an additional advantage to be gained. In general, there is far less in the psychoanalytic literature about the role of the father in early life than about that of the mother. In studies of gifted individuals in particular, the primary role of the mother is often taken for granted in theoretical formulations or, at very least, not discriminated from the possible influences of the father. In the case of Charles Ives, we are afforded a unique opportunity to investigate the nature of the father-child relationship and its influence in a particular gifted individual. This will remain the focus in this study.

Resuming the thread of Charles Ives's earlier life against this background, we may attempt to gain some picture from his own account (and those of others) of a boyhood in a small town among immediate and extended family, endowed, challenged, and perhaps burdened by a gift which was both shared and cultivated by his father. What little is known of Charles's earliest life may be of significance. He was born on October 20, 1874, in the old Ives family house on Main Street. The bank had long since been moved nearby, but his grandparents still lived in the house. George and Mollie had married the previous January, and they occupied the upstairs bedroom where Charles was born and, sixteen months later, his brother Moss (Joseph Moss Ives II). It was said to be a full, active household, and George, especially in the months when Mollie was pregnant with Moss, would go to the barn to practice the violin, one of several instruments he played, usually taking Charles with him. As described by a cousin ten years older, "Charlie, who was under two, was sent along where he sat happily in Uncle Joe's buggy playing with the whip while his father practiced" (Amelia Merritt Van Wyck, in Perlis, 1974, pp. 3–4). Actually Charles would have been a little more than a year old.

When Charles was five, the family was displaced by George's assertive older sister Amelia who wanted to return to the old house to live. George, therefore, had to move his family nearby for a few years but later fixed up the barn which was directly behind the old house and returned to live there. "So," Charles's cousin relates, "when Charlie practiced piano when he was growing up, it was in the same place where he'd sat in the buggy and raised his whip some years before." And where, we would add, he watched and listened to his father make music. These were no doubt among Charles's earliest experiences and memories.

It seems likely, owing to the irregular and uncertain hours of George's employment, that he was more available for child care and companionship and, judging from the nature of his later involvement with the boys, that he would not shun it on the grounds that it was "woman's work." Moreover, in George's own earlier history there is a distinct caring trend: When George was twenty and the band was stationed not far from Richmond, Virginia, he had been drawn to a little ten-year-old boy, the son of his laundress, who liked to listen to the band rehearse. George wrote to his mother about the boy, Anderson Brooks, and after the war brought him home to Danbury for a time. Ives (1972) notes in his *Memos* that "Father taught him to read and write (both English and music)" (p. 53). Thus, whatever the homoerotic impulse awakened in George, it was channeled in this way at the time. It was to continue in fatherhood, as is often the case, comprising the tender element in paternal love for the boy. Along with the reciprocal love engendered in the boy, however, he may well have experienced guilt and anxiety, related to attendant problems in sexual identification—ultimately the fear of castration. Intense affects may be the inevitable cost of such an erotic attachment.

Charles's account of his own early life is a celebration of boyhood—of his own, of his father's (still implicit in the sounds and sights of a town rapidly changing but still imbued with a post-Civil War atmosphere), and of boyhood in general. There was a reverence in Ives's use of the term, *we boys*, which only intensified as he later idealized these earlier years. He appears to have experienced his boyhood as if shared not only by his younger brother Moss and his contemporaries but by his father as well. Much of the boy remained in George Ives the man—much of the curiosity of latency as well as the heightened narcissism and social thrust of adolescence. Above all, he could still play, and many of Ives's earlier reminiscences of his father were of their playing together in the exciting close-to-real manner that is the joy of childhood. For example, George participated actively in an elaborate game which the boys Charles and Moss engaged in for perhaps five years from the time Charles was eleven. This was a mock grocery store in a portion of their grandmother's house with a sign reading, "Ives Bros." (Ives, 1972, p. 247; photograph after p. 160). Billheads were printed up, and there exists a page of an account book in George's writing which stems from the later period when he was clerk for Cousin Howdie.

But more important were the musical games, recreations, instruction, and experiments shared by father and son. Even among the boys' earliest "serious" games with their father music had a characteristic place. When Charles was about ten, it was "the Ives Bros. R. R. under the clothes line. . . . Father always entered into it seriously . . . at that time I remember he was practicing the violin . . . father discovered that staccato passages could be made to sound like the clicking of car wheels. . . . So he . . . rode in the rear passenger car for whole trips . . . the noise of the wheels always stopped at the stations" (Ives, 1972, p. 47). Even when they were playing "train" a musical instrument was not far from hand. Musical play blended readily to experimentation and later moved easily into formal instruction. "Besides starting my music lessons, when I was five years old, and keeping me at music in many ways until he died, with the best teaching a boy could have, Father knew (and filled me up with) Bach and the best of the classical music and the study of harmony and counterpoint, etc. And musical history" (Ives, 1972, p. 44). Ives (1972) devotes an entire section of his memoirs *(Memos)* in the *Scrapbook* (pp. 42–48) to his father. This is only one of a number of places where his father appears in his writings in more or less explicit form. In still another portion of the *Memos, Memories*, there is a section, "My Father and My Wife," indeed the two most important objects in his life in that order (1972, pp. 114–115). Mostly it is about George. In a biographical statement which he prepared at the request of John Tasker Howard for inclusion in his *Our American Music* Ives's response to the question on "Early musical background, education, home influences, etc." gives what amounts to his father's biographical material and expresses an appreciation of him bordering on eulogy.

> My father was a musician and a teacher (in Danbury and neighboring villages) of the violin, piano, (brass and wood instruments), harmony, sight reading, (and ear training), etc. He played in and taught the brass band (and orchestra), led the church choirs, the music at the Camp Meetings, the local Choral Society. He had a reverence, devotion, and a talent for music which was unusual. His interest lay not only in what had been done but in what might be done. His study of acoustics led him to

many experiments into the character of musical instruments and of tonal combinations, and even into the divisions of the tone.

He had a belief that everyone was born with at least one germ of musical talent, and that an early application of great music (and not trivial music) would help it grow. He started all the children of the family—and most of the children of the town for that matter—on Bach and Stephen Foster. (Quite shortly after they were born—always regardless of whether they had, would have, or wouldn't have any musical gifts or sense, etc.—) he put a love of music into the heart of many a boy who might have gone without it but for him. (I feel that, if I had done anything that is good in music, I owe it almost entirely to him and his influence.) [Ives, 1972, pp. 236–237].

As if to demonstrate this last point, Professor Parker at Yale is merely noted in parentheses, and Yale College is mentioned as an afterthought.

The *Scrapbook* entry mentioned earlier contains Ives's account of his father's musical experiments and a description of his teaching methods; he was at once sensitive and respectful to his student-son while at the same time insisting on the mastery of the rules and encouraging experimentation within that framework. "Father was not against a reasonable amount of 'boy's fooling,' if it were done with some sense behind it . . . as playing left-hand accompaniment in one key and tune in right hand in another . . ." (Ives, 1972, p. 46). There is also ample reminiscence, appreciation, even apology crammed into these few rambling pages. "There was something about the way Father played hymns even if some of the choir could read music readily at the rehearsals, he always liked to play each part over with his horn, and have them get it entirely through listening, through the ear, through his phrasing tone and general style of playing. He had the gift of putting something in the music which meant more sometimes than when some people sang the words . . ." (Ives, 1972, p. 46). Ives goes on to note that this technique had given him the idea of writing songs for an instrument with the words underneath as he did in some of the *114 Songs*. We will return to this later in considering one such song which is in effect a musical memoir of his father.

George had a unique capacity for hearing some essence in the music around him. "Don't pay too much attention to the sounds," he said, "For if you do you may miss the music." The "wrong notes" sung by burly, tone-deaf but emotionally moved farmers at a prayer meeting were perceived sharply by George's sensitive ears but interpreted as those individuals' unique, hence "correct," way of expressing a music. It was this quality of hearing that father and son shared and seemed to cultivate together. Again and again, the ears come up, increasingly endowed with meaning: "Father had a kind of natural interest in sounds of every kind, everywhere, known or unknown, measured as such or not, and this led him into positions or situations . . . that made some of the townspeople call him a crank whenever he appeared in public with one of his contraptions . . ." (Ives, 1972, p. 45). The ears could make one different, even deviant.

Ives repeatedly comes back to the notion of the ears as a strong, masculine organ and makes it clear that the source of this idea lies in his boyhood training and musical experiences with his father. Father's exercises "stretched" the ears, made them grander, more encompassing, more muscular. Later Ives was to adopt an imaginary character, "Rollo," a musically effete straw man, upon whom he would vent his spleen in his prose writings and in explosive comments upon musical scores. Rollo was the personification of the faint imagination—the person who could not "hear," a symbol of the effeminate in music and/or musical impotence. Rollo's ancestor is certainly to be found in a letter of George's in which he had written of certain ("mostly German") teachers who "are gradually circumscribing a great art by these rules, rules, rules with which they wrap up the student's ears and minds as a lady does her hair—habit and custom all underneath . . ." (Ives, 1972, p. 42). (The style of these remarks is startling in its similarity to that later characteristic of Charles.) But, as noted, George was able to play, not just follow rules, and it was this combination of qualities which was to have an enduring influence on Charles's musical style. Ives later told the Cowells (1969): "What started as boy play and in fun gradually worked into something that had a serious side to it which opened up possibilities, sometimes valuable ones, as the ears got used to and acquainted with these many various dissonant sound combinations . . ." (p. 26). This "ear" of which Ives so often wrote (as did his father, earlier) was more than the metaphorical inner ear, the mental ear of the musician. It was, as we shall see, endowed with the qualities of a special organ, a fantasied one, its imagery richly elaborated. He wrote, for example, "The American ear has become a Soft-Static Co. (Limited)" (Ives, 1972, p. 41). The Ivesian "ear," on the other hand, was strong, masculine, potent, its potential boundless. It was a man's organ.

Music had become the medium of exchange in a tender relationship between boy and man. While sublimation was for the most part effective, it could be unstable at times (particularly at adolescence), exposing the erotic roots of the relationship. At such times it is clear that anxiety (and other affects, such as embarrassment) would be exacted for gratification received, and defenses were rapidly instituted. Charles's retrospective masculinization of his musical experiences with George asserts their intimacy as it denies any association with effeminacy. Yet he had in fact been much concerned with being considered a "sissy" by his contemporaries. A fortunate aptitude for sports helped buttress his presentation to self and others as unimpeachably masculine, but inevitably music was drawn into the conflict.

When he was fifteen Charles joined a baseball team, the Alerts, and a few years later was captain of the high-school football team, another sport in which he excelled. He took these activities as seriously as he did music, and they were in fact interspersed with those of a growing practicing musician such as giving recitals and playing the organ in church, a pattern which perhaps foreshadowed Ives's later double life. In an anecdote of the period, when asked by someone who had heard of his musical interest what he played, his answer was "Shortstop!" (Rossiter, 1975, p. 32). His conflict is touchingly revealed in a story of a performance of the thirteen-year-old Charlie's *Holiday Quick Step* by the band on Decoration Day. He had not taken his usual place among the snare drums. Instead, as the band came down Main Street, "playing Charlie's piece full tilt, the boy was discovered nervously playing handball against the barn door, his back to the parade" (Cowell and Cowell, 1969, p. 27). Of such experiences he was later to say, "As a boy [I was] partially ashamed of it [music]—an entirely wrong attitude, but it was strong—most boys in American towns, I think, felt the same. When other boys, Monday a.m. on vacation, were out driving grocery carts, or doing chores, or playing ball, I felt all wrong to stay in and play piano. And there may be something in it. Hasn't music always been too much an emasculated art . . . ?" (Ives, 1972, pp. 130–131).

Rossiter (1975) develops at some length the psychosocial aspects of this tension in Ives's life. He also brings to light some suggestion of a period of turmoil in Charles's later adolescence just prior to his father's death (pp. 48 ff.). This was an important and little-known period which doubtless served as background for what was to follow. Ives evidently required tutorial preparation in order to get into Yale, which was his manifest destiny in the eyes of the family. His father was already sacrificing for it. Yale was a family tradition which had been disregarded in the choices George had made. Both his grandfather and his older, more successful brother Joseph had been Yale men. In an analogous way the younger Moss, unlike Charles, was proving himself to be intellectually gifted. Uncle Lyman (the husband of George's older sister Amelia), childless, took an interest in Moss and was already grooming him for Yale Law School and for eventually taking over his successful practice. It is likely that George wished to bring both of his boys into realignment with family tradition. Aside from matters of esteem, from which he seemed to have suffered a lack in his later, clerking years, there was the risk that Charles would go his way, the way of a musician or a maverick of some kind. Already a village musician was an anachronism, and Charles had been encouraged in regular church jobs. The life of a freelance musician was equally uncertain, and an academic background would answer to both the problems of esteem and potential stability. It seems to have been taken for granted, however, that he would study music at Yale as a part of the curriculum.

Charles faced several problems. For one, he was only an average student and needed to work hard at his studies. For another, he seemed to require the extracurricular involvement in sports which asserted his masculinity, although it disturbed his father. Letters of this period cited by Rossiter (1975) reveal the alarm on the part of his parents and guilt on Charles's part. He had been enrolled in the Hopkins Academy in New Haven in the spring semester of 1883, a school which had a reputation for getting boys into Yale, but there was some question as to whether Charles would make it. It was a period of turmoil in his life which is often overlooked, perhaps owing to Ives's subsequent successful career at Yale and later idealization of his Yale years. The year and a half prior to his matriculation at Yale and George's unfortunately timed death was the most troubled in his life, and he was clearly depressed.

The conflict in Charles's mind was exacerbated by the fact that now every move was drawing him further away from George. Even in his final cramming for acceptance to Yale, it was Uncle Lyman who undertook to help him. It was a task he could not share with his father in their accustomed way and, in any event, not without ambivalence at this point. This brief shift to Lyman culminated in Charles's accompanying him as his secretary to the world's Columbian Exposition in Chicago the summer prior to his matriculation at Yale and the death of George that fall.

Without question he was moving away from his father and, sadly, with his father's anxious encouragement. In some respects it was the route he needed to go, and his involvement in sports had represented that. While feelings of guilt resulted from his wish to be separate from George, he might still have experienced anxiety and anger on feeling separated from him. There was physical distance for the first time. Moreover, separation insinuates itself in many ways—for example, in the mode of communication between the two. Gone were the everyday give and take of word and music; now letters and at times telegrams were required. The exchange of letters suggests that George followed Charles's daily activities in intimate detail, commenting negatively on any he disapproved of (such as his leading the baseball team to victory as pitcher), and on Charles's need to justify himself.

Clearly, the older Ives did not wish his beloved Charlie to turn out as he had. As he approached his fifties, he appeared to attempt to realign his own destiny closer to family tradition and in a more honorable way than when financial pressure led him to take the office job. George, the black sheep of the family, had then to put away the toys of childhood, and it must have seemed to Charles that he now as well was expected to do so, rather precipitously. But the "toys" had been those of music, shared by father and son, and, accordingly, to give them up was to give up the George of Charles's childhood. On the other hand, deep involvement in a musical mental life was now a fait accompli for Charles. What had begun as a shared experience now led a life of its own. Moreover, like it or not, Charles had become a competent professional, and music would now help pay the cost of his education. Certainly by this time Charles did not need George's physical presence to do or make music, however much a part of him may have longed for it. But there are many facets of a musical life, and composition in particular never became an absolutely autonomous activity. It was to always retain something of the shared experience with George.

Charles entered Yale in September 1894 and started work as organist at the Centre Church, New Haven, at the same time. On Sunday, November 4, George died suddenly of a stroke at the age of forty-nine. It was a blow which Charles never completely came to terms with. Many years later, Harmony Ives recalled, he would often exclaim, "How I want to see Father again" (Ives, 1972, p. 249). His subsequent life is rich in detail with regard to his ongoing relationship to his father's memory and the vicissitudes of mourning.

Even as he immersed himself in the student life of Yale which he so idealized later, he was seeking to reorient himself from the stunning blow of his father's death in his relationships with other men. These included John Cornelius Griggs, nine years his senior, a former Yale man and choirmaster at Centre Church, and Horatio Parker, Charles's music professor at Yale. Despite anecdotes which indicate a lack of rapport, certainly with reference to Ives's innovations, the latter nevertheless was to exert considerable musical influence upon him, as Perry (1974) has shown (p. 8). Both men had more than a twist of the distinctive and unusual about them, qualities of George forever recurring in Charles's later relationships, and, of course, both were makers of music. This trend was culminated in his marriage.

Ives met Harmony Twitchell through her brother David, his classmate at Yale. Charles's admiration for the entire family, in particular her father, the Reverend Joseph Hopkins Twitchell, was boundless. The couple asked for his "blessing" on Sunday, November 17, 1907, a near-anniversary of George's death. In a letter Charles sent him a few days after, he wrote: "Father died just at the time I needed him most. It's been years since I've had an older man that I felt like going to when things seemed to go wrong or something comes up when it's hard to figure out which is the best or right thing to do. . . . I hope you'll let me—*Please* do . . ." (Ives, 1972, p. 261). It was a true match; Harmony had a striking characterological similarity to Charles, as revealed in certain of her own prose writings (Ives, 1972, pp. 275–279). Just as Charles appealed to her father as a son (and the couple remained devoted to him until his death), so could Harmony have been the spiritual daughter of George. Charles proved to have little need for what he begs in the letter to her father; it was given him by Harmony.

Harmony was an extraordinary person of many parts. She had an impeccable educational and family background—a graduate of Miss Porter's School, with "prettiest girl in town" looks, she had become a registered and practicing nurse. She also wrote quite naturally for occasion and recreation and after their marriage occasionally collaborated with her husband on a song. Moreover, she was an idealist of a similar turn of mind to that of Ives. She had a strong sense of family attachment and a feeling for the past not unlike Ives's own. It was revealed, for example, in a note she wrote on visiting a ninety-six-year-old man whom she had recalled from her own childhood—a tender memoir with a curious mixture of reverence for her own girlhood and patriotism (Ives, 1972, p. 279). She was to an extraordinary degree Ives's female counterpart and, accordingly, that of his father. Late in Ives's life, when mental faculties were failing, she carried on his correspondence in a manner somewhat different from the conventional way in which one partner might do so for another. Ives might give her a written draft or some verbal notion of what he had in mind, and Harmony would cast the letter correctly and with the more subtle nuances of intent as she wrote what "Mr. Ives" meant to convey. To Ives she was wife, father, and in some sense himself too.

Harmony also reinforced that part of himself which he often doubted—and indeed the world doubted as well: was he a composer or an eccentric at best, crazy at worst? While she was not in a position to appreciate the music for various reasons, including the fact that most of it was in rough manuscript score barely discernible by the composer himself, she faithfully supported the endeavor. In this she approached the only other person in Charles's life who did so unreservedly, his father. In effect, Harmony, like George, was Charles's silent collaborator, the secret sharer of his composition. Kirkpatrick dates "the explosion . . . of his radical experimental vein" to 1906, connecting it with his courtship of Harmony (Ives, 1972, p. 277).

As noted earlier, the couple was unable to have children. Harmony's month-long hospitalization ten months after their marriage suggests some complication of pregnancy with a probable hysterectomy. Those biographical sources who had been close to the family fail to mention this. Sidney Cowell (1976, personal communication) agrees with my impression. The effect on Charles must have been profound, although he never spoke or wrote about it. Perhaps most telling is the anguished

"Like A Sick Eagle" No. 26 (1922), which has been discussed in more detail elsewhere (Feder, 1984). A child, Edith, was adopted in 1916.

The broad outlines of Charles's adult years may be sketched briefly for our purposes here. Following Ives's graduation from Yale, he embarked on the unique double life for which he is well known. With the full imprimatur of the Yale man, he began a business career in the growing insurance industry which was modest at first but which led him ultimately to senior partnership in the firm of Ives and Myrick.

Concurrently, he pursued independently and largely in artistic isolation his own musical craft, composing with day-to-day regularity from his college years onward. During the first dozen or so years of marriage, nearly all of Ives's spare time was spent composing. Social life was kept to a minimum, and what there was tended to be connected to family. These were the most active business years as well, and Ives at the same time was achieving through that endeavor a personal fortune.

With regard to composition, it was as if some powerful impetus had been organized during adolescence, had gathered force under the influence of his father, and had finally been unleashed at some point during Ives's Yale years following the death of George. Nurtured during courtship and marriage, this impetus was to continue into Ives's fourth decade and, as described earlier, to diminish and essentially spend itself before Ives reached fifty. Following the efforts related to the volume of *114 Songs* and the "Concord" Sonata with its accompanying prose *Essays* and their publication in Ives's late forties, no further major work was produced. He himself noted that he did almost no composing after 1918 when he was forty-four. The "housecleaning," as he called it, had started soon after, and a number of earlier pieces were reworked in the process of organizing the *114 Songs* for publication. Without question, by 1926, when he was fifty-two, he experienced his creative capacity as totally extinguished.

His career at the agency continued very effectively until his decision to retire when he was fifty-five, which was in part due to increasing medical problems. Meanwhile, he had met Henry Cowell two years earlier, their relationship coinciding with the new musical interest which appeared to dovetail Ives's failing creativity. This was his growing interest in the dissemination and performance of his own music (what he called "the career of the music") and, along with Cowell, the music of other composers of new music. Ives carried this out with characteristic citizenlike responsibility. He lived to be seventy-nine, outliving the composer in him as it were by more than thirty years.

THE CHILDHOOD OF THE COMPOSER: A PSYCHOANALYTIC INTERPRETATION

To explore or to attempt to reconstruct from a psychoanalytic point of view the unknown early life of this unique artist, Charles Ives, is to be confronted with yet another terra incognita: the role of the father in early human life.

Ideas about the role of the father in a child's life have had a curious history in the last century. Throughout the nineteenth century it was the father who was considered preeminent. Writing of John Stuart Mill, Mazlich (1975) comments that surrounding him and for many years subsequently "the novels and autobiographies overtly on the father–son relation became legion" (p. 15). As Greenacre (1963) points out, "Fathers and sons" (or its singular) is a common heading for the first chapter of autobiographies of this period and also served as title to works of Turgenev and Gosse, "while Dostoyevsky considered it as a possible title for *The Brothers Karamazov*" (p. 96). It was Freud's contribution to cast the entire phenomenon in a scientific context, thus opening the possibilities for its study in a more rigorous and reliable fashion without losing the potential for nuance of novel and autobiography. Moreover, in describing the Oedipus complex as a universal phenomenon, he provided a framework for the observation and study of *all* father–son relationships within the broader family context—not only those with extraordinary or dramatic features.

With the development of ego psychology in the twentieth century and its concomitant emphasis on infant and child observation, the development of ego functions, and separation–individuation, or what has been felicitously called "the psychological birth of the human infant" (Mahler, Pine, and Bergmann, 1975), it was the mother who came to play the feature role. Where some external human agent is required for the unfolding of human function, it is the mother who is emphasized in the work of Mahler, Spitz, Jacobson, Hartmann, and so on. It is as if in this first act of human life the father has not yet appeared on the stage, although his undefined presence is sensed. But one knows for sure that in at least two of the following acts—those representing the oedipal and adolescent periods—he is going to have more than one dramatic scene!

Freud (1923) himself appeared to be uncertain about the father's role in earliest development. In writing of the origin of the ego ideal, he comments that there lies hidden behind it "an individual's first and most important identification, his identification with the father in his own personal prehistory" (p. 31). In a footnote, however, he adds, "Perhaps it would be safer to say 'with the parents.'" Greenacre (1966), who has herself made many important contributions to the understanding of the position of the father in human development, has also pointed out that his role "in the first two years of life has on the whole been rather neglected" (p. 743). Among Greenacre's many contributions to the understanding of early childhood in general and that of the artist in particular is her elaboration of the concept of the "collective alternates" in several of her writings.

This notion is developed repeatedly in her writings as if it were work-in-progress, and she introduces it in *The Childhood of the Artist* (1957, p. 479) as a phrase particularly adopted to clarify in her own mind certain features of the early development of the artist (p. 490). We will return later to this concept in which early object relations and their ramifications in later life are of critical importance. Yet even here it is precisely the various aspects of the mother to which "alternates" are developed, and nowhere is specific discrimination made of where the father of the artist may fit into the paradigm. Abelin (1971) has provided an excellent review of the psychoanalytic literature on the role of the father in the first years of life, as well as his own astute observations. The quotation from Freud (1923) which is the epigraph of Abelin's paper sums up the problem: "It . . . [is] difficult to obtain a clear view of the facts in connection with the earliest object-choices and identifications, and still more difficult to describe them intelligibly" (p. 33; quoted in Abelin [1971], p. 229). And this, it should be noted, refers to *clinical* psychoanalysis; imagine its applications in biography!

Against this background of psychoanalytic thought, how are we to consider Charles Ives, who gives one the impression that he hardly had a mother?—or, if he did, that it was the result of some biological necessity for which he paid its due in the polite, distant, and responsible respect he was to show his mother later in his life. But for all humanistic intents and purposes, he presents himself as if born of man! In the biographical sketch already mentioned, which Ives provided John Tasker Howard, he makes no mention of his mother even in a category which included "home influences." She had died only the previous year in Danbury at the age of seventy-nine. Nor were there any discernible signs of a *memorialization in music* (to use Pollock's [1975b] term) which would have been so characteristic of Ives, especially with reference to his father. His answer to the first question (Born) had been a terse, "October 20, 1874, Danbury, Connecticut." In response to the second (Early musical background, education, home influences, etc.) comes what I have described as essentially a biography of George: "My father was a musician and a teacher . . . ," etc. His answer to the fifth and final question, which he rephrased as "the idiom the composer finds himself in," was so lengthy that he apologized for it at the end. It is a ramble on the old and new in music and the issue of artistic value. There is a characteristically personal statement in the final paragraph which ends quite naturally, if illogically, with a quotation from George; "My father used to say, 'If a poet knows more about a horse than he does about heaven, he might better stick to the horse, and someday the horse may carry him into heaven'" (Ives, 1972, p. 240). The verbal quotation is "framed" within Charles's statements in much the same way as musical quotations with reference to George occur in the music.

The above autobiographical picture is consistent with other presentations of himself in the collected *Memos* (the "Scrapbook" and "Memories") and elsewhere. Similarly, the reference to George, not only with regard to the presentation of fact and detail but also in terms of *representation*—a direct quotation—summons up the man's style and very sound of voice just as certain musical phrases might evoke other aspects of George, along with their associated affects within Charles. At the same time, the content (namely, the prevalence of George, particularly in the absence of reference to his mother) draws us to the question of what fantasy might underlie this curious amalgam of presentation, representation, and, indeed, misrepresentation or distortion.

The fundamental fantasy of autobiography is the family-romance fantasy first described by Freud (1909). One of its rich variants, frequently associated with artists, was described by Kris

(1952). The latter describes it in terms of a characteristic and common legend of origins which was deemed appropriate for artists in ancient biographies. In its barest outlines, a shepherd boy of extraordinary talent is discovered by a man of rank and power. Under his guidance and protection, the young artist realizes his genius in great art and thereby achieves wealth and acclaim (p. 64). In an otherwise rich discussion, Kris does not specifically point out that this artistic birth of the creator is achieved through the intercourse between two men and that the art that is the product is the ultimate issue of their congress. Two births are implied, that of the artist and that of the creative product. An analogy may be found in the doctrines of the Immaculate Conception and the Virgin Birth. It was Mary who was immaculately conceived; Christ who was born of a virgin. Kris's account of the legend of Christ as a child making clay birds into which he then breathed life would be an extension of the latter (p. 70). In this legend he reveals an identification with God, the sculptor of Man, and with his mother, his own creator without benefit of man. In either case, the opposite sex, of critical importance under ordinary human circumstance, is rendered unnecessary.

What is doctrine in theology may become distorted in popular usage, the distortion itself usually representative of some shared fantasy. Thus, an error commonly made by those without specific education in this area is that Christ was the result of *both* Immaculate Conception and Virgin Birth or that the two are synonymous. In writing in his account of the life of John Stuart Mill of a set of family circumstances which resembles that of Ives in several significant ways, Mazlich (1975) suggests in his opening paragraph that Mill's autobiographical identification of himself as "the eldest son of James Mill, the author of the History of British India, *invokes a new version of immaculate conception, in which the mother is entirely missing*" [emphasis added]. Mazlich perceptively points out that we have "book and boy," both produced by the father seemingly alone, and that in fact Mill's mother is not mentioned in the published version of the *Autobiography* (p. 3). Mazlich does not return to this point in an otherwise rich account. It remains on the level of a metaphor which engages one's attention at the outset. The author makes no attempt to bridge the gap between his observer's metaphor and what might well have been the subject's unconscious fantasy, which the observer had intuitively tapped. Could John

Stuart Mill's unconscious fantasy have, in fact, been that of the "new version of immaculate conception" (that is, the theologically erroneous popular version discussed above) applied to a man. If this was possibly the case, was it the lack of data or method which led the author to keep this important statement on the level of metaphor or some other element—perhaps some analogue to the countertransference of clinical psychoanalysis exerting its effect in applied psychoanalysis?

The family romance of Charles Ives, as distinctively and richly American as that of Mill's is British, contains elements of certain universal fantasies of origin. The gap between metaphor and true unconscious fantasy can be bridged only with appropriate data and methods of interpretation. Let us pursue that aspect of Ives's family romance which has to do with private fantasy regarding his relationship with his father and, in particular, the nature of his origins. The totality of Ives's references to his father, the exclusivity of the pair in Ives's mental life, the affects of love, reverence, and nostalgia which accompany these, and the apparent absence of the mother as an important object suggest the outlines of some fantasy of a family of two. The "family," consisting of father and son ("family" because of the generational element), had its origins in a prehistory which mirrored its later course in that women were unessential to its integrity. In such a system of fantasy men beget men. The manner in which this would be accomplished might well be shrouded by the veil of unconscious fantasy, but the conscious mind in such a case could go so far as to be aware of the incomparable love and intimacy which could be shared by men, the creative thrust which could be cultivated by this communion, and the creative products which might result. Certainly, Ives revealed that he was keenly aware of these in his writing about his father. The contribution of interpretation (for which corroboration must then be sought) would be that beyond this, in mental life, lies a fantasy of male virgin birth: the generative agent, mother-cum-father, was male as we know it rationally, but a special category of its own unique nature in fantasy. Conception would be "immaculate" in its popular, distorted sense. On the surface, women were merely unnecessary, and a respectful attitude would be reserved for them.

That this respect could be motivated by anxiety is strongly suggested by a preoccupation with masculinity and the threat of feminization which comes up repeatedly in Ives's thought—fundamentally castration anxiety. The taint of the feminine, however, could be denied and circumvented by birth without benefit of uterus, an achievement of biological patrilineage. However, the shared male organ by which this end would be achieved was not the equivalent or analogue of the uterus in any literal way. Rather the choice of organ, richly overdetermined, which would accomplish this would be the one which Ives wrote and spoke about in such copious detail, detail rich in metaphor: *the ear*, more specifically his particular mental image of the musician's "ear." In its starkest form, his fantasy of origin was that of the immaculate conception in and through this ear. We will return to this in more detail later.

Background, if not yet support, for the above interpretation may start with a contribution from history and custom. In the establishment of family, and usually personal identity, roots are commonly patrilinear and the generations measured in terms of the male. In the language of the Old Testament, it is literally male who begets male, and it is curious that one does not observe a fantasy such as that outlined above more frequently. Certainly the New England Victorian culture of Ives's boyhood was with certain exceptions male dominated, and the dramatis personae of his personal history were men.

Charles could trace his lineage back to Captain William Ives of the *Truelove* in 1635 and to the first settlers of the area. His own meaningful prehistory included a sense of involvement in the affairs of men via George and the Civil War which had ended scarcely half a dozen years before his birth. The fact that George was a youthful bandmaster notwithstanding, their lives had been peopled by the great General Grant, even by Lincoln himself. Finally, in the age of unrestricted economic expansion that was already starting, an alternative to family background was becoming increasingly romanticized—that of the self-made man. The independence of spirit so characteristic of Ives and valued by him as distinctively American appears here in a new guise. That creativity may be exercised upon oneself is in one sense an extreme view of independence and on another level an extension of the fantasy of man making man. Actually Charles's grandfather had achieved something like that in starting the bank in Danbury in a room of the family home. He was in this sense "self-made" in that estimable contemporary tradition.

Yet for many boys the inner world is peopled by men in this way, and the underlying fantasies suggested above are common coin. Let us now turn to the more individual features of Ives's childhood which I believe contributed to the development of those fantasies outlined above. One which I believe is of prime importance, yet often overlooked in psychobiographical writings, was biological endowment—that is, aside from gender and its psychosexual equipment. To begin with, there is no question that Ives, like most composers, was born with unusual musical potential. By this I mean the anlage for whatever functions were to subserve an extraordinary capacity for musical cognition and for those processes relating to affect which are an integral part of musical thought. An unusual sensitivity in the auditory sphere must certainly constitute a large part of this, but such sensitivity is in itself complex. It is a sensitivity responsive not only to the physical qualities of sound (volume, pitch, timbre, etc.) but to formal features as well, such as patterning, pace (rhythm, meter), and appreciation of the distinctive features of auditory form. Related here is the appreciation of time, in itself a complex function. A wealth of affects are generated which themselves become part of the auditory experience; for example (here with regard to patterning and time) the gratification of continuity, the shock of surprise, the pleasures of the familiar, the unpleasant of delay—all aspects of the vicissitudes of expectation. In an individual so gifted this potential may develop in different directions and to different degrees, ranging from fullest realization to rude inhibition. In the former case it is tantamount not merely to a choice of career but to a commitment to a life characterized by a particular mode of thinking. In the absence of gross inhibition of either an external or intrapsychic nature, where a genuine ability exists the bearer of such a gift experiences it as compelling; as if the alternative would be not thinking and not feeling.

George undoubtedly shared in such a biological endowment. Put another way, his father was more like himself unfolding than anyone else in his environment. Thus, from the beginning his identification with his father had more than usual intricacy. There was not only the usual biological similarity of father and son, as well as a strong physical resemblance in other respects, but, at base, significant similarity in central nervous system endowment. Later there was to be a striking congruence of cognitive style and, above all, a preeminence of the auditory sphere. This fundamental similarity was to exert its influence in every phase of development up until adolescence. At that point Charles was to come into the same conflict with the outside world that George had encountered all his life. It would involve not only loyalty to George but a loyalty to ideals the latter had already relinquished. A unique solution was called for. Despite this final developmental shake-up of identity, something had already solidified: the characterological precipitates of Charles's identification with George and, *pari passu*, an irrevocable commitment to music. It was these characteristics which were to form the background to Charles's subsequent composing career, to the persistence of George in musical memorialization, and to what was in essence the ongoing postmortem collaboration of father and son.

In addition to these biological anlagen and their fate in development, I suggest that George played a greater-than-usual role in Charles's earliest life. A brother, Moss, was born when Charles was sixteen months old. It appears that even during his wife's pregnancy George assumed many child-caring responsibilities which from the beginning involved a sharing of music. We can only speculate about the intricacies of separation–individuation. Usually seen as a process accomplished in the context of a mother–child relationship, another caretaker might lend it a different cast. While Charles may have *turned* away from his mother (or had the experience of *being* turned away with the birth of Moss), the turning *toward* his father would have compensated for it. For among "the collective alternates" of which Greenacre (1957) writes those which related to music would have been the most critical for a child of Charles's endowment. The keys to this kingdom were in his father's hands. The child's object world would consist primarily (although not necessarily exclusively) of parts of father and alternates which were related as aspects of music. The "widened area of [sensory] responsiveness" (brackets mine) would, in turn, further intensify the relationship with his father. The enriched "capacity for symbolization" (p. 497) which such a state of affairs would tend to engender would then become inextricably associated with him. The "love affair with the world" and that with his father would become indistinguishable.

The family romance in such individuals is believed by Greenacre (1957) to be particularly intense, and "an early attitude of glorification of the parents" develops "in accordance with the peculiar vibrancy and capacity for near ecstasy derived from his own body states. Fortunate is the child if the own father fulfills the need for the model with which then to identify" (p. 494). Ives's early experiences with his father would have served to "condense and consolidate" the special arena of "collective alternates" which related to audition and to music through this "special source of identification" (p. 498). This was to become apparent not only in the development of musical capacity and function but in the musical *content* as well, namely, in certain constant stylistic features relating to George. At the same time, it was to facilitate the kind of "split in self-representation, going over into even a split in the sense of identity" which Greenacre (1957) feels is frequently to be found in creative individuals: a struggle may later ensue in adult life in which "the more conventional self may be more or less guardian or enemy of the creative self" (p. 499). Ives's two careers were a manifestation of this struggle.

Ives's music contains in effect precipitates of these earliest phases of development in relation to his father. George is present in terms of emulation, imitation, frank quotation, and the evocation of early experiences in music. In the words of one of Charles's songs related to World War I (and inevitably associated in his own text to the Civil War, George's war), "He Is There!" (Ives, 1922, p. 107).

As I have shown elsewhere (Feder, 1980b), Ives reconstructed complex memories of his father in tone in his compositions for purposes of private and shared reminiscence and memorialization. More subtly, and specifically related to the separation–individuation phase, his is a style that in a sense never strayed far from father and home, radical and deviant as it may sound. It is firmly rooted in person, place, and time: George, Danbury, and the periods of George's youth and Charles's own. The affect most associated with this aspect of Ives's music is nostalgia (Feder, 1981b). Analogues to this may be found in many other areas of Charles's later life. For example, he never strayed very far in locale. He lived and worked in New York City and bought a country home in rural Redding, Connecticut, near Danbury. His suburban home after marriage, in Hartsdale, New York, was about midway between the two—if not precisely geographically, then quite close in terms of the travel time of the teen years and certainly in terms of psychological distance. Although there were favorite vacation locales elsewhere, he did not travel to Europe until he was fifty. That locale plays a prominent role in his music is evident merely from some of the titles; for example, *Three Places in New England* which are respectively "The St. Gaudens (sculpture) in Boston Common," "Putnam's Camp, Redding, Connecticut," and "The Housatonic at Stockbridge." In more subtle form spatial effects (such as sound coming from a distance or the impression of it) are frequent (Feder, 1984).

The above considerations of person, place, and distance are, I believe, related to the separation–individuation phase and its sequelae. Rose (1979) has skillfully related similar aspects of music and other arts to this phase. In Mahler's description of normal development (1965) of locomotion, and its psychological ramifications, is a critically important element. By the time of onset of the rapprochement subphase—the one that chiefly concerns us here—the practice of locomotion has already culminated in free toddling, ambling, and walking. Between fourteen and twenty-two months locomotion paradoxically subserves the development of both separateness in moving away and togetherness in the wish to share new experiences and acquisitions.

A musical form related to both aspects, and the one, of course, of which George was unquestionably the master, is the march. No doubt the march, which is a common element in child's play, had a heightened meaning for Charles, both because of his unusual responsiveness to music and his relationship with his father. It was always to play a special role in his music. To give but a single example, in the reconstructed "boyhood memory" cited above (Feder, 1980b) a large portion of a favorite march of George and Charles is quoted, which I have suggested constitutes a screen memory of George in his finest hour. As a form, the march in general was subsequently to take on richer implications, the seeds of which are already present in this early phase: those of "men moving together," the homoerotic element, and of "moving against one another," the aggressive. Body–image implications of the march may be readily observed in the expanded sense of boundaries achieved within a member of a marching unit (Kestenberg, 1978, personal communication). When Charles was later to march in George's band playing the snare drum, his probable location was at the rear of the marching mass with George at one head, both parts of some larger body moving together in space and musical time.

Connected with the march are certain characteristic affects, whose origins revert to the earliest years of life. The confident elation of the freely walking child may be commonly reexperienced, elicited by certain march forms, and projected as if inherently "in" them. Among the subtly differing varieties is the one in the Reeves's March in "Decoration Day" which has been already cited (Feder, 1980). Here in the final repeat of the "Trio" all the band's forces are marshaled as if, in Ivesian terms, proudly "marching down Main Street." Marches appear repeatedly in the work of Ives, and there are several examples even in the *114 Songs* (1922). One that is particularly notable is "Old Home Day" (p. 115), a small masterpiece of memory with words by Charles himself, in which he nostalgically evokes the objects of childhood in visual and sound images. The affect of nostalgia already cited a likewise fundamentally related to this earliest period of life, which contains the kernel of first and future object relations and the places and contexts in which they were experienced.

In addition to the special characteristics of locomotion and affect associated with the separation–individuation phase of development, one that is highly related to Ives's developmental individuality (which is after all what we are attempting to formulate) is of importance. How does the child experience the objects who participate with him through these phases? The visual, tactile, kinesthetic, and sensorimotor spheres have all been noted. Little specific attention has been given the auditory, which may be of some importance in any case and, in a child of unusual sensitivity, of central importance. Even under usual circumstances, the ear which is to become the receptor of the literal spoken word may earlier in life have become experienced and accomplished as the receptor of nonverbal communication. The earliest example would be the prenatal percept of the mother's heartbeat as described by Salk (1960). In extrauterine life, prosodic elements of speech are responded to in advance of any comprehension of the purely verbal aspects of language (Stern, 1977, pp. 14–18). Edelson (1975) has explored some possible "meanings in the music of language" in terms of the sound itself (pp. 167 ff.). If such communications are viewed as complex auditory symbols related to those we term music, the anlagen for musical cognition are present quite early, subject to cultivation or inhibition or to assimilation as a part of verbal appreciation. In the instance of a musically gifted child, the cultivation of such auditory symbols may be rich if not extreme, depending on the nature of the gift and the facilitating environment. The caring person will play a significant role, and the mutual relationship may assume special qualities owing to both the increased range of possibilities of communication, as well as a special sharing of a less-than-usual language. Mental representations of the caring person are likely to have features related to this interaction and, likewise, fantasy. Thus, music may become the mode of symbolization for early objects and experiences. In the instances of Ives, I believe it did so in a unique way.

The above considerations apply to the early relationship of Charles and his father at the time when Ives became distinctively "bilingual." The normal, expectable verbal result provided him with the common coin of communication; the musical, with a special medium of exchange shared with George. This was to serve as background to the secret sharing which I believe was the fantasy underlying Charles's career in composition—a fantasy the background to which is discussed above and which was to become an important element in the termination of the career. The earlier sharing was also the matrix out of which a related fantasy, already cited, took shape: the fantasy of the "ear." As I have suggested by way of interpretation, this "ear" was the organ of creativity in a fantasied transaction between Charles and George; the organ of "immaculate" musical conception through the ear. I would now further suggest that its roots too lay in Ives's earliest musical experiences with his father, discussed above, which took on new meaning in the oedipal period and in latency, and generated enough conflict to threaten their actual relationship in adolescence. After George's death, it was to spark Charles's composing career as a complementary fantasy to the secret sharing. As such, it participated in the mourning process in ways which will be taken up in the next section. At this point, we will consider further these related fantasies, especially that of the "ear."

Ives's *Memos* (1972), dictated when he was fifty-eight, a decade after his last major compositional efforts, starts after a few opening remarks with a bang!

Dear Sirs and Nice Ladies:
   (This is not for publication, but anybody who can read can read it.) The following statement is made, not because it's important to anything or anybody, but because there are "lilies" taking money

from newspapers and other things whose ears and brains are somewhat emasculated from dis-use. They have ears because you can see them—they may have brains, but you can't see them (in anything they write). Every so often, an article or a clipping or a "verbal massage" (sic) is sent to a name (see name on dotted line), which shows that Rollo has a job. . . . If he can hear and he doesn't know it he's a mental-musico-defective (from his neck up. . . .) [p. 26].

The foregoing is, in effect, a caricature of a fantasy more subtly rendered earlier in his life, the result of a process one occasionally sees in older people in which they become exaggerations of their former selves. The distinct paranoid drift should not be too surprising considering the content of the fantasy, the lingering ambivalence regarding composition—by now given up—and the stresses of impending physical illness. But the ear as the masculine organ of creativity is the dominant and recurrent theme.

The Ivesian ear is a shared, masculine organ; it is virile and potent yet tenderly receptive to its own kind. Both phallic and vaginal, it can give it, and it can take it. Ives (1972) writes with pleasure of a "stunt" during his Yale years with "offbeats on black keys" and notes how the men said "that it made the music stronger and better . . . it shows what the ears can handle . . . the ears have to be on their own" (p. 41). He goes on, "If more of this and other kinds of ear stretching had gone on, if the ears and minds had been used hard and harder, there might be less 'arrested development'. . . ." The "ear stretching" is closely associated with his father. In one section of his *Memos* elements of an aesthetic of music, a textbook of advanced techniques, a musical autobiography, and a tender memoir of his father are condensed within the span of a few pages. The elements intertwine, and, similarly, prose blends easily into music. Ear stretching is not only written about but given literal representation in an example of a musical theme with widely spaced intervals (p. 44). On this kind of melodic construction Ives quotes his father: "If you must play a chromatic scale, play it like a man." An interesting feature can be seen in the very form of the *Memos*: Once momentum is gained in writing about these things, Ives readily appears to drift to thoughts about his father and often includes a quotation.

At times women are not merely omitted or their feminine qualities decried, but are presented as a frank threat. A note of bitterness and fear is sounded in a comment on "the greatest (Bach, Beethoven, Brahms, etc.)"—the etcetera doubtless George, " . . . music has always been an emasculated art. . . . They couldn't exactly help it—life with them was such that they had to live at least a part of the time by the ladies' smiles—they had to please the ladies or die." To the contrary lies the promise of music in masculine potential: "Music is a nice little art just born, and they ask 'Is it a boy or a girl?'—and one voice in the back row says 'It's going to be a boy sometime'" (p. 530).

Ives was to invent the character already mentioned, Rollo. Unmistakably effeminate and phobic, he is the quintessential sissy. Moreover, he had a distinct moral taint tending toward prostitution. Ives carried on imaginary conversations with Rollo which sometimes spilled over onto the musical manuscript. Kirkpatrick (1960) catalogues seven of such conversations (p. 60). They reflect a kind of discourse on music carried on intrapsychically between the fused imagos of father and son and that aspect of the outside world represented by Rollo. No doubt Rollo too was a denied and projected portion of the self-image, defensively split. It was a part of the processes of creativity and mourning which occupied Charles throughout his productive years and which will be discussed presently.

The Ivesian "ear," highly sexualized in practice and function, was at the heart of these transactions. It was invested from many sources. The recurrent element of the spectre of disuse atrophy suggests that displacement from the male generative organs constituted one such source. "There may be an analogy between (or at least similar processes) of the ear, the mind, and arm muscles. They don't get strong with disuse" (Ives, 1972, p. 42). What appear to be fundamental are homoerotic fantasies, no doubt a contribution from the oedipal period, superimposed upon an already intensely sexualized relationship, and the consequent threat of castration and the institution of defense. While the ways in which we can find congruence with expectable developmental patterns are of interest, perhaps of greater interest are the unexpected individual examples one comes upon. For example, a defensive function, intellectualization, is energetically employed and manifested in the prose writings, some of which are appended to the actual compositions. In the latter, however, we may also find examples of intellectualization rendered in musical as opposed to verbal symbol. (A simple example would be the "stretching" of the chromatic scale cited earlier.)

The repetitive insistence that the music be masculine suggests denial in its very thrust and particularly in the recurring homoerotic context. The musical product is "going to be a boy—sometime." This is the result of a uniquely bisexual organ, the fantasied "ear." This organ of masculine give and take can conceive in two senses. It is capable of auditory imagination and of ideational generation. At the core of the latter is a variant of a pregnancy fantasy. These two aspects also represent a further aspect of bisexuality. The imagination of a sound which is potentially acoustic in that it can be physically realized by a musical instrument, thus "sent" across some space to be received by a listener, may be viewed as a phallic function. Its reception, either in this manner or internally within the composer himself, is accomplished by the same organ functioning in a different mode. Thus sound may articulate with space—outer space and inner—and ultimately to representations of the body, both male *and* female.

A word about the "masculine" qualities of the product itself: It is assertive, even aggressive in its iconoclastic nature. The use of dissonance may at times appear to be downright assaultive. Ives defends himself at times as if anticipating attack. Interestingly, Elliot Carter recalls Ives recopying a work for performance many years after it had been written, changing octaves into sevenths and nines. Carter felt he might have tended to "jack up the level of dissonance" and even later in life to give his earlier music "its last shot of polyrhythm and dissonance" (Perlis, 1974, p. 138). Above all, the music is fundamentally *new* music and, in the foregoing anecdote, new and renewed. Music is the "art, just born. . . ." In addition to the generative and regenerative functions, one notes the masculinization of the music in the answer to the doubt whether it is going to be a boy or a girl. With regard to regeneration, I believe it was not coincidence that Ives was later a benefactor of the publication *New Music*, and, as I have suggested, his relationship with its editor, Henry Cowell, shared many of the features of Ives's relationship with his father.

The descriptions above which trench upon personification in music were not quite meant to be interpretive—Ives himself tended to think of his music in these terms, maintaining a curious attitude toward all his music which defies concise description. Despite revision, quotation, integration into other works, and multiple versions of the same work, a unit of music once invented seemed to Ives to have a life of its own. Accordingly, he appeared to have what can only be described as a kind of respect for it. There is hardly anything which can be called working sketches because they were considered to be part of the body of the music. Everything was thriftily "used," just as he would use and reuse manuscript paper and, as a result, have fragments of several works from various periods on a single sheet of paper. Likewise, one knows of no instances in which he discarded works, a common practice among composers. However, this respect did not amount to reverence. A work could readily be rearranged, altered, or include an aleatory or improvisational element. Also, for much of his creative life, he appeared to have little investment in the actual musical score once it was composed. He would very nearly throw it over his shoulder as he went on to the next. The barn in Redding was filled with uncollated manuscripts, and at least one major work was retrieved from the Ives and Myrick company safe.

This strange "respect" for the music is revealed in the publication among the *114 Songs* (1912) of eight, which he indicates in a note "have little or no musical value." They are included as good illustrations of poor music, and he asks "that they be not sung, at least in public . . ." (unnumbered, after p. 259). Nevertheless, he published them! Others in the collection he felt "cannot be sung"— and if they could, perhaps they might prefer, if they had a say, to remain as they are—that is, "in the leaf'. . . . " The lengthy prose *Postface* to the *114 Songs* ends with an imaginative personification of "a song," a declaration of its rights written in a rhapsodic style:

> [A] song has a *few* rights, the same as other ordinary citizens. . . . If it feels like walking along the left side of the street—passing the door of physiology, or sitting on the curb, why not let it? . . . Should it not be free at times from the dominion of the thorax, the diaphragm, the ear, and other points of interest . . . ? Should it not have a chance to sing to itself, if it can sing? . . . If it happens to feel like trying to fly where humans cannot fly—to sing what cannot be sung—to walk in a cave on all fours—or to tighten up its girth in blind hope and faith, and try to scale mountains that are not—Who shall stop it? [It ends in a couplet:] In short, must a song always be a song? [unnumbered, after p. 259].

This imaginative flight of fantasy is a combination of a Declaration of Independence and Bill of Rights for music. It is distinctly American, even humorously patriotic, and at the same time almost some literal reductio ad absurdum of a transcendental ideal. Yet I doubt that it is completely tongue-in-cheek. I suggest music always retained some magical quality for Ives; in this instance it was delightfully magical.

The most important aspect of this was the blurred boundaries between the world of objects and the world of music. The song personified may be seen as the offspring of aural conception and birth, the product of manly intercourse and entitled to a life of its own. However, it is an earlier phase than the oedipal which supplies the magic. I would speculate that this would be the phase of separation–individuation, which has already been discussed, the phase of the dawning of the world of self and object in which music had so important a position in the early life of Ives. The music, the self, and the object—Ives's father in this case—were experientially fused in such a way that later differentiation did not completely free one from association with the others. At the very least, the composer retained access to this mode of thinking. In this regard, we are speaking in essence of transitional experience and transitional object. It is likely that the entire transitional range was deeply experienced by the child Ives in terms of music and that music always retained for Ives some of the qualities of transitional object. With this childhood background in mind, we will proceed forward to a consideration of Ives's adult life, following his father's death, and the process of mourning.

"The Fates of the Immortal Object"

In the chapter from which the title of the present section is borrowed, Schafer (1968) develops the thesis that "in psychic reality the object is immortal and [that,] therefore, it makes more psychological sense to speak of the various fates of the immortal object than to speak of object loss pure and simple" (p. 220). Although he speaks of three fates—essentially introjection, identification, and the continued actual external object relation—he makes the important point that these are not mutually exclusive alternatives. He notes, for example, that in close, lasting relationships between two people it is more the rule that "in proportion to its importance, the object whose external index is preserved will also be represented to some degree and on some level of functioning both as a presence and an identification" (pp. 234–235). This point of view suggests the rich intricacies of mourning and at the same time allows for the manifold human solutions to the inevitability of object loss.

Charles Ives's solution was complex, as the review of his biography has already indicated. It was no secret even to himself that his longing for his father never quite disappeared but was rather tempered by one or another shift in mental life as time went on. Nor was he completely unaware of a hunger for object replacement which he appears to have negotiated with better-than-average good fortune. Harmony was as close a replacement in the external world—a match for the Charles-cum-internalized-George—as could be reasonably expected in the real and heterosexual world. He did not need the Reverend Twitchell after all, although close family ties were cultivated until the latter's death. The marital relationship was close enough to surmount Harmony's inability to bear children following her (probable) hysterectomy in their first year of marriage. Later she was to appear to be in some ways as closely identified with Charles as he was with George. When his handwriting had become shaky—and perhaps even before—she became his amanuensis, answering correspondence from dictation or, later, by paraphrasing what "Mr. Ives" wished to say. While this in itself may not appear to be out of the ordinary wifely line of duties in such a case, it is striking to observe the memoranda on the manuscript of a very late adaptation of an earlier song written in the hands of both Harmony and Edith—some continuing tradition of collaboration (Kirkpatrick, 1960, p. 198).

In New Haven Ives had found a sympathetic older companion in John Griggs, the choirmaster who appreciated his music. In moments of doubt ("Are my ears on wrong?"), he had wondered why no one "with the exception of Mrs. Ives (and one or two others . . . Dr. Griggs)" liked his music (1972, p. 71). It is clear from Perry's (1974) presentation that, despite obvious differences, Ives made some connection with his apparently pedantic and unresponsive music professor Horatio Parker and that the latter was to exert some influence on Ives. Despite his strongly traditional bent, Parker could write: "If we give people weak music, they will accept it and love it. Likewise they will accept strong music" (p. 9). Later, in the years prior to his marriage, it was the company of men he respected who sustained him in "Poverty Flat." He wrote much of his music here,

Figure 8.3 Charles at age seventy-four, with Harmony. Photo Halley Erskine. Reprinted with permission of the photographer and courtesy Yale University Music Library.

sitting at a battered piano, in a much traversed living room. Finally, in Julian Myrick, he was to find a friend and business partner in an association lasting twenty-three years. Ives's ability, perhaps need, to sustain relationships with men served him well. At the same time, George was never far from mind.

In the very first full biography of Ives by Henry and Sidney Cowell (1969), it was the latter who wrote, "His father's is the influence Charles Ives most proudly acknowledges, and it is not too much to say that the son has written his father's music for him" (p. 11). From the foregoing, it should be clear that I believe a psychoanalytic study confirms and enriches Mrs. Cowell's hypothesis. In her statement she ventured in essence an interpretation based not only upon the data in the biography but upon impressions gained from the personal relationship the Cowells had with the Iveses. Charles did indeed write George's music for him; he was the agency through whom the music was realized. The activity of composition in which Ives was so fervently occupied until he approached fifty was, in effect, an intrapsychic collaboration with George.[4]

In the music and, later, the prose, a parallel may be seen in the continual reference to George in what amounts to a wide repertoire of ways. By turns, Charles assumes the roles of historian, apologist, amanuensis, memorialist, replacement, and deputy. In a eulogy to his father in the "Scrapbook" (1972), Charles wrote, "He did but little composing—a few things or arrangements for bands—in fact, he had little interest in it for himself, and it was too bad he didn't, for it would have shown these interests, and they would have been in some keepable form. He didn't write textbooks (though I have some copies of his class talks, etc.), and he didn't write many letters. He left little behind except memories of him in others" (p. 45). It was the motive of rendering George "in some keepable form" which generated the posthumous collaboration.

In the section of the *Scrapbook* preceding this memorialization (p. 42), Charles had in effect actually written a portion of his father's "textbook." Starting with a reminiscence ("When I was a boy, I played in my father's band . . ."), he describes various shared musical practices and moves easily to a textbooklike listing of

---

[4] The notion of "secret sharing" or intrapsychic collaboration, as I have called it in this case, is not uncommon in creative activity. It is a concept which firmly connects art and object. Meyer (1972) has discussed certain important examples of this among writers (pp. 381–383).

George's "testing or experimenting in the divisions of tone." It is in this section that his father's inventions (the Humanophone and the Glass Orchestra) are noted and a musical example is even written out, giving the page itself the look of a textbook. Toward the end of this section the letter of George already cited, in the authentic "Ives" style, is introduced (about the teachers who "wrap up the students' ears and minds as a lady does her hair"), a fitting albeit cranky *envoi* to a textbook. While George "didn't write many letters," Charles himself was quite a prodigious letter writer and did not hesitate to advance his philosophy, usually in a characteristically peppery style, to anyone he had a mind to, including President Wilson and Governor Coolidge, among others.

The musical manuscripts have but a few literal references to George, none addressing him directly as, for example, "Rollo" had been addressed, but, then, the argument with the latter was in itself George's own. There is only a single quotation from any of George's music, from his Fourth Fugue in B-Flat in Charles's *Children's Day at the Camp Meeting*, which was later revised as the Fourth Violin Sonata. But George appears everywhere: portions of Charles's mental representation of his father are present in essence or in fragmentary form throughout Charles's music. Thus, both the content as well as the function of the music relate to George. Examples are many, and we will consider a few at this point in a general way. Other studies focus in detail on specific works (Feder, 1980b, 1981b).

The Violin Sonatas, of which there are four, provide a good place to start, as they were written for an instrument which, like the cornet, Ives closely associated with his father. They were written in his maturity between 1902 and 1916 (age 28–42) and, as Hitchcock (1977) and others have pointed out, "form a coherent group, more unified in style and expression than any other similar group of Ives' work" (p. 57). Two features are singled out for discussion—one of content, one of style. Almost all of the dozen movements of this body of work are based on a hymn tune often developed in a highly original manner. Form subserves function as ingenious musical elaboration evokes aspects of the actual camp meetings and similar experiences with which hymn tunes were associated in Ives's mind. The third movement of the Second Sonata, for example, subtitled *The Revival*, is aptly described by Hitchcock: "[It] opens quietly ruminatively, almost prayerfully, then like a camp meeting revival service increases in intensity through a series of mounting dynamic arcs to a frenetic, shouting climax, cathartic and draining at the same time; the music then subsides quickly to a close . . . exhausted and purged" (p. 60).

Charles recalled with intense tenderness the camp meetings of his childhood and the role George played in them.

> At the outdoor camp-meeting services in Redding all the farmers, their families, field hands, and friends for miles around would come afoot or in their farm wagon. I remember how the great waves of sound used to come through the trees when things like Beulah Land, Woodworth, Nearer My God to Thee, The Shining Shore, Nettleton, In The Sweet Bye-and-Bye, and the like were sung by thousands of "let-out" souls. The music notes and words on paper are about as much like what they were at those moments as the monogram on a man's necktie may be like his face. Father, who led the singing, sometimes with his cornet or his voice, sometimes with both voice and arms, and sometimes in the quieter hymns with a violin or French horn, would always encourage the people to sing their own way . . . [Ives, 1972, p. 132].

Once his father was asked: "How can you stand it to hear old John Bell (who was the best stonemason in town) bellow off-key the way he does at the camp meetings?" His answer was: "Old John is a supreme musician. Look into his face and hear the music of the ages. Don't pay too much attention to the sounds. If you do you may miss the music . . ." (p. 132).

Most of the above tunes, in addition to others, are quoted in the Violin Sonatas. "Beautiful River," a hymn by Robert Lowry, may be singled out in particular, since it serves as the basis of the third movement of the Sonata No. 4 for Violin and Piano (Ives, 1942). The tune is given full statement only following introductory vague gropings at it, the presentation of fragments as if in attempt to recall it, to get it started. In its complete rendition (marked "At the River, Lowry" on the score), the fourth and final phrase of the refrain is distorted as if it were being sung by a tone-deaf individual lapsing into another indeterminate key.

In these works George is richly evoked both generally and specifically. The camp meetings are reminisced and memorialized in the sound itself. The tunes are not always quoted in ideal form, but rather as George literally heard and respected them. Moreover, there is a sharing of hearing. It is the transformation of the idea "we think the same way" into auditory form. As we have seen the sound of the violin had been among Charles's earliest experiences with his father, as had the tunes, either then or some time later. Interestingly, the third movement ("At The River"), according to a notation Ives made in the manuscript, was "started as Cornet + Violins Qu Piece 1905 . . ." (Kirkpatrick, 1960, p. 73)—both instruments associated with George. Later he recalled that the occasion was an evening spent with his friend and future brother-in-law Dave Twitchell at a prayer meeting while on vacation at Saranac Lake. He had made "a little tune for trumpet and piano, *Shall We Gather At the River?*, a tune Dave was very fond of—and they happened to sing it at the meeting that night" (Ives, 1972, p. 72). With the words of the song tacitly evoked on the printed page and in the phrase of music, a lingering question is left at the end of the piece which, literally speaking, does not come to a musically traditional end in the form of a cadence. There is no answer, no resolution—in effect, no ending.

Perhaps a clue to the song's significance lies in the words which suggest reunion, since the words themselves, in simple question-and-answer form, assertively provide a resolution: "Yes, we'll gather by the river that flows by the throne of God." Against this background we may wonder if this is related to the enigmatic title of another chamber work dated the same year as the earliest version of the Fourth Violin Sonata (1906), *The Unanswered Question*. This is explored in another study (Feder, 1984). It is worth noting at this point what I believe to be Ives's conscious and unconscious concern with what lies beyond life. This is the "perennial question," and it may be seen repeatedly in various guises, in particular in the "question and answer" form of certain texts and songs. Whether one views the answer on different levels as denial or optimism, the "question" is "answered" repeatedly by turns—reflectively, fervently, indignantly. The "answer" is, "yet another life," a recreation of what has been lost—reunion.

Before leaving the Violin Sonatas to go on to further examples, a comment on style. While performance requires skill and sensitivity, these are not bravura virtuoso works. One might say they are more for person than for violin. In fact, Ives revealed that this Sonata was an attempt to write a work that his then twelve-year-old nephew Moss could play. He notes that "the first movement kept to the idea, but the second got away from it, and the third ("At the River") got about in between" (1972, p. 72). Moss, the person for whom it was intended, probably had some kind of physical or mental handicap, the nature of which is unclear. However, he evidently did play the violin and was said to have a good ear for music. He lived for a time with the Iveses, and they were said to treat him like a son, taking it for granted he would not be able to make his own living and providing for him (Perlis, 1974, p. 93). Another nephew noted: "he was the one Uncle Charlie was closest to and insisted on helping him all his life . . . he came above all the others in the family" (p. 75).

In this relationship we may find a repetition and condensation of Charles's identification with George as the tender father and provider for the weak (cf. George and his black ward Henry Anderson Brooks) and a reversal of role, as father to one aspect of his father embodied in the helpless Moss who, as his tutor put it, "just couldn't come across" (Perlis, 1974, p. 93).

An exception to the stylistic straightforwardness which is cited by Hitchcock (1977, p. 57) occurs in the middle movement of the Second Sonata. The section note, while "showy" and "idiomatic," is actually an example of country fiddling. It is perhaps related to an early hero of Charles's and, if so, a displacement from George. This was the country fiddler John Starr of Brookfield, another prominent village musician of the Danbury area (Perry, 1974, p. 3). Incidentally, locale, which was so important in Ives's life, again comes up in the "camp meeting" quotation since Redding was the site. It was in nearby West Redding that Ives purchased the land for his country home in 1912.

Another work in which George is evoked, again with a set of symbols related to aspects of the mental representation, is a piece for chamber orchestra called *The Pond*. It is a "song without words" which here has the actual words written in below the lead line. It is scored for trumpet or basset horn, again two of George's instruments, but it may be sung. In his performance notes, Ives suggests that the flute play offstage: "This, in a way, is to suggest the echo over a pond, as does the final F-sharp (harmonic) in the violin, which may sound for a moment after the other instruments stop." There is manifest reference to his father in the words which were written by Charles, "A sound of a distant horn, O'er shadowed lake is borne—my father's song."

There are some remarkable features in this brief work of eleven measures. For one, the "sound of the distant horn" is rendered literally and the spatial features are emphasized in an echo. Distance is represented not only in space but in time as the horn's tune is repeated in canon by the echoing flute a measure later. At the end of the piece the first notes of Taps are heard in the distance. The tune itself is a rendition of a melody whose usual form is slowed down beyond recognition. It is an Irish love song, "Kathleen Mavourneen," about parting and death: "Kathleen Mavourneen, the grey dawn is breaking. The horn of the hunter is heard on the hill (beginning) . . . It may be for years, and it may be forever; Then why art thou silent, thou voice of my heart? (ending)."

The associations of the verbal elements above are apparent, having to do with intense longing for a lost love object. ("Mavourneen" actually means "my love.") The concentrated musical symbolization is less obvious. A part of the object is actualized in tone, affects are expressed, reminiscence accomplished, memorialization achieved—in short, it is a small model of mourning. Yet the symbols themselves are far from limited; they are richly overdetermined. For example, "the pond" itself is a rich evocation of another of Ives's heroes who perhaps more comprehensively represents the idealized father than did John Starr—namely, Henry David Thoreau and his nonconformist life at Walden Pond. (Incidentally, one of Ives's final additions to the Redding property was a pond which he had built in 1922 when he was forty-eight.)

"The Pond" is also to be found as one of the *114 Songs*, as is "Beautiful River" (titled "At The River"), as well as three other versions of hymn tunes from various works and numerous recastings and new arrangements of earlier works. The song version of "The Pond" appears as No. 12 but is retitled in the Table of Contents of *114 Songs* as "Remembrance" (Ives, 1922). It is dated here 1921, though the original version was composed in 1906. That this and similar works were related to the work of mourning is suggested by the couplet by Wordsworth given in lieu of title over the music: "The music in my heart I bore/long after it was heard no more." "The Pond" is discussed further in "Charles Ives and the Unanswered Question" (Feder, 1984).

The foregoing examples demonstrate how Charles "wrote his father's music" in terms of reminiscence and memorialization. They are at the same time a commentary on the fate of the object. In this context, two features should be noted about the music. First, the work of composition of a piece or group of related pieces frequently extends across many years. The few references given to the complex circumstances surrounding the Violin Sonatas merely scratch the surface. At very least, one may note a musical idea coming to mind in 1905 at a prayer meeting, its roots deep in the past, coming to fruition a decade later, and making its final appearance half a dozen years after that in the summing up of the *114 Songs*. As Ives experienced the actual writing, "It was all composed quickly within two or three weeks in the fall of 1916" (1972, p. 72). Similarly, I have shown elsewhere that "Decoration Day" germinated over the course of twenty-seven years (Feder, 1980). The resulting products were not quite completely finished works; rather they were reflections of an ongoing mental process which I suggest had many of the features of mourning. (A further example in the form of ongoing collaboration will be offered shortly.) Second, there is an exceedingly close relationship between music and objects—between the musical idea in auditory terms and the mental representation of objects. Specifically, we have at times seen aspects of Ives's father in some relatively literal representation or in more or less distorted or displaced form.

The underlying mental processes of incorporation and identification are discernible in their representational form. In the example of "The Pond" one may see the nucleus of an identification in which the son writes the father's music, a situation which is amplified richly in many more complex and extensive works. These processes have to do with George's experimentation in general and his spatial experiments in particular. We have noted that George had been interested in the spatial aspects of sound, such as the sound produced by two bands marching toward each other from opposite directions, passing abreast and marching on. George apparently loved both the experimental activity and the complex aural result. He was also interested in the qualities of sounds that came from a distance or from different directions. In effect, Charles attempts to carry out one of his father's experiments—at the very least in effect—in "The Pond." In an equally striking way, Charles realizes his father's interest in quarter tones ("as a boy I had heard some quarter-tone experiments of Father") by actually writing his *Three Quarter Tone Pieces*, getting them performed, and later providing some theoretical, "textbook" kind of commentary in his *Scrapbook* (Ives, 1972, pp. 108–109).

The object is never relinquished; it remains immortal in psychic life and in its manifold transformations in art. In this realm, many of the intricacies do not readily fit neatly into any single formulation, and even the three alternatives proposed by Schafer (1968) and cited above fail to do full justice to so complex an activity and product. It is illuminating to think in terms of another category of the object's fate in which the nature of immortality is stressed; that is, fantasies, images, and symbols of immortality. Their creation may be viewed as the praxis of immortality involving both self and object.

Lifton (1979) writes of five modes in which the sense of immortality may be expressed, one of which is the creative mode. Involved in this are not only the symbols created but the activity of their creation. Elsewhere (Lifton and Olsen, 1974) he speaks of "symbolic immortality . . . wherein there is a continuity and connection beyond personal death" which is viewed as neither compensatory—a result of denial—nor pathological. Pollock (1975a) elaborates on this, suggesting that "Through the immortality of the . . . aesthetic creation, the mourning process can come to conclusion." Or, put in economic terms: "in the resolution of the mourning process following the loss of an object, the freed cathexis may be used to invest an ideal or utopian fantasy" (pp. 338–340).

Ives, however, for reasons to be cited later, never achieved this kind of ideal resolution. Elsewhere, Pollock (1975b) specifically explores various expressions of mourning through music which are strikingly relevant. He suggests that "the creation of a musical composition is the mourning for the loss and transition of the composer's self as well as the creative end-product of the mourning process, and has a new vitality of its own." This occurs in the "resolutional concluding phase" of the mourning process (p. 435). Although he focuses on the musical expressions of mourning, he does not emphasize it as a singular and unique mode among other creative acts. I believe further detailed study of the same material will reveal it to be a special mode of expression owing to such factors as its relation to time and to affects.

In essence, Ives maintained a thread of connection with his father in continuing and realizing the potential of his father. In this sense, he was the solitary exponent of a private tradition. It richly involved his father's past as well as his own, and often the two seemed fused. For example, in the nostalgic works relating to boyhood, patriotic tunes of the Civil War of George's youth were as likely to be quoted as those relating to Charles's own youth. An extension of this was a strong sense of identification of their combined past with the collective past of America. The love of his father overflowed to the love of his father's country—the "fatherland"—and filial devotion became transformed into an unabashed patriotism. These two trends flourished, manifest in the same style, both having important stylistic implications in the music itself.

There is a continuous line from George's idiosyncratic experiments to the complex forms of Charles's mature works—works such as the Fourth Symphony and the Second Pianoforte Sonata, the "Concord." It was from this direction that Ives was to develop the experimental and innovative trends which characterize his music. Although the European tradition was part of his basic training from his earliest lessons with George and later with Parker at Yale, it was not the source of innovation. Often Ives was thought of as having been influenced by a tradition which did not interest him and by music which he never heard—certain works of Schoenberg, for example. But the innovations of Schoenberg were a creative outgrowth of a Viennese tradition in which the latter was deeply involved. Although Ives's innovations may at times resemble those of Schoenberg, they were arrived at from a different direction. The same may be said for similarities to other innovators in the various subtraditions of European music, Stravinsky, Bartok, Prokofiev, and so on.

The "tradition," then, in which Charles worked during his most productive years was a personal one, intricately involving his father's past while, at the same time, preserving his presence. Paradoxically, George was mourned and kept alive at the same time. To the degree in which composing—like performing—had become an autonomous activity, we may speak of identification. However, to the degree in which some unconscious, fantasied representation of George still sparked the activity, we must consider it an introject with certain implications in the work of mourning which will be discussed. But, in either instance, George would in some sense be the secret sharer of his son's compositions and the fountainhead of innovation. Charles had neither the time nor the interest to keep up with other new musical developments, and, in fact, they tended to confuse him; they "tended to throw me out of my stride," he said. "I suppose everyone is built differently and works differently! It just so happens that I felt I could work better if I kept to my own music and let other people keep to theirs" (Cowell and Cowell, 1969, p. 41).

The long years of creative work carried out weekends and evenings constituted Charles's ongoing collaboration with George, whose presence is ubiquitous in the music. The endeavor, like the source, was private, and so, for the most part, was its product. Performance did not interest Ives until later. Meanwhile, it will be recalled, Ives carried on a satisfying family life with Harmony and extended members and an active business life which was to bring him many rewards. The wish "to write his father's music" for him and in collaboration with him was largely unconscious and for the most part interpretable only in its derivative manifestations. Frank verbal reference to his father on the manuscript occurs occasionally, but he is never addressed as was, for example, Rollo. Rather, what is "George" in content underwent various kinds and degrees of primary-process transformations; what was "George" in function (i.e., the collaboration in composition) was subject to various defensive operations. Nor should it be assumed that this proceeded in any fixed way. Before going on to the waning of these creative years, an example of what amounts to an extreme of the collaboration made manifest is instructive.

Several of Charles's earliest pieces are found in George's handwriting, the result of the latter's encouragement and a precursor of the later collaboration. For his part, Charles, aside from quotation, put his hand more than once on manuscripts of his father. For example, on an ink copy of George's Fourth Fugue in B-Flat, already cited as having been quoted in the Fourth Violin Sonata, there are many pencil additions by Charles (Kirkpatrick, 1960, p. 216).

On one occasion, probably in 1897, Charles wrote a piece of his own on the reverse side of one of his father's manuscripts. It is a curious story. In 1890 or 1891 Charles had evidently worked on a Communion Service based on one of George's which is to be found in the latter's notebooks. This was no doubt meant for performance at the Baptist Church where Charles had become organist a year earlier at the age of fifteen. George apparently helped him with it, and some of the ink copies of the voice parts are in George's hand. This music of Charles, in George's hand and based on his (George's) music, seemed to have been in Charles's possession six or seven years later when he was at Yale some three years after George's death. Charles then wrote a choral piece for the Yale Glee Club entitled

"The Bells of Yale" on the back of one of these pages of the Communion Service. Although he was in the habit even in later, more affluent years of using every scrap of music paper and often would have fragments of various pieces on a single manuscript page, this was the only time to my knowledge that he felt some explanation was in order. At some later time he wrote on the bottom of the page: "This shows that in those days music was a heavy expense—This song for the Yale Glee Club was written (on back of father's copy) [sic] some six or seven years later—to save buying some new paper" (Kirkpatrick, 1960, p. 146). This gratuitous comment very likely reflects Charles's discomfort at a point when the nature of his ongoing relationship with his father had come too close to consciousness.

As life went on for Charles, he could not but have noted the parallels and contrasts of the progression of his own life and that of his father. When George entered his forties, he began to curtail his musical activities in order to earn more money as a clerk. His failure in the world of men and affairs became manifest, and humiliation was his reward. Charles had deftly averted his father's fate in his compartmentalization of music and commerce. Moreover, he had a considerable gift for business and, as he entered his forties, was at his peak in business as well as musical creativity. In contrast to George, his rewards were real, tangible, and universally respected. Interestingly, a review of his innovations and writings in the insurance field reveals similar sources to those which inspired his music. Details would deflect this study from its course, but at least one of Ives's contributions is worth noting—a booklet he wrote in 1912 called *The Amount To Carry*. It was a handbook for agents underlying a training function which he initiated in the industry and expressing a philosophy he believed in: the protection of the future and the importance of a man's independence. These latter goals, of course, reflected two of George's shortcomings (denied by Charles) at a parallel age. Before the decade of George's forties had passed, his family would be left with little more than whatever extended family might provide. (Ives as "Insurance Man" is discussed in Cowell and Cowell [1969, chapter 4].)

Charles's creative decline tracks George's in a near-uncanny way, and there is a strong suggestion that it was more than a chance occurrence. While this decline paralleled a decline in health, it certainly did not involve a loss of esteem or capacity for continued life in other spheres. For example, family life was, if anything, enriched by the adoption of a daughter when Ives was forty-one, and involvement in the business continued until his retirement in his midfifties. Moreover, there was the elegant, conscious winding up of his composing career with the publication of the "Concord" and accompanying "Essays" and the *114 Songs*. Also, as we have noted, he was later to be deeply involved in what he called "the career of music" in contrast to its composition.

The pivotal point appears to be in 1918 when in October, within a few weeks of his forty-fourth birthday, Ives sustained a heart attack. This seemed to serve as stimulus for review, revision, completion, and closure. A task was about to be completed. The heart attack had not done him in; the work of summing up and "cleaning house" after all took a good deal of energy. But his work was over: the collaboration with George had spent itself. Elsewhere (Feder, 1984), in discussing the timing of Ives's creative decline, I have considered the significance of a brief piece for chamber orchestra, "Premonitions," which was also included as a song in the *114 Songs* (1922, pp. 57–58). The selection of this text (by Robert Underwood Johnson) and its unusual setting in music calls attention to Ives's concern with aging and the spectre of death in January 1918. ("There's a shadow on the grass that was never there before/ . . . Omens that were once but jest, now are messengers of fate . . ."). He was then already experiencing the decline, although the heart attack did not occur until the following autumn. It was while recovering in Asheville, North Carolina, with Harmony nursing him, that the last creative burst of activity which was to result in the final trilogy began. Although his creative life was essentially over by the time he reached fifty, a life of generativity replaced it as Ives became involved in the advancement of new music.

I suggest that the waning of Ives's creativity is multiply determined; that physical factors were only one of several determinants; and that, among the psychological factors, those relating to Charles's ongoing relation to George—the "fates of the immortal object"—are paramount. With regard to this, I will highlight the following in concluding.

Charles's identification with George spawned his creative activity but by the same token determined its duration. Charles remained the composer during his life over the same span of time that he experienced George to have been musician in his. Charles's adolescence had coincided with his father's early forties, and in those years of unrest the idealized image of George which might have been shaken intrapsychically in any event was further shattered by the fact of his actual loss of status and esteem. The "collaboration" is thus a rewriting of musical history closer to heart's desire, a realization of his father's neglected potential and a posthumous repair of esteem. It constitutes a denial and idealization which characterized the mourning process, a process which in this case intricately involved music. Earlier in this study, in discussing "The Pond" I suggested one possible mechanism through which music articulates with the mental activity of mourning. Elsewhere (Feder, 1980b) I have shown how a constructed auditory memory (in "Decoration Day") may subserve both a memorializing and a screening function. I believe that the essential feature that renders music a particularly effective medium for mourning is its relation to affect—in this case the eliciting, binding, and symbolization of affect. Another point of contact between music and mourning, which is to be observed in Ives's work, is that of remembering; that is, the conjuring up of the past for purposes of reexperiencing and mastery and the generation of affects which is an integral part of the work of mourning. In any event the product in this instance is a body of work which may be viewed as a precipitate of memory and affect, highly transformed in the characteristic aural symbolism of music. In the final analysis it is an achievement of symbolic immortality.

As for the precise timing of the decline in this activity, who can say when one has mourned enough? At best mourning is always incomplete, its flaws a twin index of ambivalence and attachment. Perhaps as Ives entered the decade which had been his father's last, some shift occurred in his point of view—no longer the boy bereaved but now himself a father, possibly soon to die himself as his father had at age forty-nine. It was in 1916 that the Iveses formally adopted Edith, who had been with them about a year, two days before Charles's forty-second birthday. It was at about the same time that he wrote the Fourth Violin Sonata, "Children's Day at the Camp Meeting," discussed earlier, with its questioning ending, "Shall we gather at the River?" In terms of his own view of his output, he may well have later judged it to be his last major work.

Elements of guilt, which have not heretofore been stressed (with the exception of Ives's adolescent turmoil), dictated a limit to productivity. One may not survive the person who made the sacrifice. From the point of view of the superego, the "collaboration" may be thus viewed as a duty but its continuation a transgression. Mourning in this sense was flawed and revealed at length an ambivalence which had earlier in life broken through during adolescence. A measure of aggression in addition to disappointment must be considered as an expectable outgrowth of the developmental sequences outlined: Collaboration masks competition while aggressive fantasies may defensively spur idealization. There is scant evidence for the ideal mourning described by Pollock (1975b) and the "freeing" of cathexis for further investment. To the contrary, as far as composition was concerned, with his "housecleaning" and the culminating final trilogy, he was in a sense freed of a burden, however loving a burden it may have been.

The final *114 Songs* was published in 1922, the year Charles would achieve his forty-eighth birthday. The three last volumes were privately printed at Ives's expense and distributed free to libraries, music critics, musicians, and anyone who asked for them. There was no copyright. They were Charles's gift to the world. As suggested earlier, the *114 Songs*, with its scope from the pen of the fourteen-year-old boy to that of the forty-seven-year-old man, is a biography-in-miniature in music. It includes elements from nearly every aspect of Charles's life and comes close to exemplifying in a single body of work a certain philosophical point of view that Ives held related to the New England Transcendentalists: "The fabric of existence weaves itself whole. You cannot set an art off in the corner and hope for it to have vitality, reality, and substance. There can be nothing *exclusive* about a substantial art. It comes directly out of the heart of experience of life and thinking about life and living life . . ." (Cowell and Cowell, 1969, p. 97).

In these works one finds both the culmination of Charles's collaboration with George and the final flourish of a long-standing fantasy underlying their partnership in music. The gift to the world was a love gift, the issue of their relationship in life and in death. The offspring were fundamentally aural, as had been the process of its creation. They had, as Charles said in the postface, "a *few* rights, the same as any ordinary citizen." Perhaps Charles had some inkling of this fantasy of creation and birth when he asked at the climactic conclusion of the essay: "In short, must a song always be a song?"

The love gift was to be free and free of its creators as well. And, finally, as the elation of the postface may indicate, Charles himself was free of the task and burden of mourning. He was redeemed. Its product, a precipitate of the process, conceived and realized in the privacy of mind and now externalized in music, was there for the world to share.

III
Psychoanalytic Theory Applied to Musical Composition

Chapter 9

On Hearing and Inspiration in the Composition of Music

Martin L. Nass, Ph.D.

The world of the musician, particularly of the composer, is a world of sound: musical themes and sounds constantly flood his consciousness. This matrix of sound organized into music structures the composer's world and flows continuously in his life's experience. It forms the basis of his unique sensory style around which he organizes his perception of the world. In his creative endeavors the composer reaches into this stream of material and shapes his composition. He uses his auditory approach to the world as the basis for his creation and then experiences the creation as having a source outside of himself. This experience in the visual and literary arts has been studied and described by Kris (1952). I will attempt to illustrate this phenomenon as it pertains to music by presenting introspective reports of some classical and modern composers in which they reflect upon their style of composing music. While this approach presents the problem of using verbal means to describe nonverbal phenomena and involves all of the difficulties inherent in presenting early forms of thought processes by means of more structuralized forms, there is a body of biographical literature which provides some valuable information and insight into the musician's experience during inspiration. This paper focuses primarily on the inspirational phase, not on the actual details of the process of composition.

In an earlier paper (Nass, 1971) I described the "auditory style." Briefly, early listening and hearing experiences serve to develop a sensory style in certain children which is used by the ego as a means of adapting to and mastering reality. "Hearing and music may be seen as

---

The helpful suggestions of Drs. Sheldon Bach, Norbert Freedman, Mark Grunes, and Irving Steingart are gratefully acknowledged.
First published in *Psychoanalytic Quarterly*, 44:431–449, 1975. Reprinted by permission.

attempts to employ early sensitivities and early pathways in the struggles of the infant and young child to relate to and master aspects of the world. Its early use may be as a channel of contact between mother and child [A. Freud, 1963] ..." (Nass, 1971, p. 306). Such children appear to use the auditory apparatus as their primary sensory mode. In *The Psychopathology of Everyday Life*, Freud (1901) commented on sensory preference in referring to forms of memory: "Some people remember in visual images; their memories have a visual character. Other people can scarcely reproduce in their memory even the scantiest [visual] outlines of what they have experienced. Following Charcot's proposal, such people are called *auditifs* and *moteurs* in contrast to the *visuels*" (p. 47). Although Freud mentions it strictly in relation to memory, this appears to be one of the earliest statements regarding sensory preference.

There has subsequently been considerable discussion of how the preference for sound develops. A physiological hypersensitivity to sound seems to be present in some individuals, together with significant listening and hearing experiences (Bergman and Escalona, 1949; Niederland, 1958). This auditory preference, in fact, seems in some instances to have a cultural basis, suggesting that early experiences with sound are of critical importance. J. S. Carothers has discussed the role of sound in various African cultures and observes the relatively greater importance of sound experiences to sight experiences in these groups (Tanner and Inhelder, 1956). Similar observations regarding the influence of early sound experiences have been made by A. Freud (1963) and Spitz (1963). Escalona (1968) observes, however, that in infants up to eight months of age the auditory modality does not play a central role in reducing excitation but may contribute to a general soothing, involving holding and rocking. She does not indicate how these experiences may relate to a later preferred modality—a line of communication described by Anna Freud. But the connection between sound and movement has been noted by some writers (Isakower, 1939; Niederland, 1958; Nass, 1971). Sound and movement experiences relate to body rhythm and dance, and appear to originate in early rocking and holding experiences in the mother–infant relationship.

The process of musical composition has been described by several composers. In their descriptions, a consistent theme emerges. First, the auditory mode is the primary vehicle of contact, not only in the act of composing but in the overall manner of experiencing the external world. Thus, Roger Sessions (1970) states: "Composers think in terms of musical sounds, not of words or verbal concepts" (p. 107). Their world is a world of sound. Descriptions of fragments of music constantly running through their thoughts are frequent in the introspective reports of musicians and composers and in their associative material in analysis. Sound as a continuous presence is important in supplying a constant source of stimulus input in the maintenance of structure (Piaget, 1952; Rapaport, 1957) and in providing a "companion" to ward off loneliness and isolation. Much of the work in the area of sensory deprivation (e.g., Solomon, Kubzansky, Leiderman, Mendelson, Trumbull, and Wexler, 1961) as well as in the structure of the analytic situation involving silence and deprivation bears on this issue. In patients who utilize an auditory style, one frequently finds that silences are extremely difficult to tolerate. There is also a constant listening for the presence of the analyst.

The dependence upon auditory cues for the maintenance of psychic structure has been clearly shown by George Klein (1965). In an experiment demonstrating the importance of nonconflictual cues involving informational feedback, Klein interfered with his subjects' perceptions of their own voices by masking their voices. He found an increase in drive-related content when the subject was unable to hear his own voice. His findings on the function of stimuli in the maintenance of the sense of self and on their absence resulting in its disruption are in accord with other studies of sensory deprivation (Solomon et al., 1961). One central aspect of the creative act has been formulated as the building and maintenance of structure (Coltrera, 1965). The composer approaches this through his composition.

The composer's stance with respect to his experience of inspiration brings into focus issues of activity and passivity, and the issue of whether the source of inspiration is internal or external. In the majority of descriptive reports of composers, the source of inspiration is experienced as external. Kris (1952) describes this phenomenon as it appears in other art forms: "It is not the subject who speaks but a voice from out of him.... In a state similar to intoxication, elated, in a trance, not conscious of what he does ... the poet sings his song. The voice of God speaks through him to men" (p. 293).

Kris related this to the turning of activity into passivity through attributing the creation to a supernatural being, the artist thus acting as an agent. According to Kris, the tendency toward passive reception recaptures periods of longing for passive nurturance and remnants of the time when passivity was a precondition of early need gratification—the nursing period. The fantasies associated with the process of inspiration derive in content from early incorporative fantasies associated with conflicts over oedipal wishes. In Kris's patients, a passive, homosexual fantasy involving incorporation of the paternal phallus was present. In form, the inspirational act affirms a sense of incompleteness which moves toward closure. In content, it is related to fantasies of introjection and projection involving a gift-giving substance from the outside. Impregnation fantasies are frequently seen in such material. Greenacre's (1963) description of the inspirational state as involving the surrender to a power felt to be outside of the self highlights the creative person's bisexuality and his passivity in the quest for an ideal father. Arlow (1984) described a musician who, during performances, experienced inspiration as coming from the light of the sun through her body and into her fingers—a fantasy rooted in incorporative wishes.

In the discussions covered by the present paper, although the focus is on the structural characteristics of the act of inspiration, issues related to the content and to the underlying fantasies should be kept in mind. Emphasis on ego and structural aspects of a phenomenon will not exclude the important drive-related aspects (Hartmann, Kris, and Loewenstein, 1946).

In composing music, the act of inspiration is an auditory one in which the material is often experienced as heard and thus the internal theme is felt to be external. Composers frequently describe an ambiguous state during this experience which seems to be related to early cognitive experiences around hearing and the auditory modality. Audition seems to facilitate this shift to earlier modes because of its developmental closeness to movement experiences. During the process of inspiration many of these early feelings are recaptured. In attending to and working with these modes, highly organized cognitive processes are not in use initially, and the altered state of consciousness so characteristic of the creative experience is paramount (Ghiselin, 1952). It is noteworthy that this quality is described by composers. Thus, Paul Hindemith (1952) states: "The baby's own crying, whining, and playful crowing is probably the primordial material which . . . assumes a very primitive musical meaning after comparison with the already experienced feeling of general motion" (p. 38). Roger Sessions (1941) also makes this connection, stating "it is easy to trace our primary musical responses to the most primitive movements of our being—to those movements which are at the very basis of animate existence" (p. 108). The linking of movement with early experience involving body sensations is basic to Piaget's (1952) and Rapaport's (1953) formulations on the development of the sense of internal and external through action toward the object, and to formulations concerning the sense of incomplete closure in the creative individual toward which the creative act moves (Greenacre, 1958b; Coltrera, 1965).

The shift to a more loosely organized state of consciousness is characteristic of the act of musical composition. As a consequence, there is the experience of ambiguity and confusion over the internal and the external. Whether or not this needs to be conceptualized as a regressive phenomenon is questionable; some recent writers (Schachtel, 1959; Coltrera, 1965; Weissman, 1967) dispute the contention that it is regressive and hold that it may be more closely related to cognitive shifts connected with altered states of consciousness (Klein, 1959).

The creative individual thus has the capacity to call forth earlier ego states with their less structured cognitive organization and the resulting internal-external ambiguity. The shift enhances his capacity to work with earlier forms of thought which of necessity involve a more loosely organized separation between inner and outer stimulation. His own impulses are thus experienced as external in origin and he becomes the copyist and not the creator. This appears in fields other than music. Gide called it *le part de Dieu*. It involves a particular psychology which seems to be partly a response to heightened sensory awareness and an extremely close, often sensuous mother-child interaction, factors so well described in several of Greenacre's (1957, 1958a) works. The capacity to shift to more "open" states is characteristic of the creative individual and has been conceptualized as a uniquely organized apparatus of consciousness within the ego, able to distribute and pattern attention cathexis of varying modalities (Coltrera, 1965).

The attribution of the source of inspiration to the outside appears in the introspective reports of a number of nineteenth- and early twentieth-century composers who were interviewed by Arthur M. Abell (1955). Abell, who died in 1958, was a music critic, amateur violinist, and writer who was the European correspondent for the now defunct *Musical Courier*. He interviewed Brahms, Bruch, Grieg, Humperdinck, Puccini, and Richard Strauss on their subjective experiences in composing. His work is unique in providing a source of material not otherwise available. Abell's interviews were rich in anecdotal detail and contained material about these great composers that provides invaluable insights into their creative processes. The parallels between the subjective reports of these men and our observations concerning the external origin of inspiration are noteworthy. (Hebb [1974] has an interesting physiological explanation for the phenomenon, relating it to work on the split-brain procedure.)

Thus, Brahms, whose interview with Abell (1955) was transcribed stenographically, insisted that Abell not release the details of the 1896 interview for fifty years. He described his experience in composing:

> Straightway the ideas flow in upon me, directly from God, and not only do I see distinct themes in my mind's eye but they are clothed in the right forms, harmonies and orchestration. Measure by measure the finished product is revealed to me when I am in those rare, inspired moods.... I have to be in a semi-trance condition to get such results—a condition when the conscious mind is in temporary abeyance and the subconscious is in control, for it is through the subconscious mind, which is a part of Omnipotence, that the inspiration comes. I have to be careful, however, not to lose consciousness, otherwise the ideas fade away ... [pp. 21–22].

> I am in a trance-like condition—hovering between being asleep and awake; I am still conscious but right on the border of losing consciousness, and it is at such moments that inspired ideas come. All true inspiration emanates from God and He can reveal Himself to us only through that spark of divinity within— through what modern psychologists call the subconscious mind [pp. 25–26].

The conceptual model illustrated in Brahms's description is a topographic one, although it predates the formulation of the topographic theory. The description of a state of consciousness as such is the crucial factor. Applying a structural point of view, one can see that the less precise states of consciousness have a more loosely organized cognitive and perceptual character and that reaching into this material involves a high order of ego strength and flexibility. Brahms's evoking divine inspiration suggests a need to deny his own power or omnipotence and to indicate that there is only one Creator. The evocation of an ambiguous ego state is also apparent in Brahms's statement, "I felt that I was in tune with the Infinite, and there is no thrill like it" (Abell, 1955, p. 99)—a clear reference to the ambiguity encountered in the shift to a more loosely organized state of consciousness and in the recapturing of an infantile experience of bliss.

In his interview with Abell, Puccini makes a similar statement about his inspiration. In regard to Madama Butterfly he said. "The music of this opera was dictated to me by God; I was merely instrumental in putting it on paper and communicating it to the public" (pp. 156–157) and, "I know from my own experience when composing that it is a supernatural influence which qualifies me to receive Divine truths" (p. 155).

Richard Strauss, at age twenty-six, told Abell, "When in my most inspired moods, I have definite compelling visions involving a higher selfhood. I feel at such moments that I am tapping the source of Infinite and Eternal energy from which you and I and all things proceed. Religion calls it God" (p. 120). "I realize that the ability to have such ideas register in my consciousness is a Divine gift. It is a mandate from God, a charge entrusted to my keeping . . ." (p. 137).[1]

Similar statements were noted in descriptions by Wagner and Bruch, the latter composer suspending consciousness completely in his comment, "My most beautiful melodies have come to me in dreams" (p. 190).

Probably the most famous example of the appearance of the

---

[1] The evocation of God goes beyond the issue of the religious tenor of the times. Current attributions to "chance" or "luck" in explaining the source of inspiration are but more modern renderings of the same phenomenon (Kris, 1952, pp. 296–297). The passive nature of inspiration is also illustrated in Freud. In his letter to Fliess regarding the Irma dream he speculates on the marble tablet which states that " . . . the Secret of Dreams *was revealed to* Dr. Sigmund Freud" (Freud, 1887–1902, p. 322, emphasis added).

composer's inspiration in a dream comes from the eighteenth-century Paduan violinist and composer, Giuseppe Tartini. Tartini described the inspiration for his famous "Devil's Trill" sonata as follows:

> One night in the year 1713 [Tartini would have been 21] I dreamt I had sold my soul to the devil. Everything went as I had wished; my new servant anticipated my every desire. Among other things I gave him my violin to see if he could play. How great was my astonishment on hearing a sonata so wonderful and beautiful, played with such great art and intelligence, as I had never even conceived in my boldest flights of fantasy. I was so delighted, so enchanted, so bewitched that I forgot to breathe and thus awoke. I immediately grasped my violin in order to retrain, in part at least, the impression of my dream. In vain! The music which I at this time composed is indeed the best that I ever wrote, and I still call it the "Devil's Trill", but the difference between it and that which so moved me is great [Abell, 1908, p. 9].

The form of this dream presents a clear statement of the creative process so fully described in many introspective reports of composers and artists (Ghiselin, 1952). The creative impulse originates in an altered state of consciousness which is characterized by a less precise sense of inside and outside. The composer acts as a recorder and experiences the act of composition in a passive manner, as noted in the previous instances. In some experiences, the inspiration is felt to emanate from God; in Tartini's case, from the devil. Schumann experienced an alternation, particularly during his developing psychosis (Schauffler, 1945).

The factors relating to the appearance of the devil as Tartini's inspiration are of interest in relation to their content as well as form. According to biographical sources (Capri, 1945; Blom, 1954), Tartini was in hiding at the monastery at Assisi after having eloped with the daughter of a dependent of Cardinal Giorgio Cornaro.[2] The Cardinal strongly objected to the marriage when he learned of

---

[2] Several sources say that the woman, Elisabetta Premazone, was a niece of the Cardinal. However, the more recent biographical data suggest that she was the daughter of one of his workers and that the Cardinal was particularly interested in her. She studied violin with Tartini.

it and, according to the story, Tartini was forced to flee.[3] In Assisi he spent two years in hiding and studied composition and violin. His dream at the age of twenty-one, then, was dreamed in a monastery when Tartini was fleeing from a Cardinal and inspired by Satan. He reportedly found asylum at Assisi through the sexton who was a relative of his mother.

Tartini's relationship with his father was fraught with rebellion. The father, who was a landowner and a member of the staff of the Public Salt Works at Pirano, wished his son to enter the priesthood, a move the young Tartini refused to make. Instead, he initially studied law at the University of Padua and gave fencing and music lessons. He was an excellent fencer as well as an accomplished violinist. The violinist Albert Spalding (1953), in his biographical novel, *A Fiddle, a Sword, and a Lady*, captures the vivacious character of this man. The study of music alienated him from his family, who regarded him as an outcast, two of his brothers having followed the father in family pursuits. Thus, while he is living in the house of God, fleeing from an emissary of God, and rebelling against his father, who is connected with the image of the pursuing Cardinal, Tartini the fugitive constructs his greatest composition, dictated by the devil in a dream. Clearly the conflictual meaning of his rebellion emerges in the dream: the devil provides this would-be priest with the means to further his gift and thereby to extend his rebellion and alienation from his family.

The extent to which the Devil's Trill dream and Tartini's problems with passivity are related raises some additional questions regarding the passive nature of inspiration and the role of passivity in the character structure of the creative person. Rapaport (1960) and Piaget (1952, 1954) have described the human organism as stimulus-seeking and in constant need of some kind of stimulus input. This conception has followed the shift from the early topographic view of the mind as strictly a tension-discharge organization. Yet, the creative individual almost universally describes an externally focused experience and seems to deny his own role in the inspirational process. He is thus able to deny the fact that he is

---

[3] Despite the fact that this version appears in virtually every biographical source encountered, there is one writer, Capri (1945), who suggests that the evidence connecting her with the Cardinal is not definitive. I wish to express my thanks to Dr. Rachel Milano for translating substantial portions of Capri's biography.

truly creating and to maintain a passive image. Tartini copied the devil's composition; Brahms and Puccini copied God's.

A good part of the literature dealing with the creative act has followed the topographic model, viewing the creative act as close to pathological since the simplistic view of primary process thinking as pathology is locked into the theory; alternative explanations to account for the availability of shifts in mode of experience are not possible. One sees this particularly in writings on the understanding of music, in which music is explained strictly as id derivative as well as in those dealing with general issues in creative work (Montani, 1945; Michel, 1960; Eissler, 1967).

Ego psychology has made it possible to consider these issues within the normal developmental framework. This is particularly true in its application to the cognitive realm. Rapaport's (1951) and Klein's (1959) work on states of consciousness and their influence on the perceptual experience has helped to provide the basis for moving the conceptualization of the creative process into a more solid theoretical framework. This framework rests on a developmental basis that relates to the formation and maintenance of psychic structure and to the quest for stimulus nutriment. The operation of the creative act has been described as "more in accord with the economy of nonmotivational attention cathexis rather than according to those of motivational cathexis" (Coltrera, 1965, p. 670). It can be conceptualized in this connection as independent from psychopathology or regressive shifts and as operating in the service of structure building rather than exclusively as an expression of conflict and conflict resolution.

Modern composers (Sessions, 1941, 1950, 1970; Copland, 1952; Hindemith, 1952; Amram, 1968; Rosner and Abt, 1972) have described their insights in terms less animistic than those used by the earlier composers. The experience of passivity and of recapturing early ambiguous states is present. In discussing inspiration, Sessions (1970) notes that composers think in terms of musical sounds and are constantly improvising musical patterns. At times musical ideas occur in "flashes," are worked over, and elaborated. He states that the process of composing may take many different forms. The initial idea is most likely to come at a moment when it is quite unexpected, although in some manner the soil has been prepared. Thus, an idea will "seize the attention of the composer." It may "bring with it" other patterns, often contrasting: "Two extremely contrasting ideas came to me in such rapid succession that there was never any question in my mind that I must bring them together as parts of the same design" (p. 79). Here Sessions is referring to a synthetic function that brings together a higher level of integration, not unlike a good piece of analytic interpretive work. The form of these descriptions speaks to the passivity of the composer, although he does not attribute inspiration to a supernatural force. Sessions comments on the open mind in hearing music and in listening without preconceived ideas or strained effort. The analogy to Freud's (1912) description of the analyst's evenly suspended attention is noteworthy.

The auditory sensory style in composers and the fact that the ear and auditory pathways are hypersensitized in many musicians and composers require further study. Several possible determinants immediately come to mind: physiological hypersensitivity to sound, repeated exposure to sound and music, although often of a traumatic nature, or some experience with a special focus on the auditory area. The content may be related to mastery and organization of auditory trauma (Niederland, 1958), and the experiences of sound and listening may be highly libidinized. Instances of hearing disturbance or ear disease are common in the history of musicians and might be one of several factors in hypercathecting the ear. Experiences of pain in the ear and ringing or buzzing in the head during childhood appear frequently in biographical and clinical material. While this is a dimension independent of talent, it may serve to heighten auditory cathexis.

Among the world's great composers, Beethoven, Schumann, Smetana, and Fauré had serious auditory symptoms with related confusion over inside–outside differentiation. Beethoven's deafness, almost total by 1817, was progressive for about twenty years before then. In a letter to Dr. Franz Wegeler, June 29, 1801, he stated that the humming in his ears continued day and night (Beethoven, 1801). His deafness was accompanied by incessant noises, ringing, whistling. "There were ear-aches and head-aches for the rest of his life. The ear-aches being particularly troublesome every February. . . . During the bombardment of Vienna (1809) he went to the cellar and covered his ears with cushions . . ." (Cooper, 1970, p. 440).

Schumann had a history of depression and in 1844 at the age of thirty-four, suffered what was referred to as a "breakdown" following the birth of his second daughter. One of the characteristics of his illness was extreme irritation while listening to music. He stated in a letter, "For a while I could not stand listening to music. It cut into my nerves like knives" (Schauffler, 1945, p. 184). In 1854 he suffered auditory hallucinations and made a suicide attempt. Schumann described a "pronounced and painful auditory affection." He was kept awake by a single maddening tone, occasionally replaced by one other tone. This culminated in his leap from a bridge into the Rhine and his subsequent institutionalization. During the weeks between the onset of the tone and the suicide attempt he heard entire pieces of music played by full orchestra and he heard unusual instruments.

Smetana describes a similar kind of experience. According to the diary of Eliska Krasnohorska he stated:

[W]hen I look at the written music it comes to life in my imagination without any effort of will on my part, as though I could really hear the instruments and voices; only if I persist for some time, then I feel a most unpleasant vibration in my head and the ringing increases . . . the greatest torture is caused me by the almost continuous internal noise which goes on in my head and sometimes rises to a thundrous crashing. This dark turmoil is pierced by the shrieking of voices, from strident whistles to ghastly shrieks as though furies and demons were bearing down on me in furious rage . . . [Smetana, undated, p. 212].

It is conceivable that for some composers, the auditory symptoms contribute to some of the confusion between internal and external sources of inspiration. Problems in the auditory apparatus make it especially difficult to differentiate the external or internal origin of the ringing or buzzing sounds. The noises inside the head often seem to have an external origin. This distortion is associated with a more diffuse state of consciousness and a less structured cognitive organization. It is my belief that the musician is "primed" for these experiences by an auditory sensory style which builds upon his hypersensitivity to sound. Pain and other symptoms of ear disease may also contribute to a greater degree of maternal hovering and closeness; this kind of behavior has been described by Greenacre (1957) in her work on the childhood of the gifted.

The inside–outside discrimination has a further connection with the issue of Beethoven's deafness, during which time he composed his most profound works. Medical reports of his autopsy and medical discussions concerning the nature of his deafness are examined in the literature. Earlier reports suggested that his deafness was due to labyrinthitis and that his inner auditory apparatus was intact. Rolland (1929) in correspondence with a Dr. Marage, whom he describes as a specialist in the study of hearing and its variations, developed a romanticized notion that Beethoven's deafness was related to the fact that he responded more to inner cues and "overworked" his auditory apparatus. Dr. Marage suggested that although Beethoven was deaf to outer stimulation his auditory centers were "in a state of constant excitement, producing musical vibrations and hummings that he sometimes perceived with the utmost intensity" (p. 283). However, the kind of hearing he suggests does not appear to be physiologically possible. According to Edward Larkin (Cooper, 1970), the opinion most favored by otologists is that Beethoven's deafness was caused by otosclerosis, "mixed type with degeneration of the auditory nerve" (p. 440). "Otosclerosis is due to a constitutional tendency, usually hereditary, for the cartilage rim of the opening to the inner ear to turn into bone thus immobilizing the ossicle (stapes) whose base fits into the opening and transmits the sound waves" (Cooper, 1970, p. 441). Consequently, the physiological impossibility of hearing the sounds as described by Marage is clear.

It should be indicated again that difficulty with the auditory apparatus is but one of several possible sources of auditory hyperacuity in composers. The chief determinant of a low threshold for sound beginning in infancy and an auditory acuity and hypersensitivity common among musicians is probably constitutional (Noy, 1968a; Nass, 1971). The use of sound as the central vehicle of communication between mother and child is also important (A. Freud, 1963).

Characteristic of the process of musical inspiration and composition is the ability to be open, to shift into and out of a more loosely organized state of consciousness. With the few exceptions cited, most composers appear to feel that the experience is external and that they are not in charge of the process. There is a common fantasy among composers that their special gifts help them to participate in divine inspiration that floats down from above. A composer's denial of his own activity in inspiration involves the denial of his own aggression. The phenomenological experience of the self is defended against so that the composer will not feel its intensity while composing. This narcissistic defense against the aggressive self-experience has a phobic quality. For the composer to acknowledge his own separateness and control over creative impulses may be tantamount to the abandonment of early object ties, particularly those involving passive nurturance. To be able to contact this feeling and then to shift back to a more organized, active, critical state is a difficult and demanding task. The process involves an acknowledgment of a creative imagination which places one in the awesome position of making unique organizations of experience built upon a fundamental base of separateness. Greenacre's (1963) statement, "if there is to be the fullest fruition of the creative force, there must be a coming to terms with and inner acceptance of the creative ability as belonging to the individual himself" (p. 22), is relevant here. In her terms, what is involved is the resolution of the search for a powerful, idealized father. The creator's acceptance of his own creativity is facilitated by conflict resolution with diminution of guilt and self-defeating tendencies.

Similarly, Kris (1953) states that the feeling of full control mobilizes deep layers of the personality. Thus, it seems plausible to suggest that the composer's acceptance of his own creative role becomes the true statement of his independence. He can rely upon his capacity to explore the ordinarily regressed residues of past experience, contacting contents that are simultaneously unknown, awesome, and blissful. In this mobile exploration he can often recapture early experiences with sound and movement that are selectively used in the creative work.

Because of the anxiety and aggression released by contact with early experiential modes and by the shift to less organized psychic structure, however partial and temporary, it is understandable that the composer tends to stay close to the defensive experience of receiving his inspiration from outside. That this experience is not only defensive but gratifies passive wishes might be a precondition for the progression of the creative drive to artistic creation.

SUMMARY

Abundant biographic and autobiographic data from the lives of classical and modern composers lead to certain psychoanalytic inferences regarding hearing and inspiration in musical creativity.

Hearing and Inspiration in Music Composition

The composer (and gifted performer) has an increased auditory acuity, a hypersensitivity to sound and rhythm that appears to originate in the infant–mother sensorimotor relationship. The preference for sound during childhood establishes hearing as the chief sensory modality in organizing the composer's cognitive functions, his object relations, and his perception of the world. Some of the many determinants of the composer's auditory style and hypercathexis of hearing are discussed.

The composer typically experiences his inspiration as coming from without, frequently as God given. His passivity in this experience, as well as other aspects of his creativity, is strikingly similar to that of the graphic artist and writer as described by many psychoanalysts. Study of the data and the psychoanalytic literature on creativity leads the author to favor the structural theory, particularly as it pertains to ego development, in approaching an understanding of the creative process in the composer.

Chapter 10
Mourning and Memorialization through Music

George Pollock, M.D., Ph.D.

This essay will focus on musical expressions of the mourning process following object death and will specifically concern itself with compositions that range from the requiem mass, funeral music, memorial music and laments, to modern elegiac works. Particular musical compositions and what they may have meant to their composers will be used as illustrations of the thesis that mourning can occur through musical creations.

For many years I had intended to compile a list of musical compositions that dealt with death. This formidable task is no longer necessary, for the well-known British musicologist Alec Robertson (1968) has written a monumental book on the music of mourning and consolation. Although Robertson does not discuss the intrapsychic aspects of mourning music and its meaning for both creators and listeners, his is the first approach to the topic, and I am deeply grateful to him for his systematic and comprehensive study. I have made liberal use of his material in this paper without constantly quoting or giving him the great amount of credit his work deserves. In a few instances I have used data from other sources as well.

The self and its component parts is perceived by the ego as an external object with its own intrapsychic representations. The body self and the psychic self can be aspects of these component parts of

---

This research was supported by the Anne Pollock Lederer Research Fund and the Fred M. Hellman Research Fund of the Chicago Institute for Psychoanalysis.
First published in *The Annual of Psychoanalysis*, 3:423–436, 1975. New York: International Universities Press.

the self. If there are changes, losses, or transitions in these self-as-object component representations, the ego can perceive and react to them with the adaptive mourning process. Ego, the major adaptive organization in this mourning process, deals with the self as external to it, as it does with objects and their representations. Hence, whatever applies to external object relations can also apply to the self relations. This adds an additional dimension to the ego's adaptive tasks; that is, id, superego, external reality, and self. The creative resolution of the mourning for self or its components can be a self creation. In the gifted composer this may be the requiem.

My thesis is not that musical creativity depends upon object loss, but that, given such losses, the direction of musical creativity and creativity in general will be influenced by intrapsychic processes of mourning and memorialization. It may be of significance that Robertson's book, which was first published in England in 1968, bears the dedication "In loving memory of my brother, Mac Robertson, killed in action in France on 22 May 1915."

I

The Latin requiem mass had its origins in the prayers found in the catacombs, the underground cemeteries of the early Christians in Rome. In all probability, man has always had rituals dealing with death, the dead, burials, and a concept of the afterlife (Pollock, 1972a, 1974b, 1975c). In the catacombs, the Christians addressed their dead with such phrases as "Vivas in Deo" (Live in God), or "In Pace Christi" (In the Peace of Christ). Many prayers for the dead person begged forgiveness and salvation for the departed one's sins, but even more asked the dead person, who presumably was in the afterlife, to intercede for his dear ones still on earth. Robertson (1968, p. 5) cites the following examples:

> Pray for your parents.
> Pray for your children.
> May he pray for us.
> Pray for us. Pray that we may be saved.
> Pray for the child you have left behind you.
> Live in Christ and pray for us.
> Anatolius, our first-born, ours for a
> little while, pray for us.

For these early Christians, death had no finality but led to immortality. Thus "Alexander is not dead, but lives above the stars, and his body rests in this tomb, a rest that will end with a resurrection" (Robertson, 1968, p. 6).

Requiem, rest, was to become the leading theme of the mass for the dead and subsequently became the requiem mass. However, rest, sleep, and peace, the main subjects of the music sung at burial or memorial rites, directly suggested immortality and eventual resurrection.

It was not until the close of the tenth century that one could speak of a specific requiem mass. Before that time, masses for the dead were not usually distinguished from other masses. Whereas France and Spain had a dozen or more different formulas for the mass, depending on the status of the dead they celebrated, Rome had a single one for all—king, pope, peasant, or pauper.

The earliest mention of a polyphonic requiem mass was in 1474, when the Burgundian composer Guillaume Dufay directed in his will that a work composed by him be performed at his own funeral. The score of this requiem has been lost. Dufay wished his obsequies to be celebrated in Cambrai Cathedral (of which he was a canon, as well as Master of the Music), with bells, bright lights, and four candles burning before the statue of St. Anthony of Padua. On the same day, masses were to be said for the repose of his soul. He further asked that those who took part in the service receive a due reward from his estate and that bread and money be provided to the poor. For the day after these rites, he prescribed that a requiem mass be sung in the Chapel of St. Etienne by a dozen of the best singers chosen from among the vicars choral of high and low rank. After the mass had ended, after the *Requiescant in Pace* a sequential prayer chosen by them was to be performed, followed by the *De Profundis*. The requiem mass to be performed was "Missam Meam de Requiem"—a mass of his own composition—*Missa de Requiem compilata per M. G. da Fay, copiée par Simon Mellet en 1470* (Robertson, 1968, pp. 26–27).

Dufay's request to have four candles burning before the statue of St. Anthony of Padua indicated his special veneration for this saint, an affection that is further borne out by the frequent mention in his will of a mass and two motets dedicated to him. One might speculate that Dufay may have been thus beseeching his idealized saint to assure the immortality of his soul and ease his transition from life to death to afterlife.

The requiem mass of the Flemish composer Johannes Ockeghem

(c. 1420–1495) is the first known in the history of the church music of the early Renaissance. There is some evidence that Ockeghem studied with Dufay and probably was influenced by him.

Although the early requiem masses were sung, instruments were also used. An account of the mass sung on the death of Philip of Castille in 1507 mentions that organs, trumpets, trombones, fiddles, and other string instruments were played. Brumel (c. 1460–1520), a student of Ockeghem, composed a requiem that was printed in 1493, and de la Rue, also a follower of Ockeghem, wrote his requiem in 1492.

Palestrina's requiem is dated 1554. Thomas Luis de Victoria (c. 1548–1611) composed two requiem masses, one in 1585 and the other in 1603. The latter was in memory of Empress Maria, widow of Emperor Maximilian II, daughter of Emperor Charles V, and mother of two emperors. Empress Maria died on February 26, 1603, and was buried on March 1, and Victoria's requiem was presented on April 23. In his dedication he called the mass a "swan song" for the empress. However, Victoria did not publish any more works until he died on August 27, 1611. It may well have been his own "swan song"—a phenomenon that has been observed in other requiem composers, for it has been suggested that the requiem is a manifestation of the antemortem mourning of the composer for his own death. We will discuss this observation in greater detail in connection with Mozart's *Requiem*.

In 1621 Monteverdi was commissioned to compose a requiem for the late Duke of Tuscany. Alessandro Scarlatti (1660–1720) also composed a requiem mass. John Blow (1649–1708) composed an *Ode on the Death of Henry Purcell* when Purcell suddenly died at the age of thirty-six.

Michael Haydn (1737–1806), younger brother of Joseph Haydn (1732–1809), wrote a requiem mass for the funeral of Sigismund von Schrattenbach, the Archbishop of Salzburg, in December 1771. It may be that Haydn's requiem was written not only for the Archbishop but also to commemorate the death of his young daughter, who died earlier in 1771 and whose loss undoubtedly greatly grieved him. Franz Joseph Haydn's (1732–1809) *Mass in Time of War* was written in 1796 as a lament for the dead when the Imperial Armies in Italy were being routed by the French forces.

Mozart, the genius who was so prolific in his musical productivity, died at thirty-five while writing his beautiful requiem. Mozart was not unfamiliar with death. He and his sister (who was five years older) were the only survivors of their parents' seven children. Mozart, born on January 27, 1756, was to have his mother die when he was twenty-two, on July 3, 1778. On April 4, 1787, Mozart, hearing that his father was quite ill, wrote him a letter in which he expressed his thoughts about death.

> As death, when we come to consider it closely, is the time goal of an existence, I have formed during the last few years such close relations with this best and truest friend of mankind, that his image is not only no longer terrifying to me, but is indeed very soothing and consoling! And I thank my God for graciously granting me the opportunity . . . of learning that death is the key which unlocks the door to our true happiness. I never lie down at night without reflecting that—young as I am [he was thirty-one]—I may not live to see another day. Yet no one of all my acquaintances could say that in company I am morose or disgruntled. For this blessing I daily thank my Creator and wish with all my heart that each of my fellow creatures could enjoy it [Robertson, 1968, p. 64].

The question of the authenticity of Mozart's requiem has been the source of much controversy and confusion. The authenticity problem concerns the question of which parts of the work were written by Mozart himself, which were carried out by him more or less extensively and then completed by someone else, and which were composed on the basis of Mozart's outlines and sketches (Blume, 1963). Blume, in careful musical-historical detective work, concludes that the requiem was indeed substantially composed by Mozart in 1791 and that it was completed after Mozart's death by Franz Süssmayer, with the aid of Mozart's sketches and instructions.

The work was occasioned by the death of the wife of Count Franz von Walsegg, February 14, 1791. The widower conceived the idea of having a requiem mass performed on his country estate at Wiener Neustadt, and he passed the work off as his own. To preserve his secret, Walsegg used his estate manager, Leitgeb, as an intermediary, and Mozart never knew the commission came from Walsegg.

This history of the work is a dramatic one. In the last year of his life, Mozart allegedly wrote a letter in response to a request that he leave Vienna and seek employment in England. The letter, dated September, 1791, written in Italian without a named addressee and unsigned, states:

My dear Sir,
  I wish I could follow your advice, but how could I do so? I feel stunned. I reason with difficulty and cannot get rid of the vision of this unknown man. I see him perpetually; he entreats me, presses me, and impatiently demands the work. I go on writing because composition tires me less than resting. Otherwise I have nothing here to fear. I know from what I suffer that the hour is come. I am at the point of death: I have come to an end before having had the enjoyment of my talent, life indeed was so beautiful, my career began under such fortunate auspices; but one cannot change one's own destiny. No one can measure his own days, one must resign oneself, it will be as providence wills, and so I finish my death-song. I must not leave it incomplete [Robertson, 1968, p. 65].

The unknown man, Count Walsegg's emissary, was a tall, thin, grave looking man, dressed in gray from head to foot, who in July of 1791, had presented Mozart with an unsigned letter asking him to name his price for composing a requiem. Mozart agreed and asked as the entire price of the work 50 ducats, without, however, fixing the time when the work would be delivered. The messenger came once more, paid the money and promised an additional sum, stipulated that the composer was to write precisely as he wished, and only when he felt like writing, but to make no effort to discover the person who gave the commission. The mystery surrounding the commission presumably seized Mozart's mind and it is said that he looked upon it as an omen. At the same time, he was busy with *The Magic Flute* and an opera for Leopold's coronation in Prague. The mysterious messenger again approached him in August, and Mozart assured him that the requiem would be his first task. Again it is alleged that Mozart took this as a new warning not to postpone what he himself believed would be his last work. In October he worked uninterruptedly on the requiem, frequently writing until two o'clock in the morning. Although physically exhausted, he continued to drive himself on what was in essence his dying song. Constance, his wife, noticed Mozart's growing infirmity and melancholy with increasing alarm. She tried to divert him, but in November he began to speak of death, saying with tears in his eyes: "I know very well I am writing the Requiem for myself. I am too conscious of myself." Constance, exceedingly alarmed, took the score of the requiem from him, relieved now to have Mozart resting.

Soon, however, he demanded the requiem back and again became weak and melancholy. Before long, he took to bed, never to leave it, though never losing consciousness. During the afternoon that preceded his last night of life, Mozart had the score of the requiem brought to him, and several of his friends and relatives sang until they reached the Lacrimosa, when Mozart burst into tears and put the score aside. His sister-in-law Sophie came in the evening, and he said to her, "My dear, good Sophie, how glad I am you are here. You must stay to-night and see me die. I have the death taste on my tongue. I have the odor of death in my nostrils." Constance asked her sister to go for a clergyman. When she returned, she found Süssmayer at his bedside. Mozart was explaining to him how to finish the requiem, remarking as he did so: "Did I not say that I was writing it for myself?" In the evening, the crisis came and Mozart died at one o'clock in the morning on December 5, 1791. Thirty-five years after his death, his sister-in-law Sophie wrote: "The last thing he did was to endeavor to imitate the kettle drums in the Requiem." Three medical opinions assigned three different causes for Mozart's premature death—inflammation of the brain, fever, and dropsy. Since there was little money, Mozart was buried in a common unmarked grave. Of his six children—four boys and two girls—only two boys survived infancy (Holmes, 1921; Nohl, 1880; Turner, 1938).

Thus, we see how Mozart's requiem did actually become his own requiem, even though it was not sung at his pauper's funeral. Could one say that Mozart was mourning for himself? We will never know, but we do know that Mozart died while working on his requiem, and we can conjecture that he knew he was about to die.

I have indicated that not infrequently after a composer wrote a requiem composition, either he himself shortly died or he "died creatively"; that is, he no longer created music. I have suggested that this phenomenon might be explained as the composer's mourning for himself. The mourning process is related to change and transition. As such, it is a universal process. Grief, the specific reaction to the death of a significant other, is a subclass of the broader mourning process, the phases of which process I described in 1961. The loss of a particular state of oneself and the awareness of the disintegration of one's body and ego is well known to analysts from their clinical observations. I am suggesting that in Mozart's situation, as well as in that of the other composers whose mourning music was their last work, this music represented the creator's own mourning for himself and the already attempted beginning resolution of his mourning work, the emergence of a creative product that would remain, that had its own vitality. I have observed in writers, poets, painters, scientists, sculptors, and political leaders, as well as in composers of music, the use of creative works for purposes of mourning the internal loss of self- or object representations, and at the same time as the focus of redirected creative "energies." In every mourning process there is a loss to the self organization. The precipitant of the process may be an external loss, or a perception of the loss of one's body or mind. However, the mourning process, which includes attempts at resolution that may or may not succeed, may go on almost from the initiation of the process. We observe the creative product when it attains greatness, as did Mozart's requiem.

The next two major composers to write requiem masses were Cherubini and Berlioz. Cherubini's *Requiem Mass in C Minor* was commissioned in 1815 for the commemoration, in the following year, of the execution of Louis XVI. Early in 1836, Cherubini, in his seventy-sixth year, began work on a second requiem mass, this time in D Minor. He intended the work to be performed at his own funeral—which it was. Here again we may suggest that the musical composition reflects the mourning for the self before death has occurred, as well as the memorialization of the composer through his work.

Six months after Cherubini completed his *D Minor Requiem Mass*, Berlioz was commissioned by the French government to prepare a requiem to be performed on the day of the annual service celebrated for the victims of the 1830 Revolution. One might call Berlioz's requiem an anniversary mass.

Verdi's requiem, intended to be performed in the concert hall and not in the church, had deep personal meaning for the composer. Alessandro Manzoni, political figure and Italian poet, was greatly admired by Verdi. Manzoni died in Milan on May 22, 1873. His death so deeply affected Verdi that he could not attend the funeral. Verdi had read Manzoni's novel *I Promessi Sposi* when he was sixteen and summed up the deep impression it made on him when he wrote, "It's that this is a true book; as true as the truth" (Robertson, 1968, p. 100). Manzoni's book became a primer and dictionary of the emerging Italian language. Verdi saw Manzoni as

Mourning and Memorialization through Music

a saintly ideal. He wrote, "What can I say? How to describe the extraordinary, indefinable sensation the presence of the saint . . . produced in me. I would have gone down on my knees before him if we were allowed to worship men. They say it is wrong to do so and it may be: although we raise up on altars many that have neither the talent nor the virtue of Manzoni" (Robertson, 1968, p. 100). All that Verdi felt, all his reverence for the "saintly man" is expressed in the requiem—a composition that allowed Verdi not only to express his grief over the death of this idealized figure but also to honor his memory and thus immortalize the man as well as the composer. Verdi offered the requiem for performance on May 22, 1874, the first anniversary of Manzoni's death. The work, which has also come to be known as the *Manzoni Requiem*, was a great artistic and financial success.

One movement of the requiem had been written five years earlier as part of a plan to commemorate the composer Rossini on the first anniversary of his death. Verdi had announced a plan for each of thirteen Italian composers to contribute a movement for a composite mass to be performed only on succeeding anniversaries of Rossini's death. Neither composers nor performers were to receive any remuneration for their work. However, the concerts never took place, although the movements that the composers prepared are still in a library in Milan.

Musical memorial tributes were a common nineteenth-century tradition. Anton Bruckner (1824–1896) designated his Seventh Symphony "In Memoriam" for Richard Wagner. In 1876–1877, Antonin Dvořák (1841–1904) composed his deeply moving *Stabat Mater* in memory of his eldest daughter, who had just died. Modest Moussorgsky (1835–1881) memorialized his close friend, the painter Victor Hartmann, in one of his best-known works, *Pictures at an Exhibition*. After attending a memorial exhibition of Hartmann's paintings after his death in 1873 at the age of thirty-nine, Moussorgsky set ten of the artist's pictures to music as a memorial tribute to his dead friend. These piano compositions are highly descriptive and are considered masterpieces of musical characterization.

Dvořák's requiem mass, first performed in 1891, is not a mass in the customary fashion, but a full-length oratorio, and was almost contemporaneous with the requiem mass of Gabriel Fauré. Fauré composed his requiem in memory of his father, who died in 1885, but by the time it was finished, his mother had also died, and so it commemorates both of his parents. Maurice Duruflé, a French organist and composer, born in 1902, composed his requiem in 1947 and dedicated it to the memory of his father.

The personal Latin requiem mass had its origin in original prayers for and to the dead but became a vehicle for the expression of a composer's feelings following the loss of a parent, a child, or an idealized figure; as such, it can be considered an expressive, sublimated aspect of the mourning process. However, in addition, it has also been a means of publicly memorializing the dead as well as immortalizing the creator, whose musical work "lives" on after he is no longer present.

II

I turn now to other forms of music which, like the Latin requiem mass, are related to the mourning and memorialization process.

The *Stabat Mater*, a poem that vividly and poignantly pictures the Mother of Christ sorrowing at the foot of the cross as her son is dying, was frequently used as a musical text: Josquin des Prés, Palestrina, Pergolesi (who died at twenty-six, like Mozart, in such poverty that he was cast into the common burial pit of the poor), Alessandro Scarlatti, Caldara, Rossini, Dvořák (whose *Stabat Mater* was born of grief at the death of one of his children), Verdi, Gounod, Berkeley, Szymanowski, and Poulenc all composed music devoted to this theme. In 1936, moved by the tragic death of a friend in a car accident, François Poulenc made a pilgrimage to the shrine of Our Lady of Rocamadour, a pilgrimage that inspired his first religious work, *Litanies à la Vierge Noir*, and led to further religious pieces, culminating in 1949 with the *Stabat Mater*. In the dedication of this work, Poulenc commends the soul of his friend, Christian Berard, to Our Lady of Rocamadour. Poulenc had considered composing a requiem mass when his friend was killed, but felt unequal to dealing with the Day of Judgment. The *Stabat Mater*, the lamentations of the Holy Week Office of Tenebrae (which symbolizes the darkness that covered the earth from the sixth to the ninth hour after Christ died and were composed by Palestrina, Victoria, Lassus, Tallis, and Byrd), and Liszt's *Via Crucis* (Stations of the Cross), which also depicts the last hours of Christ's life, all deal with the grief and acute mourning for the dying and dead Christ.

Prayers asking that the dead may rest in peace are absent from both the official Lutheran and Anglican Services. The Lutheran reformers taught that souls freed from sin by faith in Christ alone and without any deeds were saved and went directly to heaven. Luther and his followers rejected Purgatory, masses for the dead, and many other Roman Catholic practices. The concept of "rest" was retained, but was referred to as "rest in the Lord." At a funeral service in the church, a concluding *Traüerlied* (funeral cantata) was performed. Heinrich Schütz wrote such a piece, which was published in 1636, for the concluding funeral service for his good friend and patron, Prince Heinrich. These funeral cantatas were called German requiems.

Henry Purcell wrote music for the funeral of Queen Mary (wife of William of Orange), who died of smallpox on December 28, 1694. Eight months after the funeral of Queen Mary, Purcell, himself, died at the age of thirty-six.

Johann Sebastian Bach's mother and father both died within nine months of each other when he was nine to ten years old. He also had to bear the sorrow of the loss of seven of his thirteen children, and of his first wife when he was thirty-five years of age. Bach deals directly with death in many of his cantatas. In fact, Schweitzer, cited by Robertson (1968, p. 201), indicates that the totality of Bach's thought was transfigured by a serene longing for death. Whenever the text afforded the least pretext for it, Bach voiced this longing in his music, and nowhere is his musical speech so moving as in the cantatas in which he focuses on the release of the body from death, an experience with which he had early and frequent contact.

Brahms presumably called his greatest choral work *A German Requiem* to disassociate it from the Latin requiem mass and to make it clear that the text came from the Lutheran Bible, although Christ's name is never mentioned in the text. Brahms's requiem, completed in 1866, was inspired by the deaths of Robert Schumann in 1856, and of his own mother in 1865. The work ends with a solo, "Now hath man sorrow but yet I shall again behold you and fill your heart with rejoicing," to which the chorus responds with "Oh Yea, I will give you comfort as one whom his mother comforts"—a reference that may refer to Brahms's grief over his mother's death and his hope to once again be with her. The catalog of Brahms's works shows ample evidence of his intense preoccupation with death. In 1858, when he was twenty-five years old, he composed a funeral hymn. The majority of the *Eleven Chorale Preludes*, completed in the year before his own life ended, are also concerned with death. The final one is a most moving setting of words to melody. It states, "O Welt ich muss dich Lassen" ("Oh World, I must now leave you"). The Brahms requiem is not an oratorio but a choral symphony. In it, Brahms quotes Christ when he says, "Blessed are they that mourn: for they shall be comforted" (Matthew 5:4). Brahms knew well the value of mourning through music.

III

A custom arose in the fifteenth century of writing laments for recently dead musicians in which they were named and in which the requiem mass was briefly quoted. These laments and memorial music were not limited to dead composers, although this may have been originally true. I shall now cite several examples of this nonreligious music, which had its origins 500 years ago but which still continues to the present: Ockeghem's lament on the death of Gilles Binchois; Josquin des Prés's *La Déploration de Jehan Ockeghem*; Jacob Arcadelt's (c. 1510–1597) lament for Alessandro dei Medici, who was brutally murdered by his cousin Lorenzino in 1537; Morley's and Weelkes's elegies on the death of Henry Noel, an amateur musician and a favorite at the Court of Queen Elizabeth I; William Byrd's two funeral songs for Sir Philip Sydney, Knight; Jeremiah Clarke's music on Henry Purcell's death; Igor Stravinsky's *In Memoriam Dylan Thomas: Dirge-Canons and Song*, composed in 1959, after Dylan Thomas's death; Stravinsky's expression of grief, through his *Funeral Song*, at the loss of Rimsky-Korsakoff, his teacher and close friend, in 1908; Benjamin Britten's *Canticle in Memory of Noel Mewton-Wood*, a young Australian pianist, who killed himself at age thirty-one in December 1953; Hugo Wolf's dedication of a group of his songs to the memory of his father, when Wolf was twenty-three; Leonard Bernstein's *Mass* for John F. Kennedy.

Richard Strauss's *Vier Letze Lieder* (Four Last Songs) were composed a year before Strauss's death in 1949 and could be considered as self-laments for his own approaching death.

The great laments of David for Saul and Jonathan, and for his son Absalom have inspired musicians such as Josquin, Weelkes, Schutz, and Tomkins (1572–1656). Especially to be noted is Handel's oratorio *Saul*, in which passionate grief is transformed into sound, particularly when the bodies of the king and his son are borne to their graves in one of the greatest of funeral marches.

Modern elegiac works, though still composed, seemingly are not as common as was true in earlier times. Mention has already been made of Bernstein's *Mass* for John F. Kennedy. Another such work is Hindemith's *When Lilacs Last in the Door-Yard Bloom'd*, subtitled "A Requiem for Those We Love." This work, commemorating the recently deceased President Franklin D. Roosevelt, and those who had fallen in World War II, takes its title and text from a poem of Walt Whitman which was published in 1865 after Lincoln's assassination on Good Friday, 1865. Whitman memorialized Lincoln in his poetry, and Hindemith memorialized Franklin Roosevelt with his music.

The end of World War I also inspired requiems and memorial musical compositions. J. C. Fould composed *A World Requiem* in 1923 to commemorate those who died in this war. Elgar's *For the Fallen* was also dedicated to the memory of men who were lost in the war. Arthur Bliss's *Morning Heroes*, a symphony for orator, chorus, and orchestra, was composed in 1930 and dedicated "To the memory of Francis Kennard Bliss, my brother, and all other comrades killed in battle."

Frederick Delius's *Requiem*, composed between 1914 and 1916, is dedicated to "the memory of all young artists fallen in the war." In 1940, Benjamin Britten composed his *Sinfonia da Requiem*, the score of which bears the inscription, "In memory of my parents." After World War II, Britten was commissioned to prepare his war requiem to celebrate the consecration of the new St. Michael's Cathedral in Coventry. Britten dedicated the war requiem "in loving memory" of four of his friends who lost their lives in World War II.

On November 26, 1973, Joseph La Croix (DeDe) Pierce, one of the outstanding jazz trumpeters and singers of Creole songs, died and had a "Jazz Funeral." DeDe Pierce was buried in front of three brass bands, composed of musicians who had been his friends. The three bands escorted the coffin and the mourning family to the church, where a fourth band waited inside to play a jazz mass, and then finally to the cemetery, playing dirges. Playing jazz at a funeral was a New Orleans innovation that began during the nineteenth century.

Music, the expressive form closest to the human voice, has probably been used to express grief and mourning from the time of man's beginnings. Initially an expression of affect, it became linked to prayer and a concept of the afterlife. For the listener such music may not have the same significance as for the creator, who may express his mourning through a creative and sublimated process that memorializes himself as well as the departed; for as long as his music exists he thereby achieves immortality.

The mourning process is a universal adaptational process to loss, change, and transition. It is an intrapsychic process having distinct stages and phases. Bereavement, one class of this process, has as its precipitant the loss of a meaningful external object. Mourning can also be initiated by other losses as well, such as changes and transitions reflecting bodily and psychic alterations. Mourning for the loss of self-organization may follow the same path as that seen and experienced following the external loss of the meaningful other. However, the mourning process is intrapsychic and includes the resolutional concluding phase, which may yield a creative product. In this essay I have suggested that the creation of a musical composition is the mourning for the loss and transition of the composer's self as well as the creative end-product of the mourning process, and has a new vitality of its own. This mourning creation may take the form of a new object tie, a new self-organization, a poem, a novel, an artistic production—such as a painting, a scientific advance, the fulfillment of a political ideal, or some other form which will be determined by the premourning personality organization.

Chapter 11

Form Creation in Art: An Ego Psychological Approach to Creativity

Pinchas Noy, M.D.

The psychoanalytic theory of artistic creativity has repeatedly been blamed for its one-sidedness—for the fact that it places all its emphasis on the attempt to uncover latent meaning, thereby overlooking almost all the central issues necessary for understanding the way in which art is actually created. Susanne Langer (1942) criticized psychoanalytic theory as follows:

> I do not think this theory (though probably valid) throws any real light on those issues which confront artists and critics and constitute the philosophical problem of art. For the Freudian interpretation, no matter how far it be carried, never offers even the rudest criterion of artistic excellence. It may explain why a poem was written, why it is popular, what human features it hides under its fanciful imagery; what secret ideas a picture combines, and why Leonardo's women smile mysteriously. But it *makes no distinction between good and bad art*. . . . it can look only to a hidden *content* of the work, and not to what every artist knows as the real problem—*the perfection of form*, which makes this form "significant" in the artistic sense [pp. 207–208].

And Hacker (1953) has stated: "it is equally undeniable that psychoanalysis, while eliciting many details of artistic production, and answering many peripheral questions of art, has missed or avoided the central problem. . . . In short, our science has clarified everything concerning art but art itself" (p. 129).

First published in *Psychoanalytic Quarterly*, 48/2:229–256, 1979. Reprinted by permission.

It would be unfair to blame Freud for this one-sidedness, as he purposely abstained from proposing any theory regarding artistic creativity. In his *Autobiographical Study* (1925), he wrote about the psychoanalytic theory of art: "It can do nothing towards elucidating the nature of the artistic gift, nor can it explain the means by which the artist works—artistic technique" (p. 65). And a little later, he admitted: "Before the problem of the creative artist analysis must, alas, lay down its arms" (1927, p. 177).

In his studies Freud approached art as a medium through which the artists succeed in expressing, in a sublimatory manner, their hidden wishes and conflicts. Freud therefore used art as another "royal road to a knowledge of the unconscious activities of the mind" (1900, p. 608), alongside the dream and the joke. Thus, he was more interested in utilizing the intuitive knowledge of the creative artist to understand the depths of the human mind than in applying his knowledge of depth psychology to understanding the phenomenon of artistic creativity. As a matter of fact, most of his classic papers on art, such as those on Leonardo da Vinci (1910) and Dostoevsky (1927), are studies on "psychosexuality," "parricide," and so on, more than they are studies on art.

The psychoanalytic study of the creative process proper began only with the development of ego psychology. This development shifted the focus of interest from the latent content of the mind to the mechanisms which process these contents, thereby allowing psychoanalysis gradually to begin tackling the crucial problems of artistic creativity: the process of creativity, the structure of the creative personality, creativity and psychopathology, and the artist's most pressing problem—the perfection of form.

The aim of the present paper is to examine artistic creativity from the point of view of form, to attain an understanding of the process of form creation, the function of "good form," the search for the "perfect form," and the difference between neurosis and creativity insofar as they are revealed in the study of form.

Aestheticians in the eighteenth and nineteenth centuries spent their time discussing "content versus form." On one side was the group of philosophers who, basing their work on the tradition of Plato, Plotinus, and Longinus, regarded form as the mere outer mask of the content, of an "idea" that by its verity shines through even the roughest form *(splendor veri)*—Hegel, for instance, who stated that form is only the manifestation of the idea. On the other side were those who, basing their concepts on the tradition of Augustine *(splendor ordinis)* and Thomas Aquinas *(splendor formae)*, regarded form as the dominant element for determining the aesthetic value of art; for example, Herbart, the creator of *Formenwissenschaft*, who believed that beauty in art is only to be found in form, or Schiller, who regarded form as so dominant that it is able by its very charm to demolish content.

While psychoanalysis has never taken an explicit stand in the debate about content versus form, it does seem to suit implicitly the approach expressed by those who regard form as the decisive element in determining the aesthetic value of art. Freud's main contribution to the study of art was in showing that the analysis of *any* work of art always reveals that it contains a latent meaning which is reducible to the basic motives and conflicts common to all human beings: the oedipal conflict, homosexual problems, and so on. The difference between Freud and those among his pupils who developed their own independent theories on art is found mainly in the basic conflicts to which they connected artistic activity, as in the case of Rank (1909), who related artistic activity to the infantile struggle for independence, or Klein (1929), who related it to the striving to overcome the depressive position.

According to this approach, every art is merely a sublimated expression of the same limited number of basic human themes, and the difference between the thousands and thousands of works of art is to be found only in the way these themes are handled by the artist. Therefore, there is nothing creative in the content of art, but only in the form, in the endless ways that these redundant themes are elaborated and represented in the various artistic media.

But before discussing the psychoanalytic approach to "form," we have to define the terms *content* and *form*. The classical definition of content and form, as used in philosophy from the days of the ancient Greeks, cannot be adapted to the psychoanalytic conceptualization. Freud showed in his dream studies that the latent content of a dream may be represented in a form as well as in the manifest content; for example, a triangle which may represent the oedipal conflict in a dream. While stressing the fact that the manifest dream is only a façade which has almost no significance as an organized form in itself, Freud (1915–1917) reminded us: "There are other occasions when this façade of the dream *has* its meaning, and reproduces an important component of the latent dream-thoughts with little or no distortion" (p. 181). In his studies of Leonardo da Vinci (1910) and Michelangelo (1914a), Freud showed that meanings may be expressed by elements of form, not only in the dream, but also in art.

Some modern schools of aesthetics hold a similar opinion, in that they regard form as one of the ways to express content, especially in the case of the "contentless" arts, such as architecture, ornamentation, and particularly music. Both C. C. Pratt, whose concepts stem from Gestalt psychology, and Susanne Langer, whose work is based on symbolic logic, arrived independently at the assumption that form can be a direct expression of emotion because of the similarity between the formal patterns in music and the patterns of human emotion. Langer (1953) wrote: "The tonal structure we call 'music' bears a close logical similarity to the forms of human feeling. . . . Music is a total analogue of emotive life" (p. 27). Pratt (1952) stated that "music sounds the way emotions feel" (p. 24) and explained (1954) that "only in music is the meaning of the form identical with the form itself. Here content and form are one—whatever that phrase means" (p. 289).

These modern objections to the classical distinction between content and form require us to reformulate the two concepts. For the present study I would define form as *the means used to express, represent, or organize meanings*. The creativity of the artist manifests itself mainly in the *form* of his art, in his ability to search out and find the best means to convey the meanings he is interested in expressing and, if no such means already exist, to create them. As Pepita Haezrahi (1965), the late lecturer in aesthetics at the Hebrew University, has written:

> From the viewpoint of the artist everything is content or material or mental aesthetic elements: the subject of his creation; the medium in which he works; the technique he uses; the genre he chooses; his talent, style, inspiration—everything *except the creative activity itself*. On the other hand, for the artist form is nothing more than the solution of the problem, or, more exactly, the problem-solving activity itself. If the solution of the problem is efficient, elegant and economical, it will appear successful and endowed with that aesthetic charm which is called beauty [pp. 120–121].

In spite of the similarity in formulation between the approach of the aesthetician and the psychoanalyst, there is an essential difference. For the aesthetician "content or material or mental ... element" consists of all the manifest material at the disposal of artists when they begin to shape their creations, while for the psychoanalyst "content" also includes the unconscious material pressing for expression, about which artists rarely have any knowledge before they begin and, very often, even after they have completed their work. Therefore, while for the aesthetician the activity of form creation is mainly a technique, an expression of the artist's craftsmanship and problem-solving ability, for the psychoanalyst form creation encompasses the entire gamut of mental functions involved in the control and the discharge of unconscious wishes and motives, in the regulation and adaptation of inner needs to the requirements of reality, in mastering emotions and experience—in short, in all the functions which we call ego functions. This is the reason why most modern students of form, such as Waelder (1965), Bush (1967), Moses (1968), Slochower (1974), and Niederland (1976), have approached form and form creation from the viewpoint of ego psychology. To quote Bush (1967): "The psychoanalysis of form seems to eventually reduce itself to the psychology of the ego. . . . Almost every function of the ego (defense, discharge, neutralization and binding of energy; mastering reality; etc.) has been attributed to form in a work of art. The basic paradigm is that form stands to content as the ego stands to the id, the superego and reality" (pp. 27–28). And Moses (1968) thinks that art and ego psychology may cross-fertilize one another; that not only can we use the knowledge of ego psychology to understand the formal aspect of creation, but also the study of form "can be expected to deepen our understanding of the practical implications of ego psychology and to expand its theoretical basis" (p. 220).

The approach that regards form creation in art as an expression of the ego functions will be adopted in the present study. An attempt will be made to explain:

1. "Good form" as the means used by the ego to facilitate the expression and communication of latent meanings.
2. "Perfect form" as the means used by the ego to order disparate mental elements and to reconcile opposing wishes, ideas, and emotions as a part of the ego's efforts to maintain the integration and cohesion of the self.
3. The difference between creativity and neurosis as two different ways for the ego to solve the same underlying problems.

The Function of "Good Form"

It is common for psychoanalysts to cite a dream as "creative" in their case presentations and discussions. From the strict definition such a citation would be erroneous because dreams are generally not communicable. Common to all modern definitions of creativity is the condition that creative products must, to some extent, be communicable to or sharable with others; for example, the definition of Kahn and Piorkowski (1974) who wrote: "Creativity denotes the ability to produce unique syntheses in reality-oriented, communicable forms" (p. 233).

But even if we disregard this reservation, what do psychoanalysts mean when they speak about a "creative dream"? Certainly they cannot consider the content itself to be creative, since they know that the latent meanings of a dream always represent the same limited number of universal themes and conflicts. They do not even regard the form of most dreams as creative, since they regard the transformational devices of condensation, displacement, symbolization, and so on, to be regular activities of the dream work. When they do find themselves impressed by the "creativity" of the dream work, it is usually because a particular dream uses outstandingly clever or elegant tactics to deceive the censor by finding an extraordinarily intricate way to express its meanings as blatantly as possible, despite the various defenses and controls that endeavor to prevent this. The dream is seen in psychoanalysis as the product of a dynamic interplay between the latent content pressing for expression (or at least for representation on the inner mental screen) and the opposing forces of defenses, shame, guilt, and reality considerations attempting to prevent such expression. In this "catch-as-catch-can" interplay, anything is considered fair, and the dream work may use any trick possible to enable it to represent its latent meanings on the manifest dream screen as faithfully as possible. These tactics are not limited to the dream proper, but to everything surrounding it, such as the general atmosphere in which the dream occurs (boredom, interest, enlightenment, etc.), the manner in which it is remembered, and all the various comments made by the dreamer when he or she is relating the dream ("what a funny dream"). A common example of one such tactic, presented by Freud, is the dream inside the dream, which enables the dreamer to express contents which would not otherwise be allowed to enter the manifest dream, because they are perceived by the dream itself as "only a dream."

A patient, a professional woman who speaks four languages fluently (Hebrew, Rumanian, English, and German) presented a dream in which the analyst appeared as "Dr. Tief." "I could immediately understand the reason why the dream changed your name to Dr. Tief," she explained. "I felt that your interpretation of the last session penetrated *tief* into me [*tief* in German means "deep"], and this gave me a good feeling." After additional associations, all of which led in the direction of sex, she came to understand that *"tief"* might have the additional meaning of expressing her wish to be penetrated "deeply" sexually. At the beginning of the next session she declared: "I couldn't stop marveling at how elegantly the dream succeeded in concealing my sexual wishes with an ordinary and legitimate meaning, in using the double meaning of the word *fit*." It was now the analyst's turn to be taken aback, because he had no idea of what double meaning might be concealed in the word *fit*. Without being aware of the fact that she inverted the word *tief*, she continued to explain: "Fit describes your interpretation, which was so right and exactly *fit* my problems, and *fut* which means 'to screw' in Rumanian."

We may assume that the inverted second version of the next session was the one which originally appeared in the dream. The dream used the double meaning of the word *fit* to conceal a prohibited sexual wish by emphasizing the seemingly innocent meaning. But even in this innocuous form, the word *fit*, alluding to a vulgar word like *fut*, could not be allowed access to conscious memory. Therefore, the patient's unconscious arrived at the creative idea of inverting the word to *tief*, an inversion which keeps the same double meaning but presents it in a more acceptable manner. Only after these meanings were legitimized by the analyst could she return in her memory to the original word and express her wish openly.

We could say that the dream work is always confronted with the problem of how to enable the dream to fulfill its functions in the best way, in opposition to the various forces that strive to repress its contents, to distort its meanings, and to eradicate its images from waking memory. When the dream work succeeds in expressing its meaning by finding an especially intricate form, we are so impressed by the solution that we feel called upon to label it creative.

Creative artists are faced with the same problem. They must find the best form with which to express their contents as faithfully as possible. But the problem is far more complicated than that of the dreamer in that artists strive to create a communicable message that will have some significance for others. Not only must they overcome the resistance of their own censor, they must also attract the attention of others, stir their imagination, arouse their emotions, satisfy their wishes, and provide them with a stimulating experience.

Freud described the problem of the creative artist as that of how to make daydreams communicable. In his *Introductory Lectures on Psycho-Analysis* (1915–1917) he outlined the task of the artist:

> In the first place, he understands how to work over his daydreams in such a way as to make them lose what is too personal about them and repels strangers, and to make it possible for others to share in the enjoyment of them. He understands, too, how to tone them down so that they do not easily betray their origin from proscribed sources. Furthermore, he possesses the mysterious power of shaping some material until it has become a faithful image of his phantasy; and he knows, moreover, how to link so large a yield of pleasure to this representation of his unconscious phantasy that, for the time being at least, repressions are outweighed and lifted by it [p. 376].

Many psychoanalytic studies of art inspired by this approach have tried to analyze works of art that are characterized by an extraordinarily unusual form, in order to show that these forms hide a device that enables their creators to express their hidden wishes and conflicts with the least possible disguise. A good example of this is provided by the studies of Kligerman (1962) and Wangh (1976) on Pirandello's *Six Characters in Search of an Author*. Both studies showed that Pirandello created a "dream within a dream" by creating an inverted dramatic structure in which the main characters in his play search for their author, rather than the usual situation in which the author is the one who presents his characters. By ensuring that "no event is allowed to unfold uninterrupted, no feeling to be expressed, no thought pursued to its conclusion" (Wangh, 1976, p. 325), an emotional distance is created which allows the author to express his innermost conflicts almost completely without disguise.

The problem of the creative artist is how to find the best form to transmit the meaning inherent in the work of art from its origin in the deepest layer of the artist's mind to its final destiny, and deepest layer of the mind of the consumer. Along this route there are three censor stations that the artist must cross: his own inner defenses and controls; the surface protective barrier of the perceptual apparatus of the consumer; and the inner defenses and controls of the consumer. What is called "good form" in art is that form which succeeds in getting the artist's message across these three censor stations with minimal resistance and minimal distortion of the original meanings. The first and the third of these three censors are the same as those active in the dream, and the tactics used to overcome them are similar to those used by the dream work. The second censor is the only one exclusive to art. The crucial problem of any art creation is how to cross the superficial defenses of the perceptual apparatus, a precondition for its message being admitted into the deeper levels of the mind.

The surface layer of the perceptual apparatus, which operates according to the logical secondary processes, tends to organize all the perceptual input in terms of the preestablished categories of logical thought and language and the rules of "Gestalt" (see also, Ehrenzweig [1953]). The activity of these preset programs enables the perceptual apparatus to organize, in the shortest time and in a semiautomatic manner, all the scattered elements of input into meaningful information and at the same time to act as a filter to exclude all elements of input that do not fit into its network. Almost all words that cannot be structured into grammatical sentences, ideas that do not submit to the rules of logic, images that cannot be organized into established Gestalts, are automatically rejected as being "chaotic" or "nonsense," without any examination by our surface perception. In the case of art, a book will simply be put down, music on a radio shut off, or a picture by-passed.

One of the major concerns of the creative artist is how to prevent his work from being ignored, how to pass the filter of the perceptual apparatus in order to convey the latent symbolic meanings and to arouse a response in the deeper layers of the mind. This protective barrier, the same as any defenses of the ego, cannot simply be by-passed or penetrated, but can yield when its cooperation is ensured in some way. To my mind, most of the creative endeavors of the artist are manifested in the way he shapes his artistic material into a form that will be seized upon by the protective barrier and allowed to enter into the deeper layers. Artistic style and technique can be perceived as means of attracting, deceiving, circumventing, or outmaneuvering the structural defenses inherent in the protective barrier, in order to be allowed access into the deep mind without arousing resistance and rejection.

The first one to analyze artistic style from this viewpoint was Ehrenzweig (1953). He pointed out that the arts of painting and sculpture had been subordinated for hundreds of years to the law of realistic representation; that is, an image portrayed on canvas had to fit, in a reasonable way, its appearance in reality. But, as he went on to show, deeper symbolic meanings are conveyed not in realistic representation but in distortion, discoloration, and other deviations from it. Therefore, the problem of the painter is to find a way of distorting a figure or any part thereof without violating the law of realistic representation—in other words, to represent the irrational in a seemingly rational manner. Ehrenzweig showed that the discovery, in the *quattrocento*, of perspective and the later discovery of chiaroscuro were good examples of how painters found creative solutions to this problem. To quote Ehrenzweig (1953): "the discovery of perspective was not a coolly rational achievement but, like all creative efforts, served in the first place to express an irrational symbolism" (p. 181). By using perspective, the painter may distort any part of the image, change any proportion or sizes, and always find a logical excuse, such as: "You are correct when you claim that I have portrayed this man with a big head and small body, but if you view a man from above you will see that this is exactly the way he appears." The same is true for chiaroscuro, in which the painter may discolor any part of a figure in the most fantastic way and always use the excuse: "It appears that way due to the play of light and shadow." And Ehrenzweig explained: "The discovery of perspective is hailed as a rational achievement of art enriching our knowledge of nature. Psychologically, it is nothing of the sort. It allowed the full ambiguity prevailing in the depth-mind to intrude into the well-ordered and rational world of thing-constancies" (p. 182).

The same problem, that of how to cross the protective barrier, also pertains to music. Taylor and Paperte (1958), in their survey of the various theories explaining the effects of music on human behavior, presented the psychoanalytic theory:

> [M]usic because of its abstract nature detours the ego and intellectual controls and, contacting the lower centers directly,

stirs up latent conflicts and emotions which may then be expressed and reactivated through music. Music produces in us a state that operates somewhat like a dream ... [The] main weakness [of this formulation] is its failure to indicate how music accomplishes this aim [p. 252].

Without dwelling here on the various theories of how music "stirs up latent conflicts and emotions," it is my opinion that it successfully "detours the ego and intellectual controls" (the protective barrier) not only "because of its abstract nature," but because of the use of a variety of formal means to deceive or bribe these controls and defenses.

According to Ehrenzweig (1953), music, like any other art, is based on Gestalt-bound structures amenable to the rational requirements of "surface perception." In music most of the means used to pass the protective barrier are based on an attempt to deceive the defenses by presenting a seemingly ordinary Gestalt organization, while the latent symbolic meanings are smuggled into the depth mind by the formless Gestalt-free elements lurking beneath the surface Gestalt forms. To my mind, the latent meanings are conveyed not in Ehrenzweig's "formless elements," but in the "good form," which is itself structured so as to deceive the censor.

The best example of this can be found in the form of the fugue. The fugue, with its extremely complicated, multivoiced arrangement, forces the ear to abandon its attempts to organize the tones into recognizable Gestalts (except for the few specially trained musicians who are able to organize even the most complicated fugues) and thereby thrusts the listener back into a kind of primary, chaotic, unorganized mode of experience. But, if we examine how this goal (which is in some degree the goal of all art) is achieved, we see that it is only due to the ability of the fugue form to deceive the defenses, which otherwise would never allow us to enjoy unorganized and chaotic music. At first a melody—which, according to the rules of the fugue, must always be a simple and "Gestalt-bound" form—is presented to the perceptual censor and is of course permitted to pass without any resistance. Then a second voice appears, which by its contrapuntal placement begins to disturb the "good Gestalt" organization. However, when the censor endeavors to interfere, it is evaded by something like: "What's bothering you? This is nothing but exactly the same simple melody that has already been approved." Then the melody appears a third and a fourth time, and, in many fugues, even eight times; each time the censor is forced to yield because it is clear that "it is exactly the same simple melody." But the trick in the fugue is in the placement of the melody each time it enters the composition. Because every entrance occurs in the middle of the course of the former entrance, the contrapuntal structure becomes more complicated with each new entrance, so that finally, the average musical ear can no longer organize this music into recognizable, rational Gestalts. Every sensitive music lover listening to a fugue has had the marvelous experience whereby, after succeeding for a time to organize the tones into recognizable structure, he or she suddenly, without any warning, seems to be swept away by a huge wave that flings the listener back into a kind of "oceanic" experience in which structure and order cease to exist. It is at this point that the censor, which has up to this time been deceived by the Gestalt-form, finally yields and allows the mind to enjoy freely the activity of its primary processes.

The above example demonstrates the thesis presented in this section: the creative aspect of form in art, the striving for "good form," is found in the efforts to use or to invent the best means for transmitting the meanings inherent in the work of art, from its origin in the depth mind of the creator to its destination, the depth mind of the art consumer. What is called "good form" in art is the form that succeeds in dissolving the resistance of all three censor stations outlined above, and in establishing a direct channel of communication between the depth mind of both of the parties involved in the artistic experience.

The problem of how to overcome the resistance of the censors is common to artists in all the fields of art. Therefore, if one artist succeeds in finding a new creative solution, it is certain to be taken over and used by all other artists coping with the same problem and to become a permanent technique or style of that particular art and of the culture at large.

Gombrich (1972) explained how Cezanne became "the father of modern painting." He described the problem Cezanne managed to cope with for many years and the creative solution he finally arrived at as follows:

> We know that he was interested in the achievement of a balanced design. . . . In his tremendous effort to achieve a sense of depth

without sacrificing the brightness of colours, to achieve an orderly arrangement without sacrificing the sense of depth—in all the struggles and gropings there was one thing he was prepared to sacrifice if need be: the conventional "correctness" of outline. He was not out to distort nature; but he did not mind very much if it became distorted in some minor detail provided this helped him to obtain the desired effect.... He hardly realized that this example of indifference to "correct drawing" would start a landslide in art [pp. 432–433].

Cezanne never thought that by his withdrawing, however hesitantly, from the rule of "realistic representation" he solved a formal problem that had occupied the visual arts for hundreds of years and, with this, opened the new era in art which is today called "modern painting."

The course of development in art is such that every creative invention that results in a new form in one of the arts paves the way for a whole generation of artists to convey their message to the depth mind of their public. However, as Ehrenzweig (1953) showed, with time the defenses, having adapted themselves to the new revolutionary form, once against exert their control, so that the new form becomes "the classic style," and the artist must renew his efforts to invent new and creative formal solutions to achieve the same effect—and so on. Not only do the defenses that keep the message of the artist from reaching the public change from time to time, but also the psychological needs of the public that the artist has to satisfy, which change from one historical period to the other and from one culture to the other. In addition to the basic universal needs that are satisfied by art, every period and culture is characterized by its specific needs and patterns of defenses. This requires that the creative artists continually renew their tactics and keep searching for new means to fulfill their main function, that of addressing themselves to the depth mind of the public and satisfying their psychological needs.

Thus the search for creative forms becomes a never-ending endeavor which will continue as long as human beings continue to create art.

The Function of "Perfect Form"

The aim of all art is to find the "perfect form," and the true artist, the genius in his field, invests much of his time and energy in the never-ending search for the kind of form which, by its supreme inner order, harmony, and balance, will allow him to feel a union with eternity. "Perfect form" is regarded as the essence of aesthetic beauty, and for many schools of aesthetics, beauty is nothing more than perfect form. What are the psychological functions of perfect form? What psychological needs does it fulfill?

It is my thesis that in the realm of the ego functions, perfect form is mainly related to the organizing and ordering functions of the ego vis-à-vis the self, that is, the inner efforts to maintain the integrity and cohesion of the self.[1] The self is always divided into many dimensions ("actual self," "ideal self," "social self"); into levels of maturation ("infantile self," "mature self"); and into foci of identification (object representations). The amazing thing is how, in spite of the many dimensions, levels, and foci of identification of the self, and in spite of the fact that ever-changing reality requires us to react differently all the time and to continually change our attitudes, each one of us generally succeeds, as Erikson (1968) put it, in perceiving our "selves as continuous in time and uniform in substance" (p. 218).

There is no doubt that an enormous and constant inner organizational effort is needed in order to maintain the cohesion and integrity of the self against all the forces that pull it in various directions, threatening to tear it apart. Normally we pay little attention to these efforts, whose complexity can be appreciated only when we are confronted in clinical practice with the many psychopathological syndromes that stem from the failure of such ego efforts.

The search for "perfect form" in art, including its elements of order, symmetry, harmony, and balance, is a part of the organizational effort, and it reflects the activities of the ego in ordering the disparate parts of the self, in reconciling the opposites that may threaten to tear the self apart, and in enabling the maintenance of a stable self-image.

In several of my earlier papers (Noy, 1969, 1973, 1978) I advanced the theory that the maintenance of the self, the assimilation of experience into the self, the accommodation of the self to

---

[1] The relationship between the ego and the self is still unsettled in psychoanalytic metapsychology. I tend to agree with the approach formulated by Frances, Sacks, and Aronoff (1977): "We regard the self as an intrapsychic structure and the ego as a group of functions that differentiates and integrates the self . . . " (p. 330).

Form Creation in Art

changing experience, and the safeguarding of the self's cohesion and integrity are all functions of the primary processes. These activities are carried out in dream, contemplation, fantasy, and artistic activity, as well as in the constant stream of unconscious organizational activity that goes on alongside the reality-oriented waking activity (Kubie, 1966; Arlow, 1969).

Here, we must stress the differences between artistic activity and all other primary-process dominated mental activities: while the latter are mostly carried out between the self and itself, art is an activity which is based on the communication of experience between the self and others. Because of its communicable nature, art (the same as many other "quasi-artistic" productions such as jokes, puns, etc.) cannot be limited to the primary-process activity alone, as are the other self-centered activities, but must always be based on an operational *synthesis* between the primary and secondary processes (Arieti, 1976; Noy, 1978). This synthesis between the self-centered primary process and the reality-oriented secondary process reflects the special function of art as a bridge between the self and reality. The two factors—communicable form and synthesis between the primary and secondary processes—are the reasons why artistic activity holds a special place among all the self-centered ego activities: art serves the needs of the self for self-definition vis-à-vis the object, for adapting reality to the self and the self to reality, and for communicating and sharing self-experiences with other selves.

Let us begin with a short developmental survey of the self, to see how art, through its formal elements, reflects the central developmental tasks of the self in each successive state. The most basic core of the self-image is the "body–self," the image everyone has of his or her own body. This image, which develops in the first years of life, requires that children master the principles of symmetry. They must learn that all their main body parts are doubly arranged and that each part of one side of the body is reflected inversely on the other side. Later, when they begin to differentiate the body–self from that of an object, they must learn that an object is also structured symmetrically, but that its symmetry is inverse in relation to their own: that what is on the right side of their bodies is on the left side in that of the object, and vice versa. Then, in a third phase, when they begin to perceive themselves as an object among other objects, they have to discover their mirror image and learn that, although it is opposite to that of their own image, it is inverted as well in relation to that of other objects standing opposite.

We can see that one or more of these three elements of symmetry—simple, inverted, and mirror symmetry—form the basis of every "perfect form" in art. To my mind, they reflect the never-ending effort of the ego to cope with its body–self image (simple symmetry), its relation to the object (inverted symmetry), and to its social self, the reflection of the self in the eyes of others (mirror symmetry). In the highest forms of art, such as the great architectonic musical creations of Bach, Mozart, and Beethoven, all three forms of symmetry are integrated into a unified contrapuntal structure, an achievement which reflects the successful integration of the various dimensions of the self into one cohesive self.

Beginning in the second year of life, with the development of symbolic processes, imagery, reflective thought, and the ability to define and articulate emotions and experiences, the rudimentary body–self widens gradually to encompass the wishes, feelings, experiences, images, and object representations that make up the inner mental world of the child. The organization of the memory provides the sense of "continuity in time" and the differentiation between the self and the object, the sense of "sameness" and "uniformity in substance" (Erikson, 1956, 1968).

With the passage of time the ever-broadening self becomes a more and more complicated structure, subdivided into many dimensions and role identifications. This brings about the continuous efforts, which will occupy the ego throughout its life, to organize the disparate parts of the self and to reconcile opposing motivations and contradictory feelings and emotions that may endanger the wholeness of the self. The stubborn search of creative artists to find the "perfect form" is part of their ego-organizing efforts, the search for a formula which will enable them to arrange the parts of themselves into perfect order and to unite the opposites within themselves into one integrated structure.

"Perfect form" in art is always a *dialectical form* which represents opposing ideas or feelings and reconciles them into a unity in the most simple and economical manner. "Perfect form" always conveys a sense of inevitability, as it gives one the feeling that it is the only possible way in which any particular parts could be combined, and that no word, tone, line, or color could be changed or displaced without destroying the whole. Storr (1972), who calls the form of art "symbols of integration," quoted Harrison Gough's dictum: "Somehow, a creative product must give a sense of reconciliation, of having resolved in an aesthetic and harmonious way the discords and disharmonies present in the original situation." Storr added that "by identifying ourselves, however fleetingly, with the creator, we can participate in the integrating process which he has carried out for himself" (p. 236).

Although every art is bound to its specific medium, means of representation, and rules of composition, the endeavor to create the perfect form, which will enable the reconciliation of all opposites into one unity, is common to all of them.

Hopper (1965) wrote about *poetry*: "The poem occurs at the point of intersection where the dynamic opposites contained in the chosen scope of cosmos of the poem's postulation meet and choir or orchestrate together" (p. 17).

And Storr (1972) wrote about *music*: "Music . . . provides bridges between the external and the internal, and by making a whole out of apparently disparate elements, provides a paradigm of that substantive unity of experience towards which we all aim, but from which we are so often and so inevitably deflected" (p. 239).

A good *drama* presents a group of characters who in their deeds, thoughts, hopes, and interactions, represent the gamut of human wishes, emotions, ideas, and conflicts. "Perfect form" in drama resides in the plot, which provides the frame within which the contradictory motives and actions of the characters are organized into a unity in which every character moves toward his inevitable destiny as though he were being directed by a supreme power. Each of the characters in a drama represents a personification of one part of the creator's own self- and inner object representations. The "perfect form" serves the artist as well as the public as a means of restoring inner order and of consolidating his split-off parts into one whole and cohesive self.

To demonstrate how "perfect form" reconciles opposites, let us take two examples from music, the art that is regarded by most psychoanalysts as "the purest expression of art" (Coriat, 1945, p. 410).

Example 1

Two of the forms of music—the fugue and the unisono—may be regarded as antithetical in terms of what they express. While the fugue is the most elaborated, complicated, and sophisticated form developed in music, unisono is used when a simple, forceful, and univalent message is required (as in the "Chorus of the Slaves" in Verdi's *Nabucco*). In the finale of the second act of Mozart's *Magic Flute* we can see an extraordinary example of how these opposing forms can be combined: two singers, a tenor and a bass (the "two men in armor"), sing in unisono, while the orchestra accompanies them with a classically constructed fugue, its theme based on a chorale by Luther. The contrapuntal combination of these polar musical forms is experienced as a magnificent aesthetic accomplishment, achieved by reconciling these opposites into a single harmonious structure.

It is interesting to examine the text of the libretto for which Mozart composed this piece of music. As part of his trial, Tamino, the hero of the story, must pass between two mountains, one of which contains a raging waterfall and the other a fiery furnace. Mozart, with his inimitable genius, combined the fugue and the unisono to express in the language of music the opposition between water and fire.

Example 2

The principal theme of the first movement in Mozart's Symphony No. 40 is regarded as one of the most beautiful themes ever written. An examination of various popular "guides to the listener" shows that there are some critics who describe this theme as cheerful and happy, while others describe it as gloomy and tragic. It seems to me that the greatness of this simple theme lies exactly in the fact that it conveys both feelings at the same time. If one compares this theme and that of the aria *"Non piu andrai"* in *The Marriage of Figaro*, it is clear that their rhythmical frames are almost identical, except for some minor differences in emphasis. In the Symphony No. 40, Mozart used the rhythmic frame of his lively aria, but invested it with a minor, nearly chromatic, melody which sounds almost like a cry. These two extremes, the exhilarating and happy rhythm and the sad and tragic melody, are combined in such an ingenuous and seemingly simple manner that it is impossible to imagine anything being changed in the structure of these themes, or its components being divided again.

Although both the piece from *The Magic Flute* and the theme from the Symphony No. 40 represent characteristics of "perfect form," and, in both, two musical forms represetive of opposing emotions are reconciled in a highly felicitous manner, only in the Symphony No. 40 does the form convey the sense of inevitability. In Example 1, while in *The Magic Flute* the two opposites are combined in a perfect way, they can be separated, that is, the unisono melody and the orchestral fugue are entities in themselves and each can be played and understood separately;[2] in the Symphony No. 40 the opposites are reconciled in such a perfect way that they can never be separated again. A second difference between the two pieces is that while the first is complicated and can be appreciated only by educated music lovers, the second is so simple that anyone can whistle it.

Students of aesthetics have struggled for hundreds of years with the problem of *quality* in form and have attempted to establish criteria to rank various expositions of form to distinguish between those that are mediocre, good, or excellent. Psychoanalytic ego psychology has helped to alleviate this problem by approaching form creation as an ego activity of problem-solving. Waelder (1965), in his book, *Psychoanalytic Avenues to Art*, wrote:

> The "ego," in the later psychoanalytic model, is a problem-solving agent.... Quality of performance lies, first, in the fact that a solution has been found when the task had seemed unsolvable, or would have been unsolvable by ordinary human efforts; second, in the perfection of a solution; and finally in the elegance, the economy of means.... We consider it a "beautiful" solution of a problem if everything has been achieved that we had set out to achieve and, in particular, if this has been done with a minimum of efforts [p. 44].

The *problem* that confronts the ego of the creative artist is how to find the best form through which he can order the independent and often disparate wishes, ideas, and emotions he expresses in his artistic medium. The quality of the *solution*—which is, for the art critic, the indicator of the aesthetic value of the creative product, and, for the psychoanalyst, the indicator of the efficiency of the

---

[2] Ferrucio Busoni (1866–1924) wrote a piano piece (in *Six Pieces for the Study of the Polyphonic Style*) which is based on the accompanying fugue alone.

ordering processes of the creative ego—is dependent on the following three characteristics, as outlined by Waelder:

1. The ability to solve successfully a problem which would seem unsolvable to the ordinary mind.
2. "The perfection of solution"; that is, the degree to which the form created really succeeds in ordering and harmonizing all the components of the original problem, and the degree to which this solution convinces us that it is the best possible one.
3. "The economy of means," which is the degree to which the creator succeeds in solving the problem in the most simple way, using the minimum of necessary artistic means.

The more the form created as a solution arouses in us the feeling that the solution achieved is beyond our capabilities, the more it convinces us of its inner necessity; and the more it seems simple and economical, the closer it approaches the artistic ideal of "perfect form." According to these criteria, Mozart's Symphony No. 40, by accomplishing the seemingly unachievable task of reconciling two opposite emotions in one theme, by its seeming inevitability, and by its simplicity of theme enabling it to be sung by any child, must be regarded as closer to "perfect form" than the complicated and sophisticated example from *The Magic Flute*.

The never-ending efforts of the ego to arrange its disparate and contradictory motives, ideas, and emotions into some pattern of order and inner harmony is the prerequisite for safeguarding its self-identity and maintaining the integration of the self vis-à-vis the object and outer reality. The search for the best formulas to accomplish this task is therefore a universal human endeavor common to all people.

The creative artist belongs to the small group of human beings, which also includes creative scientists, philosophers, and originators of religions and ideologies, who are endowed with the talent to supply the needed formulas. While all the members of this group cope with the same human problems, they are able to supply only those parts of the solutions which fit their own particular frames of reference and personal talents. Creative artists can offer only the formulas confined to their specific artistic medium, and only those "consumers" who are sensitive to the particular art, perceptive to its latent meanings, and able to respond emotionally to its message can benefit by using these formulas to help solve their own inner problems. Although the nature of "perfect form" differs from one art to another, according to the medium involved, the contents handled, the kind of symbols used, and the technical problems specific to that art, the essential attributes of "perfect form" are always the same.

Each of the attributes of "perfect form," such as harmony, balance, symmetry, and the reconciliation of opposites, represents one of the ego functions vital to the maintenance and maturation of the self through its various developmental states. "Perfect form" itself serves these ego functions as a formula for ordering the disparate parts of the self into an integrated unity and for securing the contact between the self, its objects, and reality.

CREATIVITY AND NEUROSIS

One of the long-standing issues in the psychology of creativity is the relationship between creativity and neurosis. The views expressed in the scientific literature vary from those that tend to equate creativity with neurosis and to explain creativity as an expression of deep psychopathology to those that view creativity as the supreme expression of mental health and of the human endeavor for self-realization and actualization (Maslow, 1962; Rogers, 1954). The many and disparate approaches to this subject stem partly from the variety of basic approaches taken by students of the phenomenon of creativity. While the psychoanalyst—who is interested mainly in the latent motives for creativity and in the developmental background of the creative personality—is impressed by the deep psychopathology revealed, the academic psychologist, who focuses on the creative processes themselves, is convinced, by the flexibility, fluency, independence, and productivity of the creative mind's thought processes, that creativity is the expression of ego strength and integrity.

Most psychoanalysts today tend to combine the above two approaches and regard the creative personality as being characterized by a deep basic psychopathology, overlaid by a strong and efficient ego. Storr (1972) gave expression to this view:

> [W]e are all divided selves, and ... this is part of the human condition. Neurotics, because of a deficiency in the controlling apparatus (a weak ego), suffer from neurotic symptoms, as all

may do at times. Creative people may be more divided than most of us, but, unlike neurotics, have a strong ego; and, although they may periodically suffer from neurotic symptoms, have an especial power of organizing and integrating opposites within themselves without recourse to displacement, denial, repression and the other mechanisms of defence [p. 229].

This view is basically in line with that of Freud, who thought that neurotics and creative artists differ not in their basic psychopathology, but rather in the way they succeed in coping with it. In 1924 he wrote: "The artist, like the neurotic, [has] withdrawn from an unsatisfactory reality into [the] world of imagination; but, unlike the neurotic, he [knows] how to find a way back from it and once more to get a firm foothold in reality" (p. 64).

Conclusion

The recent development of ego psychology has enabled us to go into more detail regarding the mechanisms common to neurosis and creativity, as well as to define their differences. Form in art is a means for: (1) overcoming the resistances and defenses of the artist and the public, in order to enable the expression and facilitate the communication of the latent wishes, emotions, and experiences of both parties; and (2) aiding the ego in its efforts to order its disparate motives and emotions in order to maintain the integration and cohesion of the self.

The creative aspect of form creation in art resides in artists' continuous efforts to find new and original ways to attain their goals: more efficient means of expression, better ways of communication, and higher levels of integration.

The solution found by creative artists is the exact dynamic opposite of the neurotic solution. Neurosis is an attempt to restore inner order and equilibrium at the cost of preventing the free expression of dangerous wishes, splitting, and the "active maintaining apart of identification systems with opposite valences" (Kernberg, 1966, p. 248).

Neurosis is characterized by redundancy and repetition, by the tendency to freeze the situation and to resist change, while creativity is characterized by never-ending attempts to renew and reorganize its forms, to search constantly for new solutions to old problems. Neurosis is a regressive solution, an attempt to restore

Form Creation in Art

inner equilibrium and adjust to reality by regressing to the infantile patterns of adaptation that have proved successful in the past, while creativity is a progressive solution, an attempt to create new and daring patterns of adaptation which have never before been tried out.

This does not mean that creativity *is* mental health, nor that a creative artist may not be neurotic, borderline, or even psychotic, but rather that neurosis and creativity represent two antipodal *attempts* to solve the same underlying problems. And, as in any attempt to solve an inner mental problem, the creative solution may also require a compromise; that is, a suboptimal solution at the cost of using defenses, producing symptoms, and so on.

In actuality the creative solutions are never perfect solutions. Thus the creative ego may succeed, through a new form created, in solving a problem in one of its mental spheres while repressing, isolating, or dissociating the problems in other spheres. There may also be a dynamic fluctuation between the neurotic and creative states, so that a problem solved in a creative way at one time, may be handled by neurotic mechanisms at another. However, the creative solution, contrary to the neurotic solution, is a step in the *direction* of mental health. When artists create new forms, they always strive to find new means that will keep them from being forced to deny, repress, distort, or compartmentalize, and that will enable them to be free to express, feel, and communicate without endangering their inner unity and integrity.

And when artists succeed in creating a new form that fulfills all their aims, that form ceases to be the possession of its creator alone and becomes the property of all those who wish to partake in the enjoyment of it, a formula to be used by all those who can allow themselves to choose the direction toward mental health.

Chapter 12
The Nostalgia of Charles Ives: An Essay in Affects and Music

Stuart Feder, M.D.

That there is some relation between music and the affective life of man appears to be well established, although its precise nature has proven to be elusive. This relation has been noted in the earliest writings in the aesthetics of music and continues to engage theoreticians even today. In *The New Grove Dictionary of Music and Musicians* (Sadie, 1980) it is noted that "musical aesthetics has been dominated by a single theme: the nature and import of that powerful yet indeterminate emotional impact that music has or is thought to have" (Vol. 1, p. 121). On a more everyday level, it is common coin that there is some intrinsic association of affect and music, and it is frequently observed in such notions as "music expresses emotions" or "music is the language of the emotions."

Although this concept reached its musicological apogee during the romantic period when it became linked with the personal expression of individual composers which trenched on the autobiographical, its roots were fixed firmly in the earlier baroque period and in its classical background. A prevalent aesthetic concept of the seventeenth century which provided a bridge between ancient and contemporary theoreticians was the *doctrine of the affections (Affektenlehre)*, which held that composers employ means comparable to those of the classical oratory and rhetoric of Cicero and Aristotle in order to "control and direct the emotions of their audiences" (Sadie, 1980, vol. 1, p. 135). The composer would thus attempt to express in some sense that emotional state (affection) which seemed appropriate to a particular text. The *stile rappresentativo* which this theoretical perspective gave rise to flourished in the music of the Florentine *camerata* of the seventeenth century. By the late nine-

First published in *The Annual of Psychoanalysis*, 10:301–332, 1982.

teenth century it was perhaps the excesses of theoreticians of music rather than the composers themselves that fostered a point of view most clearly advanced by Eduard Hanslick (1854) which critically drew into question and argued against "the widely accepted doctrine that the office of music is 'to represent feelings' " (p. 4).

Psychoanalysis, itself an offspring of the romantic period and as closely concerned with human affect as any humanistic endeavor of its time, has had virtually nothing to say about this particular aspect of human experience. The limitations of the sparse psychoanalytic literature on music have been adequately demonstrated by Sterba (1965), and subsequent writings, though of interest in some instances, have not satisfactorily approached the issue of the relation between music and affects in any specific way. This state of affairs may reflect, among other things, the relative neglect in general of affect theory within psychoanalysis, which will be discussed later. Even the notable articles by Kohut (1957) and Kohut and Levarie (chapter 1) are limited in this regard. In the latter, for example, perhaps because of their historical role in psychoanalysis, it is predominantly anxiety and its mastery which are discussed. In both, the authors are quick to identify one or another aspect of music as an example of the functioning of psychological structures. While the structural theory provides a useful framework for conceptualization, it should not in itself substitute for a demonstrated relation between mental function and musical phenomenon. It is noteworthy that these articles, reflecting the general trend of such studies, contain scant and superficially worked-out musical examples in the context of a highly refined and sophisticated psychoanalytic framework.

The most ambitious investigation of music and psychoanalysis to date is to be found in a five-part study by Noy (1966, 1967a, b, c, d). This work consists in part of a useful comprehensive review of a wide spectrum of the psychoanalytic literature that might have some relevance to music. One of its limitations, however, is to be found in the author's attempt to unite points of view which are often divergent in content (as well as heterogeneous in other ways, such as historical period) into a single unified theory of music and psychoanalysis. In the unstated underlying assumption that within this heterogeneous literature some psychoanalytic theory of music must exist, a certain amount of leveling rather than sharpening of individual authors occurs in some attempt to fuse a compromise of views. Still other nonanalytic authors (such as Langer) suffer in that their use of language may not be congruent with psychoanalytic terminology. Later Noy seems to abandon this endeavor, and with good reason, as he demonstrates in his final critique certain omissions, errors, and failures in the literature which would not make a "unified" approach feasible at this time. Neither in his review nor in his critique does Noy place any particular emphasis on questions of the relation of music and affects.

One of the failures of the literature which Noy's review reveals but his critique does not emphasize is a particular bias in the application of psychoanalysis to music which I have already noted in the above remarks on Kohut and Levarie. In this literature there is frequently an assumption bordering on the arrogant that psychoanalysis may be usefully "applied" regardless of the analyst's competence in another field. Nowhere does one find an approach primarily from the point of view of the music itself (which would be analogous to considering actual clinical data in clinical analysis), in which the primary data of the music itself is given due consideration. Studies tend to be theoretically top-heavy and superficial in applying musical data, a condition which would not be acceptable in a parallel clinical study. In his concluding comments, which have ramifications for many important issues in psychoanalysis and aesthetics, Noy (1967d) raises a question that I share with him in connection with the present study: "May the study of music contribute to psychoanalytic knowledge in general?" (p. 120).

It might be argued that if a field such as this—namely the relationship of affect and music—remains undeveloped, there is no great loss to either psychoanalysis or music. But some reflection suggests a potential value to such an enterprise which merits exploration. To begin with, careful study might shed some light on the mental life of the creative artist when it is developed within a biographical context (Feder, 1978, 1980a, 1981a, b). Generalizations might result from this which could lead to some statements about the nature of representation in the auditory sphere, in effect, auditory symbolism. Most intriguing of all is the possibility that psychoanalysis might be informed by music rather than the opposite; that a study of how affect achieves auditory representation might say something about the nature of the affect itself in mental life.

The following study is devoted to a beginning of such an exploration. In its biographical aspects it is part of an ongoing study of the life and work of the composer Charles Ives. It is natural for the other issues noted above to arise in the course of such a study, and what follows represents an initial approach to them.

Yearning for Yesterday

The works of the American composer Charles Ives are permeated with a sense of the distinctive amalgamation of memory and affect which we call nostalgia. The longing for a past forever lost which characterizes nostalgia pervades both the music and, in the case of the songs, the texts, many of which were written by Ives himself, as well. The manifestations are varied, ranging from the obscure and arcane to expressions that are disarming in their naïveté and in the frankness of their presentation. In certain characteristic musical examples diffuse, dissonant musical textures may be heard which characteristically tend to be identified by listeners as "dreamlike." Perhaps "daydreamlike" is more apt.

In any event not only affect but mood and mental state are connoted. These examples may accompany a text such as: "Scenes on my childhood are with me . . ." (Ives, 1922, No. 51) or "Songs!— Visions of my homeland, come with strains of childhood, Come with tunes we sang in school-days with songs from mother's heart . . ." (No. 55). In other examples the foregoing *invocation* gives way to an ingenuous *evocation* of a time, place, or person which appears to be almost artless: the "Village Square" and "Main Street" as they once were; "Aunt Sarah," "my uncle," and, in a single significant reference, "my father." Music is intrinsically bound in these nostalgic references, whether in a concrete fashion within the texts, or simply qua music. Aunt Sarah appears "humming gospels" (No. 43); the uncle, too, is humming a tune described in the text as if it were some tangible object, "as threadbare as that 'old red shawl,' It is tattered, it is torn, it shows signs of being worn, It's the tune my Uncle hummed from early morn . . ." (No. 102b). And Ives's father is materialized in a complex song of only nine measures whose text is: "A sound of a distant horn, O'er shadowed lake is borne—my father's song" (No. 12, see also Feder [1984]). But beyond the use of words, nostalgia is expressed in the nonverbal, nonrepresentational forms of music itself with rich variety and inventiveness and often with a high degree of specificity with regard to the nature of memory and nuance of affect.

The Nostalgia of Charles Ives

Despite the longing to experience the past which is characteristic of nostalgia and inherent in much of the music of Ives, the places and objects of that past are fixed in time. Consciously one knows there is no return. Furthermore, the wish may persist with considerable intensity despite the fact that few would want it realized even if it were to be possible! The solution to this apparent paradox lies in the concept of mental representation in which the wish and its derivatives are bound within the matrix of a particular time which is itself a part of the representation. In this "amber" of mental function, the present is like a foreign body, and the processes of change which have forged the present are painfully threatening to the integrity of the mental representation. In more human terms we can observe this in a touching vignette of Charles Ives revisiting the scenes of his childhood as a man of sixty-five. It will serve as an introduction to Ives's biography perceived as it were *in medias res*, as well as an introduction to the natural history of nostalgia. His nephew, Bigelow Ives, relates:

> We didn't see a great deal of Uncle Charlie in Danbury because he was reluctant to come back to his boyhood town and kept himself pretty much in the circle between New York and West Redding. I can recall his coming to our house only once. Danbury recalled a past that could not be recalled, and he got quite emotional whenever he came into town. I remember very late in his life, after my own father died, he did come up to the old house where he had spent so much time as a boy. The house had been moved back away from Main Street up onto Chapel Place, and the visit was probably the first one back to the old place in maybe fifteen or twenty years. Uncle Charlie spent the night there and wandered through the old house and spoke very feelingly about the north parlor, and recalled how changed it all was. I went out walking with him late that evening, and we went up as far as the Civil War monument in the City Hall Square. That was only about half a block from the old house. He actually moaned aloud when he got up there and saw how it had all changed from his recollection of it. There were no longer any elms, and there were strange new buildings not very compatible with his vision of the old town. He leaned up against a sandbox which was on the corner by the curb, and he buried his head in his hands and moaned. "I'm going back," he said, "You can't recall the past." And he turned around and went back to the old house and said he was sorry he had gone out at all. From that I had an inkling of

how deep his love was for a bygone way of life that he apparently had nurtured ever since having left Danbury as a boy [Perlis, 1974, pp. 81–82].[1]

We will explore further the nature of nostalgia and attempt to understand how it achieves representation in art form—in this case music. The life and work of Charles Ives constitute an appropriate field in which to pursue this investigation. Following a critical review of terms and concepts related to nostalgia within a review of psychoanalytic literature, we will turn our attention to a single song of Charles Ives. It is selected primarily as a point of departure for the above considerations and will be studied here from musical and psychological viewpoints, in both instances within a biographical context. Appropriate biographical details will be outlined. The interested reader is further referred to several readily available primary and secondary biographical sources (Cowell and Cowell, 1969; Ives, 1972; Perlis, 1974) and to a few psychoanalytic articles (Feder, 1980b, 1984).

THE NOSTALGIC MOOD AND THE SYNTHETIC SOLUTION

Glover's (1938) observation of over forty years ago on the "comparative neglect of the problem of affect" (p. 298) remains relatively valid today in spite of the significant contributions that have been made since that time. In that interim, others, including Jacobson (1971, pp. 3–4), who was herself responsible for major contributions, have made similar observations. In Jacobson's historical survey of the metapsychology of affects, a paradox emerges, namely, that in the course of at least two of Freud's major theoretical thrusts it was the general theory of affects which remained relatively impoverished. Freud (1920, 1926) himself had been well aware of the scope of the topic as well as the limitations of psychoanalytic knowledge. In turning his attention to the question, however, it was anxiety that became the key psychoanalytic affect, spawning theoretical developments in ego psychology at the expense perhaps of affect theory in general. Earlier, a comparable bifurcation had taken place in the consideration of the vicissitudes of instinct. Here psychic representations manifested in ideation assumed preeminence over those of the affective sphere of mental life (Freud, 1915).

[1] Reprinted with permission of Yale University Press and Vivian Perlis.

Yet it may be questioned, as Glover (1938) did, whether the entire explanation is to be sought in the history of psychoanalysis. He points out that "not only is ideational content easier to grasp than the more labile and impermanent expressions of affect, but the exploration of affect tends to arouse greater subjective resistances" (p. 297). He also underlines the exclusive focus of psychoanalytic attention on affects associated with pathological states. It is small wonder, then, that there should be such a paucity of literature on other, individual affective states, particularly those usually encountered in the normal range.

Along with theoretical contributions of recent years which have tended in the direction of closing the gap in our understanding of affects (and apart from major clinical considerations of depression and elation), there have appeared scattered studies of individual affects, some occurring in large measure within the range of normal. A group of these have been collected by Socarides (1977). Among them are articles on enthusiasm (Greenson) and faith (Isaacs et al.); smugness (Arlow), sarcasm (Slap) and arrogance (Bion); even bitterness (Alexander) and vengeance (Socarides). Boredom seems to have been of particular interest, discussed in a small literature of its own from Fenichel (1934) onward, and most recently reviewed in the contribution of Esman (1979). And love itself has not eluded scrutiny in recent studies of Bergmann (Socarides, 1977) and others. In a similar vein, interest in the normative developmental aspects of affect has been shown by investigators such as Mahler (1966) and Emde (1977) and Pine (1977).

In the course of these events, a small body of literature has accumulated on nostalgia. Prior to the last decade much of it was so unsatisfying in its psychoanalytic superficiality as to tempt one to designate it small and insignificant. In the present writer's judgment only four contributions have been significant: those of Kleiner (1970) and Werman (1977) on nostalgia proper and that of Castelnuovo-Tedesco (1978) on reminiscence which touches importantly on the subject. In a well-detailed case study Freedman (1956) reveals important aspects of nostalgia through its relation to phobia. A comprehensive review of other psychoanalytic literature is provided jointly by Kleiner and Werman and will not be undertaken here merely for purposes of completeness. Fenichel (1945) makes mention of nostalgia only twice and offers as explanation the wish to return to the preoedipal mother (pp. 405, 561).

Two other sources of knowledge of the phenomenology and function of nostalgia should be noted, however. The first is its exploration in literature, the outstanding example of which is, of course, Proust's *Remembrance of Things Past*. It is unlikely that any psychoanalytic study could tap the range of subtlety of the phenomenon of nostalgia as skillfully as Proust, though perhaps by treating it more concisely and scientifically investigators could make nostalgia available for articulation with other aspects of mental function germane to psychoanalysis. Curiously, a study by Miller (1956), called *Nostalgia* and subtitled *A Psychoanalytic Study of Marcel Proust*, reveals little about the nature of nostalgia that might potentially be discovered in a consideration of this unique subject. Although this reference is obligatory to any bibliography of nostalgia, it is truer to its subtitle than to its professed subject. It remains a most interesting study of the man rather than a significant exploration of his affective life in general, much less of nostalgia in particular. From a psychoanalytic point of view, Miller's work is not to be considered a failure so much as an unrealized opportunity.

The second source of data on nostalgia can be already found within the psychoanalytic literature, though sometimes in other, scattered contexts. The most important example of this is the subject of the role of nostalgia in the mourning process. Although usually not explicit, it may be highlighted in the works of Freud, Jacobson, and others. A single contribution in the French literature by Geahchan (1968) purports to deal with this specifically in adumbrating a particular variety of "nostalgic relationship." These papers will be taken up in more detail later.

Kleiner (1970) states the essence of nostalgia to be "a wish to return to an idealized past" (cited in Socarides, 1977, p. 473). As is the case in most definitions, an affect ("yearning") is associated with a particular range of memories ("of home and family . . ."). Both affect and memory are of and for childhood, and "recollection brings a bittersweet pleasure" (p. 479). He distinguishes the true nostalgic from the homesick individual and the sentimentalist. In the case of the homesick, reunion may lead to relief on the one hand or, where ambivalence prevails, to sadness on the other. With the sentimentalist, the emotion that is so in excess is shallow and short-lived. In either instance, a yearning and longing which are unaffected by any actuality of reunion are absent. Likewise absent is that mixture of pleasure and sadness associated with the nostalgic's reminiscences. These features are also absent in the "romantic" individual who satisfies his wishes not in a world of the past but in fantasy, "falsifying the present, idealizing the past, and glorifying the future" (p. 497). In his discussion of an earlier case study by Sterba (1940) Kleiner presses a further distinction, questioning whether the patient, a child, was truly nostalgic or simply in a state of bereavement. In any event, he is in agreement with "all" authors on the "importance of the preoedipal mother in the emotional development of nostalgics" (p. 481).

However, in considering the clinical case that Kleiner develops at length, one suspects that further distinctions are in order. The patient, a woman who was fundamentally depressed, often experienced moods in which she would have the recurrent thoughts: "What has happened to all those years? Where have they gone? What a waste." They would be followed by pressing although quiet and cozy childhood reminiscences of home and parents. At times she would regard these as "foreign bodies," although at other times these memories would be treasured. Elucidation of the dynamics with severe disappointment in her husband, attendant aggression, and guilt over the death of a brother—as well as other narcissistic wounds—point to depressive pathology. If true nostalgia were indeed prominent, it would have been present as if imbedded in the structure of a depression. But the description leaves the matter open to question since the nostalgic's characteristic reminiscences are not generally compulsive, forced, or ego alien. They are more likely cherished, the experience frequently sought but not obsessively pursued or experienced as compulsion.

It seems to me, rather, that another shading of affect is suggested in Kleiner's case: namely, *regret*. This attitude which the present holds toward the past is different from the one characteristically seen in nostalgia. It is not one of active, conscious, current longing for a past that may have in fact been valuably rich. Instead, it says more simply, "I'm sorry." It mourns the "something bad" that happened in the past as well as the very passage of time and its lost potential. If anything, the past is devalued. Thus regret is closer to depression and quite distinct from nostalgia. Finally, Kleiner postulates episodes of true nostalgia as representing the "untroubled" state of the first year of his patient's life prior to her brother's death and mother's depression, hence confirming the early, maternal, preoedipal roots identified by other authors. However, his own clinical material appears sparse on this account, as one might well expect such material relating to the first year of life to be!

Kleiner may well be correct, but I am inclined to judge his case unproven. On the other hand, rich material would tend to confirm an oedipal source with the disappointing husband and idealized father as the warp and woof about which the fabric of nostalgia is woven. A somewhat similar condition prevailed in the life of Charles Ives, as we shall see presently. In his case, while intuition, conjecture, and theory may support the association of the affect of nostalgia with a preoedipal mother, most, if not all of the available, studied data point to the father, both oedipal and preoedipal.

In Freedman's (1956) case of a young composer nostalgic memories were first used in the analysis as a resistance. Later, the patient "developed phobic reactions *for the very locales* which had been the object of previous nostalgic feelings" (p. 84; emphasis added). Nostalgia here was seen to serve a counterphobic function. It enabled the patient to maintain the positive side of an ambivalent relationship toward his father by fostering repression of his aggressive wishes. Freedman suggests that "the presence of destructive drives in the nostalgic complex can account for the air of depression which permeates nostalgic feelings" (p. 91). The depressive component of nostalgia in this case resulted from "a passive subjugation to the father and a redirection of the death wish towards the self" (p. 92). While Freedman agrees with Fenichel and others that nostalgia represents "a return to the pre-Oedipal situation," he no doubt means a regression, since he views it in terms of "the repression of the Oedipal death wish toward the father" (p. 92). This formulation has considerable relevance to Ives's nostalgia. The ambivalent element in the latter's relationship to his father is considered elsewhere (see chapter 8). There is no doubt that Ives's tie to the people, places, and objects of the past had, among other elements, a defensive component.

Werman (1977), in his study of "Normal and Pathological Nostalgia," defines nostalgia as an "ambivalently felt, affective-cognitive experience" (p. 392), a human experience which he regards as not only ubiquitous but, for the most part, normal. He distinguishes it from fantasy in that it is not a substitute for a wish but is valued as an experience in itself. In effect the wish is intrinsic to the experience; in yearning for the past one does not desire actually to return, nor would one be likely to find the fulfillment of such a wish gratifying. Werman explores the borderland of normal and pathologic nostalgia. The most elegantly elaborated example of the latter may be seen in the case of Proust, where the working through of mourning for his mother was avoided, thus the lost object retained. "His work became the aesthetic crystallization of his nostalgia," and "the past, like a fossil, lives on in the amber of his great novel" (p. 394). In less distinguished cases, an idealization of the past may serve to master and disguise feelings of rage and guilt attendant upon rejection. Through the twin mechanisms of "denial and idealization associated with bittersweet feelings" a condition "analogous to a screen affect" (p. 395) may result. Other defensive uses of nostalgia include the "counterphobic" in which the yearning of nostalgia masks underlying "destructive tendencies to objects" (p. 396).

Werman further develops Geahchan's work (1968) on the role of nostalgia as a substitute for mourning. His summary of the core ideas in this otherwise far-ranging and discursive French study is quoted: Geahchan

> [D]escribes a "nostalgic relationship" to the lost object which avoids both internalizing the object and the work of mourning, and safeguards the subject from psychosis. While fantasy seeks to fulfill a desire, nostalgia repetitively tends toward a fantasy that never takes place. In this way the "desire" is fulfilled by not being realized, and so the subject is safe from the loss of the object, and the object is guarded by being kept in the nostalgic relationship [p. 391].

Werman spells out what would be a full clinical picture of such a failure of mourning and also cites certain "normal" aspects, thus pointing to the probability that mourning is an ideal concept which is never totally accomplished and that "it is natural that a part of the object be retained" (p. 396). The object may be displaced to the places with which it was associated in a context of nostalgic memories. Werman is impressed with the "relative absence of a conscious representation of objects in nostalgic memory" (p. 397) and sees this as a defensive displacement that serves to avoid psychic pain, one of a range of defensive operations that depend upon the nature of unconscious strivings toward the object and the degree of ambivalence. Nostalgia is seen as having the potential of serving as screen affect or screen memory.

An interesting implication in the above work relates to the

nostalgic work of art and merits clarification. Although in general I see neither clinical nor theoretical necessity for advancing the notion of an avoidance of internalization in the above formulation, the concept of an *organized mental structure* (here, the "nostalgic relationship") which is an elaborate compromise formation, yet at the same time is in some way isolated from other aspects of mental function, is an intriguing one. Thus isolated, with mourning avoided and the object preserved—fixed as it were in time, and tending toward "a fantasy that never takes place"—it would seem to constitute a condition of mental life conducive to the invention of some related work of art. Such a work, not merely isolated (in its psychological sense) but externalized and fully separate from the mind that created it, might be endowed in terms of form as well as content with displaced elements of object and fantasy. Thus it would reflect mental structure and be, from a formal point of view, congruent with and parallel to the mental condition that engendered it.

It may well be that it was in this sense that the great accomplishment of Proust may be said to represent "the aesthetic crystallization of his nostalgia." The frequency with which artists have been occupied with nostalgia in their work has often been noted. Freedman (1956), for example, cites Thomas Wolfe and others (p. 84).

In a study of reminiscence and internal objects, Castelnuovo-Tedesco (1978) attempts to discriminate reminiscence as a phenomenon in itself from the type of remembering characteristic of nostalgia. Stressing the "-algia" aspect of the derivation of the term, he emphasizes its painful nature and believes it to be basically "a regressive state and a form of depression" (p. 22). The feeling tone "is bathed in conflict." It would seem, then, that he believes all nostalgic states to be pathological ones. "By contrast," he writes, "during reminiscence the mood may be neutral or even joyful, as one savours the finding that the past has not vanished but is still available and serviceable." Because the past exists immutable in mental representation, one can yearn for it and contemplate its presence at will and with pleasure. The activity is conflict-free. Moreover, this activity subserves the cohesiveness of the self and its continuity in time by maintaining contact with internalized objects, that is with self and object representations.

Castelnuovo-Tedesco does not address the question of whether nostalgia, too, might be a mental activity with a similar function.

There is a feature in the work of all the authors I have mentioned which, while obvious enough on reflection, might easily be overlooked if not stressed. That is, in every instance cited the affect of nostalgia appears to be defined in terms of two distinct components. One is the ideational element, the other some "feeling" element that at times is designated to be the affect itself. However, it is clear enough in context that the affect is constituted by *both* the "feeling" and the ideational element. Werman (1977), for example, tends toward his more rigorous and inclusive definition of nostalgia as an "affective cognitive experience" (p. 392). Kleiner (1970), however, tends to designate the affect (yearning) as separate from but associated with ideation.

Brenner (1974) has clarified these important distinctions in the context of his unified theory of affects. He writes: "Affects are complex mental phenomena which include (a) sensations of pleasure, unpleasure, or both, and (b) ideas. Ideas and pleasure/unpleasure sensations together constitute an affect as a mental or psychological phenomenon" (p. 540). The sensations of pleasure and unpleasure, associated with drive tension or discharge, stem from the earliest phases of life and constitute the "undifferentiated matrix from which the entire gamut of the affects of later life develop." Only as ideas gradually become associated with such sensations, which in and of themselves are not affects, do the affects of later life develop. Brenner stresses that the affect consists of *both* sensations *and* ideas.

Such a view emphasizes the rich possibilities of affective experience in human life since affects are individually unique experiences and "are never precisely the same in any two individuals" (p. 544). At the same time it deciphers these often elusive experiences along familiar psychoanalytic lines: "In clinical work 'an affect' is a particular constellation of sensations of pleasure and unpleasure together with ideas, both conscious and unconscious, whose content, origins, and functional role must be determined in the usual analytic way . . ." (p. 546). While Brenner does not deal specifically with nostalgia in this or subsequent contributions, it is clear that his work may provide a framework for its consideration which has both developmental and structural implications. Brenner (1975) does take up the broad spectrum of depressive affects into which nostalgia would doubtless fall. Emphasizing the unpleasure aspect of depressive affect, he points out that, like anxiety, it may have a signal function which is capable of instituting defense and psychic conflict (p. 13). The conceptual framework which this line of thought provides in no way excludes a consideration of nostalgia. To the contrary, it can account for some of its paradoxes. For example, in nostalgia, the ideational nuance which lends the affect its particular flavor lies in the paradox that, while "something bad" has happened, it succeeds the "something good" which earlier prevailed. Thus, from the point of view of the pleasure–unpleasure component, the affect is marked by both elements to varying degrees. Nor does the paradox of "something bad" coexisting with "something good" necessarily imply psychic conflict. Affects may incorporate such tensions and may indeed still be considered to be in the normal range of human behavior and experience.

Jacobson (1971) touched on this in her paper "On the Psychoanalytic Theory of Affects." In offering a classification of affects that is basically a structural one, she uses the term *tensions* with respect to intrasystemic conditions and reserves the term *conflict* for the intersystemic. One implication of her work is to stress the fact that affects are normal psychic manifestations. She is critical of the psychoanalytic terminology which "might easily tempt us to regard emotions as altogether pathological or exceptional phenomena" (p. 6), with its further implication that the neurotic is an "emotional" person. Jacobson, however, did not view affects along the lines of Brenner's "unified theory" and, along with many psychoanalytic writers, thought in terms of some separation of the "feeling" component from other aspects of affect. For example, she suggested that the terms *affect* or *emotion* might be applied to the general range of affective phenomena and the term *feeling* best reserved for subjectively felt experience.

In her study on normal and pathological moods Jacobson (1957) distinguishes moods from other affective states. Again in structural terms, she outlines "a cross-section through the entire ego, lending a particular uniform coloring to all its manifestations for a longer or shorter period of time" (p. 68). Unlike other affective states which result from specific tensions, definite ideational representations and specific objects, moods "find expression in specific qualities attached to all feelings, thoughts and actions." It will be noted that here, speaking of both affect and moods, Jacobson comes close to Brenner's concept of affect as consisting of sensation and ideational components. An affect state may become a mood. It may "spread out and dominate the whole field of the ego" (p. 69). While she views moods as temporary states, "temporarily fixated modifications of the concepts of self and the world, based on generalized interferences and transferences from the past," they may become chronic and "enduringly fixated." While at first she tended to emphasize the primitive nature of moods in general, especially (from an economic point of view) in contrast to the well-developed, secondary-process management of affect, she revised this in the light of Weinshel's (1970) work, accepting his belief that not all moods are aspects of archaic functioning and that stability may be provided by what Weinshel emphasizes is mood structure.

Quite in passing, Jacobson (1957) fixes the normal role of nostalgia in mourning. The "nostalgic search for lost happiness" is part of a circular process characterized by affective discharge and promoted by reality testing in which there is a reactivation of sad memories of what happened and happy ones of what was lost. "Pleasure is mixed with pain because what is searched for and lost" (pp. 82–83). In mourning without trace of depression (and accordingly lacking the aggressive component) self-esteem is unshaken. One wonders whether Jacobson would have considered the same to be true in pure nostalgia.

Weinshel's thoughtful consideration of moods (Panel, 1968; Weinshel, 1970) includes in its substance some ongoing dialogue with Jacobson who, he demonstrates, falls short of considering moods as psychic structures despite her otherwise richly structural approach. Jacobson acknowledged this and certain other "neglected points" in a revision (1971) of a paper she had written in 1957. She found herself here in "full agreement" with Weinshel's (1970) principal refinements and formulation: "[Moods] are psychological structures, of varying complexity, reflecting a certain degree of synthesis and organization, and depending on contributions from all three psychic systems. . . . In the mood we can observe a mixture of affects as well as the products of varying defensive activities directed against the affects" (p. 315).

Weinshel repeatedly stresses a conceptualization of mood as a psychic structure "in which the behavioral and cognitive components cannot be ignored" (p. 315). He sees them, however, as separate, not fused, with the affective component lending the mood "its distinctive emotional coloring." He thinks it likely that, in turn, the mood structure serves to bind affect. Yet the "affective discharge associated with moods" is not necessarily archaic and may "reflect the development of highly differentiated affect channels and subtly differentiated structures." He writes of "archaic elements" within the vast range of mood structures rather than seeing them, as did Jacobson, as the result of the normal ego preserving "the use of this primitive economic modality" (p. 317). Emphasizing normal function himself, Weinshel points to the regulatory function of mood structures observing the "more organized discharge patterns of secondary process" and "tension maintenance as well as peremptory discharge." Finally, he writes of the "stability" or "quasi-stability" of these structures that endow the mental apparatus with an effective ongoing means of discharge and notes the "elegance with which the ego is often able to combine diverse psychic elements" (p. 318) within such structures. Citing Hartmann (1939), he emphasizes the adaptive role of such a blending of "the archaic with the highly developed, the irrational and the rational, the primary process with the secondary, the undifferentiated with the differentiated" (p. 318). These issues relate not only to the integrative function of the ego per se but to important ramifications such as creative activity and style. They reflect, notes Weinshel, what Hartmann (1939) terms "the synthetic solution to complex psychological problems" (p. 77).

Thus are we drawn from this excursion into the relevant psychoanalytic literature on nostalgia, affects in general, and moods in particular, full swing, back to a consideration of the mind of the artist and the central focus of this study, Charles Ives and nostalgia. I have stressed elsewhere (Feder, 1980b, see also chapter 8) the creative solutions to both conflict and the normative problems of life which Ives found in his pursuit of musical composition. Such solutions in life and in art cannot merely be chalked up to manifestations of the archaic or the pathological. Nor does Kris's (1953) concept of "regression in the service of the ego" (p. 177) do them full justice. Broader structural concepts such as Weinshel's (1970) begin to probe the complexity of mental function in this regard. Certainly simplistic psychoanalytic "explanations" of artistic products do not reflect well on either science or art. Hartmann (1939), too, observes a "multiple layering" in the creation of art similar to that which he "demonstrated in thinking" (I would be inclined to amend the phrase to "demonstrated in other forms of thinking"). He goes on to say that art "is not a mere archaic residue" (p. 77). In fact, its very origins provide for "varied possibilities for synthetic solutions." In what I would consider to be a crucial analogy to mental structuralization and the integrative and synthetic functions of the ego, Hartmann writes of the "tendency toward order inherent in every work of art, even when its content or intent represents 'disorder.' " He isolates the essential position of art in mental function, delineating it from mere fantasy: *"The process of artistic creation is the prototype of synthetic solution"* (p. 77; emphasis added).

With the foregoing in mind we return to the questions raised earlier regarding the purpose of this study which may now be stated more specifically: (1) How can affect achieve representation in art, here music? (2) What is its structure; its anatomy and physiology, as it were? (3) What relation does such a piece of work bear to the mind of the artist of which it is a product, and how do the two articulate with each other? (4) Can the product, the work of art—here, more specifically, the artistic representation of an affect—reveal anything about the functioning of that mind? Obviously, such questions are too ambitious to be approached in any single study, yet they may serve as a frame of reference as we proceed. More modestly, and appropriately, we will go on to a consideration of a brief song which is intended as no more than a point of entry into these complex issues. Shifting focus, but against the background of the foregoing psychoanalytic review, we will first attempt some preliminary musical analysis before moving on to a further study of the mind of the man who created it.

"THE THINGS OUR FATHERS LOVED"

Charles Ives composed "The Things Our Fathers Loved" (Ives, 1922, Number 43) in 1917 when he was forty-three years of age (Fig. 12.1). It is a brief song of only 22 measures written for voice with piano accompaniment. It had been adapted from a *Piece for Small Orchestra & Organ*, now lost, which was probably written in 1905 (Kirkpatrick, 1960, pp. 43, 201). It was characteristic of Ives to work and rework musical ideas over some period of time and to produce different versions, individual pieces thus appearing in whole or part in different form. The at least twelve-year gestation period of this song, then, was not unusual. Ives's (1905) comments on the manuscript page frequently veered from matters of dating and bibliographic orientation toward diaristic marginalia. Thus, at

250   Psychoanalytic Explorations in Music

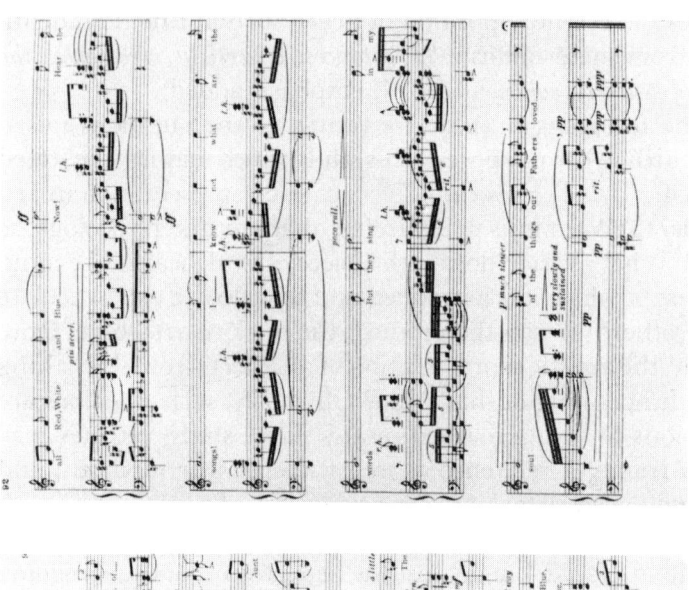

Figure 12.1. "The Things Our Father Loved (and the greatest of these was Liberty)" by Charles Ives, ©1955 by Peer International Corporation. International copyright secured. All rights reserved including the right of public performance for profit. Used by permission. Reprinted with permission of Presser & Co.

the end of the ink fair copy of this piece made by a copyist's hand, Ives scrawled the commentary: "This was arranged for V & piano—from a score for organ, trumpets Trombone Clar Fl Strings as a kind of brass band outdoors organ indoors and shown to Franz Kaltenborn, when we were living at 65 C.P.W. NY But F.K. wouldn't play it" [sic]. Typically, the boundaries of music, life, and even individual pieces were flexible. A further example is seen in sketches of this song to be found on a few available spaces of manuscript paper which was principally devoted to a set of ragtime pieces of 1902 to 1904 (Kirkpatrick, 1960, p. 40).

The text of "The Things Our Fathers Loved" was written by Ives himself (1922, No. 43, pp. 19–92):

> I think there must be a place in the soul all made of tunes, of tunes of long ago; I hear the organ on the Main Street corner, Aunt Sarah humming Gospels; Summer evenings, the village cornet band, playing in the square. The town's Red, White and Blue, all Red, White and Blue. Now! Hear the songs! I know not what are the words. But they sing in my soul of the things our Fathers loved.

Appropriate to the words, the music itself is in some literal sense "made of the tunes of long ago." Not only are many actual musical quotations incorporated into its musical structure, but in addition there are musical fragments that sound as if they *ought* to be portions of old tunes. Further, there are more subtle allusions, as we shall see presently, to "tunes of long ago," such as certain characteristic accompaniment figures. Finally, personal allusions abound which can be traced in the mental life of the composer. Above all, it should be borne in mind that, despite the foregoing, this is not a medley or random pastiche. It is a tightly fashioned work of art whose affective features are highly condensed in representation and intense in quality. I would venture that in this it is a miniature masterpiece and, as such, a good, if not exaggerated example of a style frequently encountered in this composer.

The listener may or may not be of a generation or culture for whom the specific tunes or old-fashioned musical features have any meaning. Similarly, the specific small-town references in the text may be lost to such an auditor. Strictly speaking, if one did not have some sense of small-town life in post-Civil War America, many of the referents would appear to be merely sentimental, quaint at best. However, the degree to which certain elements of these times and places still persist in some form in modern popular culture is remarkable; as is the meaningfulness of the generalized ideas, even where they do not specifically exist in the individual experience. Most important, it is striking how little historical orientation it might take to appreciate that this music is universally "about" times which are past, places which have changed, and people who thus persist only in memory. The words alert us to this at the outset: the locus is in inner life, "a place in the soul." The music, through its various devices which we shall examine in detail, likewise discloses the inward quality characteristic of private mental experience. For example, no tune achieves anything approaching full performance; only snatches, fragments, vague allusions are perceived as they might exist—not "memorized," but *in* memory, a recollection suffused with affect and a manifestation of mental structure peculiarly its own. Its progress in time resembles free association. These elements are reflected in the music, although in no simple way. Before this can be developed further, it becomes necessary to study the music in detail.

The song opens with a melodic line which may well be a typical *incipit* for hymns, folk songs, and sentimental tunes. At the same time, it is one of the several musical quotations in the song noted by Kirkpatrick (1960, p. 264), namely, "Dixie Land." It is rendered much more slowly than its usual tempo, lending a dragging, doleful quality to the music which is associated with the first phrase: "I think there must be a place . . ." Similarly, it may be noted that further on, in the second full phrase at the words, "The village cornet band . . . ," though the melody outlines the quotation of a portion of one of Ives's favorite songs. "The Battle Cry of Freedom," it is at the same time some general prototype of the kind of sprightly tune one may have heard many times over (like "Polly-Wolly-Doodle," etc.). Incidentally, just considering these two elements alone, banal as the manifest musical ideas may seem, a formal principle is apparent: they are essentially inversions of each other musically.

Such tunes, specific and prototypic simultaneously, invoke the kinds of ideas with which their words are characteristically associated. Usually they are of the places, people, things, and times gone by which characterize nostalgia. For example in "Dixie Land": "I wish I was in the land of cotton / Old times there are not forgotten. . . ." Later (measures 7–8) the same musical figure will be revealed as the hymn tune "Nettleton" bearing the words, "Aunt Sarah humming Gospels." Nostalgic references are enriched while, at the same time, from a musical viewpoint, a formal principle obtains as we observe a variant of the first tune. Further, in purely formal principle the tunes themselves may carry nostalgic association in such musical elements as tempo, rhythm, and characteristic melodic contour.

A word about the overall form is in order before continuing with details. The fundamental, underlying structure is deceptively simple, a two-part song consisting of two sections of eight measures each—as straightforward overall as any individual tune quoted within. However, modifications lead to apparent complexities and disjunctions which are interestingly sophisticated within this basically simple framework. The two principal parts are to be found in measures 1–9 and 11–22. Measure 10 is a transitional insert, and, if one takes into account that measures 15–22 represent an augmentation in time (the eight measures actually an expanded four), one finds the basic structure. This consists essentially of two complementary eight-measure phrases comprising a simple two-part form (A—measures 1–9; B—measures 11–14 plus expanded measures 15/16, 17/18, 19/20, 21/22).

Within this framework are introduced fragments of tunes as if they belonged where situated from a formal point of view in the phrase. For example, to the words, "I hear the organ on the Main Street corner, Aunt Sarah humming Gospels . . ." is set the balancing, "answering" phrase to the first eight measures. But its first portion ("I hear . . .") quotes "On the Banks of the Wabash, Far Away," in the music while the second ("Aunt Sarah . . ."), the hymn tune "Nettleton." The former ("Wabash") is also miraculously reminiscent of "My Old Kentucky Home" (measure 5) in both melodic outline and characteristic rhythm.

The transitional measure (measure 10, "Summer evenings . . .") may be heard melodically as if it were some inner fragment of a tune, perhaps again some prototypic one penultimate to a cadence such as in "Massa's in the Cold, Cold Ground." It is also the occasion musically for the kind of dissonant, polytonal chord progression which imbues the "dreamy," far-away character mentioned earlier.

The second part of the song (starting at measure 11 at "The village cornet band . . .") is based primarily on fragments of "The Battle Cry of Freedom" and its melodic homologues to the Gospel hymn, "In the Sweet Bye and Bye." It opens with a quotation of the melody appropriate to the words of the former, "Yes, we'll rally 'round the flag, boys, we'll rally once again. . . ." A syncopated figure bridging measures 11 and 12 distorts it slightly, and a few notes are deleted, but the harmonic implications of the outline of the tune remain intact. In the following measure (measure 13, "The town's . . .") the quotation is explicit as the tempo quickens ("in a gradually excited way"), and a crescendo briefly builds to the climax of the song, *fortissimo* at the words, "Now! Hear the songs!" Here, in the notes of longest duration in the melodic line so far, there is a sense of broadening which parallels the rhythmic augmentation of the melody. Although here reminiscences of prominent features of both "Battle Cry" ("The Union forever . . .") *and* "Sweet Bye and Bye" ("In the sweet etc. . . .") may be sensed (all incidentally on the same—dominant—note of the scale), yet another tune is alluded to strongly, "The Marseillaise"! Its words, "Aux armes, citoyens!" are as if superimposed upon "The Union forever" as well as "In the sweet bye and bye," all fixed within the melodic context of the climax of the Ives song and its associated words, "Now! Hear the songs!"

One is suddenly aware of the significance of the immediately preceding words which may have seemed somewhat loose logically or of a different, more metaphorical and poetic nature from the earlier concrete imagery: "The town's Red, White and Blue, all Red, White and Blue—." Packed into this revealing musical moment are multisensory allusions to experiences that include the physical congruities of the tricolor and the American flag, the visual as well as auditory features of the "the village cornet band playing in the square," and associated affects of a rather complex nature. These last are signaled in the conventional composer's instructions *crescendo* and "in a gradually excited way." In the same moment, historical allusion is rich, including the Civil War and both the French and American revolutions. The latter related appropriately to the subtitle Ives gave to "The Things Our Fathers Loved": "and the greatest of these was Liberty." The climactic moment is realized harmonically with a peculiarly Ivesian usage of a common musical device, contrary motion. As the melodic line ascends to its highest point, the bass moves in the opposite direction, the intervening harmonies handled in various ways. This device bears mention in that the "opening" and "quickening" quality which may be thus achieved is one that Ives had often used with texts associated with fervent hopefulness and with an image of the future that touches on personal eternal life or social utopias (Feder, 1984).

The musical "moment" mentioned above requires in fact only a few seconds of actual duration—perhaps a dozen at most from the transitional measure through "Now! Hear the songs!" The rich ideational allusion and potential affective concomitants in this passage, which the above account barely taps, are nothing short of astonishing. Infinitely more time is required to explicate and develop (as above) what the composer condensed into seconds, a rich portion of which the responsive listener may experience. The simultaneity of impression is, of course, an important part of this experience, and it is not the composer's intent that his music be slowed down for an analysis of its "information." Though it does, however, "inform," this is a special kind of knowledge, one in which a complex structure of idea, affect, memory, and experience is formed in word and tone. It consists of a musical structure of diverse elements. This is analogous in many respects to that mental structure postulated earlier as characteristic of moods. While it reveals itself over the course of a period of time, the presentation of simultaneous elements is characteristic. We will return to this later in the discussion.

The foregoing example is interesting not merely with reference to certain general types of music, but also with specific reference to Ives himself. There is *nothing* in the foregoing musical analysis that requires anything more of the listener than relaxed attention, a reasonable knowledge of the English language, and average formal and cultural education. No musical, much less musicological, training is necessary, nor are there any arcane historical references. Although this may be less true for the current generation than it would have been for an audience of Ives's time, perhaps a half-century ago, when the tunes quoted were more commonly known and historical references were more familiar, it is nevertheless still the case to a significant degree. Beyond the implications for understanding the present study, Ives is making a statement about the nature of the composer and his audience. Despite his contemporary musical idiom, experienced as forbidding by many even sophisticated listeners, Ives basically considered his music to have been written for the common man, who—average as he was—was to be respected as individual. This feature in itself—of a nature both aesthetic and ethical—relates to the music at hand, for it embodies the values implicit in popular beliefs about both the Revolutionary and Civil wars as well as the trajectory of American history. The heart of Ives's patriotism was reflected by the fact that for his music the common man was a competent listener.

Returning now to the song, we may complete the present analysis of its components. So far, it has been the melodic line that has been chiefly emphasized. Other elements, such as accompanying figures, tonality, prosody, and the text proper, remain to be considered, although it should be clear at this point that exhaustive analysis of even this brief song is unfeasible and a practical selectivity must be exercised. At the climactic measure 15, an accompanying figure in the piano introduces successively three phrases of the "Battle Cry of Freedom" ("The Union forever...," repeated) with accents displaced, in such a way as to end in a high-pitched, ghostly reminiscence of the phrase associated with the words, "Hurrah boys, Hurrah!" The latter is sounded as if to echo the end of the vocal phrase "I know not what are the words..." (measure 18). Actually a variation of this had already begun in the accompaniment (measure 11) at the words "The village cornet band" where a literal march version is found.

The final vocal phrase starts with a literal quotation of "In the Sweet Bye and Bye" which at this summating point in the song may draw one's attention to the musical fact that inherent in this simple tune is the first motif and its inversion, the melodic lines associated with the initial two sections of the song. The first descends ("I think there must be a place..."); the second ascends ("The village cornet band..."). A descending bass figure emphasizes the pause (measure 20) which prepares us for the final cadence which seems to be clearly aiming for the key of G major, the key of the last quotation, "But they sing in my soul—." But the cadence is deceptive, and the song (which, incidentally started in the key of C major) ends in a somewhat unstable inversion of the tonic chord—not of G—but of G-sharp major. To the listener the end sounds not only uncertain but as if frankly out-of-tune, a not infrequent Ives device (see chapter 8).

Briefly, other elements of accompanying figures may be noted. At the structurally central points of this seemingly "naïve" piece a skilled, expressive, contemporary yet personal style prevails: the transition (measure 10), the climax (measures 14–15), through most of the last section, and the final cadence (measure 21). For the rest, there is a virtual anthology of devices associated with sentimental, folk, march, and homemade music in general. Several might be pointed out in illustration: (1) the simple "parlor piano" beginning, in which the singer is started off with chord and note (measure 1); (2) the arpeggio and syncopated chord style (measures 5–9); (3) march rhythms (measures 11–14); (4) canonlike imitations of melody (measures 2–3), and so on.

As we shift our attention to the text, it should be noted that, much like the tunes, the words are never forced into a metric straitjacket and are preserved in their natural, spoken rhythms. Deviation occurs only for purposes of emphasis (". . . all *made* of tunes . . ."). The words, it will be recalled, are Ives's own. Perhaps the most strikingly obvious feature of the text is that, with the exception of the title, which is also the text for the final phase, it is entirely in the present tense. In its climax it is the "Now!" which is emphasized, a pressured immediacy. Only in the last line is it made explicit that these vivid experiences evoked with so strong a sense of presence belong to the past. This is underlined musically in the deceptive cadence that introduces this revelation. Here, in the fabric of word and music, is that peculiar tension of past and present which we have seen to be characteristic of nostalgia.

Earlier, the brief sequence of experiences had somehow revealed themselves to have been past experiences through their association musically with "the tunes of long ago." Further, they are presented in a *style* of spontaneous reminiscence in which they appear to be recollected, episode following episode, without benefit of conjunction or preposition: "I hear the organ . . . Aunt Sarah humming . . . Summer evenings . . . The village cornet band . . . The town. . . ." The music perhaps more subtly portrays its pastness through affective attitudes objectified in musical form. Fragments of tunes, in addition to conjuring up places (for example, "home" in the condensation of "The Banks of the Wabash" and "My Old Kentucky Home") at the same time cast an image of emotion—the longing association with places in these sentimental songs. It is as if the experiences were artistically pared down to some musical essential analogous to a few brushstrokes. There is no question in the listener's mind that these episodes exist only in the "Now!" of memory. Despite the literalness of musical thematic quotation and even the "quotation" of other stylistic devices, it is clear that the artist has constructed an *image* of the past, not an imitation or parody in the old style. An intrinsic element in this structure is the emotion associated with the past as if it were a commentary on it, realized in the materials of music. Despite the apparent literalness, as we have seen, there is often a profound ambiguity that opens vistas of allusion with regard to the historical past. *Thus, the possibility exists through this ambiguity for some generalization, by means of which the specific nostalgia of others may be elicited, although its details may differ.*

It is time, place, and person—as well as certain associated emotions—that this work is "about" in both isolated text and fully formed composition. The element of time is apparently the most ambiguous of all. However, one knows the answer to the riddle of whether events belong to the "then" or the "now." The key lies in the fact that all mental events occur in the present and that memories of the past comprise one such group of events. The "events" are fundamentally events of mental representation. Thus we intuitively understand the psychological truth of the poetic statement in the text of "a place in the soul all made of tunes, of tunes of long ago." There is a compelling authenticity in the words which engages us and which is simultaneously reinforced by the music. The latter is achieved manifestly by literal quotation but enriched with associated emotion and historical allusion.

Just as the text is rich in "place" and "person," so is the music. The places are specific and entirely unambiguous in the text: Main Street corner (in Danbury, Connecticut, U.S.A.) and the village square. The people, somewhat less distinct, are Aunt Sarah and, collectively, the village cornet band (of which Ives's father George was founder and bandmaster). In fact, there could have been several potential "Aunt Sarahs" in Ives's biographical dramatis personae. The references are so apparently private as paradoxically to become universal, eliciting one's own "Main Street" peopled with the objects of the past. As such they are, of course, no more or less than symbols that can accommodate literal referents as well as those of greater symbolic complexity with regard to person, place, and time. In this, the music participates richly.

For example, the past alluded to in the song which is perhaps most prominently developed, "The Battle Cry of Freedom," goes beyond the composer's personal past (see chapter 8). Although still known and sung in the post-Civil War period of Ives's childhood, and as such a part of cultural memory, it was more specifically a song of the period of the youth of Ives's father, George. The latter had been at seventeen the youngest bandmaster in the Union army. He was the idealized hero of Charles's youth and was to remain so after his death when Charles was twenty. The love of father and of country which developed within Ives constituted his unique form of patriotism and extended to the concepts, objects, and paraphernalia of patriotism including the American flag. Of all the tunes Ives quoted in his works the two used most frequently were "The Red, White and Blue: O Columbia the Gem of the Ocean" (nineteen times) and "The Battle Cry of Freedom" (sixteen times) (Kirkpatrick, 1960, p. 265).[2]

The flag as an object, the songs which celebrate it, and even the concepts with which it is associated lead us to extend the range of content from time, place, and person into things and even concepts. Ives's feelings for the past were often objectified in such things. For example, one of the most precious tangible objects which belonged to his father and which Ives kept throughout his life on a shelf in his studio was his father's cornet (Perlis, 1974; see chapter 8). Allusion to this is perhaps obscured in the present song in "the village cornet band." The concept of "Liberty" is literally referred to as the "greatest" of "the things our fathers loved" in the subtitle of the song.

Before leaving the quoted material, several facts of interest might be pointed out. A song such as "In the Sweet Bye and Bye" may be quite firmly rooted in a particular time and atmosphere. This is a Gospel tune of the immediate post-Civil War period of Charles's childhood, and he was well familiar with it. Like many such songs, and, in keeping with a theme which much interested Ives in the selection of texts for his own songs, its content touches on reunion: "In the sweet bye and bye we will meet on that beautiful shore." It starts, "There's a land that is fairer than day" (Feder, 1984). Ives

---

[2] Although Kirkpatrick (personal communication) lists "The Marseillaise" as quoted three times, he does not include "The Things Our Fathers Loved" and has expressed doubt as to whether this is in fact a quotation.

quotes this tune nine times (Kirkpatrick, 1960, p. 264). The Gospel Aunt Sarah sings is in fact sung to the very words, "Aunt Sarah singing Gospels." The hymn tune is, as indicated, "Nettleton," another favorite of Ives (ten times). He reminisced in his *Scrapbook* (after learning of its being sung by grunting black laborers in the south), "*Nettleton* was one of the Gospel and Camp Meeting Hymns, and down in the Redding Camp Meetings I heard it sung with exactly those accents, almost shouted. . . ." Here it is quite piously rendered. The Redding Meetings, incidentally, were often led by George and are the subject of other tender reminiscences in Ives's *Memos* (1972, p. 54). Again with regard to "place," Ives had a strong feeling for locale. Redding was about eight or nine miles from his boyhood Danbury. Years later, in 1912, when he was thirty-eight and four years married, he purchased country property in West Redding which was to remain his second home until his death and from which he was buried.

Individual tunes with their own particular histories and associations and Ives's feelings about them rendered them special objects, as if they were treasured "things" in themselves. Elsewhere in Ives's (1922) prose writings, in a moment of fantasy, he endows his own songs with human qualities, writing in a highly elaborated analogy that "a song has a few rights, the same as other ordinary citizens" (Postface, unnumbered). The passage ends in a couplet: "—In short, must a song / always be a song!" In the present short song, in another elaborate metaphor, "they sing in my soul"—that is, in that special "place in the soul all made . . . of tunes of long ago." Words, of course, have their own symbolism and a rich one here. However, they do not bear the entire symbolic burden, and perhaps not the most significant one. Tunes constitute a deeper knowledge of their own.

The Morphology of Nostalgia

It has been noted how frequently nostalgia and related affects seem to be associated with works of art—in particular, music. Perhaps among the arts, it is music, par excellence, which can most adequately symbolize this range of emotion. Certainly in any primitive lexicon of individual emotions gleaned from critical writings on music terms such as "longing," "yearning" (the romantic *Sehnsucht* for example) must have a prominent place. Yet the phenomenon itself has attracted little critical, much less psychoanalytic, attention. Reik (1953) explores this area sensitively in *The Haunting Melody*, a book rich in anecdote relating music and affect, especially in the nostalgic range. In a study with a complementary title, *The Haunting Lyric*, Hannett (1964) analyzes the "personal and social significance of American popular songs." She notes the prevalence of "anaclitic affects," in romantic and sentimental songs of a depressive and hostile nature, as well as in those of separation anxiety. In this category also lyrics pertain to "possessive dependence" and gratifying dreams of reunion (pp. 242–244). In specifically nostalgic references, she observes an "acknowledgment of the inability to re-create the old reality," hence the current pleasure derived from "the elaboration of nostalgic memories." She finds that in the romantic songs "the quality of longing is minimal," whereas in the sentimental songs ("in the home-and-mother frame of reference") there is a sense of urgency: "Until reunion is accomplished.... There can be no peace" (pp. 245, 251). It should be again emphasized that Hannett's study deals with the words, not the music of these songs.

Why, then, should nostalgia and associated affects be so intimately related to music? I suggest that the answer be sought in certain aspects of earliest preverbal human experience, specifically those relating to the acquisition of inner and outer orientation which result ultimately in a sense of identity. In the most elementary test of mental function performed in the assessment of "mental status" in a neurological or psychological examination, it must be determined whether an individual is oriented as to person, place, and time. To what degree can he discriminate self and important others?; what is his perception of locus, his grasp of the continuum of time? In this complex of basic orientation can be found the *content* which is invariably associated with nostalgic affects: the human and nonhuman objects as well as the places of present and past, and the sense of the continuity of self over this scale of time. Words and music encode this content in different ways, the distinguishing feature of music being the creation of expressive form. Essentially nonverbal in nature, it may most appropriately encode nonverbal (although not exclusively infantile) experience. Dealing as it does with the manifestation and manipulation of time, it may more aptly reveal aspects of time than other of the arts. Finally, one may wonder, along with Isakower (1939), at the *exceptional* position of the auditory sphere in human orientation and psychological development. The greatest refinement of this faculty is to be found in the creation, perception, and apprehension of musical form which must reflect, however elusively, other aspects of the mind that made it.

Although the subject matter of this study draws one inevitably to considerations perhaps more central to aesthetics and criticism, its principal aim continues to be psychological—and, more specifically, psychoanalytic—in its pursuit of the mental life of one man and the products (here, a single gem in miniature) of his creative life. In saying this, it is clear that other statements of value have been made literally or implicitly in the above musical analysis of its rich structure. This is not the place to attempt a review of even the relevant writings on musical aesthetics. The history is long, the documents often mutually contradictory, and above all the philosophical mode of discourse is not completely appropriate to our purposes here. However, as noted at the beginning of this essay, a consistently recurrent trend in this literature which is relevant and which has occupied writers for centuries has to do with the relation between music and emotion. There is scarcely a writer in this area who does not intuitively believe that such a relation exists and, further, that it constitutes a major source of human involvement with music. Implicit in the relation between music and emotion is the notion of communication of some kind, hence the essential expressiveness of music. Most frequently a philosopher's musical aesthetic fits more or less neatly within the framework of his particular system of philosophy. Thus there are differing views of how the acoustical phenomena of music articulate with the most private human emotional experiences.

In his study of *Symbolism in the Nonrepresentational Arts*, Stevenson (1958) has occasion to cite several of these traditional aesthetic theories as well as Suzanne Langer's particular theory of the role symbolism plays in artistic expression. Some of them are "variants of the expression theory" (p. 200), nuances as it were of the way music is "expressive." In a closely reasoned argument, Stevenson attempts to demonstrate that Mrs. Langer's specific view of music as "signifying" emotion in some iconic sense is no more plausible than other theories in which music is understood as "resembling" emotions without necessarily signifying them, or in which music is in some other way inherently associated with emotions (p. 209).

Another critic has been Peter Kivy (1980) who has addressed himself specifically to questions related to musical expressivity and affective life in a recent monograph.

In contrast, I believe Mrs. Langer's theory to be of particular value in any psychoanalytic framework that attempts to relate the mind of the artist, the work of art, and its endowment of affect. For purposes of the present study, it can help us penetrate further into meanings and affects associated with the Ives song. On the other hand, I do not think it is the only way in which aesthetics can approach these problems. It seems likely that in a given organized musical structure (a "composition," after all) affects may be represented in other ways additionally. In effect, the expressionist theories alluded to above may not be mutually exclusive. Although this point of view may be considered too all-embracing or, at least lacking in philosophical rigor, it is on the other hand more in keeping with the principles of overdeterminism and multiple function appropriate to a psychoanalytic approach.

Mrs. Langer's theory is most clearly stated in her essay *On Significance in Music* (1957, pp. 205 ff.) and will be summarized briefly for our purposes here. Proceeding from a tendency "to treat art as a *significant* phenomenon rather than a pleasurable experience" (p. 205) and citing one source of this in psychoanalytic thinking ("the discovery of a previously recognized *symbolic mode*, typified in a dream . . . ," p. 207), she goes on to consider the forms in which significance is cast. It is not the "hidden content" that is of interest and value to her in approaching the problems of art but "what every artist knows as the real problem—the *perfection of form*, which makes this form 'significant' in the artistic sense" (p. 208; emphasis added). Self-expression, "the most popular doctrine of the significance and function of music" (p. 216), leads to a paradox in that "sheer self-expression requires no artistic form." Music is not self-expression, she holds, but an "exposition of feelings." What it expresses is the composer's "knowledge of human feeling" (p. 221). She summarizes her view trenchantly: "If music has any significance, it is semantic, not symptomatic. Its 'meaning' is evidently not that of stimulus to evoke emotions, nor that of a signal to announce them; if it has an emotional content, it 'has' it in the same sense that language 'has' its conceptual content—*symbolically*. It is not usually derived *from* affects nor intended *for* them; but we may say, with certain reservations, that it is *about* them . . ." (p. 218; emphasis added).

Commenting on a statement of Wagner she underlines that, despite its romantic phraseology, it advances a principle with which she is in complete agreement: "that music is not self-expression but *formulation and representation* of emotions, moods, and mental tensions and resolutions—a 'logical picture' of sentiment, responsive life, a source of insight, not a plea for sympathy . . ." (p. 222; emphasis added).

With these principles in mind, we will return presently to Ives's music and to a final consideration of the representation of affect. I believe much can be gained by this framework in that Ives exemplifies what Langer strives to put in its purest terms. (At the same time, it should be noted, he exemplifies in many ways the opposite, that "self-expression" which Langer would no doubt consider from an aesthetic point of view to be bad art.) Again, in her own words:

> Feelings revealed in music [she speaks of an ideal music here, of course] are essential *not* "the passion, love, or longing" of such-and-such an individual inviting us to put ourselves in that individual's place, but are presented directly to our understanding, that we may grasp, realize, comprehend these feelings, without pretending to have them or imputing them to anyone else. . . . Its subject-matter is the same as that of "self-expression," and its symbols may even be borrowed, upon occasion, from the realms of expressive symptoms; yet the borrowed suggestive elements are *formalized*, and the subject-matter "distanced" in an artistic perspective [p. 222].

One of Kivy's (1980) chief criticisms of Langer stems from his understanding that Langer, in insisting that music can *only* reflect the "morphology of feelings," implies that individual emotions cannot be expressed. This goes counter, he states, to musical criticism in general and to common musical experience, including his own (p. 46). I would concur in this; however, I see nothing in her theory which precludes the reflection of the morphology of discrete affects. The fact that Langer emphasizes the lack of a fixed connotation or "dictionary meaning" only reflects the peculiar property of musical form. With regard to affect it is at once highly specific yet sufficiently ambiguous to accommodate and elicit the individual listener's personally interpretive response. An example could be seen in Ives's specific, time-fixed, place-fixed nostalgia resulting in a formal musical structure whose morphology could represent or be expressive of an affect to which the common listener could relate in terms of his own experiences.

The term "to be expressive of" in contrast to "to express" in music is a distinction for which I am indebted to Kivy and which he develops in a clear and useful manner (pp. 12–17). While space does not permit adequate exposition of his own theory in this particular study, two of its features must be noted, both highly relevant to it. They have to do with two models of musical expressiveness which, "together, account for central cases of expressiveness in music." The "'contour' theory (or model) . . . explains the expressiveness of music by the 'congruence' of musical 'contour' with the structure of expressive features and behavior." The " 'convention' theory (or model) . . . explains the expressiveness of music as a function, simply, of the customary association of certain musical features with certain emotive ones, quite apart from any structural analogy between them" (p. 77).

Charles Ives's "The Things Our Fathers Loved" is a concentrated work of art whose essential feature is the formalization and representation of an affect. The affect in this instance is nostalgia. Through the medium of auditory form with its symbolic implications, the composer achieves an organized musical structure that in some way is expressive of an affect: It both represents and communicates nostalgia. *I suggest that it does so through an intrinsic morphology which mirrors the mental organization underlying the affect*—the mental phenomena of pleasure/unpleasure and idea (Brenner) and mood structure as described earlier (Weinshel). The two are in the some sense parallel and coextensive; likewise, the formal features are isomorphic. The representation and communication of nostalgia are not achieved by mere self-expression in the activity of emoting. Rather, the crucial artistic activity is one of the creation of forms. Self-expressive aspects certainly appear in elements of content, all of which are intensely personal and some of which, in isolation, may appear quite banal. But the final result is not that of some larger nostalgic tune, the result of the "sheer self-expression" which, as Langer noted, "requires no . . . form." Rather, here the individual tunes with their endless cognitive and affective connotations are intrinsic to a formal structure.

It is this overall organization of form which is to a considerable degree isomorphic with the very mental organization through which the affect of nostalgia is constituted and generated within the mental apparatus. The affect may stimulate the artist and may even evoke spontaneous expression within a work, but this is not at the heart of a work's aesthetic effectiveness or its creator's competence. His experience of the affect may very well be a necessary stimulus and his attempt to express it necessary for the creation of what we would call a work of genius, but it would not be sufficient. It is the invention of expressive forms which is essential. I suggest that the representation of nostalgia which is thus achieved in this song is the result of a special variety of externalization of mental state and structure, one germane to art, which is accomplished symbolically by an extraordinary (and appropriately) skilled artist within the framework of the formal potential of his chosen medium—in this case music.

As I believe I have demonstrated, the product—even so brief and apparently simple a song—is a highly condensed form of knowledge. It is rich in history both personal and social and replete with examples of private and public memory. The connotations inherent in the music as well as in the words are far-reaching. The ideational content of nostalgia is comprised of persons, places, and things, and these cognitive elements are, as we have seen, highly condensed within a musical framework of brief duration. It is an inherent part of the affect which is represented and communicated in musical form. To the degree that it is isomorphic with mental structure, I suggest that it constitutes yet another kind of knowledge, the artist's intuitive, unconscious knowledge of himself, hence of other human beings, and of the nature of human feelings. A regressive state is not necessary to gain access to this knowledge. If anything, the pursuit is associated with a heightened state of awareness and realization in a work of art which is accomplished by the keenest awareness of the symbolic and formal potential of the artist's medium. Fundamentally, the artist's knowledge, as in Charles Ives's nostalgia, is that of human sentient life.

Chapter 13

The Development of Creative Imagination in Composers

Martin L. Nass, Ph.D.

During the past twelve years I have been studying various aspects of music from a psychoanalytic vantage point and more recently have attempted to understand the experience of the composer in the process of inspiration. Recent work of mine has reported on the writings and anecdotal reports of composers from the historical past (Nass, 1975). Currently, I have been speaking with contemporary composers about their work and their experiences during the inspirational phase of their work. To date, I have interviewed some twenty prominent American composers. While they varied in their capacity to articulate this complex, nonverbal experience, the material I obtained has afforded an invaluable glimpse into the creative process, a process which has received a great deal of attention in the psychoanalytic literature in recent years. The present paper should be viewed as part of a work which is ongoing and from which additional findings will emerge.

In her outstanding work on the development of the gifted, Phyllis Greenacre (1957) talks about their hyperacuity to sensory stimulation, their intense empathic ability, and their retention of sensorimotor styles which enable them to build up projective motor discharges for expressive function. I feel that this ability to retain an earlier developmental mode of understanding the world (Piaget, 1954) enables them to continue a freshness of experience, a capacity to maintain a closeness to body processes and body rhythms and to use these developmentally earlier modes to reorganize experience and present it to others via their particular gifts. Their hypersen-

---

An earlier version of this paper was presented to the New York Freudian Society, 4 February 1983.

The author wishes to express his appreciation to Stanley Grand, Ph.D., for his helpful comments and suggestions.

First published in The *International Review of Psycho-Analysis*, 11:481–492, 1984. Reprinted by permission.

sitivity and strong empathic ability quite often result in a narrowing of object distance, in increased narcissistic vulnerability, and in special self-esteem problems which become organized around their talent (Coltrera, 1965, 1981). This is not to say, as some suggest (Montani, 1945; Michel, 1960; Eissler, 1967) that giftedness and pathology are somehow linked. As Greenacre (1957) states, "Talented people are not immune from neurotic and psychotic developments under all conditions, but neither is there an intrinsic connection between talent and neurosis" (p. 60). But it does imply that there are particular early issues of development which are played out in the first months and years and around which their talent maintains a unique position and creates special developmental situations.

It is one of my purposes to explore some of these developmental issues and to show how they bear upon the phenomenology of inspiration in composers.

The tools for understanding these issues are embedded in some relatively recent work in psychoanalysis and developmental psychology. Specifically, I am referring to Winnicott's now classic findings on transitional objects and transitional phenomena (Winnicott, 1953, 1967), Mahler's work on separation–individuation (Mahler, 1968), Piaget's construction of reality (Piaget, 1954), Paul Schilder's (1950, 1964) often overlooked work on the development of the body image, and the already cited work by Greenacre. In addition, there have been some quite recent psychoanalytic writings on creativity by Rothenberg (1979b) and by Rose (1980).

According to Werner (1940), development proceeds to greater levels of differentiation following initial organizations which are more diffuse and primitive. Experiences become more integrated and specialized as development progresses. The developmental tasks which propel the child from complete dependency to greater degrees of autonomy are resolved idiosyncratically, depending upon a variety of factors which include sensorimotor styles, thresholds for stimulation, and rhythmic contact with the mother. My contention is that musicians have dealt with separation in a unique way, organizing a part of it around experiences dealing with sound or experiences which in some way have been integrated into a musical matrix. Particular developmental tasks, for example, the development and maintenance of object constancy and the maintenance of psychic structure, may be handled in a unique way by the musically gifted child by incorporating them into his special auditory sensitivity (Nass, 1971) and extending them through experiences involving sound. The musician is thus able to deal with the separation issues in a less concrete form and maintain a greater object distance. An illustration on an adult level which has inferential meaning for childhood is shown in Whitney Balliett's (1974) *New Yorker* interview with a jazz trumpeter, who said, "The times when I don't have a gig for a long time I go through an entire concert in my mind—an invented concert, note for note, right down to the lights and the applause." By so doing he is able to maintain contact with his art and provide himself with what Rapaport (1957) has called "stimulus nutriment" where in conditions of separation or sensory deprivation, psychic structures are maintained by activities which provide stimulation for their perpetuation. Some of these activities have content as well as formal meanings to them; for example, Henry Moore's description of his work on his statue called "Seated Woman" evoking memories of massaging his mother's back (James, 1966). They serve to maintain contact with the object as well as uniquely expressing the individual's creative gifts.

The importance of sensory stimulation at an early developmental level for later growth and for fostering adequate body image development is well documented (Schilder, 1950, 1964; Grand, 1982). These include visual and auditory as well as tactile stimulation (Shevrin and Toussieng, 1965).

In this connection, Schilder's work on the development of body image is most relevant since he (Schilder, 1964) ties early motility (Piaget's sensorimotor stage) with perception. He says,

> Primitive perception is a state of motion. . . . Development is in the direction of the elimination of the inner motion of the perception. Motility is one of the important factors in (the) process of the stabilization of perception [p. 8].

Schilder discusses the importance of motility for perception and toward body image stability and seems to state in another way that the creative act tends toward the building and maintenance of the psychic structure of the creator (Rapaport, 1960; Coltrera, 1965). In early development, existence is experienced as action and action is the very essence of early perception. The rhythmic qualities of early perception in visual, tactile, as well as auditory experiences are noted by Schilder (1964, p. 9). These, I feel, help provide links in the creative act to one level of the maintenance of body and self constancy and are apparent in the descriptive material of the musicians with whom I spoke. Thus, one jazz musician and composer beautifully illustrated this quality when he said:

> I think the feeling of motion—the physical feeling of motion—is really important. Some kind of joyful physical expression might be just right. . . . A lot of improvising for me is involved in a kind of fun feeling, a kind of playfulness.

The ability to be open to this kind of phenomenon is to me a central characteristic of the creative artist and is a function of his capacity to face continually and to rework early modes of experience. I will also show how this appears in the material of more classical composers.

The particular sense modality preferred by an individual has varying roots, ranging from physiological threshold to early experiences involving sensory stimulation. The fact that hearing and sound can be used as a means of separation from the mother since her presence can be maintained from a distance has been noted (Nass, 1971; Shopper, 1978). Experiences with sound can become a central basis for mother-child interaction and for the integration of body image experiences. Empathic links between mother and child in body expression have been shown to exist from the first few days of life (Meltzoff and Moore, 1977; Field, Woodson, Greenberg, and Cohen, 1982). The musician who is still open to this kind of empathic contact uses this in "tuning in" to fellow performers and has access to early forms of preverbal contact.

Experiences with sound and hearing in the musically gifted child undoubtedly play a role in the development of a sense of reality and in reality testing. The fact that the development of the body self and differentiation of surface from depth involves reality testing is shown by Lichtenberg (1978) who shows how psychic experiences with sound also provide a link with the mother through her voice and her singing. Lewis (1977) speculates that the mother's spoken words are experienced initially by the infant as tones and rhythms. Preverbal experiences involving sounds and rhythms undoubtedly form a central basis for mother-infant contact and help provide the somatosensory stimulation so essential for the development of the body image, body boundary integrity and sense of self (Grand, 1982). The form and rhythm of music sets a continuation of basic vegetative rhythms probably going back to the original in utero heartbeat. It seems to me that the potentially gifted infant builds upon these experiences through his particular sensitive apparatus and the special style of his mother which provides the unique matrix for the development of this mode of experiencing the world. Through continued experiences involving sound, sound sensitivity, music and rhythm, music emerges for him as a central mode for the expression of feeling and may assume transitional object functions in the course of separation experiences. It can be viewed as part of a developmental line leading to further musical development. Anna Freud has stated, "It is not unknown that early contact with the mother through her singing has consequences for the later attitudes to music and may promote special musical aptitude" (1963, p. 264). The use of music and sound in extending the link from mother to child is a core issue in the move toward differentiation. The fact that music can serve as a transitional phenomenon has been described by Winnicott (1953). He says that songs and tunes come "within the intermediate area as transitional phenomena along with the use of objects that are not part of the infant's body yet are not fully recognized as belonging to external reality" (p. 89). This observation has been extended by McDonald (chapter 6) to the concept of "transitional tunes" which she regards as analogous to the transitional object and as a step in musical development. This can be regarded as a connection with the mother and in instances where music has been important in development and where sound has served an organizing function, a contribution to the development of talent.

The musician thus has the capacity to continue and refine developmentally early modes of body experience and body communication. The sense of rhythmic interaction can be traced to the first days and weeks of life (Brazelton, Koslowski, and Main, 1974) and can be observed through body phenomena. Observe the mouth movements of many pianists, be they jazz or classical, as they play and you will see some of the manifestations of Hoffer's (1949) observations on eye, hand, and mouth interactions. The musician retains this capacity through his gifts and one does not need to invoke a model of pathology for explanation.

In ensemble playing, one sees the playful interaction and communication among the performers. The capacity to "read" one another through minimal cues, bodily gestures and signs, the anticipation of entrances and cut-offs all seem to center on what Schilder (1964) referred to by his statement that, "In every action, the individual must start with an orientation toward his own body and the bodies of others" (p. 210). The gifted performer then "reads" the other person and keeps the communication at a finely tuned level, in many ways approximating an open early dialogue.

An interesting example of an interference in this interaction was described to me by a jazz musician in depicting a recording session where members of his ensemble were placed in separate rooms to avoid spillage of the sound track lines and were in contact with each other only through earphones. He said:

> In this recording studio we were each stuck in little rooms so that none of your sound will leak onto the other tracks. But you couldn't see the others. We played with earphones on. Something happens that those (recording engineers) don't know about. People need to be close together and give those little signals. . . . A lot of spontaneous stuff gets killed in that kind of set-up. . . . Something about the chance, taking a chance, gets lost. Like in any conversation, if you already know what's going to be there, then the spontaneous element is gone.

Motion and physicality are most prominent in the work of jazz musicians who employ a kind of dialogue which serves to stimulate musical ideas one from the other. The communication enables the performers through their dialogue to intensify their contact. A jazz bass player said about his work in a trio,

> When things are going right, I feel we're all communicating and the audience is right there with you. I feel in touch with something deep. Something special deep inside of me that I don't get to very often.

The capacity to retain and use these early forms of expression through body rhythms and sound and give them musical shape appears to be a continuation of an early sensorimotor style. While Piaget (1952) implies that the sensorimotor phase is a way station in the development of intelligence, the musically gifted, through the incomplete closure described by Greenacre (1957), have the capacity to continue and utilize this developmentally earlier, nondiscursive mode and develop it to a higher level. The musician has the capacity to remain close to body expression and body feeling through his art form and preserve and embellish the resulting talents. The effect may be to leave him more open and less defended against narcissistic onslaughts and hence more subject to self-esteem fluctuations, but the result is also a greater accessibility to inner workings and earlier cognitive and sensorimotor modes of functioning, which are essential to his work.

How this work is effected has been the subject of a great deal of speculative inquiry, as well as a sense from some that this is not a valid area of study since one is applying verbal techniques for the study of a nonverbal process. However, if the creative process is to be studied, it is necessary to employ our technical devices, crude as they may be.

It is difficult for a composer to articulate how the musical idea is experienced and where he feels it originates. While this taps at the heart of the creative process, it demands a verbal discursive description to a nonverbal process. It has an unfair quality to it because it requires a shift in focus from process to observation. In the eighteenth century, Rameau was quoted as saying, "While composing music is not the time to recall the rules which might hold our genius in bondage" (Morgenstern, 1956, p. 42). However, fostering a greater understanding of internal process calls for a detailed articulation. Gustav Mahler (Morgenstern, 1956, p. 311) stated: "Only when I experience do I compose—only when I compose do I experience. . . . A musician's nature can hardly be expressed in words."

Despite these limits, which are very much tied to the technical limits of understanding and describing nonverbal material, a great deal can be understood about the process of inspiration.

It is important to realize that in dealing with nondiscursive projections there is a tendency to translate meaning into discursive forms. This is an error made by Noy (1968a) in reducing the attraction of the form of the fugue to a mother following a toddler, and by Rose (1980) in relating the sonata form to mother-child interaction. Nondiscursive materials need to be understood in their own terms. The attempt to translate them into discursive modes often results in both losing their meaning.

Descriptions of the inspirational process, which seem to follow a rather classical pattern, are in evidence in the literature. Interestingly enough, many of the descriptive statements come from mathematicians and many of them couch their descriptions in terms which psychologists and psychoanalysts have stressed. For example, Henri Poincaré (1952) states that the "process [of discovery] is one in which the human mind seems to borrow least from the external world. . . . It acts, or appears to act only by itself and on itself" (p. 46). Jacques Hadamard, another mathematician, in a sensitively drawn study (Hadamard, 1945) provides a clear description of the inspirational process in mathematics which has carryover to almost all creative work, and in his words, applies to invention in general.

Hadamard describes, as does Poincaré, a long germinating period of unconscious work and a sudden coming together of these processes in a rapid culmination. Incidentally, this is similar to the description of Mozart's rapid style in writing the finished product of a musical work, as contrasted to Beethoven, who labored over every phrase. In the former case, the work was done internally; in the latter, externally in sketch books. Hadamard contacted mathematicians, including Einstein, regarding descriptive material of their experiences of invention. Einstein, as will also be seen in my later description of composers, indicates that his experiences are nonverbal.

> Words or language do not seem to play any role in my mechanism of thought. The psychical entities which seem to serve as elements in thought are certain signs of muscular type. Conventional words or other signs have to be sought for laboriously only in a secondary stage [Hadamard, 1945, pp. 142–143].

It is the creator's capacity to retain earlier, nonrestrictive forms of expression which enable him to have access to and eventually shape his work. As Professor Einstein talked about the limitation of language and signs, many composers I spoke with talked about the limitation of notation in the path from internal inspiration to composition and in the fact that notations were but approximations in portraying their internal processes in composing.

An important aside in this connection is the fact that the capacity to maintain these early modes of experience and to use them in the service of creation is by no means a regressive process as had been formulated in earlier psychoanalytic writings (Sterba, 1939; Racker, 1951). In fact, the capacity to contact and employ ambiguous affective and cognitive states involves a greater degree of ego strength to experience, tolerate, and resynthesize early modes of functioning (Nass, 1971). It builds upon the previously discussed capacity to maintain contact with early body and self states and continuously to retap them. Rothenberg (1972, 1979a, b) uses the term *Janusian thinking* to describe the synthesis of opposites as one way of formulating the task of the creative individual in his capacity to employ and unify what seems to the average mind to be contradictory formulations. Rothenberg's recent uncovering of Einstein's formulation of the general theory of relativity (1979a) as an ability to synthesize an observer being at rest and in motion simultaneously is given as an example of this type of thought process. He also cautions against the use of conceptualizations using regression as the primary means of explanation of the creative process, a caution with which I am in strong agreement.

As the inspirational process has similar germinal qualities in mathematics and music, an analogous process occurs in writing as well and an extensive series of interviews with writers was conducted by the *Paris Review* (1958, 1963, 1967) and is still in progress. Here too, many similar experiences in inspiration and in the process of creative work appeared and I have noted their parallel with composers. The crucial differences are that for composers the very medium of expression is nonverbal and translating it into words shifts the meaning and utilizes a different medium. The form of experience is much closer to basic feelings (Langer, 1942) and to processes related to body rhythm. Translating them into verbal processes shifts the central expressive form, but one is left with a choice of not investigating the process at all or accepting this compromised form of expression. One can also suppose, as suggested by Beethoven in the following statement, that the initial creative impulse is similar for most creators and that the particular talent and craft of the individual helps to shape its direction.

> You may ask me where I obtain my ideas. I cannot answer this with any clarity. They come unbidden, spontaneously or unspontaneously. I may grasp them with my hands in the open air, while walking in the woods, in the stillness or night, in early morning. Stimulated by those moods which poets turn into words, I turn my ideas into tones which resound, roar and rage until at last they stand before me in the form of notes[1] [Hamburger, 1960, p. 194].

---

[1] In a recent article, Solomon (1980) questions the authenticity of this statement.

In this connection, Rothenberg's (1979b) recent work also suggests strong parallels between creativity in scientific as well as artistic fields, so that the mode of expression depends upon talent, physiological sensitivities, and preferred ways of expressing as well as experiencing early impressions. How these impressions are reexperienced by composers is a function of the composer's particular sensory style and can vary from composer to composer or from work to work of the same person. The musical idea, to my surprise and contrary to what I had learned in the past (Nass, 1975), is not necessarily experienced as a tonal or auditory pattern going through the composer's consciousness. It is experienced in a variety of ways, the auditory being but one mode. Many composers experience the musical impulse as a kinaesthetic impression, a fact that is understandable since music is so close to body rhythm and body experience (Nass, 1971).

Thus, one composer describes his work as beginning with a sense of gesture.

> The image in my mind is related to gestures. This gesture may live in my mind for months and even years before I find the opportunity to give it musical shape.... The musical ideas that I've had in my mind are related to memory experiences. They're not usually picture memory experiences but gesture memory experiences.

He does not consider the gesture as being musical until it takes on temporal qualities and extends into the dimension of time. My sense of his description of gesture is related to early body rhythm mentioned above and has previously been discussed by Hindemith (1952) in relation to music. Body movement plays a role in this man's music as well. The piece he was working on at the time of my interview with him was called "Crack the Whip," a reference to an ice skating activity from his childhood. He attempted to portray through a musical motif a visual and kinaesthetic experience of his childhood.

Another composer also reports a body sensation of a different kind:

> I can almost feel something happening physically, physiologically. I certainly can't place it, but it's a very definite physical sensation. I feel that my temperature goes up.

And another:

> Part of the process of composing for me is kinaesthetic. I think if I were put in a room without a piano, without an instrument I don't know whether I could really compose a piece . . . even the copying of the music has become part of the creative act for me. I've gotten to the point where there are certain decisions that are built into the notography.

Similarly, one composer describes a sensation of constant motion in his style of work and when it goes, "It's like a motor that won't stop."

Compare these statements with Schilder's link between motility and perception and with Piaget's discussion of sensorimotor style.

Another also senses a great deal of physicality in his music, "a kind of kinetic energy. I feel that music is highly related to bodily function. The fact that the mark on the metronome that says *moderato* happens to be the pulse beat of the human body can't be totally coincidental."

These kinaesthetic experiences of the composer tie the inspirational link back to extremely early physiological processes of motion and in his craft the composer lays out a line of development that is reexperienced by the performer and ultimately by the listener (Sessions, 1950).

I think that it is noteworthy to mention that in two instances composers told me that they developed ideas for pieces while they were riding bicycles. Also, note the statement of the composer who describes his experience at times as "a kind of texture. It's almost like having a feeling of a surface being rough or smooth." The tactile sensuality of this description and its continuity with early experience is most evident. Several people also told me about the physical enjoyment of the work of calligraphy in copying the final score and experiencing satisfaction in the actual motion.

For many composers visual imagery plays a significant role in their experiences of inspiration. It seemed to me at first to be somewhat difficult to fathom since composers work within the medium of sound and they shape sounds. However, the creative impulse can take a variety of forms. I have encountered three composers who see the entire score in their mind when they work, one described a dream of a page of a score he was planning to write out the next day, perfectly annotated in the dream. One described a visual image of a cello quintet as the letter X and used it to write out ascending and descending lines which crossed at the center. Visual imagery was also involved, incidentally, in von Kekulé's discovery of the structure of the benzene ring, as described by Koestler (1964). Generalizations in creative style within a compositional medium do not necessarily hold to the sense modality within which the artist works. I would imagine that there are some film makers who rely a great deal on auditory over visual cues, or take Frank O'Connor's description of the role of sound in his writing:

> I just notice a feeling from people. I notice particularly the cadence of their voices, the sort of phrases they'll use and that's what I'm all the time trying to hear in my head, how people word things . . . I have terribly sensitive hearing and I'm terribly aware of voices. If I remember somebody, for instance, that I was very fond of, I don't remember what he or she looked like, but I can absolutely take off the voice [*Paris Review*, Vol. 1, p. 169].

Visual imagery plays a significant part in several composers' experiences of inspiration. One says:

> I get my ideas most often walking around the streets of New York. I have a mental image. If I listen to a piece of music, particularly music I never heard before, I see the score. I keep my eyes closed and I have a picture of the score. I know very often if someone says, "Do you remember such and such a piece?", I'll summon up that visual image of what the score would have looked like.

This style also appears in the work of another who sees the score of a projected work in his mind and often proceeds to copy it, and visual imagery has influenced the work of yet another who described the inspiration for a piece when arriving in New York on a plane and being awestruck by the pattern of lights. However, the same composer will have varied experiences for different pieces, saying that, "Sometimes it's visual, sometimes auditory and sometimes even philosophical."

Visual imagery has been significant in the work of another imaginative composer. When I spoke with him he had recently completed a work based on the biblical Song of Songs and described images which he experienced based on "a forbidding dry sun that was beating down . . . a beautiful valley in the mist with drops of water." He stated that different pieces have different processes for him and that sometimes he experiences "a cloud of sound" when he works.

Another composer both hears the sound and sees it in annotated form when he works, as does one who describes both hearing "an aggregate of sounds" in his head and simultaneously seeing a full score in his mind. He describes his musical memory as a visual one, being able to summon up the image of the complete score.

What has been most impressive to me is the auditory acuity and auditory sensitivity of the composers. For the most part the musical impulse is an auditory one and is given shape, time, and dynamic value by the composer. It is also the link to the composer's past and a line of mastery of the world of sound (Niederland, 1958). Most composers I spoke with can look at a musical score and actually hear the sounds portrayed by the notes (not just imagine what they sound like). Many of them speak of constantly hearing sounds and musical phrases in their consciousness. This is true of one who from childhood had music in his head all of the time. "I realized that it was music that I couldn't identify so I knew I must have thought of it myself."

The connection between the kind of sounds used in music and an overall childhood experience is indicated by the following statement made by a composer. He said:

> Composers first draw from infancy or childhood on the sound of nature, even the particular acoustic. Appalachia happens to be a river town that sits in a valley. That's a particular acoustic which I accepted as the acoustic of the world, and I don't think there's any question but it found its way into my music, an echoing acoustic.

While the mastery and reorganization of sounds perpetuate the composer's link with the past in a variety of ways and provide a vehicle for creative expression, the particular use of the medium of sound must have special meaning, as in this case, even though in many instances the composer does not have the awareness of its meaning. It has proceeded along the developmental lines of greater differentiation and separation.

Another way of viewing the composer's development along the lines of individuation is to see that a good part of his capacity to separate involves the ability to go deeply inside himself and to take responsibility for his own production. This capacity is a most impressive accomplishment. The use of his inner workings and his "owning" them is a true mark of the artist's creative ability and goes beyond the use of technical skills. In fact, as in any creative endeavor, the mastery of technique is a given before the individual can be creative. This is true in our own field of psychoanalysis as well as artistic fields. It was reaffirmed in my discussion with a composer who said: "You have to be a master technician. Then you forget about it. It's not good either if the technique masters you. With technical mastery you can say whatever you want to say and be able to do it."

Once technical mastery has been accomplished and the accessibility to early sensory impressions is maintained, the awesome task of reimmersing oneself into the material requires a continual act of courage on the part of the composer. He must be open to his inner workings and be sensitive to them. A beautiful general description is given by one composer who told me:

> I feel like a fisherman. I feel like you throw out a line and then it goes very far and then there's this kind of distant tug that's so subtle that normal people ignore it. But the real fisherman senses that that tiny little nudge is something that one must be very cognizant of and follow it very carefully, very slowly, and sometimes zip in very fast. But the worst sin is to ignore it.

I must say that I found the parallel to picking up a ripple on the psychic surface quite strong and counteracting the tendency to ignore it is what opens the inside to the creative experience.

To begin a new piece often becomes a renewed agony for many, with attempts to arrive at short-cuts or formulas which never work in a successful piece. A way of dealing with this problem was described to me in this way:

> For me the process has been to learn enough about the way I can be productive through years of disciplining myself in certain ways, to learn to allow myself not to set up a rule about the way it's done. In each one of my projects, I've often found that I had an idea, I wrote a piece and it was successful and I did it this way, that's the way it's going to be done, and the next time comes along. . . . I'm a different person and it doesn't work that way. So what I've learned to try to do is to be responsive to who I am in any given moment and allow it to work that way. Now, that could also lead me to do nothing but goof off or play tennis or whatever, but

it doesn't. I'm sufficiently committed to the activity so that I get itchy if I don't produce something.

Beginnings are difficult for most creative artists. Their constant self-doubt and feeling that their production is not good enough is a common one (Ghiselin, 1952) and is directly related to anxieties about revealing extremely personal, private, and deep aspects of oneself which are generally untapped in most people. Thus, one stated: "In starting a piece, it takes the form of 'I can't do it. It's impossible.' I feel like I'm climbing a wall and then I start. . . . When I start writing everything feels no good at first. I throw it away. I feel it will never work."

Another said that "The first weeks and months can be a kind of agony and a torture because nothing is coming out. You can't understand how you can possibly write any music. You begin to think, 'I'm shot.' There's nothing left. I have nothing new and then little by little it begins."

One composer uses these feelings as a barometer of where he is in his work. I found the following statement of his use of his self-doubts as a gauge of his work to be extremely courageous and an indication of what I would consider a most heightened level of the creative act, because it involves the simultaneous use of self-observation and self-experience:

> I can work for many months and not feel that I understand what a piece is about. And I'm usually waiting for, I think of it as a kind of crisis. This involves doubting the sketches, doubting the quality of the ideas, doubting the concept of the form.
>
> In short, doubting whether you can make a piece at all. And then, hopefully at about that time some sort of little twist in the way of ideas coming together. It never gets easier.

This issue of overcoming the crust or resistance to work is a formidable one for many composers although several reported that they rarely experienced a dearth of musical ideas. The act of beginning work and going to internal processes is a reexperiencing of early separation issues and very often is resisted much as one sees in resistances to uncovering frightening insights. One composer said to me that he feels that writing music is like discovering or rediscovering yourself. "There are lots of times you're not going to like what you see. You really don't know yourself. It comes out of your guts and you don't like your guts at times. That's tough. If you're going to be any good you have to do it." The composer continuously has to be at the threshold of the unknown and awesome during the inspirational phase of his work if his production is to be truly original and fresh. It is this quality which I feel forms another link with early separation experiences. That is, the early use of sensory and sensorimotor capacities which have been developed from the start must be built upon through the craft and reexperienced in a variety of forms. They involve a radical kind of separation and freshness of organization. It is the true mark of the creator to be able to tap these processes each time as though it were the first time and to do it differently each time. I found this to be an articulated observation by several of the people I spoke with. One stated that, "As you write more you can feel too experienced, like you know, 'I can handle this,' and then you don't open yourself up. You're less apt to. I sense a danger in becoming too systematic or too methodical."

Another comparable statement is the following:

When I have a good idea, two things happen. They happen because I may have rejected a thousand not-so-good ideas and there's something in a composer and that's what makes him a composer that tells him, that makes him know at a given moment, "That's it!" There comes a moment when you say, "I absolutely cannot think of anything better than that." . . . A superficial composer arrives at the solution too quickly because he looks only at the easiest alternatives. He doesn't look at the path-breaking alternatives, the overwhelming alternatives, the ones you can't quite face.

This pull toward finding the easier alternative is a form of avoiding a reexperience of an intense form of separation anxiety. Separation experiences can be formulated at many levels. The creator who keeps repeating the same idea in different forms is afraid to experience another unknown or to experiment with new forms, and stays close to the safe and the familiar. New ideas involve another separation experience and a reexposure to the unknown. They involve a move away from ritualized stances and routines as a way of dealing with the anxiety of facing the new and the unknown. This, I feel, applies not only to composers of music but to all involved in work which requires creative imagination. The creative individual must of necessity continuously work at the outer edge of what is known and be open to new material. The glib, generalized interpretations sometimes given by psychoanalysts as an avoidance of dealing with materials not quite formed or understandable and which require a tolerance for the ambiguous and unknown are most pertinent here.

As a result of this investigation, I would conclude that the talented individual is able to experience and reexperience early separation trauma and face new material with courage and imagination. This capacity involves an ability to remain open to developmentally earlier modes of thought and rather than being conceptualized as regressive requires a *greater* degree of ego strength for its implementation. The talented individual has the capacity to stay open to those nonverbal experiences involving body states and body awareness and to use them in the service of his art, thus providing us with new understandings of ourself and the world through his work.

Summary

Interviews with twenty prominent American composers have resulted in the conclusion that a variety of sensory styles, not necessarily auditory, are operating during the inspirational phase of their work. These include visual, kinaesthetic, and tactile modes. In some composers, their particular style prevails in most of their work; in some, the form of inspiration varies from one work to another.

The paper discusses developmental considerations and suggests that composers organize those experiences which deal with individuation around music, sound, and listening, and have a refined capacity to retain and develop body sensitivity and body experience and to use them in the service of their art. It is the ability to retain and develop early modes of experience which is characteristic of the gifted composer.

It is suggested that the truly gifted composer has the capacity to experience and reexperience early separation trauma in order to formulate and present new ideas and is able to stay open to developmentally early modes of thought.

IV
PSYCHOANALYTIC STUDIES OF COMPOSERS

Chapter 14
On Beethoven's Deafness

Maynard Solomon

During his childhood, Beethoven often wrapped himself in a cloak of silence as a shield against both the vicissitudes of external reality and the traumatic events within his family constellation. The reports of contemporaries who knew him toward the end of his first decade repeatedly describe his withdrawal into a world of fantasy, his penchant for isolation, his monosyllabic replies to adult questioners, his happiness at being left alone by his parents, his "deafness" when a young neighbor tried to disturb his daydreams (Solomon, 1978, pp. 19–21). Silence and solitude had great utility to this lonely young genius, permitting a condition of "wakeful dreaming" within a noiseless protective world woven of his own rich fantasies (or filled with music of his own creation). In Abraham's formulation, the individual "withdraws into the depth of the night in order to know nothing of the external world, that is, in order to be alone with himself and his phantasies" (Abraham, 1913, p. 203). This region of "magical-hallucinatory omnipotence" (Ferenczi, 1913, p. 189) served another purpose as well: to isolate Beethoven from the reach of external commands and injunctions as well as from fearful sounds overheard or imagined. For the auditory sphere is "the nucleus of the super-ego" (Isakower, 1939, p. 346), a zone of conscience accessible to the verbal prohibitions and imperatives of parental and social authority. In Knapp's words, the auditory mechanism "keeps us oriented in the world of conduct" (Knapp, 1953, p. 185).

This aspect of the function of hearing was long ago perceived by Protestant theologians: they avowed that the benevolent God dwells within the heart whereas the God of wrath enters through the "open," "receptive" sense of hearing. Luther, who (like Beethoven) suffered from a tormenting buzzing in the ears, wrote: "In the Church of God nothing is demanded but hearing." Perhaps this is why Ludwig Feuerbach called the ear "the organ of terror" and asserted that "if man had only eyes, hands, and the senses of taste and smell, he would have no religion, for all these senses are organs of critique and scepticism" (Feuerbach, 1851, p. 27).

There is some evidence that sound, especially loud sounds capable of transformation into tactile sensations, produced anxieties in Beethoven. During the French bombardment of Vienna in 1809, he "spent the greater part of the time in a cellar in the house of his brother Caspar, where he covered his head with pillows so as not to hear the cannons" (Wegeler-Ries, 1838, p. 121). One might object that Beethoven was here merely protecting his sensitive organs of hearing from the cannon's roar; however, long before the first signs of his deafness appeared—toward the close of his third decade— Beethoven had abandoned playing the organ because, as he told the organist Freudenberg, "my nerves could not stand the power of the gigantic instrument" (Kerst, 1913, Vol. 2, p. 114). Does this imply that Beethoven feared what Niederland (1958, p. 498) called "auditory extinction"? Loud noises may mobilize archaic memories of fearful sounds stemming from a stage in the individual's development "when noise was something material, perhaps of an acutely threatening or . . . engulfing or devouring corporeal nature" (Niederland, 1958, p. 501).

Clinical research has also demonstrated the close association between fear of noise and the memory of being maltreated and beaten in childhood. In general, Niederland writes, many traumatic events "are accompanied by frightening and often extremely intense noises such as screaming, moaning, shouting for help, etc. This acoustic aspect of the traumatic event . . . may . . . play a much larger role than the sight of an object of anxiety" (Niederland, 1958, p. 474). (The linguistic connections between sound and beating appear in such metaphorical expressions as "beat," "strike," "blow," "bang," and "hit.") In light of our knowledge that Beethoven was repeatedly beaten by his father, and probably also by his teacher at the Bonn Tirocinium, Johann Krengel, who is known to have used "harsh corporal punishment" to correct "the smallest transgression" (Wasiliewski, 1888, Vol. 1, p. 33), it may well be that certain forms of auditory stimulation were perceived by Beethoven as threatening, reviving painful memories and reawakening the dread of physical maltreatment. As Kohut and Levarie observed, the exposure to severe auditory stimuli "must create an early, close (or 'symbolic') association between sound and the threatening external world, as opposed to quiet and security. Hence, in the regressive psychological states . . . in which hypersensitivity to noise is revived, the danger reacted to is, on the deepest level, the greatest and earliest of all: the danger of total psychobiological destruction" (see chapter 1).

In medical studies of tinnitus it has been shown that patients like Beethoven who suffer from annoying buzzing and humming sounds in their ears perceive the auditory intrusions as persecutory. Perhaps this may partially explain Beethoven's choice of metaphors re his deafness: "I should be happy, one of the happiest of mortals, if that *fiend* had not settled in my ears"; and again: "My bad hearing *haunted me everywhere like a ghost*, and I fled from mankind" (Anderson, 1961, Vol. 1, pp. 67, 270; emphasis added).

There are several routes open to one seeking to master the anxieties generated by fearful sounds: withdrawal into physical seclusion; selective hearing (i.e., the refusal to listen); retreat into daydreaming; replacement of chaotic and disturbing sounds by meaningful and pleasurable auditory experiences; and deafness. There is copious evidence that Beethoven utilized the first four of these avenues. As for the last avenue, Beethoven's deafness, whether or not it was "willed" or generated through some obscure psychosomatic mechanism (Deutsch, 1939; Knapp, 1953; Alexander, 1954), served to protect his creativity from the assaults and seductions of the external world and from the memories of a submissive past at a moment when he was about to embark upon what he termed his *new path*, a path that would lead him to transform the parameters and the procedures of the Viennese classical tradition and to establish new boundaries and norms for the future development of music.

Soon after he learned, in 1801, that his infirmity was incurable, he told his brothers and several of his intimate friends that he wished his encroaching deafness to be kept secret. However, this "great secret" (as he called it) may have been, not his deafness, but his acquiescence in the necessity of deafness as the condition of his creativity, which is to say, of his competition with God and with the omnipotent parents of archaic memory (Solomon, 1978, pp. 124–125). Max Weber described the "notion that certain kinds of suffering and abnormal states provoked through chastisements are avenues to the attainment of superhuman, i. e. magical power . . ." (Weber, 1913, p. 272). Beethoven's deafness may have been such a form of magical asceticism, a rite of passage, a prelude to an ecstatic and "holy" state from which emerged the masterpieces of his maturity.

Chapter 15
Johannes Brahms—Music, Loneliness, and Altruism

Peter Ostwald, M.D.

It has often been observed that musical creativity during the nineteenth century occurred in two great waves. The first crested at the beginning of the century, around 1810, with Mendelssohn, born in 1809, Chopin and Schumann in 1810, Liszt in 1811, Wagner and Verdi in 1813. The second wave built up after the middle of the century, beginning in 1860 with the birth of Mahler and Wolf, followed by Debussy, born in 1862, Richard Strauss in 1864, and then, a decade later Schönberg and Ives in 1874, and Stravinsky in 1882. Between these temporal concentrations of musical genius stood a solitary giant, Johannes Brahms (1833–1897).

More than just historical reasons, however, account for Brahms's singularity.[1] Something about his personality made him stand out as well. He was a Januslike figure who looked backward, seeking inspiration from the older baroque and classical traditions, while at the same time he looked forward and seemed the embodiment of modernism. A man of many contrasts, Brahms was devoted to his homeland in north Germany, but chose to live in southern Europe. He adored his parents and enjoyed family life, but never married.

---

[1] There were other midcentury composers, to be sure—Moussorgsky, born in 1839, and Tchaikovsky, in 1840, for example—but their influence upon central Europe and the mainstream of musical development was not comparable to that of Brahms.

This paper is a greatly expanded version of a talk, "Johannes Brahms, Frei Aber (nicht immer) Froh," given in 1983 at the International Brahms Symposium in the Leipzig Gewandhaus, East Germany. The author is greatly indebted to Francis Schiller, M.D., Professor of the History of Medicine, University of California, San Francisco, and to Claudio Spies, Professor of Music at Princeton University, for constructive advice regarding the present version.

He was a kind and generous man, but often adopted an extremely rude manner toward others. He was fiercely independent, yet would mourn bitterly the loss of friends and relatives. He amassed a small fortune, but always lived frugally and dressed like a poor man.

I became interested in Brahms while working on a psychobiography of Robert Schumann and trying to understand the role he played during the two-and-a-half years Schumann was hospitalized and his wife could not, or would not, see him (Ostwald, 1985, pp. 283–293). Brahms became a kind of human link between these two artists. He loved Clara and lived with her; he also loved Robert and visited him regularly in the hospital. He played the piano for both of them, spoke with one about the other, and conveyed messages back and forth. This linking function is beautifully symbolized in a composition Brahms wrote in 1854, his *Variations for Piano, on a theme by Robert Schumann*, dedicated to Clara Schumann (opus 9), which begins with a Schumann melody that Clara herself had once written variations for, and continues with variations that sometimes resemble Schumann's musical style and at other times are uniquely Brahmsian.

It occurred to me that Brahms's way of interacting with and making music for the Schumanns may have had certain characterics of what Winnicott (1971), working with mothers and children, has called the *transitional object* and Volkan (1981), observing states of bereavement, called a *linking phenomenon*. These technical psychoanalytic terms have come to denote such tangible physical items as clothing, dolls, toys, or other belongings which can carry personal meanings and thus are capable of temporarily allaying the anxieties produced by separation from a true love object. In terms of providing emotional gratification, transitional objects are less real than human objects, but they are more real than fantasized objects. Art objects in that sense can become very powerful transitional or linking phenomena, valuable not only for individuals but for entire cultures.

Music, as has been explained elsewhere (Ostwald, 1989), may be especially well suited for use as a transitional or linking phenomenon. It has a unique capacity for soothing and comforting. It has both the concreteness of real events and the abstractness of symbols. Some composers seem especially gifted in exploiting these transitional qualities of music, and I would like to suggest that Johannes Brahms is a good example of such an artist. Not only did he create effective musical links for future generations, but he also manifested certain qualities of personality that I would consider "transitional."

THE PROBLEM OF GETTING TO KNOW BRAHMS

The literature on this composer is voluminous. Max Kalbeck (1913–1922) compiled an eight-volume biography. Florence May (1981), who had been a pupil of Brahms, produced a sensitive study in two volumes. Walter Niemann (1937), Hans Gal (1963), and other scholars have contributed authoritative texts. Karl Geiringer's *Brahms* (1982) has become a classic and can be highly recommended. Thus it may seem that there ought to be few if any mysteries about this composer. Yet he remains somehow remote and unfathomable. Perhaps that is the way he wanted it to be. Brahms seems to have resisted most efforts to get close to him. Those who tried to do it were rebuffed. Even Clara Schumann had to confess that nearly fifty years of acquaintance with this musician had given her no insight into his character or ways of thinking. Here was someone who habitually kept his feelings to himself, and he deliberately destroyed many manuscripts and other personal documents that might have revealed how his mind functioned.

For the clinician, such behavior can be frustrating as well as tantalizing. Does Brahms's reserve indicate that he wanted to hide something? Or was this a way of trying to get people more interested in him. My impression is that despite his efforts at anonymity, Brahms wanted to be understood. He seems to have suffered greatly at times, and he probably had a number of depressive episodes. But the basic textbooks about illnesses of great composers are not helpful in this regard; neither Franken (1979) nor Kerner (1973) contain chapters about Brahms. In my review of the literature, I have been able to find only four authors who focus directly on his emotional condition. Lange-Eichbaum (1961) cites observations that depict Brahms as "obstinately depressive *(ein trotziger Melancholiker)* . . . sexually inhibited, immature, [and] with advancing age crochety, pedantic, and helpless in practical matters." Schauffler (1940) calls him a "schizoid personality." Hitschmann (1949) describes his "marriage inhibition." Geiringer, in the keynote address at the 1983 Library of Congress Brahms Symposium, calls him "ambivalent."

Each of these diagnostic hunches has something of merit. In addition, I would suggest that Brahms had something of the "avoidant personality" described in our modern diagnostic nomenclature, viz. hypersensitivity to rejection, unwillingness to enter into relationships that did not guarantee uncritical acceptance, social distancing, and low self-esteem. But how are all of these descriptive criteria to be understood in the context of his developmental history, particularly his musical development? In brief: he appears to have been hypersensitive and moody beginning in childhood, but thanks to music he was able to find ways of avoiding personal intimacy and thus prevent overstimulation throughout adolescence. Most of his adult life he was a loner, and he never married. Severe emotional crises were generally averted, and no serious breakdowns ever occurred. With Brahms there was also a very good fit between his personality, his talent, and his ambition—he never seriously attempted to compose an opera, for example—so that despite a number of career frustrations he always continued to work. Finally, to appreciate Brahms's generally favorable state of health, it should be pointed out that he had the advantage of a long-term relationship with an outstanding physician and surgeon, Theodor Billroth, who became his devoted admirer and undoubtedly exerted a therapeutic influence. Thus conditions that might well have become more overtly psychopathological seem to have been held in check, so that Brahms's depressive disorder and personality problems were muted, leaving residues of great music, loneliness, and altruism.

Music

There can be no doubt that Brahms's musical development in early childhood was very strongly influenced by his father, Johann Jakob Brahms (1806–1872), an enthusiastic musician who played a number of instruments including the horn, flute, viola, double bass, and drums. He was born in Heide, a farming community of 5,000 in the Ditmarsh near the North Sea, 90 kilometers from Hamburg and had rebelled against his own parental tradition of business and farming by joining the village band *(Stadtpfeiferei)* and embarking on a career as a musician. In his early twenties Johann Jakob Brahms had moved to Hamburg, hoping to find greater security there. But he found little of it. In the big city he had to eke out a meager living by playing in dance or marching bands. Marriage at the age of twenty-four had stabilized his situation somewhat; Johann Jakob chose as his bride a woman of forty-one who was an excellent cook and seamstress, Johanna Henrika Christiane Nissen (1787–1865). She was a tiny, crippled spinster who undoubtedly seized this opportunity to marry a good-looking and healthy but impoverished musician as her last hope of ever having a family of her own. Her background was more genteel than that of her husband, and it is said that she came from a family that had once been prominent. However, economic circumstances had forced her and her sister to take in boarders, and that is how she met Johann Jakob Brahms.

Their first child was a daughter named Wilhelmina Louise Elizabeth ("Elise") (1831–1892). She was in poor health for most of her life and very dependent, first on her mother and later on her brother Johannes, the second child, born in 1833, who turned out to be bright and very attractive, a musical genius, and clearly the mother's favorite. Two years later a third and last child was born, Friedrich ("Fritz") (1835–1886). Fritz also was trained as a musician, but seems to have been unsuccessful in his musical work. He gave a few concerts, worked as a piano teacher, and later lived for a while in South America. Except for his high forehead and copious hair, Fritz struck people as being very different from his famous brother, and he was often referred to as "the wrong Brahms."

It was their father's intention that both boys should help support the family by playing for money. Hamburg was, as it is now, a busy port with a large red-light district, and good opportunities for musicians in the local taverns as well as in the more respectable theater and symphony orchestras. Johannes was born in a crowded, delapidated apartment house, Speckstrasse 60,[2] near the slums. He was "delicate and often plagued by headaches" (Ehrmann, 1933, p. 9), a sensitive child who did not like to roughhouse and would prefer playing with girls. His mother adored him and pampered him with special recipes of soups, egg-nogs, and pancakes. (Some of these recipes have survived.) The two-room apartment being very crowded, she did not like to have her husband and his friends play their musical instruments there. Quarrels frequently took place

---

[2] This old wooden-frame building, along with many others in the center of Hamburg, was destroyed during the fire-bombings of World War II.

between the parents, and the father had to go elsewhere in order to make music. To what extent these conflicts affected the children is not known, but one can assume that the tension in the household may have contributed to Johannes's headaches and to his sister's respiratory distress. Perhaps even Brahms's attitude toward practicing and playing music was influenced by parental disagreement. His father is reported to have made remarks such as "shut the door, Johannes, the old woman is coming" while they were engaged in rehearsals (Hofmann, 1983, p. 14). The father was a restless and dissatisfied man. He moved his family to five different apartments while Johannes was a child, finally settling at Dammtorwall 29 when he was eight years old. He also tried with little success raising rabbits, pigeons, and chickens for money, and for a while ran a small store which also failed. At one point Brahms's father, like so many Germans at the time, considered emigrating to America. (The parents later separated, and after his wife's death, Johann Jakob married a woman eighteen years his junior.)

Significant is the fact that young Johannes chose to play the piano, which became his favorite musical instrument. Not only did the piano offer a far greater range of musical possibilities than his father's band instruments, but it also provided a psychological compromise. In their tiny apartment there was room for a small piano, an instrument that his mother was able to approve of. In fact it was she who made arrangements for the boys to take piano lessons. However, to do his practicing, and in order to take lessons (beginning at age eight), Johannes regularly went to the house of his teacher, Otto Willibald Cossel, an excellent musician who lived nearby and to whom he quickly became very attached. Cossel was amazed by the boy's precocious musical ability, and he encouraged him to perform publicly, beginning at age ten. That same year according to Niemann (1937, p. 9), the boy "suffered considerable injuries" when a carriage ran over him, but the nature of these injuries is not reported, nor do we know whether the accident took place before or after the concert or what its effects on Brahms and his family (not to mention the ambitious teacher) might have been. Presumably there were no serious physical sequelae, otherwise they would have been reported by other biographers. As for any psychological damage, one can speculate that the accident may have reinforced Brahms's already well-established reluctance to be involved in rough physical activity. Unfortunately we have no information about how he may have reacted to other environmental stresses, for example the great fire which occurred in 1842, when Johannes was nine years old, burned for three days and destroyed 5,000 houses in Hamburg.

He was surely considered to be a child prodigy. Brahms began to write music spontaneously, long before he knew about the system of notation, and it is said that he invented his own method for doing so. "I was always composing . . . my finest songs would come to me early in the morning, while I was cleaning my boots" (Niemann, 1937, p. 11). The concerts he gave were so successful that a talent scout even proposed sending the boy to America for a tour, a move that his father would have welcomed as a way of making money. But his teacher objected to this early exploitation of Brahms's talent. Instead of going to America,[3] he was given the opportunity to study with Otto Cossel's own teacher, the distinguished Hamburg pianist and composer Eduard Marxsen. Marxsen was keenly interested in the music of the seventeenth and eighteenth centuries, as well as in the German folk-song tradition, and it was undoubtedly due to the influence of this outstanding pedagogue that Brahms acquired such an extensive knowledge of these musical styles.

Again there were conflicts. Brahms's father, insisting that his talented son should be a practical musician and earn money, allowed him, beginning at the age of thirteen, to sing and play the piano in various local taverns. For this the boy would receive two Thalers and as much booze as he wanted to drink. To augment the family income, Brahms also gave music lessons and made musical arrangements for a Hamburg publisher. As May (1981, Vol. 1, p. 56) has emphasized, this "role-reversal" within his family established Brahms as a caretaker at an age when he himself needed to be taken care of. It also interfered with his education. Brahms had to quit school when he was fourteen, something he always regretted, felt uncomfortable about, and later tried to compensate for through prodigious reading. When he was sixteen, his first compositions were published, but not under his own name. (The publisher, August Cranz, preferred to have the works of unknown composers appear under the collective name G. W. Marks.) Brahms used other

---

[3] Never in his entire life did Brahms leave the European continent. He even refused to go to England when Cambridge University, in 1877, honored him with a Doctorate in Music. The excuse he gave was that the voyage would make him seasick.

pen-names as well. His favorite was Johannes Kreisler, Junior, taken from the romantic tales of E. T. A. Hoffmann. He signed this name to many of his early letters and compositions. This gives us a sense of Brahms's identification with the spirit of German romanticism, as well as his desire for anonymity. Typically, he later destroyed all of his youthful works, except for a piano duet called *Souvenir de Russie*.

A letter written by his mother, when Brahms was an adolescent, provides some information about the atmosphere in his home:

> Your father [complained] that it was taking much too long with your education [and] that you should hurry up and get out into the world; he no longer wanted to feed you; you became so excited, and both of us cried and went to bed late and Elise lay in bed and couldn't breathe, so you had to go for the doctor and get an emetic for her, it was in the middle of the night; when you returned I made a nice cup of coffee for you . . . [Hofmann, 1983, pp. 18–19].

When Brahms was nineteen he left Hamburg to go on a concert tour with Eduard Remenyi, a violinist of Hungarian origin who wanted him to be his piano accompanist. Thus Brahms was able to meet a number of prominent musicians who were to influence him in important ways. For example, in Hanover he was introduced to the violinist Joseph Joachim, who became a life-long friend. In Weimar he met Franz Liszt. Already at that time Brahms's difficult personality traits, his shyness coupled with self-confidence, his sensitivity mixed with roughness, puzzled certain musicians. The pianist Anton Rubinstein wrote to Liszt as follows: "I hardly know how to describe the impression [Brahms] made on me. He is not graceful enough for the drawing room, nor fiery enough for the concertroom, nor simple enough for the country, and not complex enough for the city. I have but little faith in this kind of person" (May, 1981, p. 201).

Joachim, whose role in Brahms's life will be discussed in greater detail, characterized him (in 1854) as:

> [T]he most dyed-in-the-wool egoist one can imagine . . . with an inconsiderateness that wounds . . . whatever doesn't fit with *his* enthusiasm, *his* experience, or *his* mood is rejected with loveless frigidity. . . . The only thing he wants is to pursue his musical

bliss, his belief in a higher, fantastical world, undisturbed . . . [Hofmann and Fürst, 1980, p. 14].

In Düsseldorf Brahms met Robert and Clara Schumann, an encounter that had profound consequences. Its importance for Brahms's musical development lay in the fact that he and Schumann had an uncanny rapport. The older composer recognized Brahms's genius. He described his piano sonatas as "veiled symphonies." In a widely read newspaper article Schumann (1883, Vol. 2, pp. 374–375) predicted that Brahms would one day "lower his magic wand where mighty masses of orchestra and chorus will lend him their power, [and] we will obtain wonderful views into the secrets of a spiritual world," a prophecy that the younger composer found embarrassing and difficult to live up to for many years. Brahms was then in what can be called a self-expressive phase of creativity, striving to forge an original, highly romantic style of music while also adhering to some of the more classical traditions. He had composed mainly for the piano, and had already completed two sonatas as well as works for piano and strings, which impressed Schumann deeply. Characteristic of this music is its rhythmic intensity, the grand, sweeping, "symphonic" use of the keyboard, a mysterious feeling-tone, short themes that soon undergo variation (they are not always easy to identify), and enormous passion. It was under the supervision of Schumann that Brahms completed his *Piano Sonata in E Minor* (op. 5), the last composition in this genre he would ever write, while Schumann, in turn influenced by Brahms, wrote his own last work for solo piano, *Songs of Early Morning* (op. 133)

Schumann attempted suicide on February 27, 1854, and he was hospitalized in Bonn-Endenich on March 3, five months after first meeting Brahms. The young friend quickly rushed back to Düsseldorf to stay with Schumann's wife, who was pregnant at the time. Deeply troubled about her husband's mental illness and the enforced separation, Clara encouraged Brahms to comfort her and to help her take care of the household, including the children. He took up residence in their house, worked in Schumann's study, reorganized his collection of books and music, did a little teaching, and kept track of financial transactions in Schumann's "Householdbook." When Clara's son Felix was born on June 11, 1854, Brahms acted in Schumann's capacity at the christening, and he became the boy's godfather.[4] Soon Clara returned to the concert stage, and Brahms would occasionally travel with her. Not surprisingly, a strong attachment developed between these two artists. "He has such a soothingly tender feeling for me," writes Clara (Litzman, 1902–1908, Vol. 2, pp. 317–318). "I am in love with her. Often I have to hold myself back forcibly from just putting my arm around her and . . . she wouldn't mind it at all," writes Brahms (Holde, 1959, p. 314). Whether they ever became lovers remains a moot point. My hunch is that some physical intimacy may have been attempted during this time of mutual infatuation. I also suspect that this turned out to be not very satisfying, and that it quickly ceased, leaving behind feelings of guilt and disappointment. Nancy Reich (1985), who has written a book about Clara Schumann, disagrees. Because so much personal correspondence has been destroyed, and neither Brahms nor Clara Schumann seems to have discussed this matter with anyone else, the whole truth will never be known.

It was during this difficult period, when Robert Schumann was in the hospital, that Brahms composed the Variations in F sharp minor (op. 9) mentioned earlier. Schumann sent Brahms a warm letter of thanks and praised him for the composition. But an unpublished draft for this letter suggests that he was probably deeply disturbed to realize how much progress Brahms was making while his own career had come to a standstill (Geiringer, 1939). Schumann may also have sensed the growing attachment between his wife and Brahms, again a moot point because we do not know what was talked about during the hospital visits.

After Schumann died (on July 29, 1856), Clara decided to dissolve the household in Düsseldorf and move to Berlin. It is possible that Brahms proposed, as he did several times over the years, to have a more permanent liaison, possibly even to marry Clara. Wanting to spare her the ordeal of a busy concert schedule, he envisioned her as a potential good *Hausfrau*, someone like his

---

[4] Rumors that Felix Schumann (1854–1879) was actually Brahms's son are difficult to support factually. It seems unlikely that Clara would have had sexual relations with Brahms in 1853, immediately after his first arrival in Düsseldorf. Also, as I have explained in more detail elsewhere (Ostwald, 1985, p. 264), Clara was having intercourse regularly with her husband during the month their last child was conceived. (Felix later became a gifted writer, and Brahms set some of his poems to music. He died tragically young, of tuberculosis.)

mother. But Clara Schumann's career as a pianist always took first place. She did not seem interested in tying herself to another man, especially someone fourteen years her junior, who in his dependency on her was beginning to resemble one of her own children, and whose fanatic need to compose was like that of her late husband. So she urged Brahms to accept a position as choral conductor in Detmold, a small principality near the Teutoburg Forest where she had friends.

Thus began the second phase of his creative career, one that might be called "experimentation." In Detmold, where he spent part of the next three years (interspersed with visits to Hamburg), he acquired the skills of orchestral and choral composition. Among his most original choral compositions during this period were the *Gesänge* (op. 17) for women's chorus, harps, and horn, with their extraordinary harmonic textures, often hovering between major and minor, giving an ambiguous, bitter-sweet mood. He completed two Serenades for Orchestra (op. 11 and 16), and, as he gained confidence, also composed notable works of chamber music, including two Quartets for Piano and Strings (op. 25 and 26), two Sextets for Strings (op. 18 and 36), and a Trio for Horn, Violin, and Piano (op. 40), the Sonata for Violoncello and Piano (op. 38), as well as a quintet for strings which later became a sonata for two pianos and still later was transformed into his Piano Quintet in F Minor (op. 34a). Brahms also tried to compose a symphony during these years, but his early effort was not successful and he converted it into the Piano Concerto in D Minor (op. 15), a work which at that time was very poorly received by the public.

It was an experimental period also as far as Brahms's life-style was concerned. He traveled a great deal, settled nowhere for long, felt rootless and often depressed. His problems in forming relationships with women will be described shortly. Clara Schumann remained his most trusted confidante, to whom he wrote long letters about their mutual interest in her husband's memory, and about his own musical activities, the joys and frustrations of being a performer (pianist and conductor) as well as a composer (Brahms, 1983).

Brahms tended to be secretive about how he went about composing music, and he would be furious if anyone tried to observe him at work. However, in a conversation with George Henschel, he once said:

There is no real *creating* without hard work. That which you would call invention, that is to say, a thought, an idea, is simply an inspiration from above, for which I am not responsible, which is no merit of mine. Yea, it is a present, a gift, which I ought even to despise until I have made it my own by right of hard work. And there need be no hurry about that, either. It is as with the seed-corn; it germinates unconsciously and in spite of ourselves [Henschel, 1907, p. 22].

For his musical "inspirations," he liked to be outdoors, walking in the country or relaxing in some beautiful scenic spot. He would save his new ideas, often for many years, and work them laboriously into a composition, usually at his desk, rarely at the piano. Max Kalbeck, who later became his biographer, once caught a glimpse of Brahms slaving over one of his scores: "[He] whined, moaned, and cried aloud like a dog. Afterwards Brahms furtively wiped his eyes with the back of his hand. He must have wept copiously . . ." (cited by Hitschmann, 1949).

A turning point, both personally and artistically, was reached at the age of thirty-two, after the death of his mother, on January 31, 1865. Years earlier, Brahms had begun to work on a large choral composition, a "German Requiem," an idea that Robert Schumann had given him. The Requiem was to be based on biblical texts in German rather than Latin, and Brahms had chosen passages to express the stern philosophy he was then developing about death, as well as the grief he had felt after Schumann's death. He had not been able to complete the work, owing perhaps to some residual ambivalence (or oedipal fear) in regard to this man whose wife he loved. Now the loss of his mother necessitated renewed mourning for Brahms, which he handled creatively by completing the work and adding two new movements, one of them dedicated specifically to his mother.[5] This makes the German Requiem (op. 45) a kind of double memorial, to the woman who had given him birth and the man who had helped make him famous. Moreover, this became Brahms's first truly successful composition. Not only did the Requiem consolidate his reputation as a major musical figure throughout the German-speaking countries of Europe, it also marked the beginning of a new phase of creative achievement, the years of "mastery."

---

[5] This is not the only composition by Brahms which memorializes his mother. Becker (1980) points specifically to the slow movement of the Horn Trio and the folksong *"Dort in der Weiden steht ein Haus,"* as compositions which serve this function.

Mastery, for Brahms, entailed the perfection of a principle of developing variations (Frisch, 1984). The uniqueness of this approach, which in certain respects can be considered one of the forerunners of modern serial techniques, lies in its ability to provide many shifting harmonic textures while never letting go of the established tonal centers. Musical ideas are continually remolded and rerepresented without ever losing their basic identity. Notable rhythmic contrasts, especially the use of double-against-triple meters, are an important feature of Brahms's style of developing variations. The impression produced by this compositional technique is one of intensely surging emotion, but emotion that is always kept under control. One hears the dynamic shifts of feeling in the music, but emotional fluctuations sound graded and often seem deliberately restrained. Rarely does a movement by Brahms explode with passion or reach a climax, as does the music of Beethoven, Wagner, or Mahler, for example.

Of greatest importance during Brahms's period of mastery—from his midthirties to early fifties—was his long-delayed debut as a composer of symphonies. He had often said "it was no laughing matter [to write a symphony] . . . when we hear the tramp of a giant like Beethoven behind us" (Niemann, 1937, p. 323). I would like to suggest that this grim fantasy of a "giant" (shared to some extent, of course, by other symphonists of the nineteenth century) may contain an introjected image of Brahms's disapproving father, who had never really forgiven him for wanting to be a composer rather than simply a performer, playing in orchestras for a living. Johannes had remained steadily devoted to his father, sending money to him in Hamburg, inviting him to visit Vienna (where Brahms was now living), maintaining essentially the "role reversal" noted earlier, of child taking care of parents. One can postulate a degree of unconscious guilt for wanting to defy the old man by breaking away from family obligations. Brahms was thirty-nine years old when his father died, on February 11, 1872, and finally the bondage to his *Heimat* seems to have loosened somewhat.[6] Sketches dating back to his twenties and ideas that had been germinating for at least fourteen years were now integrated into the Symphony No. 1 in C

---

[6] Only loosened, and never broken, however. Brahms's touching loyalty and generosity—aspects of his altruism—which he had manifested for years toward his parents was carried forward in his relationship with his sister, as well as his stepmother, and her children.

Minor (op. 68). Hans von Bülow called this majestic work "Beethoven's Tenth," a judgment that seems flattering but does not really do justice to Brahms's originality or the miraculous leap of imagination in creating a symphonic style so different from Beethoven's.

Three years later Brahms composed his sunny Symphony No. 2 in D Major (op. 73), and six years after that he wrote the heroic Symphony No. 3 in F major (op. 90). Other orchestral works produced during this phase of creative mastery were the Violin Concerto in D Major (op. 77), written for his friend Joseph Joachim (and with the violinist's very active collaboration); the Piano Concerto No. 2 in B Flat Major (op. 83), dedicated to Brahms's old teacher Eduard Marxsen in Hamburg; and the two concert overtures, *Academic Festival Overture* (op. 80), to celebrate his acceptance of an honorary doctorate from Breslau University, and the *Tragic Overture* (op. 81). The composer was by now working closely with the Meiningen Court Orchestra led by von Bülow, an excellent ensemble which performed his music throughout Germany, sometimes with Brahms himself conducting. Thus he was able to make corrections and perfect his orchestral works before they were published.

Strange as it may seem today, Brahms in his own time was a controversial composer whose music often generated violent criticism. For example, the *New York Post* (in 1880) described his first symphony as

> Poor in ideas, and the few there are want originality. They do not warm us, they do not speak to our hearts' emotions. Everything is measured, cold, and of aristocratic reserve" [cited by Slonimsky, 1965, pp. 69–70].

> Brahms's second symphony was listened to attentively but did not arouse enthusiasm. What work of Brahms ever did? Of course it is an exceedingly erudite work ... but it lacks grand sweeping ideas and is deficient in sensuous charm.... The greater part of the symphony was antiquated before it was written [*New York Post*, 1886, cited by Slonimsky, 1965, pp. 73–74].

Lest we think that such ungracious remarks came only from music critics, let us read what the Russian composer Tchaikowsky wrote in his diary, in 1886. "I've played over the music of that scoundrel Brahms. What a giftless bastard. It annoys me that this self-inflated mediocrity is hailed as a genius. Brahms's music is chaotic and absolutely empty dried up stuff" (cited by Slonimsky, 1965, p. 73).

And Richard Strauss's first reaction to Brahms's Third Symphony was that "it is so obscure and miserable in its instrumentation, that in the first and last movement I could make out only two connected ideas of four bars each" (cited by Gay, 1978, p. 240).

Historian Peter Gay has commented on the remarkable "polarity" of opinions about Brahms, who can be seen as "both a traditionalist and an innovator, both a conservative and a radical, both a craftsman and a creator . . . an emotional intellectual, without crippling conflicts, without paradox" (Gay, 1978, p. 255). Richard Wagner called him a "jewish czardas player," while Hugo Wolf characterized Brahms as using "the language of the most intensive musical impotence" (cited by Slonimsky, 1965, p. 73). Brahms himself recognized that "people don't love me—they respect me, and that is the main thing. I don't ask for more" (see Gay, p. 243).

At least some of this polarization of opinion, as well as the abuse (or lack of love) heaped upon him, was provoked, I submit, by the often incongruous features of Brahms's personality. Simultaneously appealing and repelling, yearning but self-sufficient, he could be boisterous and sarcastic, or sullen and inhibited. He was given to playing tricks on people and either sulked in silence or made devastatingly sarcastic remarks. As a young man, Brahms had often seemed impulsive and tactless. Early in his career, by signing a "declaration" that publicly condemned "the leaders and disciples of the so-called neo-German school," he had managed to antagonize Liszt, Wagner, and other musicians who wanted to be identified with the "music of the future" (Niemann, 1937, p. 78). Androgynous in appearance—"the delicate maidenly profile of an exceptionally beautiful man" (Schneider, 1974, p. 118)—and speaking with a high, piping voice, he managed to remain exceptionally youthful, even physically immature, well into his forties. Upon entering middle age, Brahms decided suddenly to change his appearance and behavior. He forced his voice into a lower register until it sounded hoarse, and he grew a beard—"with a shaven chin one is taken for an actor or a parson" (Niemann, p. 170). He began putting on weight, acted in a more reserved fashion, and in his eartly fifties embarked on what was to be the final phase of his creativity, a period of "turning inwards."

Songs and chamber music again predominated. He also wrote two important orchestral works that bear witness to the composer's successful achievement of certain artistic and personal goals. The

Fourth Symphony in E Minor (op. 98) integrates contrastive moods of sadness and joy. Beginning *Allegro non troppo* in the pensive key of E minor, the symphony moves to the contrasting key of E major in a mysterious and subdued *Andante moderato*, before giving vent to aggressive merriment in the Scherzo, *Allegro giocoso*. In the Finale, *Allegro energico e passionato (Passacaglia)*, Brahms demonstrates great ingenuity in solving the problem of how to fuse an outdated form, the *Passacaglia*, with his own uniquely "neoclassical" romantic style. He returns to the home key of E minor, and uses a sparse, scalelike theme as the "obstinate" bass line *(basso ostinato)* for thirty-two consecutive variations. An extraordinary range of styles and feelings is thus expressed within the mathematically precise form of a Bachlike structure.[7]

The Double Concerto for Violin and Violoncello (op. 102), his last orchestral work, offers a similar kind of aesthetic solution, in that certain features of the baroque *concerto grosso* are incorporated into the modern orchestral sound. One also senses a more personal solution behind this work, having to do with Brahms's mixed feelings about the violinist Joseph Joachim. Their friendship, which will be discussed in more detail shortly, had continued over the years. Joachim did everything in his power to help promote Brahms's music, and to perform it in public. However, as certain "suppressed passages" from their correspondence indicate, Brahms objected to Joachim's possessiveness and other "unfortunate character-trait[s]" (Holde, 1959). He felt it necessary to keep a certain distance from the violinist and refused, for example, ever to live in the same city with him. In the course of time, Joachim had married a singer whom Brahms greatly admired and preferred as the interpreter of his songs. A crisis arose when Joachim suddenly developed the fixed idea (probably a delusion of jealousy) that his wife Amalie was having an affair with Fritz Simrock, Brahms's publisher and financial advisor in Vienna. Proclaiming her innocence, Amalie appealed to Brahms for help, which the composer gladly gave in the form of a very frank and personal letter critical of Joachim's behavior. Amalie decided to use this letter as evidence against her husband during a bitter court battle which in 1884 led

---

[7] Brahms was a great admirer of Johann Sebastian Bach, whose Chaconne in D minor for solo violin he had once transcribed for the piano, left hand alone.

to a divorce (Moser, 1910, Vol. 2, p. 228). That of course cooled the relationship between Brahms and Joachim considerably.

Brahms describes his Double Concerto as a "curious . . . [and] happy inspiration," and in correspondence with Joachim he betrays eagerness for a more harmonious relationship with his alienated friend (Brahms, 1983, pp. 225–230). (Brahms also regretted that writing music for the cello was not as "pleasant and intelligent" as composing for the piano, an instrument he knew much better.) Perhaps it was proving to be more frustrating than he had at first imagined to bring the lower-pitched, more masculine-sounding cello voice into harmony with Joachim's higher-voiced, more feminine-sounding violin. In the first movement, the two instruments enter separately, each spinning a *cadenza*, but they soon come together, and in the second movement sing *unisono*, then dance merrily in the Finale. No doubt Brahms also had Joachim in mind when he composed his mellifluous Sonata for Violin and Piano in D minor (op. 108), with its wild, gypsylike ending. He had sent the manuscript to Clara Schumann, hoping she would perform this work with Joachim.

By now Brahms looked like a grizzled, bearded, and "rotund little gentleman" (Jenner's observation, cited by Niemann, 1937, p. 170) and was behaving more eccentrically, with little apparent concern for the feelings of others. He appeared unduly sad and was lacking in self-confidence. "I never expect that a new piece of mine will please anyone" (Brahms, 1983, p. 236). At the age of fifty-eight he seemed truly depressed, complaining that he had nothing more to say as a composer and that his life was finished. He wrote a will and prepared to die. This may have been an involutional melancholia. But for Brahms it was also a kind of "creative malady" (Pickering, 1974). In the throes of it he had discovered a new love, for the sound of the clarinet as played by Richard Mühlfeld, first clarinettist of the Meiningen Orchestra. Brahms called him "Fräulein Mühlfeld, my *prima donna*," and with this musician in mind he composed a wistful Trio for Clarinet, Piano, and Violoncello (op. 114), two Sonatas for Clarinet and Piano (op. 120), and the haunting Quintet for Clarinet and Strings (op. 115). A spate of new piano compositions soon followed: Fantasias (op. 116), Intermezzi (op. 117), and Piano Pieces (op. 118 and 119). These are introspective works, experimental in their complex rhythms and daring harmonies, unrewarding for many listeners and intended to be studied in private rather than played in a concert hall. About his Intermezzo (op. 119, no. 1) Brahms wrote Clara "this little piece is exceptionally melancholic, and *'sehr langsam spielen'* doesn't say enough. Each measure and each note must sound ritardando, as if one wants to suck melancholia out of every single one, with voluptuous pleasure . . . "(Brahms, 1983, p. 253).

LONELINESS

All his life Brahms had a way of avoiding intimate relationships with other people. Already as a child he was solitary and reclusive, preferring to be at the piano or to play with his favorite collection of toy soldiers, an interest that may have combined his need for order with sublimated aggression (as well as his love for his father, who belonged to a military band). Incidentally, Brahms's interest in military matters never subsided. All his life he was very patriotic. Enthusiastic about the Franco-Prussian war of 1870, he wanted to be sure "that the French [would] get a good beating" (Brahms, 1983, p. 151), and he composed a *Song of Triumph for Chorus and Orchestra* (op. 55) when they did. Brahms greatly admired Bismarck, and knew many of his speeches and much of his writing by heart.

Solitary pursuits, in particular reading, occupied much of his time. One of his favorite books was the Bible, from which he also could quote at length. He was widely read in the classics, history, legends, Rennaissance art, biographies of musicians, and poetry. Brahms resented bitterly any allusions to his lack of formal education, and he was proud of his ability to discuss literature and the arts with some of the leading German-speaking intellectuals (Pascal, 1983). He was an avid collector of rare books, musical manuscripts, and original autographs, including works by Mozart and Schumann. Over the years this came to be a valuable collection, over which he fussed like an orderly librarian, conscientiously keeping track of every sheet of music he ever lent out.

Some of the negative impressions Brahms made on others may be attributed to the difficulty he had in using words. He often acknowledged this fault in letters containing apologies for the rough or clumsy way he would express himself—"I can't write letters, also can't write diplomatically" (Brahms, 1983, p. 137). He was often angry and self-critical for saying the wrong thing, and he would mock himself cruelly. Those who came to know Brahms well gradually came to realize that "his mockery and anger and humour were nothing but a 'lightning conductor,' a protection against his own soft-heartedness, of which he was afraid" (Niemann, 1937, p. 178).

A man of rigid habits, Brahms rose very early (at 5 A.M. in the summer), brewed many cups of strong, black coffee for himself, and worked without stopping until midday. He then went to a restaurant, always the same one for the last fourteen years of his life in Vienna, *Der Rote Igel* (The Red Hedgehog). Then he would go for a long walk, preferably in the country. Toward the evening, he prepared himself to go to a concert or the opera. Afterwards he had supper, often with friends, and usually in an informal setting such as a beer-hall. He could easily take a cat-nap and seldom seemed tired. It was difficult for others to keep up with Brahms; for example, while traveling he always had to be on the go, to walk faster, climb higher, and explore more places than anyone else. Like Beethoven, he moved around a great deal, frequently changing his residence until he finally settled down at Karlsgasse 4, in a small furnished apartment. Yet his bags were always kept packed for a trip, and he would spend long stretches of time each year away from home. Brahms always preferred older houses, and when traveling he would stay in simple, modest inns where he could relax unobserved, mingle with the help rather than the guests, and not have to dress up. His tendency to wear ill-fitting clothes, to forget his tie and collar, and to look rumpled if not disheveled (but never dirty), was noticed already in his twenties, at the Detmold court, where Brahms sometimes appeared in public and even conducted concerts dressed in a way that would draw attention to his "bad manners" and thus offend his patrons. Later, in Vienna, he habitually wore trousers that were too short, and instead of an overcoat would drape a green blanket around his shoulders, held in place with an oversize safety-pin.

To account for these character traits, and others yet to be described, I would like to suggest two possibilities, fully recognizing that proving or disproving such explanations will be impossible, considering that our subject cannot be brought into the laboratory for biological study or into the consultation room for a thorough psychological evaluation.

1. *Bioenergetic factors*: I assume Brahms to have been afflicted with some type of mood disorder, possibly a bipolar or cyclothymic

disturbance that he tried to control, more or less successfully, through strenuously compulsive musical activities, playing the piano, studying scores, composing, and conducting. We know this to be a not uncommon problem among exceptionally productive and creative individuals (Richards, 1981), and I have described the pattern in several other nineteenth-century composers (Ostwald, 1985, 1987, 1988). These people have unusually high levels of energy and are easily aroused. Unless contained through activity and work, their abundant vigor and interest can spill over into uncomfortable states of ("hypomanic") excitement, as it probably threatened to do when Brahms would become overly abrasive, jocular, and irritating. At the other extreme are states of exhaustion and fatigue. Brahms used caffeine and nicotine to cope with them. A certain narrowing of interest may also conserve energy, and I suspect that after a long and exhausting day of struggling with musical problems, insufficient energy remained for him to attend to the "less important" matter of social conformity.

2. *Psychological conflict*: Brahms may have been torn between disobedience and conformity. This polarization undoubtedly reflected the influence of his parents, who were so widely discrepant in age, social background, and cultural attitudes (Stephenson, 1973). In regard to his habits of dress, one of my favorite anecdotes is about Brahms leaving home as a teenager. His mother gave him a sewing kit, with careful instructions on how to use it. He never did. Any holes in his clothes he would mend with sealing wax! This was his way of rebelling, through simultaneous protest and submission. Indeed, it has been noted that in contrast to the carelessness in his physical appearance, Brahms manifested the utmost scrupulosity in polishing his musical compositions. No gap was ever permitted in the fabric of a work; there were never any "loose threads." Furthermore, I would suggest as an explanation for Brahms's deportment some internalization of the life-style and personal characteristics of Ludwig van Beethoven[8] and Franz Schubert, two composers he tended to idealize. Beethoven's slovenliness, rudeness, and disregard of social convention have been discussed psychoanalytically (Solomon, 1978). Schubert's fluctuating sociability and withdrawal, his incessant involvement in things musical, and his ambivalence

---

[8] The identification with Beethoven was brought home to me by Alessandra Comini's excellent demonstration, "The Visual Brahms" (Comini, 1983).

regarding women are also well-known (Deutsch, 1947). Brahms's early infatuation with Robert Schumann, and his life-long interest in Clara Schumann, may also have led to a degree of identification with these musicians. If that was the case, then the internalized influence of Schumann would probably have had a balancing effect, tending to neutralize Brahms's identification with the lonely, eccentric, unmarried "mad genius" prototype. And that Clara did not permit a closer union and in the long run would not let him step into Robert's shoes, reflects, perhaps, her good judgment in recognizing that such a move would have been destructive to Brahms's great talent, which had to be nurtured in solitude and seemed to require certain eccentricities.

Needless to say, regular employment proved to be impossible for this artist who valued freedom and needed independence to do his creative work. Brahms used to say that he wanted to be appointed as Director of the Hamburg Philharmonic Society—Geiringer (1982) calls this a "self-delusion," probably based on the composer's wish to please or placate his father—and he felt rebuffed and embittered when Julius Stockhausen (a singer and friend of Brahms) obtained the prestigious post instead. But every time an equivalent position in Berlin, Cologne, or another major city was offered to Brahms, he would find various reasons for turning it down, and when the Hamburg post finally was made available for him, he claimed lamely that it was now too late to accept it. Brahms did accept employment on a few occasions, but only briefly. At age thirty, he served as conductor of the Vienna *Singakademie*; ten years later he became artistic director of the *Gesellschaft der Musikfreunde* but resigned after three years. By that time he no longer needed a salary. Brahms was now earning sufficient income by giving concerts, and he gradually became fairly wealthy through the sale and publication of his compositions.

Self-imposed bachelorhood was another reason for his loneliness. Brahms would speak regretfully about this at times, and his song, "*Kein Haus, keine Heimat!*" (op. 95, no. 5) expresses very well the unhappiness of a lonesome man who, in the words of Friedrich Halm, has "no house, no home, no wife, no child. I'm like a straw blown by the wind." But there also were times when he tried to make a virtue of bachelorhood. For example, when offered the Directorship of the Music Society in Düsseldorf (a post held earlier by Mendelssohn and Schumann), Brahms declined. In explaining why, he wrote to Doctor Billroth:

My main objections are of a rather childish nature, and I must remain silent about them. Perhaps the good taverns and restaurants in Vienna, the disagreeable, rough rhenish tone (generally in Düsseldorf), and—and—in Vienna one can remain a bachelor without any hindrance. In a smaller city an old bachelor is a caricature. Marriage is something I no longer want and—I do have some reasons to be afraid of the fair sex [Brahms, 1983, p. 176].

No friendship did more to reduce Brahms's loneliness than that with Joseph Joachim, the violinist and composer who was two years his senior (and outlived him by a decade). "Free But Lonely *(Frei Aber Einsam)*" was Joachim's personal motto; its initials FAE make a musical pattern. Schumann had used this for his FAE Sonata for Violin and Piano, and Brahms too employed the theme, for example in the first movement of his String Quartet in A minor (op. 51, no. 2). His own, related, motto was FAF, "Free But Happy *(Frei Aber Froh)*," heard in a whole series of compositions from the Second Piano Ballade (op. 10) to the first movement of the Third Symphony (op. 90) and beyond.

Brahms and Joachim often gave concerts together, and they maintained a lively correspondence for more than forty-one years, commenting on many musical matters as well as personal ones, such as their mutual dislike of gossip and their concerns about mental illness. Brahms held Joachim in very high esteem as a composer; in his typically ambivalent fashion he would regularly ask for technical advice, but just as regularly reject it. One source of difficulty in the relationship, alluded to earlier, was Brahms's discomfort with the violinist's need for physical expressions of affection. Apparently Joachim would try to embrace him, and while lying in bed would shed tears and beg his "dear Johannes" to come over to show his love (Schwarz, 1983). An unconscious homosexual element in the relationship is also suggested by Joachim's delusion about his wife having an affair with Brahms's friend Simrock. Early in the course of the troubled Joachim marriage, Brahms had written a cradle song for the couple's son, who in his honor was named Johannes. This song Brahms later incorporated into his moving Songs for Contralto, Viola, and Piano (op. 91). He had hoped that the music would bring about a reunion between Joachim and Amalie. It did not.

Sexuality clearly seems to have been a problem for Brahms. He was able to be affectionate with women, even demonstrative at times (as suggested by photographs, although these are mostly of the older Brahms and tend to show the women hugging him rather than vice versa). His habitual caution if not abhorrence in regard to physical intimacy may reflect traumatic childhood experiences, with parents who were unhappily married, often at cross-purposes, and perhaps abusive at times. His reserve toward women may also have been conditioned by the climate of sexual promiscuity in the Hamburg taverns where Brahms had worked as teenager. Hitschmann (1949) described it this way:

> Too early he came to know the active, frivolous, purchasable sexuality of the prostitute. He once told of scenes he had witnessed: of the sailors who rushed into the inn after a long voyage, greedy for drinks, gambling, and love of women, who, half-naked sang their obscene songs to his accompaniment, then took him on their laps and enjoyed awakening his first sexual feelings.

One would have to assume that unconscious and even conscious fantasies have been incorporated into such reminiscences. Nevertheless, Hitschmann's imagery suggests that young Brahms may have been seduced into playing the role of an aphrodisiac puppet, a go-between whose physical androgeny might be stimulating to men as well as women. And at a very critical period in his life he entered into the sexually complicated relationship between Robert and Clara Schumann, trying to satisfy both partners, as well as himself, in a marriage that had failed. "I dream and think only about the marvellous time when I will be able to live with both of you" he wrote on October 24, 1854 (Brahms, 1983, p. 41). Two months later: "I wish the doctor would employ me as an attendant or male nurse . . . I could write to you about him every day, and I could talk to him about you all day" (Litzmann, 1973). And finally, as we know, he was in love with Clara: "I think I can no longer love an unmarried girl—at least, I have completely forgotten them; they only promise the skies, whereas Clara shows it to us open" (Holde, 1959, p. 314).

Geiringer (1982, p. 52) suspects that while "Clara embodied in every respect Johannes's ideal of womanhood . . . the artist in him dimly felt that he must not definitely bind himself." Economic considerations were also important. Brahms had no regular income, and Clara had seven children to support. Ten years later, when his financial situation was considerably improved, he invited her to join him in Vienna (Brahms, 1983, pp. 129–130). But in the same letter he criticized her for always wanting to earn money by concertizing, and this offended Clara. She refused Brahms's offer. (Clara's incessant desire to travel and give concerts had also been a source of friction in her relationship with Schumann.) An additional factor in her unwillingness to live with Brahms may have been her attraction to the composer Theodor Kirchner (1823–1903), with whom Clara probably had a brief love affair (Reich, personal communication). From his lingering affection for Clara, Brahms drew inspiration for many of his greatest compositions. For example, his song "*Wie bist Du, meine Königin*" (op. 32 no. 9) expresses his veneration for her, while the Piano Quartet in C minor (op. 60) is said to be a musical dramatization of suicidal despair—in the manner of Goethe's *Werther*—felt after Clara rejected his marriage proposal.

Brahms did attract other women. Several members of a female choir he conducted in Hamburg adored him, and a singer from Vienna named Berta Porubsky may even have encouraged him to move to that city. The relationship did not continue. However, when Berta later married and had a child, Brahms composed his famous *Lullaby* (op. 49, no. 4) for her. A more substantial romance was with Agathe von Siebold, the daughter of a professor in Göttingen, introduced to him by Joachim. Brahms is said to have given her an engagement ring, and when Clara Schumann found out about this, she warned him not to marry Agathe. Brahms soon terminated this relationship, but not without considerable anguish, which he symbolized by means of an agitated theme spelling her name A-G-A-D-E in the first movement of his Sextet for Strings in E flat major (op. 18).

Brahms often teased Clara about possibly marrying one of her daughters, but he found excuses: "If [Eugenie] retains only a tiny scar on her pretty face [from a minor injury], then surely I can't marry her, and nothing will tie me down" (Brahms, 1983, p. 71). Julie Schumann, probably the prettiest of the girls, also interested Brahms for a while. When she got married, in 1867, to the Italian Count Marmorito, he felt embittered and angry, unjustly, since he had never declared any intention to marry Julie. Brahms had recently composed his melancholic Rhapsody for Alto Solo, Male Choir, and Orchestra (op. 53), and he now made a point of saying that this is "a bridal song for the Countess Schumann, but with rage do I write such things—with anger!..." (Hofmann and Fürst, 1980, p. 24). Another attractive woman in his life was Elizabeth von Herzogenberg, and again Brahms's avoidance of physical intimacy is apparent. She had been his piano student, and he broke off the relationship after noticing himself to be uncomfortably sexually aroused in her presence. They remained on good terms, however, and he regularly sought to please Elizabeth by sending her his "trifles," as he mockingly called compositions like the "tiny little Piano Concerto [in B♭ major], written with a small, delicate Scherzo" (Brahms, 1983, p. 202). (Between these lines the alert psychoanalytic reader might hypothesize some fear about the size of Brahms's genitalia.)

He also befriended a couple of contraltos. One was the buxom Hermine Spiess, whom Brahms referred to jokingly as "Hermione without an O." She premiered many of his most beautiful songs. The other was Alice Barbi, a friend in his old age. These must have been exceptional women to put up with his derisive, self-disparaging remarks, to the effect that any woman who could find him appealing must be out of her mind! Brahms liked to pose for photographs as a presumably happy bachelor surrounded by attractive women. In unguarded moments, however, his eccentricities became only too apparent, and many of his casual remarks sound utterly disillusioned: "I have no friends! If anyone says he is a friend of mine, don't believe it" (Niemann, 1937, p. 180). It is often said that he frequented prostitutes. In Vienna Brahms was occasionally observed in the company of a streetwalker whom he seemed to know on a first-name basis. Whether such contacts actually led to physical intimacy is anyone's guess. I find myself in sympathy with the historian Alessandra Comini's opinion (personal communication) that after pleasurably chatting and gossiping with these women for a while, Brahms probably went home to satisfy himself in private.

Altruism

One of his most active defenses against isolation was a highly developed feeling of responsibility. The sense of obligation Brahms displayed toward his own family and in his relationship with Robert and Clara Schumann has already been mentioned. His generosity in financial matters knew no bounds. He supported his parents, his siblings, his stepmother, and her children. He gave money lavishly to anyone, friend or stranger, who so much as requested it or seemed to be in need. Ruthless as he was toward mediocrity, he never stinted praise or direct helpfulness when it came to other musicians. He was genuinely impressed with the talent of Antonin Dvořák, found ways to get his compositions published, and even went to the trouble of copying scores for him. In the case of Richard Wagner, who on several occasions had made scurrilous statements about Brahms, he always behaved with utmost decency. Not that he had any sympathy for Wagner's extremism. On the contrary, Brahms had taken an early public position against the Liszt–Wagner camp. (He was also one of the few German composers who at that time did *not* make anti-Semitic remarks.) It was simply that Brahms respected Wagner as a composer of operas, the only musical form in which he himself had made no progress.[9] Despite Clara Schumann's condemnation of *Tristan und Isolde*, Brahms judged this to be a "magnificent work" (Brahms, 1983, p. 158), and he even assisted Wagner in a practical way, by copying orchestral parts for his *Die Meistersinger* premiere in Vienna.

In his thirty-year relationship with Theodor Billroth one also observes Brahms's altruism. These men had much in common: their background in northern Germany, their loyalty to their parents, their energy and creativity, as well as their abhorrence of emotional display. Billroth habitually condemned moodiness, which he thought was a form of stupidity. Like Brahms, he firmly believed that the best way to handle one's emotions was through disciplined work. But Billroth and Brahms also had their differences: the surgeon was a tall, stately man, eloquent in speech, socially tactful and gracious, as compared to the short, awkward composer with his shabby appearance and impossible manners. "They seemed to have an older–younger brother relationship" (Strohl, 1970).

Professor Billroth was an accomplished pianist, a passable violist, and an amateur composer. He had written three trios, a string quartet, and a piano quartet, all of which he destroyed. To please his mother, Billroth had studied medicine instead of music. He was the most daring and innovative surgeon of his day, pioneering such

---

[9] Interestingly, Brahms's favorite opera was *Uthal*, an obscure work written in 1806 by Méhul, which is based on what Musgrave (1983) has described as "a primitive world of family rivalry and conflict."

operations as radical mastectomy, total thyroidectomy, and various gastrointestinal procedures. His marriage was not a happy one, however, and that may have been a factor in his sensitive understanding of the lonely, sexually inhibited Brahms. Both men adored children, and Billroth was heartbroken when his first son turned out to be a deaf, mute, and possibly autistic child. (The boy died when Billroth was thirty-seven; that was the year he befriended Brahms.) They took many vacation trips together, and in Vienna saw as much of each other as the busy surgeon's schedule would permit. Brahms regularly invited Billroth to his rehearsals, and he offered him many new compositions to be premiered in his home. Needless to say, Billroth championed Brahms's music with utmost enthusiasm (Barkan, 1957).

The friendship began to deteriorate after Brahms learned from an old letter that Billroth had made disparaging remarks about his lack of formal education—a touchy point. He then discovered that Billroth committed the unforgivable sin of applying his surgical technique to the manuscript of a string quartet Brahms had dedicated to him. (In his worshipful attitude, Billroth had cut Brahms's signature from the title page and glued it onto his portrait.) For someone who revered original manuscripts as much as Brahms did, this was a sacrilege that justified the end of a long friendship. (Their relationship would have ended soon enough anyway, for Billroth had become ill, and died in 1894. Brahms wanted to publish Billroth's musical compositions in a posthumous edition, but the surgeon's wife objected to this plan.)

Nowhere is Brahms's generosity more apparent than in his behavior toward the old Clara Schumann.

> It angers me [he wrote her in 1888] that [among other things] you have these [money worries]—while I swim in money without even noticing it and without having any pleasure because of it. I cannot live otherwise, don't want to, and will not . . . and where my heart demands it, I can be helpful . . . and do good without being aware of it. After my death, however, I won't have any responsibilities or special wishes [Brahms, 1983, p. 232].

Thus Brahms offered to send Clara 10,000 Marks for the support of her children. "Just think what a great pleasure [it would] give me were you simply and nicely to say 'yes' " (Brahms, 1983, p. 233). Clara, characteristically, said "no." But Brahms found a way to give her the money anyway, by making an anonymous contribution to the Schumann Memorial Fund. He also took endless pains in helping Clara to edit her husband's complete works. That project led to many pathetic disagreements, caused partly by Clara's wish to suppress, and in some instances even to destroy, compositions by Schumann which she considered to be unworthy.[10] Brahms was able to rescue Schumann's D minor Symphony from such a fate by having the original score published alongside its later, more thickly orchestrated, version (op. 120). That infuriated Clara, whose coldness toward Brahms made him feel utterly rejected. "It is hard, after 40 years of loyal service (or whatever you might wish to call my relationship to you) to be [thought of as] nothing more than a bad experience" (Brahms, 1983, p. 249).

They soon forgave each other, however, and agreed to remain friends. Clara's terminal illness following a stroke in 1896 was heartbreaking for Brahms, and her death left him totally bereft. He said that she was "the only person [he] had ever really loved" (Niemann, 1937, p. 175). "Is life worth living when one is *so alone* . . . the only real immortality is in one's children" (Niemann, 1937, p. 155).

On the way to Clara's funeral in Bonn, Brahms became confused and boarded a train going in the opposite direction, thus missing the formal ceremony, although he did make it to the graveside just before her entombment (next to Schumann). His *Four Serious Songs* (op. 121) were conceived as a memorial to Clara, and he did not want them to be performed in public. They symbolize his deepest grief, as well as his own yearning for death. On returning to Vienna, Brahms himself became ill and was found to have obstructive jaundice, discovered later to be the result of a malignancy. (His father had succumbed to carcinoma of the liver.) While stoically awaiting the death he had so often thought about, Brahms continued to be as active as possible, attending concerts, putting his affairs in order, willing his property to family and friends, destroying notes, letters, and unfinished manuscripts, and composing Eleven Choral Preludes for the Organ (op. 122). These are new settings of traditional church chorales. They symbolize not only the

---

[10] In the case of Schumann's violin concerto, Clara's judgment unfortunately prevailed—she was supported by Joachim's negative opinion—with the result that this astonishing work was lost for nearly a century.

composer's typical way of seeking original solutions to old problems, but also represent his final symbolic link to external reality. "Oh World, I must leave you" is the title of the last prelude, written shortly before Brahms died on April 3, 1897.[11]

CONCLUSIONS

One cannot measure a man of genius with the same yardstick used for normal people. Brahms may have had a depressive disorder and an avoidant personality. He often displayed obsessive–compulsive habits and an irritability and impulsivity that was upsetting to people. He became more eccentric as he grew older, and in the homes of his friends he was pampered like an overgrown child. An involutional melancholia in his midfifties probably interfered with both his creativity and his well-being, but he recovered with the sounds of "Miss Muehlfeld's" clarinet ringing in his ears, only to be stressed beyond endurance by the death of his one and only Clara Schumann.

In terms of the theory of "transitional objects" which is so useful in explaining the childhood origins of shared pleasure, I would propose that there may also be "transitional personalities," people who do not attach themselves firmly to anyone, but who allow themselves to be used for purposes of aesthetic gratification by everyone. These individuals are able to endure great loneliness and even isolation without becoming psychotic. They may seem to be dualistic, and their behavior is paradoxical. One notices, for example, their brittleness and their integrity, their ruthlessness and their amiability, their vulnerability and their security. The art (or science, or other original things) they produce are meant to create linkages, to establish new connections between people, even across generations and cultures.

Brahms may have been such a transitional figure. He rose from rags to riches but never outgrew the rags. He was complicated and intellectual, but also simple and boorish. While he remained a stranger to many people, he was also a friend, able to transcend his painful loneliness through altruistic acts. As a composer of difficult music that is easy to enjoy, Brahms seems to have mastered "the

---

[11] Joseph Breuer had been one of Brahms's medical consultants, and it was Breuer's son, soon to enter medical practice, who was the last physician to treat him in his small Karlsgasse apartment.

interplay between originality and the acceptance of tradition [that is] the basis for inventiveness" (Winnicott, 1967). He was the kind of person who immerses himself so fully in his creative work that there is little time or energy left over for intimacy and the formation of families. One thinks of other geniuses for whom the whole world became a family, Beethoven, for example, or Michelangelo. Such men can change civilization. They give us new sounds, new visions, and new meanings. They achieve truths that become eternal.

Chapter 16
Mourning through Music: Gustav Mahler

George Pollock, M.D., Ph.D.

Gustav Mahler was born in Kalischt, Bohemia (near the Moravian border), on July 7, 1860. In December 1860, the family moved to the town of Iglau (Jihlava), not far from Kalischt, and it was here that Mahler spent most of his childhood and early adolescence. Of his father, Bernard, who was known to have a violent temper, Mahler wrote in a letter:

> My father (whose mother previously supported the family as a peddlar of drapery) had the most diverse phases of making a livelihood behind him and, with his usual energy had more and more worked himself up [the social scale]. At first he had been a waggoner, and while he was driving his horse and cart, had studied and read all sorts of books—he had even learnt a bit of French, which earned him the nickname of "waggon scholar." Later he was employed in various factories, and subsequently he became a private coach *[Hauslehrer]*. On the strength of the little estate in Kälischt, he eventually married my mother—the daughter of a soap manufacturer from Leddetsche—who did not love him, hardly knew him prior to the wedding, and would have

---

First published in *The Mourning-Liberation Process*, International Universities Press, 1989.

This research was supported in part by the Anne Pollock Lederer Research Fund of the Chicago Institute for Psychoanalysis.

I am particularly indebted to the published works of Gabriel Engel (1970) and Donald Mitchell (1955, 1958) for the many details I have used in this presentation.

Material from *And the Bridge Is Love*, copyright © 1958, 1986 by Alma Mahler Werfel, reprinted by permission of Harcourt Brace Jovanovich, Inc.

Material from *The Haunting Melody* by Theodore Reik, copyright © 1953 by Theodore Reik, reprinted by permission of Farrar, Straus and Giroux, Inc.

Material from *Gustav Mahler: Memories and Letters* by Alma Mahler, reprinted by permission of Marina Wahler.

preferred to marry another man of whom she was fond. But her parents and my father knew how to bend her will and to assert his. They were as ill-matched as fire and water. He was obstinacy itself, she all gentleness. And without this alliance, neither I nor my third [Symphony] would exist... [cited in Mitchell, 1958, p. 5].

Bernard Mahler was also born at Kalischt, on August 2, 1827. Mahler's mother, Marie, was born on March 3, 1837, of a Jewish family having higher social status than that of his father. Mitchell suggests that Bernard Mahler chose her in order to acquire "culture in the shape of a refined wife of a good family. The prize would have flattered his vanity, soothed his feelings of inferiority, and swelled his self-esteem" (Mitchell, 1958, p. 6). Marie Frank, being lame from birth, had a delicate constitution, and suffered from a "weak heart." Since the man she loved was not interested in her, she was resigned to an unhappy marriage, which it was. Bernard Mahler treated his wife roughly, at times violently, and the young Gustav saw the suffering his mother had to endure as a result of his father's brutality. Gustav Mahler's wife, Alma, indicates that she "never heard Mahler say an affectionate word of his father, but his love for his mother had the intensity of a fixation, then and always" (Mahler, 1969, p. 8).

Despite her physical weakness, Marie Mahler bore fourteen children. Five of Gustav's brothers died at an early age, mainly of diphtheria. Isadore, born in 1858, two years before Gustav, died from an accident when a child. I have been unable to find his age at death. The second child, Gustav, born in 1860, was the eldest surviving child. Arnold (born 1868), Friedrich (born 1871), Alfred (born 1872), and Konrad (born 1879) all died very young. Gustav's younger brother, Ernst, born in 1861, died in 1874 of a chronic heart condition after a long illness. Ernst's death was a very intense experience for Gustav Mahler. "He loved his brother Ernst and suffered with him all through his illness up to the end. For months he scarcely left his bedside and never tired of telling him stories. To all else he was blind (Mahler, 1969, p. 7). The remaining siblings who played a part in Mahler's later life were Leopoldine, Gustav's eldest sister, who was born in 1863, married unhappily, and died in 1889 of a brain tumor (in later years "Mahler reproached himself, as though he were partly to blame for her unhappiness" [Mahler, 1969, p. 9]); Justine, born in 1868, who, after the deaths of Mahler's parents in 1889, joined Gustav Mahler's household—she died in Vienna in 1938; Emma, born in 1875 and died in Weimar in 1933; Otto, born in 1873 and shot himself to death in 1895; and Alois (Louis), born in 1876.

Justine married Arnold Rosé (1863–1946), a leading member of the Vienna Philharmonic Orchestra, and a friend and close colleague of Mahler. He left for Britain in 1938, I assume after his wife's death, and died in London in 1946. Emma married Eduard Rosé, Arnold's brother, and a distinguished cellist. He was deported by the Nazis to Theresienstadt in the fall of 1942 and died there of starvation at age eighty-four in January 1943.

Justine had peculiar fantasies as a child. Alma Mahler mentions that "while still a child, she stuck candles all around the edge of her cot. Then she lay down and lit the candles and firmly believed she was dead" (Mahler, 1969, p. 9). Since Orthodox Jewish practice after death includes placing candles around the body of the deceased, one wonders if this morbid act did not relate to the number of dead siblings she had seen in such a position. As I expect to demonstrate more clearly later in this essay, the impact of the many sibling deaths during Mahler's childhood also left him with lifelong psychological scars. He was second, but became first when his brother Isadore died. Perhaps the great involvement with his dying brother, Ernst, reflected a displacement of his guilt over survival with overcompensatory defenses.

Theodor Reik (1953), writing in another connection, provides us with some evidence to support the idea that Mahler suffered from guilt over his childhood sibling deaths and, I would point out, over his successes as a conductor. Reik indicates that the last concert of the 1894 season was to be dedicated to Hans von Bülow who had just died. Richard Strauss was to direct the concert, but he became ill at the last moment and Mahler took his place. The young musician wrote then to his sister Justine: "It is strange that someone always has to become ill to make it possible for me to conduct a symphony" (cited in Reik, 1953, p. 346). Reik indicates that he felt Mahler believed that such a replacement opportunity was not due to change but was "fateful or preordained, . . . as if the illness of his predecessor were the only possible way that his wish to conduct a symphony concert could be fulfilled" (Reik, 1953, p. 346). I interpret this fantasy of Mahler as relating to his childhood replacement experience. When the first sibling-son dies, then he, the second in line, takes over the first position. The preferred becomes ill or dies and then his place is taken by Mahler. Reik considers this chain of events as indicating a concealed belief where the thoughts of the successful rival are responsible for the removal of his predecessor. This may be so, but Mahler's genius extended to two musical areas—conducting and composing. In his conducting, which he viewed as interfering with his composing, competition for position could and did occur, but I believe this competition was connected with his sibling relationships.

Reik cites instances in Mahler's career where he advanced after someone became ill. Hans von Bülow was forced to quit as conductor of the Hamburg Orchestra after a serious illness, leaving Mahler as substitute conductor until after Bülow's death, when Mahler became the permanent leader. Prior to Hamburg, he owed his early position as conductor in Olmütz to the death of the conductor there. Since 1886, Mahler had functioned as the second conductor in Leipzig. In February 1887, the first conductor became ill and Mahler took over for several months. When the primary conductor recovered, Mahler left as he felt he could not get this position. Then Alexander Erkel, the director of the Royal Opera in Budapest, became ill and Mahler was appointed director in his place. After the Hamburg post, Wilhelm Jahn, the director of the Vienna opera for seventeen years, became ill. Wanting to ease his burden, he engaged Mahler as assistant director. Jahn became further incapacitated through an eye disease, being unable to read a score; Mahler became his successor and led the Royal Theater to a phase of great artistic achievement. The same pattern was repeated with Hans Richter; he became ill and Mahler took his place as conductor of the Vienna Philharmonic Orchestra, at the same time that he was director of the Vienna Opera. Mahler never hesitated to take the place vacated by a rival's illness. There was no evidence of conscious guilt feelings in these situations, but Reik believes, and I agree with his formulation, that Mahler feared for his own replacement. He frequently quoted the phrase *vita fugax* (life is transient). He seemed to fear that his own end was not far away. This is understandable when we remember the number of his siblings who died early and almost regularly.

In 1907, Mahler left Vienna for New York where he was conductor at the Metropolitan Opera. The concert master, whom Mahler admired, told Mahler that he planned on being a conductor after he fulfilled his obligations as violinist to the orchestra. Reik notes that Mahler remarked, "Well, I have to become ill in order to give you the opportunity" (1953, p. 349). Mahler feared retribution by becoming the victim of those competitive and destructive wishes of others against him. However, we must also consider that Mahler may have felt from early childhood that his days would be very few. When Mahler was a little boy, he was asked what he wanted to be, and he replied, "A martyr." Mitchell (1958) interprets this reply as the overwhelming expression of his identification with his mother's martyrdom. I would see it additionally as an identification with his dead siblings.

To return to Mahler's two brothers, Otto and Alois, for a moment. "Alois [who] later called himself Hans, because it sounded less Jewish, ran into debt, forged notes and finally had to flee to America" (Mahler, 1969, p. 10). Otto showed great musical talent, and Gustav acted as his mentor helping him in every way possible. Otto failed at the jobs Gustav obtained for him and in February 1895, killed himself, leaving a note behind saying that life no longer pleased him and so he handed back his ticket. In Otto's desk were found two symphonies, a number of songs with orchestration, three books of *lieder*, and a nearly completed third symphony (Mitchell, 1958).

Mahler's musical abilities appeared early. Around the age of five, on a visit to his maternal grandparents, he could not be found. He was finally discovered in the attic playing on an old piano. From that period on, his parents were convinced that he was destined to be a musician and they encouraged him in this goal. Mahler himself claimed that from the age of four onward he was both making music and composing, even before he could play scales. He supposedly could sing over two hundred folksongs, learned from servants, between the ages of four and six. It is also claimed that at age four he could correctly play on an accordian all of the march tunes used in the neighboring barracks (Engel, 1970). Mahler started piano lessons at five. He learned rapidly and at age eight had a pupil of his own, aged seven. On October 13, 1870, the ten-year-old Gustav Mahler made his piano debut at a concert in Iglau before a large audience. The weekly newspaper wrote: "The great success the future virtuoso achieved with his audience did him honor; one could only wish that for his excellent playing he had had an equally good instrument at his service" (Mitchell, 1958, p. 19).

The young Mahler was now in demand. He played piano, accompanied choirs, and played at local patriotic occasions; for example, the celebration of the silver wedding of the Emperor and Empress of the Austro-Hungarian Empire on April 24, 1879.

In 1871, when Mahler was eleven, he spent the winter term at the Gymnasium in Prague. This did not work out well, and he returned to Iglau, at whose gymnasium he remained until he left for Vienna in 1875, where he enrolled at the Conservatory at the age of fifteen. Because of poverty, his days at the Conservatory were not easy. In addition to his studies at the Conservatory, Mahler continued to study for his school-leaving examinations, which he passed in 1877, after which he enrolled at the University of Vienna, studying philosophy, history, and the history of music.

He progressed rapidly at the Conservatory, and at the end of his first year, on June 23, 1876, he was unanimously awarded first place in the piano-playing competition. He also won first prize in the composition competition on July 1, 1876, for the first movement of a piano quartet. In addition, he received the highest grades in his three courses—piano playing, harmony, and composition. At the close of the next year, on June 21, 1877, he again won the first prize in the piano competition.

Mahler completed his work at the Conservatory in 1878. He was granted his matriculation and also was honored by being awarded a Diploma, for which the requirements were very stringent. In 1879, Mahler continued with his studies at the University of Vienna, spending much time with Hugo Wolf, the composer, who had tutored the children of Josef Breuer from 1873 to 1883. The relationship with Wolf, its ambivalence, and final dissolution, though interesting, will not be discussed further here. At this time, Mahler developed his friendship with Anton Bruckner, although they were separated by a wide age gulf (Mahler was seventeen and Bruckner was fifty-three). Mahler's devotion to Bruckner and his music was lifelong.

Mitchell notes that after he became a great conductor and composer, Mahler's piano playing, which played so prominent a role in his childhood, youth, and student days, "died so complete a death in later years, but for spasmodic domestic returns to the keyboard; and in his maturity as a composer, the instrument had no role at all" (1958, p. 83). Mahler was known to play his compositions on the piano in private and also to play for purely recreational purposes in the company of congenial musicians (e.g., piano-duet playing in private with Bruno Walter).

It is interesting to note that in his last years at the Conservatory, Mahler's pattern of moves from house to house was an "endless succession of removals from one lodging to another, in search of cheap, yet decent and quiet 'diggings,' where he could work at his music in peace. Between September 1876 and May 1879 . . . there are recorded no fewer than twenty-one addresses where he occupied rooms" (Mitchell, 1958, p. 83). One can wonder about the meaning of these many moves and Mahler's later moves from city to city.

I now turn to two early works composed by Mahler as I believe they illustrate themes connected with Mahler's mourning. The first, an opera composed in 1877–1878, is entitled *Herzog Ernst von Schwaben*. The second, a cantata for soprano, contralto, and tenor soloists, mixed chorus, and large orchestra, *Das klagende Lied (Song of Woe)* was composed from 1878 to 1880. Mahler finished *Das klagende Lied* in 1880, at which time he undertook his first engagement as a conductor at Bad Hall in upper Austria. His career as a composer actually antedates the beginning of his career as a conductor.

By March 1878, Mahler had completed the text of *Das klagende Lied*, having laid aside *Herzog Ernst von Schwaben* in the same year. Mahler clearly associated the memory of his much loved younger brother, Ernst, who died in 1874, to the *Herzog Ernst von Schwaben* work. Mitchell feels the connection lies in the similarity of the names. In fact, he believes that the name is influential "in such matters as the choice of opera libretto or text for a song" (1958, p. 130). I feel one must go further and ask, What does this mean? Does it serve the purpose of remembering the dead brother? Does it represent an attempt at immortalizing the dead brother? Or, does it represent a continuation of the mourning process for the dead brother?

"In the summer of 1901, Mahler composed the music for some songs by the German poet Friedrich Rückert, amongst them the first three poems known as *Kindertotenlieder* ('Songs on the Death of Infants'). Rückert had lost two children, Ernst and Luise, and wrote as many as four hundred forty-eight songs expressing his grief" (Reik, 1953, p. 315). Mahler was not married at the time of the composition of these three songs,* and had no child. Reik asks why Mahler chose those songs. He asserts that something in the wording and atmosphere of the *Kindertotenlieder* must have appealed to Mahler and suggests that an intense mourning was reawakened by memories of terrible loss and of the past when the children were still alive.

The Rückert poems speak of the death of two children. Reik asserts that it was the unconscious remembrance of the past that made Mahler compose these sad songs. At the time of the composition of the *Kindertotenlieder*, Mahler said that "he felt sorry for himself while he composed them and felt sorry for the world which would hear them" (Reik, 1953, p. 317). Reik, I believe, correctly connects the Rückert poems with conscious or unconscious memory traces of revived grief and sorrow for two lost children from his childhood: Isadore, who preceded Gustav, and Ernst, one year younger than Gustav, who died in 1874. But Reik attributes the grief and mourning to Mahler's parents. I would add the more significant mourning was that of Gustav himself. I would suggest that Gustav felt survivor guilt toward both of these dead siblings. One of Rückert's dead children was named Ernst, as was Mahler's own dead brother. So when Mahler felt sorry for himself while composing the *Kindertotenlieder*, he was still expressing his mourning for his brothers, especially for Ernst, whom he knew, loved, and cared for. The feelings which were not fully expressed, and the words which he could not say, came out in the music to the Rückert poems. Reik points out that

> children whose siblings have died and who witness the mourning and grief of their parents feel vivid emotions akin to envy and jealousy toward their dead brother or sister, as if they wished they themselves had died or that their parents would mourn for them in such a deeply felt manner. It is easy to recognize in this reaction the feelings of rivalry and competition with the sibling when he was alive. More intense than this tendency is perhaps the wish to be loved and mourned by the parents as much as the child who has died. Here is yet another process of unconscious identification, that with the dead brother [Reik, 1953, pp. 318–319].

---

*In fact, he had not even known Alma when he wrote the *Kindertotenlieder* cycle (Taylor, personal communication, 1987).

When five years later Mahler's beloved daughter died, he connected the composition of the dirge with the possibility of a prophetic anticipation. Could it not instead be that his guilt was such that he felt he had to have done to his child what was done to both his immediately older and younger siblings? The music and the texts were still aspects of Mahler's mourning work for his childhood losses. Mahler expected tragedy to be with him constantly, and unfortunately this was the true state of affairs. He himself died at age fifty-one of the same illness as his mother who died at fifty-two. By moving about, working hard, destroying his early works as a possible means of destroying the past, Mahler may have tried to avert what he felt to be his destiny—but to no avail.

When a fellow student at the Conservatory, Hans Rott (1859–1881), whom he had beaten in the composition competition, died in 1881, Mahler wrote:

> What music has lost in him cannot be estimated. Such is the height to which his genius already soars in this first symphony, which he wrote as a twenty-year-old youth and which makes him—I am not exaggerating—the founder of the new symphony as I see it. To be sure, what he wanted is not yet quite achieved. It is as if somebody raised his arm for the farthest possible throw and, still clumsy, falls far short of the target. But I know where he aims. Indeed, he is so near to my innocent self that he and I seem to me like two fruits from the same tree which the same soil has produced and the same air nourished. He could have meant infinitely much to me and perhaps the two of us would well-nigh have exhausted the content of this new time which was breaking out for music [cited in Mitchell, 1958, p. 95].

Do we read here the mourning for what was and what would never be? Is this mourning for a sibling with whom Mahler feels like "two fruits from the same tree which the same soil has produced and the same air nourished" or for himself?

When we turn to *Das klagende Lied*, we are confronted with data that may give us a clue as to why Mahler chose the fairy tale for this cantata and how he changed it to suit his needs. The text of this work has been traced by Mitchell to a tale of Grimm and to one by Ludwig Bechstein. Mahler's version is as follows:

> Part I. A proud queen declares that whosoever shall find a certain red flower growing in the forest shall win her hand. Two brothers

go in search of the flower, the younger of a sweet disposition, the elder evil in character. The younger brother finds the flower, sticks it in his hat, and stretches out to rest. He is discovered asleep by his elder brother, who, jealous of his success, strikes him dead with a sword, steals the flower, and claims the queen as his bride. The younger brother lies buried under leaves and blossoms beneath a willow tree.

Part II. . . . introduces the minstrel, who picks up a gleaming white bone, fashions it into a flute and plays upon it—when he is astonished to hear the flute pour forth its tale of murder, "sorrow and woe." The minstrel ventures forth to seek out the king and his bride.

Part III. . . . brings us to the castle. It is the queen's wedding day and a feast is in progress. The minstrel enters the castle hall and plays his flute; it repeats once more the story of the murder. The guilty king leaps to his feet, seizes the flute and scornfully places it to his lips: the bone sings again its sorry tale of fratricide. The queen collapses to the ground, the guests flee, and the castle walls begin to crumble [Mitchell, 1958, pp. 142–143].

In Ludwig Bechstein's fairy tale, the contenders for the flower are not brothers but brother and sister; and the prize is not marriage but succession to the queen's throne. The princess, the firstborn, finds the flower and lies down to sleep, whereupon she is murdered by her jealous brother. In later years a peasant boy picks up a bone and makes a flute from it; he is startled when a child's voice issues forth and tells the manner of the sister's death.

A knight takes possession of the flute and appears at the castle where the guilty brother is king and his mother still mourns her lost daughter. It is to the old queen alone that the flute reveals the terrible truth. She then takes the instrument and herself plays it to her son before a festive assembly in the castle hall. The story ends on this note of chilling catastrophe, in which the mother is the final instrument of her son's doom [Mitchell, 1958, p. 143].

In the Grimm tale, "we find two brothers competing for a wife, a rivalry which ends in fratricide. The circumstances of the competition and the murder are quite different from those we find in the cantata, but the loquacious bone flute and details of the denouement are as we know them in Mahler's text" (Mitchell, 1958, p. 143).

Mahler combined these two tales. He eliminated the mother who destroys her guilty son, and substituted two brothers for Bechstein's brother-sister rivalry. Mitchell correctly but incompletely asserts that "it must be that the roots of Mahler's variations of Bechstein's story lay in his own psychological makeup, that the changed relationships were conditioned by emotional attitudes of Mahler towards members of his family" (1958, p. 144). I would ask if it was too close to Mahler's inner fears that a mother can destroy the surviving son after the first has died. Fratricide, evil as it is, is safer than filicide at the hands of the mother. And yet, it was the same cardiac illness that destroyed not only the mother but Ernst and eventually Gustav. Did Mahler suffer from survivor guilt in regard to Ernst and Isadore? Did he fear that his music (the flute) might reveal this? Was there a fear of his own death? Mahler's music may reflect his pathological mourning and inevitable, tragic end. One can speculate about the meanings of the text Mahler chose for his cantata, though there is no definite proof. The evidence points toward unresolved problems and unfinished business connected with his childhood siblings' deaths.

While working on *Das klagende Lied*, Mahler's concerns with death emerged in two letters, both written in 1879. In the first, dated June 18, 1879, he writes:

> Oh my beloved earth, where, oh when, wilt thou take the abandoned one unto thy breast? Behold! Mankind has banished him from itself, and he flees from its cold and heartless bosom to thee, to thee! Oh care for the lonely one, for the restless one, Universal Mother [Mitchell, 1958, p. 88].

In the second letter, also written in 1879, about the time of his brother Konrad's death and while working on *Das klagende Lied*, Mahler states: "The highest ecstasy of the most joyous strength of life and the most burning desire for death: these two reign alternately within my heart; yes, oftentimes they alternate within the hour" (Mitchell, 1958, p. 89).

Engel reports that while Mahler was working day and night to finish *Das klagende Lied*, the composer kept raising his tired eyes to watch a certain shadowy corner of the room. "All at once it seemed to him that the wall was coming to life. Someone was struggling furiously to come through it into the room. Now he could see the apparition's face contorted with the agony of hopeless struggle. Suddenly he knew it was his own face! Terror-stricken Mahler rushed from the room" (Engel, 1970, p. 32).

Ten years later, while working out the funeral march in his symphony, he had a similar experience.

> One night . . . he was very weary and lifted his eyes gradually from the intricate web of notes which he had just written. His tired gaze wandered about the room, finally coming to rest upon the wreaths of flowers, trophies of the "Three Pintos" [Mahler's successful completion of Weber's unfinished musical manuscript], heaped in profusion upon the table in the center. A moment later he attempted once more to concentrate upon the music, but an uncanny feeling had stolen upon him and again he looked up. Suddenly the appearance of the table had changed. It seemed to him as if it were now surrounded by weirdly flickering candles! And on the center, among the wreaths lay a shape,—a corpse! The features were his own! Horrified he rushed from the room [Engel, 1970, p. 63].

The similarity of Justine's early action with the candles is striking. One can surmise that the meaning of this hallucination dealt with Mahler's anxiety about his own survival—a manifestation of his early childhood concerns over his own death.

To jump ahead in time, in February 1889, Mahler's father died (at age sixty-two), to be followed by the death of his mother in October of that year (at age fifty-two). The household at Iglau was abandoned and the three eldest dependent children, Justine, Emma, and Otto, moved to Vienna where Mahler assumed the burden of providing a home for them. As indicated earlier, this was also the year that his oldest sister, Leopoldine, died. Mahler was beset by financial difficulties in meeting his new responsibilities. In the next few years, he began to work on his second symphony, entitled *Death and Resurrection*, whose opening movement is entitled "Death-celebration," a funereal composition during which the dead hero is carried to his grave. The death music is "subjective and out of its sombre depths rise the ultimate human questions: Why have you lived? To what end have you suffered? Is it just a great, terrible jest? We must somehow answer this to prove life worth while, and death life's most magnificent step towards fulfillment" (Engel, 1970, p. 93).

Reik, for personal reasons, has extensively discussed Mahler's Second Symphony. He quotes a letter from Mahler:

> I know that as far as I can shape an inner experience in words, I certainly would not write any music about it. My need to express

myself musically and symphonically starts only where the dark emotions begin, at the door leading to the "other world," the world in which things are not any more separated by time and place [1953, p. 252].

Mahler describes the last movement of the Second Symphony to another friend:

> It starts with the cry of dying and now comes the solution of the terrible problems of life, at first as faith and church shaped it in the beyond. A trembling moves over the earth. Listen to the roll of the drums and your hair will stand on end! The Great Summons sounds. The graves open and all creatures emerge from the soil, shrieking and with chattering teeth. Now they all come a-marching: beggars and wealthy men, common people and kings, the ecclesia militans, the popes. With all of them the same anxiety, shouting and quivering with fear, because none is just before God. Between it again and again—as if from the other world—from beyond the Great Summons. Finally, after all had cried out in the worst turmoil, only the long-lasting voice of the death-bird from the last grave. It also becomes silent at last. And now nothing of all that which was dreaded comes; no last judgment, no blessed and no damned. None is good, none bad—no judge, low and simple the chorale sets in: Rise, yes, rise [Reik, 1953, pp. 253–254].

Mooney, who has also studied Mahler's life and works, commented that "Mahler's conscious preoccupation with problems of life and death is reflected in some way in almost every composition" (1968, p. 88). Mahler was frequently preoccupied, with understandable reason, with his own death and questions about the meaning of life, why there was so much suffering, if there was a reward or punishment in the "beyond," or even if there was a "beyond." Each of his symphonies was a new attempt at an answer. "And when he had arrived at an answer, the same question rose soon anew as an unquenchable cry of longing. He could not—such was his nature—hold positions conquered, because he was not constant" (Bruno Walter, cited in Reik, 1953, p. 257).

Mahler could not solve the problem of a finale to the Second Symphony. In a letter to Arthur Seidl (February 17, 1897) he related the experience which brought him his answer.

> Bülow died, and I attended the memorial service for him. . . . The mood in which I sat there and thought of the departed one

was exactly that of the work which, at that time, occupied me constantly—at that moment, the chorus near the organ intoned the Klopstock chorale Aufersteh'n! It struck me like a bolt of lightning and everything stood clear and vivid before my soul. The creator waits for this bolt of lightning; this is his "Holy Annunciation." What I then experienced, I had now to shape into tones. And yet, if I had not carried that idea with me, how could I have experienced it? There were a thousand people with me in the church at that moment [cited by Reik, 1953, p. 264].

It is significant that the funeral celebration for a man who had helped Mahler and who suggested that he should become his successor stimulated and sparked the solution of the finale. The funeral, undoubtedly, reminded him of other very personal funerals he had attended from childhood onward. Resurrection was the answer he sought. "Rise, yes, rise wilt thou, my dust" [Mahler's words].

The last movement, the musical exposition of Resurrection, inspired by the choral setting of Klopstock's Ode on Resurrection, which was given a choral setting at Bülow's funeral, was the answer to Mahler's questions. I believe, however, the three family deaths in 1889 served as the stimulus for this work and were in part Mahler's musical mourning for his parents and sister.

Gustav Mahler married Alma Marie Schindler on March 9, 1902, the day before his sister Justine was married. On November 3, 1902, the Mahlers had their first child, a daughter, named Marie after his mother. The name Marie was very important to Mahler. Mahler's "first impulse" was to convince Alma to change her own name to Marie after their marriage (Mahler, 1969, p. 175). This obviously did not occur, even though Alma's middle name was Marie. The second child, also a daughter, named Anna, was born on June 15, 1904.

Mahler was very attached to his daughter Marie. Alma Mahler writes:

> Our elder child used to go to Mahler's studio every morning. They held long conversations there together. Nobody has ever known what about. I never disturbed them. We had a fussy English nurse who took her to his door, as clean and neat as a new pin. By the time Mahler brought her back she was usually smeared with jam from top to toe. It was my job to pacify the English nurse. But they were so happy together after their talk that I took a secret pleasure in these occasions.

She was his child entirely. Her beauty and waywardness, and her unapproachability, her black curls and large blue eyes, foretold that she would be a danger later on. But if she was allowed only a short life, she was chosen to be his joy for a few years, and that in itself is worth an eternity. It was his wish to be buried in her grave. And his wish was fulfilled [1969, p. 105].

Marie died of complications resulting from scarlet fever and diphtheria, the disease that was so fatal for Mahler's siblings, on July 5, 1907. In addition to this blow, from which Mahler never recovered, the confirmed diagnosis of his own serious heart condition (from which he died on May 18, 1911), and his resignation of his Vienna post, all occurred in 1907. After Marie's death, Mahler then turned to the melancholy poems, *The Chinese Flute*, which answered his own deep grief and from these he wrote *Das Lied von der Erde* a year later. There is a clear connection between his mourning for Marie and this magnificent symphony. Alma Mahler notes that "he expressed all his sorrow and dread in this work—The Song of the Earth. Its first title was 'The Song of the Sorrow of the Earth'" (1969, p. 139).

Mahler's later Fifth, Sixth, and Seventh Symphonies form a trilogy dealing with death. The Fifth opens with a grim, long trumpet call in a minor key preceding a funeral march. The Sixth Symphony, called the "Tragic," is followed by the Seventh, conjuring up secrets and mysteries of goblins' spirits. As already indicated, the Ninth Symphony, *Das Lied von der Erde*, was composed after the death of his beloved child Marie. "Mahler had always been superstitious about a ninth symphony" (Mooney, 1968, p. 91). And he did not wish to call his work the Ninth Symphony as he felt he might die after its completion since Beethoven, Schubert, and Bruckner had died after writing a ninth. Although Mahler almost finished another symphony afterwards, the "Farewell Song" closing *Das Lied von der Erde* has been almost universally regarded as his own farewell to the world.

Mahler's heart condition, diagnosed by chance after Marie's death, marked the beginning of the end. Initially he was very anxious about his health, feeling his pulse, ascertaining whether his heartbeat was clear, rapid, or regular. The beginning of the end came in New York in 1911. He insisted on conducting what was his last concert on February 21, 1911. Among the works he conducted that night was the first public performance of Busoni's "Cradlesong at the Grave of My Mother." He steadily went downhill, traveling from New York to Paris and finally to Vienna, where he died on May 18, 1911. The burial, close to that of his beloved child, Marie, in the nonsectarian cemetery at Grinzing may have had deeper significance. In some way he perhaps felt the reunion was not only with Marie, his dead daughter, but also with Marie, his dead mother.

Mitchell (1958) has said, "The state of mind in which the Tenth Symphony was composed must have approximated very closely a private hell." Mahler has left evidence to indicate this in his exclamations on the manuscript, Third Movement (Purgatorio):

> "Compassion! O God! O God, why hast thou forsaken me? Death! Transfiguration!"

Fourth movement title page: "The devil leads me in a dance. Demolish me that I may forget my being! That I may cease to exist. . . . End of movement (muffled drum): None but you knows what it signifies! . . . Fare thee well, my lyre! Farewell, Farewell, Farewell." Fifth movement, Finale: "To live for thee! To die for thee! Almschi!"

Alma Mahler tells us what the muffled drum signifies. In 1907 to 1908, at the Hotel Majestic in New York,

> hearing a confused noise, we leaned out of the window and saw a long procession in the broad street along the side of Central Park. It was the funeral cortege of a fireman, of whose heroic death we had read in the newspaper. The chief mourners were almost immediately beneath us when the procession halted, and the master of ceremonies stepped forward and gave a short address. From our eleventh-floor window we could only guess what he said. There was a brief pause and then a stroke on the muffled drum, followed by a dead silence. The procession then moved forward and all was over.
>
> The scene brought tears to our eyes and I looked anxiously at Mahler's window. But he too was leaning out and his face was streaming with tears. The brief drum-stroke impressed him so deeply that he used it in the Tenth Symphony [1969, p. 135].

Since this scene followed the relatively recent death of Mahler's daughter, one can assume the tears were for her death and for the part of him that died with her, and for the remainder of himself that would soon join her. As Alma Mahler points out, Mahler wished to be buried in the same grave that held his little daughter, Marie. This was done. Mahler left specific instructions that not a word be said nor a note sung at the burial. In the teeming rain his coffin was lowered, but a rainbow appeared after the burial. Mahler did not live to hear either of his last two symphonies performed in concert.

POSTSCRIPT

The Freud-Mahler Consultation, 1910

It has been well documented that Mahler saw Freud in 1910, notlong before Mahler's untimely death in 1911. Mahler knew he was dying, but the ostensible reason for the consultation dealt with a marital problem.

Alma Mahler, brought to "a complete breakdown" in the summer of 1910, was in a sanitarium in Tobelbad. She was isolated and very melancholy and the head of the hospital introduced young people to her as company for her walks. One such individual was an architect, who fell in love with her. This architect wrote a letter declaring his love for Alma and stating if she had any feeling for him she should leave all and go with him. Although the letter was meant for Alma, it was addressed to Mahler. Mahler, opening the letter, was shocked and felt convinced that the architect addressed the letter to him as a way of asking Mahler to release Alma so that she could marry him. An intense discussion with Alma ensued, during which she told Mahler of the great deprivation she felt. Even though she felt Mahler, being too self-absorbed, gave her little, she reassured him she could never leave him. Mahler became ecstatic but he became jealous of everything and everybody having contact with his Alma. Oftentimes Alma found Mahler lying on the floor, weeping in his dread that he might lose her or that he had already lost her. On the floor he said he was nearer to the earth. In Alma Mahler's account, she gives details of this entire episode and points out that it was at this time "he wrote those outcries and ejaculations, addressed to me in the draft score of the Tenth Symphony" (Werfel, 1958, p. 175). Mahler realized he was very upset and decided to consult Freud who was then on holiday at Leyden in Holland. Alma Mahler reports that Freud calmed Mahler and said, " 'I know your wife. She loved her father [who died when she was thirteen] and she can only choose and love a man of his sort. Your age, of which you are so much afraid, is precisely what attracts her. You need not be anxious. You loved your mother, and you look for her in every woman. She was careworn and ailing, and unconsciously you wish your wife to be the same' " (Werfel, 1958, p. 176). Alma Mahler states that Freud was right in both of his statements. She states she always looked for "a small, slight man, who had wisdom and spiritual superiority, since this was what I had known and loved in my father" (Werfel, 1958, p. 175). She also believed Freud's suggestion that Mahler had a fixation on his mother.

Discussing only the Alma Mahler account at this point, I believe Mahler was more threatened at "losing" Alma, as a result of her hospitalization and her serious depression than by the rivalry with the architect. The appearance of another male might have recapitulated the earlier situation when his brother Ernst was born and Mahler was one year old. The loss of the "mother" to the new rival and to her depression and absence from him, in addition to his own anxiety about his health, could have produced a panic state, out of which Freud helped him. After this psychoanalytic consultation, Mahler was very affectionate and self-confident with Alma.

On the train bringing him back from seeing Freud in Leyden, Mahler wrote a poem for Alma, the first lines of which Theodor Reik has translated:

They melt, the shadows of the night.
What always tortured me as fright,
Is blown away by power of one word.
My feeling, pressing to the height,
My thoughts, in danger of the glide,
They flow together into one accord:
I love you. . . [1953, p. 341].

In 1935, Reik wrote Freud asking him about the meeting with Mahler in Leyden. Freud wrote back to Reik and in part of his letter, he states:

If I may believe reports, I achieved much with him at that time. This visit appeared necessary to him, because his wife at the time rebelled against the fact that he withdrew his libido from her. In highly interesting expeditions through his life history, we discovered his personal conditions for love, especially his Holy Mary complex (mother fixation). I had plenty of opportunity to admire the capability for psychological understanding of this man of genius [cited and translated by Reik, 1953, pp. 342–343].

Reik's researches allowed him to fix the date of the Freud consultation in Leyden as either August 26 or 27 of 1910. Mahler died on May 18, 1911. I would wonder if Mahler's libidinal withdrawal from Alma was an attempt to conserve his own biological and psychological integrity in the face of his oncoming death, which was not sudden when it occurred and in all probability was the result of streptococcal endocarditis secondary to rheumatic heart disease.

But before we leave the Mahler-Freud episode, let us have one last hearing—the report of Ernest Jones in his Freud biography. Jones (1955) writes that Dr. Nepollek, a Viennese psychoanalyst, who was a relative of Alma Mahler, suggested that Mahler consult with Freud. Three times did Mahler make an appointment with Freud and three times did he cancel same. Finally he saw Freud in Leyden. Jones repeats what has been noted above, that Mahler was closely attached to his mother. Jones writes that the "analytic talk evidently produced an effect, since Mahler recovered his potency, and the marriage was a happy one until his death" (1955, p. 80). I would question the almost total recovery that Jones writes about. That Mahler was more involved, attentive, and loving is attested to by Alma Mahler, but Mahler knew he was steadily growing weaker and finally died in less than a year. Freud gave Mahler hope—hope to live and expend libido outwards toward his wife. But libido could not fight cardiac pathology, which unfortunately won out in a short time. And now in our age of mourning and nostalgia, we find Mahler resurrected through his music and perhaps a little more here, through a bit of his life.

Chapter 17
Gustav Mahler: The Music of Fratricide

Stuart Feder, M.D.

YOUTH'S WONDROUS HORN

In the autumn of 1887 the twenty-seven-year-old Gustav Mahler came across the popular anthology of German folksong *Des Knaben Wunderhorn* by von Arnim and Brentano (1805), a volume which was to become his musical vade mecum for many years. While many scholars (for example, de La Grange, 1973, p. 171) note that this was to become "his chief source of inspiration until 1900," it would be perhaps more precise to say that it tended to organize and further develop elements which had long since been a part of Mahler's mental life. He had creatively visited the distinctive world of the *Wunderhorn* more than once: the youthful *Das Klagende Lied* written in 1880 when he was only twenty and *Lieder eines Fahrenden Gesellen* just three years later (in 1884) were already parts of this universe. Two other elements are significant with regard to the *Wunderhorn*: The first is the enduring and pervasive role the world of childhood played throughout Mahler's creative life—the experiences, poetry, philosophy, products, and even musical artifacts associated with it. The second, and for our purposes the central feature of the composer's mind, relates to the core metaphor of the anthology: the Magic Horn itself.

In the title poem of the collection, *Das Wunderhorn* (von Arnim and Brentano, 1805, p. 11), a fine youth dismounts from his steed at the Empress' castle bearing a gift fashioned by the hand of a water nymph. Made from an elephant's tusk, the wondrous horn is decorated with bands of gold and precious stones. A hundred golden bells gleam as the boy tells her that with a squeeze of her finger there will sound a sweeter music than was ever heard in

First published in the *International Review of Psycho-Analysis*, 8:257–284, 1981.

heaven or in nature. And at the touch of her finger the beauteous, brilliant sound is heard. The songs follow.

In what is the most undisguised rendering of this metaphor in Mahler's music, a minstrel wandering in the forest sees a bone glistening among the dead leaves. He fashions it into a flute and, playing it, hears the disembodied voice of a slain brother, revealing a tale of fratricide. His is the plaintive voice of the central section of *Das Klagende Lied*, to which we will return later. In a literal realization of the metaphor, it is the orchestral flute which is associated with the accusatory voice. At one point Mahler entertained the possibility of having a boy's voice "from afar" joining that of a contralto delivering the commentary on the flute's narration (Mitchell, 1958, p. 165).

In essence the metaphor of the Magic Horn refers to the sources and meanings of music, the composer's "voice." Fundamentally, it is an image of the composer's mind, whether its product is the guilt-tainted *Das Klagende Lied* or the musical cornucopia of *Des Knaben Wunderhorn*.

Mahler himself, like many romantic composers and perhaps more than most, never questioned the autobiographical sources of his work. On the other hand, he could not have been in a position (any more than any other human being—artist or not) to be consciously aware of its deepest sources which are ordinarily repressed in unconscious mental content and function. To the contrary, his *apparent* awareness of them may be misleading, as I hope to demonstrate later in a consideration of his Second Symphony. Nevertheless, he acknowledges music's debt to the human being in the composer numerous times. For example:

> My whole life is contained in my two symphonies. In them, I have set down my experience and suffering, truth and poetry in words. To anyone who knows how to listen my whole life will become clear, for my creative works and my existence are so closely interwoven that if my life flowed as peacefully as a stream through a meadow I believe I would no longer be able to compose anything [de La Grange, 1973, p. 272].

As we shall see, there was little likelihood of either, although there were times when Mahler longed for peace. Indeed, Mahler leaves little question in our minds as to where *he* considers the core biographical material to be. Again:

Gustav Mahler: The Music of Fratricide

We are faced with the essential question of knowing how or even why, the contents of a musical work should be defined in words.... Allow me to state briefly my point of view: I know for my part, that as long as I am able to express my experience in words, I would never do so in music. My need to express myself musically, symphonically, begins only in the realm of obscure feelings, at the gate leading to the "other world" where things are no longer destroyed by time and space [de La Grange, 1973, p. 357].

There are few composers, even of his extraordinary period, whose music is so apparently and intimately intertwined with other manifestations of the current of mental life as revealed in other biographical sources. In fact, his character and times make him the unique subject for study from this point of view. Therefore, one of the aims of this and related studies (Feder, 1978, 1980a) is to draw into the pool of psychological material on Mahler that which can be understood only from a consideration of the music itself within the context of the composer's life. Reciprocally, another goal is served; namely, to understand Mahler the man as richly as our tools of inquiry will permit. In effect, Mahler invites one into an alliance, to participate with him in a psychological study of his life and work. He himself was a person of a marked psychological turn of mind and curious about the workings of his own mind and the minds of others. Freud himself commented on this in reference to their now famous consultation in Leyden. He wrote to Reik (Reik, 1953): "I had plenty of opportunity to admire the capability for psychological understanding of this man of genius . . ." (pp. 343–344). The life of his mind is generously revealed to us through letters, memoirs, personal communications, musical commentary, and, above all, in his music.

The focus of the present study will be certain aspects of Mahler's mind as revealed in family relationships, particularly those with his siblings. The central psychological issue to be considered is that of his ambivalence as expressed in fratricidal fantasy. Character and underlying elements of conflict will be stressed, but pathography per se is of little interest here. Mahler's psychopathological propensities range within the areas of the obsessional, the depressive, and the psychosomatic. What will interest us more specifically are those motivational elements which, lying at the core of the psyche, and, therefore, capable of giving rise to symptom, may also be a source of creative activity and accordingly imbue the creative product, the music, with its distinctive specific character.

Gustav Mahler was an extraordinarily complex man, replete with contradiction, paradox, and mercurial shifts. While he could on one hand be aggressive, exacting, hostile, bitter, ironically sarcastic, and readily moved to a smoldering rage, he was also capable of loyalty, generosity, tenderness, and playfulness. He could be both tyrannical and nurturing in relation to those subordinate or otherwise junior to him, all manifestations of a characterological bisexuality which proved to be usefully adaptive in his tasks as conductor and music director. In the world of his fantasies, he was Job and Christ as well as St. Anthony the teacher, the god Apollo, and the eternal youth of the *Wunderhorn*.

THE FAMILY MAHLER

Gustav Mahler was born on July 7, 1860, in Kalisch in Bohemia, a village of little more than five hundred people where his father Bernhard kept a *Wirtshaus*, a tavern. In December 1860, the ambitious Bernard crossed the Moravian border into Iglau with his wife, Maria, and the three-month-old infant, Gustav. Iglau's twenty-five thousand inhabitants could boast schools, theater, concerts, a newspaper—these for the child and those to come—and a large military center, an exciting potential source of profit for the publican himself. A nursing infant was appropriate to the sense of a new promising life with which they arrived. Gustav was not the first child. Isidor (b. March 22, 1858; d. ?date, 1859) would have been close to two years of age had he not been killed in an accident earlier that year, the nature of which has never been revealed. It is likely that this too spurred the move: a new life, a new land, the parents sealing over their mourning of a beloved first son with the birth of a second and the promise of a new future. The parents were young and vigorous, Bernard thirty-three, Maria ten years younger. Gustav was to be his parents' replacement for Isidor, a figure defined vaguely by a date or two, yet one who was to cast a long shadow over the Mahler family.

Thirteen children were to follow. By the time the twelfth and the last boy Otto was born in June, 1873, Maria, only thirty-six, was already worn with marital strife, childbirth, and the illness and death of five more of the children, all boys. Otto was to restore the balance of the living to the dead, joining Gustav thirteen, Ernst twelve, Leopoldine (Poldi) ten, Alois six, and Justine (Justi) five. Born into a house of mourning, the year-old Alfred having died a month earlier, Otto too perhaps bore the unspoken obligation of the replacement. Before the year was out the chronically ill Ernst had died. Maria was already pregnant with Emma who was born the following October. The last child, Konrad, who survived only twenty-one months, was born in April 1879. In all, there had been fourteen children, eight of whom, all boys, had died by the time the oldest survivor, Gustav, was approaching the age of nineteen. A decade later, as we shall see presently (around the time one of the three sisters, Poldi, died), he was to assume the role of head of the family for the then remaining four children, Alois, Justi, Otto, and Emma.

Maria had been a frail girl, lame in one leg, whose quiet withdrawal at the side of her husband may have been misconstrued as arrogance by their neighbors who called her "die Herzogin," the Duchess. By now her face had taken on a look that Gustav was to describe as "stricken." She was a woman, away from the only home she knew, who had been taken in marriage by a man who aspired to her slightly elevated background, but who remained a stranger to her. She may have been expected to turn to her children in loneliness.

Bernhard, their father, fared better. By the time of Otto's birth he had overcome the economic trials of Gustav's early years. At first the man who by dint of relentless work had achieved petit bourgeois status in Kalisch sustained repeated difficulty reestablishing himself in Iglau. However, the very year Otto was born, 1873, marked a proud milestone for the father: he was appointed a *Bürger*, a citizen of the town. The certificate hung among the books of a small but carefully selected library Bernhard had long aspired to collect, in the Mahler parlor. He by now owned a distillery and a few related branches of the business. Now the family moved from the house it had occupied since the move to Iglau into the house next door, which was purchased from the former landlord. At the point when Otto was about to be born, Bernhard had reason to feel he had done well for his children.

Like many such men, by character and by economic circumstances, Bernhard mistook property for nurture. His children seem to have found it difficult to muster a kind word about him, and he is described as an irascible, hostile man lacking in humor and in human understanding. A few anecdotes repeatedly recounted in the Mahler literature suggest he was a brutal man as well. However, the sources and circumstances of these stories leave them open to question. A caricature has developed which fails to take into account the many sides of Mahler's father. For example, recognizing the boy's gift, he permitted Gustav to enter the Vienna Conservatory of Music, yielding his own wish that Gustav get a university degree and enter the distillery, harboring perhaps some updated and enriched revision of himself in the days when he was an itinerant peddler who read books. People had referred to him then as "the wagon-scholar." Perhaps the prospect of the reflected glory of a family intellectual and artist exerted an overriding attraction considering his own Jewish cultural background. At the same time it could be an investment of sorts.

Then, too, he may have correctly perceived his own determination and stubbornness in Gustav, who from early in life had been the undisputed star of the family. His resolve to become a professional musician was clear, and he had already brought a great deal of satisfaction and some degree of acclaim to the family Mahler. In April of 1873, for example, only two weeks before Alfred's death and two months before Otto's birth, Gustav had been acclaimed at the Iglau Theater, where he had played the piano at a gala concert in honor of the wedding of the Archduchess Gisela to Prince Leopold of Bavaria. Only a few months previously he had again performed at a festival honoring Schiller's birth at the Kaiserlich Königliches Obergymnasium before 800 townspeople, and received excellent critical comments in the Iglau newspaper which did not fail to point out that he received "an interminable and wildly enthusiastic ovation." Such success was bound to be seductive to Bernhard and at the same time helped forge Gustav's personal identity and pave the way toward his leaving his family, which in any event would soon become a geographical necessity. Bernhard had been unwitting accomplice to this trend when he had sent the eleven-year-old Gustav to Prague because of its better schools. Later, pressed by the fourteen-year-old to attend the Vienna Conservatory, he gave in, although the future of the Mahler enterprises would now be in doubt. With six boys dead, Ernst dying, Gustav committed to music, and the remaining boy Alois already declaring himself by his strange behavior to be incompetent, Otto would now be the only possible candidate to follow in his father's footsteps. He had the misfortune to be born into a strong father's strong expectations.

BROTHERS IN APOLLO: OTTO AND GUSTAV

Many years later Mahler wrote a dedication on the sketch of the third movement of his Ninth Symphony: "Meinem Bruder in Apoll." Despite his reputation as a stern, authoritarian taskmaster in music there was another side to him, and he was capable of warm, although demanding, friendship. Where ambivalence did not prevail, there could be devoted, even tender brotherhood. His relationships with Bruno Walter and Arnold Schönberg reveal this; that with Richard Strauss, on the other hand, whom he admired and respected, was "a friendship of reason" (de La Grange, 1973, p. 290). The razor's edge of brotherhood was forged in family relationships with siblings living and dead. A more tender side may be glimpsed at in Mahler's relationships with certain friends such as Josef Steiner, his collaborator in adolescence, and, above all, in his relationship with his brother Ernst which was characterized by a protective, almost maternal quality. This aspect of Mahler's character will have to await another study. Relevant here is the ambivalent underbelly of brotherhood, in its starkest form consisting of fratricidal fantasies, their derivatives, and defenses against the wish. While, as we shall see, these had a place in Mahler's mental life from early in life, a not uncommon event, they were later to be strongly stimulated, and assumed varied forms. These wishes came to focus in Mahler's relationship with his brother Otto and to a lesser degree Alois. In Otto, also a musician, he saw a strange and unfortunate *Doppelgänger* to himself. As Apollo, the shepherd, was god of both healing and of music, Mahler struggled to nurture and create and not to destroy.

Otto's birth could not have had much of an effect on Gustav's life except perhaps to deflect from him briefly, as had the infant Alfred's death, the family's customary attention. Besides, the focus of Gustav's family attachment at this time was upon Ernst who had entered his last year of life at about the same time as Otto entered his first. Gustav had a close attachment to Ernst who was about a year younger than himself. He was later to say that no death had ever affected him so deeply. They were especially close that last year, spending many hours together in conversation and in games which the two of them made up. Ernst died, probably of rheumatic or congenital heart disease, on April 13, 1874, which may have been the very day of his thirteenth birthday. By the following autumn, the fourteen-year-old Gustav had left Iglau to study at the Vienna Conservatory.

In a very real sense, indeed that sense that has to do with psychic reality and the meanings that relationships have, Otto and Gustav did not cross paths again until the summer of 1889 when Otto was now well into his own adolescence and Gustav, twenty-nine years old, began his private struggle to bring into balance ambivalent fraternal love (already intricately burdened since Ernst's death) with the new role in loco parentis to which he found himself called.

The details of Otto's first sixteen years are not well known. The day-to-day events of family life would now have a more immediate and different effect upon him than it would upon his oldest brother. Thus, the birth of Emma when Otto was two ended his briefly held tenure as youngest in a house without Gustav. When he was six, the last of the fourteen Mahler children was born, Konrad, who died two years later. The following year Poldi married and left the city. When Otto was ten and Gustav twenty-three, both parents developed symptoms of the heart disease from which they were to suffer for the next six years until their deaths in 1889. It may be guessed that Otto would be offered all the opportunities for education that had been given Gustav—music, gymnasium, later university, although with regard to the Conservatory, Bernhard may have taken quite a different stand with the last son who might continue the family business. In any event it was Gustav who took responsibility for the guiding of Otto's musical education, and it was he who sent Otto to the Conservatory after their parents died.

Otto chose a difficult path from any point of view. But even if he had followed in the steps of his father in business, he could not have escaped Gustav. He would have had to grow up with and live with the family legends of the favorite: how Gustav, irritable as an infant, could be soothed only by music, how he could hum a tune in his first year of life, how he played the concertina at three, took piano lessons at five, gave them at seven—the hallmarks of genius retold as family legend—and, of course, how he had composed his first piece at the age of six. Otto was bright and, no doubt, even gifted musically, but not of this caliber. Therefore, in the adolescent struggle for what he would be and do, to choose music would necessarily engulf him in conflict. His identification with Gustav had rivalrous elements of both a sibling and generational nature in that Gustav was thirteen years older as well as a leader now by profession. His own choice of career had very different sources from that of Otto. It subserved different functions in his mental life and was to last a lifetime. Otto may well later have felt betrayed by fate in a choice which carried with it naïve expectations of the success his brother had achieved. We can only wonder at the hazards of following someone to the edge of a precipice only to find that he is equipped for survival, even flight!

At sixteen then, when his father died on February 13, 1889, Otto was a music student in Iglau and in barely stable psychological equilibrium. Gustav, now Director of the Royal Budapest Opera, was summoned by telegram. He arranged for the funeral and spent a few days in Iglau setting the family in order, showing himself to be no less an administrator than their father. Otto was to be sent to Vienna to live with their sister Poldi (who had married when he was nine) and her family, and to enter the Conservatory there.

Life for Otto, living with the Ludwig Quittners and their two children in Vienna, could not have been very comfortable. Ludwig was not a very successful businessman, and the family was poor. It was generally agreed that Poldi had not made a very good marriage, for which Gustav characteristically blamed himself, although he had been only twenty-two at the time, Poldi nineteen, and their parents still alive. Soon Poldi began to develop symptoms which were diagnosed as a nervous complaint. Consequently, Gustav removed Otto and rented a room for him with Fritz and Uda Lohr, old family friends. Meanwhile, their mother's condition was worsening in Iglau, and Justi (the older of the two remaining sisters) was exhausted from the arduous task of nursing her second patient. Gustav himself was not well, suffering from hemorrhoids, and required an operation, which was performed in July. By September their mother's condition worsened, and he had gone to see her for what he might correctly have felt was the last time. He himself was in pain and taking morphine.

In Vienna, Poldi's condition now worsened. Now called a neuralgia, it soon became clear that she was suffering from a brain tumor, and she died on September 27. Two weeks later, on October 11, 1889, their mother died. It is not known if Otto attended the funeral; Gustav could not, it was said, because of work. Gustav had worriedly awaited his mother's death, in Budapest, unable to leave and still taking morphine for his own pain in order to get through rehearsals. He had begged Lohr's wife "if the worst should happen . . ." to go to Iglau for a day or two "to support my sister" (Martner, 1979, p. 121). Following Maria Mahler's death both Justi and Emma, the youngest, stayed briefly with the Lohrs, Mahler much concerned with their comfort during what he thought could be a "brief transitional period." In a final retrenchment, Emma was to remain there, along with Otto, while the exhausted Justi came to set up a new household with Gustav in Budapest. He admitted to Fritz, "I cannot suppress a slight groan," in contemplating sending him money regularly for "the two children." He was particularly anxious about Otto and wrote to Fritz, "Please do get Otto whatever he needs,—I thought Otto had a winter coat; I no longer have mine—so if it is absolutely necessary, please get him that as well . . . Please write and tell me what Otto's health is like now—and what sort of effort he is making" (Martner, 1979, p. 122).

The coat may have been in anticipation of a visit Fritz and Otto were shortly to make to Budapest for, in the midst of all this turmoil in the lives of the Mahlers that autumn, Gustav was preparing the premiere of his symphonic poem, the First Symphony. It was a milestone in his life—the first public performance of an orchestral work! In an article in the *Pester Lloyd* the critic Abrányi wrote, clearly from the notes recently furnished by Mahler himself, that the Symphonic Poem might be called *Life*, illustrating as it does the life of one "who sees, who feels, who experiences that life which throws earth's marvels into the path of youth," and which, with "the first breath of autumn, takes back pitilessly everything that has been given earlier" (de La Grange, 1973, p. 203).

Fragments of letters to Lohr reveal the following months as difficult ones: "There's always one of us ill in bed . . . have to bottle up so much vexation that I am incapable of writing!—How is Otto turning out? . . . Write soon to your careworn, Gustav" (Martner, 1979, p. 124). But glimmers of hope are to be found in plans for the following summer which he was able to bring to fruition. The fragments of family were briefly reunited at Hinterbrühl, sharing a villa with the Lohrs in the Wienerwald. It was finally to be not merely retrenchment but retreat, their first peaceful moments together after the turmoil of the past year and a half. Gustav, Justi, Otto, and Emma, the tattered survivors, all struggled to regain strength and equilibrium. (It is doubtful whether Alois joined them, although Gustav was still assuming financial responsibility for him as well.) During this summer Gustav and Otto swam together each morning, even when it rained. They now had to get to know each other in a new way. Many of the conversations were on music, Otto frequently provocative in his comments, Gustav at times lecturing. Late in August, when Gustav had to return to Budapest, he left Justi in Vienna to set up a household for Otto and Emma.

And so, in the fall of 1890, Otto at seventeen found himself in a home with his younger sister Emma, now fifteen, his twenty-two-year-old mother–sister–housekeeper Justi, and a maid and cook in the Breitegasse in Vienna. Gustav at thirty, the tyro paterfamilias, was back in Budapest and soon to be in Hamburg. Only the elusive Alois remained for the moment unaccounted for. At first Mahler seemed to be gratified to a degree with having achieved such an arrangement after so much chaos. He wrote to Lohr, "I lead an existence directed entirely towards others. Thus I have accomplished many useful things and have experienced many joys." Perhaps in this we have a glimpse of what this mastery of a seemingly insurmountable domestic situation may have meant to him. He had managed to accomplish in life what he daily did in the Opera theater, the marshaling and organization of many independent, often unpredictable forces toward the end of order, even beauty. At the same time, his father's man in this sense, he had skillfully reorganized his family and had hopes of holding it in his grasp even in absentia. This might help us to understand to a small degree the puzzling statement about his Budapest years made some time after, that "it was the happiest period of my life"—unless, of course, he meant it ironically—because in so many ways it had been dramatically quite the opposite.

To his sorrow, real people tend not to take stage directions like just so many tenors and sopranos, and, despite the appearance of life settling down, Otto was not doing well. His work at his studies was inconsistent, and he often skipped his classes at the Conservatory. Consequently, his grades wavered, and private tutors had to be engaged for him. Nor would any kind of future be assured even if he had been an excellent student, and graduated with a diploma. Conservatory training provided the basis for competent musicianship, nothing more. It could not assure a career and, as was the case with Gustav, not even equip the student as a competent conductor.

One had to seek one's fortune later, as he had done, scrounging for opportunities in country concert halls and spas. Nor could it promise one would be a "performed" composer—as if one could earn a living in that endeavor in any event. Of course, Otto well knew it could be somewhat different for him having an older brother who was a rising Kapellmeister, although that would create other problems. Then, too, the prospect of military service loomed.

As 1891 wore on, Gustav's letters were increasingly demanding, critical, and complaining. In particular, he was concerned about money. Few of the details of life in Vienna which were written to him by Justi escaped his notice and comment. His tone was often biting, and Otto had reason to feel hurt considering the promise of what had been their first adult talks as potential colleagues the previous summer. Gustav's gratified fulfillment of parental trust, and assumption of the parental role was soon met in kind with Otto's adolescent rebellion. The promise of the past summer gave way to a bitter struggle.

In truth, for Gustav to say he had led an existence directed *entirely* toward others would have been an exaggeration. Life held many gratifications for him, and he had a knack of finding his needs met in others in spite of adversity. In the very next line of the same letter, for example, he goes on to speak of his first meeting with Johannes Brahms, who had embraced him warmly and praised his performance of *Don Giovanni* lavishly. He was deeply involved in his conducting and, despite numerous problems, was finding a great deal of artistic satisfaction. However, he never ceased to resent the necessity, as he saw it, of having to do it *for* his family.

At this time Gustav again demonstrated what was his extraordinary capacity of landing squarely on his feet whenever life gave him a toss into the air. No sonner had Justi been dispatched to Vienna than Natalie Bauer-Lechner made her appearance in Budapest, and their relationship was greatly cultivated by Mahler. He gallantly invited her to be his guest in his apartment and moved to other quarters for the duration of her visit. She was to become a close friend, companion, and, above, all, chronicler of his life and amanuensis for his conversations. As far as is known, they were never to be lovers, although it is clear that Natalie at some point desired marriage strongly. It is likely from what we know about Gustav that the services she did perform were very important to him indeed, perhaps more than any other. After Natalie left,

Gustav's artistic relationship with the Wagnerian soprano, Lilli Lehman, engrossed him. Later, in the spring, after he had already left Budapest for his new post in Hamburg, he had the good fortune to gain the friendship of a woman even as he was seeking lodging, an attractive and cultured widow, Adele Marcus, who was six years his senior.

As far as we know, Otto lacked these resources so characteristic of Gustav, the sensitive responsiveness to adversity which often turned it to advantage. But, ever the pale reflection of his brother, he may have sought Nina Hoffman under these circumstances, at whose home he was later to commit suicide. Moreover, Otto's identification with Gustav was rapidly accruing to itself new layers. Whereas formerly it was with the favored child, the romantic figure, the guide who knew the route from Iglau and the stifling brewery to the promised land, it was now with Gustav the aggressor. But Gustav had that rare capacity of being able to focus his considerable aggression in a finely modulated stream which could be directed at will. Moreover, his capacity for sublimation was remarkable although not inexhaustible. Otto's expression tended to be more diffuse, disorganized, and inwardly directed. Perhaps Gustav's body suffered the more for his style—a reaction to massive yet exquisite control—his severely disabling migraines and the delicately unspeakable hemorrhoids from which he was later to fear bleeding close to death. We do not know what Otto may have suffered physically (although it is known that he was blind in one eye), but it soon became evident that he was prone to severe depression. The effects of this may in itself have retarded the pace of his studies and blunted concentration. However, none of these positions—active struggle, passive aggression, depressed inactivity—were positions Gustav could readily understand or tolerate. They would all be interpreted as insolent ungratefulness and pure laziness. "Krankheit ist Talentlosigkeit," he would say, sickness is the lack of talent. Gustav too suffered depression, but he did not permit it to interfere with his work. On the contrary, he frequently was to find that work could both stave off and bind his depression. The activity warded it off, just as the expressive content of the music encoded it. Thus, one must wonder at the similarities as well as the polarities of the two brothers. They were curious *Doppelgängers* to one another, Otto the pale image in a dark glass.

By the following summer of 1891, Gustav felt helplessly exasperated and angry. That very summer was one of the few periods of Gustav's life when defenses failed and depression did in fact impede work. During the two years preceding the calamitous family events, the summers were clearly beginning to be earmarked as the time for composing, as they were later to be regularly. During the summer preceding his father's death (1888), he had worked on the *Totenfeier* which was later to become the first movement of the Second Symphony. It lay dormant for the two summers of '89 and '90 and now for a third. As Gustav perceived it, it was purely "family matters" in the broadest sense—his need to earn their support as a conductor and the time and aggravation his responsibilities entailed—which impeded his strong drive to compose. He resented this deeply. He felt strongly the need to get away from this situation, and the summer of 1891 was the only time of his life he spent such a period alone, wandering abroad. This vacation lasted only two weeks, and he chose Scandinavia. Despite the newsy letters he wrote from time to time to Justi, he returned depressed. To Freund, however, he had written:

> What you have gathered from my letters about my "mood" is right enough. I have been through so much in the last few weeks— without any evident material cause—the past has caught up with me—all I have lost—the loneliness of the present—all sorts of things—you know these moods of mine from earlier years—when I would be overcome by sadness even while among my friends— when I was still all youth, vigour and stamina—so you can well imagine how I spend these long *lonely* afternoons and evenings here—*no one* with whom I have anything in common—whether a share in the past or shared hopes for the future [Martner, 1979, p. 140].

Although he was aware of his rising resentments, in particular as it affected composition, Gustav lets us know in this letter that he himself is not fully aware of the scope of influence of his family involvements in his inner life. Like many other depressed persons, he only knows he is depressed and that somehow something from the past has been lost, something reevoked. As if he were becoming aware of the secret silence depression keeps, he continues to Lohr:

> It was there when I was up in Norway, roaming about for weeks on end without speaking to a living soul—*and that after already having had my fill of keeping silence*—and now back in this atmo-

sphere in which I cannot get so much as a single breath of fresh air [Martner, 1979, p. 140; emphasis added].

Silence is attributed to both inner and outer worlds—to the very locale of his wanderings the previous summer. Silenced was Mahler's growing rage which was to take an uncertain course from this point on, by turns suppressed, repressed, disguised, deflected, transformed, denied, sublimated, or similarly transformed along the lines of several other mechanisms of defense. Its immediate objects were his living siblings; its genetic roots would encompass those dead as well, the echoes of earlier relationships reverberating in current intrapsychic life. In this broader context the primary wish in its most naked form would be that of fratricide manifested in defended form by fantasy and other derivatives. Finally, the aggression mobilized, which is revealed in affect and in content alike, may manifest itself in still another way. In common parlance such aggression may spur activity; in psychoanalytic terms, it is itself bound *through* activity. Of the several functions music had in Mahler's life one which was specifically related to composition was the binding of aggression. Conversely, aggression and drive derivatives thereof in affect and fantasy lay among the sources of what, for want of a better term, we call *inspiration*. Its mark is to be found both in the activity itself and in the content of its product.

In the letter to Lohr which prompts these remarks, aggression is too stifled by silence for the moment, and after Mahler writes of having had his fill of keeping silent with its expectable *sequela*, he notes the sensation of feeling stifled ("this atmosphere in which I cannot get so much as a single breath of fresh air"). There follows an "outburst" of suppression (and reaction formation), at least for the time being:

> *Don't show this letter to Justi!* [Mahler's italics] I do not need to tell you I should *gladly* make any sacrifice—but I assure you I cannot bear this much longer. I have had to economize here more than I ever had to since Vienna. Otto *must* take his examination this year! He seems to be still pretty green. . . .

That fall of 1891 Mahler had assumed a new post in Hamburg. It was here that he fully experienced the loneliness of which he wrote and which was so much a part of his depression at this time. Still troubled by his family, he continued nevertheless to struggle toward some solution, the mind nimbly and without conscious awareness trying this or that solution. In October Gustav sent the following letter to Justi in Vienna:

> Your recent letters have told me a lot of things that pleased me. I can see that you are slowly developing into a more alert human being and starting to look around for yourself. But at the same time they have given me an insight into your way of life which does not satisfy me. Please try to be a little more explicit on this subject; it seems to me that your mutual relationships are very confused. Even if something bothers you, please trust me and tell me about it frankly.
>
> However, there is one thing I beg of you: don't ever imagine that you have any knowledge of human nature! The real deep-down truth is as follows: as long as you consider yourself to be different from the others it is all right. But if believing this you do not stop demanding from others what is possible only for yourself, everything will go wrong. Never forget that each human being represents a world of his own, of which we know a large part, but only to the extent that we carry this part within ourselves; the remainder will always be a secret. If one wishes to set up new laws, these will only be valid for that particular part of the others that we know, because it is within ourselves.
>
> But this might carry us too far! Please do not fight or mistrust each other. Enjoy what you have in common, don't blame what you cannot understand in someone else, and do not try to impose your laws on the "whole of humanity." To God, you are naturally all alike! But, in the eyes of men, each one remains an unknown world for his fellow-men, with that part in common to which comprehension is limited. Try to remain united thanks to this part and beware not to destroy this bond lightly! . . .
>
> But I have forgotten the most essential point of my sermon: what particularly exasperates us in others is 99% of the time that which we are ourselves capable of. This goes for mistakes common to men as a whole: we recognize our own world in others, and this reflected image infuriates us so much that we would like to break the mirror immediately.

This remarkable letter to Justine has an obvious preaching tone, and Gustav clearly identifies it as a "sermon." In fact, by the time he does so, one is half expecting the next line to be, "and this, above all, to thine own self be true." Indeed, his literary heroes had long been Shakespeare, Wagner, and Goethe. (At this time he was also engrossed in Nietzsche. The latter, whom he refers to in a preceding Lohr letter, was later to influence him strongly in the writing of the Third Symphony, its seeds already germinating as Mahler worked on his Second.) The literary tone of this letter, a tone which Gustav was later to disavow in his writing, may have been a convention of the time but tells us much more, since he did not employ it in every letter. Mahler wanted this letter preserved! Perhaps not so much for posterity or even for the brothers and sisters but for Mahler as he attempted to work something out for himself in its content. It is a letter to himself and it becomes touchingly revealing to look upon the pompous Polonius in league with the pious St. Anthony advising a humbler part of Gustav rarely seen. Reaching through his disappointment and rage, he tries to come to terms with his family, preaching understanding and tolerance. Although one may detect grandiosity here, a note of sarcasm there, the self-sermon is a plea for brotherhood. He redundantly makes the same point as if some elusive insight he does not want to lose. He is trying to separate himself a bit from the fray and perhaps, like a good parent, let his children be, by tempering his aggression and sparing them from it.

The metaphorical reference to the mirror in the last redundant afterthought would make us wonder about Mahler's own *Doppelgänger* fantasy regarding Otto. It confirms what is suggested in the preceding thoughts, namely some specific awareness of the Otto in himself as well as the more obvious reverse. Was it the "laziness" he deplored, the lethargy of depression which was interfering with his own work, or perhaps some deeper potential within himself of the course he may already have begun to fear in Otto. As he noted to Freund, more than once despair had come over him. He had spoken of suicide to his friend Steiner when he himself was about Otto's age. In a letter reminiscent in its literary style to the "sermon," he had written of "a consuming yearning for death.... One thing I know: I can't go on like this much longer!... What way out is there but self-annihilation!' (Martner, 1979, p. 54). Just as we have seen evidence of the "Gustav" Otto had within him (the complex mental representation of all he had ever experienced with Gustav and the fantasies engendered by these experiences), so the reverse was true—the "Otto" within Gustav. For both brothers the question of "what might have been" would be a painful one. Gustav may have seen his darker side in Otto, an aspect of which emerges in the latter with the wish "to break the mirror." Here suicide and fratricide briefly merge in mental flow. Driven at times by enormous pressure to compose, and frustrated in his view by the demands of his brothers, it would not be difficult to understand that he might wish he did not have this burden, that they might never have been born, that they might yet be blotted out, die. These wishes, which were hardly new ones, would be rekindled in his mind from earlier times when it took all his considerable ability to retain supremacy with the repeated birth of siblings—twelve times!—and, each time, with the uncomfortable awareness that even the oldest is vulnerable at any moment as Isidor had been. Perhaps this also sheds some light upon why this older brother, who might have been thought by his family as having everything, could at times feel so deprived. With regard to being held back from composing, Mahler was beginning to find himself in an ever tightening bind. For just as he sought expression in letters, inevitably he would do so in music, whose flow he had experienced as restrained. At this point of his life much of the expressive content of both was rooted in his aggressive feelings and fantasies. A few years earlier the critic Steinitzer suggested he might become a writer, comparing him with Goethe, to which Mahler had replied, "No hope of that, my dear Eckermann, I *must* compose." Composition of two types may be distinguished at this time: One was related to new musical ideas; another to the refinement, development, and completion of those already formed. Where he was to experience inhibition, it was *invention* that faltered; he might still be working at completing, orchestrating, etc. At such times, as we shall see presently, he might even resume work on a score of many years earlier.

Sermons and St. Anthony will reappear as themes in Mahler's thought throughout this period. During these first two Hamburg years Mahler found himself in a state of creative inactivity with regard to composition, save for one exceptional brief period during January to February, 1892. It was then that within the course of a few weeks during a lull in the orchestra's activity he wrote five new songs on *Wunderhorn* texts (de La Grange, 1973, p. 249), this after nearly four years of almost no new composition. Nor would he write during the following summer of 1892 which was devoted to a conducting tour in England in order to earn more money for the family's needs. Troubled, that August he would discuss in detail with Natalie this failure of creative activity. Nor would anything of significance be accomplished the entire season following until the ensuing summer of 1893 which was one of the most productive of his entire creative lifetime. While family problems were not the only ones facing him during this period, their relentless, inescapable, and aggravating qualities were of a special nature, and his angry preoccupation with them appeared to have an inverse relationship to invention.

At the same time it seems clear that a work is not composed at a single sitting, even if it is notated rapidly; that some preparatory period of unconscious as well as conscious activity antecedes its apparent creation and is very much a part of the process of composition. (An example may be found in one of these very songs of the winter of 1892 which Mahler immediately earmarked for his Third Symphony, the Second existing only in part at the time.) Thus, a period of blockage may be at the same time a period of germination. We may keep this in mind in following the events of these first two Hamburg seasons from the fall of 1891 to the summer of 1893, a period during which the family problems related so far were brought to a pitch.

During this period the anthology *Des Knaben Wunderhorn* continued to permeate Mahler's mental life. He had sent to Vienna for his copy and the five songs noted above were drawn from them. Throughout this period, the *Wunderhorn* was with him in more ways than one. On the wall of his study in Hamburg he had an etching which was an illustration to one of the poems: *Des Antonius von Padua Fischpredigt*, St. Anthony's sermon to the fish. Mahler's curious identification with St. Anthony, heralded in the "sermon" letter above, will become more apparent later when in the fruitful summer of 1893, to which we shall come presently, he set this poem to music and, carried along by some impetus which inspired it, expanded it into a key movement of the Second Symphony. By then he found himself in a position to view with more humor what was the dismal failure of St. Anthony. He would tell Natalie:

> A somewhat sweet-sour humour reigns in the "Fischpredigt." The blessed Anthony preaches to the fishes, but his speech sounds completely drunken, slurred (in the clarinets), and confused. And what a glittering multitude! The eels and the carps and the sharp nosed pikes, whose stupid expression as they look at Antonius, stretching their stiff, unbending necks out of the water,

I can practically see it in my music, and I nearly burst out laughing. Then, the sermon over, the assembly swims away in all directions

The Sermon has pleased
They remain as ever!

not an atom the wiser, although the saint has performed for them! Only a very few people will understand the satire on humanity in this story!

The *Wunderhorn* songs of the winter of 1892 were written during a period of apparent respite from family pressures which was accompanied by a lifting of Mahler's depression of the previous autumn. It persisted well into the spring, concurrent with Mahler's pleasure in completing the scoring. He saw these works as an expression of "humor" in the best and truest sense of the word, writing to Justi, "I am in a very good mood, despite my recent attacks of biting (professional) insults; perhaps these very attacks are being transmuted into a symphony" (de La Grange, 1973, p. 250).

But certainly at this point sermons went unheeded. In the spring, family pressures once again mounted, this time in the form of repeated requests from Justi for extra money for various purposes. In her requests she now assumed something of Gustav's style in writing repeatedly of her own privations, which apparently upset Mahler all the more, causing him to respond, perhaps with guilt, that he only wished her to take care of herself and to enjoy life. Otto inevitably became the culprit for whom all were sacrificing, since a portion of the additional money was for his lessons. It is also likely that it was convenient for Justi to imply this, since there is no evidence that she had much competence at twenty-three in running a household, and it was unlikely that she would, knowing Gustav as she did, expose herself to his criticism. Gustav had written back to her in irritation at Otto, "Believe me, the teacher is a secondary question—it is the student who matters." His bitterness overflowed onto Lohr, whom he felt was giving up on Otto with an apparent attitude of fatalism:

> Fritz does not seem to me to worry much about Otto. On that point too he is probably a fatalist! In truth, that is the point of view of all the people who are too lazy to follow an affair through

to its conclusion. And it is characteristic of this fatalism that it exists usually at the expense of others and what they possess. As soon as those others aren't there, the fatalism disappears. . . . I am not myself a fatalist until something is completed. While it is unfinished, fatalism is nothing but cowardice and indignity . . . [Quoted in de La Grange, 1973, p. 254].

It is not difficult to understand why Justi would have been anxious to avoid the ire of a man who could so readily turn on so old and helpful a friend as Lohr. Of course, Lohr had only just abandoned the Mahler family for several months while he sojourned in Italy. In any event, now it is Lohr himself who is guilty of the unpardonable laziness and neglect, as a result of which both Gustav and Otto were joint victims. But the comment on "people who are too lazy to follow an affair through" seems to have been predictive of its true object, Otto, for unbeknownst to Gustav, Otto had already withdrawn from the Conservatory in April. Justi evidently feared to tell Gustav. Meanwhile, Alois too appeared to be in endless trouble, and Gustav lamented that Alois was unable to make use of the Hamburg business contacts Gustav was now in a position to provide. Rather, "He had just barely escaped being sent to debtor's prison!" (Quoted in de La Grange, 1973, p. 254).

After the Hamburg season, Gustav was again to renounce a summer's composition in order to go to London on tour. He was to make it clear in later negotiations in which he asked a high fee that such commitments were only to be made when they were made worth his while. Before leaving for London, he wrote sarcastically to Justi that his salary was not elastic: "The more one subtracted from it, the more it diminished." Afterwards, with barely three weeks' vacation and the start of the new season delayed because of an outbreak of cholera in Hamburg, he was in no mood for more pressure from Vienna. He was also anxious at such times, since he feared that he might be particularly vulnerable because of his unrelenting gastrointestinal disturbances.

In the fall Gustav's preoccupation with Otto resumed and intensified. He continued to worry about his military service and exams. Mahler may still not yet have known about the Conservatory. Letters reveal his continued concern, while the now diffuse accusations of others betray guilt-ridden frustration: "His education in Vienna was ruined from the start, due to excessive spoiling of the young girls [Lohr's unmarried sisters], by Fritz, and then by

Nina Hoffman." Meanwhile, Alois, now in Hamburg after accumulating numerous debts, was finally enrolled in a business school which might lead to a job. But in October he started spitting blood and tuberculosis was diagnosed. A trip to the Tyrol was called for, and Gustav sent Justi with Alois. There, he not only accepted Gustav's life-restoring trip but characteristically soon sustained debts in Merano and asked him for even more money. Gustav had written to Justi in October:

> I am really in a furiously bad temper. I mean inwardly for I seem perfectly calm. Everything seems to cross me! I really deserve some consideration from you, for when one is obliged, as I am, to fight and bleed for every inch of ground, life is really no joke.

But now, as frustration and rage mounted, his feelings toward the relentlessly psychopathic Alois may have spilled over onto Otto. He wrote to Lohr's sister:

> Those gentlemen, my brothers, never cease causing me sorrow and worries. I have nothing more to do with Alois: one cannot help him, and I do not understand where he got his character. In all my life I have never seen anyone so inconsistent, so thoughtless and, even less still, so deceitful. That is really what makes the cup run over. . . . As for Otto, he is also boldly taking flight into the world as you doubtlessly know too! For him there is no solution other than to be taught by life itself. My sole consolation is that at last Justine's health has improved. Everyone confirms this; it will turn out to be the only comfort of the year, which otherwise has not strewn many roses along my path.

The sarcasm of "those gentlemen" soon gave way to the rancour of "rascal" in writing of Alois, and, again, the distinction between the two brothers breaks down before Gustav's mounting anger.

> I have written this rascal in very strong terms. In the face of such thoughtlessness, such falseness, indulgence would be a great mistake. What will those two fellows do next to annoy me? . . . I am curious to see whether Alois will obey my order. If he does not, I shall take no more interest in him! I am tired of being dragged up hill and down dale hitched to the reins of those winged stallions, my noble brothers. I no longer wish to follow their impetuous flights. I am still young and in no mood to become a morose moralist. I still want to enjoy life, and I am not

yet ready to groan beneath the cares of a bitter old man. God knows I have my own flight to follow [Quoted in de La Grange, 1973, p. 266].

In this manner, Mahler reveals the tail wagging dog: It is he who has now become the dependent, the oppressed; master has become servant. It is Gustav who is now suffering the sadism of fate and of his brothers while he cries out in masochistic woe. Family bonds have become the bonds of torture from which he wishes to break out. Thoughts of aging and the imminence of death appear, perhaps in response to emerging fratricidal wishes. Unconscious wish borders on impulse, as he considers abandoning the brothers. Otto would be subjected to the rough handling of life and, perhaps, with the military threatening, to the potential suffering of war and its consequences. By now, Gustav had given up, resigned to the fatalism he previously deplored in Lohr. His denial betrays an inner perception of himself: the morose moralist but, as ever, no less for himself as for others.

> I believe I made a serious mistake in being always so forgiving and trusting toward these boys . . . [Otto] must not imagine that I am going to continue supporting him during [his military service] in the same way as before. I have done everything in my power to spare him, as well as myself, this sacrifice. He wouldn't listen. Let him face the consequences! Perhaps the only salvation for him is to find out for himself what life means and to be obliged to struggle and battle on his own.

Alois' response to this could well have spoken for both brothers, who were now increasingly being lumped together by Gustav, thus squeezing out of his relationship with Otto the special quality of colleague which had been so gratifying to the latter. Alois wrote, "My heart is so full of bitterness that I'd like to write twenty pages but prefer to keep silent" (Quoted in de La Grange, 1973, p. 266). It suggests too another side of the story.

Mahler complained of not being able to compose that winter because of the foregoing preoccupation. It is unlikely that it was time alone which prevented him, since the previous January (of 1892), during the orchestra's winter break, he had written the five *Wunderhorn* songs. Now, with the preoccupation of this period which Mahler has let us know involves his own cascading aggressive feelings and impulses, he had not been in what he considered a proper frame of mind to compose.

Thus was the period of creative stagnation in composition further prolonged. It had begun during the Budapest conducting years (from 1888) and paralleled Mahler's increasing concern, preoccupation, and frustration with his family from the time of his father's illness and death to the approaching summer of 1893. This period was barren of new work; however, as already noted, it would be inaccurate to give the impression of no work at all in composition. Rather there was some reworking of earlier material in the season prior to the summer of 1893: The final orchestration of *Lieder eines fahrenden Gesellen* and the start of a revision of "Titan" to become the First Symphony.

Frustration and rage characterized Mahler's mental state by this point and were fast reaching a pitch. The healer in Apollo had been tested to the maximum and his cure found lacking. The family had in some sense been preserved and the two sisters were surviving reasonably well. Of the brothers two more were failing, not in health at this point but in other elements of survival. Mahler himself had had enough, his rage causing him to entertain the thoughts of abandonment so abhorrent to him earlier. Soon the fine distinction of survival through health of body and mind would blur as Otto approached his suicide. At this juncture Apollo the Healer and Apollo the Musician were locked in combat, the functions of the one preempting and blocking that of the other. The musician–*conductor* continued to flourish for many reasons, in part because he had to, economics too playing a role in survival. The thrust of this function then need not be impeded. A compromise could be made, satisfying the need to make music and the need to make money. Excellence need not be compromised in any event. But the musician–*composer* was being stifled, as Mahler saw it, stifled from the outside owing to the pressure of his family commitments which absorbed endless time and energy. From within, the block was not quite so straightforward, involved as it was with powerful affects and fantasies. In either case, the Healer had opposed the Musician. Now a shift in balance was about to take place in a solution in which the composer was to achieve expression.

Fraternity, Fratricide, Resurrection (1893/1894)

Caesuras, inhibitions, blocks in creative pace in general have many patterns and sources. With some artists, they are the rule rather than the exception, and work is characterized by fits and starts, the pattern of creative pace often bearing a distinctive personal mark. In some instances, such as the present one, we may come to understand the motivational underpinnings of creative pace. Where inhibition occurs, not only will the *flow* of creative activity be affected, but those motivational elements underlying inhibition will cast their mark on the *content*. Thus, content as well as pace may bear the distinctive fingerprint of the artist, both rooted in identical elements in mental life and parts of a style that characterize art and life.

The shifts and lurches in creative pace are often surprising. In the summer of 1893 we find the Mahler family comfortably and tranquilly installed in five rooms of an inn by the shore of Lake Atter looking onto gently rolling green hills against the backdrop of the Alps! For ten weeks Gustav, Justi, Otto, Alois, and Emma lived in apparent harmony and order while Gustav daily composed in a simple room furnished with a grand piano. Natalie, who helped select the site with Justi, joined them there. This astonishing interlude comes as if a mounting orchestral crescendo were to be precipitously followed by a hushed silence. In it Mahler had managed a psychological tour de force second to none of his operatic productions. He had suddenly turned the photograph of his life from negative to positive: where previously creative energy faltered and emotional life was heavily laden with outer family strife and inner rage, now the latter seemed quelled for the moment and creative life burst forward.

Now, in one extraordinary summer he wrote two of his most important and unique songs, the already mentioned *Fischpredigt* and *Irdische Leben*; developed the former into the Scherzo of the Second Symphony, and also wrote the Andante of the second and worked on portions of the Finale. He also recopied the "Bluemine" movement of the First Symphony, which was the one he had been thinking of deleting. As we shall see later, energy ebbed only as he confronted the proposed theme of what was to be the vocal section of the last movement of the Second: the theme of Brotherhood!

We do not know if Otto composed that summer. He is known to us at that point only as the third brother, brought to vacation with the family by the prominent conductor as part of his entourage, accommodating himself to the composer's schedule. The family would wait for the day's work to be completed before luncheon would be served—

sometimes toward late afternoon! When a major section was completed, for entertainment Mahler would organize a hike, which he much enjoyed, in which everyone would be expected to join.

The respite of the summer was short-lived. Soon after Gustav returned to Hamburg a cholera outbreak occurred, and he was so severely stricken that Justi came to nurse him. She was convinced from his state when she arrived that he was going to die, and she ate from the same spoon in a kind of sisterly *Liebestod*! This is one of the first of several times when the actual circumstances of life reinforced his growing anxiety and fear of death. Soon after his recovery the hemorrhoidal bleeding started again to such a degree that he required treatment with iron pills.

Friction between Otto and Gustav soon redeveloped. We know of it only through its reflection in a letter Otto sent Gustav by registered mail in December, telling him how deeply wounded he felt by him. Gustav's triple response was to dispatch a fuming letter to Justi, who was in Italy, to stew privately about Otto's arrogance yet to entrust Otto to the care of Natalie in Vienna, so that he would not feel abandoned. He wrote to her, "Oh dear God, if only I could have a little peace within my family."

At this point, he turned his attention to another early work of his, written more than a dozen years previously, which he now found himself drawn to reevaluate, *Das Klagende Lied*, a symphonic cantata in three parts. It had been written between 1878 and 1880, and now Gustav marveled at how "so strange and powerful a work could come from a young man, twenty." Otto, now exactly twenty years old himself, may well have felt Gustav's enthusiasm to be salt in his wounds. Gustav wrote of his astonished admiration of his own earlier work to both Natalie and Justi, a rare moment of open self-congratulation. He judged it "already entirely original" and went on to say, "I see that the only progress I have made since then is technical, but the essentials, all the 'Mahler' whom you know was revealed at one single stroke. What surprises me most is that, even in the instrumentation, nothing has to be altered; it is all so characteristic and new. . . ." This from the ever-critical composer who was constantly revising, reorchestrating up to the last minute of performance. One cannot escape the feeling that, uncharacteristically, he is laying it on rather thickly. Within weeks a revision was complete, and he wrote drily, "it can be added to my library" (Quoted in de La Grange, 1973, p. 285).

Thus the previous summer the crust had broken, and the Second Symphony was taking shape stemming from an elaboration of the *Fischpredigt* with its ironic sermonizing. Elaborated into a symphonic movement, the scaffolding for the larger work was forming within Mahler's mind. It would include soloists and chorus in the Finale, hence a shift to the addition of verbal expression to musical. It was here that the thrust faltered as he considered the theme of brotherhood and its associations with Beethoven's choral symphony, his Ninth. He searched in reading, in conversation, and within his own mind "to find the words, the texts or sense of words to the *Second Symphony*" (Quoted in de La Grange, 1973, p. 277). The influences of his greatest heroes, Shakespeare, Wagner, and Beethoven, were reviewed. He was also steeped in Nietzsche at the time. The theme of brotherhood might appeal yet inevitably lead to associations of, if not comparison with, Beethoven, in a choral symphony.

Now, in a creative pulling back after the summer, reflection displacing invention and reconsidering earlier works, he moved from thoughts of *Bruderschaft* (brotherhood) to those of *Brudermord* (fratricide). Indeed, the ballad upon which the text of *Das Klagende Lied* had been based was well known to Mahler from childhood. According to one source, Holländer (1931), "Even as a child he had heard the *Ballade vom Brudermord* as told by a kitchen-maid, to whom he listened with unwearying zest" (p. 453).

The essential plot of *Das Klagende Lied* which Mahler had written himself from various sources (discussed in detail by Mitchell [1958, p. 141ff.]) is that of a good brother and a bad brother who murders him. For the moment it is no less dramatic that Mahler should "accidentally" happen upon his earlier score at this point in his life. In that secret stream of thought which is the source of creative content, we find erupting through the ideas of brotherhood, in the attempted realization of the Second Symphony the previous summer, the music of fratricide. Mahler has channeled his rage, now of murderous proportion, through the medium of music. At the same time the revised work itself is an innocent instrument of aggression against the brother—at once a prize, an object lesson in creativity, and a declaration of supremacy. The words Gustav wrote about *Das Klagende Lied* were to Natalie, but the *message* meant for Otto was in the music itself in the following way. Otto had long served as Gustav's archivist in Vienna. When Gustav wished to resume work on one score or another, he would send "home," and, evidently, Otto knew just where they were. Thus a secret communication between the brothers existed with music itself the medium of the message. Otto was in effect librarian of the "library" to which Gustav had so drily consigned the finished work. We can only guess the effect this could have had on the increasingly tormented Otto.

But he who calls the tune must pay the piper, and, once again, as with the "Blumine" movement of the First Symphony, Mahler considered a deletion in his work—this time the entire first section of the three of *Das Klagende Lied*, called *Waldmärchen*, itself a work of some seventy pages of manuscript and half an hour of music. This is an example of the private pacts and superstitions seen in Mahler's handling of omissions and titles, in this instance, an expiation for an evil brother's wishes toward the young Otto. In general, Mahler's revisions leaned toward the addition of material, and he was never one to be concerned about the length of a work if in his judgment it was artistically correct. But elements of emotional conflict can readily modify this judgment. With regard to length in the works of Mahler, it is of interest to note that some of them, such as the Second Symphony, at the very time in the process of gestation, leaves little room on the program for another work! The composer is the star of the evening, and there is only a little time for attention to anyone else. Thus a childhood wish may be satisfied in the handling of an essential feature of music, its course in time. Only very few times did Mahler consider cuts in his music, and, in the instance of *Das Klagende Lied*, it is related to the growing sense of guilt accompanying emerging feelings toward his brothers. The deletion of *Waldmärchen* may be viewed as an expiatory measure which in effect undoes the aggression the work expresses and binds. Jack Diether (1969), a music critic who has made many contributions to Mahlerian scholarship, is to be credited with first pointing out the possibility of the conflictual sources of the deletion of *Waldmärchen*.

In the spring of 1894, Otto, who by now had been rejected for military service, left for Leipzig where Gustav had obtained temporary musical work for him at the Opera. In September he would begin a new post there. For Otto it may have seemed like a shaky triumph to work as Chordirektor and second conductor, a job obtained for him by his brother's good offices in a city in which the latter had held the spotlight for two years. Yet Otto would be self-supporting for the first time in his life and earning more in each of the succeeding three years of his contract. The future was beginning to open up for Otto with some certainty, perhaps even promise. Gustav, with more bitterness than relief, commented, "His debuts will be much easier than mine," adding as if prophetically, "but all to no purpose unless he himself shows some enthusiasm."

In May, Gustav picked Otto up in Leipzig on his way south to Weimar where Richard Strauss had prepared the orchestra for a performance of "Titan," the First Symphony. The performance was greeted with booing and weak applause, while the critical notices were mixed. Mahler summed up this experience with his brother thus: "My brother was present—quite content over this half failure as I am over his half success." Yet even Gustav's occasional successes were sour grapes to Otto who stated that any work that wins public acclaim must be worthless.

Otto returned to Leipzig, and Gustav to Hamburg, where, before proceeding to Steinbach for vacation, he was introduced to the new assistant the Intendant Pollini, had hired. This was the eighteen-year-old Bruno Schlesinger, later Walter. We do not know if Mahler was aware of such an opening, nor if he ever interceded for Otto for the post in the Hamburg Opera. In any event, Schlesinger was everything Otto was not—extraordinarily gifted as opposed to merely competent, literate, and, above all, highly responsive to Gustav, whom he had long admired from afar. This unabashed admiration stood in strong contrast to Otto's attitude and was to Gustav closer to heart's content in the way of everyday brotherhood. Interestingly, Schlesinger was noted to look strikingly like Otto (de la Grange, 1973, p. 360). A close relationship was to develop between the two. He was one of several "brothers in Apollo" whom Mahler cultivated, fellow musicians toward whom he assumed a caring and responsible attitude. Regrettably, he could not share this less ambivalent part of himself with Otto, and, in their musical transactions, Mahler tended to pontificate. Otto could not have been unmoved by the growing relationship between his brother and the appealing Bruno Schlesinger, clearly the favorite.

In Mahler's own judgment certain other events early in 1894 had led him to the resolution of the formal problems he had encountered in his Second Symphony at the end of the previous summer. He retreated to his "Häuschen" with a clearer notion of musical and textual ideas which were to be the nucleus of the Finale. This had come about, Mahler said, as a result of an experience he had had after von Bülow's death earlier in the year. Von Bülow had died on February 11, 1893, and Mahler had various immediate professional duties as well as future conducting prospects as a result. A memorial service held at the Michaeliskirche in Hamburg on March 29 served as background to Mahler's experience:

> The way in which I received inspiration for the *Finale* is deeply indicative of the essence of musical creation. For a long time I had been considering the idea of introducing a chorus into the last movement, and only the fear that this might be interpreted as a servile imitation of Beethoven made me hesitate so long. Then von Bülow died, and I attended his funeral. The atmosphere in which I found myself and the thoughts I dedicated to the dead man were very much in the spirit of the work I was then carrying within me. All of a sudden the choir accompanied by the organ intoned Klopstock's chorale, *Auferstehn*. It was as if I had been struck by lightning; everything suddenly rose before me clearly! Such is the flash for which the creator waits, such is sacred inspiration!
> After that I had to create in sound what I had just experienced. Nonetheless, if I had not already been carrying the work within me, how could I have experienced this moment? Weren't thousands of other people with me in the church? That's how it always is with me. I only compose when I truly experience something, and I only experience it when I create [Quoted in de La Grange, 1973, p. 294].

This is the famous episode that Theodore Reik (1953) addressed himself to, taking Mahler literally at his word. It was rare for Mahler to offer such an explicit autobiographical exegesis, as de La Grange points out. We may justifiably ask, what made him do so here? The thrust of Reik's discussion leads us to Mahler's relationship with von Bülow who had once responded to a hearing of *Totenfeier* by holding his hands over his ears as if in pain. In essence, Reik's psychological calculations lead him to the following deathwish formulation: "As my unconscious wish that you who rejected me as a composer should die has been fulfilled, so my symphony will be finished and will be a masterwork." Without for the moment disputing the validity of this, acknowledging the overdetermined even in artistic choice, let us turn our attention to another psychological vector—the very one Mahler's gratuitous "explanation" deflects us from, the death wishes toward Otto that had been gathering momentum during the months prior to Gustav's experience in the Michaeliskirche! These wishes, which were to have been transformed to the brotherhood of Beethoven's Ninth and which flared up briefly in less disguised fashion a few months earlier during the revision and partial disavowal of *Das Klagende Lied*, now found resolution in Mahler's idea of resurrection. It was a very personal and idiosyncratic notion he developed. Never one to refrain from putting his own mark on another's work, Mahler continues Klopstock's simple verses with his own fervent commentary.

Klopstock:
Though shalt arise, yea, rise,
Dust of my body, after a brief rest,
Immortal life shall He
Who called thee, give thee.

Again to blossom thou art sown,
The Lord of Harvest goes forth
Collecting sheaves:
We who have died.

Mahler: (continuing)

Have faith my heart, for nought is lost to thee.
All that thou longed for shall be thine,
What is gone shall rise again
Have faith, thou was not born in vain,
Thy life, thy suffering were not in vain.

All that has grown must perish,
What perishes will rise again.
Be not afraid!
Prepare thyself to live!

All pervading pain I have escaped thee
All conquering death, now thou art conquered.
On wings that I have won I shall rise up again
I die to live again.

Thou shalt rise yea, rise, My heart instantly.
Whatever strength was thine shall carry thee to God.

Mahler's verses take off from the gentle sense of Klopstock as if with a powerful centrifugal force. It moves from self-reassurance to self-exhortation; from ecstatic escape from the inevitable—death, pain, perhaps in its context, judgment—to the denial of death; the death of death itself! It evokes a biographical image of Mahler, on one hand guilty, on the other righteous. With regard to the former, there are overtones of *Das Klagende Lied* in the benign lines of the Klopstock verses which Mahler, in the particular state of mind he described, may have been responsive to. In Mahler's version of the story after the younger brother is slain, a period of time elapses before the scene of Part Two, sufficient for the body to decay. A minstrel then finds a glistening bone ("ein Knöchlein blitzen") which he fashions into a flute. Playing it, the ballad of the murder is revealed in the language of music! In the Klopstock verse, "Thou shalt rise . . . dust of my body after a brief rest . . ." this scene is reevoked but not for purposes of retribution but rather reward. The reward of the righteous is earned by "ardent toil and love" and won only by exertion and by struggle. Its ultimate form is resurrection: rebirth and a place in the lap of God. Mahler's solution in this work is at once a moving human document and staggering musical statement—not the least because of its personal flight-of-ideas from the simple Klopstock poem. Psychologically, it is whistling in the dark on an epic scale.

There are other reverberations of *Das Klagende Lied* in the Second Symphony, the presence as it were of derivatives of the fantasy of fratricide within the context of resurrection. One is particularly noteworthy as it not only gives some insight into Mahler's thought processes in solving larger problems of form but also ties in the *Wunderhorn* which serves as the ubiquitous creative backdrop throughout this period. At some point during the conception of the Finale, Mahler decided to orchestrate one of the *Wunderhorn* songs already composed some time prior to 1892 and to incorporate it into the Second Symphony to be inserted as an additional movement before the Finale and serving, in effect, as introduction to it. This is the *Urlicht* or "Primeval Light" which begins, 'O Röschen rot!'—'Oh red rose!' In the text of *Das Klagende Lied* it had been, of course, the red flower which was the prize for which one brother murdered the other ("Im Wald eine rote Blume stand, Ach so schön wie die Königin"). As if a meditation on *Das Klagende Lied*, it is not the minstrel who is encountered on the forest path ("Ein Spielmann zog einst des Weges daher . . .") but an angel on a broad pathway ("Da kam ich auf einem breiten Weg"), who would light the way to eternal blissful life ("Wird leuchten mir bis in das ewig selig Leben").

Such considerations and others suggest determinants in the solution of the Finale which are more compelling than Reik's hypothesis about von Bülow. Mahler's own skirmish with death earlier in the season should not be overlooked. When the possibility of death as punishment is entertained in fantasy, it may, of course, exert a powerful enough effect upon mental activity; when reality itself nudges with a reminder of mortality, the ensuing anxiety may be powerful indeed. To put it in terms of Reik's psychological paradigm, it is as if Mahler in the spring and summer of 1894 is reassuring himself in denial of what he now fears most: "You *shall not* die because you wish your brother's death; in fact, there is no death because it has been conquered with your sacrifice and devotion."

Ideas of death and rebirth inevitably lead us to those whom Gustav loved and lost—perhaps loved ambivalently as was the case with Otto. His psychological preparedness for the message of the Klopstock ode lay in the fact that this occurred during a season of public mourning for von Bülow which included the fifth anniversary of Bernhard Mahler's death. Von Bülow died on the 12th of February, Gustav's father on the 18th. It must have been an eerie experience for Mahler to replace von Bülow on his own podium on the 16th, hidden behind a bust of the conductor surrounded by greenery, as he conducted Beethoven's Eroica in the memorial concert. So had he taken over the family when his father died five years before. This element would, of course, tend to support Reik's more oedipal point of view.

But another, perhaps more significant, anniversary was approaching as he sat in the Michaeliskirche on March 19. Twenty years earlier in Mahler's recollection, during the Easter season, the beloved Ernst had died. (It was actually the nineteenth anniversary, but, taking Alma Mahler's date, we may assume that Gustav distorted the year of Ernst's death, as incidentally he did his own birthdate.) An entirely different side of Gustav's character is revealed in his relationship to Ernst, the tender, nurturing side noted earlier. Memories of Ernst, as revealed in letters, were often accompanied by a feeling of "Sehnsucht"—a nostalgic, depressed longing akin in Mahler's case to the feelings of prolonged mourning.

The events of the following summer and fall were to prove what may have been Gustav's feeling that, now, he had lost both brothers. His fear, perhaps wish, was that Otto would not prove equal to the task despite the track he had now been set on. Both losses were blows to Gustav's considerable narcissism. Von Bülow had once presented Gustav with a baton inscribed: "To the Pygmalion of the Hamburg Opera." But his "ardent toil" during the Hamburg years as Pygmalion to Otto were doomed to failure.

THE MUSIC OF FRATRICIDE

It would be beyond the scope of the present study to attempt to develop exhaustively those musical ideas which relate to the biographical and literary themes already developed. Several have been touched upon in the foregoing account, such as the musical character of the *Fischpredigt* and its elaboration into a symphonic movement which had important formal implications in the realization of the entire Second Symphony. Also noted has been the function of music as message, for example, in the actual score of *Das Klagende Lied*, as it was presented to Otto who was at the time the keeper of Mahler's "drawer" of music. In a more penetrating way, we have been struck with how in this work the revelation of the murder is made *in* music and *by* musical means. However, by and large, it has been the biographical trends which have been emphasized along with considerations of their effect on creative pace as well as their reflection in certain literary themes related to the actual music. For example, it might be noted that the relationship between *Das Klagende Lied* and *Urlicht* in the red flower (which to the best of my knowledge has not been noted in the literature) appears to be a literary one. (Although one might expect to find a musical relationship sui generis as one usually does in such cases in Mahler's music, in this particular instance my own study up to this point fails to reveal one.)

What will follow in this concluding portion of the present study will be several selected examples of how the music itself relates to the foregoing, that is, not the verbal idea or creative process, but the musical idea itself as can be readily re-created at any moment in tone or form. It may be achieved in imagination or in physical actuality, its potential inherent in the symbols of the musical score. A fundamental assumption made here is that the essentially nonrepresentative forms so described have coherence and multiple meanings. On one level there may be encoded elements of human experience which are accessible through other means. Thus its content may be "tapped," as it were, through a consideration of verbal and biographical parallel.

This would appear to be particularly appropriate to the music of Mahler where the entire early period is inspired by, and permeated with, the welded word and music of *Des Knaben Wunderhorn*, the *Wunderhorn Years* as Mitchell (1975) has called them. I have suggested elsewhere (1980) that these (and the later songs as well) virtually provide a musical Rosetta Stone which aids us in seeking connections and parallels. Perhaps, after all, this is best put in the words of Mahler himself which were quoted earlier when he spoke of his entire life to date being contained in his first two symphonies: "To anyone who knows how to listen, my whole life will become clear."

Let us consider a fragment of musical thought, perhaps the single most significant one if any could be so artificially isolated from so vast a work, in the Second Symphony. This is the entrance of the a capella chorus in the Finale intoning the words, "Aufersteh'n, ja aufersteh'n wirst du, mein Staub, nach kurzer Ruh!" (at No. 31, p. 186 in Kalmus score). This moment has been carefully prepared in numerous respects, not least of which is the presence of the seated and waiting mixed chorus throughout close to an hour of orchestral music. The section which precedes Mahler marked on the autograph score, "Der Grosse Appell," often translated as "The Last Trump" (at No. 29, in Kalmus score). Elaborate directions on the score in these sections indicate the disposition of the orchestra—some of it off-stage in "Der Grosse Appell"—and various other stage directions. For example, the chorus is to be seated at its musical entrance, and the orchestra players who must resume their place are admonished to do so with care so as not to disturb the a capella singing with their noise ("Nehmen wieder ihren Platz im Orchester ein; doch mit Bedacht darauf, nicht durch Geräusch den 'a capella' Gesang zu stören"). Thus, in addition to the usual musical directions inherent in the notes and other markings, Mahler includes rather elaborate stage directions, perhaps more than in any other of his works. He never wrote an opera as such, although his job was to direct and conduct them. (Actually one of his earliest projected works from the age of fourteen or fifteen was an opera evidently connected with Mahler's idealization of the recently dead Ernst. It was called *Herzog Ernst von Schwabe* after Uhland's heroic verse drama.) Here, however, are some elements of opera, or at least of drama, without specific plot. With further regard to the preparation of the choral entrance, the insertion of the introductory *Urlicht* movement may also be cited, with its solemnly intoned brass chorale. Also, Mahler had indicated his intent that the singer in this song should use "the tone and vocal expression of a child who thinks he is in heaven" (Quoted in de La Grange, 1973, p. 790). (It should be noted that the chorus at von Bülow's funeral which inspired Mahler so much was one of children's voices.) Finally, in the second preceding the chorus, there will have been a decrescendo from the frantic blares of the trumpet ("schmetternt") into a sustained chord marked "sich verlierend"—sounds dying away.

The choral entrance is marked, 'Langsam, Misterioso' (see Figure 17.1) and the dynamics noted triple piano. The impression thus is that of a massive whisper. Its careful preparation suggests that Mahler wished the listener to become aware that the chorus had begun its entrance only gradually during the course of the first few measures. (Some conductors strive deliberately for this effect, and I believe this discussion will support that this was the composer's intent.) For what Mahler has re-created is a musical representation of the moment of awakening. From a child's point of view, it consists of those moments both before and after the daily dawn of consciousness. In essence, it is the transitional state writ large and rendered audible. Gradually one becomes aware of the voice of the awakener, "aufersteh'n—wake up" and consciousness takes hold. It is the mother's gentle reveille as perceived by a very small person. Audible form lends authenticity to the experience, since this is perhaps the most common form of awakening: one's eyes are closed, and the first stimuli are auditory. In a delicately poised balance a shift in cathexis is accomplished from inner to outer world.

Figure 17.1   Reproduced by permission of The James Marshall and Marie-Louise Osborn Collection, Beinicke Library, Yale University.

The representation of awakening is both rich and authentic psychologically, as it contains in symbolic and audible form its opposite, namely the state of falling asleep. For lullabys are similarly crooned, and in the second and third measures of the motive one may detect a quote from Brahm's famous lullaby (with meter changed) whether or not with conscious intent. (The fragment occupies the same relative position in Brahms's melody from the anacrusis or "upbeat" to the second measure to the end of the third.) In this sense we are drawn to the notion of mother as the inductress of sleep and the awakener: the guardian of the gates of life and death.

The particular quality of the sound triple piano emitted by the massive chorus will emphasize both the act of breathing and the nature of breath. This relates to concepts of birth, particularly that of the imparting of the breath of life. While the biblical connotations may lead to the Old Testament and God the Father's instillation of breath into the nostrils of man, breath has other, more quotidian qualities. As Jones (1914) points out, breath has the following attributes: blowing movement, sound, invisibility, moisture, warmth, and odor (p. 279). These are qualities of body contact which turn our attention more toward the mother, although Jones as well as Lewin (1968, pp. 26–32) speaks of father as the wakener.

On a grander scale, here actually the manifest of the program of the work, sleeping and waking are related to death and birth, actually the rebirth of resurrection. Our attention may thereby be drawn to the experiences of birth and death in Mahler's early life. There were abundant examples of each, as we have seen. In the musical idea of "aufersteh'n" we find a highly condensed statement in which there may be said to be encoded memories and experiences related to birth and death, their everyday psychological equivalents in sleep and awakening, and separation and reunion—all in auditory terms—through the voice of the mother.

On some quite literal level many of these experiences may have seemed to Mahler to have been, in fact, fused early in life. Births and deaths fairly tumbled upon one another regularly throughout his childhood years. One would wonder what this stimulated in the fantasy life of the dreamy older sibling that Mahler was—for example, what fratricidal fantasy might be stimulated in a child of one, three, four, five, seven, eight, nine, eleven, twelve, and thirteen—Mahler's age at the birth of each of his younger siblings through to Otto.

One would also wonder about the experience of actual birth which took place at home. The careful musical preparations for the entrance of the breathing chorus suggests the anticipation of arrival as the admonitions to the orchestra not to make noise suggests, "Don't wake the baby!" The mysteries of life and death merge as they do in the child. Things are happening offstage, far away, dimly perceived, poorly understood, and feared. A sense of mystery and awe prevails. Later, in Mahler's adolescence a clearer discrimination between these events could supervene, hence be, therefore, available to an ironic attitude rather than a confused one. For example, condensed in his experience of his fourteenth year were, in fact, the elements of birth, death, and separation: it was the first year of Otto's life, the last of Ernst's and, for Gustav, who was about to leave home, the final year of childhood.

Musical representation of this highly condensed complex of ideas of birth and death, sleep and awakening, separation and reunion occur repeatedly in Mahler's music. An example much later in his life as he in fact began to face his own death has been discussed in a consideration of the song "Um Mitternacht" (Feder, 1980a). In *Das Klagende Lied*, of course, the fair, younger brother falls asleep in the forest never to wake again, although his accusatory voice is resurrected in the minstrel's bone flute. The music which represents his peaceful falling asleep and rest ('zur Ruh . . . zur Ruh . . .') is quoted and developed in one of Mahler's later songs of the *Lieder eines fahrenden Gesellen* of 1884 *(Songs of a Wayfarer)* and in the First Symphony. In the former, in the final song "Die zwei blauen Augen von meinem Schatz," the despairing, wandering lover seeks solace in sleep under a linden tree. The linden, or lime tree as it is known in Europe, was rich in symbolism of which Mahler was surely aware. In Central European mythology it represented immortality, and in Germany and the Tyrol it was the tree of judgment under which magistrates of old were said to sit in its shade and pass judgment (Leach, 1972, p. 624). In the artful ambiguity of Mahler's song it is left to the imagination whether the lover finds solace in sleep or in suicide. In this instance sleep is associated with separation, abandonment, and suicide.

The issue of guilt and judgment brings us round to another aspect of the music of the Second Symphony cited earlier. This is the music of "The Last Trump." A program provided by Mahler is instructive although too lengthy to quote here in its entirety (de La

Grange, 1973, p. 786). Of striking interest is its personal, indeed idiosyncratic blend of Old and New Testament notions, of Christian and Jewish elements, and those related to neither. It is neither Jewish in that it includes the literal notion of resurrection, nor Christian in that it disavows sin and judgment. One line in particular is noteworthy in its surprising resemblance to a traditional Jewish high holiday prayer, *U-netanneh Tokef* (*Encyclopedia Judaica*, Vol. 15, p. 153). The musical realization of this program is worthy of detailed analysis, of which only a few highlights will be covered here (Kalmus score, No. 29, p. 185). It is a free meditative passage notated in a mere two dozen measures for offstage brass and flute and piccolo in the orchestra. The predominant motive, as stated in the horn, consists of an open fifth which is immediately extended to the octave. A more complex triplet figure follows in the trumpets. The characteristics of brass instruments exploited here are precisely those which the shofar or ritual ram's horn is capable of. The latter can produce only a few tones corresponding to the fifth and octave (sometimes the fourth) but is capable of some rhythmic flexibility (Idelsohn, 1948, p. 9). The section of "The Last Trump" may be understood as a highly sophisticated exploration of the limited musical possibilities of this instrument, while it embodies all its awesome religious associations. The very least one can point out is the association of the blowing of the shofar with the annual Jewish penitential season. Although the means are sophisticated, a primitive effect is achieved, or perhaps a musical image perceived, through the ears of a child—in essence a representation of memory. In response to the distant portentous brass sounding judgment day, one hears the quivering piccolo marked "wie eine Vogelstimme," a literal representation of the "distant nightingale" of Mahler's program, "a last tremulous echo of earthly life" (de La Grange, 1973, p. 786). At the same time it renders in auditory imagery the picture evoked by the prayerbook description of judgment day. There is little question that, as a child, Mahler had experiences in the synagogue. Although their exact nature is not known, recent studies suggest that the Mahler family enjoyed a greater connection with the Jewish life than it had been previously thought the "free thinking" Bernhard would permit (Blaukopf, 1976, Fig. 13; Feder, 1980a, p. 19; Mitchell, 1958, pp. 271–272). The prayer cited was one in the Ashkenazi tradition, as practiced in the late nineteenth century by the Jews of Moravia and Bohemia. The symbolism of the

Day of Atonement would serve as an organizing element connecting sin, aggression, guilt, atonement, and forgiveness which, condensed, might be put to creative use. The concept of resurrection was the Christian element, and the massive denial of judgment, sin, and punishment were Mahler's own in a highly personal eschatology and perhaps a grandiose influence of Nietzsche.

The single outstanding Christian musical symbol for death, the dies irae, recurs repeatedly in Mahler's music of this period, prominently in *Das Klagende Lied* and at an important point in the Second Symphony. It is the portion of the Requiem Mass most consistent with the fearful passages above and in fact is drawn from the fire-and-brimstone call for repentence of pre-Christian times already mentioned in Zephania (Robertson, 1968, p. 16). Its verses certainly suggest common psychological, if not historical, roots, and in its third verse (tuba mirum . . .) the trumpet of judgment appears: "A trumpet first shall rend the skies/And all, wherever laid, must rise/and come unto the bar in prisoner's guise" (Robertson, 1968, p. 17). The opening motive of this plainsong chant has been quoted numerous times, particularly, although not exclusively, in romantic music where it has come to represent a memento mori in tone.

This motive is intricately woven into the second and third parts of *Das Klagende Lied* with telling dramatic effect. (The interested reader is referred to the analysis by Diether [1969].) It is likewise important in the extended first movement of the Second Symphony, called originally *Totenfeier*, or "Funeral Rites," a portion which we have not so far considered in this study. At its climax it appears in the horns in choralelike fashion only to be followed by a theme in the trumpets which presages, what will later become clear, the music associated with life, rebirth, resurrection in the Finale. This nucleus of a musical idea receives extensive treatment in the Finale. Not only is the dies irae incorporated and developed there, but I believe it would be accurate to say that it receives its most thorough treatment in the romantic literature: it is made intrinsic, not merely quoted as an emblem.

It should be stressed once again that these examples are intended to be illustrative of certain mental trends of the composer and do not pretend to be comprehensive in any musical-analytic sense. Thus we may select one more feature of the *Totenfeier* to note: It is the second time that a funeral rite is incorporated into a Mahler symphony. Mahler acknowledges this in one of his several programs: "it is the hero of my First D Major Symphony who is being carried to his grave and whose life I imagine I can see reflected in a mirror from a high watchtower . . ." (Quoted in de La Grange, 1973, p. 784). Specifically, in the First Symphony, the third movement is a funeral march, although, in its ironic turns, strictly speaking it can hardly be called a dirge. It was said to have been inspired by an engraving by the French artist Jacques Callot—actually it was Mauritz von Schwind—in which a funeral procession of animals bears the coffin of the hunter. The coffin, identified by the hunter's gun, is carried by stags. The procession is led by the cats carrying standards and playing instruments. Following the coffin are foxes, deer, and birds weeping copiously, some into large handkerchiefs (Blaukopf, 1976, Fig. 77). The enigmatic and apparently satirical interpretation Mahler gives to this stimulus is revealing. The childhood round "Frere Jacques" (known to Mahler as "Bruder Martin") is played in the strained upper register of the double bass. The movement in general is rich in childhood associations in both musical and literary content. The engraving itself is the equivalent of a "comic strip" and in this sense may be understood to be not only of childhood and for children but *about* children as well. In the same sense as in the dream, small animals may represent small children, particularly, as Freud (1900) points out, "undesired brothers and sisters" (p. 357). In the solution to unconscious fratricidal wishes found here, the hunted are burying the hunter. The artist is ultimately his own hero, and the funeral is his. As we have seen, in the Second Symphony yet another solution is sought.

The above serves as an example of a common trend, apparently encountered by many authors in writing about Mahler and his music. There is, as it were, a centripetal pull toward childhood, toward some center in his life and past. Mahler's very first composition, written when he was six, was called "Polka with Introductory Funeral March" (Polka mit einem Trauermarsch als Einleitung) (de La Grange, 1973, p. 18). Up to Mahler's sixth birthday, four siblings had been born, and the only death had been that of his brother Isidor prior to his own birth. In that year, the two most recently born boys died as infants. It seems likely that the deaths and rituals associated with mourning (the Mahlers were a part of the Iglau religious community at this time) served as stimulus, at least to the manifest content of the piece. What had become masterful irony in the adult artist is exposed in the child at its source. It is not merely denial. It may also be an overstimulation of affects of contradictory nature which are not as yet in fully developed form which makes the child laugh instead of cry—elements of undifferentiation, ambivalence, and confusion.

From a musical point of view, the above suggests an intriguing possibility which perhaps merits speculation. Just as Mahler's childhood seems to exert a magnetic pull, so do the trends originating there appear to extend continuously into later life. This, of course, is as might be expected psychologically, but its reflection in the music is what is of interest here. As we have seen, it is often possible to trace the vicissitudes of a musical idea over a period of time. Might it be possible that some fragment of a musical idea of this lost earliest piece survives in some form in the context of a mature work? If so, this funeral march of the First Symphony would seem a likely candidate. It is noteworthy that a dance tune of an apparently Slavic nature [Gartenberg (1978, p. 256) says "Chassidid"; Cooke (1980, p. 35) 'cheap band music'] intrudes during the course of the movement. This movement incidentally contains another look backward related to a music we have already discussed. A middle, "trio" section quotes no less than thirty measures of the song *Die zwei blauen Augen von meinem Schatz*, which, as we have seen, had its musical origin in *Das Klagende Lied*. There it had been associated with the words *zur Ruh*; in the song, as the despairing lover sought solace in sleep under the lime tree, forgetting his bitter pain, everything good once again, the words are "alles wieder gut. Alles! Alles! Lieb' und Leid! Und Welt und Traum."

Before leaving this discussion of certain musical elements, we will consider briefly but in more detail certain aspects having to do with the forming of the Second Symphony which were only touched on earlier. It was noted that at the very height of Mahler's frustration and rage at his brothers he had managed during the summer of 1893 to have one of the most productive times of his creative life. It will be recalled that whatever inhibition he experienced had to do with new work, as he continued to refine and complete other current work as well as look backward in reworking such earlier scores as *Das Klagende Lied*. Once again it was a song that served as germ to a symphonic movement, this time the *Fischpredigt* with the literary implications already discussed of the preacher sermonizing to dumb faces, deaf ears, and Mahler's own identification with St. Anthony. An impetus was generated in this context which not only gave rise to the song and symphonic movement but bridged the gap between the already completed first section *(Totenfeier)* and the Finale which was yet to come. Although in one program Mahler views the three inner movements (of the five) as "intermezzi" (de La Grange, 1973). I believe a strong case could be made for the middle movement, the *Fischpredigt* Scherzo, to be central in formal and conceptual terms as well as in position. This impetus, fundamentally aggressive in nature, could not be contained in a song no matter how sophisticated. Expanded and developed, the song would require greater duration, expanded and contrasting sections, a wider range of dynamics, and the resources of a full symphony orchestra, in particular percussion. Of the impetus Mahler experienced in composing that summer, he would write years later to Natalie: "I am amazed that I was able to write this that summer in Steinbach! It was only thanks to the long interruption that had been forced upon me, after which the waters gushed forth, as they do from an obstructed pipe. . . ." The autograph score (1894) reveals that Mahler first intended a longer tympani introduction but crossed out four measures. Two other aspects of percussion are of interest, perhaps symbolically. Mahler employs a rarely used percussion device which he uses in only one other place, namely the orchestrated song version of the *Fischpredigt* as it appears in *Des Knaben Wunderhorn*. This is the "Ruthe" or "Rute" which consists essentially of a bundle of birch branches which when used on a drum (usually the bass drum) gives a particular effect. Its rare use is no doubt due to the fact that related effects may be achieved in numerous other ways. It is of interest to us here in that the *Rute* is, of course, the German term for the switch or rod, specifically birch rod as in the idiom "einem Kind die Rute geben," literally to give the child the rod, or to beat the child. Any wish this reference may harbor would certainly not be acceptable to St. Anthony! At the very end of the orchestral version of the song, Mahler employs a device used with such telling effect in only one other song as to suggest some particular symbolism. That is at the close of the *Wunderhorn* song, "Irdische Leben," where the single stroke of the muffled cymbal announces the death of a starving child. "Irdische Leben" was also one of the fruits of the summer of 1893 and something of a companion piece to the *Fischpredigt* in that it was written at about the same time (Mitchell, 1975, p. 128). Its content is unique in Mahler's songs and perhaps (with the exception of Schubert's "Erlkönig") in all vocal literature: A child is starved to death as it is seductively urged to wait by the crooning mother, here the bearer of death. Elsewhere, I have discussed its music and pointed out a much later relationship to the Tenth Symphony (Feder, 1978, p. 145). It might be noted that in the latter, a near-identical musical symbol (a muffled drum stroke) explicitly represents death (p. 142). Of interest to us here is that the orchestrated song, *Fischpredigt*, ends with the same muffled cymbal as "Irdische Leben." The larger movement which it gave rise to does not. Mitchell (1975) in his description of the autograph score points out some "enigmatic marks" in Mahler's hand. In blue crayon he "drew a vertical line that exactly coincides with the penultimate bar line.... Thus isolating—detaching as it were—the final bar itself" (p. 272). He makes some cogent speculations about its musical, actually formal, function. I would wonder if among the many vectors here leading to an artistic act an unconscious one might have been the avoidance of the death blow.

The foregoing examples are intended to provide hints of the background to these works in the mental life of its composer. They are isolated examples which do not pretend to take into account the larger emotional thrust of the work, much less make a statement on its artistic merit. However, there is little question as to the intrinsic nature of the *Fischpredigt*, its amplification and roots in Mahler's mental life during this time. A fact of a purely musical nature which tends to support this is that both the symphonic movement and song are in the key of C minor, the tonal center of the symphony. An amusing example of the St. Anthony in Mahler might be cited before concluding this discussion of the music. At one point (Kalmus score, at No. 38, p. 96) Mahler has the lower strings enter in parallel with a figure in the violins causing four consecutive "parallel fifths" which are considered to be errors of voice leading according to the rules of harmony of the common practice era. Mahler marked the autograph score with a large asterisk, referring to a footnote on the score: "sind verboten! Ich weiss!" (It is forbidden! I know!). Beneath this, in parentheses: "Note for the Judge." On the score itself he had noted the transgression with connecting dotted lines after the fashion of the pedant. Since Mahler's musical idiom might be judged to contain many comparable "errors," this is surely a private joke stimulated perhaps by his own awareness of having written a studentlike fugato in developing one of the themes. (A passage which could well be a quote or imitation of Bach follows.) Perhaps too it is a private ironic reference to an earlier event when he failed to win the Beethoven Prize of the Gesellschaft der Musikfreunde for *Das Klagende Lied*. He had always remembered this wound with bitterness and with several distortions, believing that the course of his life would have been completely different and that he would not have been "condemned to the Hell of the theatre" in order to earn a living (Quoted in de La Grange, 1973, p. 80). He believed that it had been owing to the hostility of the "conservatives" Brahms and Hanslick that he had failed to win the prize.

While Mahler might later have relegated the importance of the Scherzo to one of a mere "intermezzo," we know from Natalie Bauer-Lechner, who was with him that summer of 1893, that this was inconsistent with the circumstances of its composition. He was described as being "in an almost pathological state" while working on the central movements. He worried about the response people would have, whether the "message" would be conveyed. "What terrible problems will the Scherzo, for instance, present to those who hear it?" (Quoted in de La Grange, 1973, pp. 274–275).

As for the Finale, the following summer Mahler experienced the triumph of life over death—of creativity over aggression, the process of composition itself identified in his own mind as a life-giving process. This was consistent with some of Mahler's own fantasies about the act of composition itself. He likened it to a pearl, "that treasure offered to the world only after having caused the oyster severe pain" (Quoted in de La Grange, 1973, p. 274). Completing the Finale on June 29, 1894, he wrote to Fritz Lohr:

> Beg to report safe delivery of a strong, healthy last movement to my Second. Father and child both doing as well as can be expected—the latter not yet out of danger. At the baptismal ceremony it was given the name 'Lux lucet in tenebris'. Silent sympathy is requested. Floral tributes are declined with thanks. Other presents, however, are acceptable. Yours, Gustav. These are my birthday greetings to you [Martner, 1979, pp. 154–155].

Mahler was here referring to his own thirty-fourth birthday on July 7, the following week. Thus he identified himself not only as the giver of life, but as its gift in fantasied reenactment of his own birth—the second child.

DISCUSSION: MUSIC AND AGGRESSION

The deaths of children and of youths is the theme which permeates the literary and musical aspect of Mahler's entire oeuvre from first to last. Long before the literal deaths of children in *Kindertotenlieder* it had been a preoccupation from the earliest "Funeral March" and the hero of "Herzog Ernst" and those of the first two symphonies. The youths of the *Wunderhorn* died, too, killed in war or hung by order of the military tribunal. In one song, a child dies of starvation. Only in the later works, in the final trilogy of the last two symphonies (the Ninth and Tenth) and *Das Lied von der Erde* do we have hints of the youth aging and that the man facing death is Mahler himself. If the parting friends of *Der Abschied* are not literally reaching the ends of their lives, the weary, crepuscular, and valetudinal atmosphere which prevails makes them appear to be. In the Ninth Symphony it becomes increasingly apparent that it is the composer who is coming to terms with death (Diether, 1963), and in the unfinished Tenth it is explicit, death literally scrawled across the manuscript page (Feder, 1978).

The power of this theme and its endurance throughout Mahler's creative lifetime comes from three sources in his life—here biography and mental life. The first is the repeated experience of child mortality, especially that which he experienced as a loss, as in the death of Ernst, and that which could only have been a shadowy threat, the dead older brother Isidor. The second is Mahler's relentless anxiety regarding his own death. This is particularly important here in terms of that aspect that has to do intrapsychically with punishment. This touches on the third which has been the focus of interest in this study: Death as the harshest retribution for aggressive acts and unacceptable aggressive fantasies. The central underlying fantasy that has been our focus here has been the fantasy of fratricide.

I have tried to suggest some of its early roots, but, whatever they may have been, the structure of Mahler's psyche was such that the resultant conflicts could not settle into the relative comfort of minor psychopathology or character trait which is often the fate of early neurotic pattern. Two external factors contribute. One was Mahler's extreme success, with its attendant triumph over others. This was not only the case in his family. Many friendly rivals and frank competitors fell by the wayside and not only into mediocrity but (as with some of his Conservatory companions) into psychosis and suicide. The second element, exposed in detail in the present study, was the continuing stimulation of earlier conflict by life circumstances which Mahler could not help but be responsive to. Thus, following the deaths of his parents, he found himself thrust into a maelstrom of conflict which, under other circumstances, he might have been able to avoid or at least deal with in the attenuated way characteristic of adulthood.

Mahler's growing rage and the circumstances that fostered it served, as I have tried to show, as backdrop to the "music of fratricide" of this period. Expectably, there were antecedents in the music and sequelae as well. But this period is characterized by an exacerbation which puts its mark on every aspect of creative life, including its pace and the form and content of its product.

To study this is instructive from another point of view, certainly with regard to understanding Mahler, and perhaps as a vantage point from which to wonder about certain aspects of musical function in mental life. Speaking of Mahler as composer, not conductor in this instance, we may wonder what psychological functions composing subserved. In raising this question, it is not to be interpreted that this purports to exhaust the possible functions. On the contrary, there is good evidence beyond the scope of the present essay to suggest that, to an enormous degree, music-making activity in composers is an autonomous one. However, where it is not conflict-free, as in the present instance, we may be in an advantageous position to explore a certain portion of man and music. Studies in the life of Mahler and his music have suggested to me that there are four interrelated functions involved in composition which, to a greater or lesser degree, *may* be the result of conflict, the first two very likely, the third not necessarily, and the fourth only at times:

1. The binding of aggression is the function most clearly seen in this study. Here we have seen how the identical source might be inhibitory or stimulating and how form, content, and every aspect of related action may bear its mark.

2. Composition may contribute to the mastery of trauma. (This has been advanced as a general proposition by Kohut, 1957.)

3. The role played by mourning and memorialization in musical composition is an important one in the case of Mahler (see chapter 16). Everything depends here upon the nature of the memorialization from an intrapsychic point of view: it may facilitate mourning, avoid it, or prolong it. With Mahler we find at various times elements of all three.

4. Finally, we come to a function which, for want of a better term, I would call a *conceptualizing* function. This is one of the fundamental capacities of the composer—to "think" in tonal, formal, temporal, and, essentially, nonrepresentational terms. As such, it is a unique mode of thinking, but, like the commoner varieties of cognition, a kind that the composer may employ in his coming to terms with the world. Just as other modes of thinking have an adaptive side, so does this. It should be made clear that I speak here not of the verbal aspects of music, the ones I have called literary which are so prominent in the music discussed, but the purely musical aspect. This function relates to each of the three previous. It is a way of thinking, hence of coming to terms with the inner and outer world, which includes aggression, trauma, and loss.

Epilogue

An abrupt disappearance of references to Otto descends upon the correspondence after the summer of 1894, suggesting censorship by some hand. By the end of July Otto was returning depressed from the summer post he never fulfilled in Bremen, nor did he ever return to Leipzig to assume his new post there. He wrote to Justi on August 15 saying that he had arrived in Bremen exhausted and "half mad." In February 1895, as Otto put it, he turned in his ticket, committing suicide in a shared atmosphere of Dostoevskian gloom at the home of a family friend, Nina Hoffman.

The following month, on March 11, 1895, Gustav had to conduct the final symphonic concert of the season. He selected a work he had not conducted since his Prague days in 1886 but which, as we have seen, had a great deal of meaning to him, the Ninth Symphony of Beethoven. Its message of brotherhood was one Mahler had struggled to come to terms with in the composition of the recently completed Second Symphony, before he had been drawn to the theme of resurrection. He may have felt this would be an appropriate work for the end of the concert season as well as the Easter season. Characteristically, he made some revisions in the orchestral score. He even entertained the possibility of an off-stage ensemble in the Finale of the Beethoven in order to initiate a stunning crescendo. His comment reveals how very much his fantasies continued to reverberate with the spirit of his own Second Symphony: The crescendo was to suggest "the approach of a vast legion of enraptured, ecstatic beings, a jubilant hosanna on their lips, as on the first of all Palm Sundays." Palm Sunday, the Sunday preceding Easter, commemorates Christ's triumphal entry into Jerusalem. In keeping with this grandiose sense of triumph, the triumph perhaps of the survivor, Mahler had built for himself a high, wooden platform from which to conduct. Its rationale was the enlarged orchestra and the number of volunteers for the chorus. The carpenter had taken Mahler's orders for the structure too literally, as well he might have done, knowing the conductor's reputation for exactness, and he built the podium an entire story high! Mahler, mounting the platform, experienced a sudden attack of vertigo and came close to losing his balance. Witnesses described him as if pawing the wooden platform in order to plant himself firmly once he gained a footing. Characteristically, pulling himself together magnificently, he conducted the entire symphony without moving from that position (de La Grange, 1973, p. 323). Natalie Bauer-Lechner (1923, p. 53) described the structure as a "Podiumgerüste," a scaffolding, "from which one could break one's neck." Assuming that this imagery, as usual, came from her conversations with Mahler and, therefore, in turn, from his fantasies, we would wonder if for Mahler the podium had become the gallows.

As far as is known, Mahler had a recurrence of this symptom on one other occasion, at the premiere of his Second Symphony in Berlin the following December. He had arrived with a migraine that nearly incapacitated him. At the performance, he had to mount a high platform similar to the one he had had built for his performance of the Beethoven Ninth earlier that year. Bruno Walter (1966) describes him on the podium as pale as death and attempting to conquer his pain and to marshal the assembled forces in the Second (p. 24). It was Walter's opinion that this critical performance marked the emergence of Mahler as a composer.

Summary

In this musical–psychoanalytic study of Gustav Mahler, certain of the sources of the composer's creativity are considered; namely, those related to fratricidal fantasy. In connection with this, the relationship of the content of art to the biography of the artist is studied, and therefore the role of conflict in the realization of an art form.

Against the background of childhood, Mahler's relationship to his thirteen living and dead siblings is taken up, in particular that with a pair of surviving brothers, one of whom, like himself, was a musician. This study focuses on the period of the composer's early thirties when, following the deaths of both parents and his assumption of a role in loco parentis, there was a resurgence of earlier fratricidal fantasy and impulse.

The relationship of this mental trend to the music is demonstrated in analyses of the Second Symphony of this period, certain related songs of *Des Knaben Wunderhorn*, and the earlier *Das Klagende Lied*, a cantata based on the tale of fratricide. The role of aggression in music is discussed.

Chapter 18
Mozart: A Study in Genius

Aaron H. Esman, M.D.

The enigma of creative genius is perhaps the most fascinating of problems to students of the human mind. There have been many psychoanalytic contributions to the understanding of this mystery, among them Freud on Dostoevsky (1928) and Leonardo (1910), Sharpe on Shakespeare (1946), Bonaparte on Poe (1949), Lee on the creative mind (1947), and Bergler on writing (1950), but the genesis of creative genius remains virtually unsolved. Freud stated, "The nature of artistic attainment is psychoanalytically inaccessible to us ... [psychoanalysis] can do nothing toward elucidating the nature of the artistic gift ..." (1925, p. 65). It is nevertheless tempting to seek in the life and work of an artist clues that may lead to just such an elucidation.

Perhaps the greatest in his field, Wolfgang Amadeus Mozart's genius was at once unique and so extraordinary that it fairly cries out for investigation. We are comforted by the assurance that whether or not we reach any general conclusions about creative genius, we can learn much of interest about one of the supreme figures of Western art.

DEVELOPMENT AND CHARACTER

Certainly the most striking feature of Mozart's very brief but incredibly productive career was his precocity. The story of his surreptitious pianistics at the age of four is too well known—if not too apocryphal—to bear retelling. Surreptitious or not, it is well established that Mozart was musically active before most children are able to read, and was composing short pieces for the clavier at the age of five.

Outstanding in Mozart's development was his relationship with

First published in the *Psychoanalytic Quarterly*, 20:603–612, 1951.

his father, Leopold. The father, unquestionably the dominant figure in the Mozart home, was a prominent Salzburg musician, author of an internationally known treatise on violin playing, and from all accounts an effective, sober, rigid authoritarian,[1] but a warm person with a sharp sense of reality and a keen eye for commercial advantage. Emily Anderson, the editor of the letters of Mozart and his family, describes Leopold as "an indefatigable correspondent, a collector of information, a keeper of lists and diaries . . . an overmethodical, rather pedantic, and perhaps too inquisitive parent" (1938, pp. xi, xii)—an excellent capsule description of an anal character. He was extremely religious, and constantly adjured his son to Catholic piety and churchly devotion. He regarded hard work as a cardinal virtue, and was not entirely insensible of the considerable material advantage that might accrue to him from the application of this ethic to his children.[2]

Anna Maria Mozart, Wolfgang's mother, is a rather shadowy figure. She appears to have been a warm, devoted mother, of considerably less intellectual stature than her husband, friendly, more tolerant than Leopold. Their marriage was an eminently happy and successful one. "Wolfgang loved her dearly, and had not the slightest respect for her authority" (Quoted in Einstein, 1945, pp. 11–12).

Wolfgang's musical precocity led inevitably to his father's taking him under his wing. The fact that he never went to school and never had any teacher other than Leopold, either in musical or general studies, gave Wolfgang more than the usual opportunity to incorporate his father's ideas and principles, and to identify with him. He has frequently been quoted as having said in childhood, "After God, Papa" (Turner, 1938, p. 182). In his early years he was an unquestioning devout Catholic, and in many other areas submitted to his father's authority. The orderliness and meticulousness of Leopold is clearly reflected in Wolfgang's music which, more than any other of the generally orderly classical period, is distinguished by its clarity, precision, and economy.

---

[1] "These passages are for practice. The more distasteful they are, the better I shall be pleased. I have striven to make them so." *Leopold's Violinschule*, quoted in Turner (1938, p. 16).
[2] "You know my children are accustomed to work. Should they become used to idleness, my whole edifice is overthrown." Leopold, quoted in Turner (1938, p. 52).

If we look further we can see many indirect consequences of this submission and identification. As Wolfgang matured, and particularly as he traveled about Europe without his father, signs of rebellion became increasingly evident. Even as he was composing the delicate, precise music of his late adolescence, he was writing to his female cousin in Augsburg the famous "Bäsle" letters. These fascinating documents throw a great deal of light on Mozart's character. They are replete with nonsense, neologisms, wordplay, and innumerable references to feces, defecation, the anus and buttocks, reiterated lovingly and interminably.[3] Granted the greater freedom of the eighteenth century in permitting such expressions, these letters are nonetheless unusual, and it is difficult to doubt the evidence of a marked anal preoccupation, breaking through the reaction formations imposed by his rigid, anal father and representing the first sign of restiveness.

When he was twenty-two his mother died while she and Wolfgang were in Paris. In his correspondence with his father, which reveals his personal sense of loss and his sensitive consideration for the absent Leopold, there appears an interesting passage: "I had never seen anyone die", he writes, "though I had often wished to" (Quoted in Anderson, 1938, Vol. 2, p. 865). One may speculate about the possible connection between this remark and one quoted by Leopold: "When a child you said you would put me in a glass case and protect me from any breath of air, so that you might always have me with you and honor me" (Quoted in Anderson, 1938, Vol. 2, p. 701). It is not difficult to see in this childish expression of devotion an unambiguous undercurrent of hostility. In such a glass case Leopold would, of course, have suffocated—and who was it that Wolfgang had often wished to see die, and why?

During the succeeding period, in which for the first time he was independent of parental domination and was perforce compelled to manage his own affairs (in addition to sending money home to Salzburg, a duty of which Leopold never wearied of reminding him), Wolfgang conceived innumerable financial schemes, all grossly unrealistic and impractical. Leopold received each of them with expressions of dismay, incredulity, and displeasure. Each such

---

[3] "Muck! Sweet word! Muck, suck—! Oh, charmante! Muck, suck. That's what I like, muck, chuck, and suck. Chuck muck and suck muck." (Quoted in Anderson, 1938, Vol, 2, p. 741).

rebuke was greeted by Wolfgang with wounded *amour-propre*—and another, even more impractical scheme. It is difficult to imagine anything he might have thought of that could have irritated his father more, except an unsatisfactory marriage into which he managed to enter somewhat later. One who accepts the principle of unconscious determinism will see in such behavior a compulsion on Wolfgang's part to act out his unconscious hostility toward his father. By presenting these absurd plans he struck his father at a particularly vulnerable point, and he subsequently bribed his superego therefor by accepting his father's rebukes. Superego thus appeased, he could act out his rebellion as he saw fit.

In 1785, Mozart was initiated into the Freemason's Lodge in Vienna at the age of twenty-nine. The Masonic order, then as now, was opposed by the Church of Rome, and was vigorously attacked from the Vatican. But in his travels, and as he became increasingly independent of his father, Mozart's religious observances became more and more heterodox. He openly expressed disdain for the church rules of fasting, and rejected the church's concepts of death and the life hereafter, finding in the doctrines of Freemasonry ideas more congenial to his own independence, fatalism, and spiritual resignation. Though he never left the church, his religious observances became increasingly perfunctory (here we may recall Leopold's strictures on this point) and, significantly, from the time of his initiation until shortly before his death, he wrote no religious music, though Masonic music abounds, capped by his great opera, *The Magic Flute*.[4]

Mozart's drifting from religious orthodoxy was paralleled by his rupture with his priestly patron, the Archbishop Hieronymus Colloredo of Salzburg. This tyrannical cleric never appreciated the genius of his young court organist and concertmaster, and Mozart and his father were in perpetual conflict with him. Wolfgang had tried to break away when he was twenty-one; had, in fact, resigned his place, and was induced to return only by the importunities of his father. In 1781, when he was twenty-five, he was subjected to a series of indignities, insults, and physical assaults by the Archbishop and his courtiers. His proud spirit could not support such treatment; against this authority he could express his resentment

---

[4] It should be noted that Leopold joined the Freemasons avowedly through his son's influence. [Ed.]

openly, and he did. He resigned his position, this time for good, not without a series of reproving letters from his father. Fully aware of his genius, Mozart sensed that in this act he had achieved his maturity and his independence, and the tone of his subsequent letters to Salzburg reflect the cooling of his feelings for his father. Leopold's death in 1787 he accepted with notable equanimity, advising his father in a letter shortly before the event to accept death as a friend, without fear but with great expectations. And it was in this spirit that he himself died four years later.[5]

Mozart's confident awareness of his remarkable talents, though reflecting his emotional stability and harmonizing strikingly with Rank's description of the creative personality,[6] served him in poor stead in a society in which the artist was wholly dependent on the favor of wealthy patrons. Mozart could not toady. He had small respect for authority. He realized well enough that he was his father's artistic master and one of the greatest musicians of his time, and his frank, often caustic comments on the work of other musicians (well justified in the light of history) won him many enemies, the number of whom was added to by those who were envious of him. It has long been regarded in musical circles as a mystery that Mozart could get no court position or steady patronage. But a man who had only recently emerged successfully from the struggle to liberate himself from his father and the Archbishop would scarcely have been likely to adopt behavior that would endear him to paternalistic noblemen. Thus we see that Mozart's achievement of emotional maturity proved his economic ruin in a society not yet emerged from feudalism. It is no coincidence that such a man chose to set to music Da Ponte's libretti, *Don Giovanni* and *The Marriage of Figaro*, in each of which the decline of feudalism is symbolized by the frustration and defeat of a concupiscent nobleman at the hands of menials.

In Mozart's relations with women one can trace the pattern of his emotional development. He was, according to his own testimony, a virgin to the day of his marriage. He expressed in his letters to his father (who repeatedly warned him against the dangers of injudi-

---

[5] Mozart died in a state of deep depression: "I feel certain I shall not be long; someone has poisoned me. I cannot shake off the idea." *Groves Dictionary of Music and Musicians*. New York: The Macmillan Co., 1936, Vol. 3. [Ed.]

[6] "The precondition of the creative personality is not only its acceptance, but its actual glorification of itself." (Rank, 1932, p. 27).

cious marriage and illicit sexuality) recurrent assurances that he had not succumbed to temptation, and emphasized his anxiety lest he acquire a disease were he to do so. All his love affairs, and there were several, were chaste flirtations with idealized women (if we except the literary anal erotism lavished on the Bäsle). It was not until he had successfully completed his rebellion that he married— without waiting for his father's consent—a girl of whose limitations he was quite aware and with whom he was probably not in love, but on whom he became quite dependent and with whom he was sexually active, as his six children and one of his letters[7] make abundantly clear.

THE ARTIST AND SUBLIMATION

In his brief span of thirty-five years Mozart composed an almost unbelievable quantity of music, much of which has been lost. The catalogue of his works that are extant numbers over six hundred compositions, ranging from short clavier pieces to operas, symphonies, and masses. There was no field of composition at which he did not try his hand, and none at which he did not excel. He repeatedly indicated in his letters his single-minded absorption in composition, the sole intellectual activity from which he derived real gratification. He worked with tremendous speed and incredible industry; his manuscripts rarely show changes or erasures. Though he led an active social and musical life, it seems that he was driven by an irresistible impulse to compose, independently of the economic pressures that compelled him to do so.

Before considering Mozart's creative drive, however, it may be profitable to review the contributions of some psychological and psychoanalytic writers on the subjects of sublimation and of artistic creation, which is but one form of it. Sharpe (1930 pp. 11–12, Quoted in Róheim [1945, p. 118]) speaks of sublimation as "a reparation, a control, a nullification of anxiety." Róheim (1945, p. 111) describes it as "the repetition of an infantile situation ... the happy union of mother and child." Lee (1947, p. 281), who has written extensively on art and creativity, states that art arises out of a neurotic depression produced by an upsurge of destructive rage

---

[7] "Arrange your dear sweet nest very daintily, for my little fellow deserves it indeed ... and is only longing to possess your sweetest ... [word deleted by his wife]" (Quoted in Anderson [1938, vol. 3, p. 1382]).

that is turned on the self. The artist seeks to cure the depression by restoring (symbolically) the hated object in the form of a work of art, in order to reinstate himself with the pitying, loving, maternal elements in the superego.

Otto Rank regards the creative urge as deriving from the need of the artist to immortalize himself due to the "fear of death" (1932, p. 12). Rank leaves the matter here; he fails to consider the fact, pointed out by Freud (1915b), that in the unconscious there is no conception of death as such. To the child (and the unconscious) "death" is equated with loss of maternal love and consequent exposure to the hostile forces of the environment. Thus we see that the logical extension of Rank's thesis leads us to the view that creation represents the artist's effort to reassure himself of continued love and protection from the mother—a conclusion strikingly similar to Róheim's.

A further consideration arises here, however. Freud states (1915b) that fear of death is frequently a representation of fear of castration. Thus, again, by extension of Rank's point, the artistic urge may represent a device for the allaying of castration anxiety, as suggested by Sharpe. Parenthetically, it may be that in this fact lies a partial explanation for the far greater incidence in our culture of artistic creativity among men than women.

Let us now see how these theoretical constructions may be reconstructed in Mozart's life and work. As we have previously noted, Mozart's mother was a warm, affectionate, quiet person, to whom Mozart was deeply devoted. We have adduced ample evidence of his ambivalent feelings toward his father, and the determining quality of the hostile component. These hostile feelings arose, we must assume, not only from his resentment against his father's domination, but also out of the competitive striving for the mother. Not only did Mozart, in his pursuit of music, identify with his father (aggressor), but, in addition, he sought to outdo him, to win this vital competition. In order to do this, he had to be not merely a musician like his father, but a greater and more productive musician. Thus his insatiable urge to compose, thus the driven and compelling nature of his creative activity.

A curious fact about Mozart's creative activity leads us to further speculation. It has frequently been noted that Mozart (not to mention other composers) wrote some of his gayest, brightest, most beautiful and cheerful music during periods of his life that were, to say the least, trying. In this fact can be seen striking confirmation of Lee's theory of creativity and of Róheim's and Sharpe's conceptions of the function of sublimation. The depression Mozart tells of having suffered during these periods[8] was accompanied by outbursts of creative activity, in which he sought unconsciously to restore the infantile situation of complete bliss at the mother's breast, much as, Freud (1905, p. 236) tells us, we all do when we resort to wit and humor: "The euphoria . . . is nothing but the state of a bygone time . . . the state of our childhood in which we did not . . . need humor to make us happy" (Anderson, 1938, p. 803). In these depressions Mozart had turned his destructive rage inward. Unconsciously the rage was equated with his aggressive impulses toward his father. By diverting his aggression into creative work, and by restoring the hated object by means of musical creation, he unconsciously denied his hostile impulses toward his father, thus allaying the danger of castration, and regained the approval of the maternal elements of his superego.

CONCLUSION

The study of Mozart's creativity confirms and provides a partial synthesis of published theories of sublimation. Some sources of Mozart's creative impulse are traced. Motivations are presented to account for his need to create, for certain aspects of his work, for the tremendous pressure his muse imposed upon him, and for their functions in terms of psychic economy. But these leave unexplained the peculiar greatness of Mozart's music. Lee (1948, p. 281) serves us here, in part, by equating the achievement of beauty in art with the symbolic restoration of the ambivalent object in idealized form.

Perhaps the answer to this question lies, as Freud suggested, outside psychoanalysis—in the realm, perhaps, of Gestalt psychology, which will explain Mozart's superior capacity for combining tones into organized, meaningful patterns of sound, or yet of the geneticist, who will demonstrate the hereditary transmission of Mozart's innate talent. For such or other contributions we may devoutly hope. Meanwhile, we must be content with having found

---

[8]"If people could see into my heart, I should feel almost ashamed. To me everything is cold as ice . . . everything seems so empty" (September 30, 1790), "a kind of emptiness . . . a kind of longing . . . which increases daily . . ." (July 7, 1791) (Quoted in Einstein, 1945, p. 69.)

in the life of one great artist data which throw light on the problem of artistic creation, and with having suggested some of the necessary if not wholly determining factors that made Mozart the man he was, and the artist whose music we can but hear with wonder, admiration, and delight.

Chapter 19
Mozart's Zoroastran Riddles

Maynard Solomon

On February 19, 1786, during the Viennese Carnival, a masquerader, cloaked in the robes of an Oriental philosopher, proceeded to the Redoutensaal of the Hofburg, where festivities were in progress. There, he passed out copies of a broadside sheet containing eight riddles and fourteen proverbs, entitled "Excerpts from the Fragments of Zoroaster" and printed for "the edification of the masked ball" (Bauer, Deutsch, and Eibl, 1962–1975, Vol. 3, pp. 506–507). The masquerader and author was Mozart. Copies of the broadside have not survived, but Mozart sent one to his father, who found many of its thoughts commendable; he, in turn, forwarded it to his daughter, Nannerl:

> Your brother sent this printed enclosure to me. The first seven riddles were immediately solved on sight. The eighth is more difficult. The *Fragments* [i.e., the proverbs] are really *good* and *true* from *first* to *last* and should really be taken to heart.... Please return the sheet to me [Bauer, Deutsch, and Eibl, 1962–1975, p. 521 No. 943].

However strained the relationship between father and son may have been at this time, Leopold Mozart was unable to conceal his delight in his son's creative accomplishments; and that is how one of the riddles and seven of the proverbs were preserved: Leopold Mozart placed them at the disposal of his friend Lorenz Hübner, editor of the Salzburg *Oberdeutsche Staatszeitung*, who published them in the issue of March 23, 1786, without mentioning Mozart's name. Evidently, Hübner did not regard the materials to be quite as edifying as did Mozart's father. While he gave them some faint praise, he also reported that they were included because the newspaper was, as he delicately put it, "short of more important matters" (Deutsch, 1965, p. 268).

First published in *American Imago*, Winter, Vol. 42, No. 4. pp. 345–369, 1985.

The proverbs are Mozart's own formulations of standard European and classical proverbs on matters of behavior and morality, concentrating on such familiar dualities as vice/virtue, poverty/riches, hypocrisy/honesty, and diligence/laziness:

1) Talk much—and talk badly; but this last will follow of itself: all eyes and ears will be directed towards you.
4) I prefer an open vice to an equivocal virtue; it at least shows me where I stand.
5) A hypocrite anxious to pretend to virtue can imitate it only with watercolours.
10) It is not seemly for everybody to be modest; only great men are able to be so.
11) If you are poor but clever, arm yourself with patience, and work. If you do not grow rich, you will at least remain a clever man.—If you are an ass, but wealthy, take advantage of your good fortune and be lazy. If you do not become poor, you will at least remain an ass.
12) A woman is praised in the surest and most tender fashion by abuse of her rivals. But how many men are not women in this respect?
14) If you are a poor dunce, become a C[leric]. If you are a rich dunce, become a tenant. If you are a noble but poor dunce—become what you can, for bread. If you are a wealthy noble dunce, become what you like; only—pray—not a man of sense.

Leopold Mozart was pleased by such sentiments, which harmonized with his own outlook on life. "The riddles are only for fun," he wrote to Nannerl Mozart on March 28, but the proverbs "are really for the improvement of morality" (Bauer, Deutsch, and Eibl, Vol. 3, p. 524, No. 946). He especially liked his son's apparent devotion to the performance principle: "Every sensible person must work, so long as he lives . . . ," he wrote to his daughter, a sentiment which he had often tried to impress on his son.

The *Oberdeutsche Staatszeitung* printed only one of the riddles, followed by the putative "solution" which Mozart had anagrammatized beneath it:

One can possess me without seeing me.
One can carry me without feeling me.
One can give me without having me.
    s.h.n.o.r., i.e. "Horns"
            (*D.e.e.h.i.n.ö.r.r.*, i.e., *Die Hörner*)

In the absence of the other riddles, this "solution" seemed innocuous enough. But the recent discovery of the remainder of Mozart's Zoroastran riddles indicates that the entire matter was considerably richer in its implications than it had seemed to the composer's father at the time.

A quarto sheet in Mozart's hand [see Figs. 19.1 and 19.2], presently in the Berlin Staatsbibliothek Preussischer Kulturbesitz (collection Hermann Härtel), contains drafts of the other seven riddles,[1] two of which have been rendered quite illegible, evidently by Georg Nissen, Constanze Mozart's second husband, who also defaced parts of Mozart's correspondence which he considered objectionable.

[1.] We are many sisters; it is painful for us to unite as well as to separate. We live in a palace, yet we could rather call it a prison, for we live securely locked up and must work for the sustenance of men. The most remarkable thing is that the doors are opened for us quite often, both day and night, and still we do not come out, except when one pulls us out by force.

[2.] I am an altogether patient thing, I let myself be used by everyone. Through me the truth, the lie, erudition and stupidity are proclaimed to the world. He who wants to know everything need only come and ask me, for I know everything. Since everybody needs me I am told everything. Money changers can well use me; I also serve barbers sometimes. I am inevitably necessary to the [illegible word] and [illegible word]. Through me are the most important affairs of state arranged, wars conducted, and lands conquered. Through my endurance the sick receive health, also frequently death. In brief, happiness, unhappiness, life, and death often depend upon me. One would imagine that so many superior qualities would make me happy; O no! My death is generally terrifying—painful, and when it happens gently, base and contemptible. Nevertheless, should I die in the last manner at the hand of a beautiful woman, so shall I take that consolation with me to the grave, that I have seen some things which not everyone gets to see.

[3.] I am an unusual (sonderbares) thing; I have no soul and no body; one cannot see me but can hear me; I do not exist for

---

[1] The rediscovery of the riddles was announced in 1970 and they were first published in 1971 in the appendix to the second "Commentary" volume of the Bauer-Deutsch edition of *Mozarts Briefe und Aufzeichnungen*, as well as in a journal article by Eibl (1970). Mozart's putative "solutions" do not appear in the autograph; the solution to Riddle 3 was given by him in a letter to his father (see n. 5 below).

404   Psychoanalytic Explorations in Music

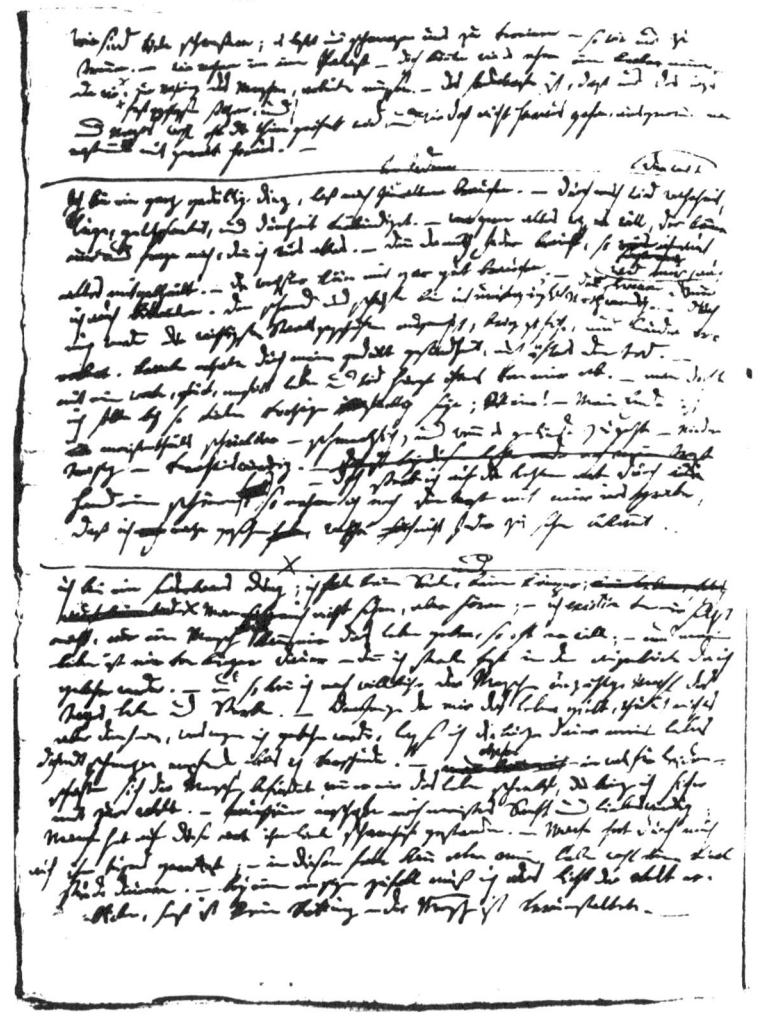

Figure 19.1. Mozart. Zoroastran Riddles, p. 1. Berlin, *Staatsbibliothek Preussischer Kulturbesitz, Musikabteilung.*

myself: only a human being can give me life, as often as he wishes; and my life is only of short duration, for I die almost at the moment in which I am born. And so, in accordance with men's caprice, I may live and die untold times a day. To those who give me life I do nothing—but those on whose account I am born I leave with painful sensations for the short duration of my life until I depart. Whatever passions a man finds himself in at the

Figure 19.2. Mozart. Zoroastran Riddles, p. 2. *Berlin, Staatsbibliothek Preussicher Kulturbesitz, Musikabteilung.*

time when he grants me life I will surely bring those along into the world. For the most part, women produce me gently and amiably; many have modestly confessed their love in this way. Many have also saved their virtue through me; in these cases, however, my life can scarcely endure a quarter of an hour. I must come into the world by a singular stroke of fortune: otherwise there is no outlet—the man is deformed.

[4.] I serve many as an ornament, many as a mutilation. However, I am highly necessary to everyone. Sometimes it would be better if I were not there; sometimes, on the other hand, it is a blessing (Wohltat) that I am there. Frequently even entire [illegible word] are uncovered through me. Frequently many men are even freed of [illegible word] insults through me. Men regard me as a good recommendation to women. I serve old people also, beyond my obligations; on that account [two illegible words] people who become old [illegible word] take care of me, so that I am not spoiled, let alone die before my time.

[5.] We are created for man's pleasures. How can we help it if an accident befalls by which we become the opposite of them? If he is lacking one of us, then he is—defective.

My main concern here is not with the solutions of the riddles but with some of the possible meanings hidden within this biographical datum. For, although a riddle's symbolic import can be unravelled, its mystery does not disappear when the decoding has been accomplished. Paul Ricoeur notes that the dream and its analogues, such as the riddle, are "set within a region of language that presents itself as the locus of complex significations where another meaning is both given and hidden in an immediate meaning," and that the making of a riddle "does not block understanding but provokes it," for it calls attention to "double meaning, the intending of the second meaning in and through the first" (Ricoeur, 1970, pp. 7, 18).

Riddling involves a game of wits. The riddler's strategy is to offer a "roundabout description of an unnamed object" (Friedreich, 1860, p. 2), so worded as to lead us to draw inferences that will finally be shown to be false (de Filippis, 1948, p. 14). Aristotle placed the riddle under the rubric of metaphor. He stressed its use of deception, which arouses a "sense of surprise at the way in which the sentence ends and the soul seems to say, 'Quite true, and I had missed the point.' " (Quoted in Tupper, 1910, pp. xii–xiii). By way of example, Mozart's "Horns" riddle:

One can possess me without seeing me.
One can carry me without feeling me.
One can give me without possessing me,

combines several commonplace traditional riddles. The experienced riddler will anticipate the usual solutions, such as "A Name," or "Your Word" for all three lines, or "Your Heart," "A Thought," "Death," or "Blood" for one or more of them. Mozart's "Horns" solution defeats the reader's expectations by a novel yet appropriate answer which strikes a comic, slightly absurb note, thus evoking the delight and surprise—mixed with chagrin—of a successfully wrought jest.

The pleasure is heightened by the more than faint—and less than accidental—phallic implications of Mozart's solution, which is resonant of Falstaff's remark: "Well, he may sleep in security, for he hath the horn of abundance, and the lightness of his wife shines through it" (Shakespeare, 2 *Henry IV*, Act I, Sc. ii, 48–50). It is also reminiscent of a riddle that Mozart once posed to his merry female cousin from Augsburg (called "Bäsle") in a letter of December 2, 1777 (Letter 256*). Pretending that he was referring to his handwriting, he asked her to choose between an article which is "fair, straight and serious" or "untidy, crooked and jolly." He insisted on her rapid reply: "So all depends now on what you prefer. You must make the choice (I have no medium article to offer you)...." However, the phallic connotation of the "Horns" riddle collides with the other main implication, the horns of cuckoldry, a contradiction which cannot be fully resolved because the word *horns* can symbolize power or inadequacy, honor or disgrace, and even—as in the horns of Moses and Lucifer—extremes of good and evil (Elworthy, 1900; Mellinkoff, 1970, pp. 121–124). We come to realize that the unmasking of the riddle's double meaning by a strategy of symbolic interpretation does not exhaust all possibilities. Indeed, Mozart's double meaning in turn has a double meaning.

Another rapid example: the intended solution of the riddle about the many sisters who live in a palace/prison and cannot go out unless one of them is pulled out by force, is "Teeth." It is common in riddles to personify the teeth as sisters or maidens, for example the Westphalian riddle about "Thirty-two maidens dressed in white," or the Javanese, "The front teeth are six sisters..." (Taylor, 1951, pp. 316–317). Here Mozart's strategy is to suggest erotic activity, perhaps in a brothel from which the occupants cannot escape. The unambiguously correct, "innocent" solution then frustrates these vaguely formed inferences. Thus, for a moment, the riddle temporarily suspends moral inhibition, leading to the discharge of repressed psychic energy, and then restores the balance by denying that any moral infraction has taken place. Ernst Kris (1952,

---

*Letter designations are from Anderson (1966).

p. 182) observes that "the comic originates in the conflict between instinctual trends and the superego's repudiation of them," occupying a position "midway between pleasure and unpleasure."

However, this double-edged character survives the riddle's solution, for, as in the "Horns" riddle, we again have an "innocent" answer which, closely examined, revives the bawdy overtones of the imagery. For, in German slang, "to pull out a tooth" (sich einen Zahn aufreissen) strongly suggests sexual intimacy with a woman, and a "Zahn" may signify a "bride" or a "bed partner."

Mozart's riddles, then, belong to the tradition of salacious or obscene riddling, which, originating in primitive rites, took on new life in the Renaissance, when practitioners of the rarefied literary riddle became extraordinarily proficient at constructing indecent riddles while simultaneously protesting their innocence. *Honi soit qui mal y pense* was the motto of such riddlers, many of whose works nevertheless ended up on the *Index librorum prohibitorum* (de Filippis, 1948, p. 66). So far as we know, Mozart's interest in riddling was aroused solely in its role as social recreation and entertainment. (I say "so far as we know," because further research may show a tradition of riddling in Freemasonry contributing to his interest.) In this, he was far from unusual: Goethe, Schiller, Voltaire, and Rousseau—to name only a few of his contemporaries—all wrote riddles for entertainment, and riddling burgeoned in popularity in Europe particularly during the 1780s.[2] However, though the plain motivation of Mozart's Zoroastran riddles surely was to amuse and confound his friends, the underlying connection to the archaic levels of riddling—to the mythic, the sacred, and the dangerous—is not wholly lost in them.

One such link is provided by the Feast of Carnival. On the surface, Carnival was a time to have fun, to adopt a new persona, to startle, frighten, and amuse. And the celebration of Carnival in this sense goes far back in Mozart's life and music (See, for example, Letter 80, February 17, 1770; Letter 82a, March 3, 1770; Letter 293, February 28, 1778). At an early age, we find him attending Carnivals in major cities of Austria, Germany, and Italy; and five of his operas, including *Mitridate re di Ponto*, *Lucio Silla*, and *Idomeneo*,

---

[2] Although only a few collections of German riddles had appeared in the preceding thirty years, the decade commencing in 1779 saw a spate of such publications, with more than twenty separate books of riddles issued in the major German and Austrian cities. See Hayn (1890, pp. 526–528).

were specifically written for Carnivals in Milan, Munich, or Vienna. Furthermore, for Mozart, as a virtuoso keyboard artist, the pre-Lenten concert season was the most active season of the year, making Carnival a time to exercise his creativity as well as to participate in the festivities.

More fundamentally, the modern Carnival retains the imprint of the ancient seasonal festivals (the Roman Saturnalia, the French Feast of Fools, the English Lords of Misrule) of which it is a survival. Sir James Frazier explained the festivals as "an annual period of license, when the customary restraints of law and morality are thrown aside, when the whole population give themselves up to extravagant mirth and jollity, and when the darker passions find a vent" (1922, p. 583). Elaborating the implications of Frazier, Freud regarded the institution of Festivals as a periodic lifting of the "renunciations and limitations imposed upon the ego" (1921, p. 131). A complementary hypothesis holds that the main purpose of the Festivals, rather than ritualized overthrow of authority, is to safeguard the person of the king through vicarious sacrifice of a surrogate masquerader (Bourboulis, 1964, pp. 7-37). The characteristic verbal and literary mode of the festivals is satire—mockery, ridicule, burlesque. It is a time of derision and profanation, when things are turned topsy-turvey and inside out, when lower and higher are interchanged. Obscenity, sexual wordplay, and double-meaning are the natural language of Carnival, in the *Fastnachtspiele* (Catholy, 1961, 1966), as in Mozart's riddles. Thus, it is a time when Mozart's well-known propensities for the bawdy, the riotous, and the scatological can be revealed to society at large. Mozart's brother-in-law, Joseph Lange, noted how Mozart "took delight" in "sudden outbursts of vulgar platitudes . . ." (Deutsch, 1965, p. 503).

It is at *Fastnacht* that the performance principle is momentarily set aside and the *Spieltrieb* holds sway. In modern Carnivals the original festive element has been narrowed down, but it has not disappeared. The feast remains a time of defiance and reversal, when beggars become princes and scapegoats kings. In Bakhtin's words, "It is a temporary transfer to the utopian world" (1968, p. 287). It is a holiday from conformity. And it is also what Kris calls "a holiday from the superego" (1953, p. 182).

That may be why we sense that many of Mozart's long-standing preoccupations merge to create the Carnival riddles of 1786. We have his penchant for codes and ciphers, which he used in many letters, primarily to his father; and his love for secret tongues: in 1772, he even learned the sign language of the deaf. There is Mozart's attachment to secret societies and orders—and not only to the Masonic lodges. As a child, he founded an imaginary kingdom which he called "The Kingdom of Back" (Das Königreich Rücken) which he visited more than once even after he was grown up. In his last years, he hoped to found his own secret society, called "The Grotto," about which his wife reported rather reticently after his death. Mozart's attraction to a Zoroastran orientalism is in the tradition of the Masonic lodges and reading societies, which were hotbeds of interest in the exotic, the oriental, and the miraculous. (Not suprisingly, Zoroaster is later reincarnated as "Sarastro" in Mozart's mythic/Masonic opera, *Die Zauberflöte*.) And we have Mozart's love for wordplay of every kind, including neologisms, transpositions, reversals, puns, rhymes, word-salads, and the like. If *Fastnacht* derives from "faseln"—to talk nonsense—it was a holiday season designed for Mozart, for nonsense was the mother-tongue of his Kingdom of Rücken. Last, there is Mozart's antic disposition, revealed particularly in his bawdy letters to his Bäsle cousin, his outrageous first-person entries in his sister's personal diary for 1783, and in his obscene canons of the 1780s.

What these tendencies and preoccupations have in common, of course, is the play principle; but, beyond that, a longing for the secret and the forbidden, as well as for the power that they represented to Mozart. In the Vienna Carnival of 1786, Mozart does publicly what he dares not attempt in private: he violates taboos, without conscious expectation of punishment. For Carnival is precisely the time when ritual laughter can be directed against the gods, when the overthrow of the primal fathers is licensed. During the "fire festival" that marked the climax of the Roman Carnival, shouts of "Death to you!" were heard everywhere, as each person contended with stranger and friend alike to blow out his lighted candle, the symbol of flesh and mortality. Goethe was particularly entranced to see a young boy blow out his father's candle, crying "Sia ammazzato, il signor Padre!"—Death to you, Sir Father! (Goethe, 1786–1788, pp. 542–543). Mozart, as the carnivalesque son, takes the place of the father by donning the robes of a powerful, exotic lawgiver and by formulating apodictic proverbs and obscure, grandiose riddles. He has seized the trappings of divinity and wisdom, has fashioned himself as an oracle, as one who can penetrate final mysteries. He has transformed himself from the supplicant Oedipus into the all-knowing Sphinx, the maker of riddles. More, he has taken both roles—simultaneously posing riddles and offering their solutions. The mythic hero addresses questions to destiny; Mozart addresses questions to himself as well.

However, Mozart addressed his riddles not only to himself and to fate, but to at least one other person. He sent them to his father and, in effect, dared him to solve them. Thereby his riddling became a heavy wager, a critical test risking a grave forfeit.

Neither distance nor silence could free Mozart from a lifelong paternal domination of overwhelming intensity. On one important level, Mozart's biography is the story of the intricate mechanisms and maneuvers by which he tries to reach an accommodation with the man who had not only fathered him, but had been his primary instructor in all matters and had sought to control his every action through relentless mental pressure alternating with seductive benevolence. Mozart's drive to achieve a degree of relief from this torturing relationship led to a series of crises which he handled with dignity and reserve. Responding, in February 1778, to his father's reproaches, he wrote: "Those days when, standing on a chair, I used to sing to you . . . and finish by kissing you on the tip of your nose, are gone indeed; but do I honour, love and obey you any the less on that account? I will say no more" (Letter 288, February 19, 1778). Several of Mozart biographers have observed, not without reason, that Mozart arranged to leave Salzburg in 1780, first for Munich, and then Vienna, in full flight from a suffocating atmosphere. Mozart was never forgiven for what his father perceived as a reckless abandonment; and he burdened his son with guilt, blaming him for his own "trying circumstances": "Wolfgang," he wrote, "is aware of the degradations I am suffering in Salzburg, since he must realize that both morally and materially I am being punished for his conduct. . ." (Letter 460, August 23, 1782).

This was not a momentary expression of Leopold Mozart's anger, but part of an ongoing tactic by which he sought to ensnare Mozart in a web of guilt: "You know what I have endured for more than five years," he wrote in 1778, "and what a lot I have had to swallow on your account. The Prince's conduct can only bend me, but yours can crush me. He can only make me ill, but you can kill me" (Letter 290).

The issue was plain: Leopold Mozart proposed to maintain his son in a perpetually dependent state. He warned him against giving his love to women, or his friendship to men, for no one was to be trusted. He fiercely opposed, and never reconciled himself, to Mozart's marriage. He constantly urged Mozart to keep one goal in mind: "You must not lose sight of your main object, which is to make money" (Letter 222, October 15, 1777).

During the acrimonious months following his moving to Vienna, Mozart pleaded with his father for mercy (the phrase is not too strong). He wrote: "I implore you, dearest, most beloved father, for the future to spare me such letters. I entreat you to do so, for they only irritate my mind and disturb my heart and spirit; and I, who must now keep on composing, need a cheerful mind and a calm disposition" (Letter 409, June 9, 1781).

His father's complaints were more than he could bear: "I *have often thought I should go crazy,*" he tells Count Arco of his reaction to Leopold Mozart's letters (Letter 408, June 2, 1781).

Despite his father's fears, Mozart remained most productive. And he made a good deal of money as well, certainly more than his father had ever anticipated. However, with the passage of time, a curious and painful fact became increasingly clear: the fulfillment of his father's stated goals did not bring parental approval. Indeed, Leopold Mozart's recriminations seemed to multiply with Mozart's accomplishments. To put it briefly: I suggest that Leopold Mozart's unspoken grievance was that Mozart had surpassed his expectations. Thus, the rejection went beyond Mozart's alleged character flaws and his perceived abandonment: It extended to his creativity.

The matter reached its most poignant expression one year before the composition of the riddles, at Carnival time 1785, during Leopold Mozart's lengthy visit to Vienna. There he was subjected to a vivid and unrelenting demonstration of his son's success as a performer, composer, and impresario. Mozart gave numerous concerts, including some half-dozen for his own benefit within a space of only six weeks, and he performed a piano concerto in the presence of the Emperor, who "waved his hat and called out 'Bravo, Mozart!'" In addition, Leopold Mozart was daily witness to his son's warm acceptance by the highest levels of Viennese society, attending parties, balls, and banquets as part of Mozart's entourage, visiting the Masonic "Wohltätigkeit" (Beneficence) Lodge and securing membership under his son's sponsorship. It was during his first days in Vienna that Joseph Haydn told him what any father, even one who was himself a composer and court musician, should have longed to hear—that his son was "the greatest composer known to me either in person or by name" (Letter 523, February 16, 1785, Leopold Mozart to Nannerl Mozart).

It is against this backdrop that the father's ability to bear his son's limitless triumph finally gave way. In a letter of March 12 to his daughter, he writes: "We never get to sleep before one o'clock in the morning, we never get up before 9 o'clock, and we eat at 2 or half-past 2. Horrible weather!" (Letter 525).

These are reasonable complaints for an elderly man, one who was moreover coming down with a cold. But his next words indicate that he was more than just physically weary of the constant round of events: "Daily concerts, constant lessons, music, composing, etc. How shall I bear it! If only the concerts were over: it is impossible to describe the constant vexation and restlessness (Schererey und Unruhe)" (Letter 525).

From early on, Mozart equated praise of his music with love for his person. Leopold Mozart's approval, in particular, was his justification for being. Thus, one can imagine his bewilderment and hurt when his father withheld approval. Doubtless, the threat of his father's disapproval had long been used to compel Mozart's compliance, but it is only in his adult years that we find evidence touching on this sensitive issue. In a crushing, quite pathological letter of February 1778, Leopold Mozart wrote his rebellious son: "My one great delight—to hear your compositions—is gone! Everything around me is dead!" (Letter 291, February 25–26, 1778). Four years later, to demonstrate the depth of his opposition to Mozart's impending marriage, Leopold Mozart pointedly refrained from praising *Die Entführung aus dem Serail*, the score of which he had just received. Mozart did not let this slight pass; he wrote: "I received today your letter of the 26th, but a cold, indifferent letter, such as I could never have expected in reply to my news of the good reception of my opera. . . ." Warming to the sense of his father's injustice, he continued: "I thought . . . that you would hardly be able to open the parcel for excitement and eagerness to see your son's work which . . . is making such a sensation in Vienna. . . . But you—have not had the time" (Letter 456, July 31, 1782).

Leopold Mozart left Vienna on April 25, 1785. He never saw his son again, and we have only one letter from Mozart to him after this date. I hypothesize that it was at or about this time that Mozart glimpsed the full extent and nature of his father's competition with him. This realization was devastating. He now sensed that his father was not merely opposed to his marriage and his wife, to his independence, and to perceived flaws in his character, but to his creativity as well. If I read the evidence correctly, Mozart's responses to these implications shaped the balance of his short life. It seems to me that in the aftermath of his father's visit to Vienna, a realignment of Mozart's personality got under way as he strove to expel the deeply rooted residues of his father's character and values. The repudiation had to be incomplete, of course, for his identification with Leopold Mozart had until then supported his sense of worth and mission. The disentanglement could never be wholly achieved. But the strains of the effort took their toll on Mozart in the fourth and final decade of a short life. In his last years, desolated at being sundered from his father, guilt-ridden at rejecting him, Mozart— by wasting his money, his body, and perhaps his very being—set out to prove the old man right. In the process, he succeeded in destroying the only thing which really mattered to Leopold Mozart.

That Mozart worked assiduously to bring his father's resentments to the surface is quite clear. Mozart put on a demonstration of his success, affluence, and musical achievements sufficient to arouse the envy of Saint Cecilia. Heedless of his father's advanced age and weakened physical condition, he insisted on his presence at every concert and festivity: it was as though he had staged this triumphant panorama—this Mozart Carnival—for the purpose of finally putting his father's reproaches to rest. And, let it be said plainly, of demonstrating his own superiority and vitality at the expense of a lonely old widower. There was castration in the air at the Viennese Carnival of 1785.

And that may help explain why a striking cluster of images in Mozart's Zoroastran riddles—written in the aftermath of, and on the first anniversary of Leopold Mozart's Viennese visit—center on themes of deformity and mutilation. The concentrated references indicate Mozart's preoccupations: "the man is deformed" (Riddle 3); "I serve many as an ornament, many as a mutilation" (Riddle 4); "people who become old take care of me, so that I am not spoiled" (Riddle 4); "if an accident befalls ... and [a man] is lacking one of us, then he is—defective" (Riddle 5). Even the "Teeth" riddle carries similar overtones, with its fusion of aggressive orality and implied dangerous sexuality; further, as Karl Abraham has observed, the loss of a tooth in dreams is a "symbolic occurrence which typified both fear of castration and of an object-loss . . ." (Abraham, 1924, p. 465).[3]

The imagery of genital mutilation mingles with the imagery of death. In Riddle 2, the grandiose oracle claims to be an ambassador of death; he tells us that "life and death" depend on him and he describes his own death as "generally terrifying" and "painful"; the remarkably insubstantial and soulless being of Riddle 3 dies "untold times a day" and lives for only the shortest period of time: "I die almost at the moment in which I am born"; the narrator of Riddle 4 fears that he will "die before [his] time." Of course, in the language of venery, the verb "to die" is also a metaphor for various sexual and bodily processes (Partridge, 1960, p. 101). (Robert Rogers [1978] observes that "to die," in linguistic metaphor, "refers to death of the body, flatus, and orgasm . . ." [p. 101]). Mozart's "should I die . . . at the hand of a beautiful woman" is the closest kin to Benedict's words to Beatrice: "I will live in thy heart, die in thy lap, and be buried in thy eyes" (Shakespeare, *Much Ado About Nothing*, Act V, Sc. ii, 99–101).

With a few swift strokes, the riddles plunge from a comic, ironic surface to a center where fear of death and castration dominate. While seeking to assuage anxiety, the comic impulse has inadvertently brought it into being.[4] Seeking to establish superiority over his father, Mozart succeeds in quickening his own sense of dread. The riddles are the hieroglyphics of a secret discourse, a deadly play between a father and his son. However, this is no abstract contest for supremacy. The surface is comic, the undercurrent is terror, the "answers" are phallic, but the subject is Mozart's mother, Leopold's wife. She is the prize for whom the contest is waged; she herself is a

---

[3] On the verso of one of the pages containing the riddles Mozart has doodled a caricature of a deformed male figure (see Figure 19.3).

[4] Previously, Mozart's comic impulse had found its outlet in scatological anal obscenity, perhaps, in part, as his refutation of his father's cash- and morality-centered outlook. Riddle 3, whose unsatisfactory, "innocent" solution is "Die Maulschelle"—The Box on the Ear (see Leopold Mozart to Nannerl Mozart, letter of May 22, 1786), but whose obscene solution is "a fart," shows that Mozart's wit remains at its best in anal humor. But phallic/genital humor predominates in the other riddles, a kind of braggadocio overlaying issues of potency, castration dread, and fear of homosexual incorporation. In the parallel case of Goethe, Eissler regards such humor as mainly signifying fixation to the phallic phase (Eissler, 1963, Vol. 2, pp. 1341, 1352).

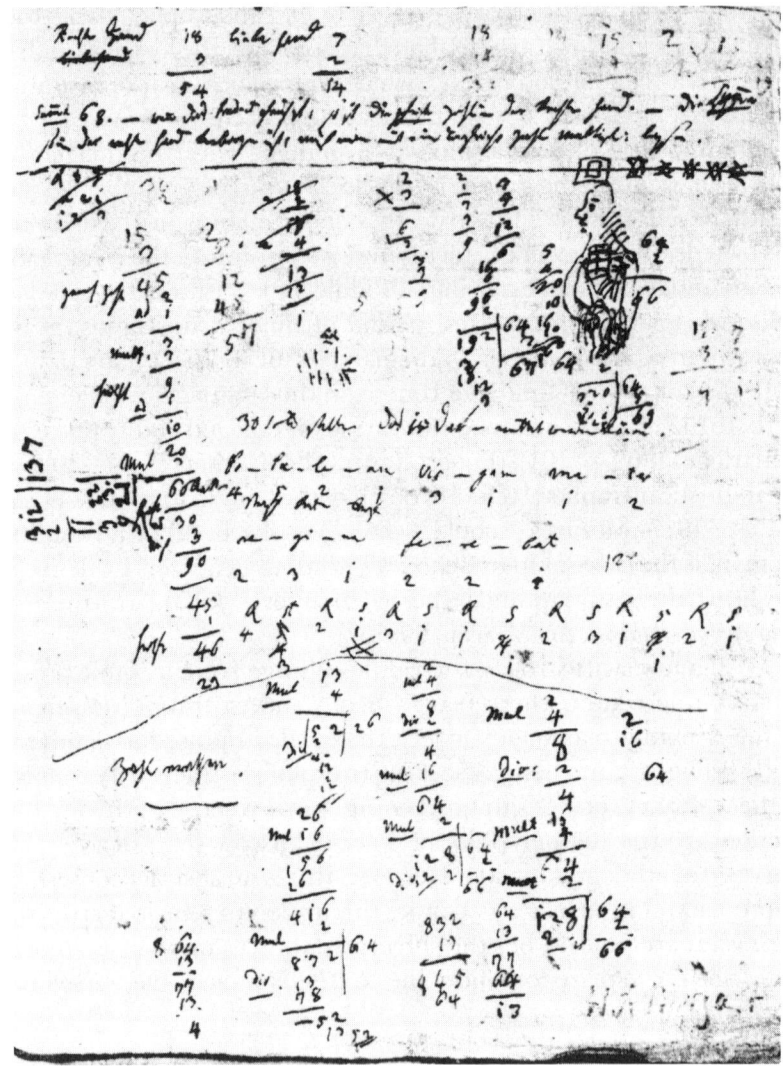

Figure 19.3. Mozart. Caricature. *Berlin, Staatsbibliothek Preussicher Kulturbesitz, Musikabteilung.*

riddle whose secret is to be solved at all costs. In life, she had been Mozart's shield against punishment, mutilation, and death; in death, she became the focus of Mozart's guilt, for his father had charged him with causing her death by his negligence. Because the stakes are so high, the feminine becomes a zone of danger: In the first riddle, she is the fanged temptress, *vagina dentata*; in the "horns" riddle, she betrays her husband. A masquerading virility continues in Riddle 2, where the lover is quite ready to "die at the hands of a beautiful woman," content to know that his flesh has seen something "which not everyone gets to see." In Riddle 3, the woman temporarily preserves her chastity by surrounding herself with noxious odors. The misogyny is only partly feigned, for Mozart could not remain altogether immune to his father's cautionings: "I shall say nothing about women," wrote Leopold Mozart, even as he proceeded to say a great deal about them:

> [F]or where they are concerned the greatest reserve and prudence are necessary, Nature herself being our enemy. Whoever does not use his judgement to the utmost to keep the necessary reserve with them, will exert it in vain later on when he endeavours to extricate himself from the labyrinth, *a misfortune which most often ends in death* [Letter 282, February 5, 1778].

And, perhaps fearing that a warning against the dangers of illicit sexuality might be misread by his son as a recommendation for conjugality, he makes himself equally clear about the consequences of matrimonial sexuality:

> Now it depends solely on your good sense and your way of life whether you die as an ordinary musician, utterly forgotten by the world, or as a famous Kapellmeister, of whom *posterity* will read—whether, captured by some woman, you die bedded on straw in an attic full of starving children, or whether, after a Christian life spent in contentment, honour and renown, you leave this world with your family well provided for and your name respected by all [Letter 285, February 11–12, 1778].

Mozart's own misogynous tendencies, his sexual jealousy, and morbid fear of being betrayed by his wife (a fear entwined with a desire for precisely such a betrayal), all represent submission to his father's attitudes. In the riddles' equations of pleasure and mutilation, sex and death, orgasm and annihilation, we have echoes of Leopold Mozart's warnings against the ensnaring, labyrinthian, contaminating woman, warnings by which he unconsciously aimed both to separate Mozart from his mother and to keep Mozart for himself.

However, it is, or should be, an essential principle of reading a text that its plainest meaning not be overlooked. That, at least, was the lesson of "The Purloined Letter." And here, too, the most obvious fact about Mozart's riddles may be the most difficult to perceive: All of them are written in the first person, singular or plural. To write and distribute the riddles was not only to ask questions but to make a statement. To send them to Leopold Mozart was to write him a coded letter, just as in the old days. Beneath the witty surface, beneath the literary convention, beneath the aggressive implications and the taunting double entendres, Mozart may have sent to Salzburg a plain confession and a call for help. The first riddle conveys his feeling of captivity in a palace which is really a prison, where he must work for the benefit of others rather than for his own gratification or fulfillment. The second tells of his genius, his sense of greatness: "One would imagine that so many superior qualities would make me happy; O no! My death is generally terrifying [and] painful. . . ." In the third riddle, an uncanny sense of dissociation overcomes the narrator: "I have no soul and no body. One cannot see me but can hear me." (We may now acknowledge the musical implications of this phrase: incorporeal, the narrator/composer exists only in the sounds which he produces.) His very being is in question: "I do not exist for myself." He owes his life to another: "Only a human being can give me life, as often as he wishes"; he has a foretaste of doom: "my life is only of short duration" and depends wholly upon "the caprice of men." He is overcome with guilt: "To those who give me life I do nothing—but those on whose account I am born I leave with painful sensations for the short duration of my life. . . ."

Similar themes echo through the fourth riddle: "I serve many as an ornament, many as a mutilation . . . Sometimes it would be better if I were not there, sometimes . . . it is a blessing that I am there. . . ." He knows of his power to discover and to heal, but his pathetic wish is to be of service to others in the hope that they may reciprocate with kindness: "I serve old people also, beyond my obligations; on that account, people who become old take care of me, so that I am not spoiled, let alone die before my time." This glimmer of hope dissolves in Riddle 5, the most despairing and aggressive of the set: We are "created for man's pleasures. How can we help it if an accident befalls by which we become the opposite? If he is lacking one of us, then he is—defective."

Mozart's riddles oscillate between concealing and revealing, between mystery and clarity, between asking and waiting for an answer. And this is not only in the nature of riddling: it is in the nature of Mozart's needs. Though he cannot overcome the anxiety aroused by his father's imperatives, he will not submit; he cannot restore the old relationship of domination/humiliation without undermining his creativity. He turns aside the homosexual blandishment of a perpetual childhood under the protection of a compassionate omnipotent father. Fearing punishment, he becomes a masquerader; to avoid discovery, one can flee or one can hide. But the phallic pretense of the maimed clown is insufficient to neutralize his fear or to delude the punishing superego. So he plainly needs to confess the extent of his woundedness. He needs Leopold Mozart's help but cannot openly ask for it.

And so the real riddle is posed: "Who is it that is deserving both of your punishment and of your forgiveness?" Unfortunately, Leopold Mozart had insufficient patience for his son's studied obscurity of expression. Almost ten years earlier, Mozart had playfully teased his father:

> In my next letter I may perhaps be able to tell you something *very good* for you, but only *good* for me, or something *very bad* in your eyes, but *tolerable* in mine; or it may be something *tolerable* for you, but *good, precious and valuable* for me! [Letter 247, November 22, 1777].

Mozart insisted that though this might be "obscure," and even "rather in the style of an oracle," yet it was "intelligible." His father disagreed strongly. *"Blast your oracular utterances . . . !"* (Letter 252, December 1, 1777). He wrote back, asking for a plainer explanation.

At Carnival 1786, the oracle-harlequin once again asked Leopold Mozart to investigate; but the eighteenth-century Deputy Kapellmeister, secure in his rationality and righteousness, failed to perceive a mystery.

I have discussed Mozart's Zoroastran riddles in the hope that they can help us understand something about his personality and even, perhaps, something about his creativity. In a very fundamental sense, raw materials, such as these, are better suited for psychological analysis than are structured works of art. In artistic creativity, the process of sublimation retains its etymological meaning: to refine, to elevate, to purify, that is, to convert into a higher form. Thus, the artist's personal motivations, experiences, and drives may be so thoroughly absorbed, or objectified, in a successful creation that the retrieval of autobiographical data can scarcely be accomplished without his close cooperation, if at all. In his work, the artist finds ways symbolically to repair psychic injuries and object losses, to neutralize anxieties. But he does this by means of socially developed techniques and forms of art, so that what had been private and opaque becomes a shared communication. The artist, remarked Freud in a famous passage, "understands how to elaborate his day-dreams, so that they lose that personal note which grates upon strange ears . . . ; he knows too how to modify them sufficiently so that their origin in prohibited sources is not easily detected" (1915–1917, p. 376).

To put this somewhat differently: The work of art mediates between an archaeology and a teleology. The productive imagination brings into being objects which have sources in current and archaic materials but which nevertheless have never previously existed in these individual forms. Thus, in Paul Ricoeur's splendid formulation, we can say that: "the work of art goes ahead of the artist; it is a prospective symbol of his personal synthesis and of man's future, rather than a regressive symbol of his unresolved conflicts" (1970, pp. 175, 521).

If the sublimated transformations and symbolic disguises which lie near the core of artistic creativity are not sufficient to daunt the investigator of links between biography and art, consider the additional difficulty for the music historian, who deals with materials that are largely nonverbal and even preverbal. I do not envy those investigators their task, though I always envy their daring and, occasionally, their insights. I have no doubt that, in the process of creation, the originating impulses are preserved precisely at the same time that they are mastered. Something of a composer's personality and experience flows into his works and perhaps even constitutes an important ingredient of his artistic individuality, his style. The difficulty lies in reading the runes.

It is less difficult to read Mozart's riddles. For, apart from their being verbal rather than musical productions, they are incomplete, even unsuccessful sublimations. And it is precisely failed actions, whether those of daily life or works of art and science, which give us a glimpse of the interior. Here, the original libidinal impulse has not been wholly transmuted, let alone mastered in form. In his riddles, Mozart lets his guard down, unaware that the riddles are anything other than literary exercises written purely for the fun of it. He believes that his riddles convey a clear set of objective signals which require only rational decoding for their significance to be grasped and enjoyed. He is unaware that the riddles are also free associational products of his imagination, symbols to which are bonded fragments of a hidden life.

Chapter 20
Rossini: A Psychoanalytic Approach to "The Great Renunciation"

Daniel W. Schwartz, M.D.

Gioacchino Rossini remains unique in the history of serious music. At thirty-seven, at the height of his fame and unquestionably the most celebrated and most widely performed opera composer in the world, he suddenly stopped writing. During the next thirty-nine years of his life he composed only two masses and a number of small pieces, but never again did he write in the medium that had brought him such renown that Stendhal (1824) called him "the greatest living artist of our time" (p. 407).

Many explanations have been offered by many people, including the composer himself, but none seems sufficient. Newman (1930) summarizes some of them:

> It is said that he was piqued by the failure of the public to take to its heart what he knew to be the best of his works; that he was jealous of the growing vogue of Meyerbeer; that he had made so much money (he was given many a good Stock Exchange tip by his friends the Rothschilds) that he could indulge his natural bent towards indolence; that he wanted, in the years following the production of *William Tell*, to live in Italy with his old father, who, not knowing a word of French, would have been unhappy in Paris; and so on [p. 235].

The "and so on" includes a suggestion that he was just being

Adapted from a paper presented at the Annual Meeting of the American Psychoanalytic Association in Los Angeles on May 2, 1964.

The author wishes to thank the many people who offered helpful advice and encouragement in the preparation of this paper, most particularly Dr. Nathaniel Ross.

First published in the *Journal of the American Psychoanalytic Association*, 133:551–569, 1965.

perverse after having made his decision. Toye (1947) emphasizes Rossini's poor health almost immediately after *William Tell* and even suggests that "some of Rossini's troubles were of venereal origin," citing his later symptoms, disease of the bladder and urinary tract and his premature baldness and toothlessness. Further possibilities mentioned by other authors (Edwards, 1881; Cross and Ewen, 1953) include his failing inspiration, his "neurasthenia," his inability to find adequate singers, and his sense of futility at working in a period of political turmoil.

None of the above-mentioned explanations is really sufficient. All of them can be either easily refuted or shown to be quite inadequate for such a momentous decision. Nor are the explanations offered by Rossini himself, as cited by Toye (1947), any more satisfactory: that "the sentiment and ideals of the present day are wholly concerned with steam, rapine and barricades" (p. 167); that his silence proceeded partly from a dislike of having to follow the evil tendencies of the day, partly from a desire to give a good example; that "Music needs freshness of ideas; I am conscious of nothing but lassitude and crabbedness" (p. 167); his lack of a son; and the absence of any singers capable of interpreting his music, due to the disappearance of the castrati. Rossini himself was reluctant to discuss the matter and it is most likely that all he could offer were these rationalizations for a decision that was largely unconsciously determined. But perhaps we can find a more satisfactory explanation from a fuller understanding of the composer's personality, returning to Rossini's explanations for the renunciation as part of a study of his life history and a psychoanalytic approach to some of his operas, particularly his two best, *The Barber of Seville* and *William Tell*.

The question may be raised: how much of a composer's personality are we entitled to infer from an opera's libretto, when it is the music through which he expresses himself? And, in the case of Rossini, this point may be even more cogently argued, since he had no choice of plot in so many of his operas. In answering this question I think we are justified in assuming that, when a composer does write his best music for a certain plot, that story has a particular valence for him; in other words, not only that operatic composition in general is an important sublimation for him but, further, that the particular librettos he cathects enough to write his greatest music for have a greater than average resonance with his particular unconscious conflicts.

The Barber of Seville, moreover, was written under circumstances particularly favorable for Rossini to have the greatest possible influence on the libretto. It was Rossini himself who suggested the subject and he was not, as in many other operas, handed a finished book. According to Edwards (1881), the composer and his librettist, Sterbini, "were always together during the composition of the opera; ready mutually to suggest and profit by suggestions." Together, they decided what in Beaumarchais' comedy should be adopted. "Sterbini was a most accommodating poet. He was quite prepared to carry out the composer's ideas, and did not object to alter, curtail or add to his verses with a view to increasing the effectiveness of Rossini's music."

William Tell, besides being considered by many to be his masterpiece, maintains a position of singular importance, inasmuch as it is the last opera he ever wrote. It would seem reasonable to examine such a work for a possible understanding of the dynamics leading to his renunciation of this form of musical expression. Furthermore, Newman (1930) writes that Rossini took an unusual amount of pains over the composition of *William Tell*, retiring to a friend's country house for six months to write the piano portion, leaving the orchestration to be added on his return to Paris. The shortest estimate of how long he actually took for the complete composition would probably be somewhere in the neighborhood of nine months; the actual length of time is probably even longer, for he is known to have decided on the subject some time previously. This is in striking contrast to the three days required to write his first opera and the two weeks needed for *The Barber*. In this opera, as in no others, he fought bitterly with his librettists until it took the shape with which he was satisfied. Rossini apparently felt the need to express himself most precisely in *William Tell* as he had never done before.

I am well aware of the difficulties and dangers in "analyzing" someone in absentia. We lack the individual's associations and affects, his resistances to and confirmations of our constructions and interpretations, and a real appreciation of his ego structure. What we are forced to fall back on, to a great extent, is a symbolic interpretation of unconscious drives and defenses, an interpretation that may be true in the general but inappropriate in the specific, and an interpretation that must always remain highly speculative without real confirmation. The attempt has been made often enough with other historical figures and sometimes quite effectively, especially where there is enough detailed biographic or autobiographic material available, particularly in the form of letters, to provide a sound basis for careful analytic thinking. Here, unfortunately, I have little such material available as yet. Nevertheless, I think the attempt in this paper is worth while, if for no other reason than that it may stimulate others to take an interest in Rossini. His life was truly fascinating. What I intend to present here, then, is certainly not a complete or even adequate explanation of the great renunciation but rather a partial and tentative working hypothesis of some of the unconscious drives and conflicts that may have motivated him, drawn from the plots of his operas and the known facts of the composer's life. As inadequate as the explanation may be, it cannot be any more unsatisfactory than the explanations already offered by historians.

Gioacchino Rossini was born on February 29, 1792, in Pesaro, Italy. His father, then thirty-three years old, was "an impoverished and third rate horn player, a member of that fraternity of nomadic musicians who, to earn a scanty living, wander from fairground to fairground" (Stendhal, 1824, p. 45). Two years previously he had obtained the position of municipal trumpeter (comparable to what we would call a town crier) in Pesaro, where he also played horn and trumpet in the local theater band and acted as inspector of the public slaughterhouses. "Owing to his ingratiating ways and above all to the gay and impulsive disposition that earned him the nickname of 'Vivazza,' he soon became a very popular figure" (Toye, 1947, p. 5). An ardent republican and Francophile, he conspired with zeal and publicly boasted of his radical views and capabilities when the political situation was favorable. He was imprisoned by the Austrians in 1796, when the young Rossini was four years old, and either that year or the next lost his municipal positions.

The composer's mother, twelve years younger than her husband, was one of the prettiest girls in the town. Rossini later described her to an intimate friend as "tall and well proportioned, with a fresh, rather pale complexion, perfect teeth, and magnificent black curly hair. She was always cheerful and good-tempered, a constant smile on her lips, and on her face an expression of truly angelic sweetness" (Toye, 1947, p. 6).

She had earned her living as a dressmaker but had also been a competent *seconda donna*. Following her husband's first release from prison, the couple wandered from town to town, he playing in the orchestra and she singing on the stage, while the boy was generally left behind at Pesaro in the care of his aunt and his grandmother. In addition to accompanying her, Vivazza presumably taught her her parts because she could not read a note of music and had to learn everything by ear. There were several more political upheavals in the Romagna, during which the elder Rossini was imprisoned several times, in Bologna and finally again in Pesaro in 1799.

The younger Rossini was also having his troubles, in a somewhat similar way, for he spent most of his time getting into mischief. Left to himself by his grandmother, he was allowed to run wild and all attempts to impose discipline on him were futile. As punishment he was apprenticed to a blacksmith, but with small success, for shortly afterwards his parents felt obliged to make him come and live with them in Bologna. The family situation, however, was not much different there: his father being imprisoned, his mother earned her living as *prima donna buffa* at various theaters in the Romagna, where she was ultimately rejoined by her husband. The boy's attitude was not much different either: boarded out as an apprentice to a pork butcher, he indulged in exactly the same behavior as before and was soon given up as incorrigible. "There can be no doubt that for sheer naughtiness Rossini's boyhood is unparalleled in the annals of the great masters of music; but there was every excuse for him. So handsome as to be commonly known as 'The Little Adonis,' he was doubtless spoilt by outsiders if not by his parents, the wildly Bohemian circumstances of his boyhood being hardly compatible with discipline in any event" (Toye, 1947, pp. 9–10).

In 1802, Vivazza moved himself and his family to Lugo but the ten-year-old boy seems hardly to have improved in behavior. Again he found himself apprenticed to a blacksmith and then, for the first time, began to show signs of comparative obedience. Toye (1947) speculates that "it may well be that the influence of his mother began to make itself really felt about this time" (p. 11). Rossini "adored her to an extent that was almost abnormal" and "thought his mother the most lovely thing in all the world, alike in voice, face, and character. . . . The most poignant emotion he ever knew was undoubtedly adoration of his mother" (p. 11).

Some time in 1804 this peripatetic family moved permanently to Bologna. Here, in one of the main musical centers of Italy, the twelve-year-old boy began to make rapid progress with his new music teacher. He had made his first public appearance five years previously in Bologna as a singer. In the intervening years he had learned to play the horn from the elder Rossini and would frequently accompany his parents on tours, playing the part of second horn while his father took the part of the first horn and his mother sang on the stage. Now, in Bologna, his teacher was so pleased with him that he procured for his thirteen-year-old pupil an engagement as chorister in one of the local churches. Two years later he was competent enough to act as musical director with a traveling opera company.

At sixteen, Rossini was considered the best student in the Liceo Musicale, which he had entered only one year before, and was chosen to compose a cantata. Following this he was appointed director of the Philharmonic concerts and one year later produced his first symphony and string quartet. Historians disagree as to whether Rossini wrote his first opera when he was fourteen or seventeen; in either case, this work was not produced until he was twenty. He was only eighteen, however, when his first publicly performed opera, *La Cambiale di Matrimonio*, was produced at Venice.

In 1812 he wrote no fewer than five operas, two of which were quite popular. The following year two more successes were produced and the twenty-one-year-old composer of twelve operas found himself the idol of Venice and the most renowned opera composer in Italy. His fame began to spread rapidly throughout Europe.

In 1815 Rossini left Bologna for Naples, having signed a contract with the impresario Barbaja, a man of great power and influence. His prima donna, Isabella Colbran, was also his mistress and, if Barbaja ruled Naples, Mademoiselle Colbran ruled Barbaja and enjoyed, moreover, the special favor of the court as well. Whether or not she and Rossini knew each other before this is not certain; at any rate the two seem to have gotten on well together from the outset. His first Neapolitan opera was particularly suited to her idiosyncrasies and achieved an enthusiastic response for both the singer and the composer.

The next month Rossini took advantage of a leave-of-absence clause in his contract to go to Rome. His first opera written there was a definite failure, but the second was to be his most famous of all. Space does not permit me to go into a detailed description and analysis of *The Barber of Seville*. It is the rather light-hearted story of Count Almaviva's secretly courting and finally marrying Rosina, in the process of which he is aided and abetted by Figaro. In order to do so, he conceals his true identity from Rosina herself, blatantly bribes her music teacher several times, and repeatedly outwits her guardian, who himself has marital intentions toward the girl.

It seems to me that Rossini identified himself with the successful Count and his mother with the fair Rosina. There is readily apparent then a "love triangle" with old Doctor Bartolo representing the unwanted father who keeps his love object as secluded as possible, just as, in real life, the elder Rossini took his wife touring around the Romagna while the young composer-to-be was left behind. The similarity between the characters of Figaro and Rossini's real father is too great to go unnoticed. His public boasting of his importance, value, and resourcefulness is most reminiscent of Vivazza. That he represents a potential castration threat is further suggested by his occupation, of which he boasts so much—a barber. But here an interesting thing seems to have happened: Rossini apparently overcomes his castration anxiety by making Figaro his ally. The father image seems to be split into a potent but good figure, on the one hand, and a bad but impotent figure, on the other. Now, with a father-ally not only condoning but also aiding and abetting his plans, the young lover would have to win.

I said "love triangle" before rather than oedipal triangle because, although there are many aspects of the opera's plot that point to a phallic level of development, it is not without strong pregenital components. Anal derivatives, such as the preoccupation with bribery and money, are rampant throughout and oral fixations are just as evident. But at this point the phallic organization was most dominant in the twenty-three-year-old composer, the deeper pre-oedipal conflicts still not crippling him.

Rossini's identification with the successful Count is further suggested by the original title of the opera: *Almaviva, or the Vain Precaution*. The composer stated in a preface to the libretto that he did this out of respect for the composer Paisiello, who had written an opera entitled *The Barber of Seville* thirty-four years before. But Toye (1947) points out that this step was entirely unnecessary since Beaumarchais' story had been used for musical purposes on two other occasions before Paisiello's version, four times since, and still another in Dresden at almost exactly the same time Rossini's version was produced. In view of Rossini's excessive concern about offending Paisiello, it seems most likely that he unconsciously felt he was doing exactly the same thing in real life that he had accomplished in the opera: competing with the father and winning the mother.

Forty-four years later, in his famous interview with Wagner, Rossini further indicated that this opera had always held a great competitive significance for him. According to his own account, his remuneration consisted of 1,200 francs and a suit worth 100 francs. He analyzed this payment as working out to 100 francs a day for each of the thirteen days employed in writing the opera. It made him, he said, feel very proud, for 2½ francs a day was all that his father had ever been able to earn by playing the trumpet.

One more comment on *The Barber of Seville* is furnished by Stendhal (1824), who makes the astute observation that Rosina is not really the blushing girl of eighteen she is supposed to be. The music written for her is "devoid of the slightest suggestion of melancholy, or even, I might dare to add, of certain finer shades of fastidiousness and hesitation" (p. 103). He concludes that her love music becomes reasonable only if we think of Rosina as being *twenty-eight years old and a widow*! Stendhal is inclined to attribute this to the type of women Rossini must have been associating with each evening before coming home to write the opera. But Edwards (1881) tells us that Rossini never left his apartment during the composition of *The Barber* and, in fact, deliberately let his beard grow, ostensibly so that he would not be tempted to go out. The music written for Rosina seems much more comprehensible if we assume that, unconsciously at least, he *was* writing for a fantasied mature widow—his mother.

The next thirteen years were a period of great triumph for Rossini. His contract with Barbaja at Naples ran for another six years until 1822, during which time he produced no fewer than sixteen operas. They were not all good or successful; but enough were, so that when he left, it was in a blaze of glory—and in the company of Barbaja's former mistress and prima donna. At some time during those years, Rossini had won the affections of Isabella

Colbran, who was seven years his senior. It would seem that he had finally acted out, to a certain extent, the fantasies he had heretofore only been able to portray in music. Interestingly enough, Barbaja seems to have accepted the situation philosophically and the three people remained on very friendly terms. In fact, after stopping off in Bologna just long enough to get married, Rossini and his wife returned to work for Barbaja, who was now the new impresario at Vienna.

During his four months there, Rossini was the hero of the day. He was gay, witty, in perfect health, going everywhere and knowing everybody. "His wit, his good temper, his beautiful manners opened to him every door in Vienna. Crowds followed him wherever he went" (Toye, 1947, p. 102). In 1823, back in Venice, his popularity was unbelievable. In this one year, at least twenty-three of his operas were being performed in various countries. Stendhal (1824) was moved to write, "The glory of this man is only limited by the limits of civilization itself; and he is not yet thirty-two" (p. 407).

In the fall of that year, on his way to London, Rossini stayed in Paris for a month, just long enough to captivate all fashionable society with his immense personal charm. His triumph culminated in a brilliant dinner in his honor, the most outstanding social event of the year. In London, where he remained seven months, he again became the favorite of society. Following his interview with George IV, in which his urbanity was at its highest, no smart musical party was complete without him. He returned to Paris in August 1824, richer by 175,000 francs.

Following a short visit with his parents—the last time he was ever to see his mother alive—he assumed his duties as director of the Théâtre Italien in December, 1824. His first opera was a failure, but his next, after he had studied hard to consolidate his position as a French composer, was a huge success. The third was an even greater triumph, but at the same time disaster struck.

During the rehearsals he had heard that his mother was very ill. She finally died in February, 1827, apparently from an aneurysm. The news had to be relayed secondhand, since Vivazza could not bring himself to break the news to his son himself, "knowing his extreme, not to say pathological, sensitiveness" (Toye, 1947, p. 132). The immediate effects on the thirty-five-year-old Rossini were not outwardly noticeable except on one occasion. One month later, when taking his opening night curtain call for his operatic triumph, he was heard to murmur, "Ah, but she is dead!" This was the beginning of the ebb of his lighthearted exuberance and the onset of a profound depression which was to reach its clinical peak twenty-five years later.

He made one last attempt to turn out a comic opera in *Le Comte Ory*, produced in August, 1828. But, as Toye (1947) points out, "there is not the irresistible vitality, the uncontrollable flow of music characteristic of *L'Italiana* or *The Barber*" (p. 133). The story, as summarized by Toye, is simple enough:

> Count Ory, a regular medieval Don Juan, disguises himself as a hermit in order to further his amorous purposes, receiving in this capacity the confidences of the Countess Adele, whose husband, accompanied by all the husbands of the district, has gone on a crusade. Ory and his boon companions dress up as nuns and thus gain admittance to the castle where the Countess and her husbandless friends are trying to console themselves. The inevitable is about to happen when the return of the husbands is announced. The Countess decides to forgive Ory; he and his companions are smuggled out of a side door; that is all. The thinness of plot, the absence of cumulative interest, are obvious [1947, p. 134].

What is thin about the opera, from our point of view, is the apparently bare oedipal situation, which really does not end victoriously for the hero. His only triumph, if it can be called that, is that he manages to escape and that the Countess–mother forgives him for his intended transgression. Once again there is the predilection for disguises in Rossini's operas—mechanisms which serve to avoid open conflict and possible punishment, but which also point to a more fundamental lack of a true feeling of identity on the part of the composer. The separation of spouses is reminiscent of Rossini's youth, except that the situations are reversed; here it is the women who are left alone in the castle as the husbands are out campaigning, while in real life it was Vivazza who was left alone in jail as Anna toured the Romagna. His hero's failure to succeed in this opera already bespeaks the renunciation of genitality as a psychic organizer and the tremendous loss sustained in his mother's death. He is beginning consciously to assume the burden of guilt for her death, just as the Count is held responsible for what would have happened in the opera.

After the second performance of *Le Comte Ory*, Rossini, now the most popular figure in Paris, began to work on *William Tell*. The composition, as previously mentioned, took at least about nine months. The production was repeatedly postponed because of the composer's determination to secure a proper contract, his previous one having expired some time before. He now asked for an annual salary in perpetuity, in exchange for which he promised to write five operas during the next ten years. He was openly concerned with security for the first time in his life and, despite his promise to compose four more operas after *William Tell*, may have dimly perceived that his productive life was at an end. At one point he suspended rehearsals and threatened to withdraw the opera completely until his demands were met. Eventually this contract was agreed upon, and Rossini's last opera was finally produced on August 3, 1829.

Again, space does not permit a detailed discussion of this rather involved opera. The plot is the familiar story of how Tell yearns to free Switzerland from the Austrians, is forced by the tyrant Gessler to shoot an apple from his son's head, and ultimately leads the Switzers to victory as he himself kills Gessler. Lest this brief summary sound too heroic and Superman-ish, let me point out that Tell breaks down and cries when his skill as a marksman is put to the test, pleading to be spared the ordeal. Throughout the opera, it is his little boy who is the intrepid hero and who actually restores his father's courage. Running through the opera, contrapuntally, as it were, is an entirely different plot, that of Arnold, son of the village patriarch, who loves the Austrian princess, Mathilde, and hesitates to fight for his people's freedom until his father has been killed by Gessler. He ultimately joins Tell and plays an important part in the victory, while it is the princess who actually saves the life of Tell's son. Interestingly enough, it is for these two lovers that Rossini wrote the best music in the opera, music in which Mathilde resigns herself to a life of unhappiness and Arnold sadly laments over the loss of his father and his happy childhood days. Newman (1930) satirically remarks that the only reason for this music is that the leading soprano and tenor had their "inalienable rights," but I hardly think this explanation suffices. Rossini had broken and established enough operatic conventions before this to do anything he pleased. It seems to me that this music represented, in the opera itself, a renunciation of genitality, a theme that had been stated more humorously in the previous work. There is even the introduction of a neurotic symptom at one point when Arnold, visiting the home of his murdered father to strengthen his longing for vengeance, is unable to cross the threshold; I do not think it is too speculative to infer the instinctual drives defended against in this inhibition. The work abounds with violence and bloodshed and practically everyone longs at one time or another for the pleasures of childhood. Jemmy, Tell's son, worshipping his father and secure in the affection of the princess and his mother, is the only undisturbed and confident character in the whole story. His father in the opera is imprisoned by the Austrians, just as was Rossini's father in the composer's youth. I think that Rossini's basic identification at this point is with the child and the security such a noncompetitive, preoedipal role represents. It is interesting to note that the boy signals the patriots at the end by setting fire to his house; a fair marksman in his own right, he saves his father's bows and arrows but not his own.

William Tell is considered by musical critics to be Rossini's preeminent achievement. It contains the most striking and beautiful music he ever wrote and secured for him the Legion of Honor. The enthusiasm of contemporary musicians knew no bounds; even Berlioz, his harshest critic, wrote of it five years later with wild enthusiasm. Despite this, it was Rossini's last opera. He never again wrote in the medium that had brought him such fame and fortune.

Why? I am suggesting that "the great renunciation" was directly related to the death of Rossini's mother and his intense ambivalence toward her. He had never established a secure, maturely neutralized, and internalized image of his mother that could lead to a stable ego structure and a meaningful sense of identity, capable of sustaining her loss. In his youth, this inability to sustain her absence and control his ambivalence had already shown itself in his delinquent behavior. Later, operatic composition had served as a partial sublimation of his aggression. Even then, however, his ambivalence was clear: he always notified his mother about his failures but never informed her of his successes. This ambivalent attitude was also displaced onto female singers in general. On the one hand, he was an expert at writing arias to accommodate the specific soprano, with her range in mind, "to enhance the strong points of her singing and to disguise her weak points" (Cross and Ewen, 1953, p. 647). On the other hand, he placed unprecedented restrictions on what had previously been the singer's prerogative: "he wrote out—for the first time—the cadenza passages for his arias, rather than leaving them to the whim and fancy of the singer" (Cross and Ewen, 1953, p. 647). Now, subsequent to his mother's death, he was so threatened by the strength of his aggression that he could no longer sublimate it. Instead, he defended against it by narcissistic withdrawal, depression, and intensification of his obsessional mechanisms.[1] His inability to compose was both a defense against the anger, an unconscious attempt to control it, and also a direct instinctual expression of his aggression through obsessional withholding. Consciously, he had the most exaggerated adoration of his mother, an idealized picture that was too good to be true, while behind the glorification lay a tremendous rage that manifested itself in his obsessional character structure and depression.

Can any of this be discerned in the reasons Rossini reluctantly gave for his renunciation? I think so. Lassitude and lack of freshness of ideas are common clinical symptoms of depression. His statement that "the sentiment and ideals of the present day are wholly concerned with steam, rapine and barricades" (Toye, 1947, p. 167) and his reference to the evil tendencies of the day seem to be projections of the rage within himself, a rage that he was only dimly aware of when he referred to his own "crabbedness." His lack of a son, I think, refers primarily to his own no longer being a son, and his complaint that there were no singers capable of interpreting his music, due to the disappearance of the castrati, really is a complaint that his mother was no longer alive. As a matter of fact, after the age of twenty-one, he never wrote an operatic part for a male soprano, but his reference to them in this context, I think, once again indicates the pregenital nature of his relationship with his mother.

The remainder of Rossini's life was basically one long agitated depression. While the signs were slow in assuming pathological proportions, there had been previous indications that it was coming. Six years before, while crossing the Channel to England, he had been reduced to a state of nervous collapse which lasted for over two weeks. Now, at the time of his last opera, he was suffering from severe insomnia.

---

[1] The immediate reaction to her death was repression and denial, for he showed no outwardly noticeable signs of a normal mourning process. Just prior to the production of *William Tell* his anality and need to protect against future loss were already evident in his insistence on a salary in perpetuity.

Soon after the production of *William Tell*, Rossini and his wife returned to Bologna, where he gave some parties and helped produce several of his earlier operas. In September 1830 he returned to Paris and found that, due to the July revolution, his contract had been canceled. His obsessional pettiness and preoccupation with security were more prominent than ever, for, despite his great wealth, he spent six years of wearisome litigation to prevent the pension from being canceled.

The marriage with Isabella, which even from the beginning seems not to have gone too well, was now a definite failure. She had made the fatal mistake of quarreling with Rossini's beloved mother. Still, it was not until they settled in Paris that there was a serious breach. Isabella, always extravagant, had taken to gambling and, to pay her debts, had given singing lessons on the quiet, much to Rossini's disgust. When he returned to Paris in 1830, she was left behind in Bologna with old Vivazza.

In 1832, Rossini met a courtesan, Olympe Pélissier, and the two were immediately attracted to each other. Independently wealthy from her sexual affairs, she seems to have wanted nothing more than to look after the already failing composer and to put a little order in his life. What could be more desirable to him than such a woman of the world who wanted to mother him? Four years later, when he returned to Bologna at the age of forty-four, "he wanted quiet, quiet above all things" (Toye, 1967, p. 164). He settled up affairs with Isabella, the two of them remaining separately in Bologna and then, at his urgent request, was joined by Olympe. "Now at last she had come to give him the care and attention he so missed" (Toye, 1947, p. 165).

Just before returning to Bologna he had taken his first ride on a railroad. The effect was disastrous: he had a severe anxiety attack and required many days to recover his composure. He suffered another severe setback in January, 1838, when the Théâtre Italien was destroyed by fire and the director, who lived in the building, perished. After hearing the news, Rossini was flooded with obsessional preoccupations. His morbid imagination gave him no rest and he was prostrate for many days thinking of what might have happened if the fire had taken place when he, too, lived there. The next year was marked by an even greater depression when his father died at the age of eighty. Rossini immediately sold the house and soon sought rest in Naples. His health was so poor that his doctors refused to let him make the trip to Paris, where hospitality had been offered by an old friend.

It was not until ten months later that his health allowed him to devote any serious attention to work and then he threw himself into it with tremendous zeal. He worked furiously as director of the Liceo in Bologna, with a degree of energy that he had never shown in Paris. He apparently was in an agitated state, a kind of manic denial, desperately fighting off the ever-present depression. His generosity in helping friends and young musicians was outstanding and continued, whenever his health permitted, for the rest of his life. The only thing he appeared to be completely uninterested in was writing music on his own account. His only effort in this field, perhaps significantly, was to complete the *Stabat Mater* he had started ten years previously. It was finally performed in 1842, but the fifty-year-old Rossini would not travel to Paris to see it produced.

Soon afterwards he arranged to have the work performed in Bologna, but he had to ask Donizetti to conduct it for him. At the conclusion of the final rehearsal Rossini slipped away, fell into a chair and, gazing at his mother's picture on the wall, burst into tears. He refused to attend any of the performances and, even when Donizetti had finally prevailed upon him to come to the last one, he refused to sit in the hall itself but remained in a neighboring room with one or two friends. As they laughed together about an unfavorable review, the man formerly so indifferent to adverse criticism suddenly began to tremble and break into a heavy sweat. When Donizetti finally left, Rossini wept as he embraced him and repeatedly murmured, "Do not abandon me, dear friend" (Toye, 1947, p. 188).

The next ten years were marked by a progressive withdrawal and morbid fears of death. His condition was exacerbated in 1845 when Isabella Colbran died. Although he had not seen her in many years, the event undoubtedly revived associations to his mother's death, for his depression was severe. A year later, at the age of fifty-four, he married Olympe. They left Bologna in 1848, after twelve years, following a revolutionary outburst in which he was accused of being a rich reactionary by a hostile mob and Olympe became quite frightened. Most likely, the experience of seeing mob violence and its effect on the woman he was so dependent upon exacerbated his fear of losing control over his own precariously repressed aggression. He never lived there again and never forgave Bologna, "the home of aggression and sausages," as with persistent bitterness he called it thirteen years later (Toye, 1947, p. 198).

It was in 1852 that the sixty-year-old Rossini, now living in Florence, began to go from bad to worse. He was in a psychotic depression for the next three years and was obsessed with thoughts of being forgotten and despised by the world. His anorexia and insomnia were extreme and sometimes, standing before a mirror, he would berate himself for being too cowardly to commit suicide. His delusions of poverty, a common enough depressive symptom, may have had a special significance for the composer. Forty-three years previously he had written an opera in which the hero pretends ruin and poverty in order to test his girl's love and, after this apparent ruin, the advances are all from her side.

Finally persuaded by Olympe to move back to Paris, he could hardly walk or talk in other than an unfragmented way for many months. He suffered from a peculiar symptom at that time: he could not listen to any note without compulsively imagining the major third. It was so upsetting that the porter had a special fund to keep away barrel organs and other street musicians. It is interesting to speculate on the meaning of this compulsion. Musically defined, what he imagined was "the harmonic combination of two tones a third apart." Taking this concretely, we might speculate that, in his loneliness and depression, he unconsciously thought of his parents together in death and himself, the "third," still apart from them.[2]

Gradually he began to improve and by the fall of the following year he seemed like a different man. True, he still had certain neurotic symptoms. He was still timid and quite secretive, extremely anxious when driving in a carriage, and absolutely phobic about gas lighting and railroad trains. But, in general, he was able to substitute obsessional defenses. His house was unbelievably orderly and his daily schedule was planned down to the last minute. As long as he never varied from the prescribed routine, he was able

---

[2] When this paper was presented, several discussants offered further speculations on this interesting symptom. It was pointed out by one that, since the major third contains a silent note between two others, this configuration may have been genetically associated to a little boy lying quietly in bed between his parents. Still another discussant made the observation, in conjunction with Rossini's precarious ego structure and his view of a crumbling inner and outer world, that the third is the most stable configuration in music.

to function. His dependence on Olympe was complete and she, in turn, suited his needs perfectly. With all her heart, mind and strength, we are told, she served the man who "has always been to me like a god" (Toye, 1947, p. 193).

By 1857 he had improved to the extent that he was able to write a small composition for his wife, the first time in over twenty years that he had written music because of a genuine desire to do so. In the next ten years he wrote 186 miniature pieces, mostly satirical or grotesque, which he called *Sins of My Old Age*. Macalpine and Hunter (1952), in their paper dealing with one of these miniatures, have pointed out that the separate headings of one of them suggest that Rossini was still expressing what they consider to be his central conflict, namely, his unconscious longing for, and terror of, union with his mother.

With time he seemed to grow even stronger: in 1863, at the age of seventy-one, he wrote the *Petite Messe Solenelle* (which was anything but *petite*) and in 1867 a mammoth composition for chorus and orchestra for the Paris Exhibition. He died the following year at the age of seventy-six from septicemia, following surgery for a rectal fistula. His *Petite Messe Solenelle* was one of the most remarkable pieces Rossini ever produced, if for no other reason than for the notes he appended to the original score, the first of which runs as follows:

> Petite Messe Solenelle in four parts, with accompaniment for two pianos and a harmonium, composed for my summer stay in Passy. Twelve singers of three sexes, men, women and *castrati*, will suffice for its performance, that is to say, eight for the chorus and four for the solos; twelve Cherubim in all. May God forgive me the following comparison. Twelve in number also are the Apostles in the celebrated fresco by Leonardo called *The Last Supper*. Who would believe it? Among thy disciples there are some capable of singing wrong notes! Lord be reassured, I guarantee that there will be no Judas at my luncheon, and that all mine will sing accurately and *con amore* Thy praises, as well as this little composition, which is, alas! the last mortal sin of my old age.— Passy, 1863 [Toye, 1947, p. 225].

SUMMARY

Gioacchino Rossini, when only thirty-seven years old and at the pinnacle of success, permanently ceased his career as an opera composer. A psychoanalytic approach to "the great renunciation"—

unique in the annals of serious music and heretofore only inadequately explained—suggests that the crucial factor was the death of the composer's mother two years previously. From his earliest years, which were punctuated by frequent separations from her, he had never established a secure, maturely neutralized, and internalized image of his mother which could lead to the formation of a stable ego structure and a meaningful sense of identity. Throughout his life, Rossini continued to act out his infantile and highly ambivalent attachment to her; operatic composition itself was a precariously sublimated and insufficiently neutralized expression of his aggression.[3] This intense ambivalence toward his mother made it impossible for him to mourn her in a healthy way, and his refusal to compose was the ultimate expression of his unconscious anger at her for having deserted him. Most of the remaining thirty-nine years of Rossini's life were basically one long agitated depression, which at times reached psychotic proportions. Only when he had established sufficient obsessional defenses and a stable enough dependent, sadomasochistic relationship with his second wife (and perhaps, too, when the instinctual energies involved had sufficiently diminished in intensity with old age) could he compose music, again, albeit still not opera; but even then he seems to have had some awareness of the aggression involved, for he called these compositions "sins" and, by negation, identified himself with Judas. While he had always consciously maintained an exaggerated adoration of his mother, it was in attempting to master the unconscious aggression toward her that he had originally written such beautiful music; and it was his inability to neutralize this aggression sufficiently that, unfortunately, led to "the great renunciation."

---

[3]The fascinating question of the general relationship between musical composition and the expression of anal aggressive drives would take us far beyond the scope of this paper. Just to mention one example from our own time, the great folk singer Woody Guthrie composed much of his music while on the toilet each morning.

Chapter 21
Robert Schumann and Clara Wieck—A Creative Partnership

Anna M. Burton, M.D.

On December 4, 1837, Robert Schumann made a heartfelt request in a letter to Josef Fischhof, the Vienna correspondent for his music journal, the *Neue Zeitschrift*:

> And now for another favor. Clara Wieck will probably be with you just now. You will see her, admire, and love her. Will you always send me word by post, as quickly as possible, whether she gains ground in Vienna as an exponent of the Romantic School—how she and her concerts succeed. . . . She is sure to play some of my compositions, so you will hear them *at their very source* [May, 1888, Vol. 1, p. 135, emphasis added].

This essay explores what lay behind Schumann's metaphoric placing of Clara's playing "at the very source" of his music. Original sources (diaries and letters) and the definitive biographies (Litzmann [1973], Reich [1985], etc.) provide copious data with which to analyze this participatory process, in which Clara Wieck progressed from being a "partner in performance" with her teacher-father (see chapter 7), to being a "partner in creativity" with Robert Schumann.

Curiosity about creative people and the mysteries of creation holds a fascination analogous to the curiosity of children about parents, and the mysteries of procreation. Many have dared to explore, and some have desisted, protesting that the task is impossible, and even that it springs from a certain unwise hubris. Actually, creativity presents an entire spectrum: at one end are the great "obligatory" creators—one thinks of Beethoven, Shakespeare—whose creativity is rarely interrupted. At the other end are those who, like some adolescents, are moved to create at specially favorable moments. While pathographies at either end of the spectrum explain nothing of the nature of the creative act, it remains possible that exploring a psychological partnership will illuminate familiar phenomena in a different light.

Using the term *creative partnership* I am following a path cleared by Bernard C. Meyer, whose elegant study of Joseph Conrad, Conrad's inner objects, and his "secret sharer" has stimulated many related projects (1967). Secret sharing may be found in association with genius in many areas. In the history of psychoanalysis, for instance, Sigmund Freud's correspondent and secret sharer was Wilhelm Fliess. In music, one thinks of the relationship between Tchaikowsky and Mme. Nadejda von Meck, except that, as will be made plain, the bond between Clara and Robert Schumann was far more complex, and richly based on shared history, life experiences, and creative play. Indeed, Clara Wieck contributed more germinally to her partner's music than is so with other "musical couples."

In this relationship, as with others, it would seem that separation modifies the affects, both positive and negative, and intensifies the object representations. Moreover, conditions of alternating togetherness and apartness seem to favor the integration of overlapping and idealized self and object representations. Within Schumann's mental life, the ever-present image of Clara served such an integrating function in ways which are fascinating to pursue.

Like most artists, Schumann did not try to explain creativity— his own or that of others. Although he was an intrepid explorer of his own psyche, and a wonderfully expressive writer, he explained nothing; his approach was the Romantic one, pointing with analogy and poetry toward distant, unreachable meanings. He never ceased writing, and when words did not go far enough, he depended on his music. Conversely, when the musical impulse faltered, he reverted to poetry and prose. And in all creative outlets, he revealed the seminal importance of the image of Clara Wieck.

This was especially clear in the early piano compositions. Schumann credited her, for instance, with the inspiration for the piano cycles: "I dare say the struggles I have endured about Clara are to a certain extent reflected in my music. . . . The concerto, the sonata, *Davidsbündlertänze*, *Kreisleriana*, and *Novelletten* were almost entirely inspired by her . . ." (September 5, 1831). And in 1839, Schumann wrote ebulliently: "I have revelled in the thought of you, and have loved you as I never did before. I sat at the piano all week, and composed and wrote, and laughed and cried, all at once; you will find all this fairly depicted in my Opus 20, the great *Humoreske* . . ." (Quoted in Litzmann, 1913, Vol. 1, pp. 203–204).

At the time of these letters, Clara Wieck (later Clara Schumann) was not yet twenty and already well launched on a long and influential career as one of nineteenth-century Europe's greatest pianists and teachers. She had already earned fame and signal honors throughout Germany and Austria and was far better known than her fiancé. Her father, Friedrich Wieck, was Robert's teacher. Since Clara's eleventh, and Robert's twentieth years, their lives had been closely intertwined. How it came about that Wieck esteemed Schumann as a composer and a writer, yet stubbornly refused him as a son-in-law, becomes clearer with an understanding of the father–daughter bond. It nearly blighted the courtship, which resembled a four-year obstacle course. Schumann, who had already suffered several depressions, went through at least four more such episodes, two of them rather serious.[1] He also had brief states of

[1] This chronology of Robert Schumann's depressions derives from data in his *Early Letters* (May, 1888), Slater and Meyer's pathography (1959), and from Litzmann's biography of Clara Schumann (1972). The depressive episodes described were superimposed on a personality which was generally melancholic. As an eighteen-year-old, his "predominant mood [was] melancholic" (Slater and Meyer, 1959, p. 72), and suicidal impulses appear amongst deeply introspective ruminations. Moreover, as can be seen from his letters, Schumann's mood was always volatile, so that each week, or even each day, had its own depressive moments.

a. In 1830 Robert was reported as melancholy and complaining of indecisiveness.

b. In the spring of 1831, he was irritable and melancholic. There was a noticeable reduction in the flow of letters; later that year, he was agitated, had suicidal ideas, developed a phobia (about cholera), and then progressed to depressed apathy, which lifted as the year ended.

c. In early 1832, however, Robert's spirits sank again. While Clara was away on tour, he wrote in February that he felt "depressed and leaden."

d. In October 1833, another depression began, as before, with fears and nightmares. He was afraid of heights, and of an impulse to throw himself from a window; this was relieved after a friend moved in with him. He described the "terrible night of October 18th, 1833," in a letter written to Clara on November 2. (Earlier that year Robert had suffered three significant losses: the deaths of his brother and his sister-in-law, and the fateful injury of his finger.) Again, the depression was reported to be lifting in January of 1834.

e. Summer 1836 began another long depressive period, lasting into January of 1837.

f. In the fall of 1837, his depression recurred, this one perhaps a reaction to Clara's doubts about their marriage plans. A letter of November 28 describes Robert's urge to throw her ring into the water and follow it himself.

g. In March 1838, deep presentiments of death occurred while Robert hypomania. His surges of productivity in the years between 1836 and 1839 created the great piano cycles, which came to full development at the climax of Clara's struggle to free herself from her father.

Much has been written about the early piano compositions, their musical imagery, spontaneity, intensity, and introspection, and musical renderings of Clara's image. Sometimes Schumann used Clara's themes (as in the first of the *Davidsbündler* pieces, op. 6); sometimes he quoted themes they had shared. He also made thematic allusions to his feelings about her, as in the Fantasie in C Major (op. 17), through a quotation from a Beethoven song cycle. The girl-woman, Clara, gazes out from her portraits in the *Davidsbündlertänze* and the *Carnaval* (op. 9)—works which amaze and delight, as they show how fully Schumann had developed his youthful games of musical portraiture. The entire *Novelletten* (op. 21), Schumann wrote, contained "images of you in every possible setting and harmony, and in other ways in which you are irresistible!" (Quoted in Litzmann, 1913, Vol. 1, p. 241).

Schumann also realized the possibilities of allowing a "singable" melody to sound through the surrounding figuration (Dale, 1952). In parts of the *Humoreske*, this melody is located on the page between the treble and bass staves and labeled "Innere Stimme" (inner voice). For Clara and Robert, the "inner voice" signified the voice of spirit, the voice of the beloved, and the expression of their union. Clara wrote: "Ah! Words fail me so completely. I feel so much and can say so little—an inner voice must say it to you" (Quoted in Litzmann, 1913, Vol. 1, p. 116).

Schumann symbolically "spoke" the name of Clara endlessly, in its musical translation, indulging his proclivity for musical anagrams of various kinds. Several writers have noted a theme of falling notes associated with Clara (Rehberg and Rehberg, 1969), and Eric Sams, in particular, has tirelessly detected a five-note

---

Schumann was composing *Nachstücke für Pianoforte* (op. 23). On July 7, he wrote of his "grave sin" in coming between Clara and her father, and expressed thoughts of his death. This became another long depression, lasting from June through the summer; in September, he was still in a "critical mental state."

h. In late 1839 and early 1840 (the months of bitter attacks from Wieck, before winning the legal battle to marry) Robert's depression and withdrawal was profound. He came out of this despair as he took strong legal action himself, and at the same time began a new kind of composition.

"Clara" theme in its many guises (1972). These and other motto-themes apparently became an integral part of Schumann's musical vocabulary and implicit to his contribution to Romantic music.

All of Schumann's revolutionary musical ideas appear within these pre-piano works: the harmonic innovations, rhythmic freedom, experiments with structure, reliance on motives, the evocative sound images, violent contrasts, and literary and poetic allusions. After 1840, Schumann's path led away from the solo piano. Thus the years 1836 to 1840, the crisis years of the courtship of Clara, represent a first and novel peak of creativity. In order to trace the remarkable series of interlocking relations and functions between Clara and Robert which underlay their creative partnership, I shall sketch their developmental highlights and personalities; and in the case of Clara, draw from a fuller psychoanalytic study of her personality.

Childhood of a Virtuoso

Clara Wieck was born into a vocation preassigned by the dominating man of music and business who was her father. Her education was unique; she wrote notes and understood rhythm before reading and writing. Friedrich Wieck was a "progressive" teacher, who suited his practical method to the individual student. In Clara's case, her "ear" was the means of instruction. Wieck composed suitable exercise pieces for his daughter and used her intrinsic pleasure in the music as the reward.

Clara's mother, Marianne, was an accomplished singer who came to study piano and theory with Wieck, and remained to marry him and bear five children. Under his determined tutelage, she became a teacher and keyboard performer in her own right. Thus Clara was surrounded by singing and piano music, with a mother who was always either pregnant, teaching or performing—a pattern of life which she clearly internalized and later followed faithfully.

The calendar of Marianne Wieck's productions of both babies and performances gives "hard" data suggesting a degree of maternal deprivation, especially between the ages of twenty-two and twenty-six months. This age usually sees the rapid development of motor and sphincter control, locomotion, and speech. Clara's development was apparently normal, except for her verbal communication. Even at four, Clara did not seem to understand speech, and her first, indistinct words were uttered well after that.[2] This localized failure in the development of a crucial ego function is presumed by the author to have resulted mainly from separation-individuation difficulties.

Clara's delayed speech has also been attributed to the fact that she was cared for by a taciturn maidservant. Indeed, it is difficult *not* to speculate that association with the silent Johanna favored nonverbal modes of communication, and an inattention to the spoken word. Nonverbal channels for this toddler would have become more significant than for others, carrying life-sustaining and nurturing messages implicit in her mother's music and Johanna's silent modes of child-rearing. Moreover, within the context of the bustling, probably stormy life in the Wieck home, music could provide a safe territory for private recovery and play, while to use words might mean taking sides in a terrible dispute. When Clara finally did speak, it was with and to another child, in a small piano class.

It was interesting to discover, in a special study of Clara Schumann's personality, that in her writings, the metaphoric expressions she employed had mostly to do with conflict over speaking; for example, expressing a sense of wordlessness, or an inability to speak her feelings.[3] Such "speech-inhibited" metaphors occur, from the earliest to the final years, and so regularly as to be characteristic. Furthermore, she often linked by contiguity the idea of being unable to express herself, and the idea of being understood without words. (The reader will note from what follows how these characteristic thoughts corresponded with elements in Schumann's per-

---

[2] This data comes from the first entry in Clara's Diary, written by Friedrich Wieck himself, using the first person, as though impersonating his daughter. The entry also gives a good characterization of Wieck, unblushing in his appropriation of Clara's personality, unempathic, and blunt (Litzmann, 1913, Vol. 1, pp. 1–2).

[3] The psychological significance of an individual's choice of metaphor was demonstrated by Ella Freeman Sharpe, who concluded from clinical observations that metaphor evolves from the displacement of emotions onto perceptions of the body, especially those associated with sphincter control. In adult life, the spontaneous use of a metaphor evokes "the epitome of a forgotten (important) experience," and the study of an individual's metaphors reveals something of her early perceptions of environment and her instinctual tensions. Thus, characteristic choices of metaphor derive from, and indicate the periods of development most fraught with anxiety (Sharpe, 1940).

sonality.) Both ideas appeared in a context of nostalgic reference to a childhood which clearly contained much unhappiness.

We know little of the Wieck home atmosphere, except that it ended in divorce. Clara was permitted one last summer with her mother, and then, at age five, returned to her father to become the object of his career design. The study of Clara Schumann's personality (see chapter 7) shows how she resolved the conflict of loyalties. As a child she became tool and servant to her father—her only viable parent and sole teacher. But he allowed her to compare her repertoire with that of her mother; his general crudeness and lack of empathy were softened in one realm—that of the keyboard. At the piano, Clara could work successfully with her father and express affects pertaining to her earlier experiences with her mother. Apparently she managed an enduring maternal identification centred on music and that which is expressible through music.

Thus Clara identified strongly with a woman who bore children, performed, and had the strength to break away from a dominating, possessive man. The covert identification with her mother became manifest only when Clara broke free of her father at nineteen.[4] Until then her personality was powerfully and overtly marked by her father's characteristics.

Wieck's regimen fostered a new one-to-one relationship of great intensity, since Clara had won an unfortunate oedipal "victory." Not only was she, for several years, the only woman of the house, but she now also occupied the same place in Wieck's musical world from which her mother had fled. Clara's development was thus inescapably funnelled into, and organized around her piano career, with her mother's example and the earlier faulty individuation preparing the way for her father's enthusiastic takeover. This overdetermined identification with Wieck was to color the oedipal issues of Clara Schumann's life.

From the spring of 1830, when Clara was ten-and-a-half years old, for a period of eight years, Wieck toured with his daughter for weeks and months at a time. The letters he sent home to his second wife give a vivid picture of his hypomanic pace, his callousness and adroitness at capitalizing on Clara's budding career. Wieck wrote

---

[4] Clara's identification with her mother was again in evidence years later, when she shouldered the same burdens as Marianne did in her second marriage—caring for an ailing husband and supporting a family through music.

"criticism," collected endorsements, and sold engravings of Clara, and pianos on the side. Once, a damper became stuck and he had to manually depress it, as he wrote, "a few hundred times during the concert." Thus, while Clara played, her father, in effect, functioned as part of her instrument (Wieck, 1830, p. 48). This scene, as depicted by Wieck, is emblematic of their life during those eight years. Through mingling experiences, thoughts and activities in pursuit of one great shared purpose, Clara's tastes, affective style, and priorities were profoundly patterned upon those of her father.

Once, in a rush of narcissistic excitement, Wieck revealed what his daughter signified to him, in these lines: "It cannot be described what a sensation both of the monkeys from the Leipzig menagerie are making here! . . . (people) are too dense . . . ever to conceive what an extraordinary child Clara is, and even less, that your Fritz from Pretzsch possesses and moulds her. . ." (Wieck, 1830, p. 27).

What he had created, he now possessed, and to this Clara raised no objections. She became troubled only when her performances did not measure up to their standard. Apparently Clara functioned as a "phallic extension" of her father and had already begun to personify his ego ideal (a factor of importance in her later relationship with Robert Schumann). She internalized her father's precepts and carried the responsibility for upholding his standards as a teacher. She had also integrated his work attitudes such as moderation, naturalness, and regularity of exercise. Writings by the mature Clara Schumann show a thorough identification with those values pertaining to work and art—such as truthfulness to the spirit of the music, wholeness, good proportion, and the placing of art above material gain. She became, like her father, a resilient and resourceful person. However, in the earning and handling of considerable sums of money, her scrupulousness reflected only the "better" side of her father's character, and though never violent as he sometimes was, she could be harsh in upholding principles, even toward her own children. (Reich has best depicted Clara Schumann as a mother [1985].)

Clara Wieck's personality was relatively insulated against change by her innate gifts, the pattern and deficiencies of her mothering, and intrusive management by her father. Her personality had a fixed, unchanging quality, despite some gains in adolescence. One sees this in Clara Schumann's well-rooted musical life. While she was always eager for new music, whether from Chopin, Schumann,

Mendelssohn, or Brahms, she unfailingly approached it from those interpretive referents learned in childhood. Her tastes changed slowly, and her technic and ideals, virtually not at all. What attracted Robert Schumann then was a young woman who had developed a highly integrated and stable personality, who was not truly autonomous, but who was oriented toward performance, and a performer's version of love, marriage, and motherhood.

THE YOUNG SCHUMANN

Robert Schumann's double gifts in music and literature bloomed early. In contrast to Clara Wieck, Robert was at the other end of the sibling progression, the youngest of five. His father's second career as writer–publisher–bookseller provided Schumann's literary background, and Robert hewed to his father's life pattern, both in the changing of careers, and in his lifelong writing.[5] Schumann's father endorsed his music education, but did not live to complete it, with the result that certain deficiencies remained—deficiencies which drew Robert strongly toward Wieck and his impeccably trained daughter.

Robert's mother was an amateur singer. From their letters, we learn that she knew a great many songs, but was often silenced by depressions. Both mother and son were stricken by the death, first, of Robert's older sister, when he was fifteen, and, a year later, of his father. A guardian arranged with Schumann's mother for Robert to study law.

The correspondence between mother and son, after Robert left home, is expressive and revealing. Typical adolescent conflicts over dependence and shared grandiose plans abound, with transparent oedipal longings. On one vacation, he wrote to his brother (July 18, 1832): "[a] little Italian village fascinated me like an old, old memory. Mother will tell you why. Oh, that Autumn could always be like May, only more mature and beautiful!"

Schumann's Opus 1 (the Abegg Variations) was dedicated to his brothers' wives, and the score was enclosed in a letter to his mother,

---

[5] Even at the last, when he was institutionalized and had deteriorated mentally, Schumann ruminated over anthologies and played with his alphabetical lists. Despite some questions, and apart from his depressive illness, the likeliest explanation of Schumann's organicity and steady decline after the mid-1840s is the diagnosis of general paresis, secondary to syphilis (Slater and Meyer, 1959).

redolent with love-gift and oceanic allusions. Dependent–erotic attachments to older women were characteristic of the young Schumann. Immersing himself in the musical life of Leipzig, especially at the home of Dr. Carus, Robert became close to Carus's attractive and musical wife. Agnus Carus may certainly be classed, along with Robert's beloved sisters-in-law, as a strongly idealized oedipal object. The essence of Robert's relationship toward such idealized female figures appeared in his writings as early as the age of nineteen, as in the following:

> Imagine a perfectly ideal woman, proudly and gracefully curbing a raging panther which she rides in the full consciousness of her beauty and power. The panther seems inclined to resent it, and yet fawningly rubs his head against her hand, while her head is thrown back, and she looks proudly towards heaven. What a beautiful idea it is that beauty can tame everything, even the most savage nature! [May 5, 1829].

It was probably at the Caruses' that Robert had the fateful meeting with the Wiecks. Friedrich Wieck instructed Robert for less than a year, but the eager pupil continued to pursue him through the mails. Particularly drawn to friendships with older men, Robert soon wrote to him at length about his self-doubts, artistic hopes, and beliefs (Schumann, November 6, 1829, December 22, 1837). Thus it was merely one further step in this direction when Wieck was drawn into corresponding with Robert's mother about the critical choice Robert had to make between law and music. Through his bold quarantee to make Robert into a great virtuoso, and his grasp of Robert's somewhat mercurial nature, Wieck assumed the mantle of parental authority.

A six-month trial period followed, during which the discipline and musical regimen of the Wieck home enveloped Robert. He became part of the household, the studies and practice sessions, and he played and wrote exercises together with Clara and other students. Routine daily walks were suited to Robert's sensitivity to the moods of nature, which became the organizing ideas for some of his compositions. After a fiery dispute over switching teachers, Robert knew just how jealous and possessive Clara's father could be. In response, Robert's diary records a kind of filial ambivalence toward Wieck, as well as almost daily entries concerning Clara.

The one-and-a-half years as Clara's fellow-pupil represented almost all of Robert's advanced training—a less complete education than Clara's, of course. Yet Clara's biographers agree that she received from Robert a very special kind of richness. From the very first, these two played at the keyboard, sharing musical ghost stories, fables, and riddles with the light romantic fantasy which was Robert's specialty. He initiated games concerning "doubles"; thus, when Clara was away, their letters would plan for their "doubles" to meet (if each played the same music at an appointed time). Spiritual communion was entirely possible: Robert wrote in January 1832, "I hear music in my dreams—you are composing!" Theirs was a world where the soul could have doubles, and these doubles could form unions with those of other souls. Word- or note-phrases used to exchange such ideas provided a language for shared creative work to come. Robert contributed his consensual modes of perceiving and expressing; his fancies combined words, images, and tones, while his writings intuitively bridged musical and literary ideas.

The novels of Jean Paul, and the plays of E.T.A. Hoffman, with their doubled or split characters, inspired a creative solution to Schumann's need to integrate the various parts of his personality: the feminine and masculine, the literary and the musical, the active and the dreaming. By creating his two personae (as Ostwald has pointed out [1985]), Schumann reified his two opposite self-representations—Florestan, the active, passionate one, and Eusebius, the gentle, feminine dreamer. Robert's circle of friends, including the Wiecks, could then freely interrelate with both "characters." Furthermore, all became figures within Schumann's "Davidsbund": Clara as "Chiarina," Mendelssohn as "Felix Meritas," and Friedrich Wieck as "Meister Raro." Stories by or about "Florestan" and "Eusebius" appeared in the *Neue Zeitschrift für Musik*. Schumann took prime responsibility for the journal after its second year of publication, but he always sought the counsel of Friedrich Wieck. Even three years later, in 1837, he wrote to Wieck: "When I am in full swing, the most I shall ask of you is to put on the curb; when you get excited, I will do the same by you, but if I should grow slack, you must lend me your wings. That is only fair" (p. 208).

"Raro" was Schumann's condensation of the last two letters of Clara's name with the first two of his own. Most significantly, here is an imaginary character whose name "marries" parts of both Clara's and Robert's, and condenses it with the stern and powerful figure of Wieck himself, possessor of wisdom and "superego" attributes.[6] From these data comes the thesis that Wieck played a key role in the late-adolescent development of Robert Schumann's superego and ego ideal, a development which was necessary for his subsequent creative work.

Robert's prolonged and painful late adolescence was marked by periodic depressions. He associated these with a vernal cycle, but also confessed that the absence of Friedrich Wieck rendered him more vulnerable (Schumann, April 28 and May 8, 1832). Another morbid development was the well-known crippling of Schumann's right third finger. According to different theories, this disability may have resulted from self-prescribed overexercise, from trauma, from a pressure-paralysis, or from mercury treatment for syphilis. As different remedies failed, Schumann acknowledged, by degrees, that his virtuoso hopes were ended. The result was a fateful shift: from performer and composer, Schumann became composer and critic. The lost performing career seemed to augment his vicarious pleasure in Clara's steady development, and, if anything, deepened his investment in the person of Friedrich Wieck.

Meanwhile, Robert's letters to the traveling Wieck revealed deep personal curiosity, as he sought points of identification (Schumann, January 11, 1832). Wieck's imprint—his explicit ethic regarding work, discipline, and musical standards—was added to Robert's ideal image, built from memories of his father and figures from literature and music. No matter that Friedrich Wieck often fell short of such ideals in practice; he had succeeded brilliantly in implanting them for life in his daughter. Thus, like so many others, Robert began to idealize the thirteen-year-old artist as a kind of priestess of art.

In this way Clara became both external object and embodiment of an artistic inheritance, endorsed by Robert's own father and transmitted through her father–teacher, encompassing all the great masters whose works she interpreted so beautifully. Representations of Clara and her father affected Schumann's creative process in a formal and profound way. In creative activity with its mingled primary and secondary thought processes, the mental representa-

---

[6] "We were all very anxious to hear Meister Raro's judgment on Chopin, for he is often all too Sebastian Bachish toward young men, and a born enemy of everything half-baked, dull, morbid, aesthetic. He understands how to cool down the spirit without jesting and converts the fire of passion into a holy, clear flame. In short, he hurts us . . ." (Quoted in Reik, 1952, p. 10).

tions of Clara would function as an organizing principle: the ear to which his music was attuned, the instrumental hands, and the listening–judging faculty of their shared traditions.

The complex intertwining of Robert with the two Wiecks is reflected musically in his *Impromptu* based on Clara's theme, and dedicated to Wieck (Litzmann, 1913, Vol. 1, p. 58). How Schumann was drawn from his tie to the father into a more profound relationship with Clara is beautifully expressed in his diary entry of May 3, 1832: "Now I have him back again. Whether this was due to absentmindedness or exhaustion, he appeared weaker to me in every respect than before: only his arrogance, his fire and rolling eye were the same. Clara has become prettier, taller and stronger and easier in her manner . . ." (Quoted in Litzmann, 1913, Vol. 1, pp. 43–44).

Toward the end of 1835, the courtship proper began, with all the tangles and crises that have been chronicled. By far the worst shocks for Robert in this saga came when he faced the shattering of his hopes for Clara and his illusions about her father. His moral bewilderment, the loss of precious guidelines, and the terrible narcissistic blow he sustained, are conveyed in these despairing lines, written to Clara:

> What now, then, what now? . . . In vain I seek for an excuse for your father, whom I have always considered as a noble, humane man . . . believe me, he would throw you to the first comer who had enough money and rank. Beyond this, he has no higher idea than concert-giving and travelling. For this, he saps your life and shatters my strength. . . . Make every effort to find out what has to be done. I will follow like a child. . . . The roots of my life are withered [Quoted in Litzmann, 1913, Vol. 1, pp. 108–109].

Just before another separation, Robert caught a forbidden glimpse of Clara, and wrote her of his "one thought," which he wished "to portray everywhere in great letters and chords" (Quoted in Litzman, 1913, Vol. 1, p. 111). The "one thought" was the echo of his overdetermined dependence on Clara. Robert was holding fast to Clara, to his sense of self-worth, and to the Jovian figure of Wieck. In a letter dated January 2, 1838, he wrote:

> In truth, I have my terrible hours too when even your image forsakes me . . . your father's treatment of me is the cause of all

these questions and doubts. A man easily thinks himself what others think him.... But my turn will come some day—and then he shall see how I love him and you. For, let me whisper it in your ear, I love and honour your father for his many great and noble qualities, as, except for you, no one else can prize him, it is a peculiar, innate attachment on my part, a submission which I feel towards him, as I do towards all energetic natures... [Quoted in Litzmann, 1913, Vol. 1, p. 135].

March 1837 turned rose-colored because Wieck raised false hopes. Schumann's *Novelletten* (op. 21) was written at this time, with its images of Clara and wedding references, as well as the *Kinderscenen* (op. 15). In April, the bubble burst, hopes faded, and Robert confessed to procrastinating and missing a sense of *Clara's* discipline. *Kreisleriana* (op. 16) expressed an opposite mood, with gloomy, bizarre images, associated with angry thoughts. At this juncture, Schumann induced a hallucination of the distant Clara— and then panicked when he "heard" her voice (letter dated April 14, 1838, Quoted in Litzmann, 1913, Vol. 1, p. 154). The episode heralded another full-blown depression.

Schumann's dilemma, during all his courtship years, was that Clara was sometimes far away and sometimes accessible, sometimes incommunicado and sometimes a warm correspondent. He held the claim to her, but could never be sure of the possession. This is poetically rendered in Robert's letter of March 17, 1838:

> As I read your letter..., I feel as the first man may well have felt when his angel led him through the new, young creation, from height to height, where one beautiful view was continually lost in another still more beautiful, and at last the angel said to him: "All this shall be yours." Shall all this be mine? [Quoted in Litzmann, 1913, Vol. 1, pp. 142–143].

Wieck's false hopes, Clara's waverings, and his own despairs, all forced Schumann to summon his reparative functions again and again. He had suffered many losses: a sister, a father, a brother, and sister-in-law. But more pertinent to his composing were the fresh losses of the courtship years, during which he also lost his mother, a second brother, and lived under intermittent threat of losing Clara. These were the conditions during which Robert Schumann created his great early compositions: Clara struggling most intensely to free herself from her father, Robert inhabiting a world in which she was more often a shadow than a real presence, but still his constant preoccupation.

Gradually, Clara's commitment to him deepened; she even made her own independent entries into the *Diary*, and it seemed that Father Wieck was gradually being displaced. From a low point in his self-esteem, Robert revived a bit, and instead of composing, this time, wrote poetry to Clara (Litzmann, 1913, Vol. 1, pp. 173–176). The little verses were inscribed on four tiny pages, decorated with miniature sketches, and both the size and the dedication reveal his self-abnegating, submissive mood. The dedication read: "To Clara from R.S.: To a certain Bride who will have no man in the Twenties for her Husband."

These were the words of a man whose suit is deferred, and who may still be rejected. Of these poems, the first written since his childhood, the first five deal with real frustrations: for two mature people, after years of courtship, waiting any longer might be "fatal." Verses 6 through 9 idealize Clara, and 10 through 12 proclaim her power to uplift his spirits. Thus, verses 6 through 12 pin Robert's hopes for happiness completely on his "Klärchen."

The hostility emerges in verses 13 to 18. "Florestan" is jealous, wild, and threatening at Clara's delays. Unable to integrate "Florestan" and "Eusebius," Robert calls upon Clara to do so for him—to "take them together" or to choose one and disown the other.[7] Then, in the nineteenth verse, Robert reveals that his soul mirrors hers; she may look inside him and find herself—although some parts (his depression and anxiety) he must hide from her. The remaining verses express his attempt at resolution and restored confidence.

These poems, while never as evocative or powerful as Schumann's music, add the specificity of words to our understanding of his inner world, as the tide turned in his courtship of Clara Wieck. For despite the pitfalls yet to appear, their marriage was now inevitable.

---

[7] Verse 16: "Jealous in truth is Florestan, Eusebius trusts in his brother-man. Which of the twain shall be dearest to thee? Who most true to himself and his love shall be."

[7] Verse 18: "Then lead we thee with pageant to the throne. And humbly take our place on either side. If one of us thou'rt ready to disown, Will a like fate the other too, betide?"

An Analysis of the Creative Partnership

It was the intrinsic drama of the Clara–Robert story which originally suggested the term *creative partnership*. Such a partnership can be conceptualized on several levels. First of all, it rests on a functioning relationship in the real, external world (which may be termed "object-relatedness"). Second, the inner worlds of Robert and Clara were in resonance through the strong, elaborated mental representations each had of the other. Mental representations, being complex entities which incorporate elements of ego and superego functioning, by the same token must contribute to the expression of ego and superego functions. Thus there is a third and "deepest" level of the creative partnership: through the process of internalization, change may be effected in personality structure.

Surveying the real-world partnership, the reader has already seen an array of forces uniting these two people. To begin with, the reciprocal of Clara Wieck's trouble with spoken language was her remarkable natural access to the "language" of music. Although her father understood that language, he spoke it but poorly. Hence it was Robert Schumann who could express Clara's feelings at the piano just as she did, inaugurating their communicating partnership. Over a period which lasted some sixty-six years, Clara became his link to the public, as well as to students of the piano. A perusal of her letters, notably those of August 30 and November 25, 1938, shows that this activity was no less than her basic emotional sustenance; and further, that she regarded Robert's music as their exclusive domain, which she disliked sharing even with the musical elite (Litzmann, 1913, Vol. 1, pp. 160, 172). Exclusivity, even elitism, was characteristic of Robert as well. (This may also have been a rationale for his wish to retire from company, for in later years he evinced a pathological, near-mute withdrawal.)

The pragmatic aspects of Clara's role have been abundantly documented by Reich, who described her knowledge of audiences and her exquisite caution in presenting the works of Robert Schumann (Reich, 1985, chapter 12). In keeping with the family experience as oldest and most important child, Clara naturally supplied an energetic, practical direction to Robert, a last-born child who by his own admission was somewhat passive and indulged (Litzmann, 1902–1908, Vol. 1, p. 355). Finally, their functional "fit," with the keyboard forming the linking element, was cemented when Robert had to give up performing and Clara put off serious attempts to compose. These crucial choices minimized their competition and oriented them in complementary roles.

The foregoing describes object-relatedness in the external world. Within the representational world Robert's relationships with objects have been demonstrated in his visual, verbal, and musical images. We have seen how musical representations of Clara permeated the content of Robert's works, becoming fragmented, varied, reversed, and gradually integrated into Schumann's composing and writing style. Schumann wrote (March 19, 1838) that he could not correspond with Clara in writing, and at the same time, compose; one mode displaced the other (Schumann, March 19, 1838, quoted in Litzmann, Vol. 1, p. 146). But whether through letters or notes, they enjoyed a complete dialogue, made possible by a shared musical heritage, Wieck's training, and by Clara's full initiation into Schumann's poetic fantasies, consensual ideas, and new musical vocabulary. After his finger injury, another "Clara" representation was that of Robert's "right hand" (Ostwald, 1980). This apt metaphor introduces the important concept of Clara as Robert's chief executant, to whom he passed more and more responsibilities as the years passed. Frequent references to Clara as a deity or priestess signify unmistakable superego attributes. Robert wrote to her: "I am up early generally before 6 o'clock; those are my most sacred hours. My room has now become a proper chapel, the piano an organ, and your portrait—that is now the altar-piece" (Quoted in Litzmann, 1913, Vol. 1, p. 145).

When Robert was in creative ferment, additional representations of Clara as a child, mother, and lover occurred, and were sometimes expressed through simultaneous or superimposed images. The same redundancy of Clara-images appears in his writings, where she was variously "Chiarina," "Zilia," and "Beda" in the essays, while in his diary and letters appear a whole series of less well-defined representations. Suffused with the memories of his years with Wieck, these references seem to elaborate multiple symbolic meanings. Applying the widest definition of the concept of mental representation, Clara personified their art in a letter dated March 19, 1838: "for in you everything harmonizes, so that I cannot think of you without your art—and I love one thing with another" (Quoted in Litzmann, 1913, Vol. 1, p. 146). Finally, Schumann's small verses of 1839 frankly assign Clara the task of integrating his warring self-divisions, so that his soul might then mirror hers. By the same token, Clara Wieck was drawn through close empathy to regard herself as Robert did, in his glowing letters and in the Davidsbund fantasies. These colored her own self-representations and added to her identifications with mother and father, influencing her personality in many ways (discussed in chapter 7). Such mutually profound influences are the more comprehensible if one recognizes that despite their nine-year difference in age, Robert and Clara were each passing through an adolescence at the same time.

Having reviewed the functional relationship in the real world, and indicated how, through mental representations of each other, each served multiple functions within the other's psychic apparatus, we should now consider whether this creative partnership also involved true internalizations, which by definition imply some change in psychic structure. Since this conceptualizing aspires to a higher level of abstraction (and in any case, lacks the supporting first-hand data of an ongoing transference analysis), the only approach is to judge how the principles of developmental psychoanalysis contribute usefully to this material.

It is understood that the dynamic unconscious operates with and between endopsychic objects, "virtual" rather than "real," and that psychic structure is shaped with reference to the early object relationships. Conscious and unconscious fantasies develop, involving these love-objects, and these fantasies serve to organize and fix the personality. In the case of artists, there seems to be a special openness, or delayed closure of personality structure, so that it continues to resonate with and be contoured by later self and object relationships. (Many artists have subjectively recognized this aspect of themselves.)

Schumann's creativity took place "within" his particular psychic structure, of which each part was to some degree marked by his relationship with Clara, and through her, with her father. His record, like that of a psychoanalysis, is a reverberating network of conflictual dyadic and triadic attachments. The most conspicuous of these attachments are in the domain of the Oedipus complex, in both its positive and negative forms. The "Florestan" part of Robert's nature—masculine, energetic, and exhibitionistic—pursued Clara with ardor, as the idealized but forbidden woman, whom he wished to possess completely. (He enlisted intermediaries to keep his presence alive with her, and when the two met secretly in

Leipzig, using prearranged signals and romantic conspiracies, he utilized every doorway on the streets for stolen kisses.) As his beloved became more attainable, Robert assumed quite seriously the role of her teacher and father. As Robert saw it in a letter dated June 3, 1839: "With my gentle manner, [I] early made an impression on you, and I think you would have been a different girl if you had never seen and known me. Let me be happy in the belief that I have taught you love, your father, hate. (I mean it in the best sense, for one must know how to hate.)" (Litzmann, 1913, Vol. 1, p. 337).

With respect to his own music, he tried to set standards for her and even, in letters dated March 11 and December 16, 1839, addressed himself to her self-importance, with a mild lecture (Schumann, 1839). Thus he prepared himself as husband and head of household through identifying with her father, as well as his own. Viewed from her end of the growing tie between them, Robert possessed the luster of greater knowledge of music, literature, worldly affairs, and, of course, sexual matters. In the courtship, he became her new authority and the male whom she would now strive to please. (On one occasion he even served as her therapist by successfully interpreting Clara's performance anxiety.) (Litzmann, 1913, Vol. 1, pp. 271–274).

Corresponding with Schumann's strikingly bisexual identifications, Clara signified to him both positive and negative oedipal object. The first glimpse of "Eusebius," the passive–homosexual side of Robert's personality, occurs in the adolescent Schumann's description of the "panther-tamer" as his phallic-feminine ideal (see above). This gentle "Eusebius" personality was deeply harmonious with Clara's strong and active qualities. As has been seen, Robert was acquiring a young woman who had developed as a phallic extension as well as representative of her teacher–father. She had adapted to quasi-symbiotic union with such a man—a union almost physical at times (such as on the occasion cited above, of the defective concert piano). Her phallic qualities were her connection with Wieck, her own perseverance and formidable achievements, and the indispensable position she assumed as Schumann's musical representative. Robert's attachment to Clara was forged, then, through both heterosexual and homosexual emotional links—the latter only dimly conscious with respect to Wieck, and unconscious concerning that aspect of Clara which would forever reflect and transmit the Wieckian influence to Robert.

An equally strong binding force between these two was their reciprocal parent–child relationship. While one reason for Robert's persistent pull toward Clara was his need for her father, a second reason was that Clara became the object of displacement of Robert's deep bond with his mother. Clara understood this very early and responded maternally to the same narcissistically tinged needs which had tied Robert to his sisters-in-law. He had clearly "replaced" his mother with Clara when he visited her in avoidance of his mother's funeral, and he did the same metaphorically in his letters. For example, to Clara's suggestion, on November 13, 1838, that they should wait another six months to marry, Robert reacted in the metaphor of a disappointed child protesting to a cruel parent:

> Clärchen, what would you call parents who promise their children a tree and beautiful presents for Christmas, and then on Christmas Eve lead the children into a dark room and lock them in? See—that is what you have done to me; you promised me a reward if I conducted myself well, and then you put me off to an indefinite time, till 1850 or -60 when I shall long have been lying in my grave [Quoted in Litzmann, 1913, Vol. 1, p. 170].

Thus we may recognize a double dependence in Robert, for whom the figure of Clara represented both mother and father. The intensity of this overdetermined need is conveyed by Schumann's plea, written on the reverse side of one of Clara's clandestine letters to him: "Do not abandon me, you who are like no other girl. I cling to you with all my strength; if you give way I am done for!" (Quoted in Litzmann, 1913 Vol. 1, p. 108).

It is interesting that while both Clara and Robert were specially endowed, their narcissistic lines of development differed. Clara was largely free of conflict over her developing fame, her self-esteem resting securely on her supreme ability to fulfill her father's aims. That Robert was a great composer himself was another article of faith for her, and she was vicariously gratified by identifying with his music and becoming its "official" interpreter. Through many hardships, Clara did not lose her self-esteem; on the contrary, her self-therapy for depressed moments was to rededicate herself to her music.

Schumann's narcissistic balance, on the other hand, was always at risk. He had been a precocious youngster who attracted attention. The *Early Letters* display charm, easy success, and feelings of entitlement. Robert's personal goals then were originality, versatility, and hedonism, and the great attraction of Friedrich Wieck for Robert was largely the promise of fame as a virtuoso. (How dashed Robert felt when the teacher demoted him to basic finger exercises!) Schumann's self-esteem soared and crashed repeatedly with his cyclic depressions, and at least up to his thirtieth year, his spirits remained partly dependent on external reassurances.

On the more positive side, during Schumann's twenties, he carried through three achievements which were to prove firm foundations for his self-respect. These were the great piano compositions, the founding and editorship of the *Neue Zeitschrift*, and the alliance with Clara Wieck.

THE WANING OF THE CREATIVE PARTNERSHIP

The year 1840 brought the promise of marriage, and with it subtle transformations which changed and all but disrupted the uniquely creative relationship between Clara and Robert. Clara's waves of old loyalty and affection for her father were repeatedly dashed by Wieck's adamant refusals, so that her investment in Robert deepened. But Robert's vulnerability was alarming. Her dazzling successes, her doubts, and her occasional small thrusts at him set off anxious depressions, with somatic symptoms and feelings of guilt. Clara's father issued a slanderous "Declaration" which left him unmanned by its virulence and by the public loss of Wieck's regard. Schumann's "ferocious apathy," as he called it, had consumed the autumn of 1839, while Clara also developed symptoms over rupturing the union with her father. Help came from two sources. One was Clara's mother, whose Berlin home was a warm haven for the couple. The other was the upswing in Robert's mood (in February of 1840), when he finally took legal action against the slander.

In the same upsurge of energy, Schumann began a new kind of composing. The same letter which told Clara how he was striking back, contained the announcement that he now wrote songs! There was a tremendous emotional outpouring in these songs. Short and relatively simple, they intertwined the keyboard and voice in original ways. Schumann wrote in a letter of February 24, 1840:

> I cannot tell you how easily all this has come to me, and how much
> I enjoyed doing it. As a rule I compose them [songs] standing or

walking *not at the piano*. It is quite a different sort of music, *which does not come first through the fingers*—much more direct and melodious . . . [Quoted in Litzmann, 1913, Vol. 1, p. 280; emphasis added].

Thus, at the finale of the courtship period, there were two simultaneous developments: Robert's anger finally emerged into action, and he turned away from piano compositions toward song. With two "instruments," piano and voice, his world now exceeded the keyboard—the latter forever associated with the figures of Clara and Friedrich Wieck. The turn to songs may in part reflect Schumann's hard-won ability to go on living and creating without Wieck. It might also be viewed as another creative doubling, analagous to the birth of Florestan and Eusebius, or, from the more distant past, the songs of Robert's mother may be resounding in these pieces. Whatever forces produced this change, Schumann considered it vital for himself, as well as for other young composers, to whom he offered the same prescription—namely, to compose *away from the keyboard* (Schumann, 1846, in May, 1988, Vol. 2, p. 49).

The songs were largely addressed to Clara, and refer to the mixed emotions of the courtship period. While there are covert outlines of Clara, both in "her" motto-themes, and in the evocative, somewhat dominant part played by the piano, something significant has changed with the addition of the voice. The first sharing was at the keyboard. With physical union approaching, by adding the voice, Schumann obtained a kind of psychic "privacy," a new psychological distance between the mental representations of himself and Clara. I believe that Schumann's overflowing "Year of Song" represented his thrust toward individuation and differentiation from Clara, in the twilight of their true creative partnership. It was never recaptured; once married, and in the physical and mental struggles of later years, Clara figured intimately in all aspects of Robert's life *except* his composing.

To take some perspective on the relationship here called "creative partnership," one must first note its fortuitous occurrence in the Romantic period. This may be a phenomenon which is possible only within an ethereal, mystical–magical cultural atmosphere. Second, one asks, what can such an intertwining of personalities tell us about creativity? Only the following: that for Robert Schumann, the interaction with Clara Wieck in his twenties provided him with qualities of integration, and purpose, and released his flow of affective expression. Just as the complexities of Schumann's personality may be sensed as they reveal themselves in his music, the psychoanalytic approach is supremely oriented toward the appreciation of such complexities and prepared to address them without closure. Psychoanalytic theory continues to develop, from topographic, to structural, and further to poststructural concepts, some of which may be well-suited to pursue the analysis of creativity. However, that too belongs to another chapter.

Chapter 22
On Falling in Love: The Mystery of Tristan and Isolde

Richard D. Chessick, M.D., Ph.D.

[for Joy]

> The queen, for her part, all that evening ached
> With longing that her heart's blood fed, a wound
> Or inward fire eating her away.
> The manhood of the man, his pride of birth,
> Came home to her time and again; his looks,
> His words remained with her to haunt her mind,
> And desire for him gave her no rest.
>
> Virgil, *Aeneid* (trans. Fitzgerald, 1983, p. 95)

In a previous publication (1983b), I discussed *The Ring of the Niebelung* as representing Wagner's projected dream of preoedipal destruction, and I argued that in the character of Wotan it presents a classical dramatic example of what Kohut (1977) called tragic man in middle age, a man whose narcissistic dreams are turning to ashes and who is left all by himself as even his children mature and attempt to separate from him. Utilizing object-relations theory I tried to establish that the host of extreme and sometimes grotesque characters in the *Ring* represent split-off images of archaic aspects from within Wagner's unconscious that kept him boiling in an unresolved intrapsychic chaos. As in the drama of the *Ring*, for Wagner only death could finally terminate the situation and bring peace.

In the middle of writing the four long operas of the *Ring*, Wagner became increasingly dissatisfied with his life and inclined to turn more and more inward. By 1855 he had completed the full score of Acts I and II of *Die Walküre*, and in September of 1856 he began work upon *Siegfried*, making good progress, and confident that he would complete the entire *Ring* by 1858. However, in June of 1857 he informed Liszt that he would embark upon the composition of *Tristan und Isolde*, and so in that year he abandoned the

Ring and turned to the *Tristan* subject (Newman, 1933). He was forty-four years old at the time, and the precipitant of his sudden abandonment of the *Ring* project superficially appeared to be his excited reading of Schopenhauer's *The World as Will and Idea*. In 1857 he drafted the actual poem that was to become the libretto of *Tristan*, but already in 1854 he came under the spell of the Celtic legend of *Tristan and Isolda*, most probably through the translation by Herman Kurtz, published in 1844, of Gottfried von Strassburg's thirteenth-century epic.

Although his reading of Schopenhauer is often credited for the composition of *Tristan*, it is clear from a study of various biographical works (Newman, 1933; Taylor, 1979; Watson, 1979; Westernhagen, 1981) and of the opera itself that reading Schopenhauer merely brought him to a crystallization of a philosophy already latent in him. The philosophy manifest in *Tristan und Isolde* is quite different than that of Schopenhauer; in fact I am convinced that Schopenhauer would have scoffed at it. In 1859 a copy of the dramatic libretto of *Tristan* written by Wagner was sent to Schopenhauer, but the reactions of the nearly seventy-year-old philosopher to it are not known.

In this paper I will attempt to describe and to understand what Wagner was trying to express in an extraordinary work of art and quite possibly the greatest opera ever written. This portrayal has important clinical implications, for it presents the breaking forth of powerful longings that sweep away all the civilized and social restrictions of ordinary human existence, and bring about the destruction of both of the lovers—a destruction which throughout the opera they both actually long for. Only those who have experienced such powerful longings, either in themselves or empathically through others in clinical work, can understand the intensity of such passion when it breaks forth, and can empathize with the plight of the individual who becomes demoniacally held in an almost unbearable obsession. First I will present the manifest material of Wagner's opera and the philosophy it expresses; then I will discuss the deeper philosophical, psychoanalytic, and special clinical implications.

PRESENTATION

Holmberg (1983) argues that Wagner tried to save men from the self-seeking, self-destructive materialism of the nineteenth century; he viewed art as a substitute religion and the theater as its temple. Through his work he attempted to negate reason and science by turning to legends, myths, and dreams because he believed that intuition, imagination, and emotion would save man. In attempting to use art to probe the unconscious he stood between Schopenhauer and Freud. He restored seriousness of purpose to nineteenth-century drama, and for this reason he stands beside Ibsen, Strindberg, and Chekhov.

In this opera Wagner replaced plot with mood; he claimed that he wanted to uncover what is the most hidden in the heart of man. *Tristan und Isolde* is a drama of the soul, a theater of inner states. Wagner turned a romantic legend into an existential fable, not only about intimacy and love, but also about isolation and alienation.

Each act of the opera begins with anticipation, is followed by union, and ends with separation due to the brutal intrusion of the external world. Each act begins with a symbol; the sailor's song in the first act, Brangäne's torch in the second act, and the doleful tune of the shepherd in the third act. Each symbol is then, according to Westernhagen (1981), transposed onto a psychological and metaphysical plane through the music and libretto.

Wagner reduces a sprawling medieval narration of courtly love into an emotionally packed and condensed human situation, in which he selects only those moments that he needs in order to portray the internalized drama inside the souls of Tristan and Isolde.

Act I catches the ebb and flow of Isolde's shifting emotional states and shows both Tristan and Isolde unbearably tormented and internally torn up by their concepts of duty and social obligations which force them to be untrue to themselves. This act anticipates Freud's (1930) discussion of the malaise inherent in civilization in *Civilization and Its Discontents*, and it ends with the external symbol of the love potion—which dramatizes the explosion of their emotions and the consequent shattering of social responsibility and cultural facade.

The second act centers around the intense contrast between Schopenhauer's famous symbols of Night and Day. Day stands for the world of reason, society, and the socialized individual, a world that Tristan, like Nietzsche (Chessick, 1983a), recognizes as meaningless illusion. Night stands for the transcendent realm of Truth, accompanied by a state of mystical union and ecstasy that remains throughout the central issue of the opera.

The final act centers on the conflict between life and death, foreshadowing Freud's (1930) "battle of the giants"—Eros versus Thanatos. It is commonplace among interpreters to point out that this yearning of Tristan and Isolde represents an attempt to re-fuse with the mother, producing the so-called oceanic state suggested by Isolde's final "transfiguration" in the opera:

In the surging swell
In the ringing sound,
In the vast wave
Of the world's breath—
To drown,
To sink
Unconscious—
Supreme bliss [Salter, 1982].

The other central imagery of the opera emphasized by Holmberg (1983) is that of the wound. In Act I we are told how Tristan's wound brought them together and how while tending his physical wound Isolde inflicted a second psychological wound—the joy and pain of love—on both of them; the wound comes to symbolize the fundamental isolation of the individual and the only cure is to lose the self in the bliss of union. In Wagner's tortured mind, death for Tristan and Isolde is not the end but a liberation and a transformation to a higher state of being. Holmberg (1983) writes: "Isolde's transfiguration is both the most sensuous and most spiritual moment in all western drama. The flood of erotic energy released by the relentlessly building rhythms underscores the interpenetration of the sexual and the sacred—not unlike Saint Theresa of Avila's description of the mystical union" (p. 9).

This is *not* the Schopenhauer doctrine, and furthermore, Schopenhauer never believed one could find happiness with one woman only. It is common knowledge that Wagner's drama reflects his unfulfilled love for one Mathilde Wesendonk whom he idealized after they met in Zurich in 1852; but it was in 1857 that their relationship reached a peak. She was married and although she appreciated his genius she did not yield to his importunities and kept her husband fully informed. It was to Mathilde that he wrote the famous letter enclosed with the first composition sketch of the *Tristan* prelude, presented to Mathilde in celebration of the completion of Act I. This letter—I suspect due to no accident—was left in an exposed situation so that Wagner's wife opened and read it, causing a domestic explosion. Watson (1979) gives a quotation from the letter: "When this marvellous, holy glance rests upon me then everything becomes so indisputably true to me, I am so sure of myself, and I submerge myself within it. Then there is no longer any object or subject; then everything is one, united, deep, infinite harmony! Oh, that is peace, and in that peace the highest most perfect life!" (p. 154).

Wagner clearly agreed with Schopenhauer's pessimistic view of existence (Lüthi, 1982), in which the urgent passions of love and the will to live create nothing but torment, and life on earth becomes a sea of suffering. Thus the secular world loses its worth and denies fulfillment to mortals. Wagner differs from Schopenhauer in that he did not follow the Schopenhauerian solution of renouncing desire and settling into the calm of resignation—neither did Schopenhauer! Wagner produced a neurotic religion of death, in which a triumph of love brings the lovers into a mystical union in the other realm of eternal Night. In the Day world, however, the individual is isolated by its very worthlessness, a common theme in the arts of the second half of the nineteenth century (Maehder, 1982), and death represents for Wagner a release in spiritual union. This theme has often been mentioned in the psychiatric literature as a motivation for suicide in which there is the hidden fantasy of reunion with the mother in heaven. I have discussed this Wagnerian concept in the *Ring* dramas also (1983b); there Wagner portrays the price of growth and maturation as death—again a mystical overvaluation or romanticizing of death peculiar to Wagner and not found in Schopenhauer.

A prevailing, subsequent confusion was introduced by the later erroneous labeling of Isolde's final magnificent aria at the end of the opera as the *Liebestod*; it is actually properly called her "transfiguration" and was so specifically designated by Wagner. It is the Prelude to the opera that is the *Liebestod*, with the drama opening in a situation where they are separated and dying in psychic pain from their separation. The entire opera is subject to an amazing number of orchestral interpretations, varying from conductor to conductor, across a range from those who like Bernstein (Phillips) stress the theme of resignation, or those who like Kleiber (D.G.G.) stress the intense drive of the passions. I was fascinated in a study of all the available recordings by the correlation between the age of the conductor and the interpretations. In general, the older maestros slow the pace and emphasize the resignation and suffering while the younger ones dramatize the tension and longing. Watson (1979) writes that, "The extremely chromatic harmony of *Tristan* gave to Western culture a new concept of musical language, expression and tonality" (p. 149). Westernhagen (1981, p. 237) points out that the famous *Tristan* chord, the first chord of the Prelude, is already found in the Andante of Bach's A Minor violin concerto and in the Andante of Mozart's E Flat Major Quartet. What was new was the elevation of this famous chord and the chromaticism into forming a principle of an entire musical work on a large scale. The chord provides an inner dynamic which sweeps the music on from tension to relaxation to renewed tension.

Taylor (1979) quotes Wagner in his diary as writing, "What music this is going to be! I could spend my entire life just working on this music, so profound, so beautiful will it be! Never before have I done anything like this; I am totally immersed in this music, and I do not want to hear anyone else ask me when it will be finished. I shall live in this music eternally" (p. 136).

Taylor (1979) stresses the issue of responsibility and choice on which the actual drama rests. The loneliness and the isolation of the pair arise from the fact that they know they are betraying King Mark and that there can be no happy resolution: "they are human beings in a human context, gripped by passion and an awareness of guilt, by the consummation of their bliss and their agony of conscience, with no gods or supernatural spirits either to appeal to or to be judged by" (p. 137). At the basis of this longing, Wagner wrote, is the framework of sex. He explains, "The most vital human love is possible only between man and woman; all other love is merely a result, a derivate or an imitation of sexual love" (Taylor, 1979, p. 137).

For Wagner the opera represented a triumphant victory of art over life; the love between Wagner and Mathilde Wesendonk was doomed from the beginning, but in the music and the resolution of *Tristan und Isolde*, the passion is triumphant. The heart of the action and the meaning of the opera lies in the music which Taylor describes as, "Music of a kind the world had never heard, a profound disturbing music which carries the psychological movement of the work and the pessimistic fatalism of its immoral passion" (p. 138). In order to be more specific he explains:

What happens in the score of *Tristan* is something that had never happened in music before. The action and meaning of the drama are enmeshed in the web of the orchestral score. And as the lovers' passion is immoral, their self-absorption is so complete, their anguish so intense—does *passio* not mean suffering?—And their tragic fate so inescapable, so the music rests on ambiguous harmonies, half-resolved dissonances, interrupted cadences, long, soaring melodic arcs, dense orchestral textures, a ceaseless flowing, inward-looking music that expresses the ebb and flow of desire and its consummation in death [p. 138].

DISCUSSION

What do Tristan and Isolde really want? The opera idealizes death and shows how a sexualized passion can transcend all and sweep away the rules and regulations of this world as symbolized by the realm of Day. The music and the libretto are submerged in Schopenhauerian gloom and hopeless desire, and the opera attempts to explore a mysterious realm of darkness beyond everyday reality.

But death solves nothing, it just ends it all. This would even be the argument of Schopenhauer against Wagner. The power of longing produces an unusual state, abnormal in intensity, breaks loose, and destroys the bonds of civilized life. Where does this come from? Is this "beyond the pleasure principle" (Freud)? Is it "beyond good and evil" (Nietzsche)? Is death the ultimate end? Wagner's religion of death was clearly a failure and nobody followed it, but what is his art pointing to?

A PARALLEL FROM LITERATURE

Thomas Hardy (1897) claims in *The Well-Beloved*, his last novel, that this falling in love, what he describes as a state of being "powerless in the grasp of the idealizing passion" (p. 121) tends to occur not less after youth as popularly believed, but sometimes even more frequently in the third, fourth, and fifth decades of life. Only the aging process, in which some individuals sooner, and some later, reach "the calm waters of philosophy," puts an end to these episodes. So Hardy's protagonist in his sixties can finally relax with a sigh, "Thank Heaven I am old at last. The curse is removed" (p. 202). All of Hardy's novels explore this common but perplexing human paradox: with the painful desire and perpetual dissatisfaction that love brings as well as the genuine suffering it often entails, why do humans keep repeating this pattern, bringing unhappiness upon themselves and others?

The Well-Beloved portrays the curious correlation, also illustrated in the life of Wagner, between the capacity for falling in love and the capacity for artistic creativity. For Hardy's protagonist there is a wraith, a "migratory Well-Beloved" that represents a "sisterly-image" which invests one loved woman after another; when it leaves that person the love for her disappears and she is abruptly abandoned. In Hardy's extreme example we are presented with a rather clear example of Freud's (1914b) notion of narcissistic object choice, fused with brother-sister twinship incestuous desires, very similar to the love of the Volsungs Siegmund and Sieglinde in Wagner's *Die Walküre*. Thus, at the end of Act I:

Sieglinde: Are you Siegmund whom I see here?
I am Sieglinde who longed for you:
your own sister
you have won and the sword as well.

Siegmund: Wife and sister you'll be to your brother.
So let the Volsung blood increase [Mann, 1981].

In a remarkable article Updike (1963) discusses the work of Denis De Rougemont, the Swiss theologian and essayist best known as the author of *Love in the Western World* (1983). The argument of De Rougemont is that Tristan and Isolde are in love not with one another but with love itself, with their "being in love." Updike quotes De Rougemont's famous conclusion: "Their unhappiness thus originates in a false reciprocity, which disguises a twin narcissism" (p. 52). He outlines De Rougemont's elaboration of the Tristan and Isolde legend from a passionate love story into a struggle between feudal honor and unlimited passion. On this is based De Rougemont's main thesis, describing an inescapable conflict in the West between passion and marriage. He writes, "passion and marriage are essentially irreconcilable. Their origins and their ends make them mutually exclusive" (p. 277). Updike strongly disagrees with De Rougemont in a splendid literary argument too long to reproduce in this paper. The same issues have been raised in a recent novel, *Love in the Time of Cholera*, by Garciá Márquez (1988).

Psychoanalytic Contributions

Bak (1973) suggests that "being in love" is often preceded by separation or by an important object loss—real, imaginary, or threatened—"or by one of the numerous losses of object representations that lead to melancholia" (p. 1). He adds, "To these precipitating causes I might add damage to the self image and lack of fulfilment of strivings of the ideal-ego which indirectly lead to the threat of object loss" (p. 1). For Bak, "being in love" is a way of avoiding melancholia on the one hand or a regression to narcissism on the other, by means of finding a substitute object in order to undo the loss. He points out the well-known theme in history and literature where attempts to substitute another love object prove unsuccessful and the lover develops acute melancholia and even commits suicide.

The state of "being in love" emphasizes the irrational, stormy, emotional turmoil or grand passion such as that of Goethe's (1774) Werther, whose sufferings are described in a literary masterpiece. This is distinguished by Freud (for a review of Freud's comments on love see Bergmann [1980]) from the "epic" phase of love which is calmer, more rational, and durable, what we usually call mature genital object relations. Being in love, or falling in love, with its characteristic sexual overvaluation of the object is conceived by Bak (1973) as based on an attempt to undo the separation of the mother and child.

Chasseguet-Smirgel (1985) describes the "malady of the ideal" as the "*primum movens*" of psychic life. She postulates that when the infant comes to realize that the narcissistic state of perfection is impossible it sets up an image of such perfection in the ego ideal, as described by Freud. The ego ideal becomes a substitute for the lost object of primary fusion and all human beings spend the rest of their lives trying to bridge the gap between the ego and the ego ideal, in order to reinstate this primary fusion with the mother. This "malady of the ideal" becomes a central impetus for all the activities of the person, accompanied by a nostalgia for a lost state of perfection. When the person falls in love, at least at first, contrary to Freud's contention that the ego is impoverished, the radiance of the ego ideal falls on the ego, so that the first moments of love "are full of exalted joy, of an expansiveness of the ego" (p. 55). The possibility of a fusion of the two agencies produces a range of phenomena of "the ephemeral plunge into the world of primary narcissism" (p. 56), often experienced as a blinding light, a thunderbolt, and so on, magnificently portrayed by Wagner just after Tristan and Isolde drink the love potion.

Werman and Jacobs (1983), in discussing Hardy's *The Well-Beloved*, point out that although "infatuation" is common, the psychoanalytic literature pertaining to it is relatively limited. They conceive of it as "a final common pathway, arising from multiple sources and consequently having different aims" (p. 456). Thus we should avoid any simplistic interpretation of a legend with so many versions (Gediman, 1981) as the Tristan and Isolde story. Furthermore the pathological, shifting, repetitive, and compulsive "infatuations" of Hardy's protagonist are of a phenomenologically different quality than the existential, deep, profound, and unique episode of "falling in love," as Freud (1914b) called it, that overwhelmed Tristan and Isolde.

Arlow (1980) claims that "there is no clear delineation of any specific syndrome which we call loving or being in love" (p. 122). He objects to those authors (such as Bak [1973] or Bergmann [1980]) who try to trace the psychology of loving to the wish to reachieve symbiotic fusion with the mother in order to undo primordial separation. He points out that "Cultural ambience influences not only how love is expressed, but also how it is experienced" (p. 129), and that love relations integrate complex needs of individuals at a given time, so that "what happens is determined by the nature of the unconscious conflict which the individual is trying to resolve at that particular time of life" (p. 128). He reminds us that in the "oceanic feeling," or the sense of total fusion with the beloved often described by poets in the ecstasy of love, there is still a "concomitant awareness of the existence of the other person as an independent object" (p. 119).

Gediman (1975) reminds us that certain people who fall romantically in love are also capable of enduring object love, and she maintains that Kohut's (1971) position of a separate narcissistic developmental line which is never outgrown but rather transformed, rather neatly helps to explain this fact. In addition she reminds us of Kohut's comment that for the average individual, idealization as a transitional point in the development of narcissistic libido survives only in the state of being in love. Kohut adds that the gifted individual idealizes and despairs about his or her creative work as well, so for the creator, his or her work is a transitional object invested with transitional narcissistic libido (Kohut, 1966, p. 261).

Gediman draws a parallel between the twin narcissism (De Rougemont) of lovers like Tristan and Isolde, and the narcissistic elements in the core of the artist's fantasies, which are projected onto the image of an empathic, sometimes adoring audience. She sees the narcissism of Tristan and Isolde more in line with the view of Updike—which is less pejorative about passion than that of De Rougemont—and, shifting back to the classical Freudian interpretation, she interprets twin narcissism as "a term for fusion of self and object which is evocative of an early ego state common both to lovers and some creative artists" (p. 411).

Bergmann (1980) maintains that a thorough understanding of love requires (1) illumination of falling in love as a special ego state; (2) solving the problem of why a particular person is selected as a love object; and (3) explaining the capacity to maintain a sustained love relationship with one person over a long period of time, "with fidelity, maturity, and a preponderance of love over envy and aggression in the relationship" (p. 57). He also interprets falling or "being in love" as a temporary undoing of separation and individuation, and finding a way back to a state of bliss known before individuation—which he postulates to be the feeling state of the symbiotic stage.

Gediman (1981) like Arlow (1980) warns that this type of interpretation is to commit the genetic fallacy, explaining all facets of complex adult patterns of love as derivatives of impressions of the earliest infantile state and of universal fantasies. She makes the most careful analysis available of the various versions of the Tristan and Isolde myth with particular emphasis on the *liebestod* motif. Certainly Tristan and Isolde each form a selfobject for the other. She concludes:

> The "exquisite anguish" in the yielding swoon of the lovers casts its spell because it is evocative not only of sexual passion, but also of the early ego state of fusion and merging. . . . In this way, I find it useful to view the rhythms of parting and coming together, the theme of all courtly myths, as derivatives of the rapprochement rhythms of establishing distance between two people, both literally and intrapsychically [p. 620].

The common oedipal interpretation of this opera involving

Tristan, Isolde, and King Mark, seems weak and contrived. The story is not primarily sexual or triadic, and sex here is manifestly just a vehicle of preoedipal union. Could it represent, as many commentators have said, and consistent with some of the authors quoted above, a preoedipal union with the mother—a dyadic relationship? The libretto of the drama, when carefully studied, is dyadic and symbiotic over and over again. This is especially true of the second act, in which the language is almost unintelligible and "who is saying what" is so blurred together in the mystical union that only the music carries the message. It is clear that such longing is regressive when it appears and represents a turning of one's back on the frustrating world of Day. But Tristan is successful and well thought of by everyone; he is a worldly hero and a mature man. The only latent dynamite is that his needs have always been subordinated to his sense of duty throughout his adult life even long before the opera opens.

Tristan und Isolde in one sense is a paean to the power of the instincts but notice that *both* Tristan and Isolde seek the union and *both* are transfigured by death which is idealized by Wagner alone. Bliss here represents the total sudden gratification of a primordial wish, but what is the wish? Clearly it is for everlasting union and an oceanic feeling that goes with it. Tristan seeks for the wound-healing mother with magical power. Isolde seeks for a lost part of herself, and in this sense Lacan's (1977) interpretation that the child's greatest and most basic desire is to seek to become the part of the body that the mother feels she has lost, which Lacan names the phallus, seems to fit. Yet all of this is surely inadequate to explain the gripping power of this overwhelming work of art and its universal appeal.

PHILOSOPHICAL ISSUES

Another way to picture their situation is that the lovers have a passion to restore contact with Being, for falling away from Being represents daytime preoccupations—what Heidegger in *Being and Time* has labeled an immersion in the "they." Their search in this sense is existential and represents the longing for an authentic life (Chessick, 1986b), which can occur for the neurotic Wagner only in death. Indeed that is the point Wagner was trying to make in the opera, but he was carried by his art into a realm beyond his muddled philosophy. When we look at his letter to Mathilde

Wesendonk, we are struck by the longing for fusion with the maternal figure, but when we experience the sublime opera itself we are brought into a deeper philosophical preoccupation with the attempt to somehow make contact with Being—a preoccupation that Heidegger says has been the fundamental task of all metaphysics from even before the time of Plato and Aristotle.

The unanswered question here, and also central to the work of De Rougemont (1983), is whether passion of this all-consuming power can be explained on the basis of infantile longings alone or whether something transcendent is in it, such as Freud's Eros and Thanatos at work. The philosophical importance of *Tristan und Isolde* is not in solving this question but in illustrating the question in a way that no artist before or afterwards has ever been able to do. Are we simply dealing with the explosion of long-repressed and unsatisfied needs? Or have Tristan and Isolde become gripped in cosmic forces unintelligible even to themselves?

An alternative view is expressed by Magee (1983) who, in his book on Schopenhauer, devotes a long appendix to the relationship between Schopenhauer's philosophy and the operas of Wagner—especially *Tristan und Isolde*. As far as Magee is concerned, "Both as a totality and in its detail, and both in its music and in its verbal text, it is a fusion, effected at white heat, of insights from a great philosopher with the art of a consummate musical dramatist" (p. 361). This description of *Tristan* and Magee's insistence that it includes a celebration of sexual love using verbal imagery drawn straight from Schopenhauer, particularly as regards the significance of Night and Day, places Wagner more in the position of simply expressing in art form the philosophy of Schopenhauer, just as Proust is claimed by some to have expressed the philosophy of Bergson (Chessick, 1986a).

I think (with De Rougemont) that this view does a disservice to the genius of Wagner as an artist and musician and overestimates his philosophical accomplishments. On the surface *Tristan und Isolde* expresses Wagner's idiosyncratic religion of death, but something has happened in the genius of the music that has enabled Wagner to get in touch with some kind of primordial force in the human psyche, which is an anticivilization force in Freud's terminology and which, when it breaks out in a person, sweeps everything before it. Wagner through art is putting us in touch with something beyond our conscious selves.

The Oceanic Feeling

Fenichel (1945) reminds us that the regressive element in love is found both in women and men: "an archaic type of self-regard (or even of omnipotence) comes back again in an oceanic feeling of losing one's ego boundaries" (p. 86). He stresses the narcissistic gratification involved in fusing with a partner that contains the projected perfection and idealization. This explains the explosive "falling in love" that can occur during periods of chronic narcissistic wounding, such as has been repeatedly described in the aging therapist carrying on many frustrating long-term cases, and depressed in his personal life (Dahlberg, 1970).

The other, or object-relations aspect of the oceanic feeling that follows fusion and loss of ego boundaries, is, of course, reassurance against separation anxiety, but Fenichel in his references to the subject stresses the narcissistic bliss that such union brings rather than its defensive value. Ross (1968) on the other hand emphasizes "the need for the sustained eternal existence of an immutably protective loving object" (p. 269) and the "dread of object loss" as the defensively motivated basis for religious faith and phenomena, including those which, like the oceanic feeling, involve the loss of ego boundaries. He vaguely adds that "there is a case of narcissism in all religious belief" (p. 274). He does not seem to notice that his description of "loss of ego boundaries accompanied by profound ecstasy" and "detachment from the external world" is common to *both* mystical religious experience and sexual fusion with a passionately loved person, although he does note that certain religious mystical experiences, like that of St. Theresa, are "often imbued with erotic intensity" (p. 270).

It is a logical and philosophical error, however, to attribute the oceanic feeling that Romain Rolland saw as the core of religious experience, or other mystical experiences of this sort, simply to regression to early forms of narcissism or to conflict–defense formulations. This may be true in some cases but it is not necessarily true in all cases. This well-known reductionist fallacy runs throughout Freud's views of religion (Chessick, 1980); he dismisses the *Credo quia absurdum** of Tertullian in one page as believable only to those influenced by the "artifices of philosophy."

---

*"I believe because it is impossible" (*On the Body of Christ*, V).

As I pointed out (1980), "The Future of an Illusion" contains *two* sets of illusions, those Freud attributes to religion and those of Freud himself in his religion of science—already under attack by Nietzsche (Chessick, 1983a)—and it also contains a philosophical a priori premise: "But an illusion it would be to suppose that what science cannot give us we can get elsewhere" (Freud, 1927, p. 56).

The paradox in this premise is immediately manifest when *Civilization and Its Discontents* (Freud, 1930) opens with a magnificent paragraph pregnant with value judgments about aims and ideals, which certainly cannot come from science, and then proceeds to characteristize both the oceanic feeling and the state of being in love as merely regression to a primary developmental state where ego boundaries are not yet established—"the restoration of limitless narcissism" (p. 72). Freud's only philosophical argument for this explanation is that he is "inclined" to trace these phenomena "back to an early phase of ego-feeling." There is *no way* to validate such an explanation either by philosophic argument *or* by science, since early preverbal experiences are never directly reported. Our versions always represent contaminated extrapolations from later reports—contaminated both by psychic distortion and by later experiences and conflicts.

Harrison (1979), in a more recent paper, returns to this subject and stresses Freud's ambivalence about the matter of explaining "oceanic feeling." He attempts to trace the roots of this ambivalence to Freud's relationship to his mother. He writes, "One might say that Rolland denied the preoedipal 'bad mother' in a lifelong embrace, via his mysticism, of a hallucinatory formless, divine mother who represented his lost primary narcissism; whereas Freud simply isolated the most traumatizing aspects of his early life with explicit aversion" (p. 414). How to establish the scientific validity of even such a plausible psychohistorical interpretation remains a very open question.

Masson (1980) claims that he can trace the term *oceanic feeling* used by Rolland and "explained" by Freud to Sanskrit sources, a claim which may or may not be true. This kind of oceanic feeling is related to Kohut's (1978) concept of cosmic narcissism, originally used by the philosopher Gaston Bachelard (1884–1962). However, Bachelard did not worship science and was much aware of the dismal epistemological profile assumed by classical science, and of the significant subjective and creative aspects implicit in all scientific endeavor. Bachelard's statement "The subject projects his dream upon things" he insists is equally true in art and science.

Masson (1980) correctly stresses the dark side of the ocean metaphor with its implications of suicide and annihilation, and, I would add, drowning. However, Kohut (1978) distinguishes between (1) the primordial "oceanic feeling" which is experienced passively, and (2) the creative activity of an autonomous ego that produces "the acceptance of transience and the quasi-religious solemnity of a cosmic narcissism" (p. 456). This is an extremely important distinction, often confused in the literature, and misunderstood psychodynamically.

Wagner has presented the most profound statement of this cosmic narcissism in its secular form in *Tristan und Isolde*; one might argue, supported by various authorities, that in *Parsifal* he presents the same phenomena in a Chistian religious form. Masson's study of ancient Indian philosophy certainly contains convincing evidence that we are dealing with a universal human theme; indeed it was Wagner's turning to Indian philosophy, through his fascination with Schopenhauer, that precipitated a disruption of the composition of the *Ring* by his creation of *Tristan und Isolde*. Masson (1980) quotes a Vedanta text:

> You are not the body. You do not have a body.
> You do nothing and you experience nothing.
> You are pure consciousness.
> You are the eternal witness.
> Free, wander in happiness [p. 37].

Wagner, in his usual muddled fashion, has mixed up two similar but not identical phenomena. Drawing on his narcissistic need to conquer the married Mathilde Wesendonk, the genius of his art elevated this petty narcissistic neurotic problem into a universal theme of fusion of ecstatic lovers in death to produce the oceanic feeling—hence we have Isolde's "transfiguration" at the end, and the death of both the lovers.

WHY DID THEY FALL IN LOVE?

However, the outbreak of a profound narcissistic need in a man like Tristan who has always kept his nose to the grindstone and served by subordinating his needs to those of others should not be confused with the evident universal longing of mankind for fusion with God. The former is a clinical phenomenon, not rare in the treatment of aging narcissists in our time and fully explainable by concepts such as those of Kohut (1971, 1977, 1978). The latter represents a boundary beyond which science cannot pass, as Kohut (1978) implies. Explanations from religion are no less applicable to this than such speculative conceptions as Freud's "death instinct." Reductionistic psychoanalytic hypotheses are clearly applicable in such states when they appear in cases of psychopathology, but become open to much question when applied to those individuals of obvious great psychological strength from all civilizations and all ages who have reported such experiences and even found in them new sources of strength and conviction. The explanation of this puzzle remains unresolved. As Freud wrote in a 1929 letter to Romain Rolland, "Your letter of December 5, 1927, containing your remarks about a feeling you describe as 'oceanic' has left me no peace" (E. Freud, 1960, p. 388).

The important clinical contribution of Wagner's art here is to demonstrate the overwhelming power of archaic narcissistic structures when they regressively break loose under stress. Here is the significance of Tristan's "wound," which Isolde has healed before the opera opens and which has riveted them on each other. Isolde's humiliation is complete even before the opera and her narcissistic rage predominates the entire long first act, as does the empty depression of Tristan. We witness a dramatic bilateral fragmentation at the end of the first act, and mutual healing in the fusion of the lovers in the second act, completed only in their imagined permanent fusion in death at the end of the opera.

The psychology of the self (Chessick, 1985) is very helpful in understanding the disastrous situation of the lovers. Kohut (1971) explains that after a disturbance of the psychological equilibrium of primary narcissism: "the psyche saves a part of the lost experience of global narcissistic perfection by assigning it to an archaic, rudimentary (transitional) self-object, the idealized parent imago. Since all bliss and power now reside in the idealized object, the child feels empty and powerless when he is separated from it and he attempts, therefore, to maintain a continuous union with it" (p. 37).

Under overburdening adult stress, there is regression to the early configurations, and the true believer seeks mystical merger with God; the nonbeliever is more prone to outbreaks of passionate longings such as those of Tristan and Isolde. The power of this passion is explained by the need to maintain the vital bedrock of the personality, a cohesive sense of self, which is threatened with fragmentation under the pressure of severe narcissistic wounding. Thus the very psychological existence of the person is at stake and in this situation nothing else matters. Prosen, Martin, and Prosen (1972) discuss how the "middle age crisis" in men who must deny the aging process is a sufficiently noxious narcissistic wound in certain men to set off an obsessive search for an idealized woman, a search which can attain "hypomanic" intensity, and which is based on the hoped-for fusion with the vaguely remembered fantasized mother of childhood, a woman he never finds.

These situations, which can occur at any time in a person's life, have been labeled "boundary situations" by the psychiatrist-philosopher Karl Jaspers (1932). They have not received sufficient psychoanalytic exploration or metapsychological delineation. They are ultimate situations requiring the facing of existential questions and also have ethical ramifications because they require crucial choices in a person's life; they represent the crises in human existence in which conflict and its meaning become poignantly and tragically clear. Jaspers emphasizes death, suffering, and struggle or "death, chance, guilt, and the uncertainty of the world," and two more general boundary situations— (1) that of the particular historical determination of one's particular existence, and (2) the relativity of all that is real—its self-contradictory character as being always somehow what it is not. Falling in love reflects the presence of a boundary situation, as does creativity that serves the function of psychological self-repair for the artist. Silverman and Will (1986) point out, using the example of Sylvia Plath, that when such efforts at self-repair fail, suicidal violence threatens to break out. A sweeping narcissistic regression may occur, with a longing for death as a release and ultimate bliss, a death which may be self-inflicted in one way or another as an expression of that violence or narcissistic rage. Clearly we are dealing here with a clinical matter of the utmost importance.

The universal fascination and enduring aspect of the opera *Tristan und Isolde* is in the empathy it produces for the pain and suffering and rage of two wounded narcissistic people who must relieve this discomfort even if it means death. This should also help us empathize clinically with borderline patients and addicted patients, who are driven to pursue self-defeating activities at any cost and in spite of our best efforts at interpretations; with the tragic and puzzling suicide of wounded narcissistic poets so common in our time; and with what it is like to long for someone with your whole heart and soul, living in a state of continual agitation, ignoring the claims of the external world, feeling that you must fuse with that person no matter what the cost to yourself, your career, or your very life. In two forthcoming publications (1989, 1990) I will discuss the clinical situation in detail.

Afterword
The Field of Inquiry: Sharpening the Focus— Widening the Scope

With the publication of this anthology it is our hope to accomplish two things. First, to provide the interested student of either music or psychoanalysis (or both) with a selection of articles representative of the kind of work that has been done to date and of a variety which may not be readily available elsewhere. Second, and equally important, to attempt to establish a field of inquiry interdisciplinary in nature within the area of applied psychoanalysis. The latter objective cannot, of course, be achieved on the basis of casual observation or anecdote no matter what its potential. Nor can a few isolated studies or occasional articles, no matter how original or excellent, serve to establish such an area. Only a body of knowledge emerging from the studies of many over a course of time can accomplish this. And, even under the best of circumstances, this can only happen in an atmosphere of inquiry and critical dialogue. We hope in this volume to provide the impetus for such an emergent field.

We have noted (see Introduction) that psychoanalysis in its application to the arts played a seminal role in the first psychoanalytic dialogues and that explorations and extrapolations to the field of music were first conducted by musicologist Max Graf. Between 1910 and prior to 1950, only a handful of papers on some facet of music were presented at a congress or appeared in publication; however, almost without exception such presentations were first steps which did not meet the standard of quality already being established in other areas of applied psychoanalytic work let alone being on a par with papers in clinical psychoanalysis or metapsychological theory. Reviewers of the sparse literature accrued by the end of the 1950s (Sterba, 1965) and 1960s (Noy, 1966–1967) make only too clear the extremely limited development to date of a field which both authors seemed to feel had greater potential. In that context, the occasional imaginative article, such as those included in this volume, or the particularly responsive writer, stands out in sharp relief. Since that time, through the 1980s, studies of greater sophistication have emerged involving more careful attention to the musical element, and theory applicability and, with regard to the latter, a more modern view of psychoanalysis. The greatest number of contributions included in the anthology are from this period. In aggregate, however, they suggest more the opening of interesting directions than they do the presentation of any as yet cohesive body of knowledge or unified approach. At best they delineate a field of inquiry and that indeed has been one of our goals, to demonstrate the possibilities of such a field by drawing together these efforts separated in time and place and, in a few instances, written by authors of diverse background.

Both the successes and the limitations of these articles point up a common problem faced by their authors. Assuming that some meaningful relationship may exist between music and psychoanalysis, some potential area for constructive discourse, what might be appropriate points of entry? Some have approached the field with the assumption that the principles of psychoanalysis can be meaningfully applied to anything ad infinitum and accordingly have sought willy-nilly to relate metapsychology to music. Such studies tend usually to be long on analysis but short on music. Others have attempted a biographical approach closer in principle to clinical psychoanalysis. In some instances this, among other factors, has led to an undue emphasis on psychopathology in spite of the fact that the adaptational point of view of ego psychology provides a richer perspective on the life of the artist. In most instances there has been a curious reluctance to deal with the music itself in any detail. Perhaps this attitude reflects prudence more than phobia.

The feature that many find engaging and even tantalizing, analysts and nonanalysts alike, consists in the intuitive impression that music relates to human life in some as yet unarticulated manner. The relationship of music to emotions, for example, has the quality of a cliché in modern times. However, musical aestheticians two centuries ago wrote scholarly treatises on the subject. By the end of the nineteenth century it was taken as a matter of course to be a regular aspect of romantic music. Composers today might question as a naive or at least highly limited notion that the function of music is to "express emotions." However, whatever the relationship between music and affect, and whatever its relative importance in music, the question arises, what, if anything, can the psychoanalyst say about it? Equally important is the question of how he can even approach the subject in order to generate data about which he can say anything at all. Where is the point of entry? Similarly, there is an assumption in common thought that music is in some way related to other aspects of the composer's inner life—to his biography on one level, his life course on another. It is a line of thinking that analysts, nonanalysts, and even those well trained in music fall into. One has only to read the program notes at concerts or listen to the commentary introducing classical music on radio for a fair sampling of this thinking. Virtually at random at this writing, a program is at hand for a chamber music concert in which it is noted that a piano trio was written by Dvořák immediately after the death of his mother. The notes go on to say that it is the first such work to achieve "epic" proportions. Some relationship is strongly implied and left to the imagination of the listener. But what exactly is that relationship? What understanding, if any, can psychoanalysis bring to bear on such questions? And, if it can, how can the question be approached; where, again, is the point of entry?

In raising these questions, are we able to say that there is some single, irreducible principle, or set of principles, which might be said to relate music and psychoanalysis? Something, for example, on the order of "the two principles of mental function" in its own context? If so, it would appear obvious that the proper focus would be in the mental lives of the participants and be a function of them. We speak here not only of composer, performer, and auditor but of the scholar as well, for elements of mental life related to (although not identical with) the countertransferences and counteridentifications of clinical psychoanalysis inevitably come into play. Such principles would have to be related to symbolic thinking on one hand, the means of representation on the other. It may be that it would be fruitful to return to aspects of the *Interpretation of Dreams* (1900) in seeking these, wary of course of the danger of implying a relationship between the dream and the finished work of art. It was, after all, Freud's legendary affinity with the visual and relative disinterest in the auditory (some would say resistance) that led to the present state of affairs. Perhaps the best we can do at the moment is to advance the minimal but, we feel, significant point of view that discrete *elements of mental life are infinitely displaceable*; thus, whatever can be represented in one modality can be represented in another. We know, for example, that such diverse products of mind as symptom, character trait, parapraxis, joke, and dream are fundamentally related. Whatever can be represented, for example, in visual dream symbolism should be capable of achieving representation in auditory form—indeed, in the dream it sometimes does. From a psychoanalytic viewpoint this is one way that music can be approached and music as an example of auditory symbolism can be related to multiple facets of mental life associated with cognition, drive, and affect. Auditory representation in musical form, which constitutes the composer's work, requires an ego state which integrates and synthesizes both primary *and* secondary process thinking. It calls upon multiple ego functions including the most highly developed of ego-based transforming capacities. In this sense the process of composition stands in stark contrast to that of dreaming and the formed "musical idea" in contrast to the manifest "dream fragment." Yet each is representational of some latent mental element. Looked at from this vantage point, an intriguing possibility presents itself: that not only may psychoanalysis make some contribution to the understanding of music but that the reverse may also be the case—that the study of musical form may constitute another avenue toward the understanding of the human mind.

This then is the nature of the inquiry that we are endeavoring to establish here and in subsequent publications. Since in the present anthology we felt it important to include articles culled from the already published literature, it is not possible, for reasons of space, to include several appropriate contributions among those solicited or independently submitted. Some of these will appear in *Psychoanalytic Explorations in Music—Series Two*, which is being collected and edited at this writing. We anticipate there and in future periodic publications, as interest and material warrants, to publish contributions in areas not included in the present volume. One such relates to performers, the performance of music, and possibly problems in performance, although, with regard to the last, our interest is not primarily psychopathology as such. Another is the transcultural background of art as reflected in music. Further, we hope to include, and are eager to encourage, contributions from writers in music and related fields who are analytically informed. *Series Two* will include an updated, critical review of more recent work. Thus at that point a number of the studies in the present volume will come under scrutiny reflecting what we anticipate will be an ongoing dialogue and critical evaluation in a new field of inquiry.

S.F.
R.L.K.
G.H.P.

References

Abelin, E.L. (1971), The role of the father in the separation–individuation process. In: *Separation Individuation, Essays in Honor of Margaret S. Mahler*, eds. J.B. McDevitt & C. F. Settlage. New York: International Universities Press, pp. 229–252.
Abell, A.M. (1908), Famous violinists of the past. II. Giuseppe Tartini. *Musical Courier*, 57/5:8–9.
_____ (1955), *Talks with Great Composers*. New York: Philosophical Library.
Abraham, K. (1913), Restriction and transformations of scoptophilia in psychoneurotics. In: *Selected Papers on Psycho-Analysis*. London: Hogarth Press, 1927, pp. 169–234.
_____ (1913), The ear and auditory passage as erotogenic zones. In: *Selected Papers on Psycho-Analysis*. London: Hogarth Press, 1927, pp. 244–247.
_____ (1924), A short study of the development of the libido, viewed in the light of mental disorders. In: *Selected Papers on Psycho-Analysis*. London: Hogarth Press, 1927, pp. 418–501.
Alexander, F. (1954), The psychosomatic approach in medical therapy. In: *The Scope of Psychoanalysis*. New York: Basic Books, 1961, pp. 345–358.
Amram, D. (1968), *Vibrations, Adventures and Musical Times of David Amram*. New York: Macmillan.
Anderson, E., ed. (1938), *The Letters of Mozart and His Family*, 3 vols. London: Macmillan.
_____ (1961), *The Letters of Beethoven*, 3 vols. London: Macmillan.
_____ (1966), *The Letters of Mozart and His Family*, 2nd ed., 2 vols. London: Macmillan.
Antrim, D. (1943), Music in industry. *Musical Quart.*, 29: 275–290.
Anzieu, D. (1979), The sound image of the self. *Internat. Rev. Psycho-Anal.*, 6: 23–36.
Arazi, I. (1969), One plus one equals one. *Amer. String Teacher*, 19: 1, 6–10, 26.
Arieti, S. (1976), *Creativity: The Magic Synthesis*. New York: Basic Books.
Aristotle, *Politica*, Book 8. Trans. T. A. Sinclair. New York: Penguin, 1981.
_____ *Rhetoric*, 3. Quoted in *The Riddles of the Exeter Book*, ed. F. Tupper. Boston: Ginn and Co, 1910, pp. xii–xiii.
Arlow, J.A. (1969), Fantasy, memory and reality testing. *Psychoanal. Quart.*, 38: 28–51.
_____ (1980), Object concept and object choice. *Psychoanal. Quart.*, 49: 109–133.
_____ (1984), Disturbances in the sense of time. With special reference to experiences of timelessness. *Psychoanal. Quart.*, 53:13–37.
Babikian, H.M. (1983), The psychoanalytic treatment of the performing artist: Superego aspects. Paper presented at the annual meeting, American Academy of Psychoanalysis, New York.
Bach, K. (1753), *Versuch iber die wahre Art das Clavier zu spielen*, 5th ed. Berlin: F. Henning.
Bak, R. (1973), Being in love and object loss. *Internat. J. Psycho-Anal.*, 54: 1–8.
Bakhtin, M. (1968), *Rabelais and His World*. Cambridge: Massachusetts Institute of Technology.
Balliet, W. (1974), *Alex Wilder and His Friends*. New York: Houghton Mifflin.
Barkan, H. (1957), *Johannes Brahms and Theodor Billroth; Letters from a Musical Friendship*. Norman: University of Oklahoma Press.

Bauer, W.L., Deutsch, O.E., & Eibl, J.H., eds. (1962–1975), *Mozart: Briefe und Aufzeichnungen*, 7 vols. Kassel: Barenreiter Verlag.
Bauer-Lechner, N. (1923), *Erinnerungen an Gustav Mahler*. Zurich: E P. Tal.
Becker, H. (1980), Johannes Brahms. In: *The New Grove Dictionary of Music and Musicians*. Vol. 3, 6th ed. S. Sadie. London: Macmillan, pp. 155–174.
Beethoven, L. van (1801), *Letters*, ed. A. Eaglefeld-Hill. New York: E. P. Dutton, 1951.
Beres, D. (1957), Communication in psychoanalysis and in the creative process: A parallel. *J. Amer. Psychoanal. Assn.*, 5: 408–423.
Berezin, M.A. (1958), Some observations on art (music) and its relationship to ego mastery. *Bull. Phila. Assn. Psychoanal.*, 8: 49–65.
Bergler, E. (1950), *The Writer and Psychoanalysis*. Garden City, NY: Doubleday.
Bergman, P., & Escalona, S.K. (1949), Unusual sensitivities in very young children. *The Psychoanalytic Study of the Child*, 3/4:333–352. New York: International Universities Press.
Bergmann, M. (1980), On the intrapsychic function of falling in love. *Psychoanal. Quart.*, 49: 56–77.
Bernfeld, S. (1915), Zur Psychologie der Unmusikalischen. *Archiv. fur die gesamte Psychologie*, 34: 235–253.
Blaukopf, K. (1976), *Mahler, a Documentary Study*. New York: Oxford University Press.
Blom, E. (1954), *Grove's Dictionary of Music and Musicians*. 5th ed. New York: St. Martin's Press.
Blume, F. (1963), Requiem but no peace. In: *The Creative World of Mozart*, ed. P.H. Lang. New York: W.W. Norton, pp. 103–126.
Bonaparte, M. (1949), *The Life and Works of Edgar Allan Poe*. London: Imago.
Bourboulis, P.P. (1964), Ancient festivals of "Saturnalia" type. Hellenika, 16, pp. 7–37 (Thessalonike, 1964).
Bradshaw, S. (1973), A psychoanalytic view of music composition. *Confinia Psychiat.*, 16:220–237.
Brahms, J. (1983), *Briefe*. Leipzig: Reclam.
Branfman, T.C. (1955), Psychology of music and musicians: Two clinical examples. *Amer. Imago*, 12: 3–7.
Brazelton, T. B., Koslowski, B., & Main, M. (1974), The origins of reciprocity: The early mother–infant interaction. In: *The Effect of the Infant on Its Caregiver*, eds. M. Lewis & L.A. Rosenblum. New York: John Wiley, pp. 49–76.
Brenner, C. (1968), Archaic features of ego functioning. *Internat. J. Psycho-Anal.*, 49: 426–429.
————— (1974), On the nature and development of affects: A unified theory. *Psychoanal. Quart.*, 44: 532–556.
————— (1975), Affects and psychic conflict. *Psychoanal. Quart.*, 45: 5–28.
Brockway, W., & Weinstock, H. (1941), *The Opera: A History of Its Creation and Performance: 1600–1941*. New York: Simon & Schuster.
Bush, M. (1967), The problem of form in the psychoanalytic theory of art. *Psychoanal. Rev.*, 54: 5–35.
Capri, A. (1945), *Giuseppe Tartini*. Milan: Garzanti.
Castelnuovo-Tedesco, P. (1978), The mind as a stage: Some comments on reminiscence and internal objects. *Internat. J. Psycho-Anal.*, 59: 19–26.
Catholy, E. (1961), *Das Fastnachtspiel des Spatmittelters: Gestalt und Funktion*. Hermaea Germanische Forschungen, Neue Folge, Vol. 8.
————— (1966), *Fastnachtspiel*. Stuttgart: J. B. Metzler.
Chasseguet-Smirgel, J. (1985), *The Ego Ideal: A Psychoanalytic Essay on the Malady of the Ideal*, trans. P. Barrows. London: Free Association Books.
Chessick, R. (1980), *Freud Teaches Psychotherapy*. Indianapolis: Hackett.

References

———— (1983a), *A Brief Introduction to the Genius of Nietzsche*. Washington, DC: University Press of America.

———— (1983b), The Ring: Richard Wagner's dream of preoedipal destruction. *Amer. J. Psychoanal.*, 43: 361–374.

———— (1985), *The Psychology of the Self and the Treatment of Narcissism*. New York: Jason Aronson.

———— (1986a), The search for the authentic self in Bergson and Proust. In: *Psychoanalytic Perspectives in Literature and Film*, eds. J. Reppen & M. Charney. Madison, NJ: Farleigh Dickinson University Press.

———— (1986b), Heidegger for psychotherapists. *Amer. J. Psychother.*, 40: 83–95.

———— (1989), On falling in love. II: The two woman phenomenon revisited. *J. Amer. Acad. Psychoanal.*, 17: 293–304.

———— (1990), On falling in love. III: Creativity and problem-solving. *Amer. J. Psychother.* (in press).

Chijs, A., Van Der (1923), An attempt to apply objective psychoanalysis to musical composition. *Internat. J. Psycho-Anal.*, 4: 379–380.

Chissell, J. (1983), *Clara Schumann: A Dedicated Spirit*. London: Hamish Hamilton.

Coeuroy, A. (1951), Schumann et Bach. *Contrepoints*, 7: 27–33.

Coltrera, J.T. (1965), On the creation of beauty and thought: The unique as vicissitude. *J. Amer. Psychoanal. Assn.*, 13: 643–703.

———— (1981), *Lives, Events, and Other Players: Directions in Psychobiography*. New York: Jason Aronson.

Comini, A. (1983), An sichten von Brahms—Idole und Bilder. *Kongreßbericht zum III. Gewandhaus-Symposium*. Leipzig: Gewandhaus, pp. 58–65.

Cooke, D, (1980), *Gustav Mahler: An Introduction to His Music*. London: Faber.

Cooper, M. (1970), *Beethoven: The Last Decade, 1817–1827*. London: Oxford University Press.

Copland, A. (1952), *Music and Imagination*. New York: Mentor Books.

Corbin, E.I. (1974), The autonomous ego functions in creativity. *J. Amer. Psychoanal. Assn.*, 22:568–587.

Coriat, I.H. (1945), Some aspects of a psychoanalytic interpretation of music. *Psychoanal. Rev.*, 32: 408–418.

Cowell, H. (1926), The process of musical creation. *Amer. J. Psychology*, 37: 233–236.

———— Cowell, S. (1969), *Charles Ives and His Music*. London: Oxford University Press.

Craft, R. (no date), Erwartung, Notes on the Dramatic Structure. Record jacket notes, Columbia Records.

Croce, B. (1902), *Estetica come scienza dell'espression e linguistica generale*. Milan: R. Sandron.

Cross, M., & Ewen, D. (1953), *Milton Cross' Encyclopedia of the Great Composers and Their Music*. Garden City, NY: Doubleday.

Dahlberg, C. (1970), Sexual contact between patient and therapist. *Contemp. Psychoanal.*, 6: 107–124.

Dale, K. (1952), Piano music. In: *Schumann: A Symposium*, ed. G. Abraham. London: Oxford University Press, p. 63.

Darwin, C. A. (1872), *The Descent of Man and Selection in Relation to Sex*, Vol. 2. New York: Appleton.

de Filippis, M. (1948), *The Literary Riddle in Italy to the End of the Sixteenth Century*. Berkeley: University of California Press.

de La Grange, H. (1973), *Mahler*, Vol. 1. Garden City, NY: Doubleday.

De Rougemont, D. (1983), *Love in the Western World*. Princeton, NJ: Princeton University Press.

Deutsch, F. (1939), The choice of organ in organ neuroses. *Internat. J. Psycho-Anal.*, 20: 252–262.

Deutsch, O. E., ed. (1947), *A Schubert Reader: A Life of Franz Schubert in Letters and Documents* (trans). New York: W. W. Norton.
_____ (1965), *Mozart: A Documentary Biography.* Stanford, CA: Stanford University Press.
Diether, J. (1963), The expressive content of Mahler's Ninth. *Chord and Discord,* 2: 69–107.
_____ (1969), Notes on some Mahler juvenilia. *Chord and Discord,* 1: 3–100.
Douglas, A. (1977), *The Feminization of American Culture.* New York: Alfred A. Knopf.
Edelheit, H. (1965), Speech and psychic structure. *J. Amer. Psychoanal. Assn.,* 17: 381–412.
Edelson, M. (1975), *Language in Interpretation in Psychoanalysis.* New Haven, CT: Yale University Press.
Edwards, H. S. (1881), *Rossini and His School.* New York: Scribner & Welford.
Eggar, K. (1920), The subconscious mind and the musical faculty. Proceedings of the (Royal) Musical Association, 47: 23–38.
Ehrenzweig, A. (1953), *The Psychoanalysis of Artistic Vision and Hearing.* New York: George Braziller.
Ehrmann, A. (1933), *Johannes Brahms; Weg, Werk, Welt.* Leipzig: Breitkopf & Härtel.
Eibl, J.H. (1970), Mozartiana aus der Sammlung Hermann Härtel. *Musikforschung,* 23: 445.
_____ (1971), Mozart verfasst Rätsel. *Oesterreichische Musikzeitschrift,* 26: 65–71.
Einstein, A. (1945), *Mozart, His Character, His Work.* New York: Oxford University Press.
Eissler, K. (1963), *Goethe: A Psychoanalytic Study,* Vol. 2. Detroit: Wayne State University Press.
_____ (1967), Psychopathology and creativity. *Amer. Imago,* 24: 35–81.
Elkus, J. (1974), *Charles Ives and the American Band Tradition: A Centennial Tribute.* American Arts Pamphlet No. 4. Exeter, UK: University of Exeter.
Elworthy, F.T. (1900), *Horns of Honour, and Other Studies in the Bi-ways of Archaeology.* London: J. Murray.
Emde, R.N. (1977), Toward a psychoanalytic theory of affect. Presented to the Discussion Group, Affect in Theory and Practice. American Psychoanalytic Association, New York, December.
Encyclopaedia Britannica (1943), 19: 567–568.
Encyclopedia Judaica (1972), Jerusalem: Kester (High Holiday Prayer, U-netanneh Tokef), 15: 153.
Engel, G. (1970), *Gustav Mahler.* New York: David Lewis.
Erikson, E.H. (1956), The problem of ego identity. *J. Amer. Psychoanal. Assn.,* 4: 56–121.
_____ (1968), *Identity, Youth and Crisis.* New York: W.W. Norton.
Escalona, S.K. (1968), *The Roots of Individuality. Normal Patterns of Development in Infancy.* Chicago: Aldine.
Esman, A. (1979), Some reflections on boredom. *J. Amer. Psychoanal. Assn.,* 27: 423–440.
Farnsworth, P.R. (1961), Musicality and abnormality. *Confinia. Psychiat.,* 4: 158–164.
Feder, S. (1978), Gustav Mahler, dying. *Internat. Rev. Psycho-Anal.,* 5: 125–148.
_____ (1980a), Gustav Mahler Um Mitternacht. *Internat. Rev. Psycho-Anal.,* 7: 11–25.
_____ (1980b), Decoration Day: A boyhood memory of Charles Ives. *Musical Quart.,* 66: 234–261.
_____ (1981a), Gustav Mahler: The music of fratricide. *Internat. Rev. Psycho-Anal.,* 8: 257–284.

——— (1981b), The nostalgia of Charles Ives: An essay in affects and music. *Ann. Psychoanal.*, 10: 301–332.
——— (1983), The enduring father: Psychoanalysis in Ives studies. Presentation to the American Musicological Society. Louisville.
——— (1984), Charles Ives and the unanswered question. *The Psychoanalytic Study of Society*, 10: 321–351. Hillsdale, NJ: Analytic Press.
Fenichel, O. (1934), On the psychology of boredom. In: *The Collected Papers of Otto Fenichel*. New York: W.W. Norton, 1954, pp. 292–302.
——— (1945), *The Psychoanalytic Theory of Neuroses*. New York: W.W. Norton.
Ferenczi, S. (1911), On obscene words. In: *Contributions to Psychoanalysis*. London: Hogarth Press, 1952, pp. 132–153.
——— (1913), Stages in the development of the sense of reality. In: *Contributions to Psycho-Analysis*. London: Hogarth Press, 1952, pp. 213–239.
Feuerbach, L. (1851), *Lectures on the Essence of Religion*. New York: Harper & Row, 1967.
Field, T.M., Woodson, R., Greenberg, R., & Cohen, D. (1982), Discrimination and imitation of facial expressions by neonates. *Science*, 218: 179–181.
Flugel, J.C. (1936), The Tannhauser motif. *Brit. J. Med. Psychol.*, 15: 279–295.
Fraisse, P. (1963), *The Psychology of Time*. New York: Harper & Row.
Frances, A., Sacks, M., & Aronoff, M. S. (1977), Depersonalization: A self-relations perspective. *Internat. J. Psycho-Anal.*, 58: 325–331.
Franken, F. H. (1979), *Krankheit und Tod Grosser Komponisten*. New York: Witzstrock.
Frazier, Sir J. (1922), *The Golden Bough*. New York: Macmillan.
Freedman, A. (1956), The feeling of nostalgia and its relationship to phobia. *Bull. Phila. Assn. Psychoanal.*, 6: 84–92.
Freud, A. (1963), The concept of developmental lines. *The Psychoanalytic Study of the Child*, 18: 245–265. New York: International Universities Press.
——— (1965), *Normality and Pathology in Childhood*. New York: International Universities Press.
Freud, E., ed. (1960), *Letters of Sigmund Freud*. New York: Basic Books.
Freud, S. (1887–1902), *The Origins of Psychoanalysis. Letters to Wilhelm Fliess, Drafts and Notes*, ed. M. Bonaparte, A. Freud, & E. Kris. New York: Basic Books, 1954.
——— (1900), The Interpretation of Dreams. *Standard Edition*, 4/5. London: Hogarth Press, 1953.
——— (1901), The Psychopathology of Everyday Life. *Standard Edition*, 6. London: Hogarth Press, 1960.
——— (1905), Jokes and Their Relation to the Unconscious. *Standard Edition*, 8. London: Hogarth Press, 1960.
——— (1909), Family romances. *Standard Edition*, 9: 237–241. London: Hogarth Press, 1959.
——— (1910), Leonardo da Vinci and a memory of his childhood. *Standard Edition*, 11: 63–138. London: Hogarth Press, 1957.
——— (1912), Recommendations to physicians practising psycho-analysis. *Standard Edition*, 12: 111–120. London: Hogarth Press, 1958.
——— (1914), The Moses of Michelangelo. *Standard Edition*, 13: 211–238. London: Hogarth Press, 1953.
——— (1914), On narcissism: An introduction. *Standard Edition*, 14: 67–104. London: Hogarth Press, 1957.
——— (1915), Repression. *Standard Edition*. 14: 159–215. London: Hogarth Press, 1957.
——— (1915), Thoughts for the times on war and death. *Standard Edition*, 14: 275–302. London: Hogarth Press, 1957.
——— (1915–1917), Introductory Lectures on Psycho-Analysis. *Standard Edition*, 15/16. London: Hogarth Press, 1961, 1963.

——— (1917), Mourning and melancholia. *Standard Edition*, 14: 237–258. London: Hogarth Press, 1957.

——— (1919), A child is being beaten: A contribution to the study of the origin of sexual perversion. *Standard Edition*, 17: 175–204. London: Hogarth Press, 1955.

——— (1920), Beyond the pleasure principle. *Standard Edition*, 18: 3–64. London: Hogarth Press, 1955.

——— (1921), Group psychology and the analysis of the ego. *Standard Edition*, 18: 61–145. London: Hogarth Press, 1955.

——— (1923), The ego and the id. *Standard Edition*, 19: 12–66. London: Hogarth Press, 1961.

——— (1925), An autobiographical study. *Standard Edition*, 20: 7–74. London: Hogarth Press, 1959.

——— (1926), Inhibitions, symptoms and anxiety. *Standard Edition*, 20: 77–175. London: Hogarth Press, 1959.

——— (1927), The future of an illusion. *Standard Edition*, 21: 5–56. London: Hogarth Press, 1961.

——— (1928), Dostoevsky and parricide. *Standard Edition*, 21: 177–194, London: Hogarth Press, 1961.

——— (1929), Letter No. 241. In: *Letters of Sigmund Freud*, ed. E. Freud. New York: Basic Books.

——— (1930), Civilization and its discontents. *Standard Edition*, 21: 64–145. London: Hogarth Press, 1961.

Friedman, S. (1960), One aspect of the structure of music: A study of regressive transformations of musical themes. *J. Amer. Psychoanal. Assn.*, 8: 427–449.

Friedreich, J. B. (1860), *Geschichte des Rätsels*. Dresden: Kuntze.

Frisch, W. (1984), *Brahms and the Principle of Developing Variation*. Berkeley: University of California.

Gal, H. (1963), *Johannes Brahms; His Work and Personality*, trans. J. Stein. New York: Knopf.

Garciá Márquez, G. (1988), *Love in the Time of Cholera*. New York: Alfred A. Knopf.

Gardner, R. W. (1953), Cognitive styles in categorizing behavior. *J. Personality*, 22: 214–233.

——— (1962), Cognitive controls in adaptation: Research and measurement. In: *Measurement in Personality and Cognition*, eds. S. Messick & J. Ross. New York: John Wiley.

——— Jackson, D., & Messick, S. (1960), Personality organization in cognitive controls and intellectual ability. *Psychological Issues*, Vol. 2, Monograph 8. New York: International Universities Press.

Gartenberg, E. (1978), *Mahler, The Man and His Music*. New York: Schirmer.

Gay, P. (1978), Aimez-Vous Brahms? In: *Freud, Jews and Other Germans*. New York: Oxford University Press, pp. 231–256.

Geahchan, D. (1968), Devil et nostalgie. *Rev. Fran. Psychanal.*, 32: 59–65.

Gediman, H. (1975), Reflections on romanticism, narcissism, and creativity. *J. Amer. Psychoanal. Assn.*, 23: 407–423.

——— (1981), On Love, dying together, and liebestod fantasies. *J. Amer. Psychoanal. Assn.*, 29: 607–630.

Geiringer, K. (1939), New light on Schumann's last year. In: *The Listener*, ed. F. Aprahamian. London: Cassell, 1967, pp. 228–231.

——— (1982), *Brahms; His Life and Work*, 3rd ed. New York: Da Capo.

Germain, P. (1928), La musique et la psychanalyse. *Rev. Franc. Psychanal.*, 2: 751–792.

Ghiselin, B. (1952), *The Creative Process*. Berkeley: University of California Press.

References

Glover, E. (1938), The psychoanalysis of affects. In: *On the Early Development of Mind*. London: Imago, pp. 297–306.
Goethe, J. (1774), *The Sufferings of Young Werther*, trans. B. Morgan. New York: Ungar, 1954.
——— (1786–1788), Travels in Italy. In: *The Permanent Goethe, Selected and with an Introduction by Thomas Mann*, ed. T. Mann. New York: Dial, 1948, pp. 505–547.
Goldstein, K. (1948), *Language and Language Disturbances*. New York: Grune & Stratton.
Gombrich, E. R. (1972), *The Story of Art*, 12th ed. London: Phaidon Press.
Graf, M. (1911), Richard Wagner im fliegenden Hollander. Ein Beitrag zur Psychologie kunstlerischen Schaffens. *Schriften zur angewandten Seelenkunde*, 9. Vienna: Franz Deutike.
——— (1942), Reminiscences of professor Sigmund Freud. *Psychoanal. Quart.*, 11: 465–476.
Grand, S. (1982), The body and its boundaries: A psychoanalytic view of cognitive process disturbances in schizophrenia. *Internat. Rev. Psycho-Anal.*, 9: 327–342.
Greenacre, P. (1957), The childhood of the artist: Libidinal phase development and giftedness. *The Psychoanalytic Study of the Child*, 12: 47–72. New York: International Universities Press.
——— (1958a), The family romance of the artist. *The Psychoanalytic Study of the Child*, 13: 9–36. New York: International Universities Press.
——— (1958b), The relation of the impostor to the artist. *The Psychoanalytic Study of the Child*, 12: 521–540. New York: International Universities Press.
——— (1963), *The Quest for Father*. New York: International Universities Press.
——— (1966), Problems of overidealization of the analyst and of analysis. *The Psychoanalytic Study of the Child*, 21: 193–212. New York: International Universities Press.
Greenson, R.R. (1954), About the sound 'mm . . .' *Psychoanal. Quart.*, 23: 234–239.
Gutheil, E.A. (1954), Music as adjoint to psychotherapy. *Amer. J. Psychother.*, 8: 94–109.
Hacker, F. J. (1953), On artistic production. In: *Explorations in Psychoanalysis*, ed. R. Londner. New York: Julian Press, pp. 128–138.
Hadamard, J. (1945), *The Psychology of Invention in the Mathematical Field*. Princeton, NJ: Princeton University Press.
Haezrahi, P. (1965), *The Contemplative Activity: Studies in Aesthetics*. Jerusalem: Magnes Edition (Hebrew).
Hamburger, M. (1960), *Beethoven Letters, Journals and Conversations*. Garden City, NY: Doubleday/Anchor.
Hannett, F. (1964), The haunting lyric. *Psychoanal. Quart.*, 33: 226–269.
Hanslick, E. (1854), *The Beautiful in Music*, trans. B. Cohen. New York: Bobbs-Merrill, 1957.
——— (1896), *Vom Musikalisch-Schonen*, 9th ed. Leipzig: J.A. Barth.
Hardy, T. (1897), *The Well-Beloved*. London: Macmillan, 1985.
Harrison, I. (1979), On Freud's view of the infant–mother relationship and of the oceanic feeling—Some subjective influences. *J. Amer. Psychoanal. Assn.*, 27: 399–422.
Hartmann, H. (1939), *Ego Psychology and the Problem of Adaptation*. New York: International Universities Press, 1958.
——— (1939), Psychoanalysis and the concept of health. In: *Essays on Ego Psychology*. New York: International Universities Press, 1964, pp. 3–18.
——— Kris, E., & Loewenstein, R.M. (1946), Comments on the formation of psychic structure. *The Psychoanalytic Study of the Child*, 2: 11–38. New York: International Universities Press.

Hayn, H. (1890), Die Deutsche Räthsel-Litteratur. *Centralblatt für Bibliothekswesen*, 17: 526–528.
Hebb, D.O. (1974), What psychology is about. *Amer. Psychol.*, 29:71–79.
Helmholtz, L. (1865), *Die Lehre von den Tonempfindungen*, 2nd ed. Brunswick: F. Vieweg & Son.
Henschel, G. (1907), *Personal Recollections of Johannes Brahms*. Boston: Badger.
Herbert, M. (1837), *Early Letters*, trans. from R. Schumann's *Jugendbriefe*. London: G. Bell, 1888.
High Holiday Prayer Book (1948), Vol. 1. New York: Jewish Reconstructionist Foundation.
Hindemith, P. (1952), *A Composer's World*. Cambridge, MA: Harvard University Press.
Hitchcock, H.W. (1974), *Music in the United States*, 2nd ed. Englewood Cliffs: Prentice-Hall.
────── (1977), *Ives*. Oxford Studies of Composers, Vol. 14. London: Oxford University Press.
Hitschmann, E. (1949), Johannes Brahms and women. *Amer. Imago*, 6: 69–96.
Hoffer, W. (1949), Mouth, hand and ego-integration. *The Psychoanalytic Study of the Child*, 3/4: 49–56. New York: International Universities Press.
Hofmann, K. (1983), Johannes Brahms' Wirken in Hamburg bis zum Jahre 1862; eine biografische Standortbestimmung. *Kongressbericht zum III. Gewandhaus-Symposium*. Leipzig: Gewandhaus, pp. 14–25.
────── Fürst, J. (1980), *Johannes Brahms—The Man and His Work*. Detroit: Detroit Symphony Orchestra.
Holde, A. (1959), Suppressed passages in the Brahms–Joachim correspondence published for the first time. *Musical Quart.*, 45: 312–324.
Holländer, A (1931), Gustav Mahler. *Musical Quart.*, 4: 449–463.
Holmberg, A. (1983), Tristan und Isolde, a Drama of the Soul. Booklet with recording of *Tristan und Isolde*, conducted by Leonard Bernstein, Phillips No. 6769091.
Holmes, E. (1921), *The Life of Mozart*. London: J.M. Dent.
Holt, L.E., & Howland, J. (1940), *Holt's Diseases of Infancy and Childhood*, 11th ed., eds. L. E. Holt, Jr. & R. McIntosh. New York: D. Appleton-Century.
Hopper, S.R. (1965), Wallace Stevens: The sundry comforts of the sun. In: *Four Ways of Modern Poetry*, ed. N. A. Scott, Jr. Richmond: John Knox Press.
Idelsohn, A.Z. (1948), *Jewish Music in Its Historical Development*. New York: Tudor.
Isakower, O. (1939), On the exceptional position of the auditory sphere. *Internat. J. Psycho-Anal.*, 20: 340–348.
Ives, C. (1905), Manuscript sketches for "The Things Our Fathers Loved." Ives Collection, Library of the Yale School of Music, Negative 2742.
────── (1920a), Essays before a sonata. In: *Essays Before a Sonata, The Majority, and Other Writings by Charles Ives*, ed. H. Boatwright. New York: W.W. Norton, pp. 3–102.
────── (1920b), The amount to carry. In: *Essays Before a Sonata, The Majority, and Other Writings by Charles Ives*, ed H. Boatwright. New York: W.W. Norton, pp. 235–240.
────── (1922), *114 Songs*. Bryn Mawr: Merion Music.
────── (1942), *Sonata No. 4 for Violin and Piano*. New York: Associated Music Publishers.
────── (1972), *Charles E. Ives—Memos*, ed. J. Kirkpatrick. New York: W.W. Norton.
Jacobson, E. (1957), Normal and pathological moods: Their nature and functions. In: *Depression*, ed. E. Jacobson. New York: International Universities Press, 1971, pp. 66–106.

——— (1959), The "exceptions": An elaboration of Freud's character study. *The Psychoanalytic Study of the Child*, 14: 135–154. New York: International Universities Press.
——— (1971), On the psychoanalytic theory of affects. In: *Depression*, ed. E. Jacobson. New York: International Universities Press, 1971, pp. 3–46.
Jacoby, H. (1926), Mus es Unmusikalische geben? *Zeitschrift für Psychoanalytische Pädagogik*, 1: 33–38, 110–119.
Jaffe, D.S. (1983), On words and music: A personal commentary. *Psychoanal. Quart.*, 52: 590–593.
James, P. (1966), *Henry Moore on Sculpture*. New York: Viking Press.
Jaspers, K. (1932), *Philosophy*, 3 vols., trans. E. Ashton. Chicago: University of Chicago Press.
Jones, E. (1914), The Madonna's conception through the ear. In: *Essays in Applied Psycho-Analysis*, Vol. 2. London: Hogarth Press, 1951, pp. 266–357.
——— (1955), *The Life and Works of Sigmund Freud*, Vol. 2. New York: Basic Books.
Kahn, C., & Piorkowski, G. (1974), Conditions promoting creativity in group rearing of children. *The Psychoanalytic Study of the Child*, 29: 231–255. New Haven, CT: Yale University Press.
Kalbeck, M., ed. (1909), *Brahms: The Herzogenberg Correspondence*, trans. H. Bryant. London: John Murray.
——— (1913–1922), *Johannes Brahms*, 4 vols. Berlin: Deutsche Brahms-Gesellschaft.
Kalfus, M. (1984), Richard Wagner as cult hero: The Tannhauser who would be Siegfried. *J. Psychohist.*, 11:315–382.
Kant, I. (1790), *Kritik der Urteilskraft*. Berlin: Lagarde & Friederich.
Kanzer, M. (1957), Contemporary psychoanalytic views of aesthetics. *J. Amer. Psychoanal. Assn.*, 5: 514–524.
Katan, A. (1961), Some thoughts about the role of verbalization in early childhood. *The Psychoanalytic Study of the Child*, 16: 184–188. New York: International Universities Press.
Keller, H. (1957), "Die Gluckliche Hand and Other Errors." *The Listener*, 57: 961.
Kernberg, O. (1966), Structural derivatives of object relationships. *Internat. J. Psycho-Anal.*, 47: 236–260.
Kerner, D. (1973), *Krankheiten Grosser Musiker*, 2 vols., 3rd. ed. New York: Schattauer.
Kerr, W.A. (1945), *Experiments on the Effects of Music on Factory Production*. Applied Psychology Monograph 5. Stanford, CA: Stanford University Press.
Kerst, F. (1913), *Die Erinnerungen an Beethoven*, 2 vols. Stuttgart: Hoffmann.
Kierkegaard, S.A. (1843), *De unmiddelbare erotiske Stadier; eller, Det Musikalisk Erotiske*. Enten-eller, Copenhagen: C.A. Reitzel.
Kirkpatrick, J. (1960) *A Temporary Mimeographed Catalogue of the Music Manuscripts and Related Materials of Charles Edward Ives 1874–1954*. New Haven, CT: Library of the Yale School of Music.
——— ed. (1972), *Charles E. Ives—Memos*. New York: W.W. Norton.
Kivy, P. (1980), *The Corded Shill: Reflections on Musical Expression*. Princeton, NJ: Princeton University Press.
Klein, G. (1949), Adaptive properties of sensory functioning: Some postulates and hypotheses. *Bull. Menn. Clin.*, 13: 16–23.
——— (1958), Cognitive control and motivation. In: *Assessment of Human Motives*, ed. G. Lindzey. New York: Holt, Rinehart & Winston, pp. 87–118.
——— (1959), Consciousness in psychoanalytic theory: Some implications for current research in perception. *J. Amer. Psychoanal. Assn.*, 7:5–34.
——— (1965), On hearing one's own voice: An aspect of cognitive control in spoken thought. In: *Psychoanalysis and Current Biological Thought*, eds. N.S.

Greenfield & W.C. Lewis. Madison: University of Wisconsin Press, pp. 245–273.
Klein, M. (1929), Infantile anxiety-situations reflected in a work of art and in the creative impulse. *Internat. J. Psycho-Anal.*, 10: 436–443.
Kleiner, J. (1961), On a lullaby. *Bull. Phila. Assn. Psychoanal.*, 11: 183–189.
―――― (1970), On nostalgia. *Bull. Phila. Assn. Psychoanal.*, 20: 11–30.
Kligerman, C. (1962), A psychoanalytic study of Pirandello's "Six Characters in Search of an Author." *J. Amer. Psychoanal. Assn.*, 10: 731–744.
Knapp, P.H. (1953), The ear, listening and hearing. In: *The Yearbook of Psychoanalysis*, Vol. 10, ed. S. Lorand. New York: International Universities Press, 1955, pp. 177–192.
Koestler, A. (1964), *The Act of Creation*. New York: Macmillan.
Kohut, H. (1951), The psychological significance of musical activity. *Music Ther.*, 1:151–158.
―――― (1952), Review. *Psychoanal. Quart.*, 21:109–111.
―――― (1955), Some psychological effects of music and their relation to music therapy. *Music Ther.*, 5:17–20.
―――― (1957), Observations on the psychological functions of music. *J. Amer. Psychoanal. Assn.*, 5: 389–407.
―――― (1966), Forms and transformations of narcissism. *J. Amer. Psychoanal. Assn.* 145: 243–272.
―――― (1971), *The Analysis of the Self*. New York: International Universities Press.
―――― (1976), Creativeness, charisma, group psychology. In: Freud: The Fusion of Science and Humanism, eds. J. E. Gedo & G. H. Pollock. *Psychological Issues*, Monograph 34/35. New York: International Universities Press, pp. 379–425.
―――― (1977), *The Restoration of the Self*. New York: International Universities Press.
―――― (1978), *The Search for the Self*, ed. P. Ornstein. New York: International Universities Press.
―――― Levarie, S. (1950), On the enjoyment of listening to music. *Psychoanal. Quart.*, 19:64–87.
Korner, A.F. (1964), Some hypotheses regarding the significance of individual differences at birth for later development. *The Psychoanalytic Study of the Child*, 19: 58–72. New York: International Universities Press.
Kris, E. (1936), The psychology of caricature. *Internat. J. Psycho-Anal.*, 17: 285–303.
―――― (1953), *Psychoanalytic Explorations in Art*. New York: International Universities Press, 1957.
―――― Kurz, O. (1934), *Legend, Myth, and Magic in the Image of the Artist*. New Haven, CT: Yale University Press, 1979.
Kubie, L.S. (1966), A reconsideration of thinking, the dream process, and "The Dream." *Psychoanal. Quart.*, 35: 191–198.
Lacan, J. (1977), *Ecrits: A Selection*. New York: W. W. Norton.
Lange-Eichbaum, W. (1961), *Genie, Irrsinn und Ruhm: Eine Pathographie des Genies*, ed. W. Kurth. Munich: Reinhardt.
Langer, S.K. (1953), *Feeling and Form*. New York: Charles Scribner's Sons.
―――― (1957), *Philosophy in a New Key*. Cambridge, MA: Harvard University Press.
―――― (1967), *Mind: An Essay on Human Feeling*. Baltimore: Johns Hopkins University Press.
Leach, M. (1972), *Standard Dictionary of Folklore, Mythology and Legend*. New York: Funk & Wagnalls.
Lee, H. (1947), On the aesthetic states of mind. *Psychiatry*, 10: 281–306.
―――― (1948), Spirituality and beauty in artistic experience. *Psychoanal. Quart.*, 17: 507–523.

References

_____ (1949), The creative imagination. *Psychoanal. Quart.*, 18: 351–360.
Lewin, B. D. (1953), The forgetting of dreams. In: *Drives, Affects, Behavior*, ed. R. M. Lowenstein. New York: International Universities Press.
_____ (1954), Sleep, narcissistic neurosis, and the analytic situation. *Psychoanal. Quart.*, 23: 487–510.
_____ (1968), *The Image and The Past*. New York: International Universities Press.
Lewis, M. (1977), Language, cognitive development and personality. *J. Amer. Acad. Child. Psychiat.*, 16: 646–666.
Lichtenberg, J. D. (1978), The testing of reality from the standpoint of the body self. *J. Amer. Psychoanal. Assn.*, 26: 357–385.
_____ (1984), The late works and styles of Eugene O'Neill, Henry James, and Ludwig van Beethoven. In: *Psychoanalysis: The Vital Issues*, eds. J. E. Gedo & G. H. Pollock. New York: International Universities Press, pp. 297–319.
Lifton, R. J. (1979), *The Broken Connection—On Death and the Continuity of Life*. New York: Simon & Schuster.
_____ Olson, E. (1974), *Living and Dying*. New York: Praeger.
Litzmann, B. (1902–1908), *Clara Schumann: Ein Künstlerleben nach Tagebüchern und Briefe*, 3 vols. Leipzig: Breitkopf & Härtel.
_____ (1913), *Clara Schumann: An Artist's Life*, 2 vols., 4th ed., trans. & ed. & abridged, G. E. Hadow. New York: Vienna House, 1972.
_____ (1973), *Letters of Clara Schumann and Johannes Brahms* (1853–1896), trans. N. Reich. New York: Vienna House.
Lundin, R.W. (1953), *An Objective Psychology of Music*. New York: Ronald Press.
Lustman, S.L. (1968), The economic point of view and defense. *The Psychoanalytic Study of the Child*, 23: 189–203. New York: International Universities Press.
Lüthi, H. (1982), Reflections on the exterior and interior action of the work Tristan and Isolde. Booklet with recording of *Tristan und Isolde*, conducted by Carlos Kleiber, D.G.G. No. 2741006.
Macalpine, I., & Hunter, R.A. (1952), Rossini: Piano pieces for the primal scene. *Amer. Imago*, 9: 213–219.
MacDonald, M. (1976), *Schoenberg*. London: J.M. Dent.
Maehder, J. (1982), Intervallic structure and sonority in the score of Tristan. Booklet with recording of *Tristan und Isolde*, conducted by Carlos Kleiber, D.G.G. No. 2741006.
Magee, B. (1983), *The Philosophy of Schopenhauer*. New York: Oxford University Press.
Mahler, A. (1969), *Gustav Mahler: Memories and Letters*, rev. ed. New York: Viking Press.
Mahler, G. (no date), Symphony No. 2 in C Minor. Kalmus.
_____ (1984), Symphony No. 2 in C Minor. Autograph score. Osborn Collection, Yale University Library.
Mahler, M. (1965), Mother–child interaction during separation–individuation. In: *The Selected Papers of Margaret S. Mahler*, Vol. 2. New York: Jason Aronson, pp. 35–42.
_____ (1966), Notes on the development of basic moods: The depressive affect. In: *Psychoanalysis—A General Psychology*, eds. R. M. Loewenstein, L. M. Newman, M. Schur, & A. J. Solnit. New York: International Universities Press, pp. 152–168.
_____ (1968), *On Human Symbiosis and the Vicissitudes of Individuation*. New York: International Universities Press.
_____ Pine, F., & Bergman, A. (1975), *The Psychological Birth of the Human Infant*. New York: Basic Books.

Malich, B. (1975), *James and John Stuart Mill—Father and Son in the Nineteenth Century.* New York: Basic Books.
Mann, W. (1981), Libretto for Wagner's *Die Walkure,* English translation. Holland: Phillips Recording No. 6769071.
Margolis, N.M. (1954), A theory on the psychology of jazz. *Amer. Imago,* 11: 263–291.
Martin, P.A. (1966), A psychoanalytic study of the Marschallin theme from *Der Rosenkavalier. J. Amer. Psychoanal. Assn.,* 14: 760–774.
Martner, K. (1979), *Selected Letters of Gustav Mahler.* New York: Farrar, Strauss, Giroux.
Maslow, A.H. (1962), *Toward a Psychology of Being.* Princeton, NJ: Van Nostrand.
Masserman, J.H. (1955), *The Practice of Dynamic Psychiatry.* Philadelphia: Saunders.
Masson, J. (1980), *The Oceanic Feeling.* Boston: D. Reidel.
May, F. (1981), *The Life of Brahms,* 2 vols. enlarged & illus. ed. Neptune, NJ: Paganiniana.
May, H. (1888), *Early Letters.* London: G. Bell.
——— (1890), *The Life of Robert Schumann as Told in His Letters.* London: Richard Bentley.
Mazlich, B. (1975), *James and John Stuart Mill—Father and Son in the Nineteenth Century.* New York: Basic Books.
McDonald, M. (1970), The Suzuki method, child development, and transitional tunes. *Amer. String Teacher,* 20, 1:24–29.
Mellinkoff, R. (1970), *The Horned Moses in Medieval Art and Thought.* Berkeley: University of California Press.
Meltzoff, A.N., & Moore, M.K. (1977), Imitation of facial and manual gestures by human neonates. *Science,* 198: 75–78.
Metana, B. (undated), *Letters and Reminiscences,* ed. F. Bartos. Prague: Artia, 1955.
Meyer, B.C. (1967), *Joseph Conrad. A Psychoanalytic Biography.* Princeton, NJ: Princeton University Press.
——— (1972), Some reflections on the contribution of psychoanalysis to biography. In: *Psychoanalysis and Contemporary Science,* Vol. 1. New York: Macmillan, pp. 373–391.
Michel, A. (1951), *Psychanalyse de la musique.* Paris: Presses Universitaires de France.
——— (1960), *L'école freudienne devant la musique.* Paris: Les Editions du Scorpion.
Miller, M. (1956), *Nostalgia, A Psychoanalytic Study of Marcel Proust.* Boston: Houghton-Mifflin.
Mitchell, D. (1955), Some notes on Mahler's Tenth Symphony. *Mus. Times,* December.
——— (1958), *Gustav Mahler: The Early Years,* rev. ed. London: Faber & Faber, 1980.
——— (1975), *Gustav Mahler: The Wunderhorn Years.* Boulder: Westview Press.
Montani, A. (1945), Psychoanalysis of music. *Psychoanal. Rev.,* 32: 225–227.
Mooney, W. E. (1968), Gustav Mahler: A note on life and death in music. *Psychoanal. Quart.,* 37: 80–102.
Morgenstern, S. (1956), *Composers on Music.* New York: Pantheon Books.
Moser, A. (1910), *Joseph Joachim; Ein Lebensbild.* Berlin: Deutsche Brahms-Gesellschaft.
Moses, R. (1968), Form and content: An ego-psychological view. *The Psychoanalytic Study of the Child,* 23: 204–223. New York: International Universities Press.
Mosonyi, D. (1935), Die irrationalen Grundlagen der Musik. *Imago,* 21: 207–226.
Mozart, W.A. (1778), *The Letters of Mozart and His Family,* 2 vols., 2nd ed., ed. E. Anderson. London: Macmillan, 1966.

———— (1786), Excerpts from the fragments of Zoroaster. In: *Mozart: Briefe and Aufzeichnungen*, Vol. 3, eds. W.A. Bauer, O.E. Deutsch, & J.H. Eibl. Kassel, 1962–1975, pp. 506–507.
Musgrave, M. (1983), The cultural world of Brahms. In: *Brahms—Biographical, Documentary, and Analytical Studies*, ed. R Pascall. New York: Cambridge University Press, pp. 1–26.
Nass, M.L. (1964), The development of conscience: A comparison of the moral judgements of deaf and hearing children. *Child Develop.*, 35: 1073–1080.
———— (1971), Some considerations of psychoanalytic interpretation of music. *Psychoanal. Quart.*, 40: 303–316.
———— (1975), On hearing and inspiration in the composition of music. *Psychoanal. Quart.*, 44: 431–449.
Nemiah, J. (1967), Obsessive-compulsive disorder (obsessive-compulsive neurosis). In: *Comprehensive Textbook of Psychiatry*, Vol. 1, 4th ed., eds. H.S. Kaplan & B.J. Sadock. Baltimore: Williams & Wilkins, 1985, pp. 904–917.
Newman, E. (1930), *Stories of the Great Operas and Their Composers*, Vol. 2. Garden City, NY: Garden City Publishing Company.
———— (1933), *The Life of Richard Wagner*, Vol. 2. New York: Cambridge University Press.
Nickels, C. (1968), Who is Suzuki? *Amer. String Teacher*, 18, 4:4–5.
Niederland, W. G. (1958), Early auditory experiences, beating fantasies and primal scene. *The Psychoanalytic Study of the Child*, 18: 471–502. New York: International Universities Press.
———— (1976), Psychoanalytic approaches to artistic creativity. *Psychoanal. Quart.*, 45: 185–212.
Niemann, W. (1937), *Brahms*, trans. C.A. Phillips. New York: Tudor, 1968.
Nohl, L. (1880), *Life of Mozart*. Chicago: Jansen, McClurg.
Noy, P. (1966), The psychodynamics of music. *J. Music Ther.*, 3: 126–134.
———— (1967a), The psychodynamics of music. *J. Music Ther.*, 4: 7–23.
———— (1967b), The psychodynamics of music. *J. Music Ther.*, 4: 45–51.
———— (1967c), The psychodynamics of music. *J. Music Ther.*, 4: 81–94.
———— (1967d), The psychodynamics of music. *J. Music Ther.*, 4: 117–125.
———— (1968a), The development of musical ability. *The Psychoanalytic Study of the Child*, 23: 332–347. New York: International Universities Press.
———— (1968b), A theory of art and aesthetic experience. *Psychoanal. Rev.*, 55: 623–645.
———— (1969), A revision of the psychoanalytic theory of the primary process. *Internat. J. Psycho-Anal.*, 50: 155–178.
———— (1973), Symbolism and mental representation. *Ann. Psychoanal.* 1: 125–158.
———— (1978), Insight and creativity. *J. Amer. Psychoanal. Assn.*, 26: 717–748.
Olson, E (1974), *Living and Dying*. New York: Praeger.
Ostwald, P. (1980), Florestan, Eusebius, Clara, and Schumann's right hand. *19th Cent. Music*, 4 (Summer): 20ff.
———— (1983), Johannes Brahms, "Frei, aber (nicht immer) froh." *Kongreßbericht zum III. Gewandhaus-Symposium*. Leipzig: Gewandhaus, pp. 52–55.
———— (1985), *Schumann; The Inner Voices of a Musical Genius*. Boston: Northeastern University Press.
———— (1987), Anton Bruckner; musical intelligence and depressive disorder. In: *Kongreßbericht zum V. Gewandhaus-Symposium*. Leipzig: Gewandhaus.
———— (1988), Gustav Mahler; health and creative energy. In: *Rondom Mahler VIII*. Amsterdam: Concertgebouw.

———— (1989), The healing power of music; some observations on the semiotic function of transitional objects in musical communication. In: *The Semiotic Bridge*, eds. I. Rauch & G.F. Carr. Berlin/New York: de Gruyter, pp. 279–296.

Panel (1968), Psychoanalytic theory of affects, E.M. Weinshel, reporter. *J. Amer. Psychoanal. Assn.*, 16: 645–646.

Paris Review. *Writers at Work*. Series 1,2,3. New York: Viking Press, 1958, 1963, 1967.

Partridge, E. (1960), *Shakespeare's Bawdy*. New York: Dutton.

Pascal, R. (1983), *Brahms—Biographical, Documentary, and Analytical Studies*. New York: Cambridge University Press.

Peller, L.E. (1965), Language and its pre-stages. *Bull. Phila. Pyschoanal. Assn.*, 14: 55–76.

Perlis, V. (1974), *Charles Ives Remembered: An Oral History*. New Haven, CT: Yale University Press.

Perry, S.R. (1974), *Charles Ives and the American Mind*. Kent: Kent State University Press.

Peyser, J. (1971), *The New Music: The Sense Behind the Sound*. New York: Delacorte Press.

———— (1975), Style and idea. In: *Selected Writings of Arnold Schoenberg*, ed. L. Stein. New York: St. Martin's Press.

Pfeiffer, S. (1922), Problems of the psychology of music in the light of psychoanalysis. I. Psychophysiology of musical sound. *Internat. J. Psycho-Anal.*, 3: 127–130.

———— (1923), Musikpsychologische probleme. *Imago*, 9: 453–462.

Piaget, J. (1952), *The Origins of Intelligence in Children*. New York: International Universities Press.

———— (1954), *The Construction of Reality in the Child*. New York: Basic Books.

Pickering, G. (1984), *Creative Malady*. London: Oxford University Press.

Pine, F. (1977), On the expansion of the affect array: A developmental description. Presented to the Discussion Group: Affect in Theory and Practice. American Psychoanalytic Association, New York.

Plato, *The Republic*, Bk. 3, trans. R.W. Sterling & W.C. Scott. New York: W.W. Norton, 1985.

Poincaré, H. (1952), *Science and Method*. New York: Dover.

Pollock, G.H. (1961), Mourning and adaptation. *Internat. J. Psycho-Anal.*, 42: 341–361.

———— (1962), Childhood parent and sibling loss in adult patients. *Arch. Gen. Psychiat.*, 7: 295–305.

———— (1966), Mourning and childhood loss: Their possible significance in the Josef Breuer–Bertha Pappenheim relationship. *Bull. Assn. Psychoanal. Med.*, 5/4: 51–54.

———— (1968), The possible significance of childhood object loss in the Josef Breuer–Bertha Pappenheim (Anna O.)–Sigmund Freud relationship. *J. Amer. Psychoanal. Assn.*, 16: 711–739.

———— (1970), Anniversary reactions, trauma and mourning. *Psychoanal. Quart.*, 39: 347–371.

———— (1971a), On time and anniversaries. In: *The Unconscious Today*, ed. M. Kanzer. New York: International Universities Press, pp. 233–257.

———— (1971b), Temporal anniversary manifestations: Hour, day, holiday. *Psychoanal. Quart.*, 40/1: 123–131.

———— (1971c), Some historical notes on Bertha Pappenheim's idealized ancestor: Gluckel von Hameln. *Amer. Imago*, 28/3: 216–227.

_____ (1972a), On mourning and anniversaries. The relationship of culturally constituted defensive systems to intrapsychic adaptive processes. *Israel Ann. Psychiat.*, 10:9–40.
_____ (1972b), Bertha Pappenheim's pathological mourning: Possible effects of childhood sibling loss. *J. Amer. Psychoanal. Assn.*, 21/2: 328–332.
_____ (1973), Bertha Pappenheim: Addenda to her case history. *J. Amer. Psychoanal. Assn.*, 21/2: 328–332.
_____ (1974a), Mourning through music: Gustav Mahler. Presented to the Regional Conference of the Chicago Psychoanalytic Society. March 30, 1974.
_____ (1974b), On anniversary suicide and mourning. In: *Depression and Human Existence*, eds. T. Benedek & E. J. Anthony. Boston: Little Brown, 1975.
_____ (1975a), On mourning, immortality and utopia. *J. Amer. Psychoanal. Assn.*, 23: 334–362.
_____ (1975b), Mourning and memorialization through music. *Ann. Psychoanal.*, 3: 423–436.
_____ (1975c), On mourning, immortality, and utopia. *J. Amer. Psychoanal. Assn.*, 23: 334–362.
Portnoy, J. (1963), *Music in the Life of Man*. New York: Holt, Rinehart & Winston.
Pratt, C. C. (1952), *Music and the Language of Emotion*. Washington, DC: Library of Congress.
_____ (1954), The design of music. *J. Aesth.*, 12: 289–300.
Prosen, H., Martin, R., & Prosen, M. (1972), The remembered mother and the fantasized mother. *Arch. Gen. Psychiat.*, 27: 791–794.
Racker, H. (1951), Contribution to psychoanalysis of music. *Amer. Imago*, 8: 129–163.
Rank, O. (1909), *The Myth of the Birth of the Hero*. New York: Robert Brunner, 1952.
_____ (1932), *Art and the Artist*. New York: Alfred A. Knopf.
Rapaport, D. (1951), States of consciousness: A psychopathological and psychodynamic view. In: *The Collected Papers of David Rapaport*, ed. M. M. Gill. New York: Basic Books, 1967, pp. 385–404.
_____ (1953), Some metapsychological considerations concerning activity and passivity. In: *The Collected Papers of David Rapaport*, ed. M. M. Gill. New York: Basic Books, pp. 530–568.
_____ (1957), The theory of ego autonomy: A generalization. In: *The Collected Papers of David Rapaport*, ed. M. M. Gill. New York: Basic Books, 1967, pp. 722–744.
_____ (1960), On the psychoanalytic theory of motivation. In: *The Collected Papers of David Rapaport*, ed. M. M. Gill. New York: Basic Books, pp. 853–915.
Rechardt, E. (1985), On musical cognition and archaic meaning schemata. *Scand. Psychoanal. Rev.*, 8: 95–113.
Rehberg, P., & Rehberg, W. (1969), *Robert Schumann: Sein leben und sein werk*, 2nd ed. Zurich: Artemis.
Reich, N.B. (1985), *Clara Schumann—The Artist and the Woman*. New York: Cornell University Press.
Reik, T. (1952), On wings of song. *Psychoanal.*, 1:3–11.
_____ (1953), *The Haunting Melody*. New York: Farrar, Straus & Young.
Richards, R. L. (1981), Relationship between Creativity and Psychopathology: An Evaluation and Interpretation of the Evidence. *Genetic Psychology Monographs*, 103:261–324.
Ricoeur, P. (1970), *Freud and Philosophy*. New Haven, CT: Yale University Press.
Riemann, H. (1900), *Die Elemente der musikalischen Ästhetik*. Berlin: W. Spemann.
Robertson, A. (1968), *Requiem: Music of Mourning and Consolation*. New York: Praeger.

Rogers, C. R. (1954), Toward a theory of creativity. *ETC: Review of General Semantics*, 11: 249–260.
Rogers, R. (1978), *Metaphor: A Psychoanalytic View*. Berkeley: University of California Press.
Roheim, G. (1945), Sublimation. In: *Yearbook of Psychoanalysis*, Vol. 1, ed. S. Lorand. New York: International Universities Press, pp. 109–120.
Rolland, R. (1929), *Beethoven the Creator*. New York: Harper.
Rose, G. (1979), William Faulkner's *Light in August*: The orchestration of time in the psychology of artistic style. *The Psychoanalytic Study of Society*, 8: 251–276. New Haven, CT: Yale University Press.
——— (1980), *The Power of Form*. New York: International Universities Press.
Rosen, V.H. (1964), Some effects of artistic talent on character style. *Psychoanal. Quart.*, 33: 1–24.
Rosner, S., & Abt, L. E. (1972), *The Creative Experience*. New York: Delta Books.
Ross, N. (1968), Beyond "The Future of an Illusion." *J. Hillside Hosp.*, 17: 259–276.
Rossiter, F.R. (1975), *Charles Ives and His America*. New York: Liveright.
Rothenberg, A. (1972), Poetic process and psychotherapy. *Psychiatry*, 35: 238–252.
——— (1979a), Einstein's creative thinking and the general theory of relativity: A documented report. *Amer. J. Psychiat.*, 136: 38–43.
——— (1979b), *The Emerging Goddess*. Chicago: University of Chicago Press.
Rousseau, J. J. (1781), *Traités sur la musique*. Geneva.
Russell, J. (1983), "Schoenberg, the painter." *Keynote*, January: 7–13.
Sachs, C. (1929), *Geist und Werden der Musikinstrumente*. Berlin: Reimer.
Sadie, S. (1980), *The New Grove Dictionary of Music and Musicians*, 6th ed. London: Macmillan.
Salk, L. (1960), The effects of the normal heartbeat sound on the behavior of the new-born infant: Implications for mental health. *World Mental Health*, 12: 1–8.
Salter, L. (1982), *Tristan and Isolde*. Translation of libretto. D.G.G. recording conducted by Carlos Kleiber No. 2741006.
Salzer, F. (1962), *Structural Hearing*. New York: Dover.
Sams, E. (1972), Schumann and the tonal analogue. In: *Robert Schumann: The Man and His Music*, ed. A. Walker. London: Barrie & Jenkins, pp. 398–402.
Schachtel, E. (1959), *Metamorphosis: On the Development of Affect, Perception, Attention and Memory*. New York: Basic Books.
Schachter, S. (1976), Rhythm and linear analysis: A preliminary study. *The Music Forum*, 4: 281–334.
Schafer, R. (1968), *Aspects of Internalization*. New York: International Universities Press.
Schauffler, R.H. (1940), *The Unknown Brahms: His Life, Character and Works*. New York: Crown.
——— (1945), *Florestan: The Life and Work of Robert Schumann*. New York: Dover, 1963.
Schilder, P. (1950), *The Image and Appearance of the Human Body*. New York: International Universities Press.
——— (1964), *Contributions to Developmental Neuropsychiatry*. New York: International Universities Press.
Schneider, H. (1974), *Robert Schumann: Manuscripte, Briefe, Schumanniana*. Katalog Nr. 188. Tutzing: Schneider.
Schoen, M. (1940), *The Psychology of Music*. New York: Ronald Press.
Schonberg, H.C. (1963), *The Great Pianists, from Mozart to the Present*. New York: Simon & Schuster.
Schopenhauer, A. (1877), Die Welt als Wille und Vorstellung. In: *Sämmtliche Werke*, 2nd ed. Leipzig: F.A. Brockhaus.
Schumann, E. (1833), *Caecilia*, 1:253–258.

Schumann, R. (1883), *Gesammelte Schriften uber Musik und Musiker*, 2 vols. Leipzig: Breitkopf & Härtel.
Schwarz, B. (1983), Johannes Brahms and Joseph Joachim. In: *Brahms Symposium*. Washington, DC: Library of Congress.
Seashore, C.E. (1938), *Psychology of Music*. New York: McGraw-Hill.
Sechehaye, M.S. (1956)), *A New Psychotherapy on Schizophrenia*, trans. G. Rubin-Rabson. New York: Grune & Stratton.
Sessions, R. (1941), The composer and his message. In: *The Intent of the Artist*, ed. A. Centeno. Princeton, NJ: Princeton University Press, pp. 101–134.
─────── (1950), *The Musical Experience of Composer, Performer, Listener*. Princeton, NJ: Princeton University Press.
─────── (1970), *Questions about Music*. Cambridge, MA: Harvard University Press.
Sharpe, E. (1930), Certain aspects of sublimation and delusion. *Internat. J. Psycho-Anal.*, 11: 12–23.
─────── (1940), Psycho-physical problems revealed in language: An examination of metaphor. *Internat. J. Psycho-Anal.*, 21: 201–213.
─────── (1946), From "King Lear" to "The Tempest." *Internat. J. Psycho-Anal.*, 27: 19–30.
Shevrin, H., & Toussieng, P. (1965), Vicissitudes of the need for tactile stimulation in instinctual development. *The Psychoanalytic Study of the Child*, 20: 310–339. New York: International Universities Press.
Shopper, M. (1978), The role of audition in early psychic development. *J. Amer. Psychoanal. Assn.*, 26: 283–310.
Silverman, M., & Will, N. (1986), Sylvia Plath and the failure of emotional self-repair through poetry. *Psychoanal. Quart.*, 55: 99–129.
Slater, E., & Mayer, A. (1959), Contributions to a pathography of the musicians: 1. Robert Schumann. *Confinia Psychiat.*, 2: 65–94.
Slochower, H. (1974), Psychoanalysis and creativity. In: *Essays in Creativity*, ed. S. Rosner & L. E. Abt. Croton-On-Hudson: North River Press.
Slonimsky, N. (1965), *Lexicon of Musical Invective; Critical Assaults on Composers Since Beethoven's Time*, 2nd ed. New York: Coleman-Ross.
Smetana, B. (undated), *Letters and Reminiscences,* ed. F. Bartos. Prague: Artia, 1955.
Socarides, C.W. (1977), *The World of Emotions*. New York: International Universities Press.
Solomon, M. (1978), *Beethoven*. New York: Schirmer.
─────── (1980), On Beethoven's creative process: A two-part invention. *Music & Letters*, 61: 272–283.
Solomon, P., Kubzansky, P. E., Leiderman, P. H., Mendelson, J.H., Trumbull, R., & Wexler, D. (1961), *Sensory Deprivation*. Cambridge, MA: Harvard University Press.
Spalding, A. (1953), *A Fiddle, a Sword, and a Lady*. New York: Holt, Rinehart & Winston.
Spencer, H. (1902), The origin and function of music. In: *Facts and Comments*. New York: Appleton.
Spitz, R.A. (1963), Life and the dialogue. In: *Counterpoint, Libidinal Object and Subject*, ed. H. S. Gaskill. New York: International Universities Press, pp. 154–176.
─────── (1965), *The First Year of Life*. New York: International Universities Press.
Stein, H. (1976), *Peter and the Wolf*, a musical tale of individuation and the imagery of the New Soviet Man: A psychoanalytic perspective on Russian cultural history. *The Psychoanalytic Study of Society*, 7: 31–63. New Haven, CT: Yale University Press.

Stekel, W. (1911), Review. *Zentralblatt für psychoanalyse und psychotherapie*, 1:252–254.
Stendhal (1824), *Life of Rossini*. New York: Criterion Books, 1957.
Stephenson, K. (1973), *Johannes Brahms in Seiner Familie—Der Briefwechsel*. Hamburg: Hauswedel.
Sterba, E. (1940), Homesickness and the mother's breast. *Psychiat. Quart.*, 14: 701–708.
Sterba, R.F. (1939), Toward the problem of the musical process. *Psychoanal. Rev.*, 33: 37–43.
———— (1965), Psychoanalysis and music. *Amer. Imago*, 22:96–111.
———— Sterba, E. (1952), Beethoven and his nephew. *Internat. J. Psycho-Anal.*, 33: 470–478.
Stern, D. (1977), *The First Relationship: Mother and Infant*. Cambridge, MA: Harvard University Press.
Stevenson, C.E. (1958), Symbolism in the non-representational arts. In: *Introductory Readings in Aesthetics*, ed. J. Hospers. New York: Free Press, 1969, pp. 185–209.
Stevenson, O. (1954), The first treasured possession. *The Psychoanalytic Study of the Child*, 9: 199–217. New York: International Universities Press.
Storr, A. (1972), *The Dynamics of Creation*. London: Secker & Warburg.
Strohl, E.L. (1970), The unique friendship of Theodor Billroth and Johannes Brahms. *Surg., Gynecol., Obstet.*, 131: 757–761.
Stuckenschmidt, H. H. (1978), *Schoenberg, His Life, World, and Work*, ed. T. H. Searle. New York: Schirmer Books.
Stumpf, K. (1883–1890), *Tonpsychologie*. Leipzig: S. Hirzel.
Suzuki, S. (1969), *Nurtured by Love: A New Approach to Education*. New York: Exposition Press.
Tanner, J. M., & Inhelder, B. (1956), *Discussions on Child Development. A Consideration of the Biological, Psychological, and Cultural Approaches to the Understanding of Human Development and Behavior*. New York: International Universities Press.
Taylor, A. (1951), *English Riddles from Oral Tradition*. Berkeley: University of California Press.
Taylor, I. A., & Paperte, F. (1958), Current theory and research in the effects of music on human behavior. *J. Aesth. Art Crit.*, 117: 251–258.
Taylor, R. (1979), *Richard Wagner: His Life, Art and Thought*. New York: Taplinger.
Toye, F. (1947), *Rossini: A Study in Tragi-Comedy*, rev. ed. New York: W.W. Norton, 1963.
Tupper, F., ed. (1910), *The Riddles of the Exeter Book*. Boston: Ginn.
Turner, W. (1938), *Mozart: The Man and His Works*. Garden City, NY: Doubleday, 1955.
Updike, J. (1963), More love in the Western world. *New Yorker*, August 24, pp. 90–104.
Virgil, *The Aeneid by Virgil*, trans. R. Fitzgerald. New York: Random House, 1983.
Volkan, V. (1981), *Linking Objects and Linking Phenomena*. New York: International Universities Press.
Von Arnim, L.A., & Brentano, C. (1805), *Des Knaben Wunderhorn*. Berlin: Verlag der Nation, 1974.
Waelder, R. (1965), *Psychoanalytic Avenues to Art*. New York: International Universities Press.
Walter, B. (1966), *Gustav Mahler*. New York: Alfred A. Knopf.
Wangh, M. (1976), Underlying motivations in Pirandello's "Six Characters in Search of an Author": A Psychoanalytic view. *J. Amer. Psychoanal. Assn.*, 24: 309–328.
Wasiliewski, W. J. (1888), *Ludwig van Beethoven*, 2 vols. Berlin: Brachvogel & Ranst.
Watson, D. (1979), *Richard Wagner: A Biography*. New York: Schirmer.

Weber, M. (1913), The social psychology of the world religions. In: *From Max Weber: Essays in Sociology*, ed. H. H. Gerth & C. W. Mills. New York: Oxford University Press, 1958, pp. 267–301.
Wegeler-Ries, F. (1838), *Biographische Notizen über Ludwig van Beethoven*. Coblenz: Bädeker.
Weinshel, E.M. (1970), Some psychoanalytic considerations on mood. *Internat. J. Psycho-Anal.*, 51: 313–320.
Weiss, J. (1947), A psychological theory of formal beauty. *Psychoanal. Quart.*, 16: 391–400.
Weissman, P. (1967), Theoretical considerations of ego regression and ego functions in creativity. *Psychoanal. Quart.*, 36: 37–50.
Werfel, A.M. (1958), *And the Bridge Is Love*. New York: Harcourt, Brace.
Werman, D.S. (1977), Normal and pathological nostalgia. *J. Amer. Psychoanal. Assn.*, 25: 387–398.
———— & Jacobs, T. (1983), Thomas Hardy's "The Well-Beloved" and the nature of infatuation. *Internat. Rev. Psycho-Anal.*, 10: 447–457.
Werner, H. (1940), *Comparative Psychology of Mental Development*. New York: International Universities Press.
Westernhagen, C. (1981), *Wagner: A Biography*. New York: Cambridge University Press.
Whitehead, A. (1927), *Symbolism: Its Meaning and Effect*. New York: Macmillan.
Wieck, F. (1830), *Briefe aus den Jahren 1830–1838*, ed. K. Walche-Schumann. Cologne: Arno Volk Verlag, 1968.
Winnicott, D. W. (1953), Transitional objects and transitional phenomena. *Internat. J. Psycho-Anal.*, 34: 89–97.
———— (1967), The location of cultural experience. *Internat. J. Psycho-Anal.*, 48: 368–372.
———— (1971), *Playing and Reality*. London: Tavistock.
Wolff, P. H. (1960), The Development Psychologies of Jean Piaget and Psychoanalysis. *Psychological Issues*, Vol. 2, Monograph 5. New York: International Universities Press.
Wundt, W. (1911), *Einführung in die Psychologie*. Leipzig: Voigt-Lander.

Name Index

Abelin, E.L., 144, 489
Abell, A.M., 184, 185, 186, 489
Abraham, K., 40, 287, 415, 489
Abt, L.E., 188, 504
Alexander, F., 289, 489
Amram, D., 188, 489
Anderson, E., 289, 392, 393, 393n, 396n, 398, 407n, 489
Antrim, D., 11, 489
Anzieu, D., xv, 489
Arazi, I, 90, 489
Arieti, S., 223, 489
Aristotle, 489
Arlow, J.A., 182, 223, 474, 475, 489
Aronoff, M.S., 222n, 493

Babikian, H.M., xiv, 489
Bach, K., 2, 489
Bak, R., 473, 474, 489
Bakhtin, M., 409, 489
Balliet, W., 269, 489
Barkan, H., 317, 489
Bauer, W.L., 401, 402, 490
Bauer-Lechner, N., 389, 490
Becker, H., 302n, 490
Beethoven, L. van, 189, 490
Beres, D., 490
Berezin, M.A., 72, 490
Bergler, E., 391, 490
Bergman, A., 102n, 103, 143, 499
Bergman, P., 42, 44, 46, 69, 180, 490
Bergmann, M., 473, 474, 475, 490
Bernfeld, S., xv, 490
Blaukopf, K., 379, 381, 490
Blom, E., 186, 490
Blume, F., 199, 490
Bonaparte, M., 391, 490
Bourboulis, P.P., 409, 490
Bradshaw, S., xiv, 490
Brahms, J., 301, 307–308, 311–312, 314, 315, 316, 317, 318, 490
Branfman, T.C., 490
Brazelton, T.B., 271, 490
Brenner, C., 47, 245, 490
Brentano, C., 341, 506
Brockway, W., 490
Burton, A.M., 97–113, 441–463
Bush, M., 213, 490

Capri, A., 186, 187n, 490

Castelnuovo–Tedesco, P., 239, 244–245, 490
Catholy, E., 409, 490
Chasseguet–Smirgel, J., 473, 490
Chessick, R., 465–483, 467, 469, 476, 477, 478, 479, 481, 490–491
Chijs, A., Van Der, 3, 491
Chissell, J., 491
Coeuroy, A., 25, 491
Coltrera, J.T., 42, 48, 181, 183, 188, 268, 269, 491
Comini, A., 310n, 315, 491
Cooke, D., 382, 491
Cooper, M., 189, 191, 491
Copland, A., 188, 491
Corbin, E.I., xiii, 491
Coriat, I.H., 7, 225, 491
Cowell, H., xvi–xvii, 120, 123, 125n, 136, 137, 162, 171, 172, 175, 238, 491
Cowell, S., 120, 123, 125n, 136, 137, 141, 162, 171, 172, 175, 238, 491
Craft, R., 491
Croce, B., 2, 491
Cross, M., 424, 434, 435, 491

Dahlberg, C., 478, 491
Dale, K., 444, 491
Darwin, C.A., 2, 21, 491
de Filippis, M., 406, 408, 491
de La Grange, H., 341, 342, 343, 347, 350, 358, 360, 361, 363, 366, 367, 369, 370, 376, 378–379, 381, 383, 385, 389, 491
De Rougemont, D., 472, 477, 491
Deutsch, F., 289, 491
Deutsch, O.E., 311, 401, 402, 409, 490, 492
Diether, J., 368, 380, 386, 492
Douglas, A., 128, 492

Edelheit, H., 492
Edelson, M., 153, 492
Edwards, H.S., 424, 425, 430, 492
Eggar, K., 3, 492
Ehrenzweig, A., 217, 218, 219, 221, 492
Ehrmann, A., 295, 492
Eibl, J.H., 401, 402, 403n, 490, 492
Einstein, A., 392, 398n, 492
Eissler, K., 188, 268, 415n, 492

509

Elkus, J., 127, 492
Elworthy, F.T., 407, 492
Emde, R.N., 239, 492
Encyclopaedia Britannica, 492
Encyclopedia Judaica, 379, 492
Engel, G., 321n, 325, 331, 332, 492
Erikson, E.H., 222, 224, 492
Escalona, S.K., 42, 44, 46, 69, 180, 490
Esman, A., 239, 391–399, 492
Ewen, D., 424, 434, 435, 491

Farnsworth, P.R., 492
Feder, S., ix–xvii, xi, xv, 115–176, 117n, 125n, 142, 151, 152, 153, 163, 165, 167, 168, 173, 174, 233–266, 235, 236, 238, 248, 255, 259, 341–390, 343, 378, 379, 384, 386, 485–488, 492–493
Fenichel, O., 239, 478, 493
Ferenczi, S., 7, 287, 493
Feuerbach, L., 288, 493
Field, T.M., et al., 270, 493
Flugel, J.C., x, 493
Fraisse, P., 44, 493
Frances, A., 222n, 493
Franken, F.H., 293, 493
Frazier, Sir J., 409, 493
Freedman, A., 239, 242, 244, 493
Freud, A., 39, 42, 72–73, 92, 180, 191, 271, 493
Freud, E., 481, 493
Freud, S., 4, 9, 16, 19, 30, 39, 47, 49–59 *passim*, 144, 145, 180, 185n, 189, 210, 211, 212, 216, 230, 238, 381, 391, 397, 398, 420, 467, 468, 472, 474, 479, 487, 493–494
Friedman, S., 55n, 57n, 494
Friedreich, J.B., 406, 494
Frisch, W., 303, 494
Fürst, J., 299, 315, 496

Gal, H., 293, 494
Garciá Márquez, G., 472, 494
Gardner, R.W., 41, 43, 494
Gartenberg, E., 382, 494
Gay, P., 305, 494
Geachan, D., 240, 243, 494
Gediman, H., 474, 475, 494
Geiringer, K., 293, 300, 311, 313, 494
Germain, P., 67, 494
Ghiselin, B., 182, 186, 281, 494
Glover, E., 238, 239, 495

Goethe, J., 410, 473, 495
Goldstein, K., 24, 29, 35, 495
Gombrich, E.R., 220–221, 495
Graf, M., x–xi, xvii, 485, 495
Grand, S., 269, 270, 495
Greenacre, P., 46, 69, 102, 143, 144, 150–151, 182, 183, 190, 192, 267, 268, 272, 495
Greenson, R.R., 87–88, 495
Gutheil, E.A., 64, 495

Hacker, F.J., 209, 495
Hadamard, J., 274, 495
Haezrahi, P., 212, 495
Hamburger, M., 275, 495
Hannett, F., 261, 495
Hanslick, E., 2, 234, 495
Hardy, T., 471, 495
Harrison, I., 479, 495
Hartmann, H., 43, 70, 124, 182, 248, 249, 495
Hayn, H., 408n, 496
Hebb, D.O., 184, 496
Helmholtz, L., 2, 496
Henschel, G., 302, 496
Herbert, M., 496
High Holiday Prayer Book, 496
Hindemith, P., 42–43, 46, 47, 183, 188, 276, 496
Hitchcock, H.W., 125n, 128, 163, 166, 496
Hitschmann, E., 293, 302, 313, 496
Hoffer, W., 271, 496
Hoffmann, K., 296, 298, 299, 315, 496
Holde, A., 300, 306, 313, 496
Holländer, A., 367, 496
Holmberg, A., 466, 468, 496
Holmes, E., 201, 496
Holt, L.E., 4, 5, 496
Hopper, S.R., 225, 496
Howland, J., 4, 5, 496
Hunter, R.A., 72, 439, 499

Idelsohn, A.Z., 379, 496
Inhelder, B., 180, 506
Isakower, O., xiv–xv, 28, 39, 42, 45, 180, 261, 287, 496
Ives, C., 115, 117–168 *passim*, 236, 238, 249, 251, 260, 496

Jackson, D., 41, 43, 494
Jacobs, T., 474, 507
Jacobson, E., 238, 246, 247, 496–497
Jacoby, H., xv, 497

Name Index 511

Jaffe, D.S., xii, xiv, 497
James, P., 269, 497
Jaspers, K., 482, 497
Jones, E., ix–x, 40, 339, 377, 497

Kahn, C., 214, 497
Kalbeck, M., 104, 293, 497
Kalfus, M., x, xvii, 497
Kant, I., 2, 497
Kanzer, M., 497
Karmel, R.L., ix–xvii, 485–488
Katan, A., 103, 497
Keller, H., 497
Kernberg, O., 230, 497
Kerner, D., 293, 497
Kerr, W.A., 11, 497
Kerst, F., 288, 497
Kierkegaard, S.A., 2, 497
Kirkpatrick, J., 120, 123n, 125n, 128, 130–131, 141, 156, 160, 165, 171, 172, 249, 251, 252, 259, 259n, 260, 497
Kivy, P., 263, 264, 265, 497
Klein, G., 41, 43, 44, 181, 183, 188, 497–498
Klein, M., 211, 498
Kleiner, J., xv, 239, 240, 245, 498
Kligerman, C., 216, 498
Knapp, P.H., 287, 289, 498
Koestler, A., 278, 498
Kohut, H., xiii, 1–20, 21–38, 22, 52n, 57n, 68, 72, 234, 289, 387, 465, 474, 475, 479, 480, 481, 498
Korner, A.F., 74, 498
Koslowski, B., 271, 490
Kris, E., ix, 37, 63, 145–156, 179, 181, 182, 185n, 192, 248, 407–408, 409, 495, 498
Kubie, L.S., 223, 498
Kurz, O., ix, 498

Lacan, J., 476, 498
Lange–Eichbaum, W., 293, 498
Langer, S.K., 40, 209, 212, 263–264, 275, 498
Leach, M., 378, 498
Lee, H., 391, 396, 398, 498–499
Levarie, S., 1–20, 52n, 72, 289, 498
Lewin, B.D., 28, 377, 499
Lewis, M., 270, 499
Lichtenberg, J.D., xii, 270, 499
Lifton, R.J., 169, 499
Litzmann, B., 101, 104, 105, 106, 109, 110, 112, 113, 300, 313, 441,
443, 443n, 444, 446n, 453–454, 455, 456, 457, 459, 460, 462, 499
Loewenstein, R.M., 182, 495
Lundin, R.W., 68, 499
Lustman, S.L., 41, 499
Lüthi, H., 469, 499

Macalpine, I., 72, 439, 499
MacDonald, M., 499
McDonald, M., 79–95, 82, 271, 500
Maehder, J., 469, 499
Magee, B., 477, 499
Mahler, A., 322, 323, 325, 334–335, 336, 499
Mahler, G., 499
Mahler, M., 102n, 103, 143, 152, 239, 268, 499
Main, M., 271, 490
Malich, B., 500
Mann, W., 472, 500
Margolis, N.M., 64, 500
Martin, P.A., xi, 500
Martin, R., 482, 503
Martner, K., 350, 354–355, 357, 385, 500
Maslow, A.H., 229, 500
Masserman, J.H., 64, 67, 500
Masson, J., 479, 480, 500
May, F., 293, 297, 500
Mayer, A., 505
Mazlich, B., 143, 146, 500
Mellinkoff, R., 407, 500
Meltzoff, A.N., 270, 500
Messick, S., 41, 43, 494
Metana, B., 500
Meyer, B.C., 162n, 442, 443n, 449n, 500
Michel, A., xiii, 25, 41, 188, 268, 500
Miller, M., 240, 500
Mitchell, D., 321n, 322, 325, 326, 327, 329, 330, 331, 336, 342, 367, 375, 379, 384, 500
Montani, A., 41, 188, 268, 500
Mooney, W.E., 335, 500
Moore, M.K., 270, 500
Morgenstern, S., 273, 500
Moser, A., 307, 500
Moses, R., 213, 500
Mosonyi, D., 3, 500
Mozart, W.A., 16, 411–413, 417, 419, 500–501
Musgrave, M., 316n, 501

Nass, M.L., 39–48, 45, 57n, 179–193, 180, 191, 267–283, 269, 270, 274, 276, 501

Nemiah, J., 501
Newman, E., 423, 425, 433, 466, 501
Nickels, C., 79, 80, 82, 501
Niederland, W.G., 39, 42, 72, 180, 189, 213, 279, 288, 501
Niemann, W., 293, 296, 297, 303, 305, 307, 309, 315, 318, 501
Nohl, L., 201, 501
Noy, P, xii, 41, 45n, 47n, 52n, 53n, 54n, 57n, 63–77, 191, 209–231, 222, 223, 234–235, 273, 485, 501

Olson, E., 169, 501
Ostwald, P., 291–320, 292, 300n, 310, 451, 457, 501–502

Panel (1968), 247, 502
Paperte, F., 218–219, 506
Paris Review, 275, 278, 502
Partridge, E., 415, 502
Pascal, R., 308, 502
Peller, L.E., 103, 502
Perlis, V., 121, 124, 125n, 131, 132, 157, 166, 238, 259, 502
Perry, S.R., 125n, 140, 160, 166, 502
Peyser, J., 502
Pfeiffer, S., 41, 67, 502
Piaget, J., 47, 181, 183, 187, 267, 268, 272, 502
Pickering, G., 502
Pine, F., 102n, 103, 143, 239, 499, 502
Piorkowski, G., 214, 497
Plato, 502
Poincaré, H., 274, 502
Pollock, G.H., ix–xvii, 145, 169, 175, 195–208, 196, 321–339, 485–488, 502–503
Portnoy, J., 40, 503
Pratt, C.C., 212, 503
Prosen, H., 482, 503
Prosen, M., 482, 503

Racker, H., 41, 46, 64, 72, 274, 503
Rank, O., 211, 395n, 397, 503
Rapaport, D., 181, 183, 187, 188, 269, 503
Rechardt, E., xv, 503
Rehberg, P., 444, 503
Rehberg, W., 444, 503
Reich, N.B., 98, 101, 300, 314, 441, 448, 456, 503
Reik, T., xii, 261, 323, 325, 327, 328, 332–333, 334, 338–339, 343, 370, 452n, 503

Richards, R.L., 310, 503
Ricoeur, P., 406, 420, 503
Riemann, H., 2, 503
Robertson, A., 195, 196, 197, 199, 200, 202, 203, 205, 380, 503
Rogers, C.R., 229, 504
Rogers, R., 415, 504
Roheim, G., 396, 504
Rolland, R., 191, 504
Rose, G., 152, 268, 273, 504
Rosen, V.H., 69, 504
Rosner, S., 188, 504
Ross, N., 478, 504
Rossiter, F.R., 125n, 128, 130, 137–138, 504
Rothenberg, A., 268, 275, 276, 504
Rousseau, J.J., 2, 504
Russell, J., 504

Sabbeth, D., 49–59
Sachs, C., 14, 504
Sacks, M., 222n, 493
Sadie, S., 233, 504
Salk, L., 153, 504
Salter, L., 468, 504
Salzer, F., 49n, 51, 504
Sams, E., 444–445, 504
Schachtel, E., 47, 64, 183, 504
Schachter, S., 58, 504
Schafer, R., 159, 504
Schauffler, R.H., 186, 190, 293, 504
Schilder, P., 268, 269, 272, 504
Schneider, H., 305, 504
Schoen, M., 68, 504
Schonberg, H.C., 97–98, 504
Schopenhauer, A., 1, 504
Schumann, E., 101, 504
Schumann, R., 299, 441, 442, 450, 452, 459, 462, 505
Schwartz, D.W., 423–440
Schwarz, B., 312, 505
Seashore, C.E., 68, 505
Sechehaye, M.S., 34, 505
Sessions, R., 181, 183, 188–189, 277, 505
Sharpe, E., 104, 391, 396, 397, 446n, 505
Shevrin, H., 269, 505
Shopper, M., 270, 505
Silverman, M., 482, 505
Slater, E., 443n, 449n, 505
Slochower, H., 213, 505
Slonimsky, N., 304, 305, 505
Smetana, B., 190, 505

Socarides, C.W., 239, 240, 505
Solomon, M., 275n, 287–290, 289, 310, 401–421, 505
Solomon, P., et al., 181, 505
Spalding, A., 187, 505
Spencer, H., 2, 505
Spitz, R.A., 39, 64, 65, 73, 75, 180, 505
Stein, H., xvii, 505
Stekel, W., x, 506
Stendhal, 423, 426, 430, 431, 506
Stephenson, K., 310, 506
Sterba, E., xvii, 241, 506
Sterba, R.F., xii-xiii, xvii, 3, 19, 23, 46, 67, 234, 274, 485, 506
Stern, D., 153, 506
Stevenson, C.E., 262, 506
Stevenson, O., 506
Storr, A., 224–225, 229–230, 506
Strohl, E.L., 316, 506
Stuckenschmidt, H.H., 506
Stumpf, K., 2, 506
Suzuki, S., 80, 94, 506

Tanner, J.M., 180, 506
Taylor, A., 407, 506
Taylor, I.A., 218-219, 506
Taylor, R., 466, 470, 506
Toussieng, P., 269, 505
Toye, F., 424, 426, 427, 430, 431, 432, 435, 436, 437, 438, 439, 506

Tupper, F., 406, 506
Turner, W., 201, 392, 392n, 506

Updike, J., 472, 506

Virgil, 465, 506
Volkan, V., 292, 506
Von Arnim, L.A., 341, 506

Waelder, R., 213, 227, 506
Walter, B., 389, 506
Wangh, M., 216, 506
Wasiliewski, W.J., 288, 506
Watson, D., 466, 469, 470, 506
Weber, M., 289–290, 507
Wegeler-Ries, F., 288, 507
Weinshel, E.M., 247, 248 507
Weinstock, H., 490
Weiss, J., 52n, 507
Weissman, P., 47, 183, 507
Werfel, A.M., 337, 338, 507
Werman, D.S., 239, 242, 245, 474, 507
Werner, H., 268, 507
Westernhagen, C., 466, 467, 470, 507
Whitehead, A., 507
Wieck, F., 108, 109, 111, 448, 507
Will, N., 482, 505
Winnicott, D.W., 86–87, 102, 268, 271, 292, 320, 507
Wolff, P.H., 47, 507
Wundt, W., 2, 507

Subject Index

Acoustics, 21
Adaptation, 43
"Addiction" to music, 76
Aesthetics, musical, 21, 25, 212, 233, 262
Affect(s), 238–249
  Freud's theory of, 238
  and memory, 240
  music and, 233–235, 249, 260–264, 486
  structural classification of, 246
Affect theory, 234, 238, 245, 246
Aggression, 175, 191, 192, 353, 355, 363–364, 367, 386–388, 398
  artistic endeavor as sublimination of, 434, 435
Ambiguity, 44, 46
  in composing, 184, 185, 188
  internal-external, 183
Anal stage, 3, 7, 93, 393, 396, 415n, 429
Analyst, auditory style of, 45–46, 47
Anxiety, 8, 34, 56, 66, 87, 234, 238, 396
  allaying through transitional object, 292
  mastering, 289
  noise and, 288
Aphasia, 29
Applause, 16, 18
Applied psychoanalysis, x–xii, 116, 235, 485–488
Arcadelt, Jacob, 206
Archaic elements, in moods, 248
Aristotle, 1, 51
Art, 218, 260–264
  communicable nature of, 223
  nostalgia in, 244
Artistic talent, 68–77
  acquired/environmental factors in, 68, 72–75
  constitutional factors in, 68–72
  See also Musical ability
Atonal music, 12
Audience, 17. See also Listener
Audition, 44. See also Hearing; Listening
Auditory hyperacuity, 4, 5, 24, 42, 45, 72, 191, 193, 288, 289
Auditory modes, 74–75, 180–181, 182. See also "Auditory style"

Auditory pathology, 189–192
Auditory preference, 180, 193
Auditory sensitivity, 127, 149–150, 189–192, 279, 287, 288. See also Auditory hyperacuity
"Auditory style," 44–45, 179–181, 189, 193
  of analyst, 45–46
  of composers, 189–192
Auditory symptoms, 189–191
Autobiography, 145
Autonomy, primary and secondary, 21

Bach, Johann Sebastian, 25, 89n, 205, 306n, 470
Bach, Wilhelm Friedemann, 89n
Bachelard, Gaston, 479–480
Background music, 11
Baroque period, 233
Bartok, Bela, 58
Bauer-Lechner, Natalie, 352, 358, 359–360, 365, 383, 385
Beethoven, Ludwig von, 17, 18, 58, 274, 275
  auditory sensitivity of, 288
  childhood of, 287, 288
  deafness of, 189, 191, 287–290
  symphonies, 17, 18, 19, 66, 388
"Belle indifference" reaction, 81
Bereavement, 208, 241, 292. See also Mourning
Berlioz, Hector, 202, 434
Bernstein, Leonard, 206, 207
Billroth, Theodor, 294, 311–312, 316–317
Biological endowment, 149
Biological theories, 21
Bliss, Arthur, 207
Blow, John, 198
Body image, 269, 270
Body rhythm, 275, 276
"Body-self," 223, 224
Brahms, Johanna (Henrika Christiane Nissen), 295, 298, 302
Brahms, Johannes, 184–185, 205–206, 291–320, 352
  altruism of, 303n, 315–318
  androgynous appearance of, 305, 307, 313
  childhood of, 295–297, 308, 313

515

as composer, 297, 301–308, 312, 319–320
depression of, 293, 294, 301, 307, 319
friendship with Clara Schumann, 97, 98, 292, 293, 299–300, 311, 313–314, 317–318, 319
generosity of, 315–318
"German Requiem," 205–206, 302
and Joachim, 304, 306, 312
lack of formal education, 297, 308, 317
loneliness of, 308–315, 317
"Lullaby," 91, 314, 377
mood disorder of, 309–310
musical development, 294–308
personality of, 291–294, 298–299, 305, 308–311, 319
as a prodigy, 297
relationships with women, 310–311, 313, 314–315
and Robert Schumann, 292, 299, 311, 313
"role reversal" with father, 297, 303
sexuality and, 312–313, 315
symphonies, 303–304, 305, 306, 312
as a transitional figure, 293, 319
Brahms, Johann Jakob (father), 294–296, 303
Brain damage, and perception of music, 24
Breuer, Joseph (Josef), 319*n*, 326
Britten, Benjamin, 206, 207
Bruch, Max, 185
Bruckner, Anton, 203, 326
Busoni, Ferrucio, 227*n*

Canon, 67
Carnival, Feast of, 408–409, 410–411
Carter, Elliot, 157
Castration anxiety, 133, 147–148, 397, 398, 415
Catharsis, music as, 22–23, 26, 37
Censors, in creative art, 217–220
Cezanne, Paul, 220–221
Cherubini, Mario Luigi, 202
Chinese music, 14, 16
Ciaroscuro, 218
Clapping (applause), as release of energy, 16, 18
Clarke, Jeremiah, 206
"Coenesthetic organization," 65, 65, 73, 75
Cognition, 39, 40, 44

Cognitive controls, 43
Cognitive psychology, 46–48
Cognitive style, 44
Communication, 2, 74
in ensemble playing, 45, 271–272
infant, 64–66, 74
mother-child, 73–74, 75–76
music as, 42, 63, 64, 72
preverbal, 64, 73
Composer, 2, 3, 22, 57, 179, 233, 267–283
auditory pathology of, 189–191
denial in, 191–192
development of imagination in, 267–283
and inspiration, 185, 193, 267, 268, 273, 274
Composition, 13, 14, 179–193
process of, 180, 191–192
role of inspiration in, 179–182
Condensation, 59, 54, 55
Conductor, 22, 71
Conrad, Joseph, 442
Consonance and dissonance, 14, 16, 17, 24
Content, 24, 28, 75
form vs., 209–213
of music, 9, 14, 24, 151, 261
Contrary motion, in music, 254
Conversion reaction, 81
Counteridentification, 487
Counternoise, 12, 24
"Counterphobic" reaction, 243
Countertransference, xii, 99, 487
Couperin, Francois, 66
Cowell, Henry, 123, 142, 157, 162
Creative ego, 228
Creative process, 188, 267
Creativity, 209–210, 213, 214, 216, 229, 291, 391, 396–398, 441–442
as agony, 280–281
and beginning work, 281
censors in, 217
and fear of death, 397
and neurosis, 229–231
as sublimation, 396–397, 398, 420

Danger, sound as signal of, 4, 5–6. *See also* Threat
Deafness, 287–290
of Beethoven, 189, 191, 287–290
Death, fear of, and creativity, 397
Death practices, 380–381

Orthodox Jewish, 323
See also Mourning
Defense(s), 12, 43, 70
 against anxiety, 87
 of artist, 230
 of audience, 12, 17, 23, 24
 nostalgia as, 106, 243
 transitional phenomena as, 86, 87
Delius, Frederick, 207
Denial, 191, 243
des Prés, Josquin, 206
Depression
 artistic creation and, 396–397
 binding, 353
 as "creative malady," 307
 nostalgia and, 241, 242, 244
 regret and, 241
 as "unpleasure," 245–246
 (*see also* under names of composers)
Development, musical, 91–94
Developmental hierarchy, principle of, 29–36
Developmental issues, 91–92
 for gifted people, 268–269
Discharge, musical activity as, 30
Displacement, 50, 54
Dissonance, in Ives, 157. *See also* Consonance and dissonance
Doctrine of the affections, 233
Donizetti, Gaetano, 437
Drama, perfect form in, 225
Dreams, 214–215, 487–488
 "creative," 214, 215
 Freud's study of, 211–212, 487
 as source of inspiration, 186
Dufay, Guillaume, 197
Duruflé, Maurice, 204
Dvrák, Antonin, 203, 204, 316, 487

Ear, 39–40, 107, 288
 auditory pathology, 189–192
 Ivesian, 136–137, 148, 154–155, 156, 157
Ego, 2, 7, 8, 23–25, 43, 72
 and adaptive mourning, 196
 development of, 69–70
Ego boundaries, 19
Ego development, 69–70
Ego functions, 8, 20, 25, 41, 143, 213, 222, 249, 488
Ego ideal, 473
"Ego nuclei," 75
Ego psychology, ix, xiv, 41, 43, 48, 143, 188, 213, 227, 230, 238

and psychoanalytic study of creative process, 210, 486
Einstein, Albert, 274, 275
Elegaic works, 207–208
Elgar, Sir Edward, 207
Emotion. *See* Affect
Empathic ability, 267, 268, 270
Energy, liberation of through music, 8, 9, 11–12, 16, 18–19
Enjoyment, musical 3, 7, 18, 19–20, 72
Ensemble playing, 45, 271–272
Equilibrium, 42
Eroticism, kinesthetic, 7
Expressiveness, musical, 265

Family-romance fantasy, 145–146, 150–151, 155
Fantasia, 10
Fantasy(-ies)
 family-romance, 145–146, 150–151, 155
 and inspiration, 182
 nostalgia vs., 242
Fastnacht, 409, 410
Father-child relationship, 98, 132, 143–144
Fauré, Gabriel, 203–204
Fear
 of death, and creative urge, 397
 in response to noise, 4–7, 8, 20, 288–289
Feminine/masculine nature of music, 128, 136–137, 155–156, 157
Festivals, 408–409
Film making, 278
Film music, 10
Fliess, Wilhelm, 442
Flight, in response to sound, 8, 12, 24
Fischhof, Josef, 441
Form, 24, 28
 vs. content, 209–213
 "good," 213, 214–221
 musical, 15, 24, 25, 253, 265
 "perfect," 213, 221–225, 263
 quality in, 227
Fould, J.C., 207
Fratricide, music of, 374–386
Freud, Sigmund, ix–x, 28–29, 143, 144, 209, 210, 230, 442, 478–479
 affect theory, 238
 consultation with Mahler, 337–339
 dream studies, 211–212, 214–215, 487

and family-romance fantasy, 145–146
and infantile sexuality, 23
Interpretation of Dreams, 487
on psychoanalytic theory of art, 210, 211, 391
on task of artist, 216
theory of jokes, 49–59
theory of play, 16, 23–24, 56
Fugue, 15, 47n , 67, 219–220, 225–226, 273
Funeral services, 205, 207–208

Games, children's, 56–56. *See also* Play
Genetic fallacy, 475
Genetic view (of enjoyment of music), 19–20, 42
Gestalt psychology, 70, 217, 219, 398
Giftedness, 65, 68, 132, 153–154, 267, 272, 474–475
developmental issues in, 268–269
See also Musical ability; Talent
Gough, Harrison, 225
Graf, Max, x, 485
Gregorian chant, 14, 15
Grief, 201. *See also* Mourning
Griggs, John Cornelius, 140, 160
Group experience, music as, 7, 8, 22

Hallucinations, auditory, 190
Handel, George Frederick, 207
Hardy, Thomas, 471–472, 474
Harmony, 25
Haydn, Franz Joseph, 198
Haydn, Joseph, 198, 413
Haydn, Michael, 198
Hearing, 39, 41, 42, 43, 44–45, 179–180, 287–288
discriminative, 68
erotization of, 72
See also Listening
Heidegger, Martin, 476
Hindemith, Paul, 207
Hoffman, E.T.A., 298, 451
Hoffman, Nina, 353, 388
Hypersensitivity, to sensory stimulation, 4, 5, 24, 42, 45, 72, 191, 193, 267–268, 288, 289
Hypertension, 30

Id, 1, 22–23
Idealization, 107, 133, 243
Identification, 20, 168
with absent parent, 107, 168, 170
with composer or performer, 7, 8
Id psychology, and music, 22–23, 41
Imagination, development of, 267–283
Imitation, 1, 9
Immaculate Conception, 146, 148
Immortality, 169, 197
Incorporation, 168
Individuation, 101–102, 103, 279–280. *See also* Separation-individuation
Infant, 4–5, 6, 7, 47n, 70–71
communication of, 64–66
own cry of, 25, 47
response to sound, 4, 6–7, 24, 42
selective perception of, 70–71
See also Mother-child interaction
Infantile sexuality, 23
Inhibitions, musical, 27
Inspiration, 267, 273–274, 355
body sensation in, 276–277
in composition, 179–193
in a dream, 185–186
passive nature of, 182, 187–189
sources of, 181–187, 190, 191–192
visual imagery in, 277–279
Instrument(s), musical, 7, 13, 16, 20, 92–93
as a toy, 80, 93, 93n
Intellectualization, 156–157
Ives, Bigelow, 237–238
Ives, Charles Edward, 115–176, 236–238, 242
autobiographical accounts, 116, 122–123, 125n, 133–135, 137, 145, 154–155, 162–163
business career of, 117, 120–121, 142, 172
and castration anxiety, 133, 146–147, 156
as composer, 119–120, 121, 142, 154, 157–158, 160–162, 168, 173
creative decline at midlife, 120, 122–125, 172–174
early life, 125, 132–159
education, 129, 138–139, 140
Essays Before a Sonata, 120, 142, 173
family romance of, 147, 150–151, 154
importance of locale for, 151–152, 166, 260
and Ivesian "ear," 136–137, 148, 154–155, 156, 157
marriage, 119, 140–142, 160

Subject Index

and masculine/feminine qualities of music, 128, 136–137, 155–156, 157
memorialization of father in music, 116, 145, 151, 159–176
at midlife, 117–125
nostalgia in work of, 141, 153, 236–238, 242, 248, 249–260, 265–266
114 Songs, 115–117, 120, 142, 153, 158–159, 167, 173, 175
patriotism of, 256, 259
The Pond, 166–167, 168, 174
relationship with father, 116, 130, 133–139, 143–144, 147, 150, 154, 159, 170, 171, 259
relationship with mother, 130–131, 144–145
Scrapbook (Memos), 123, 133, 134, 145, 154–156, 162–163, 260
Second Pianoforte Sonata/"Concord Mass. 1840–1860," 119, 120, 142, 170, 173
style of, 120, 160, 165–166
"The Things Our Fathers Loved," 155, 249–260, 265–266
Three Places in New England, 131, 152
Violin Sonatas, 163–166, 168, 174
as writer of father's "textbook," 162–163, 168
Ives, Edith, 119, 142
Ives, George Edward, 125–130, 132–136, 139, 148–150, 164, 236, 258, 259
as black sheep, 128, 129, 139, 172
Charles' "collaboration" with, 162, 171–175
death of, 130, 140, 174
marriage of, 129, 130
memorialization of, 116, 145, 151, 159–176
musical career of, 125–129, 162–163, 171
Ives, Harmony Twitchell, 115, 123, 130, 140–142, 160
Ives, Mary Elizabeth Parmelee, 130–131
Ives, Moss (brother), 129, 138
Ives, Moss (nephew), 165–166

Jahn, Wilhelm, 324
Janusian thinking, 275
Jazz, 23, 272
"Jazz Funeral," 207–208
Joachim, Amalie, 306, 312
Joachim, Joseph, 106, 298–299, 304, 306–307, 312
Jokes
Freud's theory of, 49–59
saving energy in, 52

Kalbeck, Max, 302
Kinaesthetic experience, and inspiration, 277
Kirchner, Theodor, 314

Laments, 206–207
Language learning, and musical talent, 80, 83–84
Laughter, 16, 18
as response to complex music, 12, 24, 25
Lehman, Lilli, 353
Libidinal satisfaction, in music, 22
Libido, 7, 67
Libretto, 10
Linear (Schenkerian) analysis, 49, 49n, 55, 57, 58, 59
Linking phenomena, 292. *See also* Transitional phenomena
Listener(s), 2, 3, 4, 10, 13, 63
mastery of music by, 11–13, 16–17, 19
resistance of, 17
response to complex music, 8, 12, 24, 25
Listening, 7–8, 39, 40, 43, 44n, 72
active, 57
selective, 70
Liszt, Franz, 290
Literature, nostalgia in, 240, 244
Locomotion, development of, 152, 153
Loss, mourning and, 201–202
Love, 478
"being in," 473–474
Lullaby(-ies), 7, 88, 90–91, 92, 95

Mahler, Alma Marie Schindler, 323, 334–335, 337–339
Mahler, Bernard (Bernhard), 321–322, 344, 345–346, 349, 373, 379
Mahler, Gustav, 273, 321–339, 341–390
aggression of, 353, 355, 363–364, 367, 387
ambivalent fraternal love of, 347–364

and brother Ernst, 322, 323, 327,
  347–348, 373
and brother Otto, 325, 344–345,
  347–353 *passim*, 357, 361–362,
  366–374 *passim*
and Bruno Walter, 347, 369, 373
career of, 324–325, 346, 358–359
childhood of, 321–323, 325–326,
  344–348, 377–378, 381–382
consultation with Freud, 337–339,
  343
Das Klagende Lied, 327, 329–332,
  335, 341, 342, 366, 367, 368,
  372–373, 374, 378, 380, 390
death of, 329, 336, 337
death of daughter Marie, 329, 335,
  336–337
depression of, 353, 354–355, 357,
  360
First Symphony, 350, 364, 365, 368,
  378, 381, 382
fratricidal fantasies of, 330, 331,
  343, 347, 355, 358, 363, 371, 377,
  381, 390
frequent moves, 327, 329
health problems, 335, 349, 353, 361,
  366, 389
Herzog Ernst von Schwaben, 327, 375
identification with St. Anthony, 359,
  383, 384
Leider eines Fahrenden Gesellen, 341,
  362
marriage, 334, 337–339
Ninth Symphony, 347, 386
as replacement child, 323–324, 344
Second Symphony (*Death and
  Resurrection*), 332–334, 342, 354,
  365–382 *passim*, 388–389, 390
sibling losses, 322, 323, 324,
  327–329, 381–382
survivor guilt of, 323, 328, 329, 331,
  332, 345
Tenth Symphony, 336, 337, 359,
  384, 386
Mahler, Marie (Maria) Frank,
  321–322, 344, 345, 349–350
Mahler, Otto, 344–353 *passim*, 357,
  361, 366, 367–369
suicide of, 325, 353, 368
Marches, 152–153
Masculine/feminine nature of music,
  128, 136–137, 155–156, 157
Mastery, 23–24, 37, 72, 103
in child's play, 16, 23

as ego function, 41
of music by listener, 11–13, 16–17,
  19, 23–26
technical, 280
Mathematics, 273–274
Melancholia, 473. *See also* Depression
Memorialization in music, 145,
  195–208
Memory, 180, 240
Metaphors, significance of, 103–105,
  446
Mill, John Stuart, 143, 146–147
Monteverdi, Claudio, 198
Moods, 246–248. *See also* Affect(s)
Moore, Henry, 269
Moro reflex, 4, 24
Mother-child interaction, 42, 72–74,
  75–76, 143, 183, 270, 271
individual differences in, 73–74
and mother's singing, 73
sound and movement in, 180
Motivation, 1
Mourning, 160, 169, 175, 208
adaptive, 196
music as, 167, 174, 195–208,
  321–339, 388
role of nostalgia in, 240, 243–244,
  247
universality of, 201
Mourning music, 195–208, 321–339
elegiac works, 207–208
laments, 206–207
requiems, 196–204
Stabat Mater, 204–206
Moussorgsky, Modest, 9, 203, 291*n*
Movement, sound and, 42, 180
Mozart, Anna Maria, 392, 393, 397,
  415–417
Mozart, Constance (Constanze), 200,
  201, 403
Mozart, Leopold, 392–395, 397, 398,
  401, 402, 411–414
Mozart, Wolfgang Amadeus, 11, 58,
  81–82, 198–202, 274, 391–399,
  410, 470
and anality, 393, 396, 415*n*
and "Bäsle" letters, 393, 396, 407,
  410
death of, 395, 395*n*
depression of, 395*n*, 398
development and character of,
  391–396
and Freemasonry, 394, 410, 413
The Magic Flute, 200, 226–228, 394

Subject Index

marriage of, 396, 412, 417
misogyny of, 417
precocity of, 391, 392
proverbs of, 401, 402
rebellion of, 393, 394–395, 396
relationship with father, 391–395, 397, 398, 401, 411–417, 419
relations with women, 395–396, 417
Requiem, 199–202
Symphony No. 40, 226–228
Zoroastran riddles of, 401, 402–411, 414–421
Musical ability, 68–77, 80–81, 83, 127, 132, 153–154
   acquired, 68, 72–75
   constitutional factors in, 68–72, 76
Musical development, 91–94
Musicality, 64. See also Musical ability
Musical language, 63, 64–69, 103, 154
   elements of, 65
   origins of, 66–68
Musical processes, primary and secondary, 26–29
Myrick, Julian, 162

Narcissism, 3, 22, 473–474, 475, 482–483
Neue Zeitschrift für Musik, 441, 451, 461
Neurosis
   creativity and, 229–231
   giftedness and, 268
   organic, 30, 34
Newborn. See Infant
New Music, 157
New Music Quarterly, 123
Noise
   anxiety and, 288
   and counternoise, 12, 24
   extraneous, 11, 70–71
   hypersensitivity to, 4, 5, 24, 42, 45, 72, 191, 193, 267–268, 288, 289
   response to, 4–7, 8
   sudden, 4–6
   as threat, 6, 13, 15, 23, 24, 288–289
   use of in composition, 13
   See also Sound
Nonverbal aspects of music, 64
Nostalgia, 141, 236–266
   affect of, 245
   as defense, 106
   vs. fantasy, 242
   in Ives' music, 141, 153, 236–238, 242, 249–260

in literature, 240
morphology of, 260–266
and mourning, 240, 243–244, 247
normal/pathologic, 242–243
paradoxes in, 246
as resistance, 242
as substitute for mourning, 243
Nurtured by Love (Suzuki), 80

Object cathexis, 35
Object loss, 34, 159–160, 195
Object-relatedness, 456
Object relations theory, 144, 159–160, 196, 465, 478
"Oceanic feeling," 19, 30, 474, 478–480
Ockeghem, Johannes, 197–198, 206
Octave, 13–14
Oedipal issues, 113
O'Neill, Eugene, *The Emperor Jones*, 6, 28
Opera, 10–11
Organ neuroses, 30, 31, 34
Orthodox Jewish death practices, 323
Overcomplexity of musical task, 17–18, 24
Oversensitivity, sensory, 4, 5, 24, 42, 45, 69–72, 191, 193, 267–268
Oversimplification of musical task, 17, 18

Painting, 218
Palestrina, Giovanni, 198
Paranoia, 34
Parent(s), in Suzuki method, 80, 83, 94
   See also Father-child relationship; Mother-child interaction
Parental introjects, 27–28
Parental voice, 27–28, 39, 66
Parker, Horatio, 135, 160
Passivity, in creative process, 182, 187–189
Pathographies, 124, 441–442
Patients, musical, 74–75
Patriotism, 170, 256, 259
Peerson, Martin, "The Primrose," 51–52, 54, 56, 57, 58
Perception, 44, 64–65, 70
   autocentric, 64
Perceptual defects, 24
Perfect form, 213, 221–225
   in poetry, music, and drama, 225
Performer, 2, 3, 22, 63, 488

Personality development, and Suzuki
  system, 91–92
Perspective, 218
Philosophers, 1–2
Phobia, nostalgia and, 239
Piaget, Jean, 48
Pierce, Joseph La Croix (DeDe), 207
Pirandello, Luigi, 216
Plath, Sylvia, 482
Plato, 2
Play, 133–134
  Freud's theory of, 16, 23–24, 56
  mastery in, 16–17
  at music, 93, 94, 134
Play principle, 410
Pleasure, 6, 245–246. *See also*
  Enjoyment
Poetry, 27, 225
Popular music, 18
Poulenc, François, 204
Prayers for the dead, 196, 205
Preoedipal mother, 241, 242
Preverbal children, 53, 65
Primary and secondary processes, xiii,
  9, 26–29, 53n, 171, 223, 247,
  452–453, 488
Proust, Marcel, 240, 243, 244
Psychoanalysis
  in absentia, 425–426
  applied, x–xii, 116, 235, 485–488
  auditory orientation, 45
  and theory of art (music), 39–48,
    210, 218–219, 234–235, 463,
    485–488
  Psychoanalytic Explorations in Art
    (Kris), ix
Psychoeconomic view of enjoyment
  of music, 18–19, 20, 31, 33–34
Psychopathology, 30, 31–34
Psychosexual development, 5
Psychosis, 25, 34–36, 69
Psychotherapy, 30–31
Puccini, Giacomo, 185
Purcell, Henry, 205

Rage, 30
  creativity and, 396–397, 398
  depression and, 396–397, 398, 435
Rameau, Jean Philippe, 273
Ravel, Maurice, 9, 23
Realism, in painting, 218
Reality testing, 87
Recognition, pleasure of, 10, 51, 52
Regression, 7, 24, 30, 35, 37, 47, 289

ambiguity as, 46–47
in composition, 183
love as, 478
music and, xiii, xiv, 7–8, 19, 37,
  67–68, 248, 274, 275, 283
narcissistic, 482
nostalgia and, 242, 244
Regret, 241
Religion, 30, 67, 478–479
Reminiscence, 244. *See also* Nostalgia
Repetition, 6, 15, 24, 52, 52n, 53,
  57–58
rhythmical, 66
Requiem mass, 195, 196, 197–203, 380
  followed by death of composer,
    201–202
  of Mozart, 199–202
Resistance, 239
  in analysis, 32, 33
  of artist, 230
  listener, 17
  nostalgia as, 242
  to work, 281
Response, variations in, 69
Reunion theme, 259, 469
Rhyme, 54
Rhythm, 7, 8, 14, 23, 27, 66, 270–271
Richter, Hans, 324
Riddles and riddling, 402–408,
  417–421
Romantic style, 17, 233
Rossini, Gioacchino, 13, 18, 72, 203,
  423–440
  Barber of Seville, 424, 425, 429–430
  ceases career as opera composer,
    423–424, 434, 439–440
  Le Comte Ory, 432
  death of mother, 431–432, 434, 435,
    435n, 440
  depression of, 432, 435–438
  health of, 424, 436–437, 438
  interview with Wagner, 430
  life of, 426–432, 435–440
  marriage of, 436
  and Olympe Pelissier, 436, 437, 438, 439
  relationship with father, 426, 436
  relationship with mother, 427–428,
    431–432, 434, 435, 440
  Petite Messe Solenelle, 439
  Sins of My Old Age, 439
  Stabat Mater, 437
  William Tell, 424, 425, 433–434, 436
Rubenstein, Anton, 298
Rückert, Friedrich, 327, 328

Subject Index   523

Scarlatti, Alessandro, 198
Schenker, Heinrich, 49n
Schizoid personality, 35
Schizophrenia, 31, 34, 35–36
Schönberg (Schoenberg), Arnold, 12, 24, 170, 347
Schopenhauer, Arthur, 466, 467, 469, 477
Schumann, Clara Weick, 97–113, 299–300, 316, 318, 441, 445–449
  childhood of, 100–107, 445–449
  as composer, 109, 110, 456
  delayed speech of, 100–101, 102, 103, 111, 112, 445–446, 456
  diaries of, 99–101, 106, 108, 109, 446n, 455
  divorce of parents, 100, 101, 106, 447
  metaphoric expressions of, 103–105, 446, 446n
  as a mother, 111, 448
  mother of, 101, 102, 106, 112, 445, 447, 447n
  "oedipal victory" of, 447
  as "partner in creativity," 98, 99, 441, 442, 456–463
  performing career of, 97–98, 447–448
  personality of, 98, 112–113, 448, 459, 460
  relationship with Brahms, 97, 98, 99, 292, 299–301, 311, 313–314, 317–318, 319
  relationship with father, 99, 107–109, 110–113, 443, 444, 445, 447–448, 451, 453–455, 458–459, 462
  relationship with Schumann, 98, 103, 110, 313, 441, 443, 445, 451, 453–455, 458–459, 462
  as a young virtuoso, 97–98, 102, 107–113, 445
Schumann, Felix, 299, 300n
Schumann, Robert, 25, 97, 98, 113, 186, 190, 299–300, 312, 313, 441–445, 449–463
  bisexual identifications of, 459
  and Brahms, 292, 299–300, 313, 318
  Clara as inspiration, 442–443, 444–445, 456–461
  as composer, 444–445, 454–457, 461–462
  courtship of Clara, 110, 443, 445, 451, 453–455, 458–460, 462
  death of, 300
  depressions of, 113, 189–190, 443–444, 444n, 449, 449n, 452, 454, 461
  early years, 449–455, 460–461
  finger injury, 452, 457
  parents of, 449, 460
  psychosis of, 186, 190
  relationship with Friedrich Wieck, 113, 443, 450, 452, 453–455, 461
  suicide attempts, 190, 299
  use of Clara's themes in his music, 444, 453
Schütz, Heinrich, 205
Science, creativity in, 274–276, 278
Secondary processes. *See* Primary and secondary processes
Secret sharing, 162n, 442
Self, 222–223
  developmental survey of, 223–224
Self-as-object, 196
Self-esteem, 22
Self-expression, music and, 263–265
Self psychology, 481
Self relations, 196
Sensorimotor styles, 267
Sensorimotor theory, 47, 269, 272
Sensory deprivation, 181, 269
Sensory modalities, responses to, 69, 75
  See also Auditory modes
Sensory preference, 180, 270, 276
Sensory sensitivity, 75–76, 267–268
  auditory, 127, 149–150, 189–192, 279, 287, 288
Sentimentality, in music, 131. *See also* Nostalgia
Separation, 101–102, 139, 269, 270, 442
  and the creative process, 281–283
  mastering, 89
  separation anxiety, 83, 261, 281–282
Separation-individuation, 102, 112, 143, 150, 152, 153, 159, 268, 446
  and creative process, 283
Sexuality, 23, 470
Silence, 6–7, 13
Smetana, Bedrich, 190
Sonata, 15
Sound(s), 9, 39–40, 181, 270, 288
  fear of, 4–7, 8, 20, 288
  and mastering anxieties, 289
  and movement, 42, 180

repetitive, monotonous, 6
response to unfamiliar, 8, 12, 24
sensory preference for, 180, 193
sensitivity to, 4, 5, 24, 71–72, 75, 267–268, 288, 289
Speech, types of, 29
Stabat Mater, 204–206
Startle response, 4, 24
Steiner, Josef, 347
Stimuli, protective barrier against, 70–71
Strauss, Richard, 9, 185, 206, 305, 323, 347
Stravinsky, Igor, 14, 206
Structural viewpoint, 22–26, 41–42
Style, 17–18
Sublimation, 137, 396–398, 419
  artistic endeavor as, 2, 396–398, 424, 434, 435
Submission, as function of music, 37
Substitute formation, 50, 54, 55
Suicide, 357–358, 469, 482, 483
Superego, xiii, 25–28, 39, 45, 287
Suzuki, Shinichi, 79–85
Suzuki method, 79–85, 91–92, 93–94, 95
Symbol(s), 2
  auditory, 154, 190, 487–488
  wound as, 468, 481
Symbolism, 262
  in *Tristan und Isolde*, 467–468, 481
Symmetry, 223–224
Symptoms, auditory, 189–191

Talent, 68–77, 80–81, 127, 267–268
  acquired/environmental factors in, 68, 72–75, 76, 81
  constitutional factors in, 68–72, 75–77, 81
  neurosis and, 268
  See also Musical ability; Giftedness
Talent education, 79, 81, 93–94
Tartini, Giuseppe, 186–187
Tchaikovsky, Peter Ilyich, 291*n*, 304, 442
Technical mastery, 280
Tension
  produced by music, 11, 18
  release of, in music, 10, 11, 18, 22–23
Theme, musical, 46
Thoreau, Henry David, 167
Threat, acoustical, 6, 13, 15, 23, 24, 288–289

mastery of, 23–24, 72
Time, 261
Tinnitus, 289
Tonality, 13–14, 17
Tones, 13–14
Tonic, 14, 56
Topographical view of enjoyment of music, (ego functions), 20, 184–185, 188
Transference, 22, 99
Transformational techniques, 50, 54–55, 58
"Transitional object," 86, 268, 292, 319
  music as, 271, 292
"Transitional personalities," 319
"Transitional phenomena," 85–88, 268, 271
  auditory, 86
  as defense, 86, 87
  music as, 85, 102, 106
"Transitional tunes," 85, 88–91, 92, 94–95, 271
Tristan chord, 470
Tristan und Isolde, 17, 19, 316, 465–472, 476–477, 480–483
Twitchell, Harmony. *See* Ives, Harmony Twitchell

Unconscious conflicts, resolving, 57
Unfamiliar (complex) music, responses to, 8, 12, 23, 24, 25
Unisono, 225–226
Universality of music, 1, 68, 127

Verbalization, 9, 10
Verdi, Giuseppe, 11, 202–203
Vienna Psycho-Analytical Society, ix
Violin, Suzuki method of teaching, 79–85
Virgin birth, 146, 147
Visual imagery, 10, 277–279
von Bülow, Hans, 304, 323, 324, 370, 373, 374
von Fricken, Ernestine, 112
von Herzogenberg, Elisabet, 103–104

Wagner, Richard, x–xi, 17, 185, 305, 316, 465–483
  Ring of the Niebelung, 465–466
  Rossini interview with, 430
  Tannhauser, 112
  Tristan und Isolde, 17, 19, 316, 465–472, 476–477, 480–483
Wallfisch, Ernst, 90

Walter, Bruno (Schlesinger), 347, 369
Wednesday Society, ix–x
Wieck, Clara. *See* Schumann, Clara Wieck
Wieck, Friedrich, 97, 100–101, 107–113, 443, 445
as author of Clara's diaries, 99, 100–101, 106, 109, 446n
divorce of, 106–107
opposition to Clara's marriage, 113, 453–455, 461
as Schumann's teacher, 450–452, 461
Wieck, Marianne, 101, 107, 445, 447n
Withdrawal
regressive, 36
from unfamiliar sound, 8, 12
Wolf, Hugo, 206, 305, 326
Wolfe, Thomas, 244
Work, music and, 11–12, 94
Writers, similarity in inspirational process in, 275